Course	Corporate Finance
Course Number	**ECON 173B**
	Garey Ramey
	University of California, San Diego
	ECONOMICS

http://create.mheducation.com

Copyright 2016 by McGraw-Hill Education. All rights
reserved. Printed in the United States of America. Except as
permitted under the United States Copyright Act of 1976, no part
of this publication may be reproduced or distributed in any form
or by any means, or stored in a database or retrieval system,
without prior written permission of the publisher.

This McGraw-Hill Create text may include materials submitted to
McGraw-Hill for publication by the instructor of this course.
The instructor is solely responsible for the editorial content of such
materials. Instructors retain copyright of these additional materials.

ISBN-10: 1121408893   ISBN-13: 9781121408890

Contents

Credits

ORGANIZATION

New and Enhanced Pedagogy
A great deal of effort has gone into expanding and enhancing the features in **Fundamentals of Corporate Finance.**

WALK-THROUGH

Brealey / Myers / Marcus
Your guide through the challenging landscape of corporate finance.

Chapter Opener
Each chapter begins with an outline of the chapter and a chapter narrative to help set the tone for the material that follows. Learning Objectives are also included to provide a quick introduction to the material students will learn and should understand fully before moving to the next chapter. Useful Web sites related to material for each chapter are provided on the book Web site at **www.mhhe.com/bmm6e.**

Key Points
Located throughout the text, and presented in **bold,** these points underscore and summarize the importance of the immediately preceding material, at the same time helping students focus on the most relevant topics critical to their understanding.

Key Terms in the Margin
Key terms are presented in bold and defined in the margin as they are introduced. A glossary is also available at the back of the book.

Numbered Examples
Numbered and titled examples are integrated in each chapter. Students can learn how to solve specific problems step-by-step as well as gain insight into general principles by seeing how they are applied to answer concrete questions and scenarios.

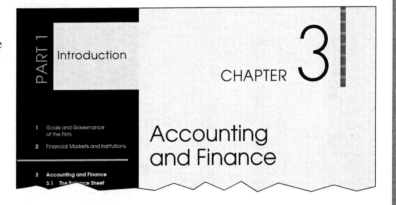

PART 1

Introduction

CHAPTER 3

Accounting and Finance

1 Goals and Governance of the Firm
2 Financial Markets and Institutions
3 Accounting and Finance
   3.1 The Balance Sheet

Table 1–1 gives for each company an example of a recent investment and financing decision. Take a look at the decisions now. We think you will agree that they appear sensible or, at least, that there is nothing obviously wrong with them. But if you are new to finance, it will be difficult to think about why these companies made these decisions and not others.

Making good investment and financing decisions is the chief task of the financial manager. Let's consider each class of decisions in more detail.

The Investment (Capital Budgeting) Decision

capital budgeting decision or investment decision
Decision to invest in tangible or intangible assets.

The **investment decision** starts with the identification of investment opportunities, often referred to as *capital investment projects*. The financial manager has to help the firm identify promising projects and decide how much to invest in each project. The investment decision is also called the **capital budgeting decision,** because most firms prepare an annual budget listing authorized capital investments.

In the distant past, "capital investments" included only investments in tangible assets, such as investment in Toyota's new automobile plants or Union Pacific's new

---

EXAMPLE 3.1 ▶ *Market- versus Book-Value Balance Sheets*

Jupiter has developed a revolutionary auto production process that enables it to produce cars 20% more efficiently than any rival. It has invested $10 billion in producing its new plant. To finance the investment, Jupiter borrowed $4 billion and raised the remaining funds by selling new shares of stock in the firm. There are currently 100 million shares of stock outstanding. Investors are very excited about Jupiter's prospects. They believe that the flow of profits from the new plant justifies a stock price of $75.

If these are Jupiter's only assets, the book-value balance sheet immediately after it has made the investment is as follows:

BOOK-VALUE BALANCE SHEET FOR JUPITER MOTORS (figures in billions of dollars)			
Assets		**Liabilities and Shareholders' Equity**	
Auto plant	$10	Debt	$4
		Shareholders' equity	6

Investors are placing a *market value* on Jupiter's equity of $7.5 billion ($75 per share times 100 million shares). We assume that the debt outstanding is worth $4

*We will show you how changing interest rates affect the market value of debt in Chapter 5.

What makes Brealey/Myers/Marcus such a powerful learning tool?

PEDAGOGY

Internet Insider Boxes

Each chapter includes boxes that highlight particular Web sites and provide students with simple activities to enhance their experience using the Internet.

INTERNET INSIDER

Understanding Financial Statements

You can find a company's financial statements on its home page, but to avoid getting entangled in a web of company promotional material it is usually easier to log on first to www.annualreports.com. Find the latest financial statements for a large nonfinancial company and draw up a simplified balance sheet, income statement, and statement of cash flows as in Tables 3–1, 3–3, and 3–4. Some companies' financial statements can be extremely complex; try to find a relatively straightforward business. Also, as far as possible, use the same headings as in these tables, and don't hesitate to group some items as "other current assets," "other expenses," and so on. Look first at your simplified balance sheet. How much was the company owed by its customers in the form of unpaid bills? What liabilities does the company need to meet within a year? What was the original cost of the company's fixed assets? Now look at the income statement. What were the company's earnings before interest and taxes (EBIT)? Finally, turn to the cash-flow statement. Did changes in working capital add to cash or use it up?

Source: IR Solutions/Annualreports.com, 2008.

Spreadsheet Solutions Boxes

These boxes provide the student with detailed examples of how to use Excel spreadsheets when applying financial concepts. Questions that apply to the spreadsheet follow and their solutions are given at the end of the applicable chapter. Denoted by an icon, these spreadsheets are available on the book Web site at **www.mhhe.com/bmm6e.**

SPREADSHEET SOLUTIONS

Using the Black-Scholes Formula

You may like to try your hand at using the Black-Scholes option-pricing formula to value the Google option. A number of Web sites include a Black-Scholes calculator (see, for example, **www.numa.com,** and look for the options calculator). But it takes only a few moments to construct your own Excel program to calculate Black-Scholes values. The following spreadsheet shows how you do it. First, type in the formulas shown on the right side of the spreadsheet in cells E2 to E8. Now enter the data for the Google June 2008 call in cells B2 to B6. Notice that the values for the standard deviation and interest rate are entered as decimals. On past evidence, the standard deviation of Google's annual returns has been about 40%, so we enter the standard deviation in

cell B2 as .40, not 40. The last two lines of the output column show that the Black-Scholes formula gives a value of $86.09 for the Google call option, fairly close to its market price in December 2007. (Don't worry about the other lines of output.)

Spreadsheet Questions

1. Use the option pricing spreadsheet to calculate the value of the call option at stock prices ranging from $500 to $900 at intervals of $25.
2. Plot the values as a function of the stock price. How does your graph compare to the plot in Figure 23–4?

e**X**cel

Please visit us at www.mhhe.com/bmm6e

	A	B	C	D	E	F	G	H	I	J
1	INPUTS			OUTPUTS			FORMULA FOR OUTPUT IN COLUMN E			
2	Standard deviation (annual)	0.4000		PV(Ex. Price)	708.749		B6/(1+B4)^B3			
3	Maturity (in years)	0.500		d1	0.197		(LN(B5/E2)+(d.5*B2^2)*B3)/(B2*SQRT(B3))			
4	Risk-free rate (effective annual rate)	0.032		d2	−0.086		E3−B2*SQRT(B3)			

Excel Exhibits

Selected exhibits are set as Excel spreadsheets. They are also available on the book Web site at **www.mhhe.com/bmm6e.**

TABLE 19–6 Dynamic Mattress's cash budget for 2010
(figures in millions of dollars)

e**X**cel

Please visit us at www.mhhe.com/bmm6e

	A	B	C	D	E
1	Quarter:	First	Second	Third	Fourth
2					
3	**A. Accounts Receivable**				
4	Receivables (beginning of period)	30.0	32.5	30.7	38.2
5	Sales	87.5	78.5	116.0	131.0
6	Collections				
7	On sales in current period (80%)	70.0	62.8	92.8	104.8
8	On sales in previous period (20%)ᵃ	15.0	17.5	15.7	23.2
9	Total collections	85.0	80.3	108.5	128.0
10	Receivables (end of period) = Rows 4+5-9	32.5	30.7	38.2	41.2
11					
12	**B. Cash Budget**				
13	Sources of cash				
14	Collections of accounts receivable (row 9)	85.0	80.3	108.5	128.0
15	Other	1.5	0.0	12.5	0.0
16	Total collections	86.5	80.3	121.0	128.0
17	Uses of cash				
18	Payments of accounts payable	65.0	60.0	55.0	50.0
19	Labor & other expenses	30.0	30.0	30.0	30.0
20	expenses	1.3	5.5		

Finance in Practice Boxes

These are excerpts that appear in most chapters, usually from the financial press, providing real-life illustrations of the chapter's topics, such as ethical choices in finance, disputes about stock valuation, financial planning, and accounting scandals.

FINANCE IN PRACTICE

What's Better in Accounting, Rules or "Feel"?

Accounting standards-setters have come under fire for producing hundreds of pages of rules that cover every conceivable situation a company could face. The much-discussed alternative is to adopt a principles-based approach, where broad-brush standards are used to govern behavior, relying on companies to reasonably apply the rules to their own situations.

The push for principles got an added boost last week, when the Securities and Exchange Commission said it may soon consider allowing U.S. companies to begin choosing between two sets of accounting rules, a move that could allow them to use an international system that is considered to be more reliant on principles, instead of U.S. generally

rules often spring up because companies ask regulators for detailed interpretations, even when guidance is based on a pretty clear-cut principle.

Backers of principles-based accounting are fond of blaming the raft of accounting rules they must follow on a legal system that makes lawsuits easy and on overzealous regulators. They argue that a principles-based system would make it easier and cheaper for them to comply with regulations, while at the same time limiting fraud.

But even groups that extol the use of broad-brush principles seem to fall back on rules. Last fall, the Committee on Capital Markets Regulation, a group of business leaders and academics whose work was backed by Treasury Secretary

Calculator Boxes and Exercises

In a continued effort to help students grasp the critical concept of the time value of money, many pedagogical tools have been added throughout the first section of the text. Financial Calculator boxes provide examples for solving a variety of problems, with directions for the three most popular financial calculators.

FINANCIAL CALCULATOR

Using Financial Calculators to Find NPV and IRR

We saw in Chapter 5 that the formulas for the present and future values of level annuities and one-time cash flows are built into financial calculators. However, as the example of the office block illustrates, most investment projects entail multiple cash flows that cannot be expected to remain level over time. Fortunately, many calculators are equipped to handle problems involving a sequence of uneven cash flows. In general, the procedure is quite simple. You enter the cash flows one by one into the calculator, and then you press the IRR key to find the project's internal rate of return. The first cash flow you enter is interpreted as coming immediately, the next cash flow is interpreted as coming at the end of one period, and so on. We can illustrate using the office block as

To calculate project NPV, the procedure is similar. You need to enter the discount rate in addition to the project cash flows, and then simply press the NPV key. Here is the specific sequence of keystrokes, assuming that the opportunity cost of capital is 7%:

Hewlett-Packard HP-10B	Sharp EL-733A	Texas Instruments BA II Plus	
–350,000 CFj	–350,000 CFi		CFi
16,000 CFj	16,000 CFi		2nd CLR Work
16,000 CFj	16,000 CFi	–350,000	ENTER ↓
66,000	466,000	16,000	ENTER ↓

Self-Test Questions

Provided in each chapter, these helpful questions enable students to check their understanding as they read. Answers are worked out at the end of each chapter.

Think about why this makes sense. In period 1, the firm expends $100 to produce the product. The product is not sold then, so the cost of producing the product is not recognized in this period; instead, the expenditure is treated as an investment in inventory, which is a negative cash flow. In period 2, the product is sold, but no cash trades hands. Instead, under accrual accounting, $150 is booked as a sale, with a corresponding investment in accounts receivable. At the same time, the $100 cost of goods sold is recognized in this period, and because the product is sold, the investment in inventories is reversed. Finally, in period 3, the cash is collected. Accounts receivable is reduced by the $150 cash inflow.

Self-Test 3.3   Consider a firm similar to the one in Example 3.2. It spends $200 to produce goods in period 1. In period 2 it sells half of those goods for $150, but it doesn't collect payment until one period later. In period 3, it sells the other half of the goods for $150, and it collects payment on these sales in period 4. Calculate the profits and the cash flows for this firm in periods 1 to 4 by completing a table like that in Example 3.2.

Global Index

The Global Index appears at the end of the text for easy reference to international material.

Global Index

Page numbers followed by n indicate material found in notes.

A&P, 620
Abitibi, 594
ABN Amro, 588
ABN Amro Mortgage Group, 6
Acciona, 588
Africa, spot/forward exchange rates, 616
Airbus Industrie, 6, 17
research and development costs, 223
Airline industry, Poland, 604
Allied Industry, 408

China, Federal Express in, 4
China National Offshore Oil Corporation, 594
Citicorp, 402
Coca-Cola Company, 615
Code of Hammurabi, 22
Coffee standard, 621
Commodity futures, 677
Competitive position, economic exposure, 629

Electric utilities, United Kingdom, 368
Endesa, Spain, 588
Enel, 418, 588
Equinox Company, 677
Erb, C., 632
Euro, 402
futures contracts, 678
Eurobonds, 402
Eurodollar deposits, 678i
Eurodollar market, 22

Financial Times, 616
Financial Times Company, 313
Financial Times Index, 313
Fisher, Irving, 624
Fixed exchange rate, 618
Ford Motor Company, 629, 632
Forecasting
exchange rates, 621–622
in international capital budgeting, 631
emerging markets, 28

End-of-Chapter Material

Summary
This feature helps review the key points and learning objectives to help provide closure to the chapter.

SUMMARY

What information is contained in the balance sheet, income statement, and statement of cash flows? *(LO1)*

Investors and other stakeholders in the firm need regular financial information to help them monitor the firm's progress. Accountants summarize this information in a balance sheet, income statement, and statement of cash flows.

The **balance sheet** provides a snapshot of the firm's assets and liabilities. The assets consist of current assets that can be rapidly turned into cash and fixed assets such as plant and machinery. The liabilities consist of current liabilities that are due for payment within a year and long-term debts. The difference between the assets and the liabilities represents the amount of the shareholders' equity.

The **income statement** measures the profitability of the company during the year. It shows the difference between revenues and expenses.

The **statement of cash flows** measures the sources and uses of cash during the year. The change in the company's cash balance is the difference between sources and uses.

Quiz, Practice, and Challenge Problems
New end-of-chapter problems are included for even more hands-on practice. Each question is labeled by topic, and learning objective, and questions are separated by level of difficulty. Answers to selected problems are provided at the back of the book.

QUESTIONS

QUIZ

1. **Underwriting.** *(LO3)*
   a. Is a rights issue more likely to be used for an initial public offering or for subsequent issues of stock?
   b. Is a private placement more likely to be used for issues of seasoned stock or seasoned bonds by an industrial company?
   c. Is shelf registration more likely to be used for issues of unseasoned stocks or bonds by a large industrial company?

2. **Underwriting.** Each of the following terms is associated with one of the events beneath. Can you match them up? *(LO4)*
   a. Shelf registration
   b. Firm commitment
   c. Right_____

PRACTICE PROBLEMS

6. **Voting for Directors.** If there are 10 directors to be elected and a shareholder owns 100 shares, indicate the maximum number of votes that he or she can cast for a favorite candidate under
   a. majority voting. *(LO3)*
   b. cumulative voting. *(LO3)*

7. **Voting for Directors.** The shareholders of the Pickwick Paper Company need to elect five directors. There are 400,000 shares outstanding. How many shares do you need to own to *ensure* that you can elect at least one director if the company has
   a. majority voting? *(LO3)*
   b. cumulative voting? *(LO3)*
   (*Hint:* How many votes in total will be cast? How many votes are required to ensure that at least one-fifth of votes are cast for your choice?)

27. **Using Financial Ratios.** For each category of financial ratios discussed in this chapter, give some examples of who would be likely to examine these ratios and why. *(LO6)*

CHALLENGE PROBLEMS

e**X**cel

Please visit us at www.mhhe.com/bmm6e

28. **Financial Statements.** As you can see, someone has spilled ink over some of the entries in the balance sheet and income statement of Transylvania Railroad. Can you use the following information to work out the missing entries? *(LO3)*

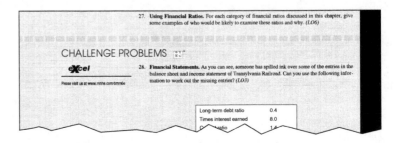

Long-term debt ratio	0.4
Times interest earned	8.0
C____ ratio	1.4

Excel Problems

Most chapters contain problems, denoted by an icon, specifically linked to Excel templates that are available on the book Web site at **www.mhhe.com/bmm6e.**

Accounts receivable	400	450
Net fixed assets†	5,000	5,800
Long-term debt	2,000	2,400
Notes payable	1,000	600
Dividends paid	410	410
Cash and marketable securities	800	300

* Taxes are paid in their entirety in the year that the tax obligation is incurred.
† Net fixed assets are fixed assets net of accumulated depreciation since the asset was installed.

28. **Book versus Market Value.** Now suppose that the market value (in thousands of dollars) of Fincorp's fixed assets in 2009 is $6,000 and that the value of its long-term debt is only $2,400. In addition, the consensus among investors is that Fincorp's past investments in developing the skills of its employees are worth $2,900. This investment of course does not show up on the balance sheet. What will be the price per share of Fincorp stock? *(LO2)*

29. **Taxes.** Turn back to Table 3–7, which shows marginal personal tax rates. Make a table in Excel that calculates taxes due for income levels ranging from $10,000 to $10 million. *(LO4)*

    a. For each income, calculate the *average* tax rate of a single taxpayer. Plot the average tax rate as a function of income.

    b. What happens to the difference between the average and top marginal tax rates as income becomes very large?

    c. Explain why, when analyzing very large firms, we may be content simply treating the corporate tax rate as 35% without worrying about tax brackets at relatively low income levels.

eXcel
Please visit us at www.mhhe.com/bmm6e

S&P Problems

Included in each chapter are problems, denoted by an icon, directly incorporating the educational version of Market Insight, a service based on Standard & Poor's renowned Compustat database.

    b. Now plot a scatter diagram of the cash ratio versus quick ratio. Do these two measures of liquidity tend to move together? Would you conclude that once you know one of these ratios, there is little to be gained by calculating the other?

STANDARD
&POOR'S

Go to Market Insight at www.mhhe.com/edumarketinsight.

1. Lowes (LOW) and The Home Depot (HD) have been in a tremendous race for the homeowner's dollar in the last few years. Who is winning? Review the company profiles (also review the industry information under the Home Improvement Retail link), financial highlights, annual ratios, profitability, and monthly valuation data reports. What company performance information supports your view as to which company is winning the race in the home improvement industry? Has the stock market picked a winner in this race?

2. Compare the sources of return on equity (using the Du Pont formula) for Abercrombie & Fitch (ANF) and Gap, Inc. (GPS). Examine both levels and trends in these variables. Review the trends in operating profit margin, total asset turnover, and leverage. What factors tend to explain the performance differential between these competing clothing retailers? How has the market reacted to their operating performance?

Minicases

Integrative minicases allow students to apply their knowledge to relatively complex, practical problems and typical real-world scenarios.

MINICASE

Old Alfred Road, who is well-known to drivers on the Maine Turnpike, has reached his seventieth birthday and is ready to retire. Mr. Road has no formal training in finance but has saved his money and invested carefully.

Mr. Road owns his home—the mortgage is paid off—and does not want to move. He is a widower, and he wants to bequeath the house and any remaining assets to his daughter.

He has accumulated savings of $180,000, conservatively invested. The investments are yielding 9% interest. Mr. Road also has $12,000 in a savings account at 5% interest. He wants to keep the savings account intact for unexpected expenses or emergencies.

Mr. Road's basic living expenses now average about $1,500 per month, and he plans to spend $500 per month on travel and hobbies. To maintain this planned standard of living, he will have to rely on his investment portfolio. The interest from the portfolio is $16,200 per year (9% of $180,000), or $1,350 per month.

Mr. Road will also receive $750 per month in social security payments for the rest of his life. These payments are indexed for inflation. That is, they will be automatically increased in proportion to changes in the consumer price index.

Mr. Road's main concern is with inflation. The inflation rate has been below 3% recently, but a 3% rate is unusually low by historical standards. His social security payments will increase with inflation, but the interest on his investment portfolio will not.

What advice do you have for Mr. Road? Can he safely spend all the interest from his investment portfolio? How much could he withdraw at year-end from that portfolio if he wants to keep its real value intact?

Suppose Mr. Road will live for 20 more years and is willing to use up all of his investment portfolio over that period. He also wants his monthly spending to increase along with inflation over that period. In other words, he wants his monthly spending to stay the same in real terms. How much can he afford to spend per month?

Assume that the investment portfolio continues to yield a 9% rate of return and that the inflation rate will be 4%.

Supplements

In addition to the overall refinement and improvement of the text material, considerable effort was put into developing an exceptional supplement package to provide students and instructors with an abundance of teaching and learning resources.

For the Instructor

Instructor's CD-ROM

ISBN 13: 9780073363455
ISBN 10: 0073363456

This CD contains the following ancillaries, as described below: Instructor's Manual, Test Bank, Computerized Test Bank, Solutions Manual, and PowerPoint presentations. We have compiled them in electronic format for easier access and convenience. Print copies are available through your McGraw-Hill/Irwin representative.

Instructor's Manual

Updated and enhanced by Sheen Liu, Washington State University–Vancouver, this supplement includes a descriptive preface containing alternative course formats and case teaching methods, a chapter overview and outline, key terms and concepts, a description of the PowerPoint slides, video teaching notes, related Web links, and pedagogical ideas.

PowerPoint Presentation System

Prepared by Matt Will, University of Indianapolis, these visually stimulating slides have been fully updated with colorful graphs, charts, and lists. The slides can be edited or manipulated to fit the needs of a particular course.

Test Bank

Ted Fu, Stanford University, has revised and added new questions and problems. Over 2,000 true/false, multiple-choice, and discussion questions/problems are available to the instructor at varying levels of difficulty and comprehension. Complete answers are provided for all test questions and problems.

Computerized Test Bank Online

A comprehensive bank of test questions is provided within a computerized test bank powered by McGraw-Hill's flexible electronic testing program EZ Test Online (**www.eztestonline.com**). EZ Test Online allows you to create tests or quizzes in this easy-to-use program!

Instructors can select questions from multiple McGraw-Hill test banks or create their own and then can either print the test for paper distribution or give it online. This user-friendly program allows instructors to sort questions by format, edit existing questions or add new ones, and scramble questions for multiple versions of the same test. You can export your tests for use in WebCT, Blackboard, PageOut, and Apple's iQuiz. Sharing tests with colleagues, adjuncts, TAs is easy! Instant scoring and feedback are provided, and EZ Test's grade book is designed to easily export to your grade book.

Solutions Manual

ISBN 13: 9780077265960
ISBN 10: 0077265963

Peter Crabb, Northwest Nazarene University, has prepared this resource containing solutions to all the end-of-chapter problems. This can also be made available to your students or packaged with the text at a discount. Please contact your McGraw-Hill/Irwin representative for more details.

DVD

ISBN 13: 9780073363653
ISBN 10: 0073363650

Our professionally produced videos showcase key topics in corporate finance, such as time value of money and capital budgeting.

For the Student

Study Guide

ISBN 13: 9780077291204
ISBN 10: 0077291204

Prepared by Matt Will, University of Indianapolis, this helpful asset contains a thorough list of activities for the student, including an introduction to the chapter, sources of business information, key concepts and terms, sample problems with solutions, integrated PowerPoint slides, and related Web links.

Online Support

Online Learning Center

Find a wealth of information online! At this book Web site, instructors have access to teaching supports such as electronic files of the ancillary materials and solutions templates for the Excel problems. Students have access to study materials created specifically for this text as well as the Excel spreadsheets, which have been denoted by an icon in the text. A link to the following support material, as described below, is also included.

Standard & Poor's Version of Market Insight

McGraw-Hill/Irwin has partnered exclusively with Standard & Poor's to bring you the educational version of Market Insight. This rich online resource provides 6 years of financial data for 1,000 companies in the renowned COMPUSTAT® database. S&P problems can be found at the end of relevant chapters of the text.

Packaging Options

Please contact your McGraw-Hill/Irwin representative for more information on the exciting packaging options available to you for your classroom use.

 **McGraw-Hill's Homework Manager®**

Are you looking for a way to spend less time grading and to have more flexibility with the problems you assign as homework and tests? McGraw-Hill's Homework Manager is an exciting new package option developed for this text! McGraw-Hill's Homework Manager is a Web-based tool for instructors and students for delivering, answering, and grading end-of-chapter problems and tests and providing a limitless supply of self-graded practice for students.

The book's end-of-chapter Quiz, Practice, and Challenge Problems are loaded into Homework Manager, and instructors can choose to assign the problems exactly as stated in the book or assign algorithmic versions of them so that each student has a unique set of variables for the problems. You create the assignments and control parameters such as whether you want your students to receive hints and whether an assignment is a graded one or practice. The test bank is also available in Homework Manager®, giving you the ability to use those questions for online tests. Both the problems and the tests are automatically graded and the results are stored in a private grade book, which

is created when you set up your class. Detailed results let you see at a glance how each student does on an assignment or an individual problem—you can even see how many tries it took the student to solve it. If you order this special package, students will receive a Homework Manager User's Guide and an access code packaged with their text.

Homework Manager Plus™

An enhanced version of McGraw-Hill's Homework Manager is available through the Homework Manager Plus package option. If you order the text packaged with Homework Manager Plus, your students will receive Homework Manager as described above, as well as an integrated online text. When students are in Homework Manager and need more help to solve a problem, a link will take them to the section of the text online that explains the concept they are struggling with. All of McGraw-Hill's media assets, such as videos and additional online quizzing, are also integrated at the appropriate places of the online text to provide students with a full learning experience. If you order this special package, students will receive

the Homework Manager Plus card packaged with their text, which gives them access to all of these products, as well as an online Homework Manager User's Guide.

McGraw-Hill's Homework Manager is powered by Brownstone.

BusinessWeek Subscription

Your students can subscribe to *Business-Week* for a special rate of $8.25 in addition to the price of the text. Students will receive a pass-code card shrink-wrapped with their new text that will refer them to a registration site to receive their subscription. Subscriptions are available in print copy or digital format.

Financial Times Subscription

Your students can subscribe to the *Financial Times* for 15 weeks at a specially priced rate of $10 in addition to the price of the text by ordering this special package. Students will receive a subscription card shrink-wrapped with their new text to fill in and send to the *Financial Times* to start receiving their subscription. Instructors, once you order, make sure you contact your sales representative to receive a complimentary 1-year subscription.

Preface

This book is about corporate finance. It focuses on how companies invest in real assets and how they raise the money to pay for these investments. It also provides a broad introduction to the financial landscape, discussing, for example, the major players in financial markets, the role of financial institutions in the economy, and how securities are traded and valued by investors. The book offers a framework for systematically thinking about most of the important financial problems that both firms and individuals are likely to confront.

Financial management is important, interesting, and challenging. It is *important* because today's capital investment decisions may determine the businesses that the firm is in 10, 20, or more years ahead. Also, a firm's success or failure depends in large part on its ability to find the capital that it needs.

Finance is *interesting* for several reasons. Financial decisions often involve huge sums of money. Large investment projects or acquisitions may involve billions of dollars. Also, the financial community is international and fast-moving, with colorful heroes and a sprinkling of unpleasant villains.

Finance is *challenging*. Financial decisions are rarely cut and dried, and the financial markets in which companies operate are changing rapidly. Good managers can cope with routine problems, but only the best managers can respond to change. To handle new problems, you need more than rules of thumb; you need to understand why companies and financial markets behave as they do and when common practice may not be best practice. Once you have a consistent framework for making financial decisions, complex problems become more manageable.

This book provides that framework. It is not an encyclopedia of finance. It focuses instead on setting out the basic *principles* of financial management and applying them to the main decisions faced by the financial manager. It explains why the firm's owners would like the manager to increase firm value and shows how managers choose between investments that may pay off at different points of time or have different degrees of risk. It also describes the main features of financial markets and discusses why companies may prefer a particular source of finance.

Some texts shy away from modern finance, sticking instead with more traditional, procedural, or institutional approaches. These are supposed to be easier or more practical. We disagree emphatically. The concepts of modern finance, properly explained, make the subject simpler, not more difficult. They are also more practical. The tools of financial management are easier to grasp and use effectively when presented in a consistent conceptual framework. Modern finance provides that framework.

Modern financial management is not "rocket science." It is a set of ideas that can be made clear by words, graphs, and numerical examples. The ideas provide the "why" behind the tools that good financial managers use to make investment and financing decisions.

We wrote this book to make financial management clear, useful, interesting, and fun for the beginning student. We set out to show that modern finance and good financial practice go together, even for the financial novice.

Fundamentals and Principles of Corporate Finance

This book is derived in part from its sister text *Principles of Corporate Finance*. The spirit of the two books is similar. Both apply modern finance to give students a working ability to make financial decisions. However, there are also substantial differences between the two books.

First, we provide much more detailed discussion of the principles and mechanics of the time value of money. This material underlies almost all of this text, and we spend a lengthy chapter providing extensive practice with this key concept.

Second, we use numerical examples in this text to a greater degree than in *Principles*. Each chapter presents several detailed numerical examples to help the reader become familiar and comfortable with the material.

Third, we have streamlined the treatment of most topics. Whereas *Principles* has 35 chapters, *Fundamentals* has only 25. The relative brevity of *Fundamentals* necessitates a broader-brush coverage of some topics, but we feel that this is an advantage for a beginning audience.

Fourth, we assume little in the way of background knowledge. While most users will have had an introductory accounting course, we review the concepts of accounting that are important to the financial manager in Chapter 3.

Principles is known for its relaxed and informal writing style, and we continue this tradition in *Fundamentals*. In addition, we use as little mathematical notation as possible. Even when we present an equation, we usually write it in words rather than symbols. This approach has two advantages. It is less intimidating, and it focuses attention on the underlying concept rather than the formula.

Organizational Design
Fundamentals is organized in eight parts.

Part 1 (Introduction)   provides essential background material. In the first chapter we discuss how businesses are organized, the role of the financial manager, and the financial markets in which the manager operates. We explain how shareholders want managers to take actions that increase the value of their investment, and we describe some of the mechanisms that help to align the interests of managers and shareholders. Of course, the task of increasing shareholder value does not justify corrupt and unscrupulous behavior. We therefore discuss some of the ethical issues that confront managers.

Chapter 2 surveys and sets out the functions of financial markets and institutions. It shows how financial managers use these markets and institutions, and it explains how markets provide useful signals to managers concerning the viability of potential investment projects.

A large corporation is a team effort, and so the firm produces financial statements to help the players monitor its progress. Chapter 3 provides a brief overview of these financial statements and introduces two key distinctions—between market and book values and between cash flows and profits. This chapter also discusses some of the shortcomings in accounting practice that became apparent in the scandals of 2001–2002. The chapter concludes with a summary of federal taxes.

Chapter 4 provides an overview of financial statement analysis. In contrast to most introductions to this topic, our discussion is motivated by considerations of valuation and the insight that financial ratios can provide about how management has added to the firm's value.

Part 2 (Value)   is concerned with valuation. In Chapter 5 we introduce the concept of the time value of money, and, since most readers will be more familiar with their own financial affairs than with the big leagues of finance, we motivate our discussion by looking first at some personal financial decisions. We show how to value long-lived streams of cash flows and work through the valuation of perpetuities and annuities. Chapter 5 also contains a short concluding section on inflation and the distinction between real and nominal returns.

Chapters 6 and 7 introduce the basic features of bonds and stocks and give students a chance to apply the ideas of Chapter 5 to the valuation of these securities. We show how to find the value of a bond given its yield, and we show how prices of bonds fluctuate as interest rates change. We look at what determines stock prices and how stock valuation formulas can be used to infer the return that investors expect. Finally, we see how investment opportunities are reflected in the stock price and why analysts focus on the price-earnings multiple. Chapter 7 also introduces the concept of market efficiency. This concept is crucial to interpreting a stock's valuation; it also provides a framework for the later treatment of the issues that arise when firms issue securities or make decisions concerning dividends or capital structure.

The remaining chapters of Part 2 are concerned with the company's investment decision. In Chapter 8 we introduce the concept of net present value and show how to calculate the NPV of a simple investment project. We also look at other measures of an investment's attractiveness—its internal rate of return, payback period, and profitability index. We then turn to more complex investment proposals, including choices between alternative projects, machine replacement decisions, and decisions of when to invest. Finally, we show how the profitability index can be used to choose between investment projects when capital is scarce.

The first step in any NPV calculation is to decide what to discount. Therefore, in Chapter 9 we work through a realistic example of a capital budgeting analysis, showing how the manager needs to recognize the investment in working capital and how taxes and depreciation affect cash flows.

We start Chapter 10 by looking at how companies organize the investment process and ensure everyone works toward a common goal. We then go on to look at various techniques to help managers identify the key assumptions in their estimates, such as sensitivity analysis, scenario analysis, and break-even analysis. We also show how managers can assess projects using NPV rather than accounting break-even analysis. We conclude the chapter by describing how managers try to build future flexibility into projects so that they can capitalize on good luck and mitigate the consequences of bad luck.

Part 3 (Risk) is concerned with the cost of capital. Chapter 11 starts with a historical survey of returns on bonds and stocks and goes on to distinguish between the unique risk and market risk of individual stocks. Chapter 12 shows how to measure market risk and discusses the relationship between risk and expected return. Chapter 13 introduces the weighted-average cost of capital and provides a practical illustration of how to estimate it.

Part 4 (Financing) begins our discussion of the financing decision. Chapter 14 provides an overview of the securities that firms issue and their relative importance as sources of finance. In Chapter 15 we look at how firms issue securities, and we follow a firm from its first need for venture capital, through its initial public offering, to its continuing need to raise debt or equity.

Part 5 (Debt and Payout Policy) focuses on the two classic long-term financing decisions. In Chapter 16 we ask how much the firm should borrow and we summarize bankruptcy procedures that occur when firms can't pay their debts. In Chapter 17 we study how firms should set dividend and payout policy. In each case we start with Modigliani and Miller's (MM's) observation that in well-functioning markets the decision should not matter, but we use this observation to help the reader understand why financial managers in practice *do* pay attention to these decisions.

Part 6 (Financial Analysis and Planning) starts with long-term financial planning in Chapter 18, where we look at how the financial manager considers the combined effects of investment and financing decisions on the firm as a whole. We also show how measures of internal and sustainable growth help managers check that the firm's planned growth is consistent with its financing plans. Chapter 19 is an introduction to short-term financial planning. It shows how managers ensure that the firm will have enough cash to pay its bills over the coming year, and describes the principal sources of short-term borrowing. Chapter 20 addresses working capital management. It describes the basic steps of credit management, the principles of inventory management, and how firms handle payments efficiently and put cash to work as quickly as possible.

Part 7 (Special Topics) covers several important but somewhat more advanced topics—mergers (Chapter 21), international financial management (Chapter 22), options (Chapter 23), and risk management (Chapter 24). Some of these topics are touched on in earlier chapters. For example, we introduce the idea of options in Chapter 10, when we show how companies build flexibility into capital projects. However, Chapter 23 generalizes this material, explains at an elementary level how options are valued, and provides some examples of why the financial manager needs to be concerned about options. International finance is also not confined to Chapter 22. As one might expect from a book that is written by an international group of authors, examples from different countries and financial systems are scattered throughout the book. However, Chapter 22 tackles the specific problems that arise when a corporation is confronted by different currencies.

Part 8 (Conclusion) contains a concluding chapter (Chapter 25), in which we review the most important ideas covered in the text. We also introduce some interesting questions that either were unanswered in the text or are still puzzles to the finance profession. Thus the last chapter is an introduction to future finance courses as well as a conclusion to this one.

Routes through the Book

There are about as many effective ways to organize a course in corporate finance as there are teachers. For this reason, we have ensured that the text is modular, so that topics can be introduced in different sequences.

We like to discuss the principles of valuation before plunging into financial planning. Nevertheless, we recognize that many instructors will prefer to move directly from Chapter 4 (Measuring Corporate Performance) to Chapter 18 (Long-Term Financial Planning) in order to provide a gentler transition from the typical prerequisite accounting course. We have made sure that Part 6 (Financial Analysis and Planning) can easily follow Part 1.

Similarly, we like to discuss working capital after the student is familiar with the basic principles of valuation and financing, but we recognize that here also many instructors prefer to reverse our order. There should be no difficulty in taking Chapter 20 out of order.

When we discuss project valuation in Part 2, we stress that the opportunity cost of capital depends on project risk. But we do not discuss how to measure risk or how return and risk are linked until Part 3. This ordering can easily be modified. For example, the chapters on risk and return can be introduced before, after, or midway through the material on project valuation.

Changes in the Sixth Edition

The most obvious changes in this new edition of *Fundamentals of Corporate Finance* are the continuing enhancement and use of pedagogical tools such as Internet resources, Excel spreadsheets, and end-of-chapter integrative cases. We have updated and expanded our Internet Insider boxes, which provide students with opportunities to explore the resources available on the Web. We also provide links to suggested Web sites online at **www.mhhe.com/bmm6e** so addresses may be kept up to date. In addition, we provide many end-of-chapter student exercises using the Web-based educational version of Standard & Poor's Market Insight. This resource provides a wide variety of financial statement data, stock market return history, and analyst coverage of hundreds of stocks, making it well suited for extended student projects on company and industry analysis.

We have also integrated more spreadsheets into the chapter material. These spreadsheets require only a basic knowledge of Excel, but they illustrate the powerful ways in which spreadsheet modeling can facilitate financial analysis. Every spreadsheet in the text is now available on the text Web site at **www.mhhe.com/bmm6e.** Where appropriate, each chapter includes a comprehensive problem that is designed to be solved using a spreadsheet.

Some of the changes in coverage reflect topics that have been highlighted by recent events. For example, the scandals of 2001–2002 and the subsequent options-backdating scandal increased interest in the issues of governance and control, while the dot-com boom and bust focused attention on behavioral finance. So you will find more emphasis in this edition on governance and behavioral finance. In fact, we introduce governance issues right up front in Chapters 1 and 2. Other topics that have received increasing emphasis in recent editions include company valuation, real options, and the role of financial institutions and markets.

In revising each chapter we have sought to improve readability and update coverage. Chapters 1 and 2 have been largely rewritten to improve interest and provide a better overview of the financial landscape. We use case histories of real firms such as FedEx and Apple to show how financial markets help infant firms grow into healthy adults. Along the way, we take a fresh look at agency and reputation issues in the context of recent scandals, and we present a nontechnical introduction to the idea of the opportunity cost of capital that provides context for the later discussion of present value.

The survey of financial institutions in Chapter 2 has been expanded to reflect the increasing importance of hedge funds and exchange traded funds.

Chapter 3 (Accounting and Finance) includes updated discussions of reporting issues informed by the accounting failures and reforms of the last few years.

Chapter 4 (Measuring Corporate Performance) was previously Chapter 17 of the text. In response to user comments, we have moved this chapter to Part 1 to accompany the previous chapter on accounting and finance. We also have extensively rewritten Chapter 4 with a sharper focus on how financial data can be used to measure contributions to firm value.

Chapters 5 to 7 have been updated and rearranged to improve logical flow. Chapter 7 (Valuing Stocks) now starts with a review of stock markets and trading procedures and motivates the following treatment of stock valuation with a small case study of an investor considering whether to purchase a particular stock, FedEx. We begin this discussion with valuation by comparables and the distinction between price and intrinsic value.

The discussion of project analysis in Chapters 8 to 10 has been streamlined and reorganized. The discussion of project cash flow has been reworked to more carefully show how each of its components can be estimated.

The overview of financing methods in Part 4 includes material on developments in the IPO market.

Part 5 on debt and payout policy also has been updated. The discussions of stock repurchases and dividend policy in particular have been rewritten to reflect recent trends and research.

Material on financial planning in Part 6 has been reorganized and updated. As noted, financial statement analysis has been moved to Part 1. In Chapter 19 (Short-Term Financial Planning), we have rewritten and updated the section on bank lending. In Chapter 20 (Working Capital Management), we have expanded the discussion of inventory management and updated the treatment of credit scoring as well as of cash management, which has changed considerably as the technology of cash transfers has advanced. We also discuss briefly the credit crunch and the value of liquidity.

Finally, Part 7, on special topics, also has been revised. For example, Chapter 21 (Mergers) has been fully reorganized, and now begins with an overview of why mergers and other forms of reorganization may make sense. Only then do we progress to the market for corporate control. The other chapters in Part 7 have been updated with new examples and data.

Assurance of Learning

Many educational institutions today are focused on the notion of assurance of learning, an important element of some accreditation standards. *Fundamentals of Corporate Finance* is designed to support your assurance-of-learning initiatives with a simple, yet powerful, solution.

In this edition we have numbered the Learning Objectives (LOs) and refer to them in the chapter summaries and end-of-chapter problems to help you see where the presented material ties into the stated objectives.

Each test bank question for *Fundamentals of Corporate Finance* maps to a specific chapter learning objective listed in the text. You can use the test bank software to easily query for learning objectives that directly relate to the learning objectives for your course. You can then use the reporting features of the software to aggregate student results in similar fashion, making the collection and presentation of assurance-of-learning data simple and easy.

OVERVIEW

CHAPTER **1**

Goals and Governance of the Firm

LEARNING OBJECTIVES

After studying this chapter, you should be able to:

1. Give examples of the investment and financing decisions that financial managers make.

2. Distinguish between real and financial assets.

3. Cite some of the advantages and disadvantages of organizing a business as a corporation.

4. Describe the responsibilities of the CFO, treasurer, and controller.

5. Explain why maximizing market value is the logical financial goal of the corporation.

6. Explain why value maximization is usually consistent with ethical behavior.

7. Explain how corporations mitigate conflicts and encourage cooperative behavior.

Related Web sites for this chapter can be found at www.mhhe.com/bmm6e.

A meeting of a corporation's directors
© Susan Moore

Corporate finance boils down to the investment and financing decisions made by corporations. Financial managers in corporations work with other managers to identify investment opportunities, to analyze and value the opportunities, and to decide whether and how much to invest. Financial managers also have to raise the money to finance the corporation's investments. Therefore we start this chapter with examples of recent investment and financing decisions by major U.S. and foreign corporations. We also review what a corporation is and describe the special roles of a corporation's top financial managers, including the chief financial officer (CFO), treasurer, and controller. Later in the chapter we will review several possible career paths in finance.

Next we turn to the financial goals of the corporation. Should it maximize value, or is it enough to survive and avoid bankruptcy? Should it strive to be a good corporate citizen? If the firm maximizes value for its stockholders, can it also be a good corporate citizen? We also consider the conflicts of interest that arise in large corporations and review the mechanisms that align the interests of the firm's managers with the interests of stockholders. Finally, we look ahead to the rest of this book and look back to some entertaining snippets of financial history.

1.1 Investment and Financing Decisions

Fred Smith is best known today as the founder of FedEx. But in 1965 he was still a sophomore at Yale, where he noted in an economics term paper that delivery systems were not keeping up with increasing needs for speed and dependability in a dawning computer age.[1] After leaving the Marine Corps in 1969, he joined his stepfather at Arkansas Aviation Sales, a struggling equipment and maintenance firm for air carriers, and shortly thereafter bought control of the company. He observed firsthand the difficulties of shipping spare parts on short notice. He saw the need for an integrated air and ground delivery system with a central hub that could connect a large number of points more efficiently than a point-to-point delivery system. In 1971, at the age of 27, Smith founded Federal Express.

Like many start-up firms, Federal Express flirted again and again with failure. Smith and his family had an inheritance of a few million dollars, but this was far from enough. The young company needed to purchase and retrofit a small fleet of aging Dassault Falcon jets, build a central-hub facility, and hire and train pilots, delivery, and office staff. The initial source of capital was short-term bank loans. Because of the company's shaky financial position, the bank demanded that the planes be used as collateral and that Smith personally guarantee the loan with his own money.

In April 1973 the company went live with a fleet of 14 jets operating out of its Memphis hub, servicing 25 U.S. cities. By then, the company had spent $25 million and was effectively flat broke, without enough funds to pay for its weekly delivery of jet fuel. In desperation, it managed to acquire a bank loan for $23.7 million. This loan had to be backed by a guarantee from General Dynamics, which in return acquired an option to buy the company (and which today surely must regret its failure to exercise that option).

In November of that year, the company finally achieved some financial stability when it raised $24.5 million from venture capitalists, investment firms that provide funds and often advice to young companies in return for a partial ownership share. Eventually, venture capitalists invested about $90 million in Federal Express. The funds were necessary, because the company continued to lose money until 1975.

After air cargo deregulation in 1977 allowed private firms to compete with the Postal Service in package delivery, Federal Express expanded its operations, which in turn required larger aircraft. It acquired seven Boeing 727s, each with about seven times the capacity of the Falcon jets. By 1978, the company was growing rapidly. But that growth called for additional investments in planes and facilities. Federal Express raised about $19 million by selling shares of stock to the general public in its *initial public offering (IPO)*. This was the first time it allowed the general public to buy shares in the firm. The new stockholders became part-owners of the company in proportion to the number of shares they purchased, and the company used the funds raised to pay for its investment outlays.

From this point on, success followed success, and the company invested heavily to expand its air fleet as well as its supporting infrastructure. It introduced the first PC-based automated shipping system in 1984 and its bar-coded tracking system in 1986. In 1994, it launched its fedex.com Web site for online package tracking. It opened several new hubs across the United States as well as in Canada, France, the Philippines, and China. In 2007 FedEx (as the company was renamed in 2000) was the world's largest airline measured by number of planes. FedEx also invested in other companies, capped by the acquisition of Kinko's for $2.4 billion in 2004. By the end of 2007, FedEx had about 280,000 employees, annual revenue of $36 billion, and a stock market value of $27 billion. Its name had become a verb—to "FedEx a package" was to ship it overnight.

---

[1] Legend has it that Smith received a grade of C on this paper. In fact, he doesn't remember the grade.

Even in retrospect, FedEx's success was hardly a sure thing. Fred Smith's idea was inspired, but its implementation was complex and difficult. It took time and considerable effort to build a customer base.

Beyond the challenges posed by its product innovation, the firm also needed to be *good at finance.* It got a long head start over potential competitors, but a series of bad financial decisions would have sunk the company.

FedEx had to make good *investment decisions.* In the beginning, these decisions were constrained. For example, used Falcon jets were the only option, given the young company's precarious financial position. Initially also, it could service only a short list of the major cities. As the company grew, its investment decisions became more complex. Which type of planes should it buy? When should it expand coverage to Europe and Asia? How many operations hubs should it build? What computer and tracking systems were necessary to keep up with increasingly complicated logistics as package volume and geographic coverage expanded? Which companies should it acquire as it expanded its range of services?

FedEx also needed to make good *financing decisions.* For example, how should it raise the money it needed for investment? In the beginning, these choices were also constrained. Available sources of financing were limited: family money and bank loans. As the company grew, its range of choices expanded. Eventually it was able to attract funding from venture capitalists, but this raised new questions. How much cash did the firm need to raise from the venture capitalists? How big a share in the firm would the venture capitalists require in return? The initial stock offering raised similar questions. How many shares should the company try to sell? At what price? As the company grew, it periodically raised more funds by selling additional stock to the public, and it borrowed money not only through bank loans but by selling publicly traded bonds to investors. At each point, it needed to decide on the proper form and terms of financing as well as the amounts to be raised.

The particulars of any company's history may differ, but, like FedEx, all successful companies must make good investment and financing decisions. Also, as with FedEx, those decisions range from prosaic and obvious to difficult, complicated, and strategically crucial.

Table 1–1 lists nine corporations. Seven are U.S. corporations. Three are foreign: BP's headquarters are in London, LVMH's in Paris,[2] and Toyota's in Japan. We have chosen very large public corporations that you are probably already familiar with. You probably have traveled on a Boeing jet, shopped at Wal-Mart, or used a Bank of America ATM, for example.

Table 1–1 gives for each company an example of a recent investment and financing decision. Take a look at the decisions now. We think you will agree that they appear sensible or, at least, that there is nothing obviously wrong with them. But if you are new to finance, it will be difficult to think about why these companies made these decisions and not others.

Making good investment and financing decisions is the chief task of the financial manager. Let's consider each class of decisions in more detail.

The Investment (Capital Budgeting) Decision

capital budgeting decision or investment decision
Decision to invest in tangible or intangible assets.

The **investment decision** starts with the identification of investment opportunities, often referred to as *capital investment projects.* The financial manager has to help the firm identify promising projects and decide how much to invest in each project. The investment decision is also called the **capital budgeting decision,** because most firms prepare an annual budget listing authorized capital investments.

In the distant past, "capital investments" included only investments in tangible assets, such as investment in Toyota's new automobile plants or Union Pacific's new

---

[2] LVMH (Moet Hennessy Louis Vuitton) markets perfumes and cosmetics, wines and spirits, watches and other fashion and luxury goods.

TABLE 1-1 Examples of recent investment and financing decisions by major public corporations

Company (2006 revenue in billions)	Recent Investment (Capital Budgeting) Decision	Recent Financing Decision
Boeing ($61.5)	Began production of its 787 Dreamliner aircraft, at a forecast cost of more than $7 billion.	Increased its dividend per share by 17%.
BP (£138, or about $274)	Committed $500 million to partnership with University of California–Berkeley to develop new sources of energy.	Returned $15 billion of cash to its stockholders by buying back their shares.
Toyota (¥23,836, or about $202)	Opened new production plants in Thailand, China, and Russia.	Increased short-term borrowing by $3 billion in 2007, much of it through debt issues in the U.S.
Citigroup ($146)	Acquired ABN AMRO Mortgage Group, a national originator and servicer of residential mortgage loans, for $3 billion.	In November 2007, sold a 4.9% stake in the firm to the Abu Dhabi Investment Authority for $7.5 billion.
Pfizer ($48.3)	Spent $7.6 billion in 2006 on research and development of new drugs.	Financed R&D expenditures with reinvested cash flow generated by sales of pharmaceutical products.
Wal-Mart ($348)	In 2007 opened more than 250 new supercenters in the U.S. and 200 new units internationally.	Issued $750 million of long-term debt, maturing in 2027 and paying interest at 5.875% per year.
Union Pacific ($15.6)	Acquired about 250 new locomotives in 2006.	Arranged bank credit lines that will allow it to borrow up to $2 billion if needed for its operations.
Bank of America ($117)	Acquired LaSalle Bank for $21 billion in 2007.	Financed the acquisition largely through borrowing.
LVMH (€15.3, or about $22.3)	Acquired the Belvedere Winery brand name in the U.S. market.	Issued a 7-year bond in 2005, raising 600 million euros.

locomotives. But you can see from Table 1–1 that the scope of the investment decision is now much broader. It includes investment in intangible assets, for example, investment in research and development (R&D), advertising and marketing of new products, or acquisition of patents and trademarks. Pfizer and other major pharmaceutical companies invest billions every year on R&D for new drugs, for example. Gillette (now part of Procter & Gamble) reportedly invested about $200 million to advertise the launch of its Fusion razor. In this case the intangible asset was brand recognition and acceptance.

The world of business can be intensely competitive, and corporations survive and prosper only if they can keep launching new products or services. In some cases the costs and risks of doing so are amazingly large. Boeing invested more than $7 billion[3] to design, test, build, and sell the new 787 Dreamliner series of aircraft. At the same time its European archrival Airbus invested more than $12 billion in the new A380 superjumbo aircraft. Each firm "bet the company" on the success of these investments.

Not all capital investments succeed. The Iridium communications satellite system, which offered its users instant telephone connections worldwide, soaked up $5 billion in investment before it started operations in 1998. It needed 400,000 subscribers to break even but attracted only a small fraction of that target number. Iridium defaulted on its debt and filed for bankruptcy in 1999. The Iridium system was sold a year later for just $25 million.[4]

---

[3] Some estimates of the total investment, including investment by suppliers and support from state, local, and national governments, run as high as $13 billion.

[4] There is a silver lining in the Iridium story, however. The private investors who bought the system have turned a profit, concentrating on aviation, maritime, and defense markets rather than retail customers. By the third quarter of 2007, revenues were running at an annual rate of almost $300 million.

The investment in Iridium, though it looks stupid with hindsight, may have been rational, given what was known in the early 1990s when the go-ahead decision was made. It may have been a good decision thwarted by bad luck. There are no free guarantees in finance. But you can tilt the odds in your favor if you learn the tools of investment analysis and apply them intelligently. We will cover these tools in detail later in this book.

Today's capital investments generate future returns. Often the returns come in the distant future. Boeing committed $7 billion to the 787 series because it believed that sales of 787s will generate cash returns for 30 years or more after the planes first enter commercial service. Those cash returns must recover the $7 billion investment and provide at least an adequate profit on that investment. The longer Boeing must wait for cash to flow back, the greater its required profit. Thus the financial manager must pay attention to the timing of project returns, not just their cumulative amount. In addition, these returns are rarely certain. A new project could be a smashing success or a dismal failure, like Iridium.

The financial manager needs a way of placing a *value* on the uncertain future cash inflows generated by capital investment projects. This value should account for the amounts, timing, and risk of the future cash flows. **If a project's value is greater than its required investment, then the project is attractive financially. An effective financial manager guides his or her firm to invest in projects that add more value than the investment required. In other words, the financial manager helps the firm to invest in projects that are worth more than they cost.**

But do not think of financial managers making major investment decisions in solitary confinement. Financial managers may work as part of a team of engineers and managers from manufacturing, marketing, and other business functions. Often the final investment decision is made by senior nonfinancial management.

Also, do not think of the financial manager as making billion-dollar investments on a daily basis. Most investment decisions are smaller and simpler, such as the purchase of a truck, machine tool, or computer system. But the objective is still to add value, that is, to find and make investments that are worth more than they cost. Most firms make thousands of small investment decisions every year. The cumulative value added by the small decisions can be just as large as the value added by occasional big decisions like those shown in Table 1–1.

The Financing Decision

financing decision
The form and amount of financing of a firm's investments.

The financial manager's second main responsibility is to raise the money that the firm needs for its investments and operations. This is the **financing decision.** When a company needs to raise money, it can invite investors to put up cash in exchange for a share of future profits, or it can promise to pay back the investors' cash plus a fixed rate of interest. In the first case, the investors receive shares of stock and become shareholders, part-owners of the corporation. The investors in this case are referred to as *equity investors,* who contribute *equity financing.* In the second case, the investors are lenders, that is, *debt investors,* who one day must be repaid. The choice between debt and equity financing is often called the **capital structure** decision. Here "capital" refers to the firm's sources of long-term financing. A firm that is seeking to raise long-term financing is said to be "raising capital."

capital structure
The mix of long-term debt and equity financing.

The financing choices available to large corporations seem almost endless. Suppose the firm decides to borrow. Should it issue debt to investors, or should it borrow from a bank? Should it borrow for 1 year or 20 years? If it borrows for 20 years, should it reserve the right to pay off the debt early if interest rates fall? Should it borrow in Paris, receiving and promising to repay euros, or should it borrow dollars in New York? (As Table 1–1 shows, LVMH borrowed euros, but it could have borrowed dollars instead.) Should it offer specific assets as collateral to back its borrowing? (For example, FedEx pledged its aircraft as collateral.) We will look at these and other choices in later chapters.

The decision to take out a 20-year loan or to issue new shares of stock obviously has long-term consequences. But the financial manager is also involved in many important short-term decisions. For example, he or she has to make sure that there is enough cash on hand to pay next week's bills and that any spare cash is put to work to earn interest. These are *short-term financing decisions* (how to raise cash to meet a short-term need) and *short-term investment decisions* (how to invest spare cash for brief periods).

The financial manager is involved in many other day-to-day activities that are essential to the smooth operation of the firm but not dramatic enough to show up in Table 1–1. For example, if the firm sells goods or services on credit, the firm has to make sure that its customers pay their bills on time. Corporations that operate internationally must constantly transfer cash from one currency to another. Manufacturing companies must decide how much to invest in inventories of raw materials and finished goods.

Businesses are inherently risky, so the financial manager has to identify risks and make sure they are managed properly. For example, the manager will want to ensure that the firm's operations will not be severely damaged by a rise in oil prices or a fall in the dollar. (Note in Table 1–1 that Toyota has increased short-term debt issues in U.S. dollars rather than in its home currency. This makes sense because of Toyota's exports to the United States. The exports generate revenues in U.S. dollars.) In later chapters we will look at how managers assess risk and at some of the ways that firms can be protected from nasty surprises.

Self-Test 1.1

Are the following capital budgeting or financing decisions? (*Hint:* In one case the answer is "both.")

a. Intel decides to spend $1 billion to develop a new microprocessor.
b. Volkswagen borrows 350 million euros (€350 million) from Deutsche Bank.
c. BP constructs a pipeline to bring natural gas onshore from a production platform in the Gulf of Mexico.
d. Budweiser spends €200 million to launch a new brand of beer in European markets.
e. Pfizer issues new shares to buy a small biotech company.

Financing and investment decisions (both long- and short-term) are of course interconnected. The amount of investment determines the amount of financing that has to be raised, and the investors who contribute financing today expect a return on that investment in the future. Thus, the investments that the firm makes today have to generate future returns for payout to investors.

Figure 1–1 traces how money flows from investors to the firm and back to investors again. The flow starts when cash is raised from investors (arrow 1 in the figure). The cash is used to pay for the real assets (investment projects) needed for the firm's operations (arrow 2). Later, if the firm does well, its operations generate cash for the firm (arrow 3). That cash is either reinvested (arrow 4a) or returned to the investors who furnished the money in the first place (arrow 4b). Of course, the choice between

FIGURE 1–1 Flow of cash between investors and the firm's operations. Key: (1) Cash raised by selling financial assets to investors; (2) cash invested in the firm's operations; (3) cash generated by the firm's operations; (4a) cash reinvested; (4b) cash returned to investors.

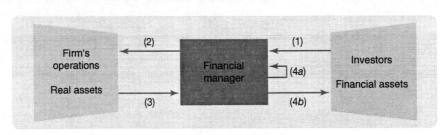

arrows 4*a* and 4*b* is constrained by the promises made when cash was raised at arrow 1. For example, if the firm borrows money from a bank at arrow 1, it must repay this money plus interest at arrow 4*b*.

You can see examples of arrows 4*a* and 4*b* in Table 1–1. Pfizer finances its drug research and testing by reinvesting earnings (arrow 4*a*). BP has decided to return cash to shareholders by buying back its stock (arrow 4*b*). In 2007, a year of very high energy prices, repurchases by BP totalled $7.5 billion.

Notice in Figure 1–1 how the financial manager stands between the firm and outside investors. On the one hand, the financial manager helps manage the firm's operations, particularly by helping to make good investment decisions. On the other, the financial manager deals with investors—not just with shareholders but also with banks and other financial institutions and with financial markets, such as the New York Stock Exchange. We will say more about financial markets and institutions in the next chapter.

real assets
Assets used to produce goods and services.

financial assets
Financial claims to the income generated by the firm's real assets.

Figure 1–1 also distinguishes **real assets** from **financial assets.** Real assets are used to produce the firm's products and services. They include tangible assets such as machinery, factories, and offices and intangible assets such as technical knowledge, trademarks, and patents. The firm finances its investments in real assets by issuing financial assets to investors. A share of stock is a financial asset, which has value as a claim on the firm's real assets and the income that those assets will produce. A bank loan is a financial asset also. It gives the bank the right to get its money back plus interest. If the firm's operations can't generate enough income to pay what the bank is owed, the bank can force the firm into bankruptcy and stake a claim on its real assets.

Shares of stock and other financial assets that can be purchased and traded by investors are called *securities*.

Self-Test 1.2

Which of the following are financial assets, and which are real assets?

a. A patent.
b. A share of stock issued by Bank of New York.
c. A blast furnace in a steel-making factory.
d. A mortgage loan taken out to help pay for a new home.
e. After a successful advertising campaign, potential customers' belief that FedEx will deliver packages promptly and reliably.
f. An IOU ("I owe you") from your brother-in-law.

1.2 What Is a Corporation?

The nine major corporations in Table 1–1 are a tiny subsample from the list of corporations operating around the world. There are about 8,000 *public companies* in the United States. "Public" means that the corporation's shares are traded in a securities market, such as the New York Stock Exchange, and therefore are available for purchase by any investor. There also are hundreds of thousands of *private corporations* whose shares are closely held by small groups of managers and investors. You can't purchase the shares of these private companies, except by negotiation with existing share owners.

corporation
A business organized as a separate legal entity owned by stockholders.

A **corporation** is a distinct, permanent legal entity. Suppose you decide to create a new corporation. You would work with a lawyer to prepare *articles of incorporation,* which set out the purpose of the business and how it is to be financed, managed, and governed. These articles must conform to the laws of the state in which the business is incorporated. For many purposes, the corporation is considered a resident of its state. For example, it can borrow or lend money and it can sue or be sued. It pays its own taxes (but it cannot vote!).

limited liability
The owners of a corporation are not personally liable for its obligations.

A corporation is legally distinct from its owners, who are called *shareholders* or *stockholders*.[5] A corporation therefore confers **limited liability:** Its owners cannot be held personally responsible for the corporation's debts. When Enron and WorldCom failed in 2002—two of the largest bankruptcies ever—no one demanded that their stockholders put up more money to cover the bankrupt companies' debts. Enron and WorldCom stockholders ended up with worthless shares and lost their entire investment in these firms but had no further liability.

EXAMPLE 1.1 ▶   Business Organization

Suppose you own a commercial building and operate a restaurant in it. You have invested in the building itself, kitchen equipment, dining-room furnishings, a computer system to keep track of supplies and reservations, plus various other assets. If you do not incorporate, you own these assets personally, as the *sole proprietor* of the business. If you have borrowed money from a bank to start the business, then you are personally responsible for this debt. If the business loses money and cannot pay the bank, then the bank can demand that you raise cash by selling other assets—your car or house, for example—in order to repay the loan. But if you incorporate the restaurant business, and the corporation borrows from the bank, your other assets are shielded from the restaurant's debts. Of course this also means that the bank will be more cautious in lending if your restaurant is incorporated, because the bank will have no recourse to your other assets.

Notice that if you incorporate your business, you exchange direct ownership of its real assets (the building, kitchen equipment, etc.) for indirect ownership via financial assets (the shares of the new corporation).

Stockholders own the corporation, but they do not usually manage it. Instead, they elect a *board of directors,* who in turn appoint the top managers and monitor their performance. The board represents stockholders and is supposed to ensure that management is acting in their best interests.

This *separation of ownership and management* is one distinctive feature of corporations. (Contrast a sole proprietor, who is both owner and manager.) Separation gives corporations permanence. If managers are fired and replaced, the corporation survives. All of today's stockholders can sell out to new investors without necessarily affecting the conduct of the corporation's business.

Corporations can, in principle, live forever, and in practice they can survive many human lifetimes. One of the oldest corporations is the Hudson's Bay Company, which was formed in 1670 to profit from the fur trade between northern Canada and England, by sea via Hudson's Bay. The company still operates as one of Canada's leading retail chains.

Large, public corporations have thousands of stockholders. An individual may have 100 shares, receive 100 votes, and be entitled to a tiny fraction of the firm's income and value. A pension fund or insurance company may own millions of shares, receive millions of votes, and have a correspondingly large stake in the firm's performance.

Given all these advantages, you may wonder why all businesses are not organized as corporations. One reason is the costs, in both time and money, of managing the corporation's legal machinery. These costs are particularly burdensome for small businesses. There is also an important tax drawback to corporations in the United States. Because the corporation is a separate legal entity, it is taxed separately. So corporations pay tax on their profits, and shareholders are taxed again when they receive dividends from the company or sell their shares at a profit.[6] By contrast, income generated by businesses that are not incorporated is taxed just once as personal income.

---

[5] "Shareholder" and "stockholder" mean exactly the same thing and are used interchangeably.

[6] The U.S. tax system is unusual in this respect. To avoid taxing the same income twice, most other countries give shareholders at least some credit for the taxes that the corporation has already paid.

Other Forms of Business Organization

This book focuses on corporations, which tend to be larger firms with many share-holders. Proprietorships are usually small "mom-and-pop" businesses. What about the middle ground? What about businesses that grow too large for sole proprietorships but don't want to reorganize as corporations?

Suppose you wish to pool money and expertise with some friends or business associates. You will form a *partnership* and enter into a partnership agreement that sets out how decisions are to be made and how profits are to be split up. Partners, like sole proprietors, face unlimited liability. If the business runs into difficulties, each partner can be held responsible for *all* the business's debts. The moral: Know thy partner.

Partnerships have a tax advantage. Partnerships, unlike corporations, do not have to pay income taxes. The partners simply pay personal income taxes on their shares of the profits.

Some businesses are hybrids that combine the tax advantage of a partnership with the limited liability advantage of a corporation. In a *limited partnership,* partners are classified as general or limited. General partners manage the business and have unlimited personal liability for its debts. Limited partners are liable only for the money they invest and do not participate in management.

Many states allow *limited liability partnerships (LLPs)* or, equivalently, *limited liability companies (LLCs).* These are partnerships in which all partners have limited liability. Another variation on the theme is the *professional corporation (PC),* which is commonly used by doctors, lawyers, and accountants. In this case, the business has limited liability, but the professionals can still be sued personally, for example for malpractice.

Most large investment banks such as Morgan Stanley, Merrill Lynch, and Goldman Sachs started life as partnerships. But eventually these companies and their financing requirements grew too large for them to continue as partnerships, and they reorganized as corporations. The partnership form of organization does not work well when ownership is widespread and separation of ownership and management is essential.

1.3 Who Is the Financial Manager?

In this book we will use the term *financial manager* to refer to anyone responsible for a significant corporate investment or financing decision. But except in the smallest firms, no *single* person is responsible for all the decisions discussed in this book. Responsibility is dispersed throughout the firm. Top management is of course constantly involved in financial decisions. But the engineer who designs a new production facility is also involved: The design determines the kind of real asset the firm will invest in. Likewise the marketing manager who undertakes a major advertising campaign is making an investment decision: The campaign is an investment in an intangible asset that will pay off in future sales and earnings.

Nevertheless, there are managers who specialize in finance, and their functions are summarized in Figure 1–2. The **treasurer** is most directly responsible for looking after the firm's cash, raising new capital, and maintaining relationships with banks and other investors that hold the firm's securities.

For small firms, the treasurer is likely to be the only financial executive. Larger corporations usually also have a **controller,** who prepares the financial statements, manages the firm's internal budgets and accounting, and looks after its tax affairs. You can see that the treasurer and controller have different roles: The treasurer's main function is to obtain and manage the firm's capital, whereas the controller ensures that the money is used efficiently.

Large corporations usually appoint a **chief financial officer (CFO)** to oversee both the treasurer's and the controller's work. The CFO is deeply involved in financial

treasurer
Responsible for financing, cash management, and relationships with banks and other financial institutions.

controller
Responsible for budgeting, accounting, and taxes.

chief financial officer (CFO)
Oversees the treasurer and controller and sets overall financial strategy.

FIGURE 1–2 Financial managers in large corporations

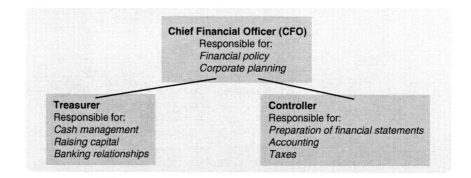

policy-making and corporate planning. He or she will have general responsibilities beyond strictly financial issues, and may join the company's board of directors.

In large corporations, a senior financial manager is responsible for organizing and supervising the capital budgeting process. However, major capital investment projects are so closely tied to plans for product development, production, and marketing that managers from these other areas are inevitably drawn into planning and analyzing the projects. If the firm has staff members specializing in corporate planning, they are naturally involved in capital budgeting too.

Because of the importance of many financial issues, ultimate decisions often rest by law or by custom with the board of directors. For example, only the board has the legal power to declare a dividend or to sanction a public issue of securities. Boards usually delegate decision-making authority for small- or medium-sized investment outlays, but the authority to approve large investments is almost never delegated.

Self-Test 1.3

Fritz and Frieda went to business school together 10 years ago. They have just been hired by a midsized corporation that wants to bring in new financial managers. Fritz studied finance, with an emphasis on financial markets and institutions. Frieda majored in accounting and became a CPA 5 years ago. Who is more suited to be treasurer and who controller? Briefly explain.

1.4 Goals of the Corporation

Shareholders Want Managers to Maximize Market Value

For small corporations, shareholders and management may be one and the same. But for large corporations, separation of ownership and management is a practical necessity. For example, Wal-Mart has about 312,000 shareholders. There is no way that these shareholders can be actively involved in management; it would be like trying to run New York City by town meetings. Authority has to be delegated.

How can shareholders decide how to delegate decision making when they all have different tastes, wealth, time horizons, and personal opportunities? Delegation can work only if the shareholders have a common objective. Fortunately there is a natural financial objective on which almost all shareholders can agree: Maximize the current *market value* of shareholders' investment in the firm.

A smart and effective financial manager makes decisions that increase the current value of the company's shares and the wealth of its stockholders. That increased wealth can then be put to whatever purposes the shareholders want. They can give their money to charity or spend it in glitzy night clubs; they can save it or spend it now. Whatever their personal tastes or objectives, they can all do more when their shares are worth more.

Sometimes you hear managers speak as if the corporation has other goals. For example, they may say that their job is to "maximize profits." That sounds reasonable. After all, don't shareholders want their company to be profitable? But taken literally, profit maximization is not a well-defined corporate objective. Here are three reasons:

1. Maximize profits? Which year's profits? A corporation may be able to increase current profits by cutting back on outlays for maintenance or staff training, but that will not add value unless the outlays were wasteful in the first place. Shareholders will not welcome higher short-term profits if long-term profits are damaged.
2. A company may be able to increase future profits by cutting this year's dividend and investing the freed-up cash in the firm. That is not in the shareholders' best interest if the company earns only a very low rate of return on the extra investment.
3. Different accountants may calculate profits in different ways. So you may find that a decision that improves profits using one set of accounting rules may reduce them using another.

In a free economy a firm is unlikely to survive if it pursues goals that reduce the firm's value. Suppose, for example, that a firm's only goal is to increase its market share. It aggressively reduces prices to capture new customers, even when the price discounts cause continuing losses. What would happen to such a firm? As losses mount, it will find it more and more difficult to borrow money, and it may not even have sufficient profits to repay existing debts. Sooner or later, however, outside investors would see an opportunity for easy money. They could buy the firm from its current shareholders, toss out existing management, and increase the firm's value by changing its policies. They would profit by the difference between the price paid for the firm and the higher value it would have under new management. Managers who pursue goals that destroy value often land in early retirement.

The natural financial objective of the corporation is to maximize current market value. Managers who consistently ignore this objective are likely to be replaced.

Ethics and Management Objectives

Crime Does Not Pay   For a public company, maximizing current market value should also maximize today's stock price. (The firm's market value is the total amount that investors are willing to pay for all of its shares.) Does that objective justify pumping up the stock price by fraud or deception? Of course not. But there will be occasional bad apples in the barrel, companies that attempt to increase market value in unethical ways.

The years 2001 and 2002 revealed an unusual number of bad apples. For example, the telecom giant WorldCom admitted that it failed to report $3.8 billion of operating expenses. (The expenses were classified as investments, contrary to the rules of accounting.) Thus WorldCom's income was overstated by $3.8 billion. In the meantime, WorldCom had run up $41 billion of debt. When the company's true profitability was discovered, it was bankrupt within a month—the largest U.S. bankruptcy ever.

The second-largest bankruptcy was Enron, the energy trading and investment company. In late 2001 it announced over $1.7 billion in losses that had previously been concealed in "special-purpose entities" (SPEs). We need not delve into Enron's SPEs here, except to say that they broke basic rules of accounting and that one of Enron's top financial executives allegedly used SPEs to pocket millions at the expense of Enron and its shareholders. The bad news came out all at once in October and November 2001, and Enron was bankrupt by year-end.

We suspect that WorldCom's and Enron's accounting misdeeds were in part a desperate attempt to stave off bankruptcy. In the end these misdeeds were the proximate cause of bankruptcy. Crime, fraud, and deceit do not pay.

The Ethics of Maximizing Value   Let us shift the focus back to the great majority of financial managers, who are honest and conscientious. Some idealists say that these managers should not be obliged to act in the selfish interests of their stockholders. Some realists argue that, regardless of what managers ought to do, they in fact look after themselves rather than their shareholders.

Let us respond to the idealists first. Does maximizing value mean that managers must act as greedy mercenaries riding roughshod over the weak and helpless? No, in most instances there is little conflict between doing well (maximizing value) and doing good.

The first step in doing well is doing good by your customers. Here is how Adam Smith put the case in 1776:

> It is not from the benevolence of the butcher, the brewer, or the baker, that we expect our dinner, but from their regard to their own interest. We address ourselves, not to their humanity but to their self-love, and never talk to them of our own necessities but of their advantages.[7]

To enrich themselves and their shareholders, businesspeople have to provide their customers with the products and services they truly desire and are willing to pay for.

Of course, ethical issues do arise in business as in other walks of life. When the stakes are high, competition is intense, and a deadline is looming, it's easy for financial managers to blunder, and not to inquire as deeply as they should about the legality or morality of their actions.

Written rules and laws can help only so much. In business, as in other day-to-day affairs, there are also unwritten rules of behavior. These work because everyone knows that such rules are in the general interest. But they are reinforced because good managers know that their firm's reputation is one of its most important assets and therefore playing fair and keeping one's word are simply good business practices. Thus huge financial deals are regularly completed on a handshake, and each side knows that the other will not renege later if things turn sour. For example, the motto of the London Stock Exchange is "My word is my bond."

Reputation is particularly important in finance. If you buy a well-known brand in a store, you can be fairly sure what you are getting. But in financial transactions the other party often has more information than you and it is less easy to be sure of the quality of what you are buying. The reaction of honest financial firms is to build long-term relationships with their customers and establish a name for fair dealing and financial integrity. Major banks and securities firms protect their reputations by emphasizing their long history and their responsible behavior when seeking new customers. When something happens to undermine that reputation, the costs can be enormous.

Consider the market-timing scandals that sullied the reputation of several mutual funds in 2003. Market timing exploits the fact that stock markets in different parts of the world close at different times. For example, if there is a strong surge in U.S. stock prices while the Japanese market is closed, it is likely that Japanese prices will increase when markets open in Asia the next day. Traders who can buy mutual funds invested in Japanese stocks while their prices are frozen will be able to make substantial profits. U.S. mutual funds were not supposed to allow such trading, but some did. After it was disclosed that managers at Putnam Investments had allowed market-timing trades for some of its investors, the company was fined $100 million and obliged to pay $10 million in compensation. But the larger cost by far was Putnam's loss of reputation. When the scandal came to light, Putnam suffered huge withdrawals of funds. Putnam mutual funds suffered outflows of $30 billion in just 2 months. If Putnam's funds charged roughly 1% of invested assets as an annual management fee (about the industry average), this loss of assets cost the company $300 million of revenue *per year.*

---

[7] Adam Smith, *An Inquiry into the Nature and Causes of the Wealth of Nations* (New York: Random House, 1937; first published 1776), p. 14.

Things Are Not Always Fair in Love or Economics

What constitutes fair behavior by companies? One survey asked a number of individuals to state whether they regarded a particular action as acceptable or unfair. Before we tell you how they responded, think how you would rate each of the following actions:

1a. A small photocopying shop has one employee who has worked in the shop for 6 months and earns $9 per hour. Business continues to be satisfactory, but a factory in the area has closed and unemployment has increased. Other small shops in the area have now hired reliable workers at $7 an hour to perform jobs similar to those done by the photocopying shop employee. The owner of the photocopying shop reduces the employee's wage to $7.

1b. Now suppose that the shop does not reduce the employee's wage but he or she leaves. The owner decides to pay a replacement $7 an hour.

2. A house painter employs two assistants and pays them $9 per hour. The painter decides to quit house painting and go into the business of providing landscape services, where the going wage is lower. He reduces the workers' wages to $7 per hour for the landscaping work.

3a. A small company employs several workers and has been paying them average wages. There is severe unemployment in the area and the company could easily replace its current employees with good workers at a lower wage. The company has been making money. The owners reduce the current workers' wages by 5%.

3b. Now suppose instead that the company has been losing money and the owners reduce wages by 5%.

4. A grocery store has several months' supply of peanut butter in stock on shelves in the storeroom. The owner hears that the wholesale price of peanut butter has increased and immediately raises the price on the current stock of peanut butter.

5. A hardware store has been selling snow shovels for $15. The morning after a large snowstorm, the store raises the price to $20.

6. A store has been sold out of the popular Beanie Baby dolls for a month. A week before Christmas a single doll is discovered in a storeroom. The managers know that many customers would like to buy the doll. They announce over the store's public address system that the doll will be sold by auction to the customer who offers to pay the most.

Now compare your responses with the responses of a random sample of individuals:

	Percent Rating the Action As:	
Action	Acceptable	Unfair
1a	17	83
1b	73	27
2	63	37
3a	23	77
3b	68	32
4	21	79
5	18	82
6	26	74

Source: Adapted from D. Kahneman, J. L. Knetsch, and R. Thaler, "Fairness as a Constraint on Profit Seeking: Entitlements in the Market," *American Economic Review* 76 (September 1986), pp. 728–741. Reprinted by permission of American Economic Association and the authors.

It is not always easy to know what is ethical behavior and there can be many gray areas. For example, should the firm be prepared to do business with a corrupt or repressive government? Should it employ child labor in countries where that is the norm? The nearby box presents several simple situations that call for an ethically based decision, along with survey responses to the proper course of action in each circumstance. Compare your decisions with those of the general public.

Self-Test 1.4

Without knowing anything about the personal ethics of the owners, which company would you better trust to keep its word in a business deal?

a. Harry's Hardware has been in business for 50 years. Harry's grandchildren, now almost adults, plan to take over and operate the business. Hardware stores require considerable investment in customer relations to become established.

b. Victor's Videos just opened for business. It rents a storefront in a strip mall and has financed its inventory with a bank loan. Victor has little of his own money invested in the business. Video shops usually command little customer loyalty.

Do Managers Really Maximize Value?

Owner-managers have no conflicts of interest in their management of the business. They work for themselves, reaping the rewards of good work and suffering the penalties of bad work. Their *personal* well-being is tied to the value of the firm.

In most large corporations the managers are not the owners, and so managers may be tempted to act in ways that are not in the best interests of shareholders. For example, they might buy luxurious corporate jets or overindulge in expense-account dinners. They might shy away from attractive but risky projects because they are worried more about the safety of their jobs than the potential for superior profits. They might engage in empire-building, adding unnecessary capacity or employees. Such problems can arise because the managers of the firm, who are hired as *agents* of the owners, may have their own axes to grind. Therefore they are called **agency problems.**

These agency problems can sometimes lead to outrageous behavior. For example, when Dennis Kozlowski, the CEO of Tyco, threw a $2 million 40th birthday bash for his wife, he charged half of the cost to the company. This of course was an extreme case of an agency conflict, as well as being illegal. In normal business dealings, agency problems commonly arise whenever managers think just a little less hard about spending money that is not their own.

Think of the company's net revenue as a pie that is divided among a number of claimants. These include the management and the work force as well as the lenders and shareholders who put up the money to establish and maintain the business. The government is a claimant, too, since it gets to tax the profits of the enterprise. It is common to hear these claimants called **stakeholders** in the firm. Each has a stake in the firm. The stakeholders' interests may not coincide.

All these stakeholders are bound together in a complex web of contracts and understandings. For example, when banks lend money to the firm, they insist on a formal contract stating the rate of interest and repayment dates, perhaps placing restrictions on dividends or additional borrowing. Similarly, large companies have carefully worked out personnel policies that establish employees' rights and responsibilities. But you can't devise written rules to cover every possible future event. So the written contracts are supplemented by understandings. For example, managers understand that in return for a fat salary they are expected to work hard and not spend the firm's money on unwarranted personal luxuries.

What enforces these understandings? Is it realistic to expect managers always to act on behalf of the shareholders? The shareholders can't spend their lives watching through binoculars to check that managers are not shirking or dissipating company funds on the latest executive jet.

A closer look reveals several arrangements that help to ensure that the shareholders and managers are working toward common goals.

Compensation Plans Managers are spurred on by incentive schemes that produce big returns if shareholders gain but are valueless if they do not. For example, Larry Ellison, CEO of the business software giant Oracle Corporation, received total compensation for 2007 estimated at between $60 and $70 million. Only a small fraction ($1 million) of that amount was salary, however. A larger amount, a bit more than $6 million, was bonus and incentive pay, and the lion's share was in the form of stock and option grants. Those options will be worthless if Oracle's share price falls from its 2007 level but will be highly valuable if the price rises. Moreover, as founder of Oracle, Ellison holds over 1 *billion* shares in the firm. No one can say for certain how hard Ellison would have worked with a different compensation package. But one thing is clear: He has a huge personal stake in the success of the firm—and in increasing its market value.

Well-designed compensation schemes encourage management to maximize shareholder wealth. But some schemes are not well designed, and in these cases, poorly performing managers may receive large windfall gains. For example, during Robert Nardelli's roughly 6-year tenure as CEO of Home Depot, the stock price fell by more than 20% while shares of its rival, Lowe's, more than doubled. When Nardelli was ousted in January 2007, he received a farewell compensation package of about $210 million. Needless to say, shareholders were not impressed by the board's generosity.

agency problems
Managers, acting as agents for stockholders, may act in their own interests rather than maximizing value.

stakeholder
Anyone with a financial interest in the firm.

Board of Directors   Boards of directors have often been portrayed as passive supporters of top management. But response to the corporate scandals of 2001–2002 has tipped the balance toward greater independence. The Sarbanes-Oxley Act requires that corporations place more independent directors on the board, that is, more directors who are not managers or are not affiliated with management. More than half of all directors are now independent. Boards also now meet in sessions without the CEO present. In addition, institutional shareholders, particularly pension funds and hedge funds, have become more active in monitoring firm performance and proposing changes to corporate governance.

Not suprisingly, more chief executives have been forced out in recent years, among them the CEOs of Dow Jones, Citigroup, Merrill Lynch, Boeing, Sun Microsystems, and Pfizer. Boards in Europe, which traditionally have been more management-friendly, have also become more willing to replace underperforming managers. The list of European departures includes senior management from Deutsche Telekom, Airbus, UBS, and Volkswagen.

If shareholders believe that the corporation is underperforming and the board of directors is not sufficiently aggressive in holding managers to task, they can try to replace the board in the next election. The dissident shareholders will attempt to convince the other shareholders to vote for their slate of candidates to the board. If they succeed, a new board will be elected and it can replace the current management team. Short of that, unhappy shareholders can attempt to elect representatives to the board to make their voices heard. In 2006, for example, dissatisfied shareholders of the H. J. Heinz food company voted in two directors proposed by an outside investor, Nelson Peltz. With over $1 trillion of assets under management, hedge funds have become increasingly aggressive and successful in pursuing this strategy.

Takeovers   Poorly performing companies are more likely to be taken over by another firm. The further a company's stock price falls, the easier it is for another company to buy up a majority of its shares. The old management team is then likely to find itself out on the street. We discuss takeovers in Chapter 21.

Specialist Monitoring   Managers are subject to the scrutiny of specialists. Their actions are monitored by the security analysts who advise investors to buy, hold, or sell the company's shares. They are also reviewed by banks, which keep an eagle eye on the progress of firms receiving their loans.

Legal and Regulatory Requirements   CEOs and financial managers have a legal duty to act responsibly and in the interests of investors. For example, the Securities and Exchange Commission (SEC) sets accounting and reporting standards for public companies in order to ensure consistency and transparency. The SEC also prohibits insider trading, that is, the purchase or sale of shares based on information that is not available to public investors. In 2002, in response to Enron, WorldCom, and other debacles of the late 1900s and early 2000s, Congress passed the Sarbanes-Oxley Act, known widely as SOX. In addition to its restrictions on board activities, SOX requires each CFO to sign off personally on the corporation's accounting procedures and results.

We do not want to leave the impression that corporate life is a series of squabbles and endless micromanagement. It isn't, because practical corporate finance has evolved to reconcile personal and corporate interests—to keep everyone working together to increase the value of the whole pie, not merely the size of each person's slice.

Agency problems are mitigated in practice in several ways: legal and regulatory standards; compensation plans that tie the fortunes of the managers to the fortunes of the firm; monitoring by lenders, stock market analysts, and investors; and ultimately the threat that poorly performing managers will be fired.

We have covered several types of constraints and incentives designed to mitigate agency costs and ensure cooperative and ethical behavior. All these mechanisms help ensure effective *corporate governance*. When scandals happen, we say that corporate governance has broken down. When corporations compete effectively and ethically and deliver value to shareholders, we are comforted that corporate governance is working properly.

Self-Test 1.5   What is an agency problem? Give two or three examples of decisions by managers that lead to agency costs.

Corporate Governance outside the United States

Ownership and control are usually separated in public U.S. corporations. But a large block of shares may give effective control even when there is no majority owner. For example, Larry Ellison's billion-plus shares in Oracle Corporation make him a 25% owner of the company as well as its chief executive. Barring some extreme catastrophe, this holding means that he can run the company pretty much as he wants to and as long as he wants to. Nevertheless, the concentration of ownership in the United States is much less than that in some other industrialized countries. The differences are not so apparent in Canada, Britain, Australia, and other English-speaking countries, but there are dramatic differences in Japan and continental Europe.

In Japan major industrial and financial companies have traditionally been linked together in a group called a *keiretsu*. For example, the Mitsubishi keiretsu contains 29 core companies including a bank, two insurance companies, an automobile manufacturer, a brewery, and a steel company. Members of the keiretsu are tied together in several ways. First, managers may sit on the boards of directors of other group companies, and a "president's council" of chief executives meets regularly. Second, each company in the group holds shares in many of the other companies. And third, companies generally borrow from the keiretsu's bank or from elsewhere within the group. These links may have several advantages. Companies can obtain funds from other members of the group without the need to reveal confidential information to the public, and if a member of the group runs into financial heavy weather, its problems can be worked out with other members of the group rather than in the bankruptcy court.

The more stable and concentrated shareholder base of large Japanese corporations may make it easier for them to resist pressures for short-term performance and allow them to focus on securing long-term advantage. But the Japanese system of corporate governance also has its disadvantages, for the lack of market discipline can allow lagging or inefficient corporations to put off painful surgery. As the Japanese economy languished in the 1990s, these disadvantages became more apparent, the links that bound keiretsus together began to weaken, and companies began to sell their shares in other members of the group.

Keiretsus are found only in Japan. But large companies in continental Europe are linked in some similar ways. For example, banks and other companies often own or control large blocks of stock and can push hard for changes in the management or strategy of poorly performing companies.[8] Thus oversight and control are entrusted largely to banks and other corporations.

In summary, while control of large public companies in the United States is exercised through the board of directors and pressure from the stock market, in many other countries the stock market is less important and control shifts to major stockholders, typically banks and other companies.

---

[8] Banks in the United States are prohibited from large or permanent holding of the stock of nonfinancial corporations.

1.5 Careers in Finance

Well over 1 million people work in the financial services industry in the United States, and many others work as financial managers in corporations. We can't tell you what each one does all day, but we can give you some idea of the variety of careers in finance. The nearby box summarizes the experience of a small sample of recent graduates.[9]

We explained earlier that corporations face two principal financial decisions: the investment decision and the financing decision. Therefore, as a newly recruited financial analyst, you may help to analyze a major new investment project. Or you may instead help to raise the money to pay for it, perhaps by negotiating a bank loan or by arranging to lease the plant and equipment. Other financial analysts work on short-term finance, managing collection and investment of the company's cash or checking whether customers are likely to pay their bills. Financial analysts are also involved in monitoring and controlling risk. For example, they may help to arrange insurance for the firm's plant and equipment, or they may assist with the purchase and sale of options, futures, and other exotic tools for managing risk.

Instead of working in the finance department of a corporation, you may join a financial institution. The largest employers are banks. Banks collect deposits and relend the cash to corporations and individuals. If you join a bank, you may start in a branch office, where individuals and small businesses come to deposit cash or to seek a loan. You could also work in the head office, helping to analyze a $500 million loan to a large corporation.

Banks do many things in addition to lending money, and they probably provide a greater variety of jobs than other financial institutions. For example, individuals and businesses use banks to make payments to each other. So if you work in the cash management department of a large bank, you may help companies electronically transfer huge sums of money as wages, taxes, and payments to suppliers. Banks also buy and sell foreign exchange, so you could find yourself working in front of one of those computer screens in a foreign exchange dealing room. Another glamorous bank job is in the derivatives group, which helps companies to manage their risk by buying and selling options, futures, and so on. This is where the mathematicians and the computer buffs thrive.

Investment banks, such as Merrill Lynch or Goldman Sachs, help companies sell their securities to investors. They also have large corporate finance departments which assist firms in mergers and acquisitions. When firms issue securities or try to take over another firm, a lot of money is at stake and the firms may need to move fast. Thus, working for an investment bank can be a high-pressure activity with long hours. It can also pay very well.

The insurance industry is another large employer. Much of the insurance industry is involved in designing and selling insurance policies on people's lives and property, but businesses are also major customers. So if you work for an insurance company or a large insurance broker, you could find yourself arranging insurance on a Boeing 787 in the United States or an oil rig in Indonesia.

Life insurance companies are major lenders to corporations and to investors in commercial real estate. (Life insurance companies deploy the insurance premiums received from policyholders into medium- or long-term loans; banks specialize in shorter-term financing.) So you could end up negotiating a $50 million loan for construction of a new shopping center or investigating the creditworthiness of a family-owned manufacturing company that has applied for a loan to expand production.

Then there is the business of "managing money," that is, deciding which companies' shares to invest in or how to balance investment in shares with safer securities, such as

---

[9] The careers are fictitious but based on the actual experiences of several of the authors' students.

FINANCE IN PRACTICE

Working in Finance

Susan Webb, Research Analyst, Mutual Fund Group

After majoring in biochemistry, I joined the research department of a large mutual fund group. Because of my background, I was assigned to work with the senior pharmaceuticals analyst. I start the day by reading *The Wall Street Journal* and reviewing the analyses that come in each day from stockbroking firms. Sometimes we need to revise our earnings forecasts and meet with the portfolio managers to discuss possible trades. The remainder of my day is spent mainly in analyzing companies and developing forecasts of revenues and earnings. I meet frequently with pharmaceutical analysts in stockbroking firms and we regularly visit company management. In the evenings I study for the Chartered Financial Analyst (CFA) exam. Since I did not study finance at college, this is quite challenging. I hope eventually to move from a research role to become a portfolio manager.

Richard Gradley, Project Finance, Large Energy Company

After leaving college, I joined the finance department of a large energy company. I spent my first year helping to analyze capital investment proposals. I then moved to the project finance group, which is responsible for analyzing independent power projects around the world. Recently, I have been involved in a proposal to set up a company that would build and operate a large new electricity plant in southeast Asia. We built a spreadsheet model of the project to make sure

that it was viable. We had to check that the contracts with the builders, operators, suppliers, and so on, were all in place before we could arrange bank financing for the project.

Albert Rodriguez, Emerging Markets Group, Major New York Bank

I joined the bank after majoring in finance. I spent the first 6 months in the bank's training program, rotating between departments. I was assigned to the Latin America team just before the 1998 Brazilian crisis when interest rates jumped to nearly 50% and the currency fell by 40%. There was a lot of activity, with everyone trying to figure out what was likely to happen next and how it would affect our business. My job is largely concerned with analyzing economies and assessing the prospects for bank business. There are plenty of opportunities to work abroad and I hope to spend some time in one of our Latin American offices, such as Argentina or Brazil.

Sherry Solera, Branch Manager, Regional Bank

I took basic finance courses in college, but nothing specific for banking. I started here as a teller. I was able to learn about banking through the bank's training program, and also by evening courses at a local college. Last year I was promoted to branch manager. I oversee the branch's operations and help customers with a wide variety of problems. I'm also spending more time on credit analysis of business loan applications. I want to expand the branch's business customers, but not by making loans to shaky companies.

the bonds (debt securities) issued by the U.S. Treasury. Take mutual funds, for example. A mutual fund collects money from individuals and invests in a portfolio of stocks or bonds. A financial analyst in a mutual fund analyzes the prospects for the securities and works with the investment manager to decide which should be bought and sold. Many other financial institutions also contain investment management departments. For example, you might work as a financial analyst in the investment department of an insurance company. (Insurance companies also invest in traded securities.) Or you could be a financial analyst in the trust department of a bank that manages money for retirement funds, universities, and charities.

Stockbroking firms help investment management companies and private individuals to invest in securities. They employ sales staff and dealers who make the trades. They also employ financial analysts to analyze the securities and help customers to decide which to buy or sell. Many stockbroking firms are owned by investment banks, such as Merrill Lynch.

Investment banks and stockbroking firms are largely headquartered in New York, as are many of the large commercial banks. Insurance companies and investment management companies tend to be more scattered. For example, some of the largest insurance companies are headquartered in Hartford, Connecticut, and many investment management companies are located in Boston. Of course, some U.S. financial institutions have large businesses outside the United States. Finance is a global business. So you may spend some time working in a branch overseas or making the occasional trip to one of the other major financial centers, such as London, Tokyo, Hong Kong, or Singapore.

Finance professionals tend to be well paid. Starting salaries for new graduates are in the region of $40,000, rather more in a major New York investment bank and somewhat

INTERNET INSIDER

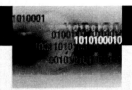

Careers in Finance

If you would like to learn about careers in finance, log on to **www.careers-in-finance.com**. This site describes jobs in commercial banking, corporate finance, financial planning, insurance, investment banking, money management, and real estate. For each area the site describes the types of jobs available, the skills and talents needed, salary ranges, and so on.

Corporate finance is the focus of this text, so we suggest you start there. Which jobs in corporate finance do you think would best suit you? Now compare the skills needed for these jobs. How do you match up? How will you match up when your education is completed?

The Web site also provides links to the job pages of major financial institutions. Log on to some of these sites and compare their descriptions of the different functions. Are these descriptions consistent with those at careers-in-finance.com?

We have listed several other useful job Web sites on our book Web site at **www.mhhe.com/bmm6e**.

Source: Careers-in-Finance, LLC. © 2008. All rights reserved.

less in a small regional bank. But let us look ahead a little: Table 1–2 gives you an idea of the compensation that you can look forward to when you become a senior financial manager (but don't assume that even department heads of large investment banking firms typically earn $70 million). The Internet Insider box for this chapter directs you to some Internet sites that provide useful information about careers in finance.

TABLE 1–2 Representative salaries for jobs in finance

Career	Annual Salary
Commercial Banking	
Loan officer	$90,000
Department manager	$200,000
Corporate Finance	
Financial analyst	$61–78,000
Credit manager	$73–92,000
Chief financial officer	$222–367,000
Investment Banking (bulge bracket)	
First-year analyst	$90–180,000
First-year associate	$200–350,000
Assistant vice president	$300–900,000
Director/principal	$500K–2 million
Managing director/partner	$600K–30 million
Department head	$1 million–70 million
Money Management	
Portfolio manager	$500,000+
Bank trust department	$60–150,000

Note: "Bulge bracket" refers to a few of the largest investment banks.

Source: Careers-in-Business, LLC.; **www.careers-in-finance.com**, **www.salary.com**, and authors' calculations. All rights reserved.

FINANCE IN PRACTICE

Finance through the Ages

Date unknown *Compound Growth.* Bacteria start to propagate by subdividing. They thereby demonstrate the power of compound growth. *(Chapter 5)*

c. 1800 B.C. *Interest Rates.* In Babylonia Hammurabi's Code established maximum interest rates on loans. Borrowers often mortgaged their property and sometimes their spouses but in these cases the lender was obliged to return the spouse in good condition within 3 years. *(Chapter 6)*

c. 1000 B.C. *Options.* One of the earliest recorded options is described by Aristotle. The philosopher Thales knew by the stars that there would be a great olive harvest, so, having a little money, he bought options for the use of olive presses. When the harvest came Thales was able to rent the presses at great profit. Today financial managers need to be able to evaluate options to buy or sell a wide variety of assets. *(Chapter 23)*

15th century *International Banking.* Modern international banking has its origins in the great Florentine banking houses. But the entire European network of the Medici empire employed only 57 people in eight offices. Today the London-based bank HSBC has more than 330,000 employees in 83 different countries. *(Chapter 14)*

1650 *Futures.* Futures markets allow companies to protect themselves against fluctuations in commodity prices. During the Tokugawa era in Japan feudal lords collected rents in the form of rice but often they wished to trade their future rice deliveries. Rice futures therefore came to be traded on what was later known as the Dojima Rice Market. Rice futures are still traded but now companies can also trade in futures on a range of items from pork bellies to stock market indexes. *(Chapter 24)*

17th century *Joint Stock Corporations.* Although investors have for a long time combined together as joint owners of an enterprise, the modern corporation with a large number of stockholders originates with the formation in England of the great trading firms like the East India Company (est. 1599). *(Chapter 15)*

17th century *Money.* America has been in the forefront in the development of new types of money. Early settlers often used a shell known as wampum. For example, Peter Stuyvesant raised a loan in wampum and in Massachusetts it was legal tender. Unfortunately, the enterprising settlers found that with a little dye the relatively common white wampum shells could be converted profitably into the more valuable black ones, which confirmed Gresham's law that bad money drives out good. The first issue of paper money in America (and almost in the world) was by the Massachusetts Bay Colony in 1690, and other colonies soon set their printing presses to producing money. In 1862 Congress agreed to an issue of paper money which would be legal tender. These notes, printed in green ink, immediately became known as "greenbacks." *(Chapters 19, 20)*

1720 *New Issue Speculation.* From time to time investors have been tempted by speculative new issues. During the South Sea Bubble in England one company was launched to develop perpetual motion. Another enterprising individual announced a company "for carrying on an undertaking of great advantage but nobody to know what it is." Within 5 hours he had raised £2000; within 6 hours he was on his way out of the country. Readers nearly two centuries later could only wonder at the naïve or foolhardy investors in these ventures—that is, until they had a chance to participate in the dot.com meltdown of 1999–2002. *(Chapter 15)*

1792 *Formation of the New York Stock Exchange.* The New York Stock Exchange (NYSE) was founded in 1792 when a group of brokers met under a buttonwood tree and arranged to trade shares with one another at agreed rates of commission. Today the NYSE is the largest stock exchange in the world, trading on average about 2 billion shares a day. *(Chapter 7)*

1929 *Stock Market Crashes.* Common stocks are risky investments. In September 1929 stock prices in the United States reached an all-time high and the economist Irving Fisher forecast that they were at "a permanently high plateau." Some 3 years later stock prices were almost 90 percent lower and it was to be a quarter of a century before the prices of September 1929 were seen again. Contrary to popular impression, no Wall Street broker jumped out the window. *(Chapter 11)*

1960s *Eurodollar Market.* In the 1950s the Soviet Union transferred its dollar holdings from the United States to a Russian-owned bank in Paris. This bank was best known by its telex address, eurobank, and consequently dollars held outside the United States came to be known as eurodollars. In the 1960s U.S. taxes and regulation made it much cheaper to borrow and lend dollars in Europe rather than in the United States, and a huge market in eurodollars arose. *(Chapter 14)*

1.6 Topics Covered in This Book

This book covers investment decisions, then financing decisions, and then a variety of planning issues that require an understanding of both investment and financing. But first there are three further introductory chapters that should be helpful to readers making a first acquaintance with financial management. Chapter 2 is an overview of financial markets and institutions. Chapter 3 reviews the basic concepts of accounting, and Chapter 4 demonstrates the techniques of financial statement analysis.

In Parts 2 and 3 we look at different aspects of the investment decision. The first is the problem of how to value assets, and the second is the link between risk and value. Our discussion of these topics occupies Chapters 5 through 13.

1971 Corporate Bankruptcies. Every generation of investors is shocked and surprised by a major corporate bankruptcy. In 1971 the Penn Central Railroad, a pillar of American industry, suddenly collapsed. Penn Central showed assets of $4.6 billion, about $21 billion in today's dollars. At that time it was the largest corporate bankruptcy in history. Enron and WorldCom have since broken Penn Central's record. *(Chapter 16)*

1972 Financial Futures. Financial futures allow companies to protect themselves against fluctuations in interest rates, exchange rates, and so on. It is said that they originated from a remark by the economist Milton Friedman that he was unable to profit from his view that sterling (the U.K. currency) was overpriced. The Chicago Mercantile Exchange founded the first financial futures market. Today futures exchanges in the United States trade over 2 billion contracts a year of financial futures. *(Chapter 24)*

1986 Capital Investment Decisions. The largest investment project undertaken by a private company was the construction of the tunnel under the English Channel. This started in 1986 and was completed in 1994 at a total cost of $15 billion. *(Chapters 8, 9)*

1988 Mergers. The 1980s saw a wave of takeovers culminating in the $25 billion takeover of RJR Nabisco. Over a period of 6 weeks three groups battled for control of the company. As one of the contestants put it, "We were charging through the rice paddies, not stopping for anything and taking no prisoners." The takeover was the largest in history and generated almost $1 billion in fees for the banks and advisers. *(Chapter 21)*

1993 Inflation. Financial managers need to recognize the effect of inflation on interest rates and on the profitability of the firm's investments. In the United States inflation has been relatively modest, but some countries have suffered from hyperinflation. In Hungary after World War II the government issued banknotes worth 1,000 trillion pengoes. In Yugoslavia in October 1993 prices rose by nearly 2,000% and a dollar bought 105 million dinars. *(Chapter 5)*

1780 and 1997 Inflation-Indexed Debt. In 1780, Massachusetts paid Revolutionary War soldiers with interest-bearing notes rather than its rapidly eroding currency. Interest and principal payments on the notes were tied to the rate of subsequent inflation. After a 217-year hiatus, the United States Treasury issued 10-year inflation-indexed notes. Many other countries, including Britain and Israel, had done so previously. *(Chapter 6)*

1993 Controlling Risk. When a company fails to keep close tabs on the risks being taken by its employees, it can get into serious trouble. This was the fate of Barings, a 220-year-old British bank that numbered the queen among its clients. In 1993 it discovered that Nick Leeson, a trader in its Singapore office, had hidden losses of $1.3 billion (£869 million) from unauthorized bets on the Japanese equity market. The losses wiped out Barings and landed Leeson in jail, with a 6-year sentence. In 2008 a rogue trader at the French bank Societé Generale established a new record by losing $7 billion on unauthorized deals. *(Chapter 24)*

1999 The Euro. Large corporations do business in many currencies. In 1999 a new currency came into existence, when 11 European countries adopted the euro in place of their separate currencies. This was not the first time that different countries have agreed on a common currency. In 1865 France, Belgium, Switzerland, and Italy came together in the Latin Monetary Union, and they were joined by Greece and Romania the following year. Members of the European Monetary Union (EMU) hope that the euro will be a longer-lasting success than earlier experiments. *(Chapter 23)*

2002 Financial Scandals. A seemingly endless series of financial and accounting scandals climaxed in this year. Resulting bankruptcies included the icons Enron (and its accounting firm, Arthur Andersen), WorldCom, and the Italian food company Parmalat. Congress passed the Sarbanes-Oxley Act to increase the accountability of corporations and executives. *(Chapters 1, 14)*

2007 Subprime Mortgages. Subprime mortgages are housing loans made to homeowners with shaky credit standing. After a decade in which housing prices had gone only up, lenders became complacent about the risks of these home loans and progressively loosened lending standards. When housing prices stalled and interest rates increased in 2007, many of these loans went bad. By early 2008, losses recognized by the major banks that purchased and packaged these loans had already topped $100 billion. *(Chapters 4, 25)*

Nine chapters devoted to the simple problem of finding real assets that are worth more than they cost may seem excessive, but that problem is not so simple in practice. We will require a theory of how long-lived, risky assets are valued, and that requirement will lead us to basic questions about financial markets. For example:

- How are corporate bonds and stocks valued in capital markets?
- What risks are borne by investors in corporate securities? How can these risks be measured?
- What compensation do investors demand for bearing risk?
- What rate of return can investors in common stocks reasonably expect to receive?
- Do stock prices accurately reflect the underlying value of the firm?

Intelligent capital budgeting and financing decisions require answers to these and other questions about how capital markets work.

Financing decisions occupy Parts 4 and 5. The two chapters in Part 4 describe the kinds of securities corporations use to raise money and explain how and when these securities are issued. Part 5 covers debt policy and dividend policy. We will also describe what happens when firms find themselves in financial distress because of poor operating performance, excessive borrowing, or both.

Part 6 covers financial analysis and planning. We cover long- and short-term financial planning and the management of working capital. *Working capital* refers to short-term assets, including cash, inventories, and money due from customers, net of short-term liabilities, such as the money that the firm has promised to pay to suppliers, banks, or other short-term lenders.

Part 7 covers three important problems that require decisions about both investment and financing. First we look at mergers and acquisitions. Then we consider international financial management. All the financial problems of doing business at home are present overseas, but the international financial manager faces the additional complications created by multiple currencies, different tax systems, and special regulations imposed by foreign institutions and governments. Finally, we look at risk management and the specialized securities, including futures and options, that managers can use to hedge or lay off risks.

Part 8 is our conclusion. It also discusses some of the things that we don't know about finance. If you can be the first to solve any of these puzzles, you will be justifiably famous.

Snippets of History

Now let's lighten up a little. In this book we are going to describe how financial decisions are made today. But financial markets also have an interesting history. Look at the nearby box, which lays out bits of this history, starting in prehistoric times, when the growth of bacteria anticipated the mathematics of compound interest, and continuing nearly to the present. We have keyed each of these episodes to the chapter of the book that discusses its topic.

www.mhhe.com/bmm6e

SUMMARY

What are the two major decisions made by financial managers? *(LO1)*

Financial management can be broken down into (1) the **investment,** or **capital budgeting,** decision and (2) the **financing** decision. The firm has to decide (1) how much to invest and which real assets to invest in and (2) how to raise the funds necessary to pay for those investments.

What does "real asset" mean? *(LO2)*

Real assets include all assets used in the production or sale of the firms' products or services. Real assets can be tangible (plant and equipment, for example) or intangible (patents or trademarks, for example). In contrast, **financial assets** are claims (such as stocks or bonds) on the income generated by real assets.

What are the advantages and disadvantages of corporate organization? *(LO3)*

Corporations are distinct, permanent legal entities. They allow for separation of ownership and control, and they can continue operating without disruption even as ownership changes. They provide **limited liability** to their owners. On the other hand, they are subject to double taxation because they pay taxes on their profits and the shareholders are taxed again when they receive dividends or sell their shares at a profit.

Who are the major financial managers? *(LO4)*

Almost all managers are involved to some degree in investment decisions, but some managers specialize in finance, for example, the treasurer, controller, and CFO. The **treasurer** is most directly responsible for raising capital and maintaining relationships with banks

www.mhhe.com/bmm6e

and investors that hold the firm's securities. The **controller** is responsible for preparing financial statements and managing budgets. In large firms, a **chief financial officer** who oversees both the treasurer and the controller will also be involved in financial policy-making and corporate planning.

Why does it make sense for corporations to maximize their market value? *(LO5)*

Value maximization is the natural financial goal of the firm. Maximizing value maximizes the wealth of the firm's owners, its shareholders. Shareholders can invest or consume that wealth as they wish.

Is value maximization ethical? *(LO6)*

Modern finance does not condone attempts to pump up stock price by unethical means. But there need be no conflict between ethics and value maximization. The surest route to maximum value starts with products and services that satisfy customers. A good reputation with customers, employees, and other stakeholders is also important for the firms' long-run profitability and value.

How do corporations ensure that managers' and stockholders' interests coincide? *(LO7)*

Conflicts of interest between managers and stockholders can lead to **agency problems.** These problems are kept in check by compensation plans that link the well-being of employees to that of the firm; by monitoring of management by the board of directors, security analysts, and creditors; and by the threat of takeover.

QUESTIONS

QUIZ

1. **Financial Decisions.** Give several examples of (a) investment decisions and (b) financing decisions. *(LO1)*

2. **Corporations.** What are the key differences between a corporation and a sole proprietorship? What is the difference between a public and a private corporation? *(LO3)*

3. **Corporations.** What is the key advantage of separating ownership and management in large corporations? *(LO3)*

4. **Limited Liability.** What is limited liability, and who benefits from it? *(LO3)*

5. **Corporations.** What do we mean when we say that corporate income is subject to *double taxation? (LO3)*

6. **Real versus Financial Assets.** Which of the following are real assets, and which are financial? *(LO2)*
   a. A share of stock.
   b. A personal IOU.
   c. A trademark.
   d. A truck.
   e. Undeveloped land.
   f. The balance in the firm's checking account.
   g. An experienced and hardworking sales force.
   h. A bank loan agreement.

7. **Financial Managers.** Which of the following statements more accurately describes the treasurer than the controller? *(LO4)*
   a. Likely to be the only financial executive in small firms.
   b. Monitors capital expenditures to make sure that they are not misappropriated.
   c. Responsible for investing the firm's spare cash.
   d. Responsible for arranging any issue of common stock.
   e. Responsible for the company's tax affairs.

8. **Value Maximization.** Give an example of an action that might increase short-run profits but at the same time reduce stock price and the market value of the firm. *(LO5)*

9. **Agency Costs.** What are agency costs? List some ways by which agency costs are mitigated. *(LO7)*

PRACTICE PROBLEMS

10. **Agency Problems.** Many firms have devised defenses that make it much more costly or difficult for other firms to take them over. How might such takeover defenses affect the firm's agency problems? Are managers of firms with formidable takeover defenses more or less likely to act in the firm's interest rather than their own? *(LO7)*

11. **Financial Decisions.** What is the difference between capital budgeting decisions and capital structure decisions? *(LO1)*

12. **Financial Assets.** Why is a bank loan a financial asset? *(LO2)*

13. **Real Assets.** Explain how investment in an R&D program creates a real asset. *(LO2)*

14. **Financial Managers.** Explain the differences between the CFO's responsibilities and the treasurer's and controller's responsibilities. *(LO4)*

15. **Limited Liability.** Is limited liability always an advantage for a corporation and its shareholders? *Hint:* Could limited liability reduce a corporation's access to financing? *(LO3)*

16. **Goals of the Firm.** You may have heard big business criticized for focusing on short-term performance at the expense of long-term results. Explain why a firm that strives to maximize stock price should be *less* subject to an overemphasis on short-term results than one that simply maximizes profits. *(LO5)*

17. **Goals of the Firm.** We claim that the goal of the firm is to maximize current market value. Could the following actions be consistent with that goal? *(LO5)*
    a. The firm adds a cost-of-living adjustment to the pensions of its retired employees.
    b. The firm reduces its dividend payment, choosing to reinvest more of earnings in the business.
    c. The firm buys a corporate jet for its executives.
    d. The firm drills for oil in a remote jungle. The chance of finding oil is only 1 in 5.

18. **Goals of the Firm.** Explain why each of the following may not be appropriate corporate goals: *(LO5)*
    a. Increase market share.
    b. Minimize costs.
    c. Underprice any competitors.
    d. Expand profits.

19. **Agency Issues.** Sometimes lawyers work on a contingency basis. They collect a percentage of their clients' settlements instead of receiving fixed fees. Why might clients prefer this arrangement? Would the arrangement mitigate an agency problem? *(LO7)*

20. **Reputation.** As you drive down a deserted highway, you are overcome with a sudden desire for a hamburger. Fortunately, just ahead are two hamburger outlets; one is owned by a national brand, the other appears to be owned by "Joe." Which outlet has the greater incentive to serve you catmeat? Why? *(LO6)*

21. **Agency Issues.** One of the "Finance through the Ages" episodes that we cited is the 1993 collapse of Barings Bank, when one of its traders lost $1.3 billion. Traders are compensated in large part according to their trading profits. How might this practice have contributed to an agency problem? *(LO7)*

22. **Agency Issues.** Discuss which of the following forms of compensation is most likely to align the interests of managers and shareholders: *(LO7)*
    a. A fixed salary.
    b. A salary linked to company profits.
    c. A salary that is paid partly in the form of the company's shares.

23. **Agency Issues.** When a company's stock is widely held, it may not pay an individual shareholder to spend time monitoring managers' performance and trying to replace poor performers. Explain why. Do you think that a bank that has made a large loan to the company is in a different position? *(LO7)*

24. **Corporate Governance.** How do clear and comprehensive financial reports promote effective corporate governance? *(LO7)*

www.mhhe.com/bmm6e

25. **Corporate Governance.** Some commentators have claimed that the U.S. system of corporate governance is "broken" and needs thorough reform. What do you think? Do you see systematic failures in corporate governance or just a few "bad apples" like Enron and WorldCom? *(LO7)*

26. **Ethics.** In some countries, such as Japan and Germany, corporations develop close long-term relationships with one bank and rely on that bank for a large part of their financing needs. In the United States companies are more likely to shop around for the best deal. Do you think that this practice is more or less likely to encourage ethical behavior on the part of the corporation? *(LO6)*

27. **Ethics.** Is there a conflict between "doing well" and "doing good"? In other words, are policies that increase the value of the firm (doing well) necessarily at odds with socially responsible policies (doing good)? When there are conflicts, how might government regulations or laws tilt the firm toward doing good? For example, how do taxes or fees charged on pollutants affect the firm's decision to pollute? Can you cite other examples of "incentives" used by governments to align private interests with public ones? *(LO6)*

28. **Ethics.** The following report appeared in the *Financial Times* (October 28, 1999, p. 1): "Coca-Cola is testing a vending machine that automatically raises the price of the world's favorite soft drink when the temperature increases . . . [T]he new machine, believed to have been tested in Japan, may well create controversy by using hot weather to charge extra. One rival said the idea of charging more when temperatures rose was 'incredible.'" Discuss. *(LO6)*

STANDARD
&POOR'S

1. This text provides you with access to a very powerful database of company information, called Standard & Poor's Market Insight. You have access via the following link (a password is provided in your book cover) to 6 years of data for 1,000 companies. The site provides several different Excel Analytics Reports including financial statements, ratios (6 years of ratios, actual and charted, with comparisons to the firm's industry), stock performance reports, and much more. Industry information (companies and profile) and company business activity are also reported.

www.mhhe.com/edumarketinsight

Enter the link above and review the introduction page. Proceed by clicking on the Continue icon, then enter your ID number, and you are in! Carefully review the *Review and Notes* Table of Contents to the right and the profile presented for each area. Take a look at the 1,000 companies in the database by clicking the *Company* icon at the top of the page, then *Population*. Select one company of interest to review. Click on the highlighted link and review the contents available from Market Insight. Look over the reports via the Table of Contents on the left. Throughout the coming chapters we will ask you to review or analyze Market Insight reports.

The *Company Profile* contains recent market valuation information and a link to the company's Web site. *Financial Highlights* provides current-quarter information on sales, market data, ratios, and so on. Click the linked terms, for example, *Employees,* and you will be provided a definition of the term, a very useful feature when getting started.

SOLUTIONS TO SELF-TEST QUESTIONS

1.1 a. The development of a microprocessor is a capital budgeting decision. The investment of $1 billion will purchase a real asset, the microprocessor design and production facilities.
   b. The bank loan is a financing decision. This is how Volkswagen will raise money for its investment.
   c. Capital budgeting.
   d. Capital budgeting. The marketing campaign should generate a real, though intangible, asset.
   e. Both. The acquisition is an investment decision. The decision to issue shares is a financing decision.

1.2   a. A real asset. Real assets can be intangible assets.
       b. Financial.
       c. Real.
       d. Financial.
       e. Real.
       f. Financial.

1.3   Fritz would more likely be the treasurer and Frieda the controller. The treasurer raises money from the financial markets and requires a background in financial institutions. The controller requires a background in accounting.

1.4   Harry's has a far bigger stake in the reputation of its business than Victor's. The store has been in business for a long time. The owners have spent years establishing customer loyalty. In contrast, Victor's has just been established. The owner has little of his own money tied up in the firm, and so has little to lose if the business fails. In addition, the nature of the business results in little customer loyalty. Harry's is probably more reliable.

1.5   Agency problems arise when managers and shareholders have different objectives. Managers may empire-build with excessive investment and growth. Managers may be unduly risk-averse, or they may try to take excessive salaries or perquisites.

CHAPTER 2

Financial Markets and Institutions

LEARNING OBJECTIVES

After studying this chapter, you should be able to:

1. Understand how financial markets and institutions channel savings to corporate investment.

2. Understand the basic structure of mutual funds, pension funds, banks, and insurance companies.

3. Explain the functions of financial markets and institutions.

4. Understand why the cost of capital for corporate investment is determined by investment opportunities in financial markets.

Related Web sites for this chapter can be found at www.mhhe.com/bmm6e.

Read this chapter before you visit the New York Stock Exchange.

Marvin E. Newman/Getty Images

If a corporation needs to issue more shares of stock, then its financial manager had better understand how the stock market works. If it wants to take out a bank loan, the financial manager had better understand how banks and other financial institutions work. That much is obvious. But the capital investment decision also requires a broader understanding of financial markets. We have said that a successful investment is one that increases the market value of the firm. How do investors value the firm? What level of profitability do investors require from the firm's capital investments? To answer these questions, we will need to think clearly about the cost of the capital that the firm raises from outside investors.

Financial markets and institutions are the firm's financial environment. You don't have to understand everything about that environment to begin the study of financial management, but a general understanding provides useful context for the work ahead. For example, that context will help you to understand why you are calculating the yield to maturity of a bond in Chapter 6, the net present value of a capital investment in Chapter 9, or the weighted-average cost of capital for a company in Chapter 13.

This chapter does three things. First it surveys financial markets and institutions. We will cover the stock and bond markets, mutual and pension funds, and banks and insurance companies. Second, we will set out the functions of financial markets and institutions. What do they do for corporations and for the economy? Third, it offers another look at why maximizing value is the natural financial objective of the corporation, and it defines the cost of capital for corporate investment.

2.1 The Importance of Financial Markets and Institutions

In the previous chapter we explained why corporations have to be good at finance in order to survive and prosper. All corporations face important investment and financing decisions. But of course those decisions are not made in a vacuum. They are made in a financial environment. That environment has two main segments: financial markets and financial institutions.

All large corporations have to go to financial markets and institutions for the financing they need to grow. When they have a surplus of cash, and no need for immediate financing, they have to invest the cash, for example, in bank accounts or in securities. Let's take Apple Computer, Inc., as an example.

Table 2–1 presents a timeline for Apple and examples of the sources of financing tapped by Apple from its start-up in a California garage in 1976 to its cash-rich status in 2007. The initial investment in Apple stock was $250,000. Apple was also able to get short-term financing from parts suppliers who did not demand immediate payment. Apple was able to get the parts, assemble and sell the computers, and then pay off its accounts payable to the suppliers. (We discuss accounts payable in Chapter 19.) Then as Apple grew, it was able to obtain several rounds of financing by selling Apple shares to private venture capital investors. (We discuss venture capital in Chapter 15.)

TABLE 2–1 Examples of financing decisions by Apple Computer

April 1976: Apple Computer, Inc., founded	Mike Makkula, Apple's first chairman, invests $250,000 in Apple shares.
1976: First 200 computers sold	Parts suppliers give Apple 30 days to pay. (Financing from accounts payable.)
1978–79	Apple raises $3.5 million from venture capital investors.
December 1980: Initial public offering	Apple raises $91 million, after fees and expenses, by selling shares to public investors.
May 1981	Apple sells 2.6 million additional shares at $31.25 per share.
April 1987	Apple pays its first dividend at an annual rate of $.12 per share
Early 1990s	Apple carries out several share repurchase programs.
1994	Apple issues $300 million of debt at an interest rate of 6.5%.
1996–97: Apple reports a $740 million loss in the second quarter of 1996. Lays off 2,700 employees in 1997.	Dividend is suspended in February 1996. Apple sells $661 million of debt to private investors in June 1996. The borrowing provides "sufficient liquidity" to execute Apple's strategic plans and to "return the company to profitability."
September 1997: Acquires assets of Power Computing Corp.	Acquisition is financed with $100 million of Apple stock.
2004: Apple is healthy and profitable, thanks to iMac, iPod, and other products.	Apple pays off the $300 million in long-term debt issued in 1994, leaving the company with no long-term debt outstanding.
2005–07	Apple's profits grow rapidly, but it pays no cash dividends. Instead it invests in short-term marketable securities, which accumulate to $15.4 billion by 2007.
From start-up to 2007	Apple stockholders reinvest $9.1 billion of earnings. Thus Apple's 2007 balance sheet shows cumulative retained earnings of $9.1 billion.

In December 1980, it raised $91 million in an initial public offering (IPO) of its shares to public investors. There was also a follow-up share issue in May 1981.[1]

Once Apple was a public company, it could raise financing from many sources, and it was able to pay for acquisitions by issuing more shares. We show a few examples in Table 2–1.

Apple started paying cash dividends to shareholders in 1987, and it also distributed cash to investors by stock repurchases in the early 1990s. But Apple hit a rough patch in 1996 and 1997, and regular dividends were eliminated. The company had to borrow $660 million from a group of private investors in order to cover its losses and finance its recovery plan. Apple was generally profitable, despite the rough years, and it financed growth by plowing back earnings into its operations. Cumulative retained earnings were $9.1 billion by 2007.

Apple is well known for its product innovations, including the Macintosh computer, the iMac, and the iPod. Apple is not special because of financing. In fact, the story of its financing is not too different from that of many other successful companies. But access to financing was vital to Apple's growth and profitability. Would we have iMac computers or iPods if Apple had been forced to operate in a country with a primitive financial system? Definitely not.

A modern financial system offers financing in many different forms, depending on the company's age, its growth rate, and the nature of its business. For example, Apple relied on venture capital financing in its early years and only later floated its shares in public stock markets. Still later, as the company matured, it turned to other forms of financing, including the examples given in Table 2–1. But the table does not begin to cover the range of financing channels open to modern corporations. We will encounter many other channels later in the book, and new channels are opening up regularly. The nearby box describes one recent financial innovation, micro-lending funds that make small loans to businesspeople in the poorer parts of the world.

2.2 The Flow of Savings to Corporations

The money that corporations invest in real assets comes ultimately from savings by investors. But there can be many stops on the road between savings and corporate investment. The road can pass through financial markets, financial intermediaries, or both.

Let's start with the simplest case of a small, closely held corporation, like Apple in its earliest years. The orange arrows in Figure 2–1 show the flow of savings from shareholders in this simple setting. There are two possible paths: The firm can sell new shares, or it can reinvest cash back into the firm's operations. Reinvestment means additional savings by existing shareholders. The reinvested cash could have been paid out to those shareholders and spent by them on personal consumption. By *not* taking and spending the cash, shareholders have reinvested their savings in the corporation. **Cash retained and reinvested in the firm's operations is cash saved and invested on behalf of the firm's shareholders.**

Of course, this small corporation has other financing choices. It could take out a bank loan, for example. The bank in turn may have raised money by attracting savings accounts. In this case investors' savings flow through the bank to the firm.

Now consider a large, public corporation, for example, Apple Computer in 2007. What's different? Scale, for one thing: Apple's annual revenues were $24 billion, and its balance sheet showed total assets of $25 billion. The scope of Apple's activities has also expanded: It now has dozens of products and operates worldwide. Because of this

---

[1] Many of the shares sold in the 1981 issue were previously held by Apple employees. Sale of these shares allowed the employees to cash out and diversify some of their Apple holdings but did not raise additional financing for Apple.

FINANCE IN PRACTICE

Micro Loans, Solid Returns

With about $200 of his own money and a $1,500 loan, Vahid Hujdur rented space in the old section of Sarajevo and started repairing and selling discarded industrial sewing machines. Hujdur now has 10 employees building, installing, and fixing industrial machinery. Hujddur didn't get his initial loan from a local bank. "They were asking for guarantees that were impossible to get," he recalls. Instead the capital came from LOKmicro, a local financial institution specializing in microfinance—the lending of small amounts to the poor in developing nations to help them launch small enterprises.

Microfinance institutions get capital from individual and institutional investors via microfinance funds, which collect the investors' money, vet the local lenders, offer them management assistance, and administer investors' accounts.

The borrowers who take out the micro loans pay relatively high interest rates because the cost of writing and administering such small loans is high and the loans are made in nations with weak currencies. Default rates on the loans run only about 4%, however. "There is a deep pride in keeping up with payments," says Deidre Wagner, an executive vice president of Starbucks, who invested $100,000 in a microfinance fund in 2003. "In some instances, when an individual is behind on payments, others in the village may make up the difference." Investors and borrowers know that when the micro loans are repaid, the money gets recycled into new loans, giving still more borrowers a chance to move up the economic ladder.

Source: Adapted from Eric Uhlfelder, "Micro Loans, Solid Returns," Business-Week, May 9, 2005, pp. 100–102.

scale and scope, Apple attracts investors' savings by a variety of different routes. It can do so because it is a large, profitable, public firm.

The flow of savings to large public corporations is shown in Figure 2–2. Notice two key differences from Figure 2–1. First, public corporations can draw savings from investors worldwide. Second, the savings flow through financial markets, financial intermediaries, or both. Suppose, for example, that Bank of America raises $300 million by a new issue of shares. An Italian investor buys 1,000 of the new shares for $60 per share. Now Bank of America takes that $60,000, along with money raised by the rest of the issue, and makes a $300 million loan to Apple. The Italian investor's

FIGURE 2–1 Flow of savings to investment in a closely held corporation. Investors use savings to buy additional shares. Investors also save when the corporation reinvests on their behalf.

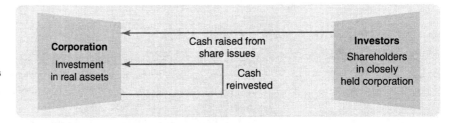

FIGURE 2–2 Flow of savings to investment for a large, public corporation. Savings come from investors worldwide. The savings may flow through financial markets or financial intermediaries. The corporation also reinvests on shareholders' behalf.

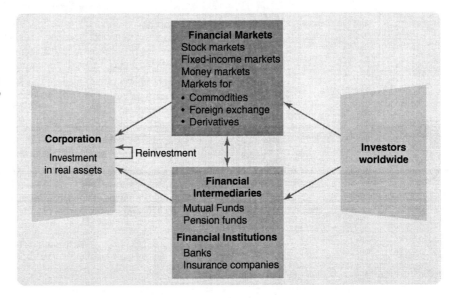

It's Not Your Grandfather's NYSE

The business of trading stocks has changed fundamentally in the last decade. In the old days, most trading was done on the crowded floor of the New York Stock Exchange (NYSE) or on the much smaller American Stock Exchange (AMEX). But by the turn of this century, most trades were routed through the NYSE's computer systems or through NASDAQ, a competing system that ties together a network of security dealers.

The trend toward electronic trading, plus rapid expansion in trading volumes, has now set off a wave of takeovers and consolidation. The NYSE, which used to be owned by a "club" of NYSE members, changed to a for-profit corporation and merged with Archipelago, which had developed an efficient electronic trading system. In 2006 the NYSE bought the European trading system Euronext, beating out the rival bidder Deutsche Borse, the German exchange. In 2008 NYSE Euronext took over AMEX.

Other exchanges joined the party. The London Stock Exchange was a perennial target of (unsuccessful) bids by the Swedish exchange OMX, Euronext (before it was acquired by the NYSE), Deutsche Borse, Macquarie Bank from Australia, and NASDAQ. NASDAQ later purchased OMX (Sweden).

"There's an obvious advantage of centralizing exchanges," says Wharton Finance Professor Richard J. Herring. Bigger exchanges have lower trading costs, which attracts more traders and listing companies. As trading volume increases, liquidity improves.

Consolidation is not limited to stock markets. Euronext was attractive to the NYSE partly because of its markets for options and commodities. The two largest Chicago commodities exchanges, the Chicago Mercantile Exchange and the Chicago Board of Trade, merged in 2007 as the CME Group. In March 2008, the CME Group announced that it would acquire the New York Mercantile Exchange in a deal to join the two largest U.S. futures exchanges.

Source: Adapted from H. Weitzman and A. Gangahar, "CME Casts Its Eye in Nymex's Direction," *Financial Times*, January 29, 2008, p. 17, and "Why Stock Exchanges Are Scrambling to Consolidate," *Knowledge@Wharton*, March 22, 2006.

savings end up flowing through financial markets (the stock market), to a financial intermediary (Bank of America), and finally to Apple.

Of course our Italian friend's $60,000 doesn't literally arrive at Apple in an envelope marked "From L. DaVinci." Investments by the purchasers of the Bank of America's stock issue are pooled, not segregated. Sr. DaVinci would own a share of all of Bank of America's assets, not just one loan to Apple. Nevertheless, investors' savings are flowing through the financial markets and the bank to finance Apple's capital investments.

The Stock Market

financial market
Market where securities are issued and traded.

A **financial market** is a market where securities are issued and traded. A security is just a traded financial asset, such as a share of stock. For a corporation, the stock market is probably the most important financial market.

As corporations grow, their requirements for outside capital can expand dramatically. At some point the firm will decide to "go public" by issuing shares on an organized exchange such as the New York Stock Exchange (NYSE); that first issue is called an *initial public offering* or *IPO*. The buyers of the IPO are helping to finance the firm's investment in real assets. In return, the buyers become part-owners of the firm and share in its future success or failure. (Most investors in the Internet IPOs of 1999 and 2000 are by now sorely disappointed, but many IPOs pay off handsomely. If only we had bought Apple shares on their IPO day in 1980 . . .) Of course a corporation's IPO is not its last chance to issue shares. For example, Bank of America went public in the 1930s, but it could make a new issue of shares tomorrow.

primary market
Market for the sale of new securities by corporations.

A new issue of shares increases both the amount of cash held by the company and the number of shares held by the public. Such an issue is known as a *primary issue,* and it is sold in the **primary market.** But in addition to helping companies raise new cash, financial markets also allow investors to trade securities among themselves. For example, Smith might decide to raise some cash by selling her Apple stock at the same time that Jones invests his spare cash in Apple. The result is simply a transfer of ownership from Smith to Jones, which has no effect on the company itself. Such purchases and sales of existing securities are known as *secondary transactions,* and they take place in the **secondary market.**

secondary market
Market in which previously issued securities are traded among investors.

Stock markets are also called *equity markets,* since stockholders are said to own the common equity of the firm. You will hear financial managers refer to the capital structure decision as "the choice between debt and equity financing."

Most trading in the shares of U.S. corporations takes place on the NYSE and on NASDAQ, which tends to attract listings from smaller, high-tech companies. The business of trading is changing rapidly, however, as the box on page 35 explains.

Now may be a good time to stress that the financial manager plays on a global stage and needs to be familiar with markets around the world. For example, the stock of Citigroup, one of the largest U.S. banks, is listed in New York but also on several European stock exchanges. Conversely, Cadbury Schweppes, Deutsche Bank, France Telecom, Nokia, Petrobras (Brazil), Sony, Toyota, Unilever, and over 400 other overseas firms have listed their shares on the NYSE. We return to the trading and pricing of shares in Chapter 7.

Agency Problems and Corporate Governance

The flow of savings to public corporations, as in Figure 2–2, requires *separation of ownership and control:* the ultimate owners of a corporation are not its managers. That creates the *agency problems* that we noted in the previous chapter. Agency problems exist because managers will consider their own interests as well as shareholders'. Corporations try to align managers' and shareholders' interests (by granting stock or options to top management, for example), but the alignment can never be perfect.

Separation of ownership and control is necessary because outside investors cannot know enough about the firm's problems and prospects to make good financial decisions. If investors did have that knowledge, they would not need managers. The investors could manage the firm on their own.

Financial markets and institutions are supposed to move financing to all firms that can invest at superior rates of return. Financing moves from investors to firms only if investors are protected. This creates the need for a system of *corporate governance,* so that financing can flow to the right firms at the right times. Good corporate governance protects investors and thus supports the development of financial markets and the financing required for economic growth. Governance includes standards for accounting and disclosure to investors, requirements for boards of directors, and legal sanctions for fraud or self-dealing by management. The Sarbanes-Oxley (SOX) Act of 2002 was an attempt to tighten corporate governance.

We discussed agency problems and governance in the previous chapter, but these topics are important and worth revisiting. Think again of the financial histories of Apple in Table 2–1 and of FedEx at the start of Chapter 1. These companies survived and grew because they had access to financing from outside investors. That financing was forthcoming because the investors trusted the companies to invest wisely. In other words, the investors trusted the U.S. system of corporate governance, and they trusted the directors and managers of the firms to try to increase shareholder value.

Other Financial Markets

Debt securities as well as equities are traded in financial markets. The Apple bond issue in 1994 was a public issue (see Table 2–1). Table 1–1 in the previous chapter also gives examples, including the debt issues by LVMH and Wal-Mart.

A few corporate debt securities are traded on the NYSE and other exchanges, but most corporate debt securities are traded *over the counter,* on a network of banks and securities dealers. Government debt is also traded over the counter.

A bond is a more complex security than a share of stock. A share is just a proportional ownership claim on the firm, with no definite maturity. Bonds and other debt securities can vary in maturity, in the degree of protection or collateral offered by the issuer, and in the level and timing of interest payments. Some bonds make "floating" interest payments tied to the future level of interest rates. Many can be "called" (repurchased and retired) by the issuing company before the bonds' stated maturity date. Some bonds can be converted into other securities, usually the stock of the issuing company. You don't need to master these distinctions now; just be aware that the debt or **fixed-income market** is a complicated and challenging place. A corporation must

fixed-income market
Market for debt securities.

Prediction Markets

Stock markets have long let traders bet on their favored stocks. Now *prediction markets* allow them to bet on almost anything else. These markets reveal the collective guess of traders on issues as diverse as the next presidential election, the winner of the Academy Awards, the amount of snow that will fall on Central Park this winter, or the severity of the next influenza season.

Prediction markets are conducted on the Iowa Electronic Market at the University of Iowa (**www.biz.uiowa.edu/iem**) and on online exchanges such as **www.intrade.com** or **www.betfair.com**. Take the 2008 presidential primary races as an example. You could bet that Barack Obama would be the Democratic candidate by buying one of his contracts. Each Obama contract would pay $1 if he won the Democratic nomination and nothing if he lost. If you thought the probability of his victory in the primaries was 55%, you would be prepared to pay up to $.55 for his contract. Someone relatively pessimistic about his chances would be happy to *sell* you such a contract, for that sale would turn a profit if Obama eventually were to lose the nomination. With many participants buying and selling contracts, the market price of a contract reveals the aggregated wisdom of the crowd.

Take a look at the accompanying figure, from the Iowa Electronic Market, which shows the prices of the three major Democratic contenders (Hillary Clinton, Barack Obama, and John Edwards) through the end of February 2008. Notice the dramatic increase in the Obama contract price after his January win in the Iowa caucuses, the equally dramatic decrease the next week when Clinton won the New Hampshire primary, and the substantial run-up in Obama's price in February as he went on to win a lengthy succession of state primaries and caucuses.

The predictive accuracy of these markets compares favorably to several major polls. This may not be surprising, since participants are putting their money where their mouths are when making their predictions. Businesses have also experimented with these markets. For example, Hewlett-Packard set up a market to predict its printer sales and plan accordingly. You can trade "weather contracts" on the Chicago Mercantile Exchange that pay off depending on average temperatures in a variety of cities. The CME has also experimented with economic prediction contracts that allow trading on macroeconomic variables such as gross domestic product or inflation rates.

Prediction markets allowed you to bet on three candidates for the Democratic nomination.

2008 US Democratic National Convention Market

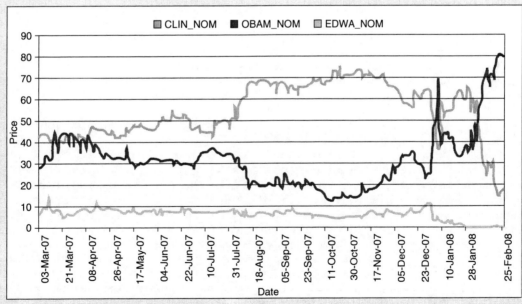

Source: Iowa Electronic Market, February 2008.

capital market
Market for long-term financing.

money market
Market for short-term financing (less than 1 year).

not only decide between debt and equity finance. It must also consider the design of debt. We return to the trading and pricing of debt securities in Chapter 6.

The markets for long-term debt and equity are called **capital markets.** A firm's *capital* is its long-run financing. Short-term securities are traded in the **money markets.** "Short term" means less than 1 year. For example, large, creditworthy corporations raise short-term financing by issues of *commercial paper,* which are debt issues with maturities of at most 270 days. Commercial paper is issued in the money market.

Self-Test 2.1

Do you understand the following distinctions? Briefly explain in each case.

a. Primary market vs. secondary market.
b. Capital market vs. money market.
c. Stock market vs. fixed-income market.

The financial manager regularly encounters other financial markets. Here are three examples, with references to the chapters where they are discussed:

- *Foreign-exchange markets* (Chapter 22). Any corporation engaged in international trade must be able to transfer money from dollars to other currencies, or vice versa. Foreign exchange is traded over the counter through a network of the largest international banks.
- *Commodities markets* (Chapter 24). Dozens of commodities are traded on organized exchanges, such as the New York Mercantile Exchange or the Chicago Board of Trade. You can buy or sell corn, wheat, cotton, fuel oil, natural gas, copper, silver, platinum, and so on.
- *Markets for options and other derivatives* (Chapters 23 and 24). Derivatives are securities whose payoffs depend on the prices of other securities or commodities. For example, you can buy an option to purchase IBM shares at a fixed price on a fixed future date. The option's payoff depends on the price of IBM shares on that date. Commodities can be traded by a different kind of derivative security called a futures contract.

Commodity and derivative markets are not sources of financing but markets where the financial manager can adjust the firm's exposure to various business risks. For example, an electric generating company may wish to "lock in" the future price of natural gas or fuel oil by trading in commodity markets, thus eliminating the risk of a sudden jump in the price of its raw materials.

Wherever there is uncertainty, investors may be interested in trading, either to speculate or to lay off their risks, and a market may arise to meet that trading demand. In recent years several new markets have been created that allow punters to bet on a single event. The nearby box discusses how prices in these markets can reveal people's predictions about the future.

Financial Intermediaries

financial intermediary
An organization that raises money from investors and provides financing for individuals, corporations, or other organizations.

A **financial intermediary** is an organization that raises money from investors and provides financing for individuals, companies, and other organizations. For corporations, intermediaries are important sources of financing. Intermediaries are a stop on the road between savings and real investment. We will start with two important classes of intermediaries, mutual funds and pension funds.

mutual fund
An investment company that pools the savings of many investors and invests in a portfolio of securities.

Mutual funds raise money by selling shares to investors. The investors' money is pooled and invested in a portfolio of securities. Investors can buy or sell shares in mutual funds as they please, and initial investments are often $3,000 or less. Vanguard's Explorer Fund, for example, held a portfolio of about 1,300 stocks with a market value of about $12 billion at the end of 2007. An investor in Explorer can increase her stake in the fund's portfolio by buying additional shares, and so gain a higher share of the portfolio's subsequent dividends and price appreciation.[2]

---

[2] Mutual funds are not corporations but investment companies. They pay no tax, providing that all income from dividends and price appreciation is passed on to the funds' shareholders. The shareholders pay personal tax on this income.

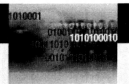

INTERNET INSIDER

Mutual Funds

Mutual Funds

Most mutual funds in the United States belong to the Investment Company Institute. Log on to its Web site at **www.ici.org**. You will find some essential information about mutual funds and a useful fact book. Make sure that you know the basic types of fund. For example, can you explain the difference between a stock fund and a money market mutual fund? Look in the fact book at the amount of assets managed by these funds. Have mutual fund assets been increasing or decreasing over the past 20 years? What are the advantages and disadvantages of investing through a mutual fund rather than doing so directly?

Choosing a Mutual Fund

Here are the Web sites for three of the largest mutual fund companies:

1. Fidelity Investments: **www.fidelity.com**
2. Putnam Investments: **www.putnam.com**
3. Vanguard Group: **www.vanguard.com**

Pick three or four funds from one of these sites and compare their investment objectives, risks, past returns, fund fees, and so on. Read the prospectuses for each of these funds; they are usually clear and informative. Who do you think should, or should not, invest in each fund? Which one would be most appropriate for a young financial executive saving for retirement?

Mutual Fund Performance

Morningstar provides data on mutual fund performance. Log on to **www.morningstar .com** and click on *Funds* and find recent returns by category of fund. Which category has performed unusually well or badly? Is it the funds investing in small- rather than large-company stocks, those investing in growth rather than value stocks, or those specializing in a particular industry? Morningstar also provides information on ETFs. ETFs are similar to mutual funds. We will explain how they work in a few pages. Look, for example, at SPDRs. How have they performed? What are the expenses of investing in SPDRs?

Source: Investment Company Institute Web site. Reprinted with permission of the Investment Company Institute. All rights reserved. © 2008 by the Investment Company Institute.

She can also sell her shares back to the fund if she decides to cash out of her investment.[3]

The advantages of a mutual fund should be clear: Unless you are very wealthy, you cannot buy and manage a 1,300-stock portfolio on your own, at least not efficiently. **Mutual funds offer investors low-cost diversification and professional management. For most investors, it's more efficient to buy a mutual fund than to assemble a diversified portfolio of stocks and bonds.**

Mutual fund managers also try their best to "beat the market," that is, to generate superior performance by finding the stocks with better-than-average returns. Whether they can pick winners consistently is another question, which we will address in Chapter 7.

---

[3] Explorer, like most mutual funds, is an *open-end* fund. It stands ready to issue shares to new investors in the fund and to buy back existing shares when its shareholders decide to cash out. The purchase and sale prices depend on the fund's net asset value (NAV) on the day of purchase or redemption. *Closed-end* funds have a fixed number of shares traded on an exchange. If you want to invest in a closed-end fund, you must buy shares from another stockholder in the fund.

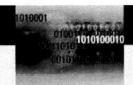

INTERNET INSIDER

Banks

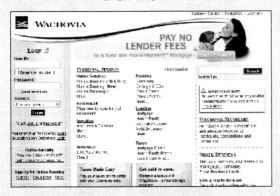

We mentioned in the last chapter that large banks have their fingers in many pies. The Web sites of the very largest banks are equally massive. Wachovia **www.wachovia.com**, and Bank of America (**www.bankofamerica.com**) are examples of banks with relatively straightforward Web sites. Use these Web sites and the company annual reports to find what services banks provide to individuals, small businesses, and large corporations.

Source: Wachovia Web site.

In exchange for their services, the fund's managers take out a management fee. There are also the expenses of running the fund. For Explorer, fees and expenses absorb about .4% of portfolio value each year. This seems reasonable, but watch out: The typical mutual fund charges more than Explorer does. In some cases fees and expenses add up to 2% per year. That's a big bite out of your investment return.

Mutual funds are a stop on the road from savings to corporate investment. Suppose Explorer purchases part of the new issue of shares by Bank of America. Again we show the flow of savings to investment by orange arrows:

Over 8,000 mutual funds operate in the United States. In fact there are more mutual funds than public companies! The funds pursue a wide variety of investment strategies. Some funds specialize in safe stocks with generous dividend payouts. Some specialize in high-tech growth stocks. Some "balanced" funds offer mixtures of stocks and bonds. Some specialize in particular countries or regions. For example, the Fidelity Investments mutual fund group sponsors funds for Canada, Japan, China, Europe, Latin America, and so on.

hedge fund
A private investment pool, open to wealthy or institutional investors, that is only lightly regulated and therefore can pursue more speculative policies than mutual funds.

Like mutual funds, **hedge funds** also pool the savings of different investors and invest on their behalf. But they differ from mutual funds in at least two ways. First, because hedge funds usually follow complex, high-risk investment strategies, access is restricted to knowledgeable investors such as pension funds, endowment funds, and wealthy individuals. Don't try to send a check for $3,000 or $5,000 to a hedge fund. The hedge fund is not in the "retail" investment business. Second, hedge funds try to attract the most talented managers by compensating them with potentially lucrative, performance-related fees.[4] In contrast, mutual funds usually pay a fixed percentage of assets under management.

Hedge funds follow many different investment strategies. Some try to make a profit by identifying *over*valued stocks or markets and selling short. (We will not go into procedures for shortselling here. Just remember that short sellers profit when prices *fall*.[5]) "Vulture funds" specialize in the securities of distressed corporations. Some hedge funds take bets on firms involved in merger negotiations, others look for mispricing

---

[4] Sometimes these fees can be very large indeed. For example, *Trader Monthly Magazine* estimated that the top-performing hedge fund manager in 2006 earned over $1.5 billion.

[5] A short seller borrows a security from another investor and sells it. Of course, the seller must sooner or later buy the security back and return it to its original owner. The short seller earns a profit if the security can be bought back at a lower price than it was sold for.)

of convertible bonds, and some take positions in currencies and interest rates. Hedge funds manage less money than mutual funds, but they sometimes take very big positions and have a large impact on the market.

pension fund
Investment plan set up by an employer to provide for employees' retirement.

There are other ways of pooling and investing savings. Consider a **pension fund** set up by a corporation or other organization on behalf of its employees. There are several types of pension plan. Here is just one example: In a *defined-contribution* plan,[6] a percentage of the employee's monthly paycheck is contributed to a pension fund. (The employer and employee may each contribute 5%, for example.) Contributions from all participating employees are pooled and invested in securities or mutual funds. (Usually the employees can choose from a menu of funds with different investment strategies.) Each employee's balance in the plan grows over the years as contributions continue and investment income accumulates. When retirement age arrives, the balance in the plan can be used to finance living expenses.

Pension funds are designed for long-run investment. They provide professional management and diversification. They also have an important tax advantage: Contributions are tax-deductible, and investment returns inside the plan are not taxed until cash is finally withdrawn.[7]

Pension plans are among the most important vehicles for savings. Private pension plans held about $5.9 trillion in assets in 2007.

Self-Test 2.2

Individual investors can buy bonds and stocks directly, or they can put their money in a mutual fund or a defined-contribution pension fund. What are the advantages of the second strategy?

Financial Institutions

financial institution
A bank, insurance company, or similar financial intermediary.

Banks and insurance companies are **financial institutions.**[8] A financial institution is an intermediary that does more than just pool and invest savings. Institutions raise financing in special ways, for example, by accepting deposits or selling insurance policies, and they provide additional financial services. Unlike a mutual fund, they not only invest in securities but also loan money directly to individuals, businesses, or other organizations.

Commercial banks lend money to corporations. (In the United States, they are generally not allowed to make equity investments in corporations, although banks in most other countries can do so.) Suppose that a local forest products company negotiates a short-term bank loan for $2.5 million. The flow of savings is:

---

[6] In a defined-contribution plan, each employee owns a portion of the pension fund and accumulates an investment balance to pay for retirement. The amount available for retirement depends on the accumulated contributions and on the rate of return earned on the invested contributions. In a *defined-benefit* plan, the employer promises a certain level of retirement benefits (set by a formula) and the *employer* invests in the pension plan. The plan's accumulated investment value has to be large enough to cover the promised benefits. If not, the employer must put in more money.

[7] Defined-benefit pension plans share these same advantages, except that the employer invests rather than the employees. In a defined-benefit plan, the advantage of tax deferral on investment income accrues to the employer. This deferral reduces the cost of funding the plan.

[8] We may be drawing too fine a distinction between financial intermediaries and institutions. A mutual fund could be considered a financial institution. But "financial institution" usually suggests a more complicated intermediary, such as a bank.

The bank provides a service to both the company and its depositors. To cover the costs of this service, it charges borrowers a higher interest rate than it pays its depositors.

Investment Banks   We have discussed commercial banks, which raise money from depositors and other investors and then make loans to businesses and individuals. *Investment banks* are different.[9] Investment banks do not take deposits, and they do not usually make loans to companies. Instead, they advise and assist companies in raising financing. For example, investment banks *underwrite* stock offerings by purchasing the new shares from the issuing company at a negotiated price and reselling the shares to investors. Thus the issuing company gets a fixed price for the new shares, and the investment bank takes responsibility for distributing the shares to thousands of investors. We discuss share issues in more detail in Chapter 15.

Investment banks also advise on takeovers, mergers, and acquisitions. They offer investment advice and manage investment portfolios for individual and institutional investors. They run trading desks for foreign exchange, commodities, bonds, options, and derivatives.

Investment banks can invest their own money in start-ups and other ventures. For example, the Australian Macquarie Bank has invested in airports, toll highways, electric transmission and generation, and other infrastructure projects around the world.

The largest investment banks are financial powerhouses. They include Merrill Lynch, Goldman Sachs, Morgan Stanley, Lehman Brothers, Lazard Freres (New York and Paris), Nomura Securities (Japan), and Macquarie Bank. In addition, the major commercial banks, including Bank of America and Citigroup, all have investment banking divisions.

Insurance Companies   In the United States, insurance companies are more important than banks for the *long-term* financing of business. They are massive investors in corporate stocks and bonds, and they often make long-term loans directly to corporations.

Suppose a company needs a loan of $2.5 million for 9 years, not 9 months. It could issue a bond directly to investors, or it could negotiate a 9-year loan with an insurance company:

The money to make the loan comes mainly from the sale of insurance policies. Say you buy a fire insurance policy on your home. You pay cash to the insurance company and get a financial asset (the policy) in exchange. You receive no interest payments on this financial asset, but if a fire does strike, the company is obliged to cover the damages up to the policy limit. This is the return on your investment. (Of course, a fire is a sad and dangerous event that you hope to avoid. But if a fire does occur, you are better off getting a return on your investment in insurance than not having insurance at all.)

The company will issue not just one policy but thousands. Normally the incidence of fires "averages out," leaving the company with a predictable obligation to its policyholders as a group. Of course the insurance company must charge enough for its policies to cover selling and administrative costs, pay policyholders' claims, and generate a profit for its stockholders.

---

[9] Banks that accept deposits and provide financing to businesses are called *commercial* banks. *Savings* banks accept deposits and savings accounts and loan the money out mostly to individuals, for example, as mortgage loans to home buyers. Investment banks do not take deposits and do not loan money to businesses or individuals, except as *bridge loans* made as temporary financing for takeovers or other transactions. Investment banks are sometimes called *merchant banks*.

Why is a financial intermediary different from a manufacturing corporation? First, it may raise money in different ways, for example, by taking deposits or selling insurance policies. Second, it invests that money in *financial* assets, for example, in stocks, bonds, or loans to businesses or individuals. The manufacturing company's main investments are in plant, equipment, or other *real* assets.

Self-Test 2.3

What are the key differences between a mutual fund and a bank or an insurance company?

Total Financing of U.S. Corporations

The pie chart in Figure 2–3 shows the investors in bonds and other debt securities. Notice the importance of institutional investors—mutual funds, pension funds, insurance companies, and banks. Households (individual investors) hold only a small slice of the debt pie. The other slices represent the rest of the world (investors from outside the United States) and various other categories.

The pie chart in Figure 2–4 shows holdings of the shares issued by U.S. corporations. Here households make a stronger showing, with 27.1% of the total. Pension funds, insurance companies, and mutual funds add up to about 58.6% of the total.[10] The rest-of-the-world slice is about 12.6%.

FIGURE 2–3 Holdings of corporate and foreign bonds, third quarter 2007. The total amount is $10.6 trillion.

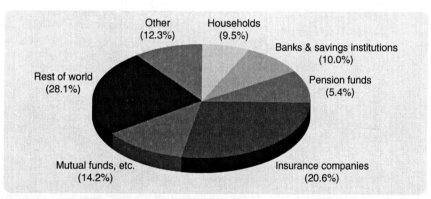

Source: Board of Governors of the Federal Reserve System, Division of Research and Statistics, *Flow of Funds Accounts,* Table L.212 (**www.federalreserve.gov**).

FIGURE 2–4 Holdings of corporate equities, third quarter 2007. The total amount is $22.4 trillion.

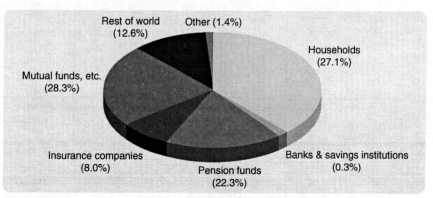

Source: Board of Governors of the Federal Reserve System, Division of Research and Statistics, *Flow of Funds Accounts,* Table L.213 (**www.federalreserve.gov**).

---

[10] Remember, banks in the United States do not usually hold stock in other companies.

The aggregate amounts represented in these figures are enormous. There is $10.6 trillion of debt behind Figure 2–3 and $22.4 trillion of equity behind Figure 2–4, (22,445,000,000,000).[11]

Chapter 14 reviews corporate financing patterns in more detail.

2.3 Functions of Financial Markets and Intermediaries

Financial markets and intermediaries provide financing for business. They channel savings to real investment. That much should be loud and clear from Sections 2.1 and 2.2 of this chapter. But there are other functions that may not be quite so obvious.

Transporting Cash across Time

Individuals need to transport expenditures in time. If you have money now that you wish to save for a rainy day, you can (for example) put the money in a savings account at a bank and withdraw it with interest later. If you don't have money today, say to buy a car, you can borrow money from the bank and pay off the loan later. Modern finance provides a kind of time machine. Lenders transport money forward in time; borrowers transport it back. Both are happier than if they were forced to spend income as it arrives. Of course, individuals are not alone in needing to raise cash from time to time. Firms with good investment opportunities, but a shortage of internally generated cash, raise cash by borrowing or selling new shares. Many governments run deficits and finance current outlays by issuing debt.

Young people saving for retirement may transport their current earnings 30 or 40 years into the future by means of a pension fund. They may even transport income to their heirs by purchase of a life insurance policy.

In principle, individuals or firms with cash surpluses could take out newspaper advertisements or surf the Web looking for counterparties with cash shortages. But it is usually cheaper and more convenient to use financial markets and intermediaries. It is not just a matter of avoiding the cost of searching for the right counterparty. Follow-up is needed. For example, banks don't just loan money and walk away. They monitor the borrower to make sure that the loan is used for its intended purpose and that the borrower's credit stays solid.

Risk Transfer and Diversification

Financial markets and intermediaries allow investors and businesses to reduce and reallocate risk. Insurance companies are an obvious example. When you buy homeowner's insurance, you greatly reduce the risk of loss from fire, theft, or accidents. But your policy is not a very risky bet for the insurance company. It diversifies by issuing thousands of policies, and it expects losses to average out over the policies.[12] The insurance company allows you to pool risk with thousands of other homeowners.

Investors should diversify too. For example, you can buy shares in a mutual fund that holds hundreds of stocks. In fact, you can buy *index funds* that invest in all the stocks in the popular market indexes. For example, the Vanguard 500 Index fund holds the stocks in the Standard & Poor's Composite stock market index. (The "S&P 500" tracks the performance of the largest U.S. stocks. It is the index most used by professional investors.) If you buy this fund, you are insulated from the company-specific risks of the 500 companies in the index. These risks are averaged out by diversification. Of course you are still left with the risk that the level of the stock market as a whole will fall. In fact, we will see in Chapter 11 that investors are mostly concerned with *market risk,* not the specific risks of individual companies.

---

[11] The total market value of shares issued by U.S. *nonfinancial* corporations is $12.5 trillion. "Nonfinancial" excludes financial institutions, such as banks and insurance companies.

[12] Unfortunately for insurance companies, the losses don't always average out. Hurricanes and earthquakes can damage thousands of homes at once. The potential losses are so great that property insurance companies buy *reinsurance* against such catastrophes.

Index mutual funds are one way to invest in widely diversified portfolios at low cost. Another route is provided by exchange traded funds (ETFs), which are portfolios of stocks that can be bought or sold in a single trade. These include Standard & Poor's Depository Receipts (SPDRs, or "spiders"), which are portfolios matching Standard & Poor's stock market indexes. The total amount invested in the spider tracking the benchmark S&P 500 index was about $75 billion by the end of 2007. You can also buy DIAMONDS, which track the Dow Jones Industrial Average; QUBES or QQQQs, which track the NASDAQ 100 index; and Vanguard ETFs that track the Vanguard Total Stock Market index, which is a basket of almost all the stocks traded in the United States. You can also buy ETFs that track foreign stock markets, bonds, or commodities.

ETFs are in some ways more efficient than mutual funds. To buy or sell an ETF, you simply make a trade, just as if you bought or sold shares of stock. To invest in an open-ended mutual fund, you have to send money to the fund in exchange for newly issued shares. If you want to withdraw the investment, you have to notify the fund, which redeems your shares and sends you a check or credits your account with the fund. Also, many of the larger ETFs charge lower fees than mutual funds. Vanguard's fee for managing its Total Stock Market ETF is .07% per year. For a $100,000 investment, the fee is only $.0007 \times 100,000 = \$70$.

Financial markets provide other mechanisms for sharing risks. For example, a wheat farmer and a baking company are each exposed to fluctuations in the price of wheat after the harvest. The farmer worries about low prices, the baker about high prices. They can both rest easier if the baker can agree with the farmer to buy wheat in the future at a fixed price. Of course, it would be difficult, to say the least, if the baker and the farmer had to contact an Internet dating service to get together to make a deal. Fortunately no dating service is needed: Each can trade in commodity markets, the farmer as a seller and the baker as a buyer.

Liquidity

liquidity
The ability to sell or exchange an asset for cash on short notice.

Markets and intermediaries also provide **liquidity,** that is, the ability to turn an investment back into cash when needed. Suppose you deposit $5,000 in a savings bank on February 1. During that month, the bank uses your deposit and other new deposits to make a 6-month construction loan to a real estate developer. On March 1, you realize that you need your $5,000 back. The bank can give it to you. Because the bank has thousands of depositors, and other sources of financing if necessary, it can make an illiquid loan to the developer financed by liquid deposits made by you and other customers. If you lend out your money for 6 months directly to the real estate developer, you will have a hard time retrieving it 1 month later.[13]

The shares of public companies are liquid because they are traded more or less continuously in the stock market. An Italian investor who puts $60,000 into Bank of America shares can recover that money on short notice. (A $60,000 sell order is a drop in the bucket, compared with the normal trading volume of Bank of America shares.) Mutual funds can redeem their shares for cash on short notice because the funds invest in traded securities, which can be sold as necessary.

Of course, liquidity is a matter of degree. Foreign exchange markets for major currencies are exceptionally liquid. Bank of America or Deutsche Bank could buy $200 million worth of yen or euros in the blink of an eye, with hardly any effect on foreign exchange rates. U.S. Treasury securities are also very liquid, and the shares of the largest companies on the major international stock exchanges are only slightly less so.

Liquidity is most important when you're in a hurry. If you try to sell $500,000 worth of the shares of a small, thinly traded company all at once, you will probably knock

---

[13] Of course, the bank can't repay all depositors simultaneously. To do so, it would have to sell off its loans to the real estate developer and other borrowers. These loans are *not* liquid. This raises the specter of bank runs, where doubts about a bank's ability to pay off its depositors cause a rush of withdrawals, with each depositor trying to get his or her money out first. Bank runs are rare, because bank deposits are backed up by the U.S. Federal Deposit Insurance Corporation, which insures bank accounts up to $100,000 per account.

down the price to some extent. If you're patient and don't surprise other investors with a large, sudden sell order, you may be able to unload your shares on better terms. It's the same problem you may face in selling real estate. A house or condominium is not a liquid asset in a panic sale. If you're determined to sell in an afternoon, you're not going to get full value.

The Payment Mechanism

Think how inconvenient life would be if you had to pay for every purchase in cash or if General Motors had to ship truckloads of hundred-dollar bills round the country to pay its suppliers. Checking accounts, credit cards, and electronic transfers allow individuals and firms to send and receive payments quickly and safely over long distances. Banks are the obvious providers of payment services, but they are not alone. For example, if you buy shares in a money market mutual fund, your money is pooled with that of other investors and used to buy safe, short-term securities. You can then write checks on this mutual fund investment, just as if you had a bank deposit.

Information Provided by Financial Markets

In well-functioning financial markets, you can *see* what securities and commodities are worth, and you can see—or at least estimate—the rates of return that investors can expect on their savings. The information provided by financial markets is often essential to a financial manager's job. Here are three examples of how this information can be used.

Commodity Prices Catalytic converters are used in the exhaust systems of cars and light trucks to reduce pollution. The catalysts include platinum, which is traded on the New York Mercantile Exchange.

In January a manufacturer of catalytic converters is planning production for July. How much per ounce should the company budget for purchases of platinum in that month? Easy: The company's CFO looks up the market price of platinum on the New York Mercantile Exchange—$1,756 per ounce for delivery in July. (This was the closing price for platinum on January 1, 2008, for delivery in July.) The CFO can lock in that price if she wishes. The details of such a trade are covered in Chapter 24.

Interest Rates The CFO of Catalytic Concepts has to raise $400 million in new financing. She considers an issue of 30-year bonds. What will the interest rate on the bonds be? To find out, the CFO looks up interest rates on existing bonds traded in financial markets.

The results are shown in Table 2–2. Notice how the interest rate climbs as credit quality deteriorates: The largest, safest companies, which are rated AAA ("triple-A"), can borrow for 30 years at a 5.71% interest rate. The interest rates for AA, A, and BBB climb to 5.78%, 6.38%, and 7.12%, respectively. Triple-B companies are still regarded as *investment grade,* that is, good quality, but the next step down takes the investor into *junk bond* territory. The interest rate for double-B companies climbs to 9.84%. Single-B companies are riskier still, so investors demand 10.82%.

TABLE 2–2 Interest rates on 30-year corporate bonds, February 2008. The interest rate is lowest for top-quality (AAA) issuers. The rate rises as credit quality declines.

Credit Rating	Interest Rate
AAA	5.71%
AA	5.78
A	6.38
BBB	7.12
BB	9.84
B	10.82

Source: Bloomberg Composite Corporate Bond Indexes.

TABLE 2-3 Calculating the total market values of Alaska Air Group and other companies in January 2008. (Shares and market values in millions. Ticker symbols in parentheses.)

	Stock Price	×	Number of Shares	=	Market Value
Alaska Air Group (ALK)	23.09	×	40.312	=	$931
Bob Evans Farms (BOBE)	25.27	×	33.509	=	$847
Callaway Golf (ELY)	15.11	×	65.113	=	$984
TransCanada Pipelines (TRP)	39.10	×	537.762	=	$21,027
General Electric (GE)	35.17	×	10,106.209	=	$355,435

Source: Standard & Poor's Market Insight (**www.mhhe.com/edumarketinsight**).

There will be more on bond ratings and interest rates in Chapter 6. But you can see how a financial manager can use information from fixed-income markets to forecast the interest rate on new debt financing. For example, if Catalytic Concepts can qualify as a BBB-rated company, and interest rates are as shown in Table 2–2, it should be able to raise new debt financing for approximately 7%.

Company Values How much was Alaska Air Group worth in January 2008? How about Bob Evans Farms, Callaway Golf, TransCanada Pipelines, or GE? Table 2–3 shows the answers. We simply multiply the number of shares outstanding by the price per share in the stock market. Investors valued Alaska Air Group at $931 million, GE at $355 *billion.*

Stock prices and company values summarize investors' collective assessment of how well a company is doing, both its current performance and its future prospects. Thus an increase in stock price sends a positive signal from investors to managers.[14] That is why top management's compensation is linked to stock prices. A manager who owns shares in his or her company will be motivated to increase the company's market value. This reduces agency costs by aligning the interests of managers and stockholders.

This is one important advantage of going public. A private company can't use its stock price as a measure of performance. It can still compensate managers with shares, but the shares will not be valued in a financial market.

Self-Test 2.4

Which of the functions described in this section require financial markets? Explain briefly.

2.4 Value Maximization and the Cost of Capital

In Chapter 1 we stated the financial objective of the firm: Maximize the current market value of shareholders' investment. This simple, unqualified goal makes sense when the shareholders have access to well-functioning financial markets and institutions. Access allows them to share risks and transport savings across time. Access gives them the flexibility to manage their own savings and investment plans, leaving the corporation's financial managers with only one task, to increase market value.

A corporation's roster of shareholders will usually include both risk-averse and risk-tolerant investors. You might expect the risk-averse to say, "Sure, maximize value, but don't touch too many high-risk projects." Instead, they say, "Risky projects are OK, *provided* that expected profits are more than enough to offset the risks. If this firm ends up too risky for my taste, I'll adjust my investment portfolio to make it safer." For example, the risk-averse shareholder can shift more of his or her portfolio to safe assets, such as U.S. government bonds. The shareholder can also just say goodbye,

---

[14] We can't claim that investors' assessments of value are always correct. Finance can be a risky and dangerous business—dangerous for your wealth, that is. With hindsight we see horrible mistakes by investors, most recently the gross overvaluation of Internet and telecom companies. On average, however, it appears that financial markets collect and assess information quickly and accurately. We'll discuss this issue again in Chapter 7.

selling off shares of the risky firm and buying shares in a safer one. If the risky investments increase market value, the departing shareholder is better off than he or she would be if the risky investments were turned down.

EXAMPLE 2.1 ▶ Value Maximization

Fast-Track Wireless shares trade for $20. It invests $3 per share in a high-risk, but potentially revolutionary, WhyFi technology. Investors note the risk of failure but are even more impressed with the technology's upside. They conclude that the possibility of very high future profits is worth $6 per share. The net value added is $6 − 3 = +$3, and the share price increases from $20 to $23.

Caspar Milquetoast, a thoughtful but timid shareholder, notes the downside risks and decides that it's time for a change. He sells out to more risk-tolerant investors. But he sells at $23 per share, not $20. Thus he captures the value added by the WhyFi project *without having to bear the project's risks.* The risks are transferred to other investors. In a well-functioning stock market, there is always a pool of investors ready to bear downside risks if the upside potential is sufficiently attractive. We know that the upside potential was sufficient in this case, because Fast-Track stock attracted investors willing to pay $23 per share.

The same principles apply to the *timing* of a corporation's cash flows, as the following self-test illustrates.

Self-Test 2.5

Rhonda and Reggie Hotspur are working hard to save for their children's college educations. They don't need more cash for current consumption but will face big tuition bills in 2020. Should they therefore avoid investing in stocks that pay generous current cash dividends? Explain briefly.

The Opportunity Cost of Capital

cost of capital
Minimum acceptable rate of return on capital investment.

Financial managers look to financial markets to measure, or at least estimate, the **cost of capital** for the firm's investment projects. **The cost of capital is the minimum acceptable rate of return for capital investment. Investment projects offering rates of return higher than the cost of capital add value to the firm. Projects offering rates of return less than the cost of capital actually subtract value and should not be undertaken.**[15]

Let's think again about the value added by risky corporate investments, for example, Fast-Track's WhyFi project. That project increased Fast-Track's overall market value and the price of each of its shares. The project was worth more than it cost because it offered a superior rate of return, even after accounting for the risks of failure.

What does "superior rate of return" mean? It means an expected rate of return higher than the return investors could achieve from alternative investments at the same level of risk. For example, suppose that the WhyFi project is just as risky as the shares of other high-tech growth companies and that the expected return on those companies' shares is 15%. If the WhyFi project offers a 20% expected return, then the project adds value. If the project offered only 10%, investing in it would destroy value, because the project return would be less than the 15% return that shareholders could obtain by investing on their own.

When the financial manager invests at a superior rate of return, stockholders applaud and stock price increases. If the financial manager invests at an inferior return, shareholders boo, stock price falls, and stockholders want their money back so that they can invest on their own.

---

[15] Of course, there are exceptions when the corporation invests for other reasons. Think of an investment in pollution control equipment for a factory. The equipment may not generate any significant cash returns, so the rate of return on investment may be negative. But firms still invest in pollution control, not to earn direct profits but to meet legal and ethical obligations.

FIGURE 2–5 The firm can
either keep and reinvest
cash or return it to investors.
(Arrows represent possible
cash flows or transfers.) If cash
is reinvested, the opportunity
cost is the expected rate of
return that shareholders could
have obtained by investing in
financial assets.

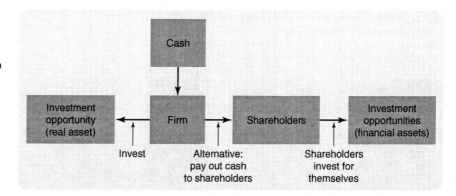

Therefore, the rates of return on investments outside the corporation set the
minimum return for investment projects inside the corporation. In other words, the
expected rates of return on investments in financial markets determine the cost of
capital for corporate investments.

Figure 2–5 summarizes this trade-off. The firm can invest, or it can pay out cash
to shareholders. Shareholders can invest for themselves in financial markets. Capital
investments by the firm should therefore offer rates of return at least as high as those
available in financial markets at the same level of risk. If they do not, the firm should
not invest. Therefore, the cost of capital for corporate investment is set by the rates
of return on investment opportunities in financial markets. You can see why financial
managers refer to the opportunity cost of capital. When the firm invests, shareholders lose the opportunity to invest that cash in financial markets.

For safe investments, you can observe the opportunity cost of capital by looking
up current interest rates on safe debt securities. For risky investments, the opportunity
cost of capital has to be estimated. That is one of the harder tasks in financial management. We will return to this task in Chapter 7 and in several later chapters.

Notice that the opportunity cost of capital is generally *not* the interest rate that
the firm pays on a loan from a bank or insurance company. If the company is making a risky investment, the opportunity cost is the expected return that investors can
achieve in financial markets at the same level of risk. The expected return on risky
securities will normally be well above the interest rate on corporate borrowing.

Self-Test 2.6

Investing $100,000 in additional raw materials today—mostly in palladium—should
allow Cryogenic Concepts to increase production and earn an additional $112,000
next year. This payoff would cover the investment today, plus a 12% return. Palladium
is traded in commodity markets. The CFO has studied the history of returns on investments in palladium and believes that investors in that precious metal can reasonably
expect a 15% return. Is Cryogenic's investment in palladium a good idea? Why or
why not?

SUMMARY

**Where does the financing
for corporations come
from?** *(LO1)*

The ultimate source of financing is individuals' savings. The savings may flow through
financial markets and **intermediaries.** The intermediaries include mutual funds, pension
funds, and financial institutions, such as banks and insurance companies.

Why do nonfinancial corporations need modern financial markets and institutions? *(LO1)*

It's simple: Corporations need access to financing in order to innovate and grow. A modern financial system offers different types of financing, depending on a corporation's age and the nature of its business. A high-tech start-up will seek venture capital financing, for example. A mature firm will rely more on bond markets.

What if a corporation finances investment by retaining and reinvesting cash generated from its operations? *(LO1)*

In that case the corporation is saving on behalf of its shareholders.

What are the key advantages of mutual funds and pension funds? *(LO2)*

Mutual and **pension funds** allow investors to diversify in professionally managed portfolios. Pension funds offer an additional tax advantage, because the returns on pension investments are not taxed until withdrawn from the plan.

What are the functions of financial markets? *(LO3)*

Financial markets help channel savings to corporate investment, and they help match up borrowers and lenders. They provide **liquidity** and diversification opportunities for investors. Trading in financial markets provides a wealth of useful information for the financial manager.

Do financial institutions have different functions? *(LO3)*

Financial institutions carry out a number of similar functions but in different ways. They channel savings to corporate investment, and they serve as **intermediaries** between borrowers and lenders. Banks also provide liquidity for depositors and, of course, play a special role in the economy's payment systems. Insurance companies allow policyholders to pool risks.

How does the financial manager identify the cost of the capital raised by a corporation? *(LO4)*

The **cost of capital** is the minimum acceptable rate of return on capital investment. It's an opportunity cost, that is, a rate of return that investors could earn in financial markets. For a safe capital investment, the opportunity cost is the interest rate on safe debt securities, such as high-grade corporate bonds. For riskier capital investments, the opportunity cost is the expected rate of return on risky securities, investments in the stock market, for example.

QUESTIONS

QUIZ

1. **Corporate Financing.** How can a small, private firm finance its capital investments? Give two or three examples of financing sources. *(LO1)*

2. **Corporate Financing.** Is it possible for an individual to save and invest in a corporation without lending money to it or purchasing additional shares? Explain. *(LO1)*

3. **Corporations.** What is meant by the separation of ownership and control for public corporations? What potential problems does this separation create? *(LO1)*

4. **Financial Markets.** The stock and bond markets are not the only financial markets. Give two or three additional examples. *(LO1)*

5. **Financial Intermediaries.** You are a beginning investor with only $5,000 in savings. How can you achieve a widely diversified portfolio at reasonable cost? *(LO2)*

6. **Financial Intermediaries.** What are the key advantages of a defined-contribution pension plan as a vehicle for retirement savings? *(LO2)*

7. **Financial Intermediaries.** Is an insurance company also a financial intermediary? How does the insurance company channel savings to corporate investment? *(LO2)*

8. **Corporate Financing.** What are the largest institutional investors in bonds? In shares? *(LO2)*

9. **Financial Markets and Institutions.** List the major functions of financial markets and institutions in a modern financial system. (*LO3*)

10. **Financial Markets.** On a mountain trek, you discover a 6-ounce gold nugget. A friend offers to pay you $2,500 for it. How do you check whether this is a fair price? (*LO3*)

11. **Financial Markets.** What kinds of useful information can a financial manager obtain from financial markets? Give examples. (*LO3*)

12. **Value Maximization.** The objective of value maximization makes sense when stockholders have access to modern financial markets and institutions. Briefly explain why. (*LO4*)

13. **Cost of Capital.** Why do financial managers refer to the *opportunity* cost of capital? How would you find the opportunity cost of capital for a safe investment? (*LO4*)

PRACTICE PROBLEMS

14. **True or False?** (*LO1*)
    a. Financing for public corporations must flow through financial markets.
    b. Financing for private corporations must flow through financial intermediaries.
    c. The sale of policies is a source of financing for insurance companies.
    d. Almost all foreign exchange trading occurs on the floors of the FOREX exchanges in New York and London.
    e. The opportunity cost of capital is the capital outlay required to undertake a real investment opportunity.
    f. The cost of capital is the interest rate paid on borrowing from a bank or other financial institution.

15. **Liquidity.** Securities traded in active financial markets are liquid assets. Explain why liquidity is important to individual investors and to mutual funds. (*LO2*)

16. **Liquidity.** Bank deposits are liquid; you can withdraw money on demand. How can the bank provide this liquidity and at the same time make illiquid loans to businesses? (*LO2*)

17. **Corporate Financing.** Financial markets and intermediaries channel savings from investors to corporate investment. The savings make this journey by many different routes. Give a specific example for each of the following routes: (*LO1*)
    a. Investor to financial intermediary, to financial markets, and to the corporation.
    b. Investor to financial markets, to a financial intermediary, and to the corporation.
    c. Investor to financial markets, to a financial intermediary, back to financial markets, and to the corporation.

18. **Financial Institutions.** Summarize the differences between a commercial and an investment bank. (*LO2*)

19. **Mutual Funds.** Why are mutual funds called financial intermediaries? Why does it make sense for an individual to invest her savings in a mutual fund rather than directly in financial markets? (*LO2*)

20. **Value Maximization.** Fritz is risk-averse and is content with a relatively low but safe return on his investments. Frieda is risk-tolerant and seeks a very high rate of return on her invested savings. Yet both shareholders will applaud a low-risk capital investment that offers a superior rate of return. Why? What is meant by "superior"? (*LO4*)

21. **Cost of Capital.** British Quince comes across an average-risk investment project that offers a rate of return of 9.5%. This is less than the company's normal rate of return, but one of Quince's directors notes that the company can easily borrow the required investment at 7%. "It's simple," he says. "If the bank lends us money at 7%, then our cost of capital must be 7%. The project's return is higher than the cost of capital, so let's move ahead." How would you respond? (*LO4*)

22. **Cost of Capital.** In a stroke of good luck, your company has uncovered an opportunity to invest for 10 years at a guaranteed 6% rate of return. What is the opportunity cost of capital? Assume interest rates as in Table 2–2. (*LO4*)

23. **Cost of Capital.** Pollution Busters, Inc., is considering purchase of 10 additional carbon sequesters for $100,000 apiece. The sequesters last for only 1 year until saturated. Then the carbon is sold to the government.

a. Suppose the government guarantees the price of carbon. At this price, the payoff after 1 year is $115,000 for sure. How would you determine the opportunity cost of capital for this investment? (*LO4*)

b. Suppose instead that the sequestered carbon has to be sold on the London Carbon Exchange. Carbon prices have been extremely volatile, but Pollution Busters' CFO learns that average rates of return from investment on that exchange have been about 20%. She thinks this is a reasonable forecast for the future. What is the opportunity cost of capital in this case? Is purchase of additional sequesters a worthwhile capital investment? (*LO4*)

STANDARD &POOR'S

1. **Information Provided by Financial Markets.** Update Table 2–3. How have these companies' market values changed? Go to Market Insight (**www.mhhe.com/edumarketinsight**), and go to the Financial Highlights page for each company. The companies' ticker symbols are given in Table 2–3.

SOLUTIONS TO SELF-TEST QUESTIONS

2.1 a. Corporations sell securities in the primary market. The securities are later traded in the secondary market.
b. The capital market is for long-term financing; the money market for short-term financing.
c. The market for stocks versus the market for bonds and other debt securities.

2.2 Efficient diversification and professional management. Pension funds offer an additional advantage, because investment returns are not taxed until withdrawn from the fund.

2.3 Mutual funds pool investor savings and invest in portfolios of traded securities. Financial institutions such as banks or insurance companies raise money in special ways, for example, by accepting deposits or selling insurance policies. They not only invest in securities but also lend directly to businesses. They provide various other financial services.

2.4 Liquidity, risk reduction by investment in diversified portfolios of securities (through a mutual fund, for example), information provided by trading.

2.5 Rhonda and Reggie need not avoid high-dividend stocks. They can reinvest the dividends and keep reinvesting until it's time to pay the tuition bills. (They will have to pay taxes on the dividends, however, which could affect their investment strategy. We discuss dividends and taxes in Chapter 17.)

2.6 It is not a good investment if the opportunity cost of capital is 15%. The investment offers only a 12% return.

CASH FLOW FORECASTING

CHAPTER 3

Accounting and Finance

LEARNING OBJECTIVES

After studying this chapter, you should be able to:

1. Interpret the information contained in the balance sheet, income statement, and statement of cash flows.

2. Distinguish between market and book values.

3. Explain why income differs from cash flow.

4. Understand the essential features of the taxation of corporate and personal income.

Accounting is not the same as finance, but if you don't understand the basics of accounting, you won't understand finance, either.

© Tom Grill/Corbis

In Chapter 1 we pointed out that a large corporation is a team effort. All the players—the shareholders, lenders, directors, management, and employees—have a stake in the company's success, and all therefore need to monitor its progress. For this reason the company prepares regular financial accounts and arranges for an independent firm of auditors to certify that these accounts present a "true and fair view."

Until the mid-nineteenth century most businesses were owner-managed and seldom required outside capital beyond personal loans to the proprietor. When businesses were small and there were few outside stakeholders in the firm, accounting could be less formal. But with the industrial revolution and the creation of large railroad and canal companies, the shareholders and bankers demanded information that would help them gauge a firm's financial strength. That was when the accounting profession began to come of age.

We don't want to get lost in the details of accounting practice. But because we will be referring to financial statements throughout this book, it may be useful to review briefly their main features. In this chapter we introduce the major financial statements: the balance sheet, the income statement, and the statement of cash flows. We discuss the important differences between income and cash flow and between book values and market values. We also discuss the federal tax system.

This chapter is our first look at financial statements and is meant primarily to serve as a brief review of your accounting class. It will be far from our last look. For example, we will see in the next chapter how managers use financial statements to analyze a firm's performance and assess its financial strength.

3.1 The Balance Sheet

balance sheet
Financial statement that shows the firm's assets and liabilities at a particular time.

Public companies are obliged to file their financial statements with the SEC each quarter. These quarterly reports (or 10Qs) provide the investor with information about the company's earnings during the quarter and its assets and liabilities at the end of the quarter. In addition, companies need to file annual financial statements (or 10Ks) that provide rather more detailed information about the outcome for the entire year.

The financial statements show the firm's balance sheet, the income statement, and a statement of cash flows. We will review each in turn.[1]

Firms need to raise cash to pay for the many assets used in their businesses. In the process of raising that cash, they also acquire liabilities to those who provide funding. The **balance sheet** presents a snapshot of the firm's assets and liabilities at one particular moment. The assets—representing the uses of the funds raised—are listed on the left-hand side of the balance sheet. The liabilities—representing the sources of that funding—are listed on the right.

Some assets can be turned more easily into cash than others; these are known as *liquid* assets. The accountant puts the most liquid assets at the top of the list and works down to the least liquid. Look, for example, at Table 3–1, which shows the consolidated balance sheet for PepsiCo, Inc., at the end of 2006.[2] ("Consolidated" simply means that the balance sheet shows the position of PepsiCo and any companies it owns.) You can see that Pepsi had $1,651 million of cash and marketable securities. In addition, it had sold goods worth $3,725 million but had not yet received payment. These payments are due soon and therefore the balance sheet shows the unpaid bills or *accounts receivable* (or simply *receivables*) as an asset. The next asset consists of inventories. These may be (1) raw materials and ingredients that the firm bought from suppliers, (2) work in process, and (3) finished products waiting to be shipped from the warehouse. Of course, there are always some items that don't fit into neat categories. So there is a fourth entry, *other current assets*.

Up to this point all the assets in Pepsi's balance sheet are likely to be used or turned into cash in the near future. They are therefore described as *current assets*. The next assets listed in the balance sheet are longer-lived or *fixed assets* and include items such as buildings, equipment, and vehicles.

The balance sheet shows that the gross value of Pepsi's property, plant, and equipment is $19,058 million. This is what the assets originally cost. But they are unlikely to be worth that now. For example, suppose the company bought a delivery van 2 years ago; that van may be worth far less now than Pepsi paid for it. It might in principle be possible for the accountant to estimate separately the value today of the van, but this would be costly and somewhat subjective. Accountants rely instead on rules of thumb to estimate the *depreciation* in the value of assets and with rare exceptions they stick to these rules. For example, in the case of that delivery van the accountant may deduct a third of the original cost each year to reflect its declining value. So if Pepsi bought the van 2 years ago for $15,000, the balance sheet would show that accumulated depreciation is $2 \times \$5,000 = \$10,000$. Net of depreciation the value is only $5,000. Table 3–1 shows that Pepsi's total accumulated depreciation on fixed assets is $9,371 million. So while the assets cost $19,058 million, their net value in the accounts is only $19,058 - \$9,371 = \$9,687$ million.

In addition to its tangible assets, Pepsi also has valuable intangible assets, such as its brand name, skilled management, and a well-trained labor force. Accountants are generally reluctant to record these intangible assets in the balance sheet unless they can be readily identified and valued.

---

[1] In addition, the company provides a statement of the shareholders' equity, which shows how much of the firm's earnings has been retained in the business rather than paid out as dividends and how much money has been raised by issuing new share or spent by repurchasing stock. We will not review in detail the statement of shareholders' equity.

[2] We have simplified and eliminated some of the detail in PepsiCo's published financial statements.

TABLE 3–1

CONSOLIDATED BALANCE SHEET FOR PEPSICO, INC., AS OF DECEMBER 31 (millions of dollars)					
Assets	**2006**	**2005**	**Liabilities and Shareholders' Equity**	**2006**	**2005**
Current assets			Current liabilities		
Cash and marketable securities	1,651	1,716	Debt due for repayment	274	2,889
Receivables	3,725	3,261	Accounts payable	5,271	5,357
Inventories	1,926	1,693	Other current liabilities	1,315	1,160
Other current assets	1,828	3,784	Total current liabilities	6,860	9,406
Total current assets	9,130	10,454			
Fixed assets			Long-term debt	2,550	2,313
Tangible fixed assets			Deferred income taxes	528	1,434
Property, plant, and equipment	19,058	16,646	Other long-term liabilities	4,624	4,323
Less accumulated depreciation	9,371	7,965			
Net tangible fixed assets	9,687	8,681	Total liabilities	14,562	17,476
Intangible fixed assets			Shareholders' equity		
Goodwill	4,594	4,088	Common stock and other paid-in capital	614	644
Other intangible assets	1,849	1,616	Retained earnings	22,591	18,803
Total intangible fixed assets	6,443	5,704	Treasury stock	(7,837)	(5,196)
			Total shareholders' equity	15,368	14,251
Total fixed assets	16,130	14,385			
			Total liabilities and shareholders' equity	29,930	31,727
Other assets	4,670	6,888			
Total assets	29,930	31,727			

Note: Column sums subject to rounding error.
Source: Derived from PepsiCo Annual Report, 2006.

There is, however, one important exception. When Pepsi has acquired other businesses in the past, it has paid more for their assets than the value shown in the firms' accounts. This difference is shown in Pepsi's balance sheet as "goodwill." Most of the intangible assets on Pepsi's balance sheet consist of goodwill.

Now look at the right-hand portion of Pepsi's balance sheet, which shows where the money to buy its assets came from. The accountant starts by looking at the company's liabilities—that is, the money owed by the company. First come those liabilities that are likely to be paid off most rapidly. For example, Pepsi has borrowed $274 million, due to be repaid shortly. It also owes its suppliers $5,271 million for goods that have been delivered but not yet paid for. These unpaid bills are shown as *accounts payable* (or *payables*). Both the borrowings and the payables are debts that Pepsi must repay within the year. They are therefore classified as *current liabilities*.

Pepsi's current assets total $9,130 million; its current liabilities amount to $6,860 million. Therefore the difference between the value of Pepsi's current assets and its current liabilities is $9,130 − $6,860 = $2,270 million. This figure is known as Pepsi's *net current assets* or *net working capital*. It roughly measures the company's potential reservoir of cash.

Below the current liabilities Pepsi's accountants have listed the firm's long-term liabilities—that is, debts that come due after the end of a year. You can see that banks and other investors have made long-term loans to Pepsi of $2,550 million.

Pepsi's liabilities are financial obligations to various parties. For example, when Pepsi buys goods from its suppliers, it has a liability to pay for them; when it borrows from the bank, it has a liability to repay the loan. Thus the suppliers and the bank have first claim on the firm's assets. What is left over after the liabilities have been paid off belongs to the shareholders. This figure is known as the shareholders' *equity.* For Pepsi the total value of shareholders' equity amounts to $15,368 million. Table 3–1 shows that Pepsi's equity is made up of three parts. A relatively small part, $614 million, has resulted from the occasional sale of new shares to investors. A much larger amount, $22,591 million, has come from earnings that Pepsi has retained and reinvested in the business on the shareholders' behalf.[3] Finally, treasury stock is a large negative number, –$7,837 million. This represents the amount that Pepsi has spent on buying back its shares. The money to repurchase them has gone out of the firm and reduced shareholders' equity.

Figure 3–1 shows how the separate items in the balance sheet link together. There are two classes of assets—current assets, which will soon be used or turned into cash, and long-term or "fixed" assets, which may be either tangible or intangible. There are also two classes of liability—current liabilities, which are due for payment shortly, and long-term liabilities.

The difference between the assets and the liabilities represents the amount of the shareholders' equity. This is the basic balance sheet identity. Shareholders are sometimes called "residual claimants" on the firm. We mean by this that shareholders' equity is what is left over when the liabilities of the firm are subtracted from its assets:

$$\text{Shareholders' equity} = \text{total assets} - \text{total liabilities} \qquad \textbf{(3.1)}$$

Self-Test 3.1

Suppose that Pepsi borrows $500 million by issuing new long-term bonds. It places $100 million of the proceeds in the bank and uses $400 million to buy new machinery. What items of the balance sheet would change? Would shareholders' equity change?

common-size balance sheet
All items in the balance sheet are expressed as a percentage of total assets.

When comparing financial statements, analysts often calculate a **common-size balance sheet,** which reexpresses all items as a percentage of total assets. Table 3–2 is Pepsi's common-size balance sheet. The financial manager might look at this common-size balance sheet and notice right away that in 2006 receivables and inventory accounted for a much higher proportion of the firm's assets than they did in the previous year. There may be good reasons for this, but the manager might wish to check that control of working capital has not become lax.

By the way, it is easy to obtain the financial statements of almost any publicly traded firm. Most firms make their annual reports available on the Web. You also can find key financial statements of most firms at Yahoo! Finance. (**http://finance.yahoo .com**). In addition, the Market Insight Web site (access comes with this text) provides Excel spreadsheets containing annual financial statements for many firms over several years. See **www.mhhe.com/edumarketinsight**.

FIGURE 3–1

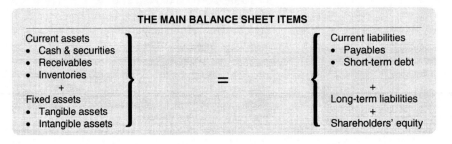

THE MAIN BALANCE SHEET ITEMS

---

[3] Here is an occasional source of confusion. You may be tempted to think of retained earnings as a pile of cash that the company has built up from its past operations. But there is absolutely no link between retained earnings and cash balances. The earnings that Pepsi has kept in the business may have been used to buy new equipment, trucks, warehouses, and so on. Typically only a small proportion will be kept in the bank. Notice that Pepsi's balance sheet lists $22,591 in retained earnings but only $1,651 in cash and marketable securities.

TABLE 3–2

COMMON-SIZE BALANCE SHEET FOR PEPSICO, INC., AS OF DECEMBER 31 (all items expressed as percentage of total assets)					
Assets	**2006**	**2005**	**Liabilities and Shareholders' Equity**	**2006**	**2005**
Current assets			Current liabilities		
Cash and marketable securities	5.5	5.4	Debt due for repayment	0.9	9.1
Receivables	12.4	10.3	Accounts payable	17.6	16.9
Inventories	6.4	5.3	Other current liabilities	4.4	3.7
Other current assets	6.1	11.9	Total current liabilities	22.9	29.6
Total current assets	30.5	32.9			
Fixed assets			Long-term debt	8.5	7.3
Tangible fixed assets			Deferred income taxes	1.8	4.5
Property, plant, and equipment	63.7	52.5	Other long-term liabilities	15.4	13.6
Less accumulated depreciation	31.3	25.1			
Net tangible fixed assets	32.4	27.4	Total liabilities	48.7	55.1
Intangible fixed assets			Shareholders' equity		
Goodwill	15.3	12.9	Common stock and other paid-in capital	2.1	2.0
Other intangible assets	6.2	5.1	Retained earnings	75.5	59.3
Total intangible fixed assets	21.5	18.0	Treasury stock	(26.2)	(16.4)
			Total shareholders' equity	51.3	44.9
Total fixed assets	53.9	45.3			
			Total liabilities and shareholders' equity	100.0	100.0
Other assets	15.6	21.7			
Total assets	100.0	100.0			

Note: Column sums subject to rounding error.
Source: Derived from PepsiCo Annual Report, 2006.

Book Values and Market Values

Throughout this book we will frequently make a distinction between the book values of the assets shown in the balance sheet and their market values.

Items in the balance sheet are valued according to **generally accepted accounting principles,** commonly called **GAAP.** These state that assets must be shown in the balance sheet at their *historical cost* adjusted for depreciation. **Book values** are therefore "backward-looking" measures of value. They are based on the past cost of the asset, not its current market price or value to the firm. For example, suppose that 2 years ago Pepsi built an office building for $30 million and that in today's market the building would sell for $40 million. The book value of the building would be less than its market value, and the balance sheet would understate the value of Pepsi's asset.

Or consider a specialized plant that Intel develops for producing special-purpose computer chips at a cost of $800 million. The book value of the plant is $800 million less depreciation. But suppose that shortly after the plant is constructed, a new chip makes the existing one obsolete. The market value of Intel's new plant could fall by 50% or more. In this case market value would be less than book value.

The difference between book value and market value is greater for some assets than for others. It is zero in the case of cash but potentially very large for fixed assets where the accountant starts with the initial cost of the fixed assets and then depreciates that figure according to a prespecified schedule. The purpose of depreciation is to allocate the original cost of the asset over its life, and the rules governing the depreciation of asset values do not reflect actual loss of market value. As a result, the market value of fixed assets usually is much higher than the book value, but sometimes it is less.

generally accepted accounting principles (GAAP)
Procedures for preparing financial statements.

book value
Value of assets or liabilities according to the balance sheet.

The same goes for the right-hand side of the balance sheet. In the case of liabilities the accountant simply records the amount of money that you have promised to pay. For short-term liabilities this figure is generally close to the market value of that promise. For example, if you owe the bank $1 million tomorrow, the accounts show a book liability of $1 million. As long as you are not bankrupt, that $1 million is also roughly the value to the bank of your promise. But now suppose that $1 million is not due to be repaid for several years. The accounts still show a liability of $1 million, but how much your debt is worth depends on what happens to interest rates. If interest rates rise after you have issued the debt, lenders may not be prepared to pay as much as $1 million for your debt; if interest rates fall, they may be prepared to pay more than $1 million.[4] Thus the market value of a long-term liability may be higher or lower than the book value. **Market values of assets and liabilities do not generally equal their book values. Book values are based on historical or *original* values. Market values measure *current* values of assets and liabilities.**

The difference between book value and market value is likely to be greatest for shareholders' equity. The book value of equity measures the cash that shareholders have contributed in the past plus the cash that the company has retained and reinvested in the business on their behalf. But this often bears little resemblance to the total market value that investors place on the shares.

If the market price of the firm's shares falls through the floor, don't try telling the shareholders that the book value is satisfactory—they won't want to hear. Shareholders are concerned with the market value of their shares; market value, not book value, is the price at which they can sell their shares. Managers who wish to keep their shareholders happy will focus on market values.

We will often find it useful to think about the firm in terms of a *market-value balance sheet*. Like a conventional balance sheet, a market-value balance sheet lists the firm's assets, but it records each asset at its current market value rather than at historical cost less depreciation. Similarly, each liability is shown at its market value. **The difference between the market values of assets and liabilities is the market value of the shareholders' equity claim. The stock price is simply the market value of shareholders' equity divided by the number of outstanding shares.**

EXAMPLE 3.1   ▶   Market- versus Book-Value Balance Sheets

Jupiter has developed a revolutionary auto production process that enables it to produce cars 20% more efficiently than any rival. It has invested $10 billion in producing its new plant. To finance the investment, Jupiter borrowed $4 billion and raised the remaining funds by selling new shares of stock in the firm. There are currently 100 million shares of stock outstanding. Investors are very excited about Jupiter's prospects. They believe that the flow of profits from the new plant justifies a stock price of $75.

If these are Jupiter's only assets, the book-value balance sheet immediately after it has made the investment is as follows:

BOOK-VALUE BALANCE SHEET FOR JUPITER MOTORS (figures in billions of dollars)			
Assets		**Liabilities and Shareholders' Equity**	
Auto plant	$10	Debt	$4
		Shareholders' equity	6

Investors are placing a *market value* on Jupiter's equity of $7.5 billion ($75 per share times 100 million shares). We assume that the debt outstanding is worth $4

---

[4] We will show you how changing interest rates affect the market value of debt in Chapter 5.

Chapter 3 Accounting and Finance

61

billion.[5] Therefore, if you owned all Jupiter's shares and all its debt, the value of your investment would be $7.5 + $4 = $11.5 billion. In this case you would own the company lock, stock, and barrel and would be entitled to all its cash flows. Because you can buy the entire company for $11.5 billion, the total value of Jupiter's assets must also be $11.5 billion. In other words, the market value of the assets must be equal to the market value of the liabilities plus the market value of the shareholders' equity.

We can now draw up the market-value balance sheet as follows:

MARKET-VALUE BALANCE SHEET FOR JUPITER MOTORS (figures in billions of dollars)			
Assets		**Liabilities and Shareholders' Equity**	
Auto plant	$11.5	Debt	$4
		Shareholders' equity	7.5

Notice that the market value of Jupiter's plant is $1.5 billion more than the plant cost to build. The difference is due to the superior profits that investors expect the plant to earn. **Thus, in contrast to the balance sheet shown in the company's books, the market-value balance sheet is forward-looking. It depends on the profits that investors expect the assets to provide.**

Is it surprising that market value exceeds book value? It shouldn't be. Firms find it attractive to raise money to invest in various projects because they believe the projects will be worth more than they cost. Otherwise, why bother? You will usually find that shares of stock sell for more than the value shown in the company's books.

Self-Test 3.2

a. What would be Jupiter's price per share if the auto plant had a market value of $14 billion?
b. How would you reassess the value of the auto plant if the value of outstanding stock were $8 billion?

3.2 The Income Statement

income statement
Financial statement that shows the revenues, expenses, and net income of a firm over a period of time.

If Pepsi's balance sheet resembles a snapshot of the firm at a particular time, its **income statement** is like a video. It shows how profitable the firm has been during the past year.

Look at the summary income statement in Table 3–3. You can see that during 2006 Pepsi sold goods worth $35,753 million and that the total expenses of producing and selling goods was $15,762 + $11,357 = $27,119 million. The largest expense item, amounting to $15,762 million, consisted of the raw materials, labor, and so on, that were needed to produce the goods. Almost all the remaining expenses were administrative expenses such as head office costs, advertising, and distribution.

In addition to these out-of-pocket expenses, Pepsi also made a deduction for the value of the plant and equipment used up in producing the goods. In 2006 this charge for depreciation was $1,406 million. Thus Pepsi's *earnings before interest and taxes (EBIT)* were

$$\begin{aligned} \text{EBIT} &= \text{total revenues} - \text{costs} - \text{depreciation} \\ &= 35{,}753 - 27{,}119 - 1{,}406 \\ &= \$7{,}228 \text{ million} \end{aligned}$$

---

[5] Jupiter has borrowed $4 billion to finance its investment, but if the interest rate has changed in the meantime, the debt could be worth more or less than $4 billion.

TABLE 3–3

CONSOLIDATED STATEMENT OF INCOME FOR PEPSICO, INC., 2006		
	$ Millions	% of Sales
Net sales	35,753	100.0
Cost of goods sold	15,762	44.1
Selling, general, and administrative expenses	11,357	32.2
Depreciation	1,406	3.9
Earnings before interest and income taxes	7,228	19.7
Interest expense	239	0.2
Taxable income	6,989	19.5
Taxes	1,347	3.8
Net income	5,642	15.8
Allocation of net income		
Dividends	1,854	5.2
Addition to retained earnings	3,788	10.6

Source: Derived from PepsiCo Annual Report, 2006.

The remainder of the income statement shows where these earnings went. As we saw earlier, Pepsi has partly financed its investment in plant and equipment by borrowing. In 2006 it paid $239 million of interest on this borrowing. A further slice of the profit went to the government in the form of taxes. This amounted to $1,347 million. The $5,642 million that was left over after paying interest and taxes belonged to the shareholders. Of this sum Pepsi paid out $1,854 million in dividends and reinvested the remaining $3,788 million in the business. Presumably, these reinvested funds made the company more valuable.

The $3,788 of earnings that PepsiCo retained, or reinvested, in the firm show up on its balance sheet as an increase in retained earnings. Notice that retained earnings in Table 3–1 increased by $3,788 million in 2006, from $18,803 million to $22,591 million. However, shareholders' equity increased by less than this amount, primarily because of Pepsi's stock repurchases during the year.

Just as it is sometimes useful to prepare a common-size balance sheet, we can also prepare a **common-size income statement.** In this case, all items are expressed as a percentage of revenues. The last column of Table 3–3 is Pepsi's common-size income statement. You can see, for example, that the cost of goods sold consumes 44.1% of revenues and that selling, general, and administrative expenses absorb a further 32.2%.

common-size income statement
All items on the income statement are expressed as a percentage of revenues.

Profits versus Cash Flow

It is important to distinguish between Pepsi's profits and the cash that the company generates. Here are three reasons why profits and cash are not the same:

1. When Pepsi's accountants prepare the income statement, they do not simply count the cash coming in and the cash going out. Instead, the accountant starts with the cash payments but then divides these payments into two groups—current expenditures (such as wages) and capital expenditures (such as the purchase of new machinery). Current expenditures are deducted from current profits. However, rather than deducting the cost of machinery in the year it is purchased, the accountant makes an annual charge for depreciation. Thus the cost of machinery is spread over its forecast life.

   When calculating profits, the accountant does *not* deduct the expenditure on new equipment that year, even though cash is paid out. However, the accountant *does* deduct depreciation on assets previously purchased, even though no cash is currently paid out. For example, suppose a $100,000 investment is depreciated by $10,000 a year.[6] This depreciation is treated as an annual expense, although the cash actually went out of the door when the asset was first purchased. For this reason, the deduction for depreciation is classified as a *noncash* expense.

To calculate the cash produced by the business, it is necessary to *add* back the depreciation charge (which is not a cash payment) and to *subtract* the expenditure on new capital equipment (which is a cash payment).

2. Consider the following stages in a manufacturing business: In period 1 the firm produces the goods; it sells them in period 2 for $100; and it is paid for them in period 3. The general rule is to recognize revenue at the time of the sale rather than when the cash is actually received. Therefore, although the cash does not arrive until period 3, the sale is included in the income statement for period 2. However, the accountant does not ignore the fact that the bills have not been paid. When the sale is made in period 2, the figure for accounts receivable in the balance sheet is adjusted to show that the company's customers owe an extra $100 in unpaid bills. This is an investment in accounts receivable, which uses cash. Thus, the net cash flow in period 2 is zero, as the following table demonstrates. Finally, when the customers pay their bills in period 3, the firm receives cash and receivables decline by $100. This may be viewed as a disinvestment in receivables that frees up cash. This payment has no impact on profits in that period. **The cash that the company *receives* is equal to the sales shown in the income statement less the increase in unpaid bills:**

Period:	2	3
Cost of goods sold	100	0
− Investment in receivables	100	(100)
= Cash received	0	+ 100

3. The accountant also tries to match the costs of producing the goods with the revenues from the sale. For example, suppose that it costs $60 in period 1 to produce the goods that are then sold in period 2 for $100. It would be misleading to say that the business made a loss in period 1 (when it produced the goods) and was very profitable in period 2 (when it sold them). Therefore, to provide a fairer measure of the firm's profitability, the income statement will not show the $60 as an expense of producing the goods until they are sold in period 2. This practice is known as *accrual accounting*. The accountant gathers together all expenses that are associated with a sale and deducts them from the revenues to calculate profit, even though the expenses may have occurred in an earlier period.

Of course, the accountant cannot ignore the fact that the firm spent money on producing the goods in period 1. So the expenditure will be shown in period 1 as an *investment* in inventories. Subsequently in period 2, when the goods are sold, the inventories would decline again.

In our example, the cash is paid out when the goods are manufactured in period 1, but this expense is not recognized until period 2 when the goods are sold. **The cash *outflow* is equal to the cost of goods sold, which is shown in the income statement, plus the change in inventories:**

Period:	1	2
Cost of goods sold	0	60
+ Investment in inventories	60	(60)
= Cash paid out	+ 60	0

---

[6] We discuss depreciation rules in Chapter 9.

EXAMPLE 3.2 ▶   Profits versus Cash Flows

Suppose a firm pays $100 in period 1 to produce some goods. It sells those goods for $150 in period 2, but it does not collect payment from its customers until period 3. The firm would "book" a $50 profit in period 2, recognizing both cost ($100) and revenue ($150) when the sale takes place. However, its cash flow in period 2 would be zero, as we see from the following table:

Period:	1	2	3
Sales	0	150	0
− Change in accounts receivable	0	150	(150)
− Cost of goods sold	0	100	0
− Change in inventories	100	(100)	0
= Net cash flow	−100	0	+150

Think about why this makes sense. In period 1, the firm expends $100 to produce the product. The product is not sold then, so the cost of producing the product is not recognized in this period; instead, the expenditure is treated as an investment in inventory, which is a negative cash flow. In period 2, the product is sold, but no cash trades hands. Instead, under accrual accounting, $150 is booked as a sale, with a corresponding investment in accounts receivable. At the same time, the $100 cost of goods sold is recognized in this period, and because the product is sold, the investment in inventories is reversed. Finally, in period 3, the cash is collected. Accounts receivable is reduced by the $150 cash inflow.

Self-Test 3.3

Consider a firm similar to the one in Example 3.2. It spends $200 to produce goods in period 1. In period 2 it sells half of those goods for $150, but it doesn't collect payment until one period later. In period 3, it sells the other half of the goods for $150, and it collects payment on these sales in period 4. Calculate the profits and the cash flows for this firm in periods 1 to 4 by completing a table like that in Example 3.2.

3.3 The Statement of Cash Flows

The firm requires *cash* when it buys new plant and machinery or when it pays interest to the bank and dividends to the shareholders. Therefore, the financial manager needs to keep track of the cash that is coming in and going out.

We have seen that the firm's cash flow can be quite different from its net income. These differences can arise for at least two reasons:

1. The income statement does not recognize capital expenditures as expenses in the year that the capital goods are paid for. Instead, it spreads those expenses over time in the form of an annual deduction for depreciation.
2. The income statement uses the accrual method of accounting, which means that revenues and expenses are recognized when sales are made, rather than when the cash is received or paid out.

statement of cash flows
Financial statement that shows the firm's cash receipts and cash payments over a period of time.

The **statement of cash flows** shows the firm's cash inflows and outflows from operations as well as from its investments and financing activities. Table 3–4 is the cash-flow statement for Pepsi. It contains three sections. The first shows the cash flow from operations. This is the cash generated from Pepsi's normal business activities. Next comes the cash that Pepsi has invested in plant and equipment or in the acquisition of new businesses. The final section reports cash flows from financing activities such as the sale of new debt or stock. We will look at these sections in turn.

TABLE 3–4

CONSOLIDATED STATEMENT OF CASH FLOWS FOR PEPSICO For the year ended December 31, 2006 (figures in millions)	
Cash Provided by Operations	
Net income	5,642
Noncash expenses	
Depreciation and amortization	1,406
Changes in working capital	
Decrease (increase) in accounts receivable	(464)
Decrease (increase) in inventories	(233)
Increase (decrease) in accounts payable	(86)
Decrease (increase) in other current assets	1,956
Increase (decrease) in other current liabilities	155
Total decrease (increase) in working capital	1,328
Cash provided by operations	8,376
Cash Flows from Investments	
Cash provided by (used for) disposal of (additions to) property, plant, and equipment	(2,412)
Sales (acquisitions) of other investments	1,479
Cash provided by (used for) investments	(933)
Cash Provided by (Used for) Financing Activities	
Additions to (reduction in) short-term debt	(2,615)
Additions to (reduction in) long-term debt	237
Dividends paid	(1,854)
Net issues (repurchases) of stock	(2,671)
Other	(605)
Cash provided by (used for) financing activities	(7,508)
Net increase (decrease) in cash and cash equivalents	(65)

Note: Column sums subject to rounding error.
Source: Derived from PepsiCo Annual Report, 2006.

The first section, cash flow from operations, starts with net income but adjusts that figure for those parts of the income statement that do not involve cash coming in or going out. Therefore, it adds back the allowance for depreciation because depreciation is not a cash outflow, even though it is treated as an expense in the income statement.

Any additions to current assets need to be *subtracted* from net income, since these absorb cash but do not show up in the income statement. Conversely, any additions to current liabilities need to be *added* to net income because these release cash. For example, you can see that the increase of $464 million in accounts receivable is subtracted from income, because this represents sales that Pepsi includes in its income statement even though it has not yet received payment from its customers. In addition, Pepsi increased inventories by $233 million. The accountant did not deduct this figure as part of the cost of the goods sold by Pepsi, even though Pepsi purchased these goods. Thus the $233 million increase in inventories must be subtracted to calculate the cash flow from operations. On the other hand, Pepsi does not pay all its bills immediately. These delayed payments show up as payables. In 2006 Pepsi had fewer bills outstanding: taxes and accounts payable *decreased* by $86 million. Paying off those bills resulted in a reduction in cash.

We have pointed out that depreciation is not a cash payment; it is simply the accountant's allocation to the current year of the original cost of the capital equipment. However, cash does flow out the door when the firm actually buys and pays for new capital equipment. Therefore, these capital expenditures are set out in the second section of the

INTERNET INSIDER

Understanding Financial Statements

Source: IR Solutions/Annualreports.com, 2008.

You can find a company's financial statements on its home page, but to avoid getting entangled in a web of company promotional material it is usually easier to log on first to **www.annual reports.com**. Find the latest financial statements for a large nonfinancial company and draw up a simplified balance sheet, income statement, and statement of cash flows as in Tables 3–1, 3–3, and 3–4. Some companies' financial statements can be extremely complex; try to find a relatively straightforward business. Also, as far as possible, use the same headings as in these tables, and don't hesitate to group some items as "other current assets," "other expenses," and so on. Look first at your simplified balance sheet. How much was the company owed by its customers in the form of unpaid bills? What liabilities does the company need to meet within a year? What was the original cost of the company's fixed assets? Now look at the income statement. What were the company's earnings before interest and taxes (EBIT)? Finally, turn to the cash-flow statement. Did changes in working capital add to cash or use it up?

cash-flow statement. You can see that Pepsi spent $2,412 million on new capital equipment. Notice that (gross) property, plant, and equipment on Pepsi's balance sheet increased by precisely this amount. On the other hand, Pepsi freed up $1,479 million by selling off other investments (this amount shows up as the change in the sum of intangible fixed assets plus other assets). Total cash used by investments was $933 million.

Finally, the third section of the cash-flow statement shows the cash from financing activities. Pepsi increased net long-term debt by $237 million but used $2,615 million to retire a good portion of its short-term debt; it used $2,671 million to buy back its stock and $1,854 million to pay dividends to its stockholders.[7]

To summarize, the cash-flow statement tells us that Pepsi generated $8,376 million from operations, spent $933 million on new investments, and used $7,508 million in financing activities. Pepsi earned and raised less cash than it spent. Therefore, its cash balance fell by $65 million. To calculate this change in cash balance, we subtract the uses of cash from the sources:

	In Millions
Cash flow from operations	$8,376
− Cash flow for new investment	− 933
+ Cash provided by new financing	−7,508
= Change in cash balance	− 65

Look back at Table 3–1 and you will see that cash accounts on the balance sheet did indeed decrease by this amount in 2006.

Self-Test 3.4

Would the following activities increase or decrease the firm's cash balance?

a. Inventories are increased.
b. The firm reduces its accounts payable.
c. The firm issues additional common stock.
d. The firm buys new equipment.

---

[7] You might think that interest payments also ought to be listed in this section. However, it is usual to include interest in the first section with cash flow from operations. This is because, unlike dividends, interest payments are not discretionary. The firm must pay interest when a payment comes due, so these payments are treated as a business expense rather than as a financing decision.

Free Cash Flow

The statement of cash flows tracks the cash flows from all the firm's activities. It shows how much cash has come from the firm's day-to-day operations and how much has come from the issue of new stock or debt. It also shows whether this cash was paid out to investors or reinvested in new plant and equipment or working capital. Often, however, you may want to know how much cash the company has available for distribution to investors after it has paid for any new capital investment or additions to working capital. This is called the firm's **free cash flow.**

free cash flow

Cash available for distribution to investors after firm pays for new investments or additions to working capital

Free cash flow has three parts. First, the cash that the firm generates from its ongoing operations is equal to

$$\text{Earnings before interest and tax (EBIT)} - \text{taxes} + \text{depreciation}$$

Not all of this cash is available to the firm's investors, however. As we've discussed, net investments in working capital, such as inventory or receivables, soak up cash. So we must subtract the change in net working capital. In addition, the firm needs to invest in fixed assets, and these investments also use cash. Thus,

$$\text{Free cash flow} = \text{EBIT} - \text{taxes} + \text{depreciation}$$
$$- \text{change in net working capital}$$
$$- \text{capital expenditures}$$

EXAMPLE 3.3 ▶ Free Cash Flow for Pepsi

We use both the income statement and the statement of cash flows to compute Pepsi's free cash flow. From the 2006 income statement, EBIT was $7,228 million, taxes were $1,347 million, and depreciation expense was $1,406 million. From the statement of cash flows (Table 3–4), the change in working capital was –$1,328 million (representing a net *dis*investment in working capital that freed up cash), and net capital expenditures were $933 million. Therefore, Pepsi's free cash flow was

$$\text{Free cash flow} = \$7{,}228 - \$1{,}347 + \$1{,}406 - (-\$1{,}328) - \$933 = \$7{,}682 \text{ million}$$

Some of this money was paid out to Pepsi's investors as interest or dividends. The remainder was used to buy back stock or repay debt.

3.4 Accounting Practice and Malpractice

Managers of public companies face constant scrutiny. Much of that scrutiny focuses on earnings. Security analysts forecast earnings per share, and investors wait to see whether the company can meet or beat the forecasts. A shortfall, even if it is only a cent or two, can be a big disappointment. Investors might judge that if you could not find that extra cent or two of earnings, the firm must be in a really bad way.

Managers complain about this pressure, but do they do anything about it? Unfortunately, the answer appears to be yes, according to Graham, Harvey and Rajgopal, who surveyed about 400 senior managers.[8] Most of the managers said that accounting earnings were the single most important number reported to investors. Most admitted to adjusting their firms' operations and investments to produce the earnings that investors were looking for. For example, 80% were prepared to decrease discretionary spending in R&D, advertising, or maintenance to meet earnings targets.

Of course, managers may not need to adjust the firm's operations if they can instead adjust their accounting methods. U.S. accounting rules are spelled out by the Financial Accounting Standards Board (FASB) and its generally accepted accounting principles (GAAP). Yet, inevitably, rules and principles leave room for discretion, and managers

---

[8] J. R. Graham, C. R. Harvey, and S. Rajgopal, "The Economic Implications of Corporate Financial Reporting," *Journal of Accounting and Economics* 40 (2005) pp. 3–73.

under pressure to perform are tempted to take advantage of this leeway to satisfy investors. In more extreme cases, managers may simply break the rules.

Here are some examples of gray areas that demand judgment calls and may tempt those who wish to conceal unflattering information to misuse any leeway in accounting rules:

- *Revenue recognition.* As we saw above, firms record a sale when it is made, not when the customer actually pays. But the date of sale is not always obvious. For example, suppose that you sell goods today but you give the customer the right to return them "if not fully satisfied." Have you made the sale when the goods are delivered or only when you can be sure that they will not be returned? Some companies have used this ambiguity to deliberately inflate their profits. For example, in 1997 the head of Sunbeam, "Chainsaw" Al Dunlap, allegedly moved millions of dollars of appliances to distributors and retailers to produce record profits. This process is termed *channel stuffing*. Between 1997 and 2001 Xerox also took an overly optimistic view of its revenues. Whenever a customer signed a long-term lease of a copy machine, Xerox booked the entire stream of future rental payments in the period that the lease contract was signed instead of spreading them over the life of the contract. In so doing, it inflated profits by around $3 billion.
- *Cookie-jar reserves.* The giant mortgage-pass-through firm Freddie Mac earned the Wall Street nickname "Steady Freddie" for its unusually smooth and predictable pattern of earnings growth. Unfortunately, it emerged in 2003 that Freddie achieved this predictability in part by misusing its reserve accounts. Normally, such accounts are intended to allow for the likely impact of events that might reduce earnings, such as the failure of customers to pay their bills. But Freddie seemed to "overreserve" against such contingencies so that it could "release" those reserves and bolster income in a bad year. Its steady growth was largely a matter of earnings management.
- *Off–balance sheet assets and liabilities.* Before its bankruptcy, Enron became infamous for its special-purpose vehicles, which allowed it to hide large potential liabilities from the public. Enron had also guaranteed the outstanding debt of other companies in which it had an ownership stake. To present a fair view of the firm, Enron should have recognized these potential liabilities on its balance sheet. But the firm created and placed paper firms—the special-purpose vehicles—in the middle of its transactions. The ambiguity of ownership resulting from these technically independent entities led Enron to exclude these liabilities from its own financial statements.

Investors worry about the fact that some companies seem particularly prone to inflate their earnings by playing fast and loose with accounting practice. They refer to such companies as having "low-quality" earnings, and they place a correspondingly lower value on the firms' stock.

The years between 2000 and 2003 were filled with a seemingly unending series of accounting scandals. Firms such as Global Crossing, Qwest Communications, WorldCom, and Fannie Mae misstated profits by billions of dollars. And this was not exclusively a U.S. phenomenon. Parmalat, an Italian dairy company, was dubbed "Europe's Enron" after it falsified the existence of a bank account to the tune of $5.5 billion and eventually entered bankruptcy. The French media and entertainment firm Vivendi Universal nearly ended up in bankruptcy after it was accused of accounting fraud.

In response to these and other scandals, in 2002 Congress passed the Sarbanes-Oxley Act, widely known as SOX. The act attempts to ensure that a firm's financial reports accurately represent its financial condition. SOX created the Public Accounting Oversight Board to oversee the auditing of public companies, and it requires that CEOs and CFOs personally sign off on the firm's financial statements.

But managers and investors worry that these reforms have gone too far. The costs of SOX and the burden of meeting detailed, inflexible regulations are pushing some

What's Better in Accounting, Rules or "Feel"?

Accounting standards–setters have come under fire for producing hundreds of pages of rules that cover every conceivable situation a company could face. The much-discussed alternative is to adopt a principles-based approach, where broad-brush standards are used to govern behavior, relying on companies to reasonably apply the rules to their own situations.

The push for principles got an added boost last week, when the Securities and Exchange Commission said it may soon consider allowing U.S. companies to begin choosing between two sets of accounting rules, a move that could allow them to use an international system that is considered to be more reliant on principles, instead of U.S. generally accepted accounting principles, which are more rules-based. Companies in Europe and parts of Asia follow international accounting standards.

One reason for telephone-book-sized rules is that people ask for them, said Robert Herz, chairman of the Financial Accounting Standards Board, which sets accounting rules in the U.S. Companies are generally fond of saying, "Give us principles, but tell us exactly what to do," he said. Detailed rules often spring up because companies ask regulators for detailed interpretations, even when guidance is based on a pretty clear-cut principle.

Backers of principles-based accounting are fond of blaming the raft of accounting rules they must follow on a legal system that makes lawsuits easy and on overzealous regulators. They argue that a principles-based system would make it easier and cheaper for them to comply with regulations, while at the same time limiting fraud.

But even groups that extol the use of broad-brush principles seem to fall back on rules. Last fall, the Committee on Capital Markets Regulation, a group of business leaders and academics whose work was backed by Treasury Secretary Henry Paulson, issued a report pushing a principles-based approach to regulation and accounting in the U.S. Instead, the committee called for the SEC to adopt a rule saying companies should only consider as important items that are greater than 5% of pretax profit. That raises the prospect that companies will engineer things so that issues fall below that number.

Source: David Reilly, *The Wall Street Journal,* April 30, 2007. © 2007 by Dow Jones & Co., Inc. Reproduced with permission of Dow Jones & Co., Inc.

corporations to return from public to private ownership. Some blame SOX and onerous regulation in the United States for the fact that an increasing number of foreign companies have chosen to list their shares in London rather than New York.

There is also a vigorous debate over "rules-based" versus "principles-based" approaches to accounting standards. The United States follows a rules-based approach, with hundreds of pages of rules governing virtually every circumstance that possibly can be anticipated. In contrast, the European Union takes a principles-based approach to accounting. Its International Financial Reporting Standards set out general approaches that financial statements should take to valuing assets but leave more room for discretion as long as firms can defend the consistency of their approach with the spirit of the standards. While this seems to give firms considerably more leeway than the U.S.'s rules-based system, critics of the U.S. approach argue that once firms find a loophole in GAAP, they are not legally bound to obey even the spirit of the rules. Europe and the United States have been engaged for years in attempts to coordinate their systems, and many in the United States have lobbied for the greater simplicity that principles-based accounting standards might offer. However, the nearby box shows how hard it can be to switch from a rules-based to a principles-based system.

3.5 Taxes

Taxes often have a major effect on financial decisions. Therefore, we should explain how corporations and investors are taxed.

Corporate Tax

Companies pay tax on their income. Table 3–5 shows that there are special low rates of corporate tax for small companies, but for large companies (those with income over $18.33 million) the corporate tax rate is 35%.[9] Thus for every $100 that the firm earns it pays $35 in corporate tax.

When firms calculate taxable income they are allowed to deduct expenses. These expenses include an allowance for depreciation. However, the Internal Revenue Service

---

[9] In addition, corporations pay state income taxes, which we ignore here for simplicity.

TABLE 3–5 Corporate tax rates, 2008

Taxable Income, $	Tax Rate, %
0–50,000	15
50,001–75,000	25
75,001–100,000	34
100,001–18,333,333	Varies between 39 and 34
Over 18,333,333	35

TABLE 3–6 Firms A and B both have earnings before interest and taxes (EBIT) of $100 million, but A pays out part of its profits as debt interest. This reduces the corporate tax paid by A.

	Firm A	Firm B
EBIT	100	100
Interest	40	0
Pretax income	60	100
Tax (35% of pretax income)	21	35
Net income	39	65

Note: Figures in millions of dollars.

(IRS) specifies the rates of depreciation that the company can use for different types of equipment.[10] The rates of depreciation that are used to calculate taxes are not the same as the rates that are used when the firm reports its profits to shareholders.

The company is also allowed to deduct interest paid to debtholders when calculating its taxable income, but dividends paid to shareholders are not deductible. These dividends are therefore paid out of after-tax income. Table 3–6 provides an example of how interest payments reduce corporate taxes.

The bad news about taxes is that each extra dollar of revenues increases taxable income by $1 and results in 35 cents of extra taxes. The good news is that each extra dollar of expense *reduces* taxable income by $1 and therefore reduces taxes by 35 cents. For example, if the firm borrows money, every dollar of interest it pays on the loan reduces taxes by 35 cents. Therefore, after-tax income is reduced by only 65 cents.

Self-Test 3.5

Recalculate the figures in Table 3–6 assuming that firm A now has to make interest payments of $60 million. What happens to taxes paid? Does net income fall by the additional $20 million interest payment compared with the case considered in Table 3–6, where interest expense was only $40 million?

When firms make profits, they pay 35% of the profits to the Internal Revenue Service. But the process doesn't work in reverse; if the firm suffers a loss, the IRS does not simply send it a check for 35% of the loss. However, the firm can carry the losses back, deduct them from taxable income in earlier years, and claim a refund of past taxes. Losses can also be carried forward and deducted from taxable income in the future.[11]

Personal Tax

Table 3–7 shows the U.S. rates of personal tax. Notice that as income increases the tax rate also increases. Notice also that the top personal tax rate is higher than the top corporate rate.

---

[10] If the company assumes a slower rate of depreciation in its income statement than the Internal Revenue Service assumes, the tax charge shown in the income statement will be higher in the early years of a project's life than the actual tax payment. This difference is recorded in the balance sheet as a liability for deferred tax. We will tell you more about depreciation allowances in Chapter 9.

[11] Losses can be carried back for a maximum of 3 years and forward for up to 15 years.

INTERNET INSIDER

Tax Rates

Source: Internal Revenue Service Web site.

The schedule of tax rates for individuals changes frequently. Check the latest schedules on either **www.irs.gov** or **money central.msn.com**. What is your marginal tax rate if you are single with a taxable income of $70,000? What is your average tax rate?

marginal tax rate
Additional taxes owed per dollar of additional income.

The tax rates presented in Table 3–7 are **marginal tax rates.** The marginal tax rate is the tax that the individual pays on each *extra* dollar of income. For example, as a single taxpayer, you would pay 10 cents of tax on each extra dollar you earn when your income is below $8,025, but once income exceeds $8,025, you would pay 15 cents of tax on each extra dollar of income up to an income of $32,550. If your total income is $40,000, your tax bill is 10% of the first $8,025 of income, 15% of the next $24,525 (i.e., 32,550 − 8,025), and 25% of the remaining $7,450:

$$\text{Tax} = (.10 \times \$8,025) + (.15 \times \$24,525) + (.25 \times \$7,450) = \$6,343.75$$

average tax rate
Total taxes owed divided by total income.

The **average tax rate** is simply the total tax bill divided by total income. In this example it is $6,343.75/$40,000 = .159 = 15.9%. Notice that the average rate is below the marginal rate. This is because of the lower rates on the first $32,550.

Self-Test 3.6

What are the average and marginal tax rates for a single taxpayer with a taxable income of $70,000? What are the average and marginal tax rates for married taxpayers filing joint returns if their joint taxable income is also $70,000?

The tax rates in Table 3–7 apply to "ordinary income," primarily income earned as salary or wages. Interest earnings also are treated as ordinary income. Other investment income is treated differently, however.

For example, dividend income for most individual investors in the United States is taxed at a 15% rate. Remember that each dollar of income that the company earns is taxed at the corporate tax rate. If the company then pays a dividend out of this after-tax income, the shareholder also pays personal income tax on the dividend, and so the company's original earnings are taxed twice, first as corporate income and then as dividend income. This treatment is commonly dubbed the "double taxation" of corporate

TABLE 3–7 Personal tax rates, 2008

Taxable Income (dollars)		
Single Taxpayers	Married Taxpayers Filing Joint Returns	Tax Rate, %
0–8,025	0–16,050	10
8,025–32,550	16,050–65,100	15
32,550–78,850	65,100–131,450	25
78,850–164,550	131,450–200,300	28
164,550–357,700	200,300–357,700	33
357,700 and above	357,700 and above	35

earnings. Suppose instead that the company earns a dollar which is paid out as interest. The dollar escapes corporate tax because the interest payment is considered a business expense that reduces the firm's taxable income, but the individual who receives the interest must pay personal tax at the rate on ordinary income. Financial managers need to worry about the tax treatment of investment income, because tax policy will affect the prices individuals are willing to pay for the company's stock or bonds. We will return to these issues in Part 5 of the text.

Capital gains are also taxed, but only when the capital gains are realized. For example, suppose that you bought Bio-technics stock when it was selling for 10 cents a share. Its market price is now $1 a share. As long as you hold on to your stock, there is no tax to pay on your gain. But if you sell, the 90 cents of capital gain is taxed. The marginal tax rate on capital gains for most shareholders is 15%.

The tax rates in Table 3–7 apply to individuals. But financial institutions are major investors in corporate securities. These institutions often have special tax provisions. For example, pension funds are not taxed on interest or dividend income or on capital gains.

SUMMARY

What information is contained in the balance sheet, income statement, and statement of cash flows? *(LO1)*

Investors and other stakeholders in the firm need regular financial information to help them monitor the firm's progress. Accountants summarize this information in a balance sheet, income statement, and statement of cash flows.

The **balance sheet** provides a snapshot of the firm's assets and liabilities. The assets consist of current assets that can be rapidly turned into cash and fixed assets such as plant and machinery. The liabilities consist of current liabilities that are due for payment within a year and long-term debts. The difference between the assets and the liabilities represents the amount of the shareholders' equity.

The **income statement** measures the profitability of the company during the year. It shows the difference between revenues and expenses.

The **statement of cash flows** measures the sources and uses of cash during the year. The change in the company's cash balance is the difference between sources and uses.

What is the difference between market and book value? *(LO2)*

It is important to distinguish between the book values that are shown in the company accounts and the market values of the assets and liabilities. **Book values** are historical measures based on the original cost of an asset. For example, the assets in the balance sheet are shown at their historical cost less an allowance for depreciation. Similarly, the figure for shareholders' equity measures the cash that shareholders have contributed in the past or that the company has reinvested on their behalf. In contrast, **market value** is the current price of an asset or liability.

Why does accounting income differ from cash flow? *(LO3)*

Income is not the same as cash flow. There are two reasons for this: (1) Investment in fixed assets is not deducted immediately from income but is instead spread (as charges for depreciation) over the expected life of the equipment, and (2) the accountant records revenues when the sale is made, rather than when the customer actually pays the bill, and at the same time deducts the production costs even though those costs may have been incurred earlier.

What are the essential features of the taxation of corporate and personal income? *(LO4)*

For large companies the **marginal rate of tax** on income is 35%. In calculating taxable income the company deducts an allowance for depreciation and interest payments. It cannot deduct dividend payments to the shareholders.

Individuals are also taxed on their income, which includes dividends and interest on their investments. Capital gains are taxed, but only when the investment is sold and the gain realized.

www.mhhe.com/bmm6e

LISTING OF EQUATIONS

3.1 Shareholders' equity = total assets − total liabilities

QUESTIONS

QUIZ

1. **Balance Sheet.** Construct a balance sheet for Sophie's Sofas given the following data. What is shareholders' equity? *(LO1)*

   Cash balances = $10,000
   Inventory of sofas = $200,000
   Store and property = $100,000
   Accounts receivable = $22,000
   Accounts payable = $17,000
   Long-term debt = $170,000

2. **Financial Statements.** Earlier in the chapter, we characterized the balance sheet as providing a snapshot of the firm at one point in time and the income statement as providing a video. What did we mean by this? Is the statement of cash flow more like a snapshot or a video? *(LO1)*

3. **Income versus Cash Flow.** Explain why accounting income generally will differ from a firm's cash inflows. *(LO3)*

4. **Working Capital.** QuickGrow is in an expanding market, and its sales are increasing by 25% per year. Would you expect its net working capital to be increasing or decreasing? *(LO3)*

5. **Tax Rates.** Using Table 3–7, calculate the marginal and average tax rates for a single taxpayer with the following incomes: *(LO4)*

   a. $20,000
   b. $50,000
   c. $300,000
   d. $3,000,000

6. **Tax Rates.** What would be the marginal and average tax rates for a *corporation* with an income level of $100,000? *(LO4)*

7. **Taxes.** A married couple earned $95,000 in 2008. How much did they pay in taxes? What were their marginal and average tax brackets? *(LO4)*

8. **Cash Flows.** What impact will the following actions have on the firm's cash balance? *(LO3)*

   a. The firm sells some goods from inventory.
   b. The firm sells some machinery to a bank and leases it back for a period of 20 years.
   c. The firm buys back 1 million shares of stock from existing shareholders.

PRACTICE PROBLEMS

9. **Balance Sheet/Income Statement.** The year-end 2008 balance sheet of Brandex Inc. listed common stock and other paid-in capital at $1,100,000 and retained earnings at $3,400,000. The next year, retained earnings were listed at $3,700,000. The firm's net income in 2009 was $900,000. There were no stock repurchases during the year. What were the dividends paid by the firm in 2009? *(LO1)*

10. **Taxes.** You have set up your tax preparation firm as an incorporated business. You took $70,000 from the firm as your salary. The firm's taxable income for the year (net of your salary) was $30,000. How much taxes must be paid to the federal government, including both your personal taxes and the firm's taxes? Assume you pay personal taxes as an unmarried taxpayer. By how much will you reduce the total tax bill by reducing your salary to $50,000, thereby leaving the firm with taxable income of $50,000? Use the tax rates presented in Tables 3–5 and 3–7. *(LO4)*

www.mhhe.com/bmm6e

Please visit us at www.mhhe.com/bmm6e

11. **Market versus Book Values.** The founder of Alchemy Products, Inc., discovered a way to turn lead into gold and patented this new technology. He then formed a corporation and invested $200,000 in setting up a production plant. He believes that he could sell his patent for $50 million. *(LO2)*
   a. What are the book value and market value of the firm?
   b. If there are 2 million shares of stock in the new corporation, what would be the price per share and the book value per share?

12. **Income Statement.** Sheryl's Shipping had sales last year of $10,000. The cost of goods sold was $6,500, general and administrative expenses were $1,000, interest expenses were $500, and depreciation was $1,000. The firm's tax rate is 35%. *(LO1)*
   a. What are earnings before interest and taxes?
   b. What is net income?
   c. What is cash flow from operations?

13. **Cash Flow.** Can cash flow from operations be positive if net income is negative? Can it be negative if net income is positive? Give examples. *(LO3)*

14. **Cash Flows.** Ponzi Products produced 100 chain letter kits this quarter, resulting in a total cash outlay of $10 per unit. It will sell 50 of the kits next quarter at a price of $11, and the other 50 kits in two quarters at a price of $12. It takes a full quarter for it to collect its bills from its customers. (Ignore possible sales in earlier or later quarters.)
   a. Prepare an income statement for Ponzi for today and for each of the next three quarters. Ignore taxes. *(LO1)*
   b. What are the cash flows for the company today and in each of the next three quarters? *(LO3)*
   c. What is Ponzi's net working capital in each quarter? *(LO1)*

15. **Profits versus Cash Flow.** During the last year of operations, accounts receivable increased by $10,000, accounts payable increased by $5,000, and inventories decreased by $2,000. What is the total impact of these changes on the difference between profits and cash flow? *(LO3)*

16. **Income Statement.** A firm's income statement included the following data. The firm's average tax rate was 20%. *(LO1)*

Cost of goods sold	$8,000
Income taxes paid	2,000
Administrative expenses	3,000
Interest expense	1,000
Depreciation	1,000

   a. What was the firm's net income?
   b. What must have been the firm's revenues?
   c. What was EBIT?

17. **Profits versus Cash Flow.** Butterfly Tractors had $14 million in sales last year. Cost of goods sold was $8 million, depreciation expense was $2 million, interest payment on outstanding debt was $1 million, and the firm's tax rate was 35%. *(LO3)*
   a. What was the firm's net income and net cash flow?
   b. What would happen to net income and cash flow if depreciation were increased by $1 million? How do you explain the differing impact of depreciation on income versus cash flow?
   c. Would you expect the change in income and cash flow to have a positive or negative impact on the firm's stock price?
   d. Now consider the impact on net income and cash flow if the firm's interest expense were $1 million higher. Why is this case different from part (b)?

18. **Cash Flow.** Candy Canes, Inc., spends $100,000 to buy sugar and peppermint in April. It produces its candy and sells it to distributors in May for $150,000, but it does not receive payment until June. For each month, find the firm's sales, net income, and net cash flow. *(LO3)*

19. **Financial Statements.** Here are the 2008 and 2009 (incomplete) balance sheets for Nobel Oil Corp. *(LO1)*

NOBEL OIL CORP. BALANCE SHEET, AS OF END OF YEAR					
Assets	**2008**	**2009**	**Liabilities and Owners' Equity**	**2008**	**2009**
Current assets	$ 310	$ 420	Current liabilities	$210	$240
Net fixed assets	1,200	1,420	Long-term debt	830	920

Chapter 3 Accounting and Finance

75

    a. What was owners' equity at the end of 2008 and 2009?

    b. If Nobel paid dividends of $100 in 2009, and made no stock issues, what must have been net income during the year?

    c. If Nobel purchased $300 in fixed assets during the year, what must have been the depreciation charge on the income statement?

    d. What was the change in net working capital between 2008 and 2009?

    e. If Nobel issued $200 of new long-term debt, how much debt must have been paid off during the year?

20. **Financial Statements.** South Sea Baubles has the following (incomplete) balance sheet and income statement.

BALANCE SHEET, AS OF END OF YEAR
(figures in millions of dollars)

Assets	2008	2009	Liabilities and Shareholders' Equity	2008	2009
Current assets	$ 90	$140	Current liabilities	$ 50	$ 60
Net fixed assets	800	900	Long-term debt	600	750

INCOME STATEMENT, 2009
(figures in millions of dollars)

Revenue	$1,950
Cost of goods sold	1,030
Depreciation	350
Interest expense	240

    a. What is shareholders' equity in 2008 and 2009? *(LO1)*

    b. What is net working capital in 2008 and 2009? *(LO1)*

    c. What are taxable income and taxes paid in 2009? Assume the firm pays taxes equal to 35% of taxable income. *(LO4)*

    d. What is cash provided by operations during 2009? Pay attention to changes in net working capital, using Table 3–4 as a guide. *(LO3)*

    e. Net fixed assets increased from $800 million to $900 million during 2009. What must have been South Sea's *gross* investment in fixed assets during 2009? *(LO1)*

    f. If South Sea reduced its outstanding accounts payable by $35 million during the year, what must have happened to its other current liabilities? *(LO1)*

The following table contains data on Fincorp, Inc., that you should use for Practice Problems 21–28. The balance sheet items correspond to values at year-end of 2008 and 2009, while the income statement items correspond to revenues or expenses during the year ending in either 2008 or 2009. All values are in thousands of dollars.

21. **Balance Sheet.** Construct a balance sheet for Fincorp for 2008 and 2009. What is shareholders' equity? *(LO1)*

22. **Working Capital.** What happened to net working capital during the year? *(LO1)*

23. **Income Statement.** Construct an income statement for Fincorp for 2008 and 2009. What were reinvested earnings for 2009? How does that compare with the increase in shareholders' equity between the two years? *(LO1)*

24. **Earnings per Share.** Suppose that Fincorp has 500,000 shares outstanding. What were earnings per share? *(LO1)*

25. **Taxes.** What was the firm's average tax bracket for each year? Do you have enough information to determine the marginal tax bracket? *(LO4)*

26. **Balance Sheet.** Examine the values for depreciation in 2009 and net fixed assets in 2008 and 2009. What was Fincorp's gross investment in plant and equipment during 2009? *(LO1)*

27. **Cash Flows.** Construct a statement of cash flows for Fincorp for 2009. *(LO1)*

www.mhhe.com/bmm6e

	2008	2009
Revenue	$4,000	$4,100
Cost of goods sold	1,600	1,700
Depreciation	500	520
Inventories	300	350
Administrative expenses	500	550
Interest expense	150	150
Federal and state taxes*	400	420
Accounts payable	300	350
Accounts receivable	400	450
Net fixed assets†	5,000	5,800
Long-term debt	2,000	2,400
Notes payable	1,000	600
Dividends paid	410	410
Cash and marketable securities	800	300

* Taxes are paid in their entirety in the year that the tax obligation is incurred.
† Net fixed assets are fixed assets net of accumulated depreciation since the asset was installed.

28. **Book versus Market Value.** Now suppose that the market value (in thousands of dollars) of Fincorp's fixed assets in 2009 is $6,000 and that the value of its long-term debt is only $2,400. In addition, the consensus among investors is that Fincorp's past investments in developing the skills of its employees are worth $2,900. This investment of course does not show up on the balance sheet. What will be the price per share of Fincorp stock? *(LO2)*

Please visit us at www.mhhe.com/bmm6e

29. **Taxes.** Turn back to Table 3–7, which shows marginal personal tax rates. Make a table in Excel that calculates taxes due for income levels ranging from $10,000 to $10 million. *(LO4)*

   a. For each income, calculate the *average* tax rate of a single taxpayer. Plot the average tax rate as a function of income.
   b. What happens to the difference between the average and top marginal tax rates as income becomes very large?
   c. Explain why, when analyzing very large firms, we may be content simply treating the corporate tax rate as 35% without worrying about tax brackets at relatively low income levels.

CHALLENGE PROBLEM

30. **Taxes.** Reconsider the data in Practice Problem 10 which imply that you have $100,000 of total pretax income to allocate between your salary and your firm's profits. What allocation will minimize the total tax bill? *Hint:* Think about marginal tax rates and the ability to shift income from a higher marginal bracket to a lower one.

STANDARD
&POOR'S

1. Find Microsoft and General Motors on Market Insight (**www.mhhe.com/edumarketinsight**), and examine the financial statements of each. Which firm uses more debt finance? Which firm has higher cash as a percentage of total assets? Which has higher EBIT per dollar of total assets? Which has higher profits per dollar of shareholders' equity?

2. Find information on two highly profitable technology firms, like Intel (INTC) and Microsoft (MSFT), and two electric utilities, such as American Electric Power (AEP) and Duke Energy (DUK), at **www.mhhe.com/edumarketsight**. Which firms have the higher ratio of market value to book value of equity? Does this make sense to you? Which firms pay out a higher fraction of their profits as dividends to shareholders? Does this make sense?

SOLUTIONS TO SELF-TEST QUESTIONS

3.1 Cash and equivalents would increase by $100 million. Property, plant, and equipment would increase by $400 million. Long-term debt would increase by $500 million. Shareholders' equity would not increase: Assets and liabilities have increased equally, leaving shareholders' equity unchanged.

3.2 a. If the auto plant were worth $14 billion, the equity in the firm would be worth $14 − $4 = $10 billion. With 100 million shares outstanding, each share would be worth $100.
   b. If the outstanding stock were worth $8 billion, we would infer that the market values the auto plant at $8 + $4 = $12 billion.

3.3 The profits for the firm are recognized in periods 2 and 3 when the sales take place. In both of those periods, profits are $150 − $100 = $50. Cash flows are derived as follows.

Period:	1	2	3	4
Sales	0	150	150	0
− Change in accounts receivable	0	150	0	(150)
− Cost of goods sold	0	100	100	0
− Change in inventories	200	(100)	(100)	0
= Net cash flow	−200	0	+ 150	+150

In period 2, half the units are sold for $150 but no cash is collected, so the entire $150 is treated as an increase in accounts receivable. Half the $200 cost of production is recognized, and a like amount is taken out of inventory. In period 3, the firm sells another $150 of product but collects $150 from its previous sales, so there is no change in outstanding accounts receivable. Net cash flow is the $150 collected in this period on the sale that occurred in period 2. In period 4, cash flow is again $150, as the accounts receivable from the sale in period 3 are collected.

3.4 a. An increase in inventories uses cash, reducing the firm's net cash balance.
   b. A reduction in accounts payable uses cash, reducing the firm's net cash balance.
   c. An issue of common stock is a source of cash.
   d. The purchase of new equipment is a use of cash, and it reduces the firm's net cash balance.

3.5

	Firm A	Firm B
EBIT	100	100
Interest	60	0
Pretax income	40	100
Tax (35% of pretax income)	14	35
Net income	26	65

Note: Figures in millions of dollars.

Taxes owed by Firm A fall from $21 million to $14 million. The reduction in taxes is 35% of the extra $20 million of interest income. Net income does not fall by the full $20 million of extra interest expense. It instead falls by interest expense less the reduction in taxes, or $20 million − $7 million = $13 million.

3.6 For a single taxpayer with taxable income of $70,000, total taxes paid are

$$.10 \times 8,025 + [.15 \times (32,550 - 8,025)] + [.25 \times (70,000 - 32,550)] = \$13,843.75$$

The marginal tax rate is 25%, but the average tax rate is only 13,843.75/70,000 = .1987, or 19.87%.

For the married taxpayers filing jointly with taxable income of $70,000, total taxes paid are

$$(.10 \times 16,050) + .15(65,100 - 16,050) + .25(70,000 - 65,100) = \$10,187.50$$

The marginal tax rate is 25%, and the average tax rate is 10,187.50/70,000 = .146, or 14.6%.

CHAPTER 9

Using Discounted Cash-Flow Analysis to Make Investment Decisions

LEARNING OBJECTIVES

After studying this chapter, you should be able to:

1. Identify the cash flows properly attributable to a proposed new project.

2. Calculate the cash flows of a project from standard financial statements.

3. Understand how the company's tax bill is affected by depreciation and how this affects project value.

4. Understand how changes in working capital affect project cash flows.

Related Web sites for this chapter can be found at www.mhhe.com/bmm6e.

A working magnoosium mine.   But how do you find its net present value?

Tyler Stableford/Getty Images

Think of the problems that Toyota's managers face when considering whether to introduce a new model. What investment must be made in new plant and equipment? What will it cost to market and promote the new car? How soon can the car be put into production? What is the projected production cost? How much must be invested in inventories of raw materials and finished cars? How many cars can be sold each year and at what price? What credit arrangements should be given to dealers? How long will the model stay in production? What happens at the end of that time? Can plant and equipment be used elsewhere in the company? All of these issues affect the level and timing of project cash flows. In this chapter we continue our analysis of the capital budgeting decision by turning our focus to how the financial manager should prepare cash-flow estimates for use in net present value analysis.

In Chapter 8 you used the net present value rule to make a simple capital budgeting decision. You tackled the problem in four steps:

Step 1.   Forecast the project cash flows.

Step 2.   Estimate the opportunity cost of capital—that is, the rate of return that your shareholders could expect to earn if they invested their money in the capital market.

Step 3.   Use the opportunity cost of capital to discount the future cash flows. The project's present value (PV) is equal to the sum of the discounted future cash flows.

Step 4.   Net present value (NPV) measures whether the project is worth more than it costs. To calculate NPV, you need to subtract the required investment from the present value of the future payoffs:

$$NPV = PV - \text{required investment}$$

You should go ahead with the project if it has a positive NPV.

We now need to consider how to apply the net present value rule to practical investment problems. The first step is to decide what to discount. We know the answer in principle: discount cash flows. This is why capital budgeting is often referred to as *discounted cash-flow*, or *DCF*, analysis. But useful forecasts of cash flows do not arrive on a silver platter. Often the financial manager has to make do with raw data supplied by specialists in product design, production, marketing, and so on, and must check and combine this information. In addition, most financial forecasts are prepared in accordance with accounting principles that do not necessarily recognize cash flows when they occur. These forecasts must also be adjusted.

We look first at what cash flows should be discounted. We then present an example designed to show how standard accounting information can be used to compute cash flows and why cash flows and accounting income usually differ.

The example will lead us to various further points, including the links between depreciation and taxes and the importance of tracking investments in working capital.

9.1 Identifying Cash Flows

Discount Cash Flows, Not Profits

Up to this point we have been concerned mainly with the mechanics of discounting and with the various methods of project appraisal. We have had almost nothing to say about the problem of *what* you should discount. The first and most important point is this: To calculate net present value, you need to discount cash flows, *not* accounting profits.

We stressed the difference between cash flows and profits in Chapter 3. Here we stress it again. Income statements are intended to show how well the firm has performed. They do not track cash flows.

If the firm lays out a large amount of money on a big capital project, you do not conclude that the firm performed poorly that year, even though a lot of cash is going out the door. Therefore, the accountant does not deduct capital expenditure when calculating the year's income but, instead, depreciates it over several years.

That is fine for computing year-by-year profits, but it could get you into trouble when working out net present value. For example, suppose that you are analyzing an investment proposal. It costs $2,000 and is expected to bring in a cash flow of $1,500 in the first year and $500 in the second. You think that the opportunity cost of capital is 10% and so calculate the present value of the cash flows as follows:

$$PV = \frac{\$1,500}{1.10} + \frac{\$500}{(1.10)^2} = \$1,776.86$$

The project is worth less than it costs; it has a negative NPV:

$$NPV = \$1,776.86 - \$2,000 = -\$223.14$$

The project costs $2,000 today, but accountants would not treat that outlay as an immediate expense. They would depreciate that $2,000 over 2 years and deduct the depreciation from the cash flow to obtain accounting income:

	Year 1	Year 2
Cash inflow	+ $1,500	+$ 500
Less depreciation	− 1,000	− 1,000
Accounting income	+ 500	− 500

Thus an accountant would forecast income of $500 in year 1 and an accounting loss of $500 in year 2.

Suppose you were given this forecast income and loss and naively discounted them. Now NPV *looks* positive:

$$\text{Apparent NPV} = \frac{\$500}{1.10} + \frac{-\$500}{(1.10)^2} = \$41.32$$

Of course we know that this is nonsense. The project is obviously a loser; we are spending money today ($2,000 cash outflow), and we are simply getting our money back later ($1,500 in year 1 and $500 in year 2). We are earning a zero return when we could get a 10% return by investing our money in the capital market.

The message of the example is this: **When calculating NPV, recognize investment expenditures when they occur, not later when they show up as depreciation. Projects are financially attractive because of the cash they generate, either for distribution to shareholders or for reinvestment in the firm. Therefore, the focus of capital budgeting must be on cash flow, not profits.**

We saw another example of the distinction between cash flow and accounting profits in Chapter 3. Accountants try to show profit as it is earned, rather than when the company and the customer get around to paying their bills. For example, an income statement will recognize revenue when the sale is made, even if the bill is not paid for months. This practice also results in a difference between accounting profits and cash flow. The sale generates immediate profits, but the cash flow comes later.

EXAMPLE 9.1 ▶ Sales before Cash

Your firm's ace computer salesman closed a $500,000 sale on December 15, just in time to count it toward his annual bonus. How did he do it? Well, for one thing he gave the customer 180 days to pay. The income statement will recognize the sale in December, even though cash will not arrive until June.

The accountant takes care of this timing difference by adding $500,000 to accounts receivable in December and then reducing accounts receivable when the money arrives in June. (The total of accounts receivable is just the sum of all cash due from customers.)

You can think of the increase in accounts receivable as an investment—it's effectively a 180-day loan to the customer—and therefore a cash outflow. That investment is recovered when the customer pays. Thus financial analysts often find it convenient to calculate cash flow as follows:

December		June	
Sales	$500,000	Sales	0
Less investment in accounts receivable	−500,000	Plus recovery of accounts receivable	+$500,000
Cash flow	0	Cash flow	$500,000

Note that this procedure gives the correct cash flow of $500,000 in June.

It is not always easy to translate accounting data back into actual dollars. If you are in doubt about what is a cash flow, simply count the dollars coming in and take away the dollars going out.

Self-Test 9.1

A regional supermarket chain is deciding whether to install a tewgit machine in each of its stores. Each machine costs $250,000. Projected income per machine is as follows:

Year:	1	2	3	4	5
Sales	$250,000	$300,000	$300,000	$250,000	$250,000
Operating expenses	200,000	200,000	200,000	200,000	200,000
Depreciation	50,000	50,000	50,000	50,000	50,000
Accounting income	0	50,000	50,000	0	0

Why would a store continue to operate a machine in years 4 and 5 if it produces no profits? What are the cash flows from investing in a machine? Assume each tewgit machine is completely depreciated and has no salvage value at the end of its 5-year life.

Discount *Incremental* Cash Flows

A project's present value depends on the *extra* cash flows that it produces. So you need to forecast first the firm's cash flows if you go ahead with the project. Then forecast the cash flows if you *don't* accept the project. Take the difference and you have the extra (or *incremental*) cash flows produced by the project:

$$\begin{array}{c} \text{Incremental} \\ \text{cash flow} \end{array} = \begin{array}{c} \text{cash flow} \\ \text{with project} \end{array} - \begin{array}{c} \text{cash flow} \\ \text{without project} \end{array}$$

EXAMPLE 9.2 ▶ Launching a New Product

Consider the decision by Microsoft to develop Vista, its new operating system. If successful, Vista could lead to several billion dollars in profits.

But are these profits all incremental cash flows? Certainly not. Our with-versus-without principle reminds us that we need also to think about what the cash flows would be *without* the new system. By launching Vista, Microsoft reduced demand for Windows XP. The incremental cash flows therefore are

$$\begin{array}{c} \text{Cash flow with Vista} \\ \text{(including lower cash flow} \\ \text{from Windows XP)} \end{array} - \begin{array}{c} \text{cash flow without Vista} \\ \text{(with higher cash flow} \\ \text{from Windows XP)} \end{array}$$

The trick in capital budgeting is to trace all the incremental flows from a proposed project. Here are some things to look out for.

Include All Indirect Effects Microsoft's new operating system illustrates a common indirect effect. New products often damage sales of an existing product. Of course, companies frequently introduce new products anyway, usually because they believe that their existing product line is under threat from competition. Even if you don't go ahead with a new product, there is no guarantee that sales of the existing product line will continue at their present level. Sooner or later they will decline.

Sometimes a new project will *help* the firm's existing business. Suppose that you are the financial manager of an airline that is considering opening a new short-haul route from Peoria, Illinois, to Chicago's O'Hare Airport. When considered in isolation, the new route may have a negative NPV. But once you allow for the additional business that the new route brings to your other traffic out of O'Hare, it may be a very worthwhile investment. **To forecast incremental cash flow, you must trace out all indirect effects of accepting the project.**

Some capital investments have very long lives once all indirect effects are recognized. Consider the introduction of a new jet engine. Engine manufacturers often offer attractive pricing to achieve early sales, because once an engine is installed, 15 years' sales of replacement parts are almost ensured. Also, since airlines prefer to limit the number of different engines in their fleet, selling jet engines today improves sales tomorrow as well. Later sales will generate further demands for replacement parts. Thus the string of incremental effects from the first sales of a new model engine can run for 20 years or more.

Forget Sunk Costs Sunk costs are like spilled milk: They are past and irreversible outflows. **Sunk costs remain the same whether or not you accept the project. Therefore, they do not affect project NPV.**

Unfortunately, managers often are influenced by sunk costs. A classic case occurred in 1971, when Lockheed sought a federal guarantee for a bank loan to continue development of the Tristar airplane. Lockheed and its supporters argued that it would be foolish to abandon a project on which nearly $1 billion had already been spent. This was a poor argument, however, because the $1 billion was sunk. The relevant questions were how much more needed to be invested and whether the finished product warranted the *incremental* investment.

Lockheed's supporters were not the only ones to appeal to sunk costs. Some of its critics claimed that it would be foolish to continue with a project that offered no prospect of a satisfactory return on that $1 billion. This argument too was faulty. The $1 billion was gone, and the decision to continue with the project should have depended only on the return on the incremental investment.

Include Opportunity Costs Resources are almost never free, even when no cash changes hands. For example, suppose a new manufacturing operation uses land that could otherwise be sold for $100,000. This resource is costly; by using the land, you pass up the opportunity to sell it. There is no out-of-pocket cost, but there is an **opportunity cost**, that is, the value of the forgone alternative use of the land.

This example prompts us to warn you against judging projects "before versus after" rather than "with versus without." A manager comparing before versus after might not assign any value to the land because the firm owns it both before and after:

Before	Take Project	After	Cash Flow, Before versus After
Firm owns land	⟶	Firm still owns land	0

The proper comparison, with versus without, is as follows:

Before	Take Project	After	Cash Flow, with Project
Firm owns land	⟶	Firm still owns land	0

Before	Do Not Take Project	After	Cash Flow, without Project
Firm owns land	⟶	Firm sells land for $100,000	$100,000

Comparing the cash flows with and without the project, we see that $100,000 is given up by undertaking the project. The original cost of purchasing the land is irrelevant—that cost is sunk. **The opportunity cost equals the cash that could be realized from selling the land now and therefore is a relevant cash flow for project evaluation.**

When the resource can be freely traded, its opportunity cost is simply the market price.[1] However, sometimes opportunity costs are difficult to estimate. Suppose that you go ahead with a project to develop Computer Nouveau, pulling your software team off their work on a new operating system that some existing customers are not-so-patiently awaiting. The exact cost of infuriating those customers may be impossible to calculate, but you'll think twice about the opportunity cost of moving the software team to Computer Nouveau.

Recognize the Investment in Working Capital **Net working capital** (often referred to simply as *working capital*) is the difference between a company's short-term assets and its liabilities. The principal short-term assets are cash, accounts receivable (customers' unpaid bills), and inventories of raw materials and finished goods, and the principal short-term liabilities are accounts payable (bills that *you* have not paid), notes payable, and accruals (liabilities for items such as wages or taxes that have recently been incurred but have not yet been paid).

---

[1] If the value of the land to the firm were less than the market price, the firm would sell it. On the other hand, the opportunity cost of using land in a particular project cannot exceed the cost of buying an equivalent parcel to replace it.

opportunity cost
Benefit or cash flow forgone as a result of an action.

net working capital
Current assets minus current liabilities.

Most projects entail an additional investment in working capital. For example, before you can start production, you need to invest in inventories of raw materials. Then, when you deliver the finished product, customers may be slow to pay and accounts receivable will increase. (Remember the computer sale described in Example 9.1. It required a $500,000, 6-month investment in accounts receivable.) Next year, as business builds up, you may need a larger stock of raw materials and you may have even more unpaid bills. **Investments in working capital, just like investments in plant and equipment, result in cash outflows.**

We find that working capital is one of the most common sources of confusion in forecasting project cash flows.[2] Here are the most common mistakes:

1. *Forgetting about working capital entirely.* We hope that you never fall into that trap.
2. *Forgetting that working capital may change during the life of the project.* Imagine that you sell $100,000 of goods per year and customers pay on average 6 months late. You will therefore have $50,000 of unpaid bills. Now you increase prices by 10%, so revenues increase to $110,000. If customers continue to pay 6 months late, unpaid bills increase to $55,000, and therefore you need to make an *additional* investment in working capital of $5,000.
3. *Forgetting that working capital is recovered at the end of the project.* When the project comes to an end, inventories are run down, any unpaid bills are (you hope) paid off, and you can recover your investment in working capital. This generates a cash *inflow.*

Remember Shutdown Cash Flows   The end of a project almost always brings additional cash flows. For example, nuclear power plants need to be decommissioned at costs measured in the hundreds of millions of dollars. Coal mines need to be closed down, and their surrounding environments often need rehabilitation. On the other hand, not all shutdown cash flows are negative. Once the project is complete, you might be able to sell some of the plant, equipment, or real estate that was dedicated to it. Also, as we just mentioned, you may recover some of your investment in working capital as you sell off inventories of finished goods and collect on outstanding accounts receivable. The important point is not to overlook these incremental cash flows.

Beware of Allocated Overhead Costs   We have already mentioned that the accountant's objective in gathering data is not always the same as the project analyst's. A case in point is the allocation of overhead costs such as rent, heat, or electricity. These overhead costs may not be related to a particular project, but they must be paid for nevertheless. Therefore, when the accountant assigns costs to the firm's projects, a charge for overhead is usually made. But our principle of incremental cash flows says that in investment appraisal we should include only the *extra* expenses that would result from the project.

A project may generate extra overhead costs, but then again it may not. We should be cautious about assuming that the accountant's allocation of overhead costs represents the *incremental* cash flow that would be incurred by accepting the project.

Self-Test 9.2   A firm is considering an investment in a new manufacturing plant. The site already is owned by the company, but existing buildings would need to be demolished. Which of the following should be treated as incremental cash flows?

---

[2] If you are not clear *why* working capital affects cash flow, look back to Chapter 3, where we gave a primer on working capital and a couple of simple examples.

a. The market value of the site.

b. The market value of the existing buildings.

c. Demolition costs and site clearance.

d. The cost of a new access road put in last year.

e. Lost cash flows on other projects due to executive time spent on the new facility.

f. Future depreciation of the new plant.

Discount Nominal Cash Flows by the Nominal Cost of Capital

The distinction between nominal and real cash flows and interest rates is crucial in capital budgeting. Interest rates are usually quoted in *nominal* terms. If you invest $100 in a bank deposit offering 6% interest, then the bank promises to pay you $106 at the end of the year. It makes no promises about what that $106 will buy. The real rate of interest on the bank deposit depends on inflation. If inflation is 2%, that $106 will buy you only 4% more goods at the end of the year than your $100 could buy today. The *real* rate of interest is therefore about 4%.[3]

If the discount rate is nominal, consistency requires that cash flows be estimated in nominal terms as well, taking account of trends in selling price, labor and materials costs, and so on. This calls for more than simply applying a single assumed inflation rate to all components of cash flow. Some costs or prices increase faster than inflation, some slower. For example, perhaps you have entered into a 5-year fixed-price contract with a supplier. No matter what happens to inflation over this period, this part of your costs is fixed in nominal terms.

Of course, there is nothing wrong with discounting real cash flows at the real interest rate, although this is not commonly done. We saw in Chapter 5 that real cash flows discounted at the real discount rate give exactly the same present values as nominal cash flows discounted at the nominal rate.

It should go without saying that you cannot mix and match real and nominal quantities. Real cash flows must be discounted at a real discount rate, nominal cash flows at a nominal rate. Discounting real cash flows at a nominal rate is a *big* mistake.

While the need to maintain consistency may seem like an obvious point, analysts sometimes forget to account for the effects of inflation when forecasting future cash flows. As a result, they end up discounting real cash flows at a nominal discount rate. This can grossly understate project values.

EXAMPLE 9.3 ▶ Cash Flows and Inflation

City Consulting Services is considering moving into a new office building. The cost of a 1-year lease is $8,000, paid immediately. This cost will increase in future years at the annual inflation rate of 3%. The firm believes that it will remain in the building for 4 years. What is the present value of its rental costs if the discount rate is 10%?

The present value can be obtained by discounting the nominal cash flows at the 10% discount rate as follows:

---

[3] Remember from Chapter 5,

$$\text{Real rate of interest} \approx \text{nominal rate of interest} - \text{inflation rate}$$

The exact formula is

$$1 + \text{real rate interest} = \frac{1 + \text{nominal rate of interest}}{1 + \text{inflation rate}} = \frac{1.06}{1.02} = 1.0392$$

Therefore, the real interest rate is .0392, or 3.92%.

Year	Cash Flow	Present Value at 10% Discount Rate	
0	8,000		8,000
1	$8,000 \times 1.03 = 8,240$	$8,240/1.10 =$	7,491
2	$8,000 \times 1.03^2 = 8,487$	$8,487/(1.10)^2 =$	7,014
3	$8,000 \times 1.03^3 = 8,742$	$8,742/(1.10)^3 =$	6,568
			$29,073

Alternatively, the real discount rate can be calculated as $1.10/1.03 - 1 = .06796 = 6.796\%$.[4] The present value of the cash flows can then be computed by discounting the real cash flows at the real discount rate as follows:

Year	Real Cash Flow	Present Value at 6.796% Discount Rate	
0	8,000		8,000
1	8,000	$8,000/1.06796 =$	7,491
2	8,000	$8,000/(1.06796)^2 =$	7,014
3	8,000	$8,000/(1.06796)^3 =$	6,568
			$29,073

Notice the real cash flow is a constant, since the lease payment increases at the rate of inflation. The present value of *each* cash flow is the same regardless of the method used to discount it. The sum of the present values is, of course, also identical.

Self-Test 9.3

Nasty Industries is closing down an outmoded factory and throwing all of its workers out on the street. Nasty's CEO is enraged to learn that the firm must continue to pay for workers' health insurance for 4 years. The cost per worker next year will be $2,400 per year, but the inflation rate is 4%, and health costs have been increasing at 3 percentage points faster than inflation. What is the present value of this obligation? The (nominal) discount rate is 10%.

Separate Investment and Financing Decisions

Suppose you finance a project partly with debt. How should you treat the proceeds from the debt issue and the interest and principal payments on the debt? Answer: you should *neither* subtract the debt proceeds from the required investment *nor* recognize the interest and principal payments on the debt as cash outflows. Regardless of the actual financing, you should view the project as if it were all equity-financed, treating all cash outflows required for the project as coming from stockholders and all cash inflows as going to them.

This procedure focuses exclusively on the *project* cash flows, not the cash flows associated with alternative financing schemes. It, therefore, allows you to separate the analysis of the investment decision from that of the financing decision. First, you ask whether the project has a positive net present value, assuming all-equity financing. Then, if the project is viable, you can undertake a separate analysis of the best financing strategy. Financing decisions are considered later in the text.

---

[4] We calculate the real discount rate to three decimal places to avoid confusion from rounding. Such precision is rarely necessary in practice.

9.2 Calculating Cash Flow

It is helpful to think of a project's cash flow as composed of three elements:

$$\text{Total cash flow} = \text{cash flows from capital investments} \qquad (9.1)$$
$$+ \text{cash flows from changes in working capital}$$
$$+ \text{operating cash flows}$$

We will look at each of these components in turn.

Capital Investment

To get a project off the ground, a company typically needs to make considerable up-front investments in plant, equipment, research, marketing, and so on. For example, development of Boeing's 787 Dreamliner is estimated to top $10 billion. This $10 billion is a negative cash flow—negative because cash goes out the door.

When the 787 program finally comes to an end, Boeing can either sell the plant and equipment or redeploy the assets elsewhere in the business. This salvage value (net of any taxes if the equipment is sold) represents a positive cash flow to the firm.

Final cash flows may also be *negative* if there are significant shutdown costs. For example, Phelps Dodge has earmarked over $300 million to cover the future costs of closing its New Mexico copper mines.

EXAMPLE 9.4 ▶   Cash Flow from Capital Investment

Slick Corporation plans to invest $800 million to develop the Mock4 razor blade. The specialized blade factory will run for 7 years until it is replaced by more advanced technology. At that point the machinery will be sold for $50 million. Taxes of $10 million will be assessed on the sale.

The initial cash flow from Slick's investment is −$800 million. In year 7, when the firm sells the land and equipment, there will be a net inflow of $50 million − $10 million = $40 million. Thus, the initial investment involves a negative cash flow, and the salvage value results in a positive flow.

Investment in Working Capital

We pointed out earlier in the chapter that when a company builds up inventories of raw materials or finished product, the company's cash is reduced; the reduction in cash reflects the firm's investment in inventories. Similarly, cash is reduced when customers are slow to pay their bills—in this case, the firm makes an investment in accounts receivable. Investment in working capital, just like investment in plant and equipment, represents a negative cash flow. On the other hand, later in the life of a project, when inventories are sold off and accounts receivable are collected, the firm's investment in working capital is reduced as it converts these assets into cash.

EXAMPLE 9.5 ▶   Cash Flow from Changes in Working Capital

Slick makes an initial (year 0) investment of $10 million in inventories of plastic and steel for its blade plant. Then in year 1 it accumulates an additional $20 million of raw materials. The total level of inventories is now $10 million + $20 million = $30 million, but the cash expenditure in year 1 is simply the $20 million addition to inventory. The $20 million investment in additional inventory results in a cash flow of −$20 million. Notice that the increase in working capital is an *investment* in the project. Like other investments, a buildup of working capital requires cash. Increases in the *level* of working capital therefore show up as *negative* cash flows.

Later on, say, in year 5, the company begins planning for the next-generation blade. At this point, it decides to reduce its inventory of raw material from $20 million to $15 million. This reduction in inventory investment frees up $5 million of cash, which is a positive cash flow. Therefore, the cash flows from inventory investment are −$10 million in year 0, −$20 million in year 1, and +$5 million in year 5.

These calculations can be summarized in a simple table, as follows:

Year:	0	1	2	3	4	5
1. Total working capital, year-end ($ million)	10	30	30	30	30	25
2. Change in working capital ($ million)	10	20	0	0	0	−5
3. Cash flow from changes in working capital	−10	−20	0	0	0	+5

In years 0 and 1, there is a net investment in working capital (line 2), corresponding to a negative cash flow (line 3), and an increase in the *level* of total working capital (line 1). In years 2 to 4, there is no investment in working capital, so its level remains unchanged at $30 million. But in year 5, as the firm begins to disinvest in working capital, the total declines, which provides a positive cash flow.

In general: **An *increase* in working capital is an investment and therefore implies a *negative* cash flow; a decrease in working capital implies a positive cash flow. The cash flow is measured by the *change* in working capital, not the *level* of working capital.**

Operating Cash Flow

Think back to Boeing's decision to develop the Dreamliner or Slick's decision to produce a new razor blade. In each case, operating cash flow consists of revenues from the sale of the new product less the costs of production and any taxes:

$$\text{Operating cash flow} = \text{revenues} - \text{costs} - \text{taxes}$$

Undoubtedly, both Boeing and Slick expect the revenues to outweigh the costs, and both therefore look forward to positive operating cash flows.

Many investments do not result in additional revenues; they are simply designed to reduce the costs of the company's existing operations. For example, a new computer system may provide labor savings, or a new heating system may be more energy-efficient than the one it replaces. Such projects also contribute to the operating cash flow of the firm—not by increasing revenues but by reducing costs. These cost savings therefore represent a positive cash flow.

EXAMPLE 9.6 ▶ Operating Cash Flow of Cost-Cutting Projects

Suppose a new heating system costs $100,000 but reduces heating costs by $30,000 a year. The firm's tax rate is 35%. The new system does not change revenues, but, thanks to the cost savings, income increases by $30,000. Therefore, incremental operating cash flow is:

Increase in (revenues less expenses)	$30,000
− Incremental tax at 35%	− 10,500
= Operating cash flow	+$19,500

Notice that because the cost savings increase profits, the company must pay more tax. The *net* increase in cash flow equals the after-tax cost savings:

$$(1 - .35) \times \$30,000 = \$19,500$$

Here is another matter that you need to look out for when calculating cash flow. When the firm calculates its taxable income, it makes a deduction for depreciation. This depreciation charge is an accounting entry. It affects the tax that the company pays, but it is not a cash expense and should not be deducted when calculating operating cash flow. (Remember from our earlier discussion that you want to discount cash flows, not profits.)

When you work out a project's cash flows, there are three possible ways to deal with depreciation.

Method 1: Dollars in Minus Dollars Out Take only the items from the income statement that represent actual cash flows. This means that you start with cash revenues and subtract cash expenses and taxes paid. You do not, however, subtract a charge for depreciation because this does not involve cash going out the door. Thus,

$$\text{Operating cash flow} = \text{revenues} - \text{cash expenses} - \text{taxes} \qquad \textbf{(9.2)}$$

Method 2: Adjusted Accounting Profits Alternatively, you can start with after-tax accounting profits and add back any depreciation deduction. This gives

$$\text{Operating cash flow} = \text{after-tax profit} + \text{depreciation} \qquad \textbf{(9.3)}$$

Method 3: Add Back Depreciation Tax Shield Although the depreciation deduction is *not* a cash expense, it does affect the firm's tax payment, which certainly is a cash item. Each additional dollar of depreciation reduces taxable income by $1. So, if the firm's tax bracket is 35%, tax payments fall by $.35, and cash flow increases by the same amount. Financial managers often refer to this tax saving as the **depreciation tax shield.** It equals the product of the tax rate and the depreciation charge:

$$\text{Depreciation tax shield} = \text{tax rate} \times \text{depreciation}$$

This suggests a third way to calculate operating cash flow. First, calculate net profit, assuming zero depreciation. This is equal to (revenues − cash expenses) × (1 − tax rate). Now add back the depreciation tax shield to find operating cash flow:

$$\text{Operating cash flow} = (\text{revenues} - \text{cash expenses}) \times (1 - \text{tax rate}) + \qquad \textbf{(9.4)}$$
$$(\text{tax rate} \times \text{depreciation})$$

The following example confirms that the three methods all give the same figure for operating cash flow.

depreciation tax shield
Reduction in taxes attributable to depreciation.

EXAMPLE 9.7 ▶ Operating Cash Flow

A project generates revenues of $1,000, cash expenses of $600, and depreciation charges of $200 in a particular year. The firm's tax bracket is 35%. Net income is calculated as follows:

Revenues	1,000
− Cash expenses	600
− Depreciation expense	200
= Profit before tax	200
− Tax at 35%	70
= Net profit	130

Methods 1, 2, and 3 all show that operating cash flow is $330:

> *Method 1:* Operating cash flow = revenues − cash expenses − taxes
> $$= 1,000 - 600 - 70 = 330$$
> *Method 2:* Operating cash flow = net profit + depreciation
> $$= 130 + 200 = 330$$
> *Method 3:* Operating cash flow = (revenues − cash expenses)
> $$\times (1 - \text{tax rate}) + (\text{depreciation} \times \text{tax rate})$$
> $$= (1,000 - 600) \times (1 - .35) + (200 \times .35) = 330$$

Self-Test 9.4   A project generates revenues of $600, expenses of $300, and depreciation charges of $200 in a particular year. The firm's tax bracket is 35%. Find the operating cash flow of the project by using all three approaches.

9.3 An Example: Blooper Industries

Now that we have examined the basic pieces of a cash-flow analysis, let's try to put them together into a coherent whole. As the newly appointed financial manager of Blooper Industries, you are about to analyze a proposal for mining and selling a small deposit of high-grade magnoosium ore.[5] You are given the forecasts shown in the spreadsheet in Table 9–1. We will walk through the lines in the table.

Cash-Flow Analysis

Investment in Fixed Assets   Panel A of the spreadsheet summarizes our assumptions. Panel B details investments and disinvestments in fixed assets. The project requires an initial investment of $10 million, as shown in cell B14. After 5 years, the ore deposit is exhausted, so the mining equipment may be sold for $2 million (cell B3), a forecast that already reflects the likely impact of inflation.

When you sell the equipment, the IRS will check to see whether any taxes are due on the sale. Any difference between the sale price ($2 million) and the book value of the equipment will be treated as a taxable gain.

We assume that Blooper depreciates the equipment to a final value of zero. Therefore, the book value of the equipment when it is sold in year 6 will be zero, and you will be subject to taxes on the full $2 million proceeds. Your sale of the equipment will land you with an additional tax bill in year 6 of .35 × $2 million = $.70 million. The net cash flow from the sale in year 6 is therefore

> Salvage value − tax on gain = $2 million − $.70 million = $1.30 million

This amount is recorded in cell H15.

Row 16 summarizes the cash flows from investments in and sales of fixed assets. The entry in each cell equals the after-tax proceeds from asset sales (row 15) minus the investments in fixed assets (row 14).

Operating Cash Flow   The company expects to be able to sell 750,000 pounds of magnoosium a year at a price of $20 a pound in year 1. That points to initial revenues of 750,000 × $20 = $15,000,000. But be careful; inflation is running at about 5% a

---

[5] Readers have inquired whether magnoosium is a real substance. Here, now, are the facts: Magnoosium was created in the early days of television, when a splendid-sounding announcer closed a variety show by saying, "This program has been brought to you by Blooper Industries, proud producer of aleemium, magnoosium, and stool." We forget the company, but the blooper really happened.

Chapter 9 Using Discounted Cash-Flow Analysis to Make Investment Decisions **269**

TABLE 9–1 Financial projections for Blooper's magnoosium mine (figures in thousands of dollars)

	A	B	C	D	E	F	G	H
1	**A. Inputs**		Spreadsheet Name					
2	Initial investment	10,000	Investment					
3	Salvage value	2,000	Salvage					
4	Initial revenue	15,000	Initial_rev					
5	Initial expenses	10,000	Initial_exp					
6	Inflation rate	0.05	Inflation					
7	Discount rate	0.12	Disc_rate					
8	Acct receiv. as % of sales	1/6	A_R					
9	Inven. as % of expenses	0.15	Inv_pct					
10	Tax rate	0.35	Tax_rate					
11								
12	**Year:**	0	1	2	3	4	5	6
13	**B. Fixed assets**							
14	Investment in fixed assets	10,000						
15	Sales of fixed assets							1,300
16	CF, invest. in fixed assets	-10,000	0	0	0	0	0	1,300
17								
18	**C. Operating cash flow**							
19	Revenues		15,000	15,750	16,538	17,364	18,233	
20	Expenses		10,000	10,500	11,025	11,576	12,155	
21	Depreciation		2,000	2,000	2,000	2,000	2,000	
22	Pretax profit		3,000	3,250	3,513	3,788	4,078	
23	Tax		1,050	1,138	1,229	1,326	1,427	
24	Profit after tax		1,950	2,113	2,283	2,462	2,650	
25	Operating cash flow		3,950	4,113	4,283	4,462	4,650	
26								
27	**D. Working capital**							
28	Working capital	1,500	4,075	4,279	4,493	4,717	3,039	0
29	*Change* in working cap	1,500	2,575	204	214	225	-1,679	-3,039
30	CF, invest. in wk capital	-1,500	-2,575	-204	-214	-225	1,679	3,039
31								
32	**E. Project valuation**							
33	Total project cash flow	-11,500	1,375	3,909	4,069	4,238	6,329	4,339
34	Discount factor	1.0	0.8929	0.7972	0.7118	0.6355	0.5674	0.5066
35	PV of cash flow	-11,500	1,228	3,116	2,896	2,693	3,591	2,198
36	Net present value	4,223						

Please visit us at www.mhhe.com/bmm6e

year. If magnoosium prices keep pace with inflation, you should increase your forecast of the second-year revenues by 5%. Third-year revenues should increase by a further 5%, and so on. Row 19 in Table 9–1 shows revenues rising in line with inflation.

The sales forecasts in Table 9–1 are cut off after 5 years. That makes sense if the ore deposit will run out at that time. But if Blooper could make sales for year 6, you should include them in your forecasts. We have sometimes encountered financial managers who assume a project life of (say) 5 years, even when they confidently expect revenues for 10 years or more. When asked the reason, they explain that forecasting beyond 5 years is too hazardous. We sympathize, but you just have to do your best. Do not arbitrarily truncate a project's life.

Expenses in year 1 are $10,000 (cell C20). We assume that the expenses of mining and refining (row 20) also increase in line with inflation at 5% a year.

straight-line depreciation
Constant depreciation for each year of the asset's accounting life.

We also assume for now that the company applies **straight-line depreciation** to the mining equipment over 5 years. This means that it deducts one-fifth of the initial $10 million investment from profits. Thus row 21 shows that the annual depreciation deduction is $2 million.

Pretax profit, shown in row 22, equals (revenues − expenses − depreciation). Taxes (row 23) are 35% of pretax profit. For example, in year 1,

$$\text{Tax} = .35 \times 3,000 = 1,050, \text{ or } \$1,050,000$$

Profit after tax (row 24) equals pretax profit less taxes.

The last row of panel C presents operating cash flow. We calculate cash flow as the sum of after-tax profits plus depreciation (method 2, above). Therefore, row 25 is the sum of rows 24 and 21.

Changes in Working Capital Row 28 shows the *level* of working capital. As the project gears up in the early years, working capital increases, but later in the project's life, the investment in working capital is recovered and the level declines.

Row 29 shows the *change* in working capital from year to year. Notice that in years 1 to 4 the change is positive; in these years the project requires a continuing investment in working capital. Starting in year 5 the change is negative; there is a disinvestment as working capital is recovered. Cash flow associated with investments in working capital (row 30) is the negative of the change in working capital. Just like investment in plant and equipment, investment in working capital produces a negative cash flow, and disinvestment produces a positive cash flow.

Total Project Cash Flow Total cash flow is the sum of cash flows from each of the three sources: Cash flow from investments in fixed assets and working capital, and operating cash flow. Therefore, total cash flow in row 33 is just the sum of rows 16, 25, and 30.

Calculating the NPV of Blooper's Project

You have now derived (in row 33) the forecast cash flows from Blooper's magnoosium mine. Suppose that investors expect a return of 12% from investments in the capital market with the same risk as the magnoosium project. This is the opportunity cost of the shareholders' money that Blooper is proposing to invest in the project. Therefore, to calculate NPV, you need to discount the cash flows at 12%.

Rows 34 and 35 set out the calculations. Remember that to calculate the present value of a cash flow in year t you can divide the cash flow by $(1 + r)^t$ or you can multiply by a discount factor that is equal to $1/(1 + r)^t$. Row 34 presents the discount factors for each year, and row 35 calculates the present value of each cash flow by multiplying the cash flow (row 33) times the discount factor. When all cash flows are discounted and added up, the magnoosium project is seen to offer a positive net present value of $4,223 thousand (cell B36), or about $4.2 million.

Now here is a small point that often causes confusion: To calculate the present value of the first year's cash flow, we divide by $(1 + r) = 1.12$. Strictly speaking, this makes sense only if all the sales and all the costs occur exactly 365 days, zero hours, and zero minutes from now. Of course the year's sales don't all take place on the stroke of midnight on December 31. However, when making capital budgeting decisions, companies are usually happy to pretend that all cash flows occur at 1-year intervals. They pretend this for one reason only—simplicity. When sales forecasts are sometimes little more than intelligent guesses, it may be pointless to inquire how the sales are likely to be spread out during the year.[6]

Further Notes and Wrinkles Arising from Blooper's Project

Before we leave Blooper and its magnoosium project, we should cover a few extra wrinkles.

---

[6] Financial managers sometimes assume cash flows arrive in the middle of the calendar year, that is, at the end of June. This midyear convention is roughly equivalent to assuming cash flows are distributed evenly throughout the year. This is a bad assumption for some industries. In retailing, for example, most of the cash flow comes late in the year, as the holiday season approaches.

Forecasting Working Capital Table 9–1 shows that Blooper expects its magnoosium mine to produce revenues of $15,000 in year 1 and $15,750 in year 2. But Blooper will not actually receive these amounts in years 1 and 2, because some of its customers will not pay up immediately. We have assumed that, on average, customers pay with a 2-month lag, so that 2/12 of each year's sales are not paid for until the following year. These unpaid bills show up as accounts receivable. For example, in year 1 Blooper will have accounts receivable of $(2/12) \times 15,000 = \$2,500$.[7]

Consider now the mine's expenses. These are forecast at $10,000 in year 1 and $10,500 in year 2. But not all of this cash will go out of the door in these 2 years, for Blooper must produce the magnoosium before selling it. Each year, Blooper mines magnoosium ore, but some of this ore is not sold until the following year. The ore is put into inventory, and the accountant does not deduct the cost of its production until it is taken out of inventory and sold. We assume that 15% of each year's expenses correspond to an investment in inventory that took place in the previous year. Thus the investment in inventory is forecast at $.15 \times 10,000 = \$1,500$ in year 0 and at $.15 \times \$10,500 = \$1,575$ in year 1.

We can now see how Blooper arrives at its forecast of working capital:

	0	1	2	3	4	5	6
1. Receivables (2/12 × revenues)	$ 0	$2,500	$2,625	$2,756	$2,894	$3,039	0
2. Inventories (.15 × following year's expenses)	1,500	1,575	1,654	1,736	1,823	0	0
3. Working capital (1 + 2)	1,500	4,075	4,279	4,493	4,717	3,039	0

Note: Columns may not sum due to rounding.

Notice that working capital builds up in years 1 to 4, as sales of magnoosium increase. Year 5 is the last year of sales, so Blooper can reduce its inventories to zero in that year. In year 6 the company expects to collect any unpaid bills from year 5 and so in that year receivables also fall to zero. This decline in working capital increases cash flow. For example, in year 6 cash flow is increased as the $3,039 of outstanding bills are paid.

The construction of the Blooper spreadsheet is discussed further in the nearby box. Once the spreadsheet is set up, it is easy to try out different assumptions for working capital. For example, you can adjust the level of receivables and inventories by changing the values in cells B8 and B9.

A Further Note on Depreciation We warned you earlier not to assume that all cash flows are likely to increase with inflation. The depreciation tax shield is a case in point, because the Internal Revenue Service lets companies depreciate only the amount of the original investment. For example, if you go back to the IRS to explain that inflation mushroomed since you made the investment and you should be allowed to depreciate more, the IRS won't listen. The *nominal* amount of depreciation is fixed, and therefore the higher the rate of inflation, the lower the *real* value of the depreciation that you can claim.

We assumed in our calculations that Blooper could depreciate its investment in mining equipment by $2 million a year. That produced an annual tax shield of $2 million $\times$ .35 = $.70 million per year for 5 years. These tax shields increase cash flows from operations and therefore increase present value. So if Blooper could get those tax shields sooner, they would be worth more, right? Fortunately for corporations, tax law allows them to do just that. It allows *accelerated depreciation*.

---

[7] For convenience, we assume that, although Blooper's customers pay with a lag, Blooper pays all its bills on the nail. If it didn't, these unpaid bills would be recorded as accounts payable. Working capital would be reduced by the amount of the accounts payable.

TABLE 9–2 Tax depreciation allowed under the modified accelerated cost recovery system (figures in percent of depreciable investment)

Year(s)	Recovery Period Class					
	3 Year	5 Year	7 Year	10 Year	15 Year	20 Year
1	33.33	20.00	14.29	10.00	5.00	3.75
2	44.45	32.00	24.49	18.00	9.50	7.22
3	14.81	19.20	17.49	14.40	8.55	6.68
4	7.41	11.52	12.49	11.52	7.70	6.18
5		11.52	8.93	9.22	6.93	5.71
6		5.76	8.92	7.37	6.23	5.28
7			8.93	6.55	5.90	4.89
8			4.46	6.55	5.90	4.52
9				6.56	5.91	4.46
10				6.55	5.90	4.46
11				3.28	5.91	4.46
12					5.90	4.46
13					5.91	4.46
14					5.90	4.46
15					5.91	4.46
16					2.95	4.46
17–20						4.46
21						2.23

Notes:
1. Tax depreciation is lower in the first year because assets are assumed to be in service for 6 months.
2. Real property is depreciated straight-line over 27.5 years for residential property and 39 years for nonresidential property.

modified accelerated cost recovery system (MACRS) Depreciation method that allows higher tax deductions in early years and lower deductions later.

The rate at which firms are permitted to depreciate equipment is known as the **modified accelerated cost recovery system**, or **MACRS**. MACRS places assets into one of six classes, each of which has an assumed life. Table 9–2 shows the rate of depreciation that the company can use for each of these classes. Most industrial equipment falls into the 5- and 7-year classes. To keep life simple, we will assume that all of Blooper's mining equipment goes into 5-year assets. Thus Blooper can depreciate 20% of its $10 million investment in year 1. In the second year it can deduct depreciation of $.32 \times 10 = \$3.2$ million, and so on.[8]

How does MACRS depreciation affect the value of the depreciation tax shield for the magnoosium project? Table 9–3 gives the answer. Notice that MACRS does not affect the total amount of depreciation that is claimed. This remains at $10 million just as before. But MACRS allows companies to get the depreciation deduction earlier, which increases the present value of the depreciation tax shield from $2,523,000 to $2,583,000, an increase of $60,000. Before we recognized MACRS depreciation, we calculated project NPV as $4,223,000. When we recognize MACRS, we should increase that figure by $60,000.

All large corporations in the United States keep two sets of books, one for stockholders and one for the Internal Revenue Service. It is common to use straight-line depreciation on the stockholder books and MACRS depreciation on the tax books. Only the tax books are relevant in capital budgeting.

---

[8] You might wonder why the 5-year asset class provides a depreciation deduction in years 1 through 6. This is because the tax authorities assume that the assets are in service for only 6 months of the first year and 6 months of the last year. The total project life is 5 years, but that 5-year life spans parts of 6 calendar years. This assumption also explains why the depreciation allowance is lower in the first year than it is in the second.

MidAmerican's Wind Power Project

In 2005, MidAmerican Energy brought into operation in Iowa one of the largest wind farms in the world. The wind farm cost $386 million, contains 257 wind turbines, and has a capacity of 360.5 megawatts (MW). Wind speeds fluctuate, and most wind farms are expected to operate at an average of only 35% of their rated capacity. In this case, at an electricity price of $55 per megawatt-hour (MWh), the project will initially produce annual revenues of $60.8 million (i.e., .35 × 8,760 hours × 360.5 MW × $55 per MWh). A reasonable estimate of maintenance and other costs is about $18.9 million in the first year of operation. Thereafter, revenues and costs should increase with inflation by around 3% a year. Conventional power stations can be depreciated using 20-year MACRS, and their profits are taxed at 35%. A project such as this one might last 25 years and entail a cost of capital of 12%.

Wind power is more costly than conventional fossil-fuel power, but to encourage the development of renewable energy sources, the government provides several tax breaks to companies constructing wind farms. How large do these

tax breaks need to be to make the wind farm viable for MidAmerican? We estimate that in the absence of any tax breaks the project would have a net present value of −$68 million. So any tax subsidy must have a value of at least $68 million to entice a private firm such as MidAmerican to undertake the project.

You can find our calculations at the Online Learning Center at **www.mhhe.com/bmm6e.** Once you're there, you might consider the following questions. Suppose the government believes that the national security and environmental benefits of being able to generate clean energy domestically are worth 25% of the value of the electricity produced. Does the subsidy make economic sense for the government? Some wind farm operators assume a capacity factor of 30% rather than 35%. If MidAmerican's plant achieves only this level of operation, how much larger would the tax subsidy need to be? If no tax breaks were available for wind farms, how high would electricity prices need to be before this plant would be viable (i.e., have a positive NPV)?

TABLE 9–3 The switch from straight-line to 5-year MACRS depreciation increases the value of Blooper's depreciation tax shield from $2,523,000 to $2,583,000 (figures in thousands of dollars).

	Straight-Line Depreciation			MACRS Depreciation		
Year	Depreciation	Tax Shield	PV Tax Shield at 12%	Depreciation	Tax Shield	PV Tax Shield at 12%
1	2,000	700	625	2,000	700	625
2	2,000	700	558	3,200	1,120	893
3	2,000	700	498	1,920	672	478
4	2,000	700	445	1,152	403	256
5	2,000	700	397	1,152	403	229
6	0	0	0	576	202	102
Totals	10,000	3,500	2,523	10,000	3,500	2,583

Note: Column sums subject to rounding error.

Self-Test 9.5

Suppose that Blooper's mining equipment could be put in the 3-year recovery period class. What is the present value of the depreciation tax shield? Confirm that the change in the value of the depreciation tax shield equals the increase in project NPV from question 1 of the Spreadsheet Solutions box.

More on Salvage Value   When you sell equipment, you must pay taxes on the difference between the sales price and the book value of the asset. The book value in turn equals the initial cost minus cumulative charges for depreciation. It is common when figuring tax depreciation to assume a salvage value of zero at the end of the asset's depreciable life.

For reports to shareholders, however, positive expected salvage values are often recognized. For example, Blooper's financial statements might assume that its $10 million investment in mining equipment would be worth $2 million in year 6. In this case, the depreciation reported to shareholders would be based on the difference between the investment and the salvage value, that is, $8 million. Straight-line depreciation then would be $1.6 million annually.

SPREADSHEET SOLUTIONS

The Blooper Spreadsheet Model

Discounted cash-flow analysis of proposed capital investments is clearly tailor-made for spreadsheet analysis. The formula view of the Excel spreadsheet used in the Blooper example appears below.

Notice that most of the entries in the spreadsheet are formulas rather than specific numbers. Once the relatively few input values are entered, the spreadsheet does most of the work. We enter only the initial investment (cell B2), the salvage value (cell B3), the initial levels of revenues and expenses (cells B4 and B5), and the other parameters in panel A.

Revenues and expenses in each year equal the value in the previous year times (1 + inflation rate), which is given in cell B6 as .05. For example, cell D19 equals C19 × 1.05. To make the spreadsheet easier to read, we have defined names for a few cells, such as B6 (Inflation rate) and B7 (Discount rate). These names can be assigned using the

Insert command and thereafter can be used to refer to specific cells.

Row 28 sets out the level of working capital, which is the sum of accounts receivable and inventories. Because inventories tend to rise with production, we set them equal to .15 times expenses recognized in the following year when the product is sold. Similarly, accounts receivable rise with sales, so we assume that they will be 2/12 times current year's revenues (in other words, that Blooper's customers pay, on average, 2 months after purchasing the product). Each entry in row 28 is the sum of these two quantities.

We calculate the discount factor in row 34 using the discount rate of 12%, compute present values of each cash flow in row 35, and add the present value of each cash flow to find project NPV in cell B36.

Once the spreadsheet is up and running, "what-if" analyses are easy. Here are a few questions to try your hand.

Formula view

	A	B	C	D	E	F	G	H
1	A. Inputs		Spreadsheet Name					
2	Initial investment	10,000	Investment					
3	Salvage value	2,000	Salvage					
4	Initial revenue	15,000	Initial_rev					
5	Initial expenses	10,000	Initial_exp					
6	Inflation rate	0.05	Inflation					
7	Discount rate	0.12	Disc_rate					
8	Acct receiv. as % of sales	=2/12	A_R					
9	Inven. as % of expenses	0.15	Inv_pct					
10	Tax rate	0.35	Tax_rate					
11								
12	Year:	0	1	2	3	4	5	6
13	B. Fixed assets							
14	Investment in fixed assets	=Investment						
15	Sales of fixed assets							=Salvage*(1-Tax_rate)
16	CF, invest. in fixed assets	=-B14+B15	=-C14+C15	=-D14+D15	=-E14+E15	=-F14+F15	=-G14+G15	=-H14+H15
17								
18	C. Operations							
19	Revenues		=Initial_rev	=C19*(1+Inflation)	=D19*(1+Inflation)	=E19*(1+Inflation)	=F19*(1+Inflation)	
20	Expenses		=Initial_exp	=C20*(1+Inflation)	=D20*(1+Inflation)	=E20*(1+Inflation)	=F20*(1+Inflation)	
21	Depreciation		=Investment/5	=Investment/5	=Investment/5	=Investment/5	=Investment/5	
22	Pretax profit		=C19-C20-C21	=D19-D20-D21	=E19-E20-E21	=F19-F20-F21	=G19-G20-G21	
23	Tax		=C22*Tax_rate	=D22*Tax_rate	=E22*Tax_rate	=F22*Tax_rate	=G22*Tax_rate	
24	Profit after tax		=C22-C23	=D22-D23	=E22-E23	=F22-F23	=G22-G23	
25	Operating cash flow		=C21 + C24	=D21 + D24	=E21 + E24	=F21 + F24	=G21 + G24	
26								
27	D. Working capital							
28	Working capital	=Inv_pct*C20+A_R*B19	=Inv_pct*D20+A_R*C19	=Inv_pct*E20+A_R*D19	=Inv_pct*F20+A_R*E19	=Inv_pct*G20+A_R*F19	=Inv_pct*H20+A_R*G19	=Inv_pct*I20+A_R*H19
29	Change in working cap	=B28	=C28-B28	=D28-C28	=E28-D28	=F28-E28	=G28-F28	=H28-G28
30	CF, invest. in wk capital	=-B29	=-C29	=-D29	=-E29	=-F29	=-G29	=-H29
31								
32	E. Project valuation							
33	Total project cash flow	=B16+B30+B25	=C16+C30+C25	=D16+D30+D25	=E16+E30+E25	=F16+F30+F25	=G16+G30+G25	=H16+H30+H25
34	Discount factor	=1/(1+Disc_rate)^B12	=1/(1+Disc_rate)^C12	=1/(1+Disc_rate)^D12	=1/(1+Disc_rate)^E12	=1/(1+Disc_rate)^F12	=1/(1+Disc_rate)^G12	=1/(1+Disc_rate)^H12
35	PV of cash flow	=B33*B34	=C33*C34	=D33*D34	=E33*E34	=F33*F34	=G33*G34	=H33*H34
36	Net present value	=SUM(B35:H35)						

Spreadsheet Questions

9.1 What happens to cash flow in each year and the NPV of the project if the firm uses MACRS depreciation assuming a 3-year recovery period? Assume year 1 is the first year that depreciation is taken.

9.2 Suppose the firm can economize on working capital by managing inventories more efficiently. If the firm can reduce inventories from 15 to 10% of next year's cost of goods sold, what will be the effect on project NPV?

9.3 What happens to NPV if the inflation rate falls from 5% to zero and the discount rate falls from 12% to 7%

Given that the real discount rate is almost unchanged, why does project NPV increase? [To be consistent, you should assume that nominal salvage value will be lower in a zero-inflation environment. If you set (before-tax) salvage value to $1.492 million, you will maintain its real value unchanged.]

Brief solutions appear at the end of the chapter. The full spreadsheet is available at the Online Learning Center for the text: **www.mhhe.com/bmm6e**.

www.mhhe.com/bmm6e

SUMMARY

How should the cash flows of a proposed new project be calculated? *(LO1)*

Here is a checklist to bear in mind when forecasting a project's cash flows:

- Discount cash flows, not profits.
- Estimate the project's *incremental* cash flows—that is, the difference between the cash flows with the project and those without the project.
- Include all indirect effects of the project, such as its impact on the sales of the firm's other products.
- Forget sunk costs.
- Include **opportunity costs,** such as the value of land that you could otherwise sell.
- Beware of allocated overhead charges for heat, light, and so on. These may not reflect the incremental effects of the project on these costs.
- Remember the investment in working capital. As sales increase, the firm may need to make additional investments in working capital, and as the project finally comes to an end, it will recover these investments.
- Treat inflation consistently. If cash flows are forecast in nominal terms (including the effects of future inflation), use a nominal discount rate. Discount real cash flows at a real rate.
- Do not include debt interest or the cost of repaying a loan. When calculating NPV, assume that the project is financed entirely by the shareholders and that they receive all the cash flows. This separates the investment decision from the financing decision.

How can the cash flows of a project be computed from standard financial statements? *(LO2)*

Project cash flow does not equal profit. You must allow for changes in working capital as well as noncash expenses such as depreciation. Also, if you use a nominal cost of capital, consistency requires that you forecast *nominal* cash flows—that is, cash flows that recognize the effect of inflation.

How is the company's tax bill affected by depreciation, and how does this affect project value? *(LO3)*

Depreciation is not a cash flow. However, because depreciation reduces taxable income, it reduces taxes. This tax reduction is called the **depreciation tax shield. Modified accelerated cost recovery system (MACRS)** depreciation schedules allow more of the depreciation allowance to be taken in early years than is possible under **straight-line depreciation.** This increases the present value of the tax shield.

How do changes in working capital affect project cash flows? *(LO4)*

Increases in **net working capital** such as accounts receivable or inventory are investments and therefore use cash—that is, they reduce the net cash flow provided by the project in that period. When working capital is run down, cash is freed up, so cash flow increases.

LISTING OF EQUATIONS

9.1   Total cash flow = cash flows from capital investments
+ cash flows from changes in working capital
+ operating cash flows

9.2   Operating cash flow = revenues − cash expenses − taxes

9.3   Operating cash flow = after-tax profit + depreciation

9.4   Operating cash flow = (revenues − cash expenses) × (1 − tax rate) +
(tax rate × depreciation)

www.mhhe.com/bmm6e

QUESTIONS

QUIZ

1. **Cash Flows.** A new project will generate sales of $74 million, costs of $42 million, and depreciation expense of $10 million in the coming year. The firm's tax rate is 35%. Calculate cash flow for the year by using all three methods discussed in the chapter, and confirm that they are equal. *(LO2)*

2. **Cash Flows.** Canyon Tours showed the following components of working capital last year: *(LO2)*

	Beginning	End of Year
Accounts receivable	$ 24,000	$23,000
Inventory	12,000	12,500
Accounts payable	14,500	16,500

   a. What was the change in net working capital during the year?
   b. If sales were $36,000 and costs were $24,000, what was cash flow for the year? Ignore taxes.

3. **Cash Flows.** Tubby Toys estimates that its new line of rubber ducks will generate sales of $7 million, operating costs of $4 million, and a depreciation expense of $1 million. If the tax rate is 35%, what is the firm's operating cash flow? Show that you get the same answer using all three methods to calculate operating cash flow. *(LO2)*

4. **Cash Flows.** We've emphasized that the firm should pay attention only to cash flows when assessing the net present value of proposed projects. Depreciation is a noncash expense. Why then does it matter whether we assume straight-line or MACRS depreciation when we assess project NPV? *(LO3)*

5. **Proper Cash Flows.** Quick Computing currently sells 10 million computer chips each year at a price of $20 per chip. It is about to introduce a new chip, and it forecasts annual sales of 12 million of these improved chips at a price of $25 each. However, demand for the old chip will decrease, and sales of the old chip are expected to fall to 3 million per year. The old chip costs $6 each to manufacture, and the new ones will cost $8 each. What is the proper cash flow to use to evaluate the present value of the introduction of the new chip? *(LO1)*

6. **Calculating Net Income.** The owner of a bicycle repair shop forecasts revenues of $160,000 a year. Variable costs will be $50,000, and rental costs for the shop are $30,000 a year. Depreciation on the repair tools will be $10,000. Prepare an income statement for the shop based on these estimates. The tax rate is 35%. *(LO2)*

7. **Cash Flows.** Calculate the operating cash flow for the repair shop in the previous problem using all three methods suggested in the chapter: (a) adjusted accounting profits; (b) cash inflow/cash outflow analysis; and (c) the depreciation tax shield approach. Confirm that all three approaches result in the same value for cash flow. *(LO2)*

8. **Cash Flows and Working Capital.** A house painting business had revenues of $16,000 and expenses of $9,000. There were no depreciation expenses. However, the business reported the following changes in working capital:

	Beginning	End
Accounts receivable	$1,200	$4,500
Accounts payable	700	300

   Calculate net cash flow for the business for this period. *(LO4)*

9. **Incremental Cash Flows.** A corporation donates a valuable painting from its private collection to an art museum. Which of the following are incremental cash flows associated with the donation? *(LO1)*

   a. The price the firm paid for the painting.
   b. The current market value of the painting.
   c. The deduction from income that it declares for its charitable gift.
   d. The reduction in taxes due to its declared tax deduction.

10. **Operating Cash Flows.** Laurel's Lawn Care, Ltd., has a new mower line that can generate revenues of $120,000 per year. Direct production costs are $40,000, and the fixed costs of maintaining the lawn mower factory are $15,000 a year. The factory originally cost $1 million and is being depreciated for tax purposes over 25 years using straight-line depreciation. Calculate the operating cash flows of the project if the firm's tax bracket is 35%. *(LO2)*

PRACTICE PROBLEMS

11. **Operating Cash Flows.** Talia's Tutus bought a new sewing machine for $40,000 that will be depreciated using the MACRS depreciation schedule for a 5-year recovery period. *(LO2)*
    a. Find the depreciation charge each year.
    b. If the sewing machine is sold after 3 years for $22,000, what will be the after-tax proceeds on the sale if the firm's tax bracket is 35%?

12. **Proper Cash Flows.** Conference Services Inc. has leased a large office building for $4 million per year. The building is larger than the company needs; two of the building's eight stories are almost empty. A manager wants to expand one of her projects, but this will require using one of the empty floors. In calculating the net present value of the proposed expansion, senior management allocates one-eighth of $4 million of building rental costs (i.e., $.5 million) to the project expansion, reasoning that the project will use one-eighth of the building's capacity. *(LO1)*
    a. Is this a reasonable procedure for purposes of calculating NPV?
    b. Can you suggest a better way to assess a cost of the office space used by the project?

13. **Cash Flows and Working Capital.** A firm had after-tax income last year of $1.2 million. Its depreciation expenses were $.4 million, and its total cash flow was $1.2 million. What happened to net working capital during the year? *(LO4)*

14. **Cash Flows and Working Capital.** The only capital investment required for a small project is investment in inventory. Profits this year were $10,000, and inventory increased from $4,000 to $5,000. What was the cash flow from the project? *(LO4)*

15. **Cash Flows and Working Capital.** A firm's balance sheets for year-end 2008 and 2009 contain the following data. What happened to investment in net working capital during 2009? All items are in millions of dollars. *(LO4)*

	Dec. 31, 2008	Dec. 31, 2009
Accounts receivable	32	36
Inventories	25	30
Accounts payable	12	26

16. **Salvage Value.** Quick Computing (from Quiz Question 5) installed its previous generation of computer chip manufacturing equipment 3 years ago. Some of that older equipment will become unnecessary when the company goes into production of its new product. The obsolete equipment, which originally cost $40 million, has been depreciated straight-line over an assumed tax life of 5 years, but it can be sold now for $18 million. The firm's tax rate is 35%. What is the after-tax cash flow from the sale of the equipment? *(LO2)*

17. **Salvage Value.** Your firm purchased machinery with a 7-year MACRS life for $10 million. The project, however, will end after 5 years. If the equipment can be sold for $4.5 million at the completion of the project, and your firm's tax rate is 35%, what is the after-tax cash flow from the sale of the machinery? *(LO2)*

18. **Depreciation and Project Value.** Bottoms Up Diaper Service is considering the purchase of a new industrial washer. It can purchase the washer for $6,000 and sell its old washer for $2,000. The new washer will last for 6 years and save $1,500 a year in expenses. The opportunity cost of capital is 16%, and the firm's tax rate is 40%. *(LO3)*
    a. If the firm uses straight-line depreciation to an assumed salvage value of zero over a 6-year life, what are the cash flows of the project in years 0 to 6? The new washer will in fact have zero salvage value after 6 years, and the old washer is fully depreciated.

b. What is project NPV?

c. What is NPV if the firm uses MACRS depreciation with a 5-year tax life?

19. **Equivalent Annual Cost.** What is the equivalent annual cost of the washer in the previous problem if the firm uses straight-line depreciation? *(LO2)*

20. **Cash Flows and NPV.** Johnny's Lunches is considering purchasing a new, energy-efficient grill. The grill will cost $40,000 and will be depreciated according to the 3-year MACRS schedule. It will be sold for scrap metal after 3 years for $10,000. The grill will have no effect on revenues but will save Johnny's $20,000 in energy expenses. The tax rate is 35%. *(LO2)*

a. What are the operating cash flows in years 1 to 3?

b. What are total cash flows in years 1 to 3?

c. If the discount rate is 12%, should the grill be purchased?

21. **Project Evaluation.** Revenues generated by a new fad product are forecast as follows:

Year	Revenues
1	$40,000
2	30,000
3	20,000
4	10,000
Thereafter	0

Expenses are expected to be 40% of revenues, and working capital required in each year is expected to be 20% of revenues in the following year. The product requires an immediate investment of $45,000 in plant and equipment. *(LO2)*

a. What is the initial investment in the product? Remember working capital.

b. If the plant and equipment are depreciated over 4 years to a salvage value of zero using straight-line depreciation, and the firm's tax rate is 40%, what are the project cash flows in each year?

c. If the opportunity cost of capital is 12%, what is project NPV?

d. What is project IRR?

Please visit us at www.mhhe.com/bmm6e

22. **Project Evaluation.** Suppose that Blooper's customers paid their bills with an average 3-month delay (instead of 2 months) and that Blooper's inventories were 20% rather than 15% of next year's expenses. *(LO4)*

a. Would project NPV be higher or lower than that in the worked example in the chapter?

b. Calculate Blooper's working capital in each year of its project.

c. What is the change in project NPV (use the Blooper spreadsheet)?

23. **Project Evaluation.** Kinky Copies may buy a high-volume copier. The machine costs $100,000 and will be depreciated straight-line over 5 years to a salvage value of $20,000. Kinky anticipates that the machine actually can be sold in 5 years for $30,000. The machine will save $20,000 a year in labor costs but will require an increase in working capital, mainly paper supplies, of $10,000. The firm's marginal tax rate is 35%, and the discount rate is 8%. Should Kinky buy the machine? *(LO2)*

24. **Project Evaluation.** Blooper Industries must replace its magnoosium purification system. Quick & Dirty Systems sells a relatively cheap purification system for $10 million. The system will last 5 years. Do-It-Right sells a sturdier but more expensive system for $12 million; it will last for 8 years. Both systems entail $1 million in operating costs; both will be depreciated straight-line to a final value of zero over their useful lives; neither will have any salvage value at the end of its life. The firm's tax rate is 35%, and the discount rate is 12%. Which system should Blooper install? (*Hint:* Check the discussion of equivalent annual annuities in the previous chapter.) *(LO2)*

25. **Project Evaluation.** The following table presents sales forecasts for Golden Gelt Giftware. The unit price is $40. The unit cost of the giftware is $25.

Year	Unit Sales
1	22,000
2	30,000
3	14,000
4	5,000
Thereafter	0

It is expected that net working capital will amount to 20% of sales in the following year. For example, the store will need an initial (year-0) investment in working capital of .20 × 22,000 × $40 = $176,000. Plant and equipment necessary to establish the Giftware business will require an additional investment of $200,000. This investment will be depreciated using MACRS and a 3-year life. After 4 years, the equipment will have an economic and book value of zero. The firm's tax rate is 35%. What is the net present value of the project? The discount rate is 20%. *(LO4)*

26. **Project Evaluation.** Ilana Industries, Inc., needs a new lathe. It can buy a new high-speed lathe for $1 million. The lathe will cost $35,000 per year to run, but will save the firm $125,000 in labor costs, and will be useful for 10 years. Suppose that for tax purposes, the lathe will be depreciated on a straight-line basis over its 10-year life to a salvage value of $100,000. The actual market value of the lathe at that time also will be $100,000. The discount rate is 8%, and the corporate tax rate is 35%. What is the NPV of buying the new lathe? *(LO2)*

CHALLENGE PROBLEMS

27. **Project Evaluation.** The efficiency gains resulting from a just-in-time inventory management system will allow a firm to reduce its level of inventories permanently by $250,000. What is the most the firm should be willing to pay for installing the system? *(LO4)*

28. **Project Evaluation.** Better Mousetraps has developed a new trap. It can go into production for an initial investment in equipment of $6 million. The equipment will be depreciated straight-line over 6 years to a value of zero, but in fact it can be sold after 6 years for $500,000. The firm believes that working capital at each date must be maintained at a level of 10% of next year's forecast sales. The firm estimates production costs equal to $1.50 per trap and believes that the traps can be sold for $4 each. Sales forecasts are given in the following table. The project will come to an end in 5 years, when the trap becomes technologically obsolete. The firm's tax bracket is 35%, and the required rate of return on the project is 12%.

Year:	0	1	2	3	4	5	6	Thereafter
Sales (millions of traps)	0	.5	.6	1.0	1.0	.6	.2	0

a. What is project NPV? *(LO2)*
b. By how much would NPV increase if the firm depreciated its investment using the 5-year MACRS schedule? *(LO3)*

29. **Working Capital Management.** Return to the previous problem. Suppose the firm can cut its requirements for working capital in half by using better inventory control systems. By how much will this increase project NPV? *(LO4)*

30. **Project Evaluation.** PC Shopping Network may upgrade its modem pool. It last upgraded 2 years ago, when it spent $115 million on equipment with an assumed life of 5 years and an assumed salvage value of $15 million for tax purposes. The firm uses straight-line depreciation. The old equipment can be sold today for $80 million. A new modem pool can be installed today for $150 million. This will have a 3-year life and will be depreciated to zero using straight-line depreciation. The new equipment will enable the firm to increase sales by $25 million per year and decrease operating costs by $10 million per year. At the end of 3 years, the new equipment will be worthless. Assume the firm's tax rate is 35% and the discount rate for projects of this sort is 10%. *(LO2)*

a. What is the net cash flow at time 0 if the old equipment is replaced?
b. What are the incremental cash flows in years 1, 2, and 3?
c. What are the NPV and IRR of the replacement project?

31. **Project Evaluation.** In the Finance in Practice box on page 273 we described a major investment in windpower by MidAmerican Energy. Suppose that the company is now contemplating construction of a gas-fired power plant. The plant is likely to last 25 years and to have no salvage value. Depreciation allowances for tax purposes on the investment of $386 million will be calculated using the 20-year MACRS schedule.

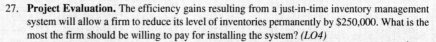
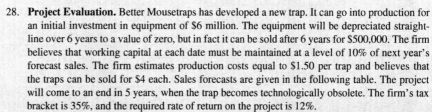
Please visit us at www.mhhe.com/bmm6e

Please visit us at www.mhhe.com/bmm6e

www.mhhe.com/bmm6e

If the plant could be operated 24 hours a day every day, it would produce each year 6.04 million megawatt-hours (MWh) of electricity. However, a more realistic estimate is that the plant will operate at an average of 60% of this notional capacity. In the first year of operation, the price of electricity is expected to average $66 per MWh, fuel costs are expected to be $38 per MWh, and labor and other costs are forecast to total $45 million. All prices and costs are expected to rise with inflation at 3% a year. The corporate tax rate is 35%. If the cost of capital is 12%, would you recommend that the company go ahead with the project? *(LO2)*

STANDARD
&POOR'S

1. Go to Market Insight (**www.mhhe.com/edumarketinsight**). Find the net capital expenditures, capital expenditures less sales of plant and equipment, and total sales for General Motors (GM) and Microsoft (MSFT). What were the ratios of net capital expenditure to sales for the last 3 years for both companies? What were the sales and net capital expenditures relative to total assets? What might explain the variation in these ratios for these two large corporations? Did the company make an investment or disinvestment in working capital in each of the 3 years?

SOLUTIONS TO SELF-TEST QUESTIONS

9.1   Remember, discount cash flows, not profits. Each tewgit machine costs $250,000 right away. Recognize that outlay, but forget accounting depreciation. Cash flows per machine are:

Year:	0	1	2	3	4	5
Investment (outflow)	−250,000					
Sales		250,000	300,000	300,000	250,000	250,000
Operating expenses		−200,000	−200,000	−200,000	−200,000	−200,000
Cash flow	−250,000	+ 50,000	+100,000	+100,000	+ 50,000	+ 50,000

Each machine is forecast to generate $50,000 of cash flow in years 4 and 5. Thus it makes sense to keep operating for 5 years.

9.2   a,b. The site and buildings could have been sold or put to another use. Their values are opportunity costs, which should be treated as incremental cash outflows.
      c. Demolition costs are incremental cash outflows.
      d. The cost of the access road is sunk and not incremental.
      e. Lost cash flows from other projects are incremental cash outflows.
      f. Depreciation is not a cash expense and should not be included, except as it affects taxes. (Taxes are discussed later in this chapter.)

9.3   Actual health costs will be increasing at about 7% a year.

Year:	1	2	3	4
Cost per worker	$2,400	$2,568	$2,748	$2,940

The present value at 10% of these four cash flows is $8,377.

9.4   The tax rate is $T = 35\%$. Taxes paid will be

$$T \times (\text{revenue} - \text{expenses} - \text{depreciation}) = .35 \times (600 - 300 - 200) = \$35$$

Operating cash flow can be calculated as follows.

a. Revenue − expenses − taxes = 600 − 300 − 35 = $265

b. Net profit + depreciation = (600 − 300 − 200 − 35) + 200 = 65 + 200 = 265
c. (Revenues − cash expenses) × (1 − tax rate) + (depreciation × tax rate) = (600 − 300) × (1 − .35) + (200 × .35) = 265

9.5

Year	MACRS 3-Year Depreciation	Tax Shield	PV Tax Shield at 12%
1	3,333	1,167	1,042
2	4,445	1,556	1,240
3	1,481	518	369
4	741	259	165
Totals	10,000	3,500	2,816

The present value increases to 2,816, or $2,816,000.

SOLUTIONS TO SPREADSHEET QUESTIONS

9.1 NPV = $4,515

9.2 NPV = $4,459

9.3 NPV = $5,741. NPV rises because the real value of depreciation allowances and the depreciation tax shield is higher when the inflation rate is lower.

MINICASE

Jack Tar, CFO of Sheetbend & Halyard, Inc., opened the company confidential envelope. It contained a draft of a competitive bid for a contract to supply duffel canvas to the U.S. Navy. The cover memo from Sheetbend's CEO asked Mr. Tar to review the bid before it was submitted.

The bid and its supporting documents had been prepared by Sheetbend's sales staff. It called for Sheetbend to supply 100,000 yards of duffel canvas per year for 5 years. The proposed selling price was fixed at $30 per yard.

Mr. Tar was not usually involved in sales, but this bid was unusual in at least two respects. First, if accepted by the navy, it would commit Sheetbend to a fixed-price, long-term contract. Second, producing the duffel canvas would require an investment of $1.5 million to purchase machinery and to refurbish Sheetbend's plant in Pleasantboro, Maine.

Mr. Tar set to work and by the end of the week had collected the following facts and assumptions:

- The plant in Pleasantboro had been built in the early 1900s and is now idle. The plant was fully depreciated on Sheetbend's books, except for the purchase cost of the land (in 1947) of $10,000.
- Now that the land was valuable shorefront property, Mr. Tar thought the land and the idle plant could be sold, immediately or in the near future, for $600,000.
- Refurbishing the plant would cost $500,000. This investment would be depreciated for tax purposes on the 10-year MACRS schedule.

- The new machinery would cost $1 million. This investment could be depreciated on the 5-year MACRS schedule.
- The refurbished plant and new machinery would last for many years. However, the remaining market for duffel canvas was small, and it was not clear that additional orders could be obtained once the navy contract was finished. The machinery was custom-built and could be used only for duffel canvas. Its secondhand value at the end of 5 years was probably zero.
- Table 9–4 shows the sales staff's forecasts of income from the navy contract. Mr. Tar reviewed this forecast and decided that its assumptions were reasonable, except that the forecast used book, not tax, depreciation.
- But the forecast income statement contained no mention of working capital. Mr. Tar thought that working capital would average about 10% of sales.

Armed with this information, Mr. Tar constructed a spreadsheet to calculate the NPV of the duffel canvas project, assuming that Sheetbend's bid would be accepted by the navy.

He had just finished debugging the spreadsheet when another confidential envelope arrived from Sheetbend's CEO. It contained a firm offer from a Maine real estate developer to purchase Sheetbend's Pleasantboro land and plant for $1.5 million in cash.

Should Mr. Tar recommend submitting the bid to the navy at the proposed price of $30 per yard? The discount rate for this project is 12%.

www.mhhe.com/bmm6e

TABLE 9-4 Forecast income statement for the U.S. Navy duffel canvas project (dollar figures in thousands, except price per yard)

Year:	1	2	3	4	5
1. Yards sold	100.00	100.00	100.00	100.00	100.00
2. Price per yard	30.00	30.00	30.00	30.00	30.00
3. Revenue (1 × 2)	3,000.00	3,000.00	3,000.00	3,000.00	3,000.00
4. Cost of goods sold	2,100.00	2,184.00	2,271.36	2,362.21	2,456.70
5. Operating cash flow (3 − 4)	900.00	816.00	728.64	637.79	543.30
6. Depreciation	250.00	250.00	250.00	250.00	250.00
7. Income (5 − 6)	650.00	566.00	478.64	387.79	293.30
8. Tax at 35%	227.50	198.10	167.52	135.72	102.65
9. Net income (7 − 8)	$422.50	$367.90	$311.12	$252.07	$190.65

Notes:
1. Yards sold and price per yard would be fixed by contract.
2. Cost of goods includes fixed cost of $300,000 per year plus variable costs of $18 per yard. Costs are expected to increase at the inflation rate of 4% per year.
3. Depreciation: A $1 million investment in machinery is depreciated straight-line over 5 years ($200,000 per year). The $500,000 cost of refurbishing the Pleasantboro plant is depreciated straight-line over 10 years ($50,000 per year).

PROJECT VALUATION and INTERNAL RATE OF RETURN

PART 2

Value

CHAPTER **5**

The Time Value of Money

LEARNING OBJECTIVES

After studying this chapter, you should be able to:

1. Calculate the future value to which money invested at a given interest rate will grow.

2. Calculate the present value of a future payment.

3. Calculate present and future values of a series of cash payments.

4. Find the interest rate implied by present and future values.

5. Compare interest rates quoted over different time intervals—for example, monthly versus annual rates.

6. Understand the difference between real and nominal cash flows and between real and nominal interest rates.

Related Web sites for this chapter can be found at www.mhhe.com/bmm6e.

Kangaroo Auto's view of the time value of money   Do you truly understand what these percentages mean? Do you realize that the dealership may not be quoting effective annual interest rates? If the dealership quotes a monthly payment on a 4-year, $20,000 car loan, would you be able to double-check the dealership's calculations?
© Myrleen Ferguson Cate/PhotoEdit

Companies invest in lots of things. Some are *tangible assets*—that is, assets you can kick, like factories, machinery, and offices. Others are *intangible assets,* such as patents or trademarks. In each case the company lays out some money now in the hope of receiving even more money later.

Individuals also make investments. For example, your college education may cost you $20,000 per year. That is an investment you hope will pay off in the form of a higher salary later in life. You are sowing now and expecting to reap later.

Companies pay for their investments by raising money and in the process assuming liabilities. For example, they may borrow money from a bank and promise to repay it with interest later. You also may have financed your investment in a college education by borrowing money that you plan to pay back out of that fat salary.

All these financial decisions require comparisons of cash payments at different dates. Will your future salary be sufficient to justify the current expenditure on college tuition? How much will you have to repay the bank if you borrow to finance your education?

In this chapter we take the first steps toward understanding the relationship between the values of dollars today and dollars in the future. We start by looking at how funds invested at a specific interest rate will grow over time. We next ask how much you would need to invest today to produce a specified future sum of money, and we describe some shortcuts for working out the value of a series of cash payments. Then we consider how inflation affects these financial calculations.

There is nothing complicated about these calculations, but if they are to become second nature, you should read the chapter thoroughly, work carefully through the examples (we have provided plenty), and make sure you tackle the self-test questions. We are asking you to make an investment now in return for a payoff later.

5.1 Future Values and Compound Interest

You have $100 invested in a bank account. Suppose banks are currently paying an interest rate of 6% per year on deposits. So after a year your account will earn interest of $6:

$$\text{Interest} = \text{interest rate} \times \text{initial investment}$$
$$= .06 \times \$100 = \$6$$

You start the year with $100 and you earn interest of $6, so the value of your investment will grow to $106 by the end of the year:

$$\text{Value of investment after 1 year} = \$100 + \$6 = \$106$$

Notice that the $100 invested grows by the factor $(1 + .06) = 1.06$. In general, for any interest rate r, the value of the investment at the end of 1 year is $(1 + r)$ times the initial investment:

$$\text{Value after 1 year} = \text{initial investment} \times (1 + r)$$
$$= \$100 \times (1.06) = \$106$$

What if you leave this money in the bank for a second year? Your balance, now $106, will continue to earn interest of 6%. So

$$\text{Interest in year 2} = .06 \times \$106 = \$6.36$$

You start the second year with $106, on which you earn interest of $6.36. So by the end of the year the value of your account will grow to $106 + $6.36 = $112.36.

In the first year your investment of $100 increases by a factor of 1.06 to $106; in the second year the $106 again increases by a factor of 1.06 to $112.36. Thus the initial $100 investment grows twice by a factor 1.06:

$$\text{Value of investment after 2 years} = \$100 \times 1.06 \times 1.06$$
$$= \$100 \times (1.06)^2 = \$112.36$$

If you keep your money invested for a third year, your investment multiplies by 1.06 each year for 3 years. By the end of the third year it will total $100 $\times (1.06)^3 =$ $119.10, scarcely enough to put you in the millionaire class, but even millionaires have to start somewhere.

Clearly, if you invest your $100 for t years, it will grow to $100 $\times (1.06)^t$. For an interest rate of r and a horizon of t years, the **future value (FV)** of your investment will be

future value (FV)
Amount to which an investment will grow after earning interest.

$$\text{Future value (FV) of } \$100 = \$100 \times (1 + r)^t \qquad (5.1)$$

Notice in our example that your interest income in the first year is $6 (6% of $100) and in the second year is $6.36 (6% of $106). Your income in the second year is higher because you now earn interest on *both* the original $100 investment *and* the $6 of interest earned in the previous year. Earning interest on interest is called *compounding* or **compound interest.** In contrast, if the bank calculated the interest only on your original investment, you would be paid **simple interest.** With simple interest the value of your investment would grow each year by .06 $\times$ $100 = $6.

compound interest
Interest earned on interest.

simple interest
Interest earned only on the original investment; no interest is earned on interest.

Table 5–1 and Figure 5–1 illustrate the mechanics of compound interest. Table 5–1 shows that in each year, you start with a greater balance in your account—your savings have been increased by the previous year's interest. As a result, your interest income also is higher.

TABLE 5–1 How your savings grow; the future value of $100 invested to earn 6% with compound interest

Year	Balance at Start of Year	Interest Earned during Year	Balance at End of Year
1	$100.00	.06 × $100.00 = $6.00	$106.00
2	$106.00	.06 × $106.00 = $6.36	$112.36
3	$112.36	.06 × $112.36 = $6.74	$119.10
4	$119.10	.06 × $119.10 = $7.15	$126.25
5	$126.25	.06 × $126.25 = $7.57	$133.82

FIGURE 5–1 A plot of the data in Table 5–1, showing the future values of an investment of $100 earning 6% with compound interest

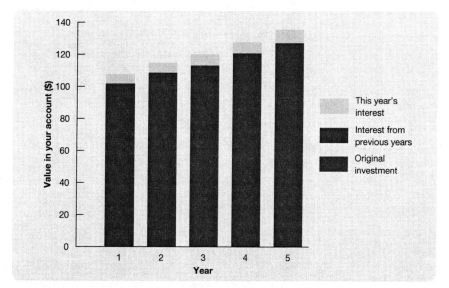

Obviously, the higher the rate of interest, the faster your savings will grow. Figure 5–2 shows that a few percentage points added to the (compound) interest rate can dramatically affect the future balance of your savings account. For example, after 10 years $100 invested at 10% will grow to $100 × $(1.10)^{10}$ = $259.37. If invested at 5%, it will grow to only $100 × $(1.05)^{10}$ = $162.89.

Calculating future values is easy using almost any calculator. If you have the patience, you can multiply your initial investment by $1 + r$ (1.06 in our example) once for each year of your investment. A simpler procedure is to use the power key (the y^x key) on your calculator. For example, to compute $(1.06)^{10}$, enter 1.06, press the y^x key, enter 10, press =, and discover that the answer is 1.7908. (Try this!)

If you don't have a calculator, you can use a table of future values such as Table 5–2. Check that you can use it to work out the future value of a 10-year investment at 6%. First find the row corresponding to 10 years. Now work along that row until you reach the column for a 6% interest rate. The entry shows that $1 invested for 10 years at 6% grows to $1.7908.

Now try one more example. If you invest $1 for 20 years at 10% and do not withdraw any money, what will you have at the end? Your answer should be $6.7275.

Table 5–2 gives future values for only a small selection of years and interest rates. Table A.1 at the end of the book is a bigger version of Table 5–2. It presents the future value of a $1 investment for a wide range of time periods and interest rates.

Future value tables are tedious, and as Table 5–2 demonstrates, they show future values only for a limited set of interest rates and time periods. For example, suppose that you want to calculate future values using an interest rate of 7.835%. The power key on your calculator will be faster and easier than future value tables. A third alternative is to use a financial calculator or a spreadsheet. These are discussed in several boxes later in this chapter.

FIGURE 5-2 How an investment of $100 grows with compound interest at different interest rates

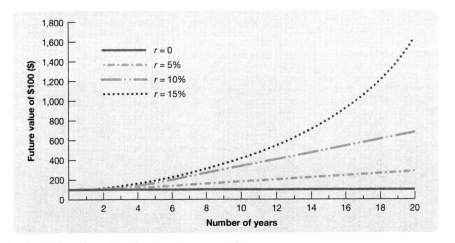

TABLE 5-2 An example of a future value table, showing how an investment of $1 grows with compound interest

Number of Years	Interest Rate per Year					
	5%	6%	7%	8%	9%	10%
1	1.0500	1.0600	1.0700	1.0800	1.0900	1.1000
2	1.1025	1.1236	1.1449	1.1664	1.1881	1.2100
3	1.1576	1.1910	1.2250	1.2597	1.2950	1.3310
4	1.2155	1.2625	1.3108	1.3605	1.4116	1.4641
5	1.2763	1.3382	1.4026	1.4693	1.5386	1.6105
10	1.6289	1.7908	1.9672	2.1589	2.3674	2.5937
20	2.6533	3.2071	3.8697	4.6610	5.6044	6.7275
30	4.3219	5.7435	7.6123	10.0627	13.2677	17.4494

EXAMPLE 5.1 ▶ Manhattan Island

Almost everyone's favorite example of the power of compound interest is the purchase of Manhattan Island for $24 in 1626 by Peter Minuit. Based on New York real estate prices today, it seems that Minuit got a great deal. But did he? Consider the future value of that $24 if it had been invested for 382 years (2008 minus 1626) at an interest rate of 8% per year:

$$\$24 \times (1.08)^{382} = \$140,633,000,000,000$$
$$= \$140.63 \text{ trillion}$$

Perhaps the deal wasn't as good as it appeared. The total value of land on Manhattan today is only a fraction of $140.63 trillion.

Though entertaining, this analysis is actually somewhat misleading. First, the 8% interest rate we've used to compute future values is quite high by historical standards. At a 3.5% interest rate, more consistent with historical experience, the future value of the $24 would be *dramatically* lower, only $24 \times (1.035)^{382} = \$12,230,000$! Second, we have understated the returns to Mr. Minuit and his successors: We have ignored all the rental income that the island's land has generated over the last three or four centuries.

All things considered, if we had been around in 1626, we would have gladly paid $24 for the island.

The power of compounding is not restricted to money. Foresters try to forecast the compound growth rate of trees, demographers the compound growth rate of population. A social commentator once observed that the number of lawyers in the United

States is increasing at a higher compound rate than the population as a whole (3.6% versus .9% in the 1980s) and calculated that in about two centuries there will be more lawyers than people. In all these cases, the principle is the same: **Compound growth means that value increases each period by the factor (1 + growth rate). The value after *t* periods will equal the initial value times (1 + growth rate)*ᵗ*. When money is invested at compound interest, the growth rate is the interest rate.**

Self-Test 5.1
Suppose that Peter Minuit did not become the first New York real estate tycoon but instead had invested his $24 at a 5% interest rate in New Amsterdam Savings Bank. What would have been the balance in his account after 5 years? 50 years?

Self-Test 5.2
In 1973 Gordon Moore, one of Intel's founders, predicted that the number of transistors that could be placed on a single silicon chip would double every 18 months, equivalent to an annual growth of 59% (i.e., $1.59^{1.5} = 2.0$). The first microprocessor was built in 1971 and had 2,250 transistors. By 2007 Intel chips contained 592 million transistors, over 263,000 times the number of transistors 36 years earlier. What has been the annual compound rate of growth in processing power? How does it compare with the prediction of Moore's law?

5.2 Present Values

present value (PV)
Value today of a future cash flow.

Money can be invested to earn interest. If you are offered the choice between $100,000 now and $100,000 at the end of the year, you naturally take the money now to get a year's interest. Financial managers make the same point when they say that money in hand today has a *time value* or when they quote perhaps the most basic financial principle: **A dollar today is worth more than a dollar tomorrow.**

We have seen that $100 invested for 1 year at 6% will grow to a future value of $100 \times 1.06 = \$106$. Let's turn this around: How much do we need to invest *now* in order to produce $106 at the end of the year? In other words, what is the **present value (PV)** of the $106 payoff?

To calculate future value, we multiply today's investment by 1 plus the interest rate, .06, or 1.06. To calculate present value, we simply reverse the process and divide the future value by 1.06:

$$\text{Present value} = \text{PV} = \frac{\text{future value}}{1.06} = \frac{\$106}{1.06} = \$100$$

What is the present value of, say, $112.36 to be received 2 years from now? Again we ask, How much would we need to invest now to produce $112.36 after 2 years? The answer is obviously $100; we've already calculated that at 6% $100 grows to $112.36:

$$\$100 \times (1.06)^2 = \$112.36$$

However, if we don't know, or forgot the answer, we just divide future value by $(1.06)^2$:

$$\text{Present value} = \text{PV} = \frac{\$112.36}{(1.06)^2} = \$100$$

In general, for a future value or payment *t* periods away, present value is

$$\text{Present value} = \frac{\text{future value after } t \text{ periods}}{(1+r)^t} \tag{5.2}$$

discounted cash flow
Another term for the present value of a future cash flow.

discount rate
Interest rate used to compute present values of future cash flows.

To calculate present value, we *discounted* the future value at the interest rate r. The calculation is therefore termed a **discounted cash-flow (DCF)** calculation, and the interest rate r is known as the **discount rate.**

In this chapter we will be working through a number of more or less complicated DCF calculations. All of them involve a present value, a discount rate, and one or more future cash flows. If ever a DCF problem leaves you confused and flustered, just pause and write down which of these measures you know and which one you need to calculate.

EXAMPLE 5.2 ▶ Saving for a Future Purchase

Suppose you need $3,000 next year to buy a new computer. The interest rate is 8% per year. How much money should you set aside now in order to pay for the purchase? Just calculate the present value at an 8% interest rate of a $3,000 payment at the end of 1 year. To the nearest dollar, this value is

$$PV = \frac{\$3,000}{1.08} = \$2,778$$

Notice that $2,778 invested for 1 year at 8% will prove just enough to buy your computer:

$$\text{Future value} = \$2,778 \times 1.08 = \$3,000$$

The longer the time before you must make a payment, the less you need to invest today. For example, suppose that you can postpone buying that computer until the end of 2 years. In this case we calculate the present value of the future payment by dividing $3,000 by $(1.08)^2$:

$$PV = \frac{\$3,000}{(1.08)^2} = \$2,572$$

Thus you need to invest $2,778 today to provide $3,000 in 1 year but only $2,572 to provide the same $3,000 in 2 years.

You now know how to calculate future and present values: **To work out how much you will have in the future if you invest for *t* years at an interest rate *r*, multiply the initial investment by $(1 + r)^t$. To find the present value of a future payment, run the process in reverse and *divide* by $(1 + r)^t$.**

Present values are always calculated using compound interest. The ascending lines in Figure 5–2 showed the future value of $1 invested with compound interest. When we calculate present values, we move back along the lines from future to present.

Thus present values decline, other things equal, when future cash payments are delayed. The longer you have to wait for money, the less it's worth today, as we see in Figure 5–3. Notice how very small variations in the interest rate can have a powerful effect on the value of distant cash flows. At an interest rate of 5%, a payment of $100 in year 20 is worth $37.69 today. If the interest rate increases to 10%, the value of the future payment falls by about 60% to $14.86.

The present value formula is sometimes written differently. Instead of dividing the future payment by $(1 + r)^t$, we could equally well multiply it by $1/(1 + r)^t$:

$$PV = \frac{\text{future payment}}{(1+r)^t} = \text{future payment} \times \frac{1}{(1+r)^t}$$

discount factor
Present value of a $1 future payment.

The expression $1/(1 + r)^t$ is called the **discount factor.** It measures the present value of $1 received in year t.

FIGURE 5-3 Present value of a future cash flow of $100. Notice that the longer you have to wait for your money, the less it is worth today.

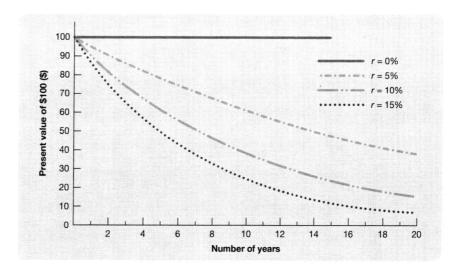

The simplest way to find the discount factor is to use a calculator, but financial managers sometimes find it convenient to use tables of discount factors. For example, Table 5–3 shows discount factors for a small range of years and interest rates. Table A.2 at the end of the book provides a set of discount factors for a wide range of years and interest rates.

Try using Table 5–3 to check our calculations of how much to put aside for that $3,000 computer purchase. If the interest rate is 8%, the present value of $1 paid at the end of 1 year is $.9259. So the present value of $3,000 is (to the nearest dollar)

$$PV = \$3,000 \times \frac{1}{1.08} = \$3,000 \times .9259 = \$2,778$$

which matches the value we obtained in Example 5.2.

What if the computer purchase is postponed until the end of 2 years? Table 5–3 shows that the present value of $1 paid at the end of 2 years is .8573. So the present value of $3,000 is

$$PV = \$3,000 \times \frac{1}{(1.08)^2} = \$3,000 \times .8573 = \$2,572$$

as we found in Example 5.2.

Notice that as you move along the rows in Table 5–3, moving to higher interest rates, present values decline. As you move down the columns, moving to longer discounting periods, present values again decline. (Why does this make sense?)

TABLE 5-3 An example of a present value table, showing the value today of $1 received in the future

Number of Years	Interest Rate per Year					
	5%	6%	7%	8%	9%	10%
1	0.9524	0.9434	0.9346	0.9259	0.9174	0.9091
2	0.9070	0.8900	0.8734	0.8573	0.8417	0.8264
3	0.8638	0.8396	0.8163	0.7938	0.7722	0.7513
4	0.8227	0.7921	0.7629	0.7350	0.7084	0.6830
5	0.7835	0.7473	0.7130	0.6806	0.6499	0.6209
10	0.6139	0.5584	0.5083	0.4632	0.4224	0.3855
20	0.3769	0.3118	0.2584	0.2145	0.1784	0.1486
30	0.2314	0.1741	0.1314	0.0994	0.0754	0.0573

FINANCIAL CALCULATOR

An Introduction to Financial Calculators

Financial calculators are designed with present value and future value formulas already programmed. Therefore, you can readily solve many problems simply by entering the inputs for the problem and punching a key for the solution.

The basic financial calculator uses five keys that correspond to the inputs for common problems involving the time value of money.

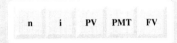

Each key represents the following input:

- *n* is the number of periods. (We have been using *t* to denote the length of time or number of periods. Most calculators use *n* for the same concept.)
- *i* is the interest rate per period, expressed as a percentage (not a decimal). For example, if the interest rate is 8%, you would enter 8, not .08. On some calculators this key is written I/Y or I/YR. (We have been using *r* to denote the interest rate or discount rate.)
- *PV* is the present value.
- *FV* is the future value.
- *PMT* is the amount of any recurring payment (called an *annuity*). In single cash-flow problems such as those we have considered so far, *PMT* is zero.

Given any four of these inputs, the calculator will solve for the fifth. (A word of advice: You should get into the habit of

clearing all inputs before beginning any new problem. You don't want leftover inputs to affect your results. Look for the "clear" or CLR key on your calculator.) We will illustrate with several examples.

Future Values

Recall Example 5.1, where we calculated the future value of Peter Minuit's $24 investment. Enter 24 into the *PV* register. (You enter the value by typing 24 and then pushing the *PV* key.) We assumed an interest rate of 8%, so enter 8 into the *i* register. Because the $24 had 382 years to compound, enter 382 into the *n* register. Enter 0 into the *PMT* register because there is no recurring payment involved in the calculation. Now ask the calculator to compute *FV*. On some calculators you simply press the *FV* key. On others you need to first press the "compute" key (which may be labeled *COMP* or *CPT*), and then press *FV*. The exact sequences of keystrokes for three popular financial calculators are as follows:*

Hewlett-Packard HP-10B	Sharp EL-733A	Texas Instruments BA II Plus
24 PV	24 PV	24 PV
382 n	382 n	382 n
8 I/YR	8 i	8 I/Y
0 PMT	0 PMT	0 PMT
FV	COMP FV	CPT FV

You should find after hitting the *FV* key that your calculator shows a value of –140.63 trillion, which, except for the minus sign, is the future value of the $24.

EXAMPLE 5.3 ▶ Puerto Rico Borrows Some Cash

In 2007, Puerto Rico needed to borrow about $2.6 billion for up to 47 years. It did so by selling IOUs, each of which simply promised to pay the holder $1,000 at the end of that time.[1] The market interest rate at the time was 5.15%. How much would you have been prepared to pay for one of these IOUs?

To calculate present value, we multiply the $1,000 future payment by the 47-year discount factor:

$$PV = \$1,000 \times \frac{1}{(1.0515)^{47}}$$
$$= \$1,000 \times .0944 = \$94.40$$

Self-Test 5.3   Suppose that Puerto Rico had promised to pay $1,000 at the end of 30 years. If the market interest rate were 5.15%, how much would you have been prepared to pay for a 30-year IOU of $1,000?

---

[1] "IOU" means "I owe you." Puerto Rico's IOUs are called *bonds*. Usually, bond investors receive a regular *interest* or *coupon* payment. The Puerto Rico bond will make only a single payment at the end of year 47. It was therefore known as a *zero-coupon bond*. More on this in the next chapter.

Why does the minus sign appear? Most calculators treat cash flows as either inflows (shown as positive numbers) or outflows (negative numbers). For example, if you borrow $100 today at an interest rate of 12%, you receive money now (a *positive* cash flow), but you will have to pay back $112 in a year, a *negative* cash flow at that time. Therefore, the calculator displays FV as a negative number. The following time line of cash flows shows the reasoning employed. The final negative cash flow of $112 has the same present value as the $100 borrowed today.

If, instead of borrowing, you were to *invest* $100 today to reap a future benefit, you would enter PV as a negative number (first press 100, then press the +/− key to make the value negative, and finally press PV to enter the value into the PV register). In this case, FV would appear as a positive number, indicating that you will reap a cash inflow when your investment comes to fruition.

Present Values

Suppose your savings goal is to accumulate $10,000 by the end of 30 years. If the interest rate is 8%, how much would you need to invest today to achieve your goal? Again, there is no recurring payment involved, so PMT is zero. We therefore enter the following: $n = 30$; $i = 8$; $FV = 10,000$;

PMT = 0. Now compute PV, and you should get an answer of −993.77. The answer is displayed as a negative number because you need to make a cash outflow (an investment) of $993.77 now in order to enjoy a cash inflow of $10,000 in 30 years.

Finding the Interest Rate

The 47-year Puerto Rico IOU in Example 5.3 sold at $94.40 and promised a final payment of $1,000. We may obtain the market interest rate by entering $n = 47$, $FV = 1,000$, $PV = -94.40$, and $PMT = 0$. Compute i and you will find that the interest rate is 5.15%. This is the value we compute directly (but with more work) on page 121.

How Long an Investment?

In Example 5.5, we consider how long it would take for an investment to double in value. This sort of problem is easily solved using a calculator. If the investment is to double, we enter $FV = 2$ and $PV = -1$. If the interest rate is 9%, enter $i = 9$ and $PMT = 0$. Compute n and you will find that $n = 8.04$ years. If the interest rate is 9.05%, the doubling period falls to 8 years, as we found in the example.

---

* The BAII Plus requires a little extra work to initialize the calculator. When you buy the calculator, it is set to automatically interpret each period as a year but to assume that interest compounds monthly. In our experience, it is best to change the compounding frequency to once per period. To do so, press [2nd] {P/Y} 1 [ENTER], then press [↓] 1 [ENTER], and finally press [2nd] {QUIT} to return to standard calculator mode. You should need to do this only once, even if the calculator is shut off.

EXAMPLE 5.4 ▶   Finding the Value of Free Credit

Kangaroo Autos is offering free credit on a $20,000 car. You pay $8,000 down and then the balance at the end of 2 years. Turtle Motors next door does not offer free credit but will give you $1,000 off the list price. If the interest rate is 10%, which company is offering the better deal?

Notice that you pay more in total by buying through Kangaroo, but since part of the payment is postponed, you can keep this money in the bank where it will continue to earn interest. To compare the two offers, you need to calculate the present value of the payments to Kangaroo. The *time line* in Figure 5–4 shows the cash payments to Kangaroo. The first payment, $8,000, takes place today. The second payment, $12,000, takes place at the end of 2 years. To find its present value, we need to multiply by the 2-year discount factor. The total present value of the payments to Kangaroo is therefore

$$PV = \$8,000 + \$12,000 \times \frac{1}{(1.10)^2}$$
$$= \$8,000 + \$9,917.36 = \$17,917.36$$

Suppose you start with $17,917.36. You make a down payment of $8,000 to Kangaroo Autos and invest the balance of $9,917.36. At an interest rate of 10%, this will grow over 2 years to $9,917.36 \times 1.10^2 = \$12,000$, just enough to make the final payment on your automobile. The total cost of $17,917.36 is a better deal than the $19,000 charged by Turtle Motors.

SPREADSHEET SOLUTIONS

Interest Rate Functions

Just as financial calculators largely replaced interest rate tables in the 1980s, these calculators are today giving way to spreadsheets. Like financial calculators, spreadsheets provide built-in functions that solve the equations linking the five variables in a time-value-of-money problem: the number of periods, the interest rate per period, the present value, the future value, and any recurring payment (the annuity). For single cash-flow problems such as the ones we've encountered so far, the recurring payment is zero. We will illustrate the use of these spreadsheets

by using Microsoft Excel™. An interactive version of this spreadsheet can be found at **www.mhhe.com/bmm6e.**

The four Excel functions relevant for single cash-flow problems are:

Future value = FV (rate, nper, pmt, PV)
Present value = PV (rate, nper, pmt, FV)
Interest rate = RATE (nper, pmt, PV, FV)
Number of periods = NPER (rate, pmt, PV, FV)

	A	B	C	D
1	Finding the future value of $24 using a spreadsheet			
2				
3	Present value (PV)	24		
4	Interest rate	0.08		
5	Payment	0		
6	Periods	382		
7				
8	Future value	$140,632,545,501,736		
9				
10				
11	The formula in cell B8 is =FV(B4,B6,B5,-B3). Notice that we enter the present value			
12	as a negative of the value in cell B3, since the "purchase price" is a cash outflow.			
13	The interest rate is entered as a decimal.			
14				
15	You can confirm for yourself that changing the entry in cell B4 to 0.035 will reduce			
16	the value to $12,229,955.			

These calculations illustrate how important it is to use present values when comparing alternative patterns of cash payment. **You should *never* compare cash flows occurring at different times without first discounting them to a common date. By calculating present values, we see how much cash must be set aside today to pay future bills.**

Finding the Interest Rate

When we looked at Puerto Rico's IOUs in Example 5.3, we used the interest rate to compute a fair market price for each IOU. Sometimes, however, you are given the price and have to calculate the interest rate that is being offered.

FIGURE 5–4 Drawing a time line can help us to calculate the present value of the payments to Kangaroo Autos.

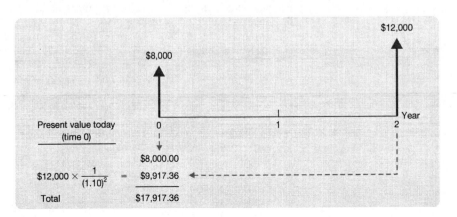

As you can see, each spreadsheet formula requires four inputs—just as financial calculators require four inputs—and provides the solution for the fifth variable. Also like most calculators, the spreadsheet functions interpret cash inflows as positive values and cash outflows as negative values. Unlike financial calculators, however, most spreadsheets require that interest rates be input as decimals rather than whole numbers (e.g., if the rate is 6%, enter .06 rather than 6). Note also the use of = signs in front of the formulas to alert Excel to the fact that these are predefined formulas. In the previous box, we saw how to use calculators to solve several problems. Let's see how we would use spreadsheets to solve the same problems.

Future Values

The figure on the facing page shows a spreadsheet that solves Example 5.1 on the future value of the $24 spent to acquire Manhattan Island. The interest rate is entered as a decimal in cell B4. The formula for future value in cell B8 takes as its last input the negative of cell B3, because the $24 purchase price is treated as cash outflow.

Present Values

We next considered an individual who wishes to accumulate a future value of $10,000 by the end of 30 years. If the interest rate is 8%, and there is no recurring payment involved, you can find the necessary investment today (the present value) by entering the formula =PV (.08,30,0,10000). If you try this, you will see that the solution is reported as a negative

value: the positive future payoff of $10,000 requires an initial payment (cash outflow) of 993.77. (Notice also that we don't use commas when entering the $10,000 future value. The spreadsheet would think that the comma was being used to separate two inputs to the function.)

Finding the Interest Rate

We showed how to use a calculator to find the interest rate on a 47-year $1,000 IOU sold today for $94.40. In Excel, we can compute =RATE(47,0,–94.40,1000) to confirm again that the interest rate is 5.15%.

How Long an Investment?

Example 5.5 asks how long it would take an investment to double if it earned interest at a rate of 9%. We treat the present value as a $1 investment (cash outflow) and the future value as a $2 cash payback. Therefore, enter =NPER(.09,0,–1,2) to find that the doubling period is 8.04 years.

Spreadsheet Questions

5.1 What was the future value of the $24 paid for Manhattan Island by 1726, that is, after 100 years of compounding? What about by 1826? What was the growth in value during the second 100 years? What was the growth in value in the last 82 years of the "investment"?

5.2 Why is the growth of value so much greater in the later years than in the earlier years?

For example, when Puerto Rico borrowed money, it did not announce an interest rate. It simply offered to sell each IOU for $94.40. Thus we know that

$$PV = \$1,000 \times \frac{1}{(1+r)^{47}} = \$94.40$$

What is the interest rate?

There are several ways to approach this. First, you might use a table of discount factors. You need to find the interest rate for which the 47-year discount factor = .0944.

Second, you can rearrange the equation and use your calculator:

$$\$94.40 \times (1+r)^{47} = \$1,000$$

$$(1+r)^{47} = \frac{\$1,000}{\$94.40} = 10.593$$

$$(1+r) = (10.593)^{1/47} = 1.0515$$

$$r = .0515, \text{ or } 5.15\%$$

In general this is more accurate. You can also use a financial calculator (see the box on pages 118–119).

EXAMPLE 5.5 ▶ Double Your Money

How many times have you heard of an investment adviser who promises to double your money? Is this really an amazing feat? That depends on how long it will take for your money to double. With enough patience, your funds eventually will double even if they earn only a very modest interest rate. Suppose your investment adviser promises to double your money in 8 years. What interest rate is implicitly being promised?

The adviser is promising a future value of $2 for every $1 invested today. Therefore, we find the interest rate by solving for r as follows:

$$\text{Future value (FV)} = \text{PV} \times (1+r)^t$$
$$\$2 = \$1 \times (1+r)^8$$
$$1+r = 2^{1/8} = 1.0905$$
$$r = .0905, \text{ or } 9.05\%$$

Self-Test 5.4   An investment of $1,000 in Amazon stock at the end of 2002 would have grown to just about $4,000 by the end of 2007. At what annual rate did the investment grow?

5.3 Multiple Cash Flows

So far, we have considered problems involving only a single cash flow. This is obviously limiting. Most real-world investments, after all, will involve many cash flows over time. When there are many payments, you'll hear managers refer to a *stream of cash flows*.

Future Value of Multiple Cash Flows

Recall the computer you hope to purchase in 2 years (see Example 5.2). Now suppose that instead of putting aside one sum in the bank to finance the purchase, you plan to save some amount of money each year. You might be able to put $1,200 in the bank now, and another $1,400 in 1 year. If you earn an 8% rate of interest, how much will you be able to spend on a computer in 2 years?

The time line in Figure 5–5 shows how your savings grow. There are two cash inflows into the savings plan. The first cash flow will have 2 years to earn interest and therefore will grow to $1,200 \times (1.08)^2 = \$1,399.68$, while the second deposit, which comes a year later, will be invested for only 1 year and will grow to $1,400 \times (1.08) = \$1,512$. After 2 years, then, your total savings will be the sum of these two amounts, or $2,911.68.

EXAMPLE 5.6 ▶ Even More Savings

Suppose that the computer purchase can be put off for an additional year and that you can make a third deposit of $1,000 at the end of the second year. How much will be available to spend 3 years from now?

Again we organize our inputs using a time line as in Figure 5–6. The total cash available will be the sum of the future values of all three deposits. Notice that when

FIGURE 5–5 Drawing a time line can help to calculate the future value of your savings.

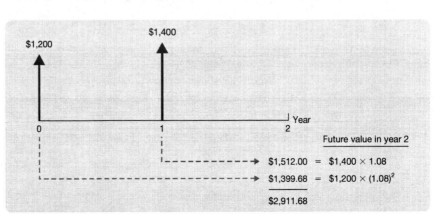

FIGURE 5–6 **To find the future value of a stream of cash flows, you just calculate the future value of each flow and then add them.**

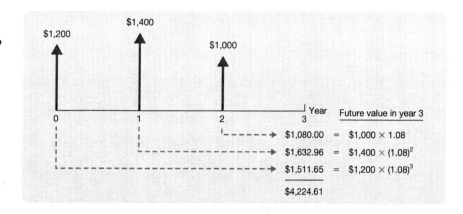

we save for 3 years, the first two deposits each have an extra year for interest to compound:

$$\$1,200 \times (1.08)^3 = \$1,511.65$$
$$\$1,400 \times (1.08)^2 = \ \ 1,632.96$$
$$\$1,000 \times (1.08) = \ \ 1,080.00$$
$$\text{Total future value} = \$4,224.61$$

Our examples show that problems involving multiple cash flows are simple extensions of single cash-flow analysis. **To find the value at some future date of a stream of cash flows, calculate what each cash flow will be worth at that future date and then add up these future values.**

As we will now see, a similar adding-up principle works for present value calculations.

Present Value of Multiple Cash Flows

When we calculate the present value of a future cash flow, we are asking how much that cash flow would be worth today. If there is more than one future cash flow, we simply need to work out what each flow would be worth today and then add these present values.

EXAMPLE 5.7 ▶   Cash Up Front versus an Installment Plan

Suppose that your auto dealer gives you a choice between paying $15,500 for a used car or entering into an installment plan where you pay $8,000 down today and make payments of $4,000 in each of the next 2 years. Which is the better deal? Before reading this chapter, you might have compared the total payments under the two plans: $15,500 versus $16,000 in the installment plan. Now, however, you know that this comparison is wrong, because it ignores the time value of money. For example, the last installment of $4,000 is less costly to you than paying out $4,000 now. The true cost of that last payment is the present value of $4,000.

Assume that the interest rate you can earn on safe investments is 8%. Suppose you choose the installment plan. As the time line in Figure 5–7 illustrates, the present value of the plan's three cash flows is:

Present Value			
Immediate payment	$8,000	=	$ 8,000.00
Second payment	$4,000/1.08	=	3,703.70
Third payment	$4,000/(1.08)²	=	3,429.36
Total present value		=	$15,133.06

FIGURE 5–7 To find the present value of a stream of cash flows, you just calculate the present value of each flow and then add them.

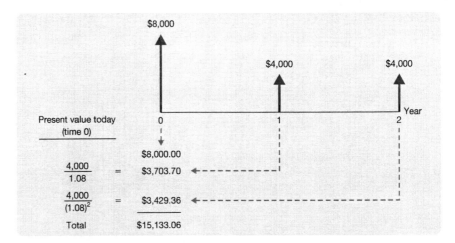

Because the present value of the three payments is less than $15,500, the installment plan is in fact the cheaper alternative.

The installment plan's present value is the amount that you would need to invest now to cover the three payments. Let's check.

Here is how your bank balance would change as you make each payment:

Year	Initial Balance	−	Payment	=	Remaining Balance	+	Interest Earned	=	Balance at Year-End
0	$15,133.06		$8,000		$7,133.06		$570.64		$7,703.70
1	7,703.70		4,000		3,703.70		296.30		4,000.00
2	4,000.00		4,000		0		0		0

If you start with the present value of $15,133.06 in the bank, you could make the first $8,000 payment and be left with $7,133.06. After 1 year, your savings account would receive an interest payment of $7,133.06 × .08 = $570.64, bringing your account to $7,703.70. Similarly, you would make the second $4,000 payment and be left with $3,703.70. This sum left in the bank would grow with interest to $4,000, just enough to make the last payment.

The present value of a stream of future cash flows is the amount you need to invest today to generate that stream.

Self-Test 5.5

In order to avoid estate taxes, your rich aunt Frederica will pay you $10,000 per year for 4 years, starting 1 year from now. What is the present value of your benefactor's planned gifts? The interest rate is 7%. How much will you have 4 years from now if you invest each gift at 7%?

5.4 Level Cash Flows: Perpetuities and Annuities

annuity
Equally spaced level stream of cash flows, with a finite maturity.

perpetuity
Stream of level cash payments that never ends.

Frequently, you may need to value a stream of equal cash flows. For example, a home mortgage might require the homeowner to make equal monthly payments for the life of the loan. For a 30-year loan, this would result in 360 equal payments. A 4-year car loan might require 48 equal monthly payments. Any such sequence of equally spaced, level cash flows is called an **annuity.** If the payment stream lasts forever, it is called a **perpetuity.**

SPREADSHEET SOLUTIONS

Multiple Cash Flows

While uneven cash-flow problems are conceptually straight-forward, they rapidly become tedious and prone to errors from "typos," even if you use a financial calculator. It really helps to use spreadsheets. The following figure is a spread-sheet solution of Example 5.7.

The spreadsheet lists the time until each payment in column A. This value is used for the number of periods (nper) in the PV formula in column C. The values for the cash flow in each future period are entered as negative numbers in the PV formula. The present values (column C) therefore appear as positive numbers.

An interactive version of this spreadsheet can be found at **www.mhhe.com/bmm6e**.

Spreadsheet Questions

5.3 Find the present value of the three payments at interest rates of 5% and 11%. Explain why the values change as they do.

5.4 Total payments over the 3 years are $16,000. What is the present value if the three payments are instead $6,000, $5,000, $5,000? Why does the present value fall? (Use an interest rate of 8%.)

	A	B	C	D	E
1	Finding the present value of multiple cash flows using a spreadsheet				
2					
3	**Time until CF**	**Cash flow**	**Present value**	**Formula in Column C**	
4	0	8000	$8,000.00	=PV(B10,A4,0,-B4)	
5	1	4000	$3,703.70	=PV(B10,A5,0,-B5)	
6	2	4000	$3,429.36	=PV(B10,A6,0,-B6)	
7					
8	SUM:		$15,133.06	=SUM(C4:C6)	
9					
10	**Discount rate:**	0.08			
11					
12	Notice that the time until each payment (nper) is found in column A.				
13	Once we enter the formula for present value in cell C4, we can copy it to cells C5 and C6.				
14	The present value for other interest rates can be found by changing the entry in cell B10.				

Please visit us at www.mhhe.com/bmm6e

How to Value Perpetuities

Some time ago the British government borrowed by issuing loans known as consols. Consols are perpetuities. In other words, instead of repaying these loans, the British government pays the investors a fixed annual payment in perpetuity (forever).

How might we value such a security? Suppose that you could invest $100 at an interest rate of 10%. You would earn annual interest of $.10 \times \$100 = \$10$ per year and could withdraw this amount from your investment account each year without ever running down your balance. In other words, a $100 investment could provide a perpetuity of $10 per year. In general,

$$\text{Cash payment from perpetuity} = \text{interest rate} \times \text{present value}$$
$$C = r \times PV$$

We can rearrange this relationship to derive the present value of a perpetuity, given the interest rate r and the cash payment C:

$$\text{PV of perpetuity} = \frac{C}{r} = \frac{\text{cash payment}}{\text{interest rate}} \tag{5.3}$$

Suppose some worthy person wishes to endow a chair in finance at your university. If the rate of interest is 10% and the aim is to provide $100,000 a year forever, the amount that must be set aside today is

$$\text{Present value of perpetuity} = \frac{C}{r} = \frac{\$100,000}{.10} = \$1,000,000$$

Two warnings about the perpetuity formula. First, at a quick glance you can easily confuse the formula with the present value of a single cash payment. A payment of $1 at the end of 1 year has a present value $1/(1 + r)$. The perpetuity has a value of $1/r$. These are quite different.

Second, the perpetuity formula tells us the value of a regular stream of payments starting one period from now. Thus our endowment of $1 million would provide the university with its first payment of $100,000 one year hence. If the worthy donor wants to provide the university with an additional payment of $100,000 up front, he or she would need to put aside $1,100,000.

Sometimes you may need to calculate the value of a perpetuity that does not start to make payments for several years. For example, suppose that our philanthropist decides to provide $100,000 a year with the first payment 4 years from now. We know that in year 3, this endowment will be an ordinary perpetuity with payments starting at the end of 1 year. So our perpetuity formula tells us that in year 3 the endowment will be worth $100,000/r$. But it is not worth that much now. To find today's value we need to multiply by the 3-year discount factor. Thus, the "delayed" perpetuity is worth

$$\$100,000 \times \frac{1}{r} \times \frac{1}{(1+r)^3} = \$1,000,000 \times \frac{1}{(1.10)^3} = \$751,315$$

Self-Test 5.6   A British government perpetuity pays £4 a year forever and is selling for £48. What is the interest rate?

How to Value Annuities

Let us return to Kangaroo Autos for (almost) the last time. Most installment plans call for level streams of payments. So let us suppose that Kangaroo now offers an "easy payment" scheme of $8,000 a year at the end of each of the next 3 years.

A level stream of cash flows that continues for a specified number of years is known as an *annuity*. The payments on the Kangaroo plan constitute a 3-year annuity. Figure 5–8 shows a time line of these cash flows and calculates the present value of each year's flow assuming an interest rate of 10%. You can see that the total present value of the payments is $19,894.82.

You can always value an annuity by calculating the present value of each cash flow and finding the total. However, it is usually quicker to use a simple formula which states that if the interest rate is r, then the present value of an annuity that pays C dollars a year for each of t periods is

$$\text{Present value of } t\text{-year annuity} = C \left[\frac{1}{r} - \frac{1}{r(1+r)^t} \right] \tag{5.4}$$

FIGURE 5–8 To find the value of an annuity, you can calculate the value of each cash flow. It is usually quicker to use the annuity formula.

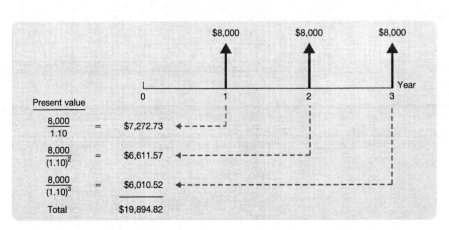

annuity factor
Present value of a
$1 annuity.

The expression in brackets shows the present value of a t-year annuity of $1 starting in period 1. It is generally known as the t-year **annuity factor.** Therefore, another way to write the value of an annuity is

$$\text{Present value of } t\text{-year annuity} = \text{payment} \times \text{annuity factor}$$

You can use this formula to calculate the present value of the payments to Kangaroo. The annual payment (C) is $8,000, the interest rate (r) is 10%, and the number of years (t) is 3. Therefore,

$$\text{Present value} = C\left[\frac{1}{r} - \frac{1}{r(1+r)^t}\right] = 8,000\left[\frac{1}{.10} - \frac{1}{.10(1.10)^3}\right] = \$19,894.82$$

This is exactly the same answer that we got by separately valuing each cash flow. If the number of periods is small, there is little to choose between the two methods, but when you are valuing long-term annuities, it is far easier to use the formula.

If you are wondering where the annuity formula comes from, look at Figure 5–9. It shows the payments and values of three investments.

Row 1   The investment in the first row provides a perpetual stream of $1 starting at the end of the first year. We have already seen that this perpetuity has a present value of $1/r$.

Row 2   Now look at the investment shown in the second row of Figure 5–9. It also provides a perpetual stream of $1 payments, but these payments don't start until year 4. This stream of payments is identical to the delayed perpetuity that we just valued. In year 3, the investment will be an ordinary perpetuity with payments starting in 1 year and will therefore be worth $1/r$ in year 3. To find the value today, we simply multiply this figure by the 3-year discount factor. Thus

$$\text{PV} = \frac{1}{r} \times \frac{1}{(1+r)^3} = \frac{1}{r(1+r)^3}$$

Row 3   Finally, look at the investment shown in the third row of Figure 5–8. This provides a level payment of $1 a year for each of 3 years. In other words, it is a 3-year annuity. You can also see that, taken together, the investments in rows 2 and 3 provide exactly the same cash payments as the investment in row 1. Thus the value of our annuity (row 3) must be equal to the value of the row 1 perpetuity less the value of the delayed row 2 perpetuity:

$$\text{Present value of a 3-year \$1 annuity} = \frac{1}{r} - \frac{1}{r(1+r)^3}$$

Remembering formulas is about as difficult as remembering other people's birthdays. But as long as you bear in mind that an annuity is equivalent to the difference between an immediate and a delayed perpetuity, you shouldn't have any difficulty.

FIGURE 5–9 The value of an annuity is equal to the difference between the value of two perpetuities.

	Year:	1	2	3	4	5	6 . . .	Present Value
1. Perpetuity A		$1	$1	$1	$1	$1	$1 . . .	$\dfrac{1}{r}$
2. Perpetuity B					$1	$1	$1 . . .	$\dfrac{1}{r(1+r)^3}$
3. Three-year annuity		$1	$1	$1				$\dfrac{1}{r} - \dfrac{1}{r(1+r)^3}$

TABLE 5–4 An example of an annuity table, showing the present value today of $1 a year received for each of *t* years

Number of Years	Interest Rate per Year					
	5%	6%	7%	8%	9%	10%
1	0.9524	0.9434	0.9346	0.9259	0.9174	0.9091
2	1.8594	1.8334	1.8080	1.7833	1.7591	1.7355
3	2.7232	2.6730	2.6243	2.5771	2.5313	2.4869
4	3.5460	3.4651	3.3872	3.3121	3.2397	3.1699
5	4.3295	4.2124	4.1002	3.9927	3.8897	3.7908
10	7.7217	7.3601	7.0236	6.7101	6.4177	6.1446
20	12.4622	11.4699	10.5940	9.8181	9.1285	8.5136
30	15.3725	13.7648	12.4090	11.2578	10.2737	9.4269

You can use a calculator or spreadsheet to work out annuity factors (we show you how later in the chapter) or you can use a set of annuity tables. Table 5–4 is an abridged annuity table (an extended version is shown in Table A.3 at the end of the book). Check that you can find the 3-year annuity factor for an interest rate of 10%.

Self-Test 5.7   If the interest rate is 8%, what is the 4-year discount factor? What is the 4-year annuity factor? What is the relationship between these two numbers? Explain.

EXAMPLE 5.8   ▶   Winning Big at the Lottery

In August 1998 thirteen lucky machinists from Ohio pooled their money to buy Powerball lottery tickets and won a record $295.7 million. (A 14th member of the group pulled out at the last minute in order to put in his own numbers.) We suspect that the winners received unsolicited congratulations, good wishes, and requests for money from dozens of more or less worthy charities, relations, and newly devoted friends. In response, they could fairly point out that the prize wasn't really worth $295.7 million. That sum was to be paid in 25 equal annual installments of $11.828 million each. Assuming that the first payment occurred at the end of 1 year, what was the present value of the prize? The interest rate at the time was 5.9%.

The present value of these payments is simply the sum of the present values of each annual payment. But rather than valuing the payments separately, it is much easier to treat them as a 25-year annuity. To value this annuity, we simply multiply $11.828 million by the 25-year annuity factor:

$$PV = 11.828 \times 25\text{-year annuity factor}$$

$$= 11.828 \times \left[\frac{1}{r} - \frac{1}{r(1+r)^{25}} \right]$$

At an interest rate of 5.9%, the annuity factor is

$$\left[\frac{1}{.059} - \frac{1}{.059(1.059)^{25}} \right] = 12.9057$$

(We could also look up the annuity factor in Table A.3.) The present value of the cash payments is $11.828 × 12.9057 = $152.6 million, much less than the much-advertised prize, but still not a bad day's haul.

Lottery operators generally make arrangements for winners with big spending plans to take an equivalent lump sum. In our example the winners could either take the $295.7 million spread over 25 years or receive $152.6 million up front. Both arrangements have the same present value.

EXAMPLE 5.9 ▶ How Much Luxury and Excitement Can $59 Billion Buy?

Bill Gates is one of the world's richest persons, with wealth estimated in 2008 at about $59 billion. We haven't yet met Mr. Gates, and so cannot fill you in on his plans for allocating the $59 billion between charitable good works and the cost of a life of luxury and excitement (L&E). So to keep things simple, we will just ask the following entirely hypothetical question: How much could Mr. Gates spend yearly on 30 more years of L&E if he were to devote the entire $59 billion to those purposes? Assume that his money is invested to earn 9%.

The 30-year, 9% annuity factor is 10.2737. Thus,

$$\text{Present value} = \text{annual spending} \times \text{annuity factor}$$
$$\$59,000,000,000 = \text{annual spending} \times 10.2737$$
$$\text{Annual spending} = \$5,743,000,000, \text{ or about } \$5.7 \text{ billion}$$

Warning to Mr. Gates: We haven't considered inflation. The cost of buying L&E will increase, so $5.7 billion won't buy as much L&E in 30 years as it will today. More on that later.

Self-Test 5.8

Suppose you retire at age 70. You expect to live 20 more years and to spend $55,000 a year during your retirement. How much money do you need to save by age 70 to support this consumption plan? Assume an interest rate of 7%.

EXAMPLE 5.10 ▶ Home Mortgages

Sometimes you may need to find the series of cash payments that would provide a given value today. For example, home purchasers typically borrow the bulk of the house price from a lender. The most common loan arrangement is a 30-year loan that is repaid in equal monthly installments. Suppose that a house costs $125,000 and that the buyer puts down 20% of the purchase price, or $25,000, in cash, borrowing the remaining $100,000 from a mortgage lender such as the local savings bank. What is the appropriate monthly mortgage payment?

The borrower repays the loan by making monthly payments over the next 30 years (360 months). The savings bank needs to set these monthly payments so that they have a present value of $100,000. Thus

$$\text{Present value} = \text{mortgage payment} \times 360\text{-month annuity factor}$$
$$= \$100,000$$

$$\text{Mortgage payment} = \frac{\$100,000}{360\text{-month annuity factor}}$$

Suppose that the interest rate is 1% a month. Then

$$\text{Mortgage payment} = \frac{\$100,000}{\left[\dfrac{1}{.01} - \dfrac{1}{.01(1.01)^{360}} \right]} = \frac{\$100,000}{97.218} = \$1,028.61$$

The mortgage loan in Example 5.10 is an example of an *amortizing loan.* "Amortizing" means that part of the monthly payment is used to pay interest on the loan and part is used to reduce the amount of the loan. Table 5–5 illustrates a 4-year amortizing loan of $1,000 with an interest rate of 10% and annual payments starting in 1 year. The annual payment (annuity) that would repay the loan is $315.47. (Confirm this for yourself.) At the end of the first year, the interest payment is 10% of $1,000, or $100. So $100 of your first payment is used to pay interest, and the remaining $215.47 is used to reduce (or "amortize") the loan balance to $784.53.

TABLE 5–5 An example of an amortizing loan. If you borrow $1,000 at an interest rate of 10%, you would need to make an annual payment of $315.47 over 4 years to repay the loan with interest.

Year	Beginning-of-Year Balance	Year-End Interest Due on Balance	Year-End Payment	Amortization of Loan	End-of-Year Balance
1	$1,000.00	$100.00	$315.47	$215.47	$784.53
2	$784.53	$78.45	$315.47	$237.02	$547.51
3	$547.51	$54.75	$315.47	$260.72	$286.79
4	$286.79	$28.68	$315.47	$286.79	$0

Next year, the outstanding balance is lower, so the interest charge is only $78.45. Therefore, $315.47 − $78.45 = $237.02 can be applied to amortization. Amortization in the second year is higher than in the first, because the amount of the loan has declined and therefore less of the payment is taken up in interest. This procedure continues until the last year, when the amortization is just enough to reduce the outstanding balance on the loan to zero.

Because the loan is progressively paid off, the fraction of each payment devoted to interest steadily falls over time, while the fraction used to reduce the loan (the amortization) steadily increases. Figure 5–10 illustrates the amortization of the mortgage loan in Example 5.11. In the early years, almost all of the mortgage payment is for interest. Even after 15 years, the bulk of the monthly payment is interest.

Self-Test 5.9

What will be the monthly payment if you take out a $100,000 fifteen-year mortgage at an interest rate of 1% per month? How much of the first payment is interest, and how much is amortization?

Annuities Due

The perpetuity and annuity formulas assume that the first payment occurs at the end of the period. They tell you the value of a stream of cash payments starting one period hence.

However, streams of cash payments often start immediately. For example, Kangaroo Autos might have required three annual payments of $8,000 starting immediately. A level stream of payments starting immediately is known as an **annuity due.**

Figure 5–11 depicts the cash-flow streams of an ordinary annuity and an annuity due. By comparing the two panels of the figure, you can see that each of the three cash

annuity due
Level stream of cash flows starting immediately.

FIGURE 5–10 Mortgage amortization. This figure shows the breakdown of mortgage payments between interest and amortization. Monthly payments within each year are summed, so the figure shows the annual payment on the mortgage.

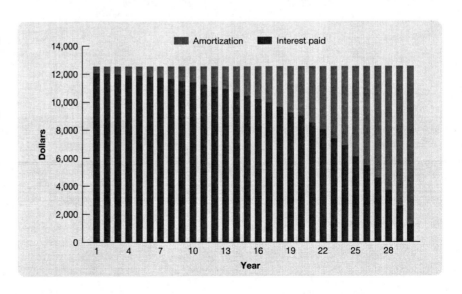

flows in the annuity due comes one period earlier than the corresponding cash flow of the ordinary annuity. Therefore,

$$\text{Present value of an annuity due} = (1 + r) \times \text{present value of an annuity} \quad \textbf{(5.5)}$$

Figure 5–11 shows that the effect of bringing the Kangaroo loan payments forward by 1 year is an increase in their value from \$19,894.82 (as an ordinary annuity) to \$21,884.30 (as an annuity due). Notice that \$21,884.30 = \$19,894.82 × 1.10.

Self-Test 5.10   When calculating the value of the Powerball lottery prize in Example 5.8, we assumed that the first of the payments occurred at the end of 1 year. However, the winners of the lottery would not in fact have needed to wait a year before receiving their first payment. They would have gotten their first installment of \$11.828 million up front, and the remaining payments would have been spread over the following 24 years. Recalculate the value of the prize.

Future Value of an Annuity

You are back in savings mode again. This time you are setting aside \$3,000 at the end of every year. If your savings earn interest of 8% a year, how much will they be worth at the end of 4 years? We can answer this question with the help of the time line in Figure 5–12. Your first year's savings will earn interest for 3 years, the second will

FIGURE 5–11 The cash payments on the ordinary annuity in panel *a* start in year 1. The first payment on the annuity due in panel *b* occurs immediately. The annuity due is therefore more valuable.

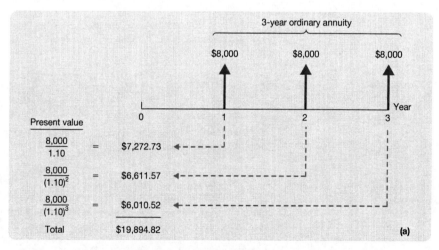

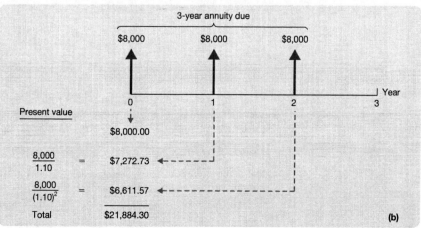

FIGURE 5-12 Calculating the future value of an ordinary annuity of $3,000 a year for 4 years (interest rate = 8%)

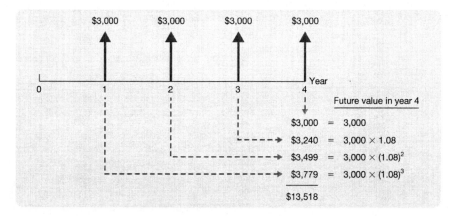

earn interest for 2 years, the third will earn interest for 1 year, and the final savings in year 4 will earn no interest. The sum of the future values of the four payments is

$$(\$3,000 \times 1.08^3) + (\$3,000 \times 1.08^2) + (\$3,000 \times 1.08) + \$3,000 = \$13,518$$

But wait a minute! We are looking here at a level stream of cash flows—an annuity. We have seen that there is a shortcut formula to calculate the *present* value of an annuity. So there ought to be a similar formula for calculating the *future* value of a level stream of cash flows.

Think first how much your stream of savings is worth today. You are setting aside $3,000 in each of the next 4 years. The *present* value of this 4-year annuity is therefore equal to

$$PV = \$3,000 \times 4\text{-year annuity factor}$$
$$= \$3,000 \times \left[\frac{1}{.08} - \frac{1}{.08(1.08)^4} \right] = \$9,936$$

Now think how much you would have after 4 years if you invested $9,936 today. Simple! Just multiply by $(1.08)^4$:

$$\text{Value at end of year 4} = \$9,936 \times 1.08^4 = \$13,518$$

We calculated the future value of the annuity by first calculating the present value and then multiplying by $(1 + r)^t$. The general formula for the future value of a stream of cash flows of $1 a year for each of t years is therefore

Future value (FV) of annuity of $1 a year = present value of annuity
of $1 a year $\times (1+r)^t$

$$= \left[\frac{1}{r} - \frac{1}{r(1+r)^t} \right] \times (1+r)^t = \frac{(1+r)^t - 1}{r}$$

(5.6)

If you need to find the future value of just four cash flows as in our example, it is a toss-up whether it is quicker to calculate the future value of each cash flow separately (as we did in Figure 5–12) or to use the annuity formula. If you are faced with a stream of 10 or 20 cash flows, there is no contest.

You can find the future value of an annuity in Table 5–6 or the more extensive Table A.4 at the end of the book. You can see that in the row corresponding to $t = 4$ and the column corresponding to $r = 8\%$, the future value of an annuity of $1 a year is $4.5061. Therefore, the future value of the $3,000 annuity is $3,000 \times 4.5061 = \$13,518$.

FINANCIAL CALCULATOR

Solving Annuity Problems Using a Financial Calculator

The formulas for both the present value and the future value of an annuity are also built into your financial calculator. Again, we can input all but one of the five financial keys, and let the calculator solve for the remaining variable. In these applications, the *PMT* key is used to either enter or solve for the cash payments of the annuity.

Solving for an Annuity

In Example 5.11, we determine the savings stream that would provide a retirement goal of $500,000 after 50 years of saving at an interest rate of 10%. To find the required savings each year, enter $n = 50$, $i = 10$, $FV = 500,000$, and $PV = 0$ (because your "savings account" currently is empty). Compute *PMT* and find that it is -429.59. Again, your calculator is likely to display the solution as -429.59, since the positive $500,000 cash value in 50 years will require 50 cash payments (outflows) of $429.59.

The sequences of key strokes on three popular calculators necessary to solve this problem are as follows:

Hewlett-Packard HP-10B	Sharp EL-733A	Texas Instruments BA II Plus
0 PV	0 PV	0 PV
50 n	50 n	50 n
10 I/YR	10 i	10 I/Y
500,000 FV	500,000 FV	500,000 FV
PMT	COMP PMT	CPT PMT

Present Value of an Annuity

In Example 5.10 we considered a 30-year mortgage with monthly payments of $1,028.61 and a monthly interest rate of 1%. Suppose we didn't know the amount of the mortgage loan. Enter $n = 360$ (months), $i = 1$, $PMT = -1,028.61$ (we enter the annuity level paid by the borrower to the lender as a negative number since it is a cash outflow), and $FV = 0$ (the mortgage is wholly paid off after 30 years; there are no final future payments beyond the normal monthly payment). Compute *PV* to find that the value of the loan is $100,000.

What about the balance left on the mortgage after 10 years have passed? This is easy: The monthly payment is still $PMT = -1,028.61$, and we continue to use $i = 1$ and $FV = 0$. The only change is that the number of monthly payments remaining has fallen from 360 to 240 (20 years are left on the loan). So enter $n = 240$ and compute *PV* as 93,417.76. This is the balance remaining on the mortgage.

Future Value of an Annuity

In Figure 5–12, we showed that a 4-year annuity of $3,000 invested at 8% would accumulate to a future value of $13,518. To solve this on your calculator, enter $n = 4$, $i = 8$, $PMT = -3,000$ (we enter the annuity paid by the investor to her savings account as a negative number since it is a cash outflow), and $PV = 0$ (the account starts with no funds). Compute *FV* to find that the future value of the savings account after 3 years is $13,518.

Calculator Self-Test Review (answers follow)

1. Turn back to Kangaroo Autos in Figure 5–8. Can you now solve for the present value of the three installment payments of $8,000 with an interest rate of 10% using your financial calculator? What key strokes must you use?
2. Now use your calculator to solve for the present value of the three installment payments if the first payment comes immediately, that is, as an annuity due.
3. Find the annual spending available to Bill Gates using the data in Example 5.9 and your financial calculator.

Solutions to Calculator Self-Test Review Questions

1. Inputs are $n = 3$, $i = 10$, $FV = 0$, and $PMT = 8,000$. Compute *PV* to find the present value of the cash flows as $19,894.82, which matches the solution given in the Example.
2. If you put your calculator in BEGIN mode and recalculate *PV* using the same inputs, you will find that *PV* has increased to $21,884.30. Alternatively, you can calculate the value of the annuity due by taking the value of the ordinary annuity, $19,894.82, and multiplying by 1 plus the interest rate, 1.10. The answer is again $19,894.82 × 1.10 = $21,884.30.
3. Inputs are $n = 30$, $i = 9$, $FV = 0$, $PV = -59,000$ million. Compute *PMT* to find that the 30-year annuity with present value of $59 billion is $5,743 million.

TABLE 5–6 An example of a table showing the future value of an investment of $1 a year for each of *t* years

Number of Years	Interest Rate per Year					
	5%	6%	7%	8%	9%	10%
1	1.0000	1.0000	1.0000	1.0000	1.0000	1.0000
2	2.0500	2.0600	2.0700	2.0800	2.0900	2.1000
3	3.1525	3.1836	3.2149	3.2464	3.2781	3.3100
4	4.3101	4.3746	4.4399	4.5061	4.5731	4.6410
5	5.5256	5.6371	5.7507	5.8666	5.9847	6.1051
10	12.5779	13.1808	13.8164	14.4866	15.1929	15.9374
20	33.0660	36.7856	40.9955	45.7620	51.1601	57.2750
30	66.4388	79.0582	94.4608	113.2832	136.3075	164.4940

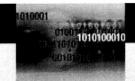

INTERNET INSIDER

Interest Rate Calculators

Source: Smart Money Web site.

Present and Future Values

There are dozens of Web sites that provide calculators to help with personal finance decisions. Two good examples are **finance.yahoo.com** and **www.smartmoney.com**. Log on first to the Yahoo! site and find the banking and budgeting calculator. Suppose that you invest $1,000 today. How much will you have after 30 years if the interest rate is 6% and you don't save another dime? Check your answer with the savings calculator.

Annuities Due

You can buy a car for $20,000, or you can lease it for 36 monthly payments of $350 each, with the first payment due immediately. At the end of the 36 months the car will be worth $10,000. Which alternative should you prefer if the interest rate is 10%? You can check your answer by logging on to the personal finance page of **www.smartmoney.com** and using the buy or lease calculator.

Mortgage Payments

In Example 5.10 we showed you how to work out mortgage payments. Log on to the personal finance page of **www.smartmoney.com** and find the mortgage payment calculator. Assume a 20-year mortgage loan of $100,000 and an interest rate of 10%. What is the amount of the payment? Check that you get the same answer when using the annuity formula. Now look at how much of the first month's payment goes to reduce the size of the mortgage. How much of the payment by the tenth year? Can you explain why the figure changes? If the interest rate doubles, would you expect the mortgage payment to double? Check whether you are right.

EXAMPLE 5.11 ▶   Saving for Retirement

In only 50 more years, you will retire. (That's right—by the time you retire, the retirement age will be around 70 years. Longevity is not an unmixed blessing.) Have you started saving yet? Suppose you believe you will need to accumulate $500,000 by your retirement date in order to support your desired standard of living. How much savings each year would be necessary to produce $500,000 at the end of 50 years? Let's say that the interest rate is 10% per year. You need to find how large the annuity in the following figure must be to provide a future value of $500,000:

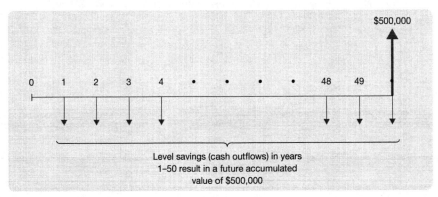

Level savings (cash outflows) in years
1–50 result in a future accumulated
value of $500,000

We know that if you were to save $1 each year your funds would accumulate to

$$\text{Future value (FV) of annuity of \$1 a year} = \frac{(1+r)^t - 1}{r} = \frac{(1.10)^{50} - 1}{.10}$$
$$= \$1,163.91$$

Annuities

By now it should be no surprise that the PMT variable in Excel's time-value-of-money functions denotes the level of an annuity. In addition, Excel provides another function to solve for annuity levels given the values of the other variables: PMT (rate, nper, PV, FV). Thus in Example 5.11, we can find the savings stream providing a future retirement goal of $500,000 after 50 years by entering =PMT(.10,50,0,500000), which results in an answer of −$429.59. Notice that we enter 0 for PV because our savings account starts with no funds.

Present Value of an Annuity

Example 5.10 examines a 30-year mortgage loan with 360 monthly payments of $1,028.61 each when the interest rate is 1% per month. The present value of this annuity is =PV(.01,360,−1028.61,0), which (except for trivial rounding error) is $100,000. We can also find the balance on the loan after 10 years, when there are 240 remaining payments, as =PV(.01,240,−1028.61,0) = $93,417.76. Notice that in both cases we entered a minus sign before 1028.61 to indicate that it was a payment.

Future Value of an Annuity

We confirmed on our calculators in the previous box that a 4-year annuity of $3,000 invested at 8% has a future value of $13,518 (see Figure 5–12). You can also confirm this value on your spreadsheet by entering =FV(.08,4,−3000,0).

Annuities Due

Excel will calculate the value of an annuity due rather than an ordinary annuity if you add an extra 1 at the end of the function. For example, we just calculated the present value of 360 monthly mortgage payments. Now assume the first payment comes immediately rather than after 1 month. In other words, the payments are an annuity due. Then the present value is found as =PV(.01,360,−1028.61,0,1), which equals $101,000, exactly 1% more than the value of the payments as an ordinary annuity. Similarly, the future value of the 4-year, $3,000 annuity that we just looked at also is higher if the first payment is made immediately. As an annuity due, the future value is =FV(.08,4,−3000,0,1) = $14,600, which is 8% higher than the future value of the ordinary annuity.

Spreadsheet Self-Test Review

In the box on page 133, we gave you three self-test review questions for your financial calculator. Now solve these problems using a spreadsheet program.

(Rather than compute the future value formula directly, you could look up the future value annuity factor in Table A.4. Alternatively, you can use a financial calculator or spreadsheet as we describe in the nearby boxes.) Therefore, if you save an amount of $C each year, you will accumulate $C × 1,163.91.

We need to choose C to ensure that C × 1,163.91 = $500,000. Thus C = $500,000/1,163.91 = $429.59. This appears to be surprisingly good news. Saving $429.59 a year does not seem to be an extremely demanding savings program. Don't celebrate yet, however. The news will get worse when we consider the impact of inflation.

Self-Test 5.11

What is the required savings level if the interest rate is only 5%? Why has the amount increased?

Remember that our ordinary annuity formulas assume that the first cash flow does not occur until the end of the first period. If the first cash flow comes immediately, the future value of the cash-flow stream is greater, since each flow has an extra year to earn interest. For example, at an interest rate of 10%, the future value of an annuity due would be exactly 10% greater than the future value of an ordinary annuity. More generally,

$$\text{Future value (FV) of annuity due} = \text{future value of ordinary annuity} \times (1 + r)$$

(5.7)

EXAMPLE 5.12 ▶ Future Value of Annuities versus Annuities Due

In Example 5.11, we showed that an annual savings stream of $429.59 invested for 50 years at 10% would satisfy a savings goal of $500,000. What savings stream would be necessary to produce $500,000 at the end of 50 years if we invested our money at the beginning rather than the end of each year?

We know from Example 5.11 that the future value of a $1 ordinary 50-year annuity at an interest rate of 10% is $1,163.91. Therefore,

$$\text{Future value (FV) of \$1 annuity due} = \text{future value of \$1 ordinary annuity} \times (1+r)$$
$$= \$1,163.91 \times 1.10 = \$1,280.30$$

We need to choose C to ensure that $C \times 1,280.30 = \$500,000$. Thus $C = \$390.53$. Notice that $390.53 equals the (ordinary) annuity we found in Example 5.11 divided by 1.10.

The nearby boxes show how to use financial calculators and spreadsheets to solve annuity problems.

5.5 Effective Annual Interest Rates

Thus far in this chapter we have mainly used *annual* interest rates to value a series of *annual* cash flows. But interest rates may be quoted for days, months, years, or any convenient interval. How should we compare rates when they are quoted for different periods, such as monthly versus annually?

Consider your credit card. Suppose you have to pay interest on any unpaid balances at the rate of 1% *per month*. What is it going to cost you if you neglect to pay off your unpaid balance for a year?

Don't be put off because the interest rate is quoted per month rather than per year. The important thing is to maintain consistency between the interest rate and the number of periods. If the interest rate is quoted as a percent per month, then we must define the number of periods in our future value calculation as the number of months. So if you borrow $100 from the credit card company at 1% per month for 12 months, you will need to repay $100 \times (1.01)^{12} = \$112.68$. Thus your debt grows after 1 year to $112.68. Therefore, we can say that the interest rate of 1% a month is equivalent to an **effective annual interest rate,** or *annually compounded rate,* of 12.68%.

effective annual interest rate
Interest rate that is annualized using compound interest.

In general, the effective annual interest rate is defined as the rate at which your money grows, allowing for the effect of compounding. Therefore, for the credit card,

$$1 + \text{effective annual rate} = (1 + \text{monthly rate})^{12}$$

When comparing interest rates, it is best to use effective annual rates. This compares interest paid or received over a common period (1 year) and allows for possible compounding during the period. Unfortunately, short-term rates are sometimes annualized by multiplying the rate per period by the number of periods in a year. In fact, truth-in-lending laws in the United States *require* that rates be annualized in this manner. Such rates are called **annual percentage rates (APRs).**[2] The interest rate on your credit card loan was 1% per month. Since there are 12 months in a year, the APR on the loan is $12 \times 1\% = 12\%$.

annual percentage rate (APR)
Interest rate that is annualized using simple interest.

If the credit card company quotes an APR of 12%, how can you find the effective annual interest rate? The solution is simple:

Step 1. Take the quoted APR and divide by the number of compounding periods in a year to recover the rate per period actually charged. In our example, the interest was calculated monthly. So we divide the APR by 12 to obtain the interest rate per month:

----

[2] The truth-in-lending laws apply to credit card loans, auto loans, home improvement loans, and some loans to small businesses. APRs are not commonly used or quoted in the big leagues of finance.

$$\text{Monthly interest rate} = \frac{APR}{12} = \frac{12\%}{12} = 1\%$$

Step 2. Now convert to an annually compounded interest rate:

$$1 + \text{effective annual rate} = (1 + \text{monthly rate})^{12} = (1 + .01)^{12} = 1.1268$$

The effective annual interest rate is .1268, or 12.68%.

In general, if an investment is quoted with a given APR and there are m compounding periods in a year, then \$1 will grow to \$1 $\times (1 + APR/m)^m$ after 1 year. The effective annual interest rate is $(1 + APR/m)^m - 1$. For example, a credit card loan that charges a monthly interest rate of 1% has an APR of 12% but an effective annual interest rate of $(1.01)^{12} - 1 = .1268$, or 12.68%. To summarize: **The effective annual rate is the rate at which invested funds will grow over the course of a year. It equals the rate of interest per period compounded for the number of periods in a year.**

EXAMPLE 5.13 ▶   The Effective Interest Rates on Bank Accounts

Back in the 1960s and 1970s federal regulation limited the (APR) interest rates banks could pay on savings accounts. Banks were hungry for depositors, and they searched for ways to increase the *effective* rate of interest that could be paid within the rules. Their solution was to keep the same APR but to calculate the interest on deposits more frequently. As interest is compounded at shorter and shorter intervals, less time passes before interest can be earned on interest. Therefore, the effective annually compounded rate of interest increases. Table 5–7 shows the calculations assuming that the maximum APR that banks could pay was 6%. (Actually, it was a bit less than this, but 6% is a nice round number to use for illustration.)

You can see from Table 5–7 how banks were able to increase the effective interest rate simply by calculating interest at more frequent intervals.

The ultimate step was to assume that interest was paid in a continuous stream rather than at fixed intervals. With 1 year's *continuous compounding*, \$1 grows to e^{APR}, where $e = 2.718$ (a figure that may be familiar to you as the base for natural logarithms). Thus if you deposited \$1 with a bank that offered a continuously compounded rate of 6%, your investment would grow by the end of the year to $(2.718)^{.06} = \$1.061837$, just a hair's breadth more than if interest were compounded daily.

Self-Test 5.12   A car loan requiring quarterly payments carries an APR of 8%. What is the effective annual rate of interest?

TABLE 5–7 These investments all have an APR of 6%, but the more frequently interest is compounded, the higher is the effective annual rate of interest.

Compounding Period	Periods per Year (m)	Per-Period Interest Rate	Growth Factor of Invested Funds	Effective Annual Rate
1 year	1	6%	1.06	6.0000%
Semiannually	2	3	$1.03^2 = 1.0609$	6.0900
Quarterly	4	1.5	$1.015^4 = 1.061364$	6.1364
Monthly	12	.5	$1.005^{12} = 1.061678$	6.1678
Weekly	52	.11538	$1.0011538^{52} = 1.061800$	6.1800
Daily	365	.01644	$1.0001644^{365} = 1.061831$	6.1831
Continuous			$e^{.06} = 1.061837$	6.1837

5.6 Inflation and the Time Value of Money

When a bank offers to pay 6% on a savings account, it promises to pay interest of $60 for every $1,000 you deposit. The bank fixes the number of dollars that it pays, but it doesn't provide any assurance of how much those dollars will buy. If the value of your investment increases by 6% while the prices of goods and services increase by 10%, you actually lose ground in terms of the goods you can buy.

Real versus Nominal Cash Flows

Prices of goods and services continually change. Textbooks may become more expensive (sorry) while computers become cheaper. An overall general rise in prices is known as **inflation.** If the inflation rate is 5% per year, then goods that cost $1.00 a year ago typically cost $1.05 this year. The increase in the general level of prices means that the purchasing power of money has eroded. If a dollar bill bought one loaf of bread last year, the same dollar this year buys only part of a loaf.

inflation
Rate at which prices as a whole are increasing.

Economists track the general level of prices using several different price indexes. The best known of these is the *consumer price index,* or *CPI.* This measures the number of dollars that it takes to buy a specified basket of goods and services that is supposed to represent the typical family's purchases.[3] Thus the percentage increase in the CPI from one year to the next measures the rate of inflation.

Table 5–8 shows the CPI for selected years. The base period for the index is 1982–1984, so the index shows the price level in each year as a percentage of the average price level during these 3 years. For example, the index in 1950 was 25.0. This means that on average $25 in 1950 would have bought the same quantity of goods and services as $100 in 1982–1984. By the end of 2007, the index had risen to 210.0. In other words, prices in 2007 were 8.40 times their level in 1950 (210.0/25.0 = 8.4).[4]

It is interesting to look at annual inflation rates over a somewhat longer period. These are shown in Figure 5–13. The peak year for inflation was 1918, when prices rose by 20%, but you can see that there have also been a few years when prices have fallen quite sharply.

As we write this in early 2008, all appears quiet on the inflation front. In the United States inflation is running at about 3.5% a year and a few countries are even experiencing falling prices, or *deflation.* This has led some economists to argue that inflation is dead; others are less sure.

EXAMPLE 5.14 ▶   The Outrageous Price of Gasoline

In early 2008 there was widespread dismay as the price of unleaded gasoline climbed to $3 a gallon. Motorists looked back longingly to 1981, when they were paying just $1.40 a gallon. But how much had the real price of gasoline changed over this period? Let's check.

In 2008 the consumer price index was about 2.3 times its level in 1981. If the price of gasoline had risen in line with inflation, it would have cost 2.3 × $1.40 = $3.22 a gallon in 2008. That was the cost of gasoline in 1981 but measured in terms of 2008 dollars rather than 1981 dollars. Thus over this time period the real price of gasoline actually *declined* nearly 7%, from $3.22 a gallon to $3.

Self-Test 5.13   Consider a telephone call to London that currently would cost $5. If the real price of telephone calls does not change in the future, how much will it cost you to make a call to London in 50 years if the inflation rate is 5% (roughly its average over the past 30 years)? What if inflation is 10%?

---

[3] Don't ask how you buy a "basket" of services.

[4] The choice by the Bureau of Labor Statistics of 1982–1984 as a base period is arbitrary. For example, the bureau could have set December 1950 as the base period. In this case the index would have been 100 in 1950 and 840.0 in 2007.

Chapter 5   The Time Value of Money   139

TABLE 5–8 **The consumer price index (CPI) shows how inflation has increased the cost of a typical family's purchases.**

	CPI	Percent Change since 1950
1950	25.0	
1960	29.8	+ 19.2%
1970	39.8	+ 59.2
1980	86.3	+ 245.2
1990	133.8	+ 435.2
2000	174.0	+ 596.0
2007	210.0	+ 740.0

FIGURE 5–13 **Annual rates of inflation in the United States from 1900 to 2007**

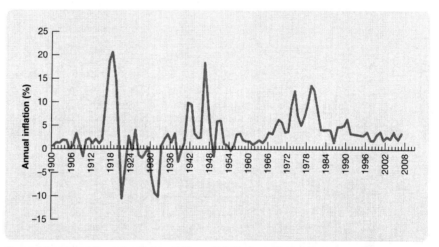

Source: Author's calculations using data from E. Dimson, P. R. Marsh, and M. Staunton, *Triumph of the Optimists: 101 Years of Global Investment Returns* (Princeton, NJ: Princeton University Press, 2007).

Economists sometimes talk about *current* or *nominal dollars* versus *constant* or *real dollars*. Current or nominal dollars refer to the actual number of dollars of the day; constant or real dollars refer to the amount of purchasing power.

Some expenditures are fixed in nominal terms and therefore *decline* in real terms. Suppose you took out a 30-year house mortgage in 1990. The monthly payment was $800. It was still $800 in 2007, even though the CPI increased by a factor of 1.57 over those years (2.10/133.8 = 1.57).

What's the monthly payment for 2007 expressed in real 1990 dollars? The answer is $800/1.57, or $509.55 per month. The real burden of paying the mortgage was much less in 2007 than in 1990.

Self-Test 5.14

If a family spent $250 a week on their typical purchases in 1950, how much would those purchases have cost in 1980? If your salary in 1980 was $30,000 a year, what would be the real value of that salary in terms of 1950 dollars?

Inflation and Interest Rates

Whenever anyone quotes an interest rate, you can be fairly sure that it is a *nominal*, not a *real*, rate. It sets the actual number of dollars you will be paid with no offset for future inflation.

nominal interest rate
Rate at which money invested grows.

If you deposit $1,000 in the bank at a **nominal interest rate** of 6%, you will have $1,060 at the end of the year. But this does not mean you are 6% better off. Suppose that the inflation rate during the year is also 6%. Then the goods that cost $1,000 last year will now cost $1,000 × 1.06 = $1,060, so you've gained nothing:

$$\text{Real future value of investment} = \frac{\$1,000 \times (1 + \text{nominal interest rate})}{(1 + \text{inflation rate})}$$

$$= \frac{\$1,000 \times 1.06}{1.06} = \$1,000$$

real interest rate
Rate at which the purchasing power of an investment increases.

In this example, the nominal rate of interest is 6%, but the **real interest rate** is zero. The real rate of interest is calculated by

$$1 + \text{real interest rate} = \frac{1 + \text{nominal interest rate}}{1 + \text{inflation rate}} \qquad (5.8)$$

In our example both the nominal interest rate and the inflation rate were 6%. So

$$1 + \text{real interest rate} = \frac{1.06}{1.06} = 1$$

$$\text{Real interest rate} = 0$$

What if the nominal interest rate is 6% but the inflation rate is only 2%? In that case the real interest rate is $1.06/1.02 - 1 = .039$, or 3.9%. Imagine that the price of a loaf of bread is $1, so that $1,000 would buy 1,000 loaves today. If you invest that $1,000 at a nominal interest rate of 6%, you will have $1,060 at the end of the year. However, if the price of loaves has risen in the meantime to $1.02, then your money will buy you $1,060/1.02 = 1,039$ loaves. The real rate of interest is 3.9%.

Self-Test 5.15

a. Suppose that you invest your funds at an interest rate of 8%. What will be your real rate of interest if the inflation rate is zero? What if it is 5%?
b. Suppose that you demand a real rate of interest of 3% on your investments. What nominal interest rate do you need to earn if the inflation rate is zero? If it is 5%?

Here is a useful approximation. The real rate approximately equals the difference between the nominal rate and the inflation rate:[5]

$$\text{Real interest rate} \approx \text{nominal interest rate} - \text{inflation rate} \qquad (5.9)$$

Our example used a nominal interest rate of 6%, an inflation rate of 2%, and a real rate of 3.9%. If we round to 4%, the approximation gives the same answer:

$$\text{Real interest rate} \approx \text{nominal interest rate} - \text{inflation rate}$$
$$\approx 6 - 2 = 4\%$$

The approximation works best when both the inflation rate and the real rate are small. When they are not small, throw the approximation away and do it right.

EXAMPLE 5.15   ▶   Real and Nominal Rates

In the United States in late 2007, long-term high-grade corporate bonds offered a yield of about 5.1%. If inflation is expected to stay at about 3%, the *real* yield is

$$1 + \text{real interest rate} = \frac{1 + \text{nominal interest rate}}{1 + \text{inflation rate}} = \frac{1.051}{1.03} = 1.0204$$

$$\text{Real interest rate} = .0204, \text{ or } 2.04\%$$

The approximation rule gives a similar value of $5.1 - 3.0 = 2.1\%$ But the approximation would not have worked in the German hyperinflation of 1922–1923, when the inflation rate was well over 100% per *month* (at one point you needed 1 million marks to mail a letter), or in Peru in 1990, when prices increased by nearly 7,500%.

---

[5] The squiggle (≈) means "approximately equal to."

Valuing Real Cash Payments

Think again about how to value future cash payments. Earlier in the chapter you learned how to value payments in current dollars by discounting at the nominal interest rate. For example, suppose that the nominal interest rate is 10%. How much do you need to invest now to produce $100 in a year's time? Easy! Calculate the present value of $100 by discounting by 10%:

$$PV = \frac{\$100}{1.10} = \$90.91$$

You get exactly the same result if you discount the *real* payment by the *real interest rate*. For example, assume that you expect inflation of 7% over the next year. The real value of that $100 is therefore only $100/1.07 = $93.46. In one year's time your $100 will buy only as much as $93.46 today. Also, with a 7% inflation rate the real rate of interest is only about 3%. We can calculate it exactly from the formula

$$1 + \text{real interest rate} = \frac{1 + \text{nominal interest rate}}{1 + \text{inflation rate}} = \frac{1.10}{1.07} = 1.028$$

$$\text{Real interest rate} = .028, \text{ or } 2.8\%$$

If we now discount the $93.46 real payment by the 2.8% real interest rate, we have a present value of $90.91, just as before:

$$PV = \frac{\$93.46}{1.028} = \$90.91$$

The two methods should always give the same answer.[6]

Remember: Current dollar cash flows must be discounted by the nominal interest rate; real cash flows must be discounted by the real interest rate.

Mixing up nominal cash flows and real discount rates (or real rates and nominal flows) is an unforgivable sin. It is surprising how many sinners one finds.

Self-Test 5.16

You are owed $5,000 by a relative who will pay it back in 1 year. The nominal interest rate is 8%, and the inflation rate is 5%. What is the present value of your relative's IOU? Show that you get the same answer (a) discounting the nominal payment at the nominal rate and (b) discounting the real payment at the real rate.

EXAMPLE 5.16 ▶   How Inflation Might Affect Bill Gates

We showed earlier (Example 5.9) that at an interest rate of 9% Bill Gates could, if he wished, turn his $59 billion wealth into a 30-year annuity of $5.7 billion per year of luxury and excitement (L&E). Unfortunately, L&E expenses inflate just like gasoline and groceries. Thus Mr. Gates would find the purchasing power of that $5.7 billion steadily declining. If he wants the same luxuries in 2038 as in 2008, he'll have to spend less in 2008 and then increase expenditures in line with inflation. How much should he spend in 2008? Assume the long-run inflation rate is 5%.

---

[6] If they don't, there must be an error in your calculations. All we have done in the second calculation is to divide both the numerator (the cash payment) and the denominator (1 plus the nominal interest rate) by the same number (1 plus the inflation rate):

$$PV = \frac{\text{payment in current dollars}}{1 + \text{nominal interest rate}}$$

$$= \frac{(\text{payment in current dollars})/(1 + \text{inflation rate})}{(1 + \text{nominal interest rate})/(1 + \text{inflation rate})}$$

$$= \frac{\text{payment in constant dollars}}{1 + \text{real interest rate}}$$

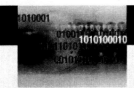

INTERNET INSIDER

Inflation

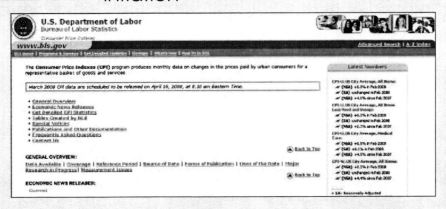

You can find data on the consumer price index (CPI) on the Bureau of Labor Statistics Web site, **www.bls.gov/cpi/home.htm**. Tables of historical data can be formatted to provide either levels of the index or changes in the index (i.e., the rate of inflation). Construct a table of annual inflation rates since 1913. When did the USA last experience a year of deflation (i.e., falling prices)? Find the inflation rate in the latest year. Now log on to **www.bloomberg.com**, and on the first page find a measure of the short-term interest rate (e.g., the 2-year rate). Use the recent level of inflation to calculate the *real* interest rate. Consider the case of Herbert Protheroe, who in 1920 was an eligible bachelor with an income of $2,000 a year. What is that equivalent to today?

Mr. Gates needs to calculate a 30-year *real* annuity. The real interest rate is a little less than 4%:

$$1 + \text{real interest rate} = \frac{1 + \text{nominal interest rate}}{1 + \text{inflation rate}}$$
$$= \frac{1.09}{1.05} = 1.038$$

so the real rate is 3.8%. The 30-year annuity factor at 3.8% is 17.720. Therefore, annual spending (in 2007 dollars) should be chosen so that

$$\$59,000,000,000 = \text{annual spending} \times 17.720$$
$$\text{annual spending} = \$3,330,000,000$$

Mr. Gates could spend that amount on L&E in one year's time and 5% more (in line with inflation) in each subsequent year. This is only a bit more than half the value we calculated when we ignored inflation. Life has many disappointments, even for tycoons.

Self-Test 5.17

You have reached age 60 with a modest fortune of $3 million and are considering early retirement. How much can you spend each year for the next 30 years? Assume that spending is stable in real terms. The nominal interest rate is 10%, and the inflation rate is 5%.

Real or Nominal?

Any present value calculation done in nominal terms can also be done in real terms, and vice versa. Most financial analysts forecast in nominal terms and discount at nominal rates. However, in some cases real cash flows are easier to deal with. In our example of Bill Gates, the *real* expenditures were fixed. In this case, it was easiest to use real quantities. On the other hand, if the cash-flow stream is fixed in nominal terms (for example, the payments on a loan), it is easiest to use all nominal quantities.

www.mhhe.com/bmm6e

SUMMARY

If you invest money at a given interest rate, what will be the future value of your investment? (*LO1*)

An investment of $1 earning an interest rate of r will increase in value each period by the factor $(1 + r)$. After t periods its value will grow to $\$(1 + r)^t$. This is the **future value** of the $1 investment with compound interest.

What is the present value of a cash flow to be received in the future? (*LO2*)

The **present value** of a future cash payment is the amount that you would need to invest today to match that future payment. To calculate present value, we divide the cash payment by $(1 + r)^t$ or, equivalently, multiply by the **discount factor** $1/(1 + r)^t$. The discount factor measures the value today of $1 received in period t.

How can we calculate present and future values of streams of cash payments? (*LO3*)

A level stream of cash payments that continues indefinitely is known as a **perpetuity;** one that continues for a limited number of years is called an **annuity.** The present value of a stream of cash flows is simply the sum of the present value of each individual cash flow. Similarly, the future value of an annuity is the sum of the future value of each individual cash flow. Shortcut formulas make the calculations for perpetuities and annuities easy.

How can we find the interest rate implied by present and future values? (*LO4*)

The present value equals the discounted value of one or more future cash flows using the appropriate interest rate. Therefore, we solve for the interest rate that makes the discounted value of the future cash flows equal to the given present value. In some cases, this may require trial and error.

How should we compare interest rates quoted over different time intervals— for example, monthly versus annual rates? (*LO5*)

Interest rates for short time periods are often quoted as annual rates by multiplying the per-period rate by the number of periods in a year. These **annual percentage rates (APRs)** do not recognize the effect of compound interest, that is, they annualize assuming simple interest. The **effective annual rate** annualizes using compound interest. It equals the rate of interest per period compounded for the number of periods in a year.

What is the difference between real and nominal cash flows and between real and nominal interest rates? (*LO6*)

A dollar is a dollar, but the amount of goods that a dollar can buy is eroded by **inflation.** If prices double, the **real value of a dollar** halves. Financial managers and economists often find it helpful to reexpress future cash flows in terms of real dollars—that is, dollars of constant purchasing power.

Be careful to distinguish the **nominal interest rate** and the **real interest rate**—that is, the rate at which the real value of the investment grows. Discount nominal cash flows (that is, cash flows measured in current dollars) at nominal interest rates. Discount real cash flows (cash flows measured in constant dollars) at real interest rates. *Never* mix and match nominal and real.

LISTING OF EQUATIONS

5.1 $\text{Future value} = \text{present value} \times (1 + r)^t$

5.2 $\text{Present value} = \dfrac{\text{future value after } t \text{ periods}}{(1 + r)^t}$

5.3 $\text{PV of perpetuity} = \dfrac{C}{r} = \dfrac{\text{cash payment}}{\text{interest rate}}$

5.4   Present value of t-year annuity $= C\left[\dfrac{1}{r} - \dfrac{1}{r(1+r)^t}\right]$

5.5   Present value of annuity due $= (1 + r) \times$ present value of annuity

5.6   Future value (FV) of annuity of \$1 a year $=$ present value of annuity of \$1 a year $\times (1 + r)^t$

$$= \left[\dfrac{1}{r} - \dfrac{1}{r(1+r)^t}\right] \times (1+r)^t = \dfrac{(1+r)^t - 1}{r}$$

5.7   Future value of annuity due $=$ future value of ordinary annuity $\times (1 + r)$

5.8 $1 +$ real interest rate $= \dfrac{1 + \text{nominal interest rate}}{1 + \text{inflation rate}}$

5.9   Real interest rate $\approx$ nominal interest rate $-$ inflation rate

QUESTIONS

QUIZ

1. **Present Values.** Compute the present value of a \$100 cash flow for the following combinations of discount rates and times: (*LO2*)
   a. $r = 8\%$, $t = 10$ years.
   b. $r = 8\%$, $t = 20$ years.
   c. $r = 4\%$, $t = 10$ years.
   d. $r = 4\%$, $t = 20$ years.

2. **Future Values.** Compute the future value of a \$100 cash flow for the same combinations of rates and times as in Quiz Question 1. (*LO1*)

3. **Future Values.** In 1880 five aboriginal trackers were each promised the equivalent of 100 Australian dollars for helping to capture the notorious outlaw Ned Kelley. In 1993 the granddaughters of two of the trackers claimed that this reward had not been paid. The Victorian prime minister stated that if this was true, the government would be happy to pay the \$100. However, the granddaughters also claimed that they were entitled to compound interest. How much was each entitled to if the interest rate was 4%? What if it was 8%? (*LO1*)

4. **Future Values.** You deposit \$1,000 in your bank account. If the bank pays 4% simple interest, how much will you accumulate in your account after 10 years? What if the bank pays compound interest? How much of your earnings will be interest on interest? (*LO1*)

5. **Present Values.** You will require \$700 in 5 years. If you earn 5% interest on your funds, how much will you need to invest today in order to reach your savings goal? (*LO2*)

6. **Calculating Interest Rate.** Find the interest rate implied by the following combinations of present and future values: (*LO4*)

Present Value	Years	Future Value
\$400	11	\$684
183	4	249
300	7	300

7. **Present Values.** Would you rather receive \$1,000 a year for 10 years or \$800 a year for 15 years if
   a. the interest rate is 5%? (*LO3*)
   b. the interest rate is 20%? (*LO3*)
   Why do your answers to (a) and (b) differ?

Chapter 5 The Time Value of Money   145

8. **Calculating Interest Rate.** Find the annual interest rate. (*LO4*)

Present Value	Future Value	Time Period
$100	$115.76	3 years
200	262.16	4
100	110.41	5

9. **Present Values.** What is the present value of the following cash-flow stream if the interest rate is 6%? (*LO3*)

Year	Cash Flow
1	$200
2	400
3	300

10. **Number of Periods.** How long will it take for $400 to grow to $1,000 at the interest rate specified? (*LO1*)
    a. 4%
    b. 8%
    c. 16%

11. **Calculating Interest Rate.** Find the effective annual interest rate for each case. (*LO5*)

APR	Compounding Period
12%	1 month
8	3
10	6

12. **Calculating Interest Rate.** Find the APR (the stated interest rate) for each case. (*LO5*)

Effective Annual Interest Rate	Compounding Period
10.00%	1 month
6.09	6
8.24	3

13. **Growth of Funds.** If you earn 6% per year on your bank account, how long will it take an account with $100 to double to $200? (*LO1*)

14. **Comparing Interest Rates.** Suppose you can borrow money at 8.6% per year (APR) compounded semiannually or 8.4% per year (APR) compounded monthly. Which is the better deal? (*LO5*)

15. **Calculating Interest Rate.** Lenny Loanshark charges "1 point" per week (that is, 1% per week) on his loans. What APR must he report to consumers? Assume exactly 52 weeks in a year. What is the effective annual rate? (*LO5*)

16. **Compound Interest.** Investments in the stock market have increased at an average compound rate of about 5% since 1900. It is now 2007.
    a. If you invested $1,000 in the stock market in 1900, how much would that investment be worth today? (*LO1*)
    b. If your investment in 1900 has grown to $1 million, how much did you invest in 1900? (*LO2*)

17. **Compound Interest.** Old Time Savings Bank pays 4% interest on its savings accounts. If you deposit $1,000 in the bank and leave it there, how much interest will you earn in the first year? The second year? The tenth year? (*LO1*)

18. **Compound Interest.** New Savings Bank pays 4% interest on its deposits. If you deposit $1,000 in the bank and leave it there, will it take more or less than 25 years for your money to double? You should be able to answer this without a calculator or interest rate tables. (*LO1*)

19. **Calculating Interest Rate.** A zero-coupon bond that will pay $1,000 in 10 years is selling today for $422.41. What interest rate does the bond offer? (*LO4*)

20. **Present Values.** A famous quarterback just signed a $15 million contract providing $3 million a year for 5 years. A less famous receiver signed a $14 million 5-year contract providing $4 million now and $2 million a year for 5 years. Who is better paid? The interest rate is 10%. (*LO3*)

PRACTICE PROBLEMS

21. **Compound Growth.** In September 2007 a pound of apples cost $1.18, while oranges cost $1.50. Ten years earlier the price of apples was only $.93 a pound and that of oranges was $.96 a pound. What was the annual compound rate of growth in the price of the two fruits? If the same rates of growth persist in the future, what will be the price of apples in 2027? What about the price of oranges? (*LO6*)

22. **Loan Payments.** If you take out an $8,000 car loan that calls for 48 monthly payments at an APR of 10%, what is your monthly payment? What is the effective annual interest rate on the loan? (*LO5*)

23. **Annuity Values.** (*LO3*)
    a. What is the present value of a 3-year annuity of $100 if the discount rate is 6%?
    b. What is the present value of the annuity in (a) if you have to wait 2 years instead of 1 year for the first payment?

24. **Annuities and Interest Rates.** Professor's Annuity Corp. offers a lifetime annuity to retiring professors. For a payment of $80,000 at age 65, the firm will pay the retiring professor $600 a month until death.
    a. If the professor's remaining life expectancy is 20 years, what is the monthly rate on this annuity? What is the effective annual rate? (*LO4*)
    b. If the monthly interest rate is .5%, what monthly annuity payment can the firm offer to the retiring professor? (*LO3*)

25. **Annuity Values.** You want to buy a new car, but you can make an initial payment of only $2,000 and can afford monthly payments of at most $400. (*LO3*)
    a. If the APR on auto loans is 12% and you finance the purchase over 48 months, what is the maximum price you can pay for the car?
    b. How much can you afford if you finance the purchase over 60 months?

26. **Calculating Interest Rate.** In a *discount interest loan,* you pay the interest payment up front. For example, if a 1-year loan is stated as $10,000 and the interest rate is 10%, the borrower "pays" $.10 \times \$10,000 = \$1,000$ immediately, thereby receiving net funds of $9,000 and repaying $10,000 in a year. (*LO5*)
    a. What is the effective interest rate on this loan?
    b. If you call the discount d (for example, $d = 10\%$ using our numbers), express the effective annual rate on the loan as a function of d.
    c. Why is the effective annual rate always greater than the stated rate d?

27. **Annuity Due.** Recall that an annuity due is like an ordinary annuity except that the first payment is made immediately instead of at the end of the first period. (*LO3*)
    a. Why is the present value of an annuity due equal to $(1 + r)$ times the present value of an ordinary annuity?
    b. Why is the future value of an annuity due equal to $(1 + r)$ times the future value of an ordinary annuity?

28. **Rate on a Loan.** If you take out an $8,000 car loan that calls for 48 monthly payments of $240 each, what is the APR of the loan? What is the effective annual interest rate on the loan? (*LO5*)

29. **Loan Payments.** Reconsider the car loan in the previous question. What if the payments are made in four annual year-end installments? What annual payment would have the same present value as the monthly payment you calculated? Use the same effective annual interest rate as in the previous question. Why is your answer not simply 12 times the monthly payment? (*LO5*)

Chapter 5 The Time Value of Money   **147**

30. **Annuity Value.** Your landscaping company can lease a truck for $8,000 a year (paid at year-end) for 6 years. It can instead buy the truck for $40,000. The truck will be valueless after 6 years. If the interest rate your company can earn on its funds is 7%, is it cheaper to buy or lease? (*LO3*)

31. **Annuity-Due Value.** Reconsider the previous problem. What if the lease payments are an annuity due, so that the first payment comes immediately? Is it cheaper to buy or lease? (*LO3*)

32. **Annuity Due.** A store offers two payment plans. Under the installment plan, you pay 25% down and 25% of the purchase price in each of the next 3 years. If you pay the entire bill immediately, you can take a 10% discount from the purchase price. Which is a better deal if you can borrow or lend funds at a 5% interest rate? (*LO3*)

33. **Annuity Value.** Reconsider the previous question. How will your answer change if the payments on the 4-year installment plan do not start for a full year? (*LO3*)

34. **Annuity and Annuity-Due Payments.** (*LO3*)
    a. If you borrow $1,000 and agree to repay the loan in five equal annual payments at an interest rate of 12%, what will your payment be?
    b. What if you make the first payment on the loan immediately instead of at the end of the first year?

35. **Valuing Delayed Annuities.** Suppose that you will receive annual payments of $10,000 for a period of 10 years. The first payment will be made 4 years from now. If the interest rate is 5%, what is the present value of this stream of payments? (*LO3*)

36. **Mortgage with Points.** Home loans typically involve "points," which are fees charged by the lender. Each point charged means that the borrower must pay 1% of the loan amount as a fee. For example, if the loan is for $100,000 and 2 points are charged, the loan repayment schedule is calculated on a $100,000 loan but the net amount the borrower receives is only $98,000. What is the effective annual interest rate charged on such a loan assuming loan repayment occurs over 360 months? Assume the interest rate is 1% per month. (*LO3*)

37. **Amortizing Loan.** You take out a 30-year $100,000 mortgage loan with an APR of 6% and monthly payments. In 12 years you decide to sell your house and pay off the mortgage. What is the principal balance on the loan? (*LO3*)

38. **Amortizing Loan.** Consider a 4-year amortizing loan. You borrow $1,000 initially, and repay it in four equal annual year-end payments. (*LO3*)
    a. If the interest rate is 8%, show that the annual payment is $301.92.
    b. Fill in the following table, which shows how much of each payment is interest versus principal repayment (that is, amortization), and the outstanding balance on the loan at each date.

Time	Loan Balance	Year-End Interest Due on Balance	Year-End Payment	Amortization of Loan
0	$1,000	$80	$301.92	$221.92
1	___	___	301.92	___
2	___	___	301.92	___
3	___	___	301.92	___
4	0	0	—	—

    c. Show that the loan balance after 1 year is equal to the year-end payment of $301.92 times the 3-year annuity factor.

39. **Annuity Value.** You've borrowed $4,248.68 and agreed to pay back the loan with monthly payments of $200. If the interest rate is 12% stated as an APR, how long will it take you to pay back the loan? What is the effective annual rate on the loan? (*LO3*)

40. **Annuity Value.** The $40 million lottery payment that you just won actually pays $2 million per year for 20 years. If the discount rate is 8% and the first payment comes in 1 year, what is the present value of the winnings? What if the first payment comes immediately? (*LO3*)

41. **Real Annuities.** A retiree wants level consumption in real terms over a 30-year retirement. If the inflation rate equals the interest rate she earns on her $450,000 of savings, how much can she spend in real terms each year over the rest of her life? (*LO6*)

42. **EAR versus APR.** You invest $1,000 at a 6% annual interest rate, stated as an APR. Interest is compounded monthly. How much will you have in 1 year? In 1.5 years? (*LO5*)

43. **Annuity Value.** You just borrowed $100,000 to buy a condo. You will repay the loan in equal monthly payments of $804.62 over the next 30 years. What monthly interest rate are you paying on the loan? What is the effective annual rate on that loan? What rate is the lender more likely to quote on the loan? (*LO3*)

44. **EAR.** If a bank pays 6% interest with continuous compounding, what is the effective annual rate? (*LO5*)

45. **Annuity Values.** You can buy a car that is advertised for $24,000 on the following terms: (a) pay $24,000 and receive a $2,000 rebate from the manufacturer; (b) pay $500 a month for 4 years for total payments of $24,000, implying zero percent financing. Which is the better deal if the interest rate is 1% per month? (*LO3*)

46. **Continuous Compounding.** How much will $100 grow to if invested at a continuously compounded interest rate of 10% for 8 years? What if it is invested for 10 years at 8%? (*LO5*)

47. **Future Values.** I now have $20,000 in the bank earning interest of .5% per month. I need $30,000 to make a down payment on a house. I can save an additional $100 per month. How long will it take me to accumulate the $30,000? (*LO3*)

48. **Perpetuities.** A local bank advertises the following deal: "Pay us $100 a year for 10 years and then we will pay you (or your beneficiaries) $100 a year *forever*." Is this a good deal if the interest rate available on other deposits is 6%? (*LO3*)

49. **Perpetuities.** A local bank will pay you $100 a year for your lifetime if you deposit $2,500 in the bank today. If you plan to live forever, what interest rate is the bank paying? (*LO4*)

50. **Perpetuities.** A property will provide $10,000 a year forever. If its value is $125,000, what must be the discount rate? (*LO4*)

51. **Applying Time Value.** You can buy property today for $3 million and sell it in 5 years for $4 million. (You earn no rental income on the property.) (*LO3*)

    a. If the interest rate is 8%, what is the present value of the sales price?
    b. Is the property investment attractive to you? Why or why not?
    c. Would your answer to (b) change if you also could earn $200,000 per year rent on the property?

52. **Applying Time Value.** A factory costs $400,000. You forecast that it will produce cash inflows of $120,000 in year 1, $180,000 in year 2, and $300,000 in year 3. The discount rate is 12%. Is the factory a good investment? Explain. (*LO3*)

53. **Applying Time Value.** You invest $1,000 today and expect to sell your investment for $2,000 in 10 years. (*LO1*)

    a. Is this a good deal if the discount rate is 6%?
    b. What if the discount rate is 10%?

54. **Calculating Interest Rate.** A store will give you a 3% discount on the cost of your purchase if you pay cash today. Otherwise, you will be billed the full price with payment due in 1 month. What is the implicit borrowing rate being paid by customers who choose to defer payment for the month? (*LO4*)

55. **Quoting Rates.** Banks sometimes quote interest rates in the form of "add-on interest." In this case, if a 1-year loan is quoted with a 20% interest rate and you borrow $1,000, then you pay back $1,200. But you make these payments in monthly installments of $100 each. What are the true APR and effective annual rate on this loan? Why should you have known that the true rates must be greater than 20% even before doing any calculations? (*LO5*)

56. **Compound Interest.** Suppose you take out a $1,000, 3-year loan using add-on interest (see previous problem) with a quoted interest rate of 20% per year. What will your monthly payments be? (Total payments are $1,000 + $1,000 × .20 × 3 = $1,600.) What are the true APR and effective annual rate on this loan? Are they the same as in the previous problem? (*LO5*)

57. **Calculating Interest Rate.** What is the effective annual rate on a 1-year loan with an interest rate quoted on a discount basis (see Practice Problem 26) of 20%? (*LO4*)

www.mhhe.com/bmm6e

58. **Effective Rates.** First National Bank pays 6.2% interest compounded semiannually. Second National Bank pays 6% interest, compounded monthly. Which bank offers the higher effective annual rate? (*LO5*)

59. **Calculating Interest Rate.** You borrow $1,000 from the bank and agree to repay the loan over the next year in 12 equal monthly payments of $90. However, the bank also charges you a loan-initiation fee of $20, which is taken out of the initial proceeds of the loan. What is the effective annual interest rate on the loan taking account of the impact of the initiation fee? (*LO4*)

60. **Retirement Savings.** You believe you will need to have saved $500,000 by the time you retire in 40 years in order to live comfortably. If the interest rate is 6% per year, how much must you save each year to meet your retirement goal? (*LO3*)

61. **Retirement Savings.** How much would you need in the previous problem if you believe that you will inherit $100,000 in 10 years? (*LO3*)

62. **Retirement Savings.** You believe you will spend $40,000 a year for 20 years once you retire in 40 years. If the interest rate is 6% per year, how much must you save each year until retirement to meet your retirement goal? (*LO3*)

63. **Retirement Planning.** A couple thinking about retirement decide to put aside $3,000 each year in a savings plan that earns 8% interest. In 5 years they will receive a gift of $10,000 that also can be invested. (*LO3*)

    a. How much money will they have accumulated 30 years from now?
    b. If their goal is to retire with $800,000 of savings, how much extra do they need to save every year?

64. **Retirement Planning.** A couple will retire in 50 years; they plan to spend about $30,000 a year in retirement, which should last about 25 years. They believe that they can earn 8% interest on retirement savings. (*LO3*)

    a. If they make annual payments into a savings plan, how much will they need to save each year? Assume the first payment comes in 1 year.
    b. How would the answer to part (a) change if the couple also realize that in 20 years, they will need to spend $60,000 on their child's college education?

65. **Real versus Nominal Dollars.** An engineer in 1950 was earning $6,000 a year. Today she earns $60,000 a year. However, on average, goods today cost 6.9 times what they did in 1950. What is her real income today in terms of constant 1950 dollars? (*LO6*)

66. **Real versus Nominal Rates.** If investors are to earn a 3% real interest rate, what nominal interest rate must they earn if the inflation rate is

    a. zero? (*LO6*)
    b. 4%? (*LO6*)
    c. 6%? (*LO6*)

67. **Real Rates.** If investors receive a 6% interest rate on their bank deposits, what real interest rate will they earn if the inflation rate over the year is

    a. zero? (*LO6*)
    b. 3%? (*LO6*)
    c. 6%? (*LO6*)

68. **Real versus Nominal Rates.** You will receive $100 from a savings bond in 3 years. The nominal interest rate is 8%.

    a. What is the present value of the proceeds from the bond? (*LO2*)
    b. If the inflation rate over the next few years is expected to be 3%, what will the real value of the $100 payoff be in terms of today's dollars? (*LO6*)
    c. What is the real interest rate? (*LO6*)
    d. Show that the real payoff from the bond [from part (b)] discounted at the real interest rate [from part (c)] gives the same present value for the bond as you found in part (a). (*LO6*)

69. **Real versus Nominal Dollars.** Your consulting firm will produce cash flows of $100,000 this year, and you expect cash flow to keep pace with any increase in the general level of prices. The interest rate currently is 6%, and you anticipate inflation of about 2%.

    a. What is the present value of your firm's cash flows for years 1 through 5? (*LO6*)
    b. How would your answer to (a) change if you anticipated no growth in cash flow? (*LO2*)

www.mhhe.com/bmm6e

CHALLENGE PROBLEMS

70. **Real versus Nominal Annuities.** Good news: You will almost certainly be a millionaire by the time you retire in 50 years. Bad news: The inflation rate over your lifetime will average about 3%. (*LO6*)

   a. What will be the real value of $1 million by the time you retire in terms of today's dollars?

   b. What real annuity (in today's dollars) will $1 million support if the real interest rate at retirement is 2% and the annuity must last for 20 years?

71. **Real versus Nominal.** If the interest rate is 6% per year, how long will it take for your money to *quadruple* in value? If the inflation rate is 4% per year, what will be the change in the purchasing power of your money over this period? (*LO1, 6*)

72. **Inflation.** In the summer of 2007, Zimbabwe's official inflation rate was about 110% per month. What was the annual inflation rate? (*LO6*)

73. **Perpetuities.** British government 4% perpetuities pay £4 interest each year forever. Another bond, 2½% perpetuities, pays £2.50 a year forever. What is the value of 4% perpetuities if the long-term interest rate is 6%? What is the value of 2½% perpetuities? (*LO3*)

74. **Real versus Nominal Annuities.** (*LO6*)

   a. You plan to retire in 30 years and want to accumulate enough by then to provide yourself with $30,000 a year for 15 years. If the interest rate is 10%, how much must you accumulate by the time you retire?

   b. How much must you save each year until retirement in order to finance your retirement consumption?

   c. Now you remember that the annual inflation rate is 4%. If a loaf of bread costs $1 today, what will it cost by the time you retire?

   d. You really want to consume $30,000 a year in *real* dollars during retirement and wish to save an equal *real* amount each year until then. What is the real amount of savings that you need to accumulate by the time you retire?

   e. Calculate the required preretirement real annual savings necessary to meet your consumption goals. Compare to your answer to (b). Why is there a difference?

   f. What is the nominal value of the amount you need to save during the first year? (Assume the savings are put aside at the end of each year.) The thirtieth year?

75. **Retirement and Inflation.** Redo part (a) of Practice Problem 64, but now assume that the inflation rate over the next 50 years will average 4%. (*LO6*)

   a. What is the real annual savings the couple must set aside?

   b. How much do they need to save in nominal terms in the first year?

   c. How much do they need to save in nominal terms in the last year?

   d. What will be their nominal expenditures in the first year of retirement? The last?

76. **Perpetuities.** What is the value of a perpetuity that pays $100 every 3 months forever? The discount rate quoted on an APR basis is 6%. (*LO5*)

77. **Changing Interest Rates.** If the interest rate this year is 8% and the interest rate next year will be 10%, what is the future value of $1 after 2 years? What is the present value of a payment of $1 to be received in 2 years? (*LO1, 2*)

78. **Changing Interest Rates.** Your wealthy uncle established a $1,000 bank account for you when you were born. For the first 8 years of your life, the interest rate earned on the account was 6%. Since then, rates have been only 4%. Now you are 21 years old and ready to cash in. How much is in your account? (*LO1*)

Please visit us at www.mhhe.com/bmm6e

79. **Real versus Nominal Cash Flows.**

   a. It is 2010, you've just graduated college, and you are contemplating your lifetime budget. You think your general living expenses will average around $50,000 a year. For the next 8 years, you will rent an apartment for $16,000 a year. After that, you will want to buy a house that should cost around $250,000. In addition, you will need to buy a new car roughly once every 10 years, costing around $30,000 each. In 25 years, you will have to put aside around

www.mhhe.com/bmm6e

$150,000 to put a child through college, and in 30 years you'll need to do the same for another child. In 50 years, you will retire, and will need to have accumulated enough savings to support roughly 20 years of retirement spending of around $35,000 a year on top of your social security benefits. The interest rate is 5% per year. What average salary will you need to earn to support this lifetime consumption plan? (*LO3*)

b. Whoops! You just realized that the inflation rate over your lifetime is likely to average about 3% per year, and you need to redo your calculations. As a rough cut, it seems reasonable to assume that all relevant prices and wages will increase at around the rate of inflation. What is your new estimate of the required salary (in today's dollars)? (*LO6*)

e**X**cel

Please visit us at www.mhhe.com/bmm6e

80. **Amortizing Loans and Inflation.** Suppose you take out a $100,000, 20-year mortgage loan to buy a condo. The interest rate on the loan is 6%, and to keep things simple, we will assume you make payments on the loan annually at the end of each year. (*LO3*)

a. What is your annual payment on the loan?

b. Construct a mortgage amortization table in Excel similar to Table 5–5 in which you compute the interest payment each year, the amortization of the loan, and the loan balance each year. (Allow the interest rate to be an input that the user of the spreadsheet can enter and change.)

c. What fraction of your initial loan payment is interest? What fraction is amortization? What about the last loan payment? What fraction of the loan has been paid off after 10 years (halfway through the life of the loan)?

d. If the inflation rate is 2%, what is the real value of the first (year-end) payment? The last?

e. Now assume the inflation rate is 8% and the real interest rate on the loan is unchanged. What must be the new nominal interest rate? Recompute the amortization table. What is the real value of the first (year-end) payment in this high-inflation scenario? The real value of the last payment?

f. Comparing your answers to (d) and (e), can you see why high inflation rates might hurt the real estate market?

STANDARD
&POOR'S

Go to Market Insight (**www.mhhe.com/edumarketinsight**).

1. Look up Abercrombie & Fitch (ANF). Calculate its 5-year growth rate in sales and net income, using annual income statement data. Next translate these results into the real growth rates. Use the "inflation calculator" provided by the Bureau of Labor Statistics at **www.bls.gov/cpi/home. htm.** You can find the actual price index data, via the Consumer Price Index link (upper left), then pull down to *Get Detailed Statistics,* and then *All Urban Consumers—Current Series.* What is the increase in the price level in the last 5 years? What is Abercrombie's growth rate of real sales and net income?

2. Look up the most recent stock prices and the prices 5 years earlier for the following firms: E-trade (ET), Sony (SNE), Georgia Pacific (GP), Toyota (TM), and Nordstrom (JWN). What was the compound growth rate of each stock price over the 5-year period? If the stock prices continue to grow at the same rates over the next 5 years, what will they be then?

SOLUTIONS TO SELF-TEST QUESTIONS

5.1   Value after 5 years would have been $24 \times (1.05)^5 = \$30.63$; after 50 years, $24 \times (1.05)^{50} = \$275.22$.

5.2   Call *g* the annual growth rate of transistors over the 36-year period between 1971 and 2007. Then

$$2,250 \times (1+g)^{36} = 592,000,000$$
$$(1+g)^{36} = 263,111$$
$$1+g = 263,111^{1/36} = 1.41$$

So the actual growth rate was $g = .41$, or 41%, not quite as high as Moore's prediction, but not so shabby either.

5.3   Multiply the $1,000 payment by the 30-year discount factor:

$$PV = \$1,000 \times \frac{1}{(1.0515)^{30}} = \$221.68$$

5.4   The $1,000 investment grew to $4,000 in 5 years.

$$
\begin{aligned}
FV &= PV \times (1+r)^t \\
4{,}000 &= 1{,}000 \times (1+r)^5 \\
(1+r)^5 &= 4.0 \\
(1+r) &= 4.0^{1/5} = 1.32 \\
r &= .32, \text{ or } 32\%
\end{aligned}
$$

5.5

Gift at Year	Present Value
1	$10,000/(1.07) = \$9,345.79$
2	$10,000/(1.07)^2 = 8,734.39$
3	$10,000/(1.07)^3 = 8,162.98$
4	$10,000/(1.07)^4 = 7,628.95$
	$33,872.11

Gift at Year	Future Value
1	$10,000 \times (1.07)^3 = \$12,250.43$
2	$10,000 \times (1.07)^2 = 11,449$
3	$10,000 \times (1.07) = 10,700$
4	$10,000 = 10,000$
	$44,399.43

5.6   The rate is 4/48 = .0833, about 8.3%.

5.7   The 4-year discount factor is $1/(1.08)^4 = .7350$. The 4-year annuity factor is $[1/.08 - 1/(.08 \times 1.08^4)] = 3.3121$. This is the difference between the present value of a $1 perpetuity starting next year and the present value of a $1 perpetuity starting in year 5:

$$PV \text{ (perpetuity starting next year)} = \frac{1}{.08} = 12.50$$

$$-PV \text{ (perpetuity starting in year 5)} = \frac{1}{.08} \times \frac{1}{(1.08)^4} = 9.1879$$

$$= PV \text{ (4-year annuity)} \qquad = 12.50 - 9.1879 = 3.3121$$

which matches the annuity factor.

5.8   You will need the present value at 7% of a 20-year annuity of $55,000:

$$\text{Present value} = \text{annual spending} \times \text{annuity factor}$$

The annuity factor is $[1/.07 - 1/(.07 \times 1.07^{20})] = 10.5940$. Thus you need $55,000 \times 10.594 = $582,670.

5.9   Fifteen years means 180 months. Then

$$
\begin{aligned}
\text{Mortgage payment} &= \frac{100{,}000}{180\text{-month annuity factor}} \\
&= \frac{100{,}000}{83.32} \\
&= \$1{,}200.17 \text{ per month}
\end{aligned}
$$

$1,000 of the payment is interest. The remainder, $200.17, is amortization.

5.10   We saw in Example 5.8 that the 25-year annuity factor for an ordinary annuity is 12.9057. Therefore, the 25-year annuity-due factor would be $12.9057 \times 1.059 = 13.6672$. The present value of the winnings would increase to $11.828 \times 13.6672 = $161.7 million. You can also put your calculator in *begin* mode; enter $n = 25$, $i = 5.9$, FV = 0, PMT = 11.828; and compute PV. Alternatively, in Excel use the formula =PV(.059,25,11.828,0,1). Starting the 25-year cash-flow stream immediately, rather than waiting 1 year, increases value by about $9 million.

5.11   If the interest rate is 5%, the future value of a 50-year, $1 annuity will be

$$\frac{(1.05)^{50} - 1}{.05} = 209.348$$

Therefore, we need to choose the cash flow, C, so that $C \times 209.348 = \$500,000$. This requires that $C = \$500,000/209.348 = \$2,388.37$. This required savings level is much higher than we found in Example 5.11. At a 5% interest rate, current savings do not grow as rapidly as when the interest rate was 10%; with less of a boost from compound interest, we need to set aside greater amounts in order to reach the target of $500,000.

5.12   The quarterly rate is 8/4 = 2%. The effective annual rate is $(1.02)^4 - 1 = .0824$, or 8.24%.

5.13   The cost in dollars will increase by 5% each year, to a value of $\$5 \times (1.05)^{50} = \$57.34$. If the inflation rate is 10%, the cost will be $\$5 \times (1.10)^{50} = \$586.95$.

5.14   The CPI in 1980 was 3.452 times its value in 1950 (see Table 5–8). Therefore, purchases that cost $250 in 1950 would have cost $\$250 \times 3.452 = \$863$ in 1980. The value of a 1980 salary of $30,000, expressed in real 1950 dollars, is $\$30,000 \times (1/3.452) = \$8,691$.

5.15   a. If there's no inflation, real and nominal rates are equal at 8%. With 5% inflation, the real rate is $(1.08/1.05) - 1 = .02857$, a bit less than 3%.
       b. If you want a 3% *real* interest rate, you need a 3% nominal rate if inflation is zero and an 8.15% rate if inflation is 5%. Note that $1.03 \times 1.05 = 1.0815$.

5.16   The present value is

$$PV = \frac{\$5,000}{1.08} = \$4,629.63$$

The real interest rate is 2.857% (see Self-Test 5.15a). The real cash payment is $5,000/(1.05) = \$4,761.90$. Thus,

$$PV = \frac{\$4,761.90}{1.02857} = \$4,629.63$$

5.17   Calculate the real annuity. The real interest rate is $1.10/1.05 - 1 = .0476$. We'll round to 4.8%. The real annuity is

$$\text{Annual payment} = \frac{\$3,000,000}{\text{30-year annuity factor}} = \frac{\$3,000,000}{\dfrac{1}{.048} - \dfrac{1}{.048(1.048)^{30}}} = \frac{\$3,000,000}{15.7292} = \$190,728$$

You can spend this much each year in dollars of constant purchasing power. The purchasing power of each dollar will decline at 5% per year, so you'll need to spend more in nominal dollars: $\$190,728 \times 1.05 = \$200,264$ in the second year, $\$190,728 \times 1.05^2 = \$210,278$ in the third year, and so on.

SOLUTIONS TO SPREADSHEET QUESTIONS

5.1

Year	Value	Increase in value
0	24	
100	52,794	52,770
200	116,134,790	116,081,996
300	255,468,811,638	255,352,676,848
382	140,632,545,501,736	140,377,076,690,098

154   **Part Two**   Value

5.2   The growth of value in the later years is very rapid because you are earning interest on interest—with a lot of compounding already behind you. For example, after 300 years, with accumulated value of $255,468,811,638, just one additional year's interest is .08 × $255,468,811,638 = $2,043,750,493.

5.3

Interest rate	Present value
5%	$15,438
8%	15,133
11%	14,850

5.4 $14,916. While the total (undiscounted) payments remain $16,000, part of the first payment in this example has been pushed to the next two years. This reduces present value.

MINICASE

Old Alfred Road, who is well-known to drivers on the Maine Turnpike, has reached his seventieth birthday and is ready to retire. Mr. Road has no formal training in finance but has saved his money and invested carefully.

Mr. Road owns his home—the mortgage is paid off—and does not want to move. He is a widower, and he wants to bequeath the house and any remaining assets to his daughter.

He has accumulated savings of $180,000, conservatively invested. The investments are yielding 9% interest. Mr. Road also has $12,000 in a savings account at 5% interest. He wants to keep the savings account intact for unexpected expenses or emergencies.

Mr. Road's basic living expenses now average about $1,500 per month, and he plans to spend $500 per month on travel and hobbies. To maintain this planned standard of living, he will have to rely on his investment portfolio. The interest from the portfolio is $16,200 per year (9% of $180,000), or $1,350 per month.

Mr. Road will also receive $750 per month in Social Security payments for the rest of his life. These payments are indexed for inflation. That is, they will be automatically increased in proportion to changes in the consumer price index.

Mr. Road's main concern is with inflation. The inflation rate has been below 3% recently, but a 3% rate is unusually low by historical standards. His Social Security payments will increase with inflation, but the interest on his investment portfolio will not.

What advice do you have for Mr. Road? Can he safely spend all the interest from his investment portfolio? How much could he withdraw at year-end from that portfolio if he wants to keep its real value intact?

Suppose Mr. Road will live for 20 more years and is willing to use up all of his investment portfolio over that period. He also wants his monthly spending to increase along with inflation over that period. In other words, he wants his monthly spending to stay the same in real terms. How much can he afford to spend per month?

Assume that the investment portfolio continues to yield a 9% rate of return and that the inflation rate will be 4%.

CHAPTER **8**

Net Present Value and Other Investment Criteria

LEARNING OBJECTIVES

After studying this chapter, you should be able to:

1. Calculate the net present value of an investment.

2. Calculate the internal rate of return of a project and know what to look out for when using the internal rate of return rule.

3. Explain why the payback rule *doesn't* always make shareholders better off.

4. Use the net present value rule to analyze three common problems that involve competing projects: (a) when to postpone an investment expenditure, (b) how to choose between projects with unequal lives, and (c) when to replace equipment.

5. Calculate the profitability index and use it to choose between projects when funds are limited.

Related Web sites for this chapter can be found at www.mhhe.com/bmm6e.

Calculating NPV can be hard work. But you've got to sweat the details and learn to do it right.

© McGraw-Hill Companies/Jill Braaten, photographer

The investment decision, also known as *capital budgeting,* is central to the success of the company. We have already seen that capital investments can sometimes absorb substantial amounts of cash; they also have very long-term consequences. The assets you buy today may determine the business you are in many years hence.

For some investment projects "substantial" is an understatement. Consider the following examples:

- By 2007, Verizon had already spent $18 billion rolling out its fiber-optic network, FiOS.
- The cost of bringing one new prescription drug to market is estimated to be $800 million.
- ExxonMobil is developing the Sakhalin Island oil and gas field in eastern Russia with a projected outlay of $20 billion.
- Toyota's research and development costs for its hybrid gas-electric engine have been about $6 billion.

- Production and marketing costs for the movie *Spiderman 3* were almost $500 million.
- The development costs of the Airbus A380 jumbo jet are estimated at around $15 billion.

Notice that many of these big capital projects require heavy investment in intangible assets. For example, almost all the cost of drug development is for research and testing. So is much of the cost of developing the hybrid auto. Any expenditure made in the hope of generating more cash later can be called a *capital investment project,* regardless of whether the cash outlay goes to tangible or intangible assets.

A company's shareholders prefer to be rich rather than poor. Therefore, they want the firm to invest in every project that is worth more than it costs. The difference between a project's value and its cost is termed the *net present value.* Companies can best help their shareholders by investing in projects with a *positive* net present value.

We start this chapter by showing how to calculate the net present value of a simple investment project. We also examine other criteria that companies sometimes consider when evaluating investments. One of these, the payback rule, is little better than a rule of thumb. Although there is a place for rules of thumb in this world, an engineer needs something more accurate when designing a 100-story building, and a financial manager needs more than a rule of thumb when making a substantial capital investment decision.

Instead of calculating a project's net present value, companies sometimes compare the expected rate of return from investing in a project with the return that shareholders could earn on equivalent-risk investments in the capital market. Companies accept only those projects that provide a higher return than shareholders could earn for themselves. This rate of return rule generally gives the same answers as the net present value rule, but, as we shall see, it has some pitfalls.

Next we turn to more complex issues such as project interactions. These occur when a company is obliged to choose between two or more competing proposals; if it accepts one proposal, it cannot take the other. For example, a company may need to choose between buying an expensive, durable machine or buying a cheap and short-lived one. We will show how the net present value criterion can be used to make such choices.

Sometimes the firm may be forced to make choices because it does not have enough money to take on every project that it would like. We will explain how to maximize shareholder wealth when capital is rationed. It turns out that the solution is to pick the projects that have the highest net present value per dollar invested. This measure is known as the *profitability index*.

8.1 Net Present Value

In Chapter 5 you learned how to discount future cash payments to find their present value. We now apply these ideas to evaluate a simple investment proposal.

Suppose that you are in the real estate business. You are considering construction of an office block. The land would cost $50,000, and construction would cost a further $300,000. You foresee a shortage of office space and predict that a year from now you will be able to sell the building for $400,000. Thus you would be investing $350,000 now in the expectation of realizing $400,000 at the end of the year. Therefore, projected cash flows may be summarized in a simple time line as follows:

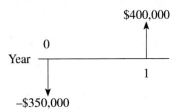

You should go ahead if the present value of the $400,000 payoff is greater than the investment of $350,000.

Assume for the moment that the $400,000 payoff is a sure thing. The office building is not the only way to obtain $400,000 a year from now. You could invest in a 1-year U.S. Treasury note. Suppose the Treasury note offers interest of 7%. How much would you have to invest in it in order to receive $400,000 at the end of the year? That's easy: You would have to invest

$$\$400,000 \times \frac{1}{1.07} = \$400,000 \times .9346 = \$373,832$$

Let's assume that as soon as you have purchased the land and laid out the money for construction, you decide to cash in on your project. How much could you sell it for? Since the property will be worth $400,000 in a year, investors would be willing to pay at most $373,832 for it now. That's all it would cost them to get the same $400,000 payoff by investing in a government security. Of course, you could always sell your property for less, but why sell for less than the market will bear?

Therefore, at an interest rate of 7%, the present value of the $400,000 payoff from the office building is $373,832.

The $373,832 present value is the only price that satisfies both buyer and seller. In general, the present value is the only feasible price, and the present value of the property is also its *market price* or *market value*.

opportunity cost of capital
Expected rate of return given up by investing in a project.

To calculate present value, we discounted the expected future payoff by the rate of return offered by comparable investment alternatives. The discount rate—7% in our example—is often known as the **opportunity cost of capital.** It is called the *opportunity cost* because it is the return that is being given up by investing in the project.

The building is worth $373,832, but this does not mean that you are $373,832 better off. You committed $350,000, and therefore your **net present value (NPV)** is $23,832. Net present value is found by subtracting the required initial investment from the present value of the project cash flows:

net present value (NPV)
Present value of cash flows minus investment.

$$\text{NPV} = \text{PV} - \text{required investment} \qquad (8.1)$$
$$= \$373,832 - \$350,000 = \$23,832$$

In other words, your office development is worth more than it costs—it makes a *net* contribution to value. **The net present value *rule* states that managers increase shareholders' wealth by accepting all projects that are worth more than they cost. Therefore, they should accept all projects with a positive net present value.**

A Comment on Risk and Present Value

In our discussion of the office development we assumed we knew the value of the completed project. Of course, you will never be *certain* about the future values of office buildings. The $400,000 represents the best *forecast,* but it is not a sure thing.

Therefore, our initial conclusion about how much investors would pay for the building is premature. Since they could achieve $400,000 risklessly by investing in $373,832 worth of U.S. Treasury notes, they would not buy your building for that amount. You would have to cut your asking price to attract investors' interest.

Here we can invoke a basic financial principle: **A risky dollar is worth less than a safe one.**

Most investors avoid risk when they can do so without sacrificing return. However, the concepts of present value and the opportunity cost of capital still apply to risky investments. It is still proper to discount the payoff by the rate of return offered by a comparable investment. But we have to think of *expected* payoffs and the *expected* rates of return on other investments.

Not all investments are equally risky. The office development is riskier than a Treasury note but is probably less risky than investing in a start-up biotech company. Suppose you believe the office development is as risky as an investment in the stock market and that you forecast a 12% rate of return for stock market investments. Then 12% would be the appropriate opportunity cost of capital. That is what you are giving up by not investing in comparable securities. You can now recompute NPV:

$$\text{PV} = \$400,000 \times \frac{1}{1.12} = \$400,000 \times .8929 = \$357,143$$
$$\text{NPV} = \text{PV} - \$350,000 = \$7,143$$

If other investors agree with your forecast of a $400,000 payoff and with your assessment of a 12% opportunity cost of capital, then the property ought to be worth $357,143 once construction is under way. If you tried to sell for more than that, there would be no takers, because the property would then offer a lower expected rate of return than the 12% available in the stock market. The office building still makes a net contribution to value, but it is much smaller than our earlier calculations indicated.

Self-Test 8.1

What is the office development's NPV if construction costs increase to $355,000? Assume the opportunity cost of capital is 12%. Is the development still a worthwhile investment? How high can development costs be before the project is no longer attractive? Now suppose that the opportunity cost of capital is 20% with construction costs of $355,000. Why is the office development no longer an attractive investment?

Valuing Long-Lived Projects

The net present value rule works for projects of any length. For example, suppose that you have identified a possible tenant who would be prepared to rent your office block for 3 years at a fixed annual rent of $16,000. You forecast that after you have collected the third year's rent the building could be sold for $450,000. The projected cash flows (denoted C) in each year are now

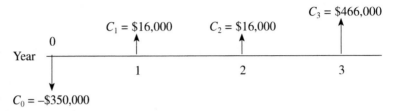

For simplicity, we will again assume that these cash flows are certain and that the opportunity cost of capital is $r = 7\%$.

Figure 8–1 shows a time line of the cash inflows and their present values. To find the present value of the project, we discount these cash inflows at the 7% opportunity cost of capital:

$$PV = \frac{C_1}{1+r} + \frac{C_2}{(1+r)^2} + \frac{C_3}{(1+r)^3}$$

$$= \frac{\$16,000}{1.07} + \frac{\$16,000}{(1.07)^2} + \frac{\$466,000}{(1.07)^3} = \$409,323$$

The net present value of the revised project is NPV = $409,323 − $350,000 = $59,323. Constructing the office block and renting it for 3 years makes a greater addition to your wealth than selling the office block at the end of the first year.

Of course, rather than subtracting the initial investment from the project's present value, you could calculate NPV directly, as in the following equation, where C_0 denotes the initial cash outflow required to build the office block. (Notice that in this example C_0 is negative, reflecting the fact that it is a cash outflow.)

$$NPV = C_0 + \frac{C_1}{1+r} + \frac{C_2}{(1+r)^2} + \frac{C_3}{(1+r)^3}$$

$$= -\$350,000 + \frac{\$16,000}{1.07} + \frac{\$16,000}{(1.07)^2} + \frac{\$466,000}{(1.07)^3} = \$59,323$$

FIGURE 8–1 Cash flows and their present values for the office block project. Final cash flow of $466,000 is the sum of the rental income in year 3 plus the forecast sales price for the building.

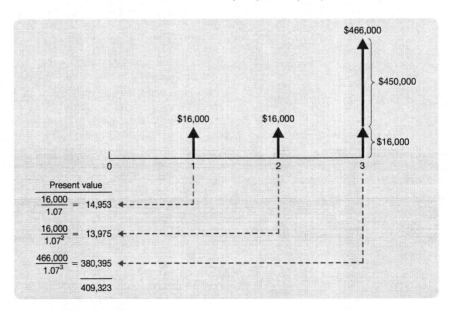

Let's check that the owners of this project really are better off. Suppose you put up $350,000 of your own money, commit to build the office building, and sign a lease that will bring $16,000 a year for 3 years. Now you can cash in by selling the project to someone else.

Suppose you sell 1,000 shares in the project. Each share represents a claim to 1/1,000 of the future cash flows. Since the cash flows are sure things, and the interest rate offered by other sure things is 7%, investors will value the shares for

$$\text{Price per share} = \frac{\$16}{1.07} + \frac{\$16}{(1.07)^2} + \frac{\$466}{(1.07)^3} = \$409.30$$

Thus you can sell the project to outside investors for $1,000 \times \$409.30 = \$409,300$, which, save for rounding, is exactly the present value we calculated earlier. Your net gain is

$$\text{Net gain} = \$409,300 - \$350,000 = \$59,300$$

which is the project's NPV. This equivalence should be no surprise, since the present value calculation is *designed* to calculate the value of future cash flows to investors in the capital markets.

Notice that in principle there could be a different opportunity cost of capital for each period's cash flow. In that case we would discount C_1 by r_1, the discount rate for 1-year cash flows; C_2 would be discounted by r_2; and so on. Here we assume that the cost of capital is the same regardless of the date of the cash flow. We do this for one reason only—simplicity. But we are in good company: With only rare exceptions firms decide on an appropriate discount rate and then use it to discount all cash flows from the project.

EXAMPLE 8.1 ▶ Valuing a New Computer System

Obsolete Technologies is considering the purchase of a new computer system to help handle its warehouse inventories. The system costs $50,000, is expected to last 4 years, and should reduce the cost of managing inventories by $22,000 a year. The opportunity cost of capital is 10%. Should Obsolete go ahead?

Don't be put off by the fact that the computer system does not generate any sales. If the expected cost savings are realized, the company's cash flows will be $22,000 a year higher as a result of buying the computer. Thus we can say that the computer increases cash flows by $22,000 a year for each of 4 years. To calculate present value, you can discount each of these cash flows by 10%. However, it is smarter to recognize that the cash flows are level, and therefore you can use the annuity formula to calculate the present value:

$$\text{PV} = \text{cash flow} \times \text{annuity factor} = \$22,000 \times \left[\frac{1}{.10} - \frac{1}{.10(1.10)^4}\right]$$

$$= \$22,000 \times 3.1699 = \$69,738$$

The net present value is

$$\text{NPV} = -\$50,000 + \$69,738 = \$19,738$$

The project has a positive NPV of $19,738. Undertaking it would increase the value of the firm by that amount.

The first two steps in calculating NPVs—forecasting the cash flows and estimating the opportunity cost of capital—are tricky, and we will have a lot more to say about them in later chapters. But once you have assembled the data, the calculation of present value and net present value should be routine. Here is another example.

EXAMPLE 8.2 ▶ Calculating Eurotunnel's NPV

One of the world's largest commercial investment projects was construction of the Channel Tunnel by the Anglo-French company Eurotunnel. Here is a chance to put yourself in the shoes of Eurotunnel's financial manager and find out whether the project looked like it would be a good deal for shareholders. The figures in column C of Table 8–1 are based on the forecasts of construction costs and revenues that the company provided to investors in 1986.

The Channel Tunnel project was not a safe investment. Indeed, the prospectus to the Channel Tunnel share issue cautioned investors that the project "involves significant risk and should be regarded at this stage as speculative. If for any reason the Project is abandoned or Eurotunnel is unable to raise the necessary finance, it is likely that equity investors will lose some or all of their money."

To be induced to invest in the project, investors needed a higher prospective rate of return than they could get on safe government bonds. Suppose investors expected a return of 13% from investments in the capital market that had a degree of risk similar to that of the Channel Tunnel. That was what investors were giving up when they provided the capital for the tunnel. To find the project's NPV we therefore discount the cash flows in Table 8–1 at 13%.

TABLE 8–1 Forecast cash flows and present values in 1986 for the Channel Tunnel project. The investment at the time appeared to have a positive NPV of £249.8 million.

	A	B	C	D	E
1			Cash Flow		
2	Year	Time	(£ million)	PV at 13%	Formula in Column D
3	1986	0	−457	−457.0	=C3/1.13^B3
4	1987	1	−476	−421.2	=C4/1.13^B4
5	1988	2	−497	−389.2	=C5/1.13^B5
6	1989	3	−522	−361.8	=C6/1.13^B6
7	1990	4	−551	−337.9	=C7/1.13^B7
8	1991	5	−584	−317.0	=C8/1.13^B8
9	1992	6	−619	−297.3	=C9/1.13^B9
10	1993	7	211	89.7	=C10/1.13^B10
11	1994	8	489	183.9	=C11/1.13^B11
12	1995	9	455	151.5	=C12/1.13^B12
13	1996	10	502	147.9	=C13/1.13^B13
14	1997	11	530	138.2	=C14/1.13^B14
15	1998	12	544	125.5	=C15/1.13^B15
16	1999	13	636	129.8	=C16/1.13^B16
17	2000	14	594	107.3	=C17/1.13^B17
18	2001	15	689	110.2	=C18/1.13^B18
19	2002	16	729	103.2	=C19/1.13^B19
20	2003	17	796	99.7	=C20/1.13^B20
21	2004	18	859	95.2	=C21/1.13^B21
22	2005	19	923	90.5	=C22/1.13^B22
23	2006	20	983	85.3	=C23/1.13^B23
24	2007	21	1,050	80.6	=C24/1.13^B24
25	2008	22	1,113	75.6	=C25/1.13^B25
26	2009	23	1,177	70.8	=C26/1.13^B26
27	2010	24	17,781	946.4	=C27/1.13^B27
28					
29	Sum:			249.8	=SUM(D3:D27)
30					
31	Instead, use Excel's NPV function			249.8	=NPV(0.13,C4:C27) + C3

eXcel

Note: Cash flow for 2010 includes the value in 2010 of forecast cash flows in all subsequent years. Some of these figures involve guesswork because the prospectus reported accumulated construction costs including interest expenses.
Source: Eurotunnel Equity II Prospectus, October 1986. Reprinted with permission.

SPREADSHEET SOLUTIONS

Present Values

Computer spreadsheets are tailor-made to calculate the present value of a series of cash flows. For example, the spreadsheet in Table 8–1, available at www.mhhe.com/bmm6e, sets up the Eurotunnel problem as an Excel spreadsheet. Cells D3 to D27 calculate the present value of each year's cash flows by discounting at 13% for the length of time given in column B. Cell D29 shows the sum of these separate present values.

Excel also provides a built-in function to calculate net present values. The formula is =NPV (discount rate, list of cash flows). So, instead of computing the present value of each cash flow separately and then summing, we could have used the NPV function in cell D31. The first entry in the function is the discount rate expressed as a decimal, in this case .13. That is followed by a list of the cash flows that appear in column C.

Why is the first entry in the cash-flow list cell C4 rather than C3, which contains the immediate cash flow, −457?

It turns out that Excel always assumes the first cash flow comes after one period, the next after two periods, and so on. If the first cash flow actually comes immediately, as in our example, we do not want it discounted, nor do we want the other cash flows discounted for an extra period. Therefore, we don't include the immediate cash flow in the NPV function, instead adding it undiscounted to the present value of the other cash flows (see cells D31 and E31).

Spreadsheet Questions

8.1 Try calculating Eurotunnel's NPV using the function =NPV(0.13,C3:C27). What do you find?

8.2 The value for NPV in Table 8–1 is exactly 1.13 times as large as the answer you should find for the previous question. Why does this make sense?

Please visit us at www.mhhe.com/bmm6e

Since the tunnel was expected to take about 7 years to build, there are 7 years of negative cash flows in Table 8–1. To calculate NPV, you just discount all the cash flows, positive and negative, at 13% and sum the results. Call 1986 "year 0," call 1987 "year 1," and so on. Then

$$\text{NPV} = C_0 + \frac{C_1}{1+r} + \frac{C_2}{(1+r)^2} + \cdots$$

$$= -£457 + \frac{-£476}{1.13} + \frac{-£497}{(1.13)^2} + \cdots + \frac{£17,781}{(1.13)^{24}} = £249.8 \text{ million}$$

We present the calculations in column D. (The nearby box provides additional discussion of how to calculate present values by using spreadsheets.) The net present value of the forecast cash flows is £249.8 million, making the tunnel a worthwhile project, though not by a wide margin, considering the planned investment of nearly £4 billion.

Of course, NPV calculations are only as good as the underlying cash-flow forecasts. The well-known Pentagon Law of Large Projects states that anything big takes longer and costs more than you're originally led to believe. As the law predicted, the tunnel proved much more expensive to build than anticipated in 1986, and the opening was delayed by more than a year. Revenues also have been below forecast, and Eurotunnel has not even generated enough profits to pay the interest on its debt. Thus, with hindsight, the tunnel was a costly negative-NPV venture. By 2007, Eurotunnel was operating under French bankruptcy law and had to be restructured. Eventually, the firm was reorganized into a new company called Groupe Eurotunnel.

Using the NPV Rule to Choose among Projects

The simple projects we have considered so far involve take-it-or-leave-it decisions. But almost all real-world decisions are either-or choices. You could build an apartment block, rather than the office block, on that vacant lot. You could build a 7-story office building or a 10-story one. You could heat it with oil or with natural gas. You could build it today or wait a year to start construction. Such choices are said to be **mutually exclusive.**

mutually exclusive projects
Two or more projects
that cannot be pursued
simultaneously.

When you need to choose among mutually exclusive projects, the decision rule is simple: Calculate the NPV of each alternative, and choose the highest positive-NPV project.[1]

EXAMPLE 8.3 ▶ Choosing between Two Projects

It has been several years since your office last upgraded its office networking software. Two competing systems have been proposed. Both have an expected useful life of 3 years, at which point it will be time for another upgrade. One proposal is for an expensive, cutting-edge system, which will cost $800,000 and increase firm cash flows by $350,000 a year through increased productivity. The other proposal is for a cheaper, somewhat slower system. This system would cost only $700,000 but would increase cash flows by only $300,000 a year. If the cost of capital is 7%, which is the better option?

The following table summarizes the cash flows and the NPVs of the two proposals:

System	\multicolumn{4}{c}{Cash Flows (thousands of dollars)}	NPV at 7%
	C_0	C_1	C_2	C_3	
Faster	−800	+350	+350	+350	+118.5
Slower	−700	+300	+300	+300	+ 87.3

In both cases, the software systems are worth more than they cost, but the faster system would make the greater contribution to value and therefore should be your preferred choice.

8.2 Other Investment Criteria

A project with a positive net present value is worth more than it costs. So whenever a firm invests in such a project, it is making its shareholders better off.

These days almost every large corporation calculates the NPV of proposed investments, but management may also consider other criteria when making investment decisions. Most commonly, they may look at the project's payback and its internal rate of return. As we describe these measures, you will see that payback is no better than a very rough guide to an investment's worth. On the other hand, when properly used, the internal rate of return will lead to the same decisions as net present value.

Payback

We suspect that you have often heard conversations that go something like this: "A washing machine costs about $800. But we are currently spending $6 a week, or around $300 a year, at the laundromat. So the washing machine should pay for itself in less than 3 years." You have just encountered the payback rule.

payback period
Time until cash flows
recover the initial
investment in the project.

A project's **payback period** is the length of time before you recover your initial investment. For the washing machine the payback period was just under 3 years. **The payback rule states that a project should be accepted if its payback period is less than a specified cutoff period.** For example, if the cutoff period is 4 years, the washing machine makes the grade; if the cutoff is 2 years, it doesn't.

As a rough rule of thumb the payback rule may be adequate, but it is easy to see that it can lead to nonsensical decisions. For example, compare projects A and B. Project A has a 2-year payback and a large positive NPV. Project B also has a 2-year payback but a negative NPV. Project A is clearly superior, but the payback rule ranks both equally. This is because payback does not consider any cash flows that arrive after the payback period. A firm that uses the payback criterion with a cutoff of 2 or more years would accept both A and B despite the fact that only A would increase shareholder wealth.

---

[1] Of course, we need to compare the alternatives on a fair basis. For example, if one heating system lasts 10 years and another 15, their different lives must also be considered. More on this later in the chapter.

Project	Cash Flows (dollars)				Payback Period, Years	NPV at 10%
	C_0	C_1	C_2	C_3		
A	−2,000	+1,000	+1,000	+10,000	2	$7,249
B	−2,000	+1,000	+1,000	0	2	−264
C	−2,000	0	+2,000	0	2	−347

A second problem with payback is that it gives equal weight to all cash flows arriving *before* the cutoff period, despite the fact that the more distant flows are less valuable. For example, look at project C. It also has a payback period of 2 years, but it has an even lower NPV than project B. Why? Because its cash flows arrive later within the payback period.

To use the payback rule, a firm has to decide on an appropriate cutoff period. If it uses the same cutoff regardless of project life, it will tend to accept too many short-lived projects and reject too many long-lived ones. The payback rule will bias the firm against accepting long-term projects because cash flows that arrive after the payback period are ignored.

Earlier in the chapter we evaluated the Channel Tunnel project. Large construction projects of this kind inevitably have long payback periods. The cash flows that we presented in Table 8–1 implied a payback period of just over 14 years. But most firms that employ the payback rule use a much shorter cutoff period than this. If they used the payback rule mechanically, long-lived projects like the Channel Tunnel wouldn't have a chance.

The primary attraction of the payback criterion is its simplicity. But remember that the hard part of project evaluation is forecasting the cash flows, not doing the arithmetic. Today's spreadsheets make discounting a trivial exercise. Therefore, the payback rule saves you only the easy part of the analysis.

We have had little good to say about payback. So why do many companies continue to use it? Senior managers don't truly believe that all cash flows after the payback period are irrelevant. It seems more likely (and more charitable to those managers) that payback survives because the deficiencies are relatively unimportant or because there are some offsetting benefits. Thus managers may point out that payback is the simplest way to *communicate* an idea of project desirability. Investment decisions require discussion and negotiation between people from all parts of the firm, and it is important to have a measure that everyone can understand. Perhaps, also, managers favor quick payback projects even when the projects have lower NPVs because they believe that quicker profits mean quicker promotion. That takes us back to Chapter 1, where we discussed the need to align the objectives of managers with those of the shareholders.

In practice payback is most commonly used when the capital investment is small or when the merits of the project are so obvious that more formal analysis is unnecessary. For example, if a project is expected to produce constant cash flows for 10 years and the payback period is only 2 years, the project in all likelihood has a positive NPV.

Discounted Payback   Sometimes managers calculate the *discounted-payback period*. This is the number of periods before the present value of prospective cash flows equals or exceeds the initial investment. The discounted-payback measure asks, How long must the project last in order to offer a positive net present value? If the discounted payback meets the company's cutoff period, the project is accepted; if not, it is rejected. The discounted-payback rule has the advantage that it will never accept a negative-NPV project. On the other hand, it still takes no account of cash flows after the cutoff date, so a company that uses the discounted-payback rule risks rejecting good long-term projects.

Rather than automatically rejecting any project with a long discounted-payback period, many managers simply use the measure as a warning signal. These managers don't unthinkingly reject a project with a long discounted-payback period. Instead, they check that the proposer is not unduly optimistic about the project's ability to generate cash flows into the distant future. They satisfy themselves that the equipment truly has a long life or that competitors will not enter the market and eat into the project's cash flows.

Self-Test 8.2

A project costs $5,000 and will generate annual cash flows of $660 for 20 years. What is the payback period? If the interest rate is 6%, what is the discounted payback period? What is the project NPV? Should the project be accepted?

Internal Rate of Return

Instead of calculating a project's net present value, companies often prefer to ask whether the project's return is higher or lower than the opportunity cost of capital. For example, think back to the original proposal to build the office block. You planned to invest $350,000 to get back a cash flow of $C_1 = $400,000 in 1 year. Therefore, you forecast a profit on the venture of $400,000 − $350,000 = $50,000. In a one-period project like this one, it is easy to calculate the rate of return. Simply compute end-of-year profit per dollar invested in the project:

$$\text{Rate of return} = \frac{\text{profit}}{\text{investment}} = \frac{C_1 - \text{investment}}{\text{investment}} = \frac{\$400,000 - \$350,000}{\$350,000}$$

$$= .1429, \text{ or about } 14.3\%$$

The alternative of investing in a U.S. Treasury note would provide a return of only 7%. Thus the return on your office building is higher than the opportunity cost of capital.[2]

This suggests two rules for deciding whether to go ahead with an investment project:

1. *The NPV rule.* Invest in any project that has a positive NPV when its cash flows are discounted at the opportunity cost of capital.
2. *The rate of return rule.* Invest in any project offering a rate of return that is higher than the opportunity cost of capital.

Both rules set the same cutoff point. An investment that is on the knife edge with an NPV of zero will also have a rate of return that is just equal to the cost of capital.

Suppose that the rate of interest on Treasury notes is not 7% but 14.3%. Since your office project also offers a return of 14.3%, the rate of return rule suggests that there is now nothing to choose between taking the project and leaving your money in Treasury notes.

The NPV rule also tells you that if the interest rate is 14.3%, the project is evenly balanced with an NPV of zero:

$$\text{NPV} = C_0 + \frac{C_1}{1 + r} = -\$350,000 + \frac{\$400,000}{1.143} = 0$$

The project would make you neither richer nor poorer; it is worth what it costs. Thus the NPV rule and the rate of return rule both give the same decision on accepting the project.

A Closer Look at the Rate of Return Rule

We know that if the office project's cash flows are discounted at a rate of 7%, the project has a net present value of $23,832. If they are discounted at a rate of 14.3%, it has an NPV of zero. In Figure 8–2 the project's NPV for a variety of discount rates is plotted. This is often called the *NPV profile* of the project. Notice two important things about Figure 8–2:

1. The project rate of return (in our example, 14.3%) is also the discount rate that would give the project a zero NPV. This gives us a useful definition: **The rate of return is the discount rate at which NPV equals zero.**[3]
2. If the opportunity cost of capital is less than the project rate of return, then the NPV of your project is positive. If the cost of capital is greater than the project rate of return, then NPV is negative. Thus the rate of return rule and the NPV rule are equivalent.

---

[2] Recall that we are assuming the profit on the office building is risk-free. Therefore, the opportunity cost of capital is the rate of return on other risk-free investments.

[3] Check it for yourself. If NPV = $C_0 + C_1/(1 + r) = 0$, then rate of return $= \dfrac{C_1 + C_0}{-C_0} = r$.

FIGURE 8–2 The value of the office project is lower when the discount rate is higher. The project has positive NPV if the discount rate is less than 14.3%.

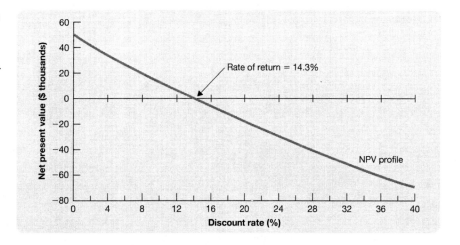

Calculating the Rate of Return for Long-Lived Projects

There is no ambiguity in calculating the rate of return for an investment that generates a single payoff after one period. Remember that C_0, the time-zero cash flow corresponding to the initial investment, is negative.[4] Thus

$$\text{Rate of return} = \frac{\text{profit}}{\text{investment}} = \frac{C_1 - \text{investment}}{\text{investment}} = \frac{C_1 + C_0}{-C_0}$$

But how do we calculate return when the project produces cash flows in several periods? Just think back to the definition that we introduced above—*the project rate of return is also the discount rate that gives the project a zero NPV.* We can use this idea to find the return on a project that has many cash flows. **The discount rate that gives the project a zero NPV is known as the project's internal rate of return, or IRR.** It is also termed the *discounted cash-flow (DCF) rate of return.*

internal rate of return (IRR) Discount rate at which project NPV = 0.

Let's calculate the IRR for the revised office project. If you rent out the office block for 3 years, the cash flows are as follows:

Year:	0	1	2	3
Cash flows	−$350,000	+$16,000	+$16,000	+$466,000

The IRR is the discount rate at which these cash flows would have zero NPV. Thus,

$$\text{NPV} = -\$350,000 + \frac{\$16,000}{1 + \text{IRR}} + \frac{\$16,000}{(1 + \text{IRR})^2} + \frac{\$466,000}{(1 + \text{IRR})^3} = 0$$

There is no simple general method for solving this equation. You have to rely on a little trial and error. Let us arbitrarily try a zero discount rate. This gives an NPV of $148,000:

$$\text{NPV} = -\$350,000 + \frac{\$16,000}{1.0} + \frac{\$16,000}{(1.0)^2} + \frac{\$466,000}{(1.0)^3} = \$148,000$$

With a zero discount rate the NPV is positive. So the IRR must be greater than zero.

The next step might be to try a discount rate of 50%. In this case NPV is −$194,000:

$$\text{NPV} = -\$350,000 + \frac{\$16,000}{1.50} + \frac{\$16,000}{(1.50)^2} + \frac{\$466,000}{(1.50)^3} = -\$194,000$$

---

[4] The *investment* in the project is therefore $-C_0 = -(-\$350,000)$, or $350,000.

FIGURE 8–3 The internal rate of return is the discount rate for which NPV equals zero.

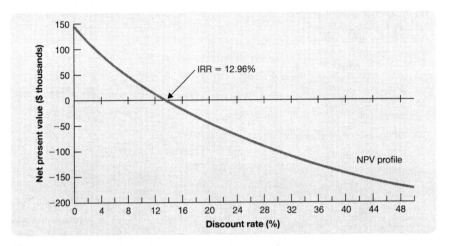

NPV is now negative. So the IRR must lie somewhere between zero and 50%. In Figure 8–3 we have plotted the net present values for a range of discount rates. You can see that a discount rate of 12.96% gives an NPV of zero. Therefore, the IRR is 12.96%. You can always find the IRR by plotting an NPV profile, as in Figure 8–3, but it is quicker and more accurate to let a spreadsheet or specially programmed financial calculator do the trial and error for you. The nearby boxes illustrate how to do so.

The rate of return rule tells you to accept a project if the rate of return exceeds the opportunity cost of capital. You can see from Figure 8–3 why this makes sense. Because the NPV profile is downward-sloping, the project has a positive NPV as long as the opportunity cost of capital is less than the project's 12.96% IRR. If the opportunity cost of capital is higher than the 12.96% IRR, NPV is negative. Therefore, when we compare the project IRR with the opportunity cost of capital, we are effectively asking whether the project has a positive NPV. This was true for our one-period office project. It is also true for our three-period office project. We conclude that **the rate of return rule will give the same answer as the NPV rule** *as long as the NPV of a project declines smoothly as the discount rate increases.*

The usual agreement between the net present value and internal rate of return rules should not be a surprise. Both are *discounted cash-flow* methods of choosing between projects. Both are concerned with identifying those projects that make shareholders better off, and both recognize that companies always have a choice: They can invest in a project, or if the project is not sufficiently attractive, they can give the money back to shareholders and let them invest it for themselves in the capital market.

Self-Test 8.3   Suppose the cash flow in year 3 is only $416,000. Redraw Figure 8–3. How would the IRR change?

A Word of Caution

Some people confuse the internal rate of return on a project with the opportunity cost of capital. Remember that the project IRR measures the profitability of the project. It is an *internal* rate of return in the sense that it depends only on the project's own cash flows. The opportunity cost of capital is the standard for deciding whether to accept the project. It is equal to the return offered by equivalent-risk investments in the capital market.

Some Pitfalls with the Internal Rate of Return Rule

Many firms use the internal rate of return rule instead of net present value. We think that this is a pity. When used properly, the two rules lead to the same decision, but the rate of return rule has several pitfalls that can trap the unwary. Here are a couple of examples.

SPREADSHEET SOLUTIONS

Internal Rate of Return

Please visit us at www.mhhe.com/bmm6e

	A	B	C	D	E	F
1		Calculating IRR by using a spreadsheet				
2						
3	Year	Cash Flow				Formula
4	0	-350,000		IRR =	0.1296	=IRR(B4:B7)
5	1	16,000				
6	2	16,000				
7	3	466,000				

Calculating internal rate of return in Excel is as easy as listing the project cash flows. For example, to calculate the IRR of the office-block project, you could simply type in its cash flows as in the spreadsheet above, and then calculate IRR as we do in cell E4. As always, the interest rate is returned as a decimal. The spreadsheet is available at www.mhhe.com/bmm6e.

Pitfall 1: Lending or Borrowing?   Remember our condition for the IRR rule to work: The project's NPV must fall as the discount rate increases. Now consider the following projects:

	Cash Flows (dollars)			
Project	C_0	C_1	IRR, %	NPV at 10%
D	−100	+150	+50	+$36.4
E	+100	−150	+50	− 36.4

Each project has an IRR of 50%. In other words, if you discount the cash flows at 50%, both projects would have zero NPV.

Does this mean that the two projects are equally attractive? Clearly not. In the case of D we are paying out $100 now and getting $150 back at the end of the year. That is better than any bank account. But what about E? Here we are getting paid $100 now but we have to pay out $150 at the end of the year. That is equivalent to borrowing money at 50%.

If someone asked you whether 50% was a good rate of interest, you could not answer unless you also knew whether that person was proposing to lend or borrow at that rate. Lending money at 50% is great (as long as the borrower does not flee the country), but borrowing at 50% is not usually a good deal (unless, of course, you plan to flee the country). When you lend money, you want a *high* rate of return; when you borrow, you want a *low* rate of return.

If you plot a graph like Figure 8–2 for project E, you will find the NPV increases as the discount rate increases. *(Try it!)* Obviously, the rate of return rule will not work in this case.

Project E is a fairly obvious trap, but if you want to make sure you don't fall into it, calculate the project's NPV. For example, suppose that the cost of capital is 10%. Then the NPV of project D is +$36.4 and the NPV of project E is −$36.4. The NPV rule correctly warns us away from a project that is equivalent to borrowing money at 50%.

When NPV rises as the interest rate rises, the rate of return rule is reversed: **When NPV is higher as the discount rate increases, a project is acceptable only if its internal rate of return is *less* than the opportunity cost of capital.**

Pitfall 2: Multiple Rates of Return   Here is a trickier problem. King Coal Corporation is considering a project to strip-mine coal. The project requires an investment of $22 million and is expected to produce a cash inflow of $15 million in each of years 1 through 4. However, the company is obliged in year 5 to reclaim the land at a cost of $40 million. At a 10% opportunity cost of capital the project has an NPV of $.7 million.

FINANCIAL CALCULATOR

Using Financial Calculators to Find NPV and IRR

We saw in Chapter 5 that the formulas for the present and future values of level annuities and one-time cash flows are built into financial calculators. However, as the example of the office block illustrates, most investment projects entail multiple cash flows that cannot be expected to remain level over time. Fortunately, many calculators are equipped to handle problems involving a sequence of uneven cash flows. In general, the procedure is quite simple. You enter the cash flows one by one into the calculator, and then you press the IRR key to find the project's internal rate of return. The first cash flow you enter is interpreted as coming immediately, the next cash flow is interpreted as coming at the end of one period, and so on. We can illustrate using the office block as an example. To find the project IRR, you would use the following sequence of keystrokes:

Hewlett-Packard HP-10B		Sharp EL-733A		Texas Instruments BA II Plus	
−350,000	CF/	−350,000	CF/		CF
16,000	CF/	16,000	CF/	2nd	[CLR Work]
16,000	CF/	16,000	CF/	−350,000	ENTER ⬇
466,000	CF/	466,000	CF/	16,000	ENTER ⬇
				16,000	ENTER ⬇
				466,000	ENTER ⬇
□	{IRR/YR}		IRR		IRR
					CPT

The calculator should display the value 12.96%, the project's internal rate of return.

To calculate project NPV, the procedure is similar. You need to enter the discount rate in addition to the project cash flows, and then simply press the NPV key. Here is the specific sequence of keystrokes, assuming that the opportunity cost of capital is 7%:

Hewlett-Packard HP-10B		Sharp EL-733A		Texas Instruments BA II Plus	
−350,000	CF/	−350,000	CF/		CF
16,000	CF/	16,000	CF/	2nd	[CLR Work]
16,000	CF/	16,000	CF/	−350,000	ENTER ⬇
466,000	CF/	466,000	CF/	16,000	ENTER ⬇
7	I/YR	7	i	16,000	ENTER ⬇
				466,000	ENTER ⬇
□	{NPV}		NPV		NPV
				7	ENTER
				⬇	CPT

The calculator should display the value 59,323, the project's NPV when the discount rate is 7%.

By the way, you can check the accuracy of our earlier calculations using your calculator. Enter 50% for the discount rate (press 50, then press i) and then press the NPV key to find that NPV = −194,148. Enter 12.96 (the project's IRR) as the discount rate, and you will find that NPV is just about zero (it is not exactly zero, because we are rounding off the IRR to only two decimal places).

To find the IRR, we have calculated the NPV for various discount rates and plotted the results in Figure 8–4. You can see that there are *two* discount rates at which NPV = 0. That is, *each* of the following statements holds:

$$NPV = -22 + \frac{15}{1.06} + \frac{15}{(1.06)^2} + \frac{15}{(1.06)^3} + \frac{15}{(1.06)^4} - \frac{40}{(1.06)^5} = 0$$

and

$$NPV = -22 + \frac{15}{1.28} + \frac{15}{(1.28)^2} + \frac{15}{(1.28)^3} + \frac{15}{(1.28)^4} - \frac{40}{(1.28)^5} = 0$$

In other words, the investment has an IRR of both 6% *and* 28%. The reason for this is the double change in the sign of the cash flows. There can be as many different internal rates of return as there are changes in the sign of the cash-flow stream.[5]

Is the coal mine worth developing? The simple IRR rule—accept if the IRR is greater than the cost of capital—won't help. For example, you can see from Figure 8–4

---

[5] There may be *fewer* IRRs than the number of sign changes. You may even encounter projects for which there is *no* IRR. For example, there is no IRR for a project that has cash flows of +$1,000 in year 0, −$3,000 in year 1, and +$2,500 in year 2. If you don't believe us, try plotting NPV for different discount rates. Can such a project ever have a negative NPV?

FIGURE 8-4 King Coal's project has two internal rates of return. NPV = 0 when the discount rate is either 6% or 28%.

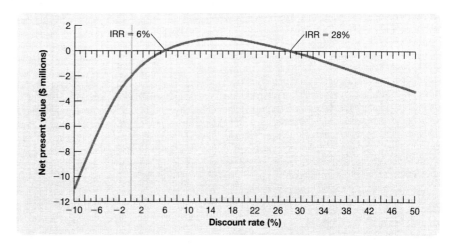

that with a low cost of capital (less than 6%) the project has a negative NPV. It has a positive NPV only if the cost of capital is between 6% and 28%.

Decommissioning and clean-up costs, which make King Coal's final cash flow negative, can sometimes be huge. Phillips Petroleum has estimated that it will need to spend $1 billion to remove its Norwegian offshore oil platforms. It can cost over $300 million to decommission a nuclear power plant. These are obvious examples where cash flows go from positive to negative, but you can probably think of a number of other cases where the company needs to plan for later expenditures. Ships periodically need to go into dry dock for a refit, hotels may receive a major facelift, machine parts may need replacement, and so on.

Whenever the cash-flow stream is expected to change sign more than once, the project typically has more than one IRR and there is no simple IRR rule. Companies sometimes get around the problem of multiple rates of return by successively combining the later cash flows into one present value until there remains only one change in sign. A *modified internal rate of return (MIRR)* can be calculated from this revised series. We illustrate by continuing the King Coal example.

EXAMPLE 8.4   ▶   Modified IRR

The cash flows for King Coal are as follows:

Year:	0	1	2	3	4	5
Cash flows	−$22	$15	$15	$15	$15	−$40

First try combining the last two cash flows into one PV calculated as of year 4. Use the 10% cost of capital to discount.

$$15 - \frac{40}{1.10} = -21.36$$

This PV is still negative, and therefore the project still entails two changes in sign. So we step back an additional year and combine the last *three* cash flows into a single PV calculated as of year 3:

$$15 + \frac{15}{1.10} - \frac{40}{(1.10)^2} = -4.42$$

This is still negative. So we step back yet another year and combine last *four* cash flows into a PV calculated as of time 2:

$$15 + \frac{15}{1.10} + \frac{15}{(1.10)^2} - \frac{40}{(1.10)^3} = 10.98$$

This value is finally positive, so if we use it in place of the last four cash flows, we will have only one change of sign. Now we can compute IRR using the *modified* cash-flow sequence:

Year:	0	1	2	3	4	5
Modified cash flows	−$22	$15	$10.98			

IRR is the discount rate at which net present value is zero:

$$-22 + \frac{15}{1 + IRR} + \frac{10.98}{(1 + IRR)^2} = 0$$

We solve to find that modified IRR = .1253, or 12.53%, which is greater than the cost of capital, 10%. The project has a positive NPV when valued at the cost of capital.

Of course, it would be much easier in cases like this one to abandon the IRR rule and just calculate project NPV.

Pitfall 3: Mutually Exclusive Projects   We have seen that firms are seldom faced with take-it-or-leave-it projects. Usually they need to choose from a number of mutually exclusive alternatives. Given a choice between competing projects, you should accept the one that adds most to shareholder wealth. This is the one with the higher NPV.

But what about the rate of return rule? Would it make sense to just choose the project that offers the highest internal rate of return? Unfortunately, no. Mutually exclusive projects involve an additional pitfall for users of the IRR rule.[6]

Think once more about the two office-block proposals from Section 8.1. You initially intended to invest $350,000 in the building and then sell it at the end of the year for $400,000. Under the revised proposal, you planned to rent out the offices for 3 years at a fixed annual rent of $16,000 and then sell the building for $450,000. Here are the cash flows, their IRRs, and their NPVs:

Project	Cash Flows (thousands of dollars)				IRR	NPV at 7%
	C_0	C_1	C_2	C_3		
Initial proposal	−350	+400			+14.29	+$24,000
Revised proposal	−350	+16	+16	+466	+12.96	+ 59,000

Both projects are good investments; both offer a positive NPV. But the revised proposal has the higher net present value and therefore is the better choice. Unfortunately, the superiority of the revised proposal doesn't show up as a higher rate of return. The IRR rule seems to say you should go for the initial proposal because it has the higher IRR. If you follow the IRR rule, you have the satisfaction of earning a 14.29% rate of return; if you use NPV, you are $59,000 richer.

Figure 8–5 shows why the IRR rule gives the wrong signal. The figure plots the NPV of each project as a function of the discount rate. These two NPV profiles cross at an interest rate of 12.26%. So if the opportunity cost of capital is higher than 12.26%,

---

[6] The other rule we've considered, payback, gives poor guidance even in the much simpler case of the accept-reject decision of a project considered in isolation. It is of no help in choosing among mutually exclusive projects.

FIGURE 8–5 The initial proposal offers a higher IRR than the revised proposal, but its NPV is lower if the discount rate is less than 12.26%.

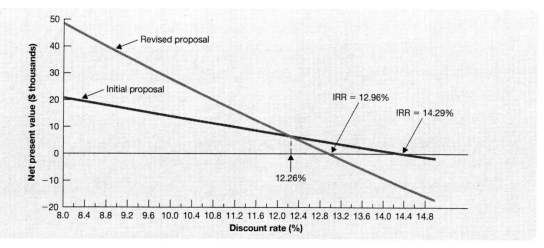

the initial proposal, with its rapid cash inflow, is the superior investment. If the cost of capital is lower than 12.26%, then the revised proposal dominates. Depending on the discount rate, either proposal may be superior. For the 7% cost of capital that we have assumed, the revised proposal is the better choice.

Now consider the IRR of each proposal. The IRR is simply the discount rate at which NPV equals zero, that is, the discount rate at which the NPV profile crosses the horizontal axis in Figure 8–5. As noted, these rates are 14.29% for the initial proposal and 12.96% for the revised proposal. However, as you can see from Figure 8–5, the higher IRR for the initial proposal does not mean that it has a higher NPV.

In our example both projects involved the same outlay, but the revised proposal had the longer life. The IRR rule mistakenly favored the quick payback project with the high percentage return but the lower NPV. **Remember, a high IRR is not an end in itself. You want projects that increase the value of the firm. Projects that earn a good rate of return for a long time often have higher NPVs than those that offer high percentage rates of return but die young.**

Self-Test 8.4

A rich, friendly, and probably slightly unbalanced benefactor offers you the opportunity to invest $1 million in two mutually exclusive ways. The payoffs are:

a. $2 million after 1 year, a 100% return.
b. $300,000 a year forever.

Neither investment is risky, and safe securities are yielding 7.5%. Which investment will you take? You can't take both, so the choices are mutually exclusive. Do you want to earn a high percentage return, or do you want to be rich? By the way, if you really had this investment opportunity, you'd have no trouble borrowing the money to undertake it.

Pitfall 3a: Mutually Exclusive Projects Involving Different Outlays A similar misranking also may occur when comparing projects with the same lives but different outlays. In this case the IRR may mistakenly favor small projects with high rates of return but low NPVs.

Self-Test 8.5   Your wacky benefactor (see Self-Test 8.4) now offers you the choice of two opportunities:

a. Invest $1,000 today and quadruple your money—a 300% return—in 1 year with no risk.

b. Invest $1 million for 1 year at a guaranteed 50% return.

Which will you take? Do you want to earn a wonderful rate of return (300%), or do you want to be rich? Safe securities still yield 7.5%.

8.3 More Examples of Mutually Exclusive Projects

Although the IRR rule can quickly lead you astray when choosing among mutually exclusive projects, the choice is easy using the NPV rule, at least in principle. As long as at least one project has positive NPV, simply choose the project with the highest NPV. But sometimes comparing project NPVs properly can be surprisingly tricky. Here are three important, but often challenging, decisions:

- *The investment timing decision.* Should you buy a computer now or wait and think again next year? (Here today's investment is competing with possible future investments.)
- *The choice between long- and short-lived equipment.* Should the company save money today by installing cheaper machinery that will not last as long? (Here today's decision would accelerate a later investment in machine replacement.)
- *The replacement decision.* When should existing machinery be replaced? (Using it another year could delay investment in more modern equipment.)

Investment Timing

Let us return to Example 8.1, where Obsolete Technologies was contemplating the purchase of a new computer system. The proposed investment has a net present value of almost $20,000, so it appears that the cost savings would easily justify the expense of the system. However, the financial manager is not persuaded. She reasons that the price of computers is continually falling and therefore proposes postponing the purchase, arguing that the NPV of the system will be even higher if the firm waits until the following year. Unfortunately, she has been making the same argument for 10 years, and the company is steadily losing business to competitors with more efficient systems. Is there a flaw in her reasoning?

This is a problem in investment timing. When is it best to commit to a positive-NPV investment? Investment timing problems all involve choices among mutually exclusive investments. You can either proceed with the project now or do so later. You can't do both.

Table 8–2 lays out the basic data for Obsolete. You can see that the cost of the computer is expected to decline from $50,000 today to $45,000 next year, and so on. The new computer system is expected to last for 4 years from the time it is installed. The present value of the savings *at the time of installation* is expected to be $70,000. Thus if Obsolete invests today, it achieves an NPV of $70,000 − $50,000 = $20,000; if it invests next year, it will have an NPV of $70,000 − $45,000 = $25,000.

Isn't a gain of $25,000 better than one of $20,000? Well, not necessarily—you may prefer to be $20,000 richer *today* rather than $25,000 richer *next year.* The better choice depends on the cost of capital. The fourth column of Table 8–2 shows the value today (year 0) of those net present values at a 10% cost of capital. For example, you can see that the discounted value of that $25,000 gain is $25,000/1.10 = $22,700. The financial manager has a point. It is worth postponing investment in the computer, but it should not be postponed indefinitely. You maximize net present value today by buying the computer in year 3.

TABLE 8–2 Obsolete Technologies: The gain from purchase of a computer is rising, but the NPV today is highest if the computer is purchased in year 3 (figures in thousands of dollars).

Year of Purchase	Cost of Computer	PV Savings	NPV at Year of Purchase ($r = 10\%$)	NPV Today	
0	$50	$70	$20	$20.0	
1	45	70	25	22.7	
2	40	70	30	24.8	
3	36	70	34	25.5	←optimal
4	33	70	37	25.3	purchase
5	31	70	39	24.2	date

Notice that you are involved in a trade-off. The sooner you can capture the $70,000 savings the better, but if it costs you less to realize those savings by postponing the investment, it may pay for you to wait. If you postpone purchase by 1 year, the gain from buying a computer rises from $20,000 to $25,000, an increase of 25%. Since the cost of capital is only 10%, it pays to postpone at least until year 1. If you postpone from year 3 to year 4, the gain rises from $34,000 to $37,000, a rise of just under 9%. Since this is less than the cost of capital, it is not worth waiting any longer. **The decision rule for investment timing is to choose the investment date that results in the highest net present value** *today*.

Self-Test 8.6

Unfortunately Obsolete Technologies' business is shrinking as the company dithers and dawdles. Its chief financial officer realizes that the savings from installing the new computer will likewise shrink by $4,000 per year, from a present value of $70,000 now, to $66,000 next year, then to $62,000, and so on. Redo Table 8–2 with this new information. When should Obsolete buy the new computer?

Long- versus Short-Lived Equipment

Suppose the firm is forced to choose between two machines, F and G. The two machines are designed differently but have identical capacity and do exactly the same job. Machine F costs $15,000 and will last 3 years. It costs $4,000 per year to run. Machine G is an "economy" model, costing only $10,000, but it will last only 2 years and costs $6,000 per year to run.

Because the two machines produce exactly the same product, the only way to choose between them is on the basis of cost. Suppose we compute the present value of the costs:

	Costs (thousands of dollars)				
Year:	0	1	2	3	PV at 6%
Machine F	15	4	4	4	$25.69
Machine G	10	6	6	—	21.00

Should we take machine G, the one with the lower present value of costs? Not necessarily. All we have shown is that machine G offers 2 years of service for a lower total cost than 3 years of service from machine F. But is the *annual* cost of using G lower than that of F?

Suppose the financial manager agrees to buy machine F and pay for its operating costs out of her budget. She then charges the plant manager an annual amount for use of the machine. There will be three equal payments starting in year 1. Obviously, the financial manager has to make sure that the present value of these payments equals the present value of the costs of machine F, $25,690. When the discount rate is 6%, the payment stream with such a present value turns out to be $9,610 a year. In other words, the cost of buying and operating machine F is equivalent to an annual charge of $9,610 a year for 3 years. This figure is therefore termed the **equivalent annual annuity** of operating machine F.

equivalent annual annuity
The cash flow per period with the same present value as the cost of buying and operating a machine.

		Costs (thousands of dollars)			
Year:	0	1	2	3	PV at 6%
Machine F	15	4	4	4	$25.69
Equivalent annual annuity		9.61	9.61	9.61	25.69

How did we know that an annual charge of $9,610 has a present value of $25,690? The annual charge is a 3-year annuity. So we calculate the value of this annuity and set it equal to $25,690:

Equivalent annual annuity $\times$ 3-year annuity factor = PV costs of F = $25,690

If the cost of capital is 6%, the 3-year annuity factor is 2.6730. So

$$\text{Equivalent annual annuity} = \frac{\text{present value of costs}}{\text{annuity factor}} \qquad (8.2)$$

$$= \frac{\$25,690}{\text{3-year annuity factor}} = \frac{\$25,690}{2.6730} = \$9,610$$

If we make a similar calculation of costs for machine G, we get:

		Costs (thousands of dollars)		
Year:	0	1	2	PV at 6%
Machine G	10	6	6	$21.00
Equivalent 2-year annuity		11.45	11.45	21.00

We see now that machine F is better, because its equivalent annual annuity is less ($9,610 for F versus $11,450 for G). In other words, the financial manager could afford to set a lower *annual* charge for the use of F. **We thus have a rule for comparing assets with different lives:** *Select the machine that has the lowest equivalent annual annuity.*

Think of the equivalent annual annuity as the level annual charge[7] necessary to recover the present value of investment outlays and operating costs. The annual charge continues for the life of the equipment. Calculate the equivalent annual annuity by dividing the present value by the annuity factor.

EXAMPLE 8.5 ▶   Equivalent Annual Annuity

You need a new car. You can either purchase one outright for $15,000 or lease one for 7 years for $3,000 a year. If you buy the car, it will be worth $500 to you in 7 years. The discount rate is 10%. Should you buy or lease? What is the maximum lease payment you would be willing to pay?

The present value of the cost of purchasing is

$$PV = \$15,000 - \frac{\$500}{(1.10)^7} = \$14,743$$

---

[7] We have implicitly assumed that inflation is zero. If that is not the case, it would be better to calculate the equivalent annuities for machines F and G in real terms, using the real rate of interest to calculate the annuity factor.

The equivalent annual cost of purchasing the car is therefore the annuity with this present value:

$$\text{Equivalent annual annuity} \times \frac{\text{7-year annuity}}{\text{factor at 10\%}} = \frac{\text{PV costs}}{\text{of buying}} = \$14,743$$

$$\text{Equivalent annual annuity} = \frac{\$14,743}{\text{7-year annuity factor}} = \frac{\$14,743}{4.8684} = \$3,028$$

Therefore, the annual lease payment of $3,000 is less than the equivalent annual annuity of buying the car. You should be willing to pay up to $3,028 annually to lease.

EXAMPLE 8.6   ▶   Another Equivalent Annual Annuity

Low-energy lightbulbs typically cost $3.50, have a life of 9 years, and use about $1.60 of electricity a year. Conventional lightbulbs are cheaper to buy, for they cost only $.50. On the other hand, they last only about a year and use about $6.60 of energy. If the real discount rate is 5%, what is the relative cost of the two products?

To answer this question, you need first to convert the initial cost of each bulb to an annual figure and then to add in the annual energy cost.[8] The following table sets out the calculations.

	Low-Energy Bulb	Conventional Bulb
1. Initial cost, $	3.50	0.50
2. Estimated life, years	9	1
3. Annuity factor at 5%	7.1078	.9524
4. Equivalent annual annuity, $, = (1)/(3)	.49	.52
5. Annual energy cost, $	1.60	6.60
6. Total annual cost, $, = (4) + (5)	2.09	7.12
Assumption: Energy costs are incurred at the end of each year.		

It seems that a low-energy lightbulb provides an annual saving of about $7.12 − $2.09 = $5.03. (By the way, Energy Star, a joint program of the U.S. Environmental Protection Agency and the Department of Energy, provides a simple calculator that works out the present value of the costs of both bulbs over the life of the longer-lived bulb. See www.energystar.gov)

Replacing an Old Machine

Our earlier comparison of machines F and G took the life of each machine as fixed. In practice, the point at which equipment is replaced reflects economics, not physical collapse. We usually decide when to replace. The machine will rarely decide for us.

Here is a common problem: You are operating an old machine that will last 2 more years before it gives up the ghost. It costs $12,000 per year to operate. You can replace it now with a new machine that costs $25,000 but is much more efficient ($8,000 per year in operating costs) and will last for 5 years. Should you replace now or wait a year? The opportunity cost of capital is 6%.

We can calculate the NPV of the new machine and its equivalent annual annuity, that is, the 5-year annuity that has the same present value.

		Costs (thousands of dollars)						
Year:	0	1	2	3	4	5	PV at 6%
New machine	25	8	8	8	8	8	$58.70
Equivalent 5-year annuity		13.93	13.93	13.93	13.93	13.93	58.70

---

[8] Our calculations ignore any environmental costs.

The cash flows of the new machine are equivalent to an annuity of $13,930 per year. So we can equally well ask at what point you would want to replace your old machine, which costs $12,000 a year to run, with a new one costing $13,930 a year. When the question is posed this way, the answer is obvious. As long as your old machine costs only $12,000 a year, why replace it with a new machine that costs $1,930 a year more?

Self-Test 8.7

Machines H and I are mutually exclusive and have the following investment and operating costs. Note that machine H lasts for only 2 years:

Year:	0	1	2	3
H	$10,000	$1,100	$1,200	—
I	12,000	1,100	1,200	$1,300

Calculate the equivalent annual annuity of each investment by using a discount rate of 10%. Which machine is the better buy?

Now suppose you have an existing machine. You can keep it going for 1 more year only, but it will cost $2,500 in repairs and $1,800 in operating costs. Is it worth replacing now with either H or I?

8.4 Capital Rationing

A firm maximizes its shareholders' wealth by accepting every project that has a positive net present value. But this assumes that the firm can raise the funds needed to pay for these investments. This is usually a good assumption, particularly for major firms that can raise very large sums of money on fair terms and short notice. Why then does top management sometimes tell subordinates that capital is limited and that they may not exceed a specified amount of capital spending? There are two reasons.

Soft Rationing

capital rationing
Limit set on the amount of funds available for investment.

For many firms the limits on capital funds are "soft." By this we mean that the **capital rationing** is not imposed by investors. Instead, the limits are imposed by top management. For example, suppose that you are an ambitious, upwardly mobile junior manager. You are keen to expand your part of the business, and as a result you tend to overstate the investment opportunities. Rather than trying to determine which of your many bright ideas really are worthwhile, upper management may find it simpler to impose a limit on the amount that you and other junior managers can spend. This limit forces you to set your own priorities.

Even if capital is not rationed, other resources may be. For example, very rapid growth can place considerable strains on management and the organization. A somewhat rough-and-ready response to this problem is to ration the amount of capital that the firm spends.

Hard Rationing

Soft rationing should never cost the firm anything. If the limits on investment become so tight that truly good projects are being passed up, then upper management should raise more money and relax the limits it has imposed on capital spending.

But what if there is "hard rationing," meaning that the firm actually *cannot* raise the money it needs? In that case, it may be forced to pass up positive-NPV projects.

With hard rationing you may still be interested in net present value, but you now need to select the package of projects that is within the company's resources and yet gives the highest net present value.

Let us illustrate. Suppose that the opportunity cost of capital is 10%, that the company has total resources of $20 million, and that it is presented with the following project proposals:

Project	Cash Flows (millions of dollars)			PV at 10%	NPV
	C_0	C_1	C_2		
J	−3	+2.2	+2.42	$ 4	$1
K	−5	+2.2	+4.84	6	1
L	−7	+6.6	+4.84	10	3
M	−6	+3.3	+6.05	8	2
N	−4	+1.1	+4.84	5	1

All five projects have a positive NPV. Therefore, if there were no shortage of capital, the firm would like to accept all five proposals. But with only $20 million available, the firm needs to find the package that gives the highest possible NPV within the budget.

The solution is to pick the projects that give the highest net present value *per dollar of investment.* The ratio of net present value to initial investment is known as the **profitability index.**[9]

profitability index
Ratio of net present value to initial investment.

$$\text{Profitability index} = \frac{\text{net present value}}{\text{initial investment}} \qquad (8.3)$$

For our five projects the profitability index is calculated as follows:

Project	PV	Investment	NPV	Profitability Index
J	$ 4	$3	$1	1/3 = 0.33
K	6	5	1	1/5 = 0.20
L	10	7	3	3/7 = 0.43
M	8	6	2	2/6 = 0.33
N	5	4	1	1/4 = 0.25

Project L offers the highest ratio of net present value to investment (0.43), and therefore L is picked first. Next come projects J and M, which tie with a ratio of 0.33, and after them comes N. These four projects exactly use up the $20 million budget. Between them they offer shareholders the highest attainable gain in wealth.[10]

Self-Test 8.8   Which projects should the firm accept if its capital budget is only $10 million?

Pitfalls of the Profitability Index

The profitability index is sometimes used to rank projects even when there is no soft or hard capital rationing. In this case the unwary user may be led to favor small projects over larger projects with higher NPVs. The profitability index was designed to select the projects with the most bang per buck—the greatest NPV per dollar spent.

---

[9] Sometimes the profitability index is defined as the ratio of present value to required investment. By this definition, all the profitability indexes calculated below are increased by 1. For example, project J's index would be PV/investment = 4/3 = 1.33. Note that project rankings under either definition are identical.

[10] Unfortunately, when capital is rationed in more than one period, or when personnel, production capacity, or other resources are rationed in addition to capital, it isn't always possible to get the NPV-maximizing package just by ranking projects on their profitability index. Tedious trial and error may be called for, or linear programming methods may be used.

That's the right objective when bucks are limited. When they are not, a bigger bang is always better than a smaller one, even when more bucks are spent. Self-Test 8.9 is a numerical example.

Self-Test 8.9   Calculate the profitability indexes of the two pairs of mutually exclusive investments in Self-Tests 8.4 and 8.5. Use a 7.5% discount rate. Does the profitability index give the right ranking in each case?

8.5 A Last Look

We've covered several investment criteria, each with its own nuances. If your head is spinning, you might want to take a look at Table 8–3, which gives an overview and summary of these decision rules.

Clearly, NPV is the gold standard. It is designed to tell you whether an investment will increase the value of the firm and by how much it will do so. It is the only rule that consistently can be used to rank and choose among mutually exclusive investments. The only instance in which NPV fails as a decision rule occurs when the firm faces capital rationing. In this case, there may not be enough cash to take every project with positive NPV, and the firm must then rank projects by the profitability index, that is, net present value per dollar invested.

For managers in the field, discounted cash-flow analysis is in fact the dominant tool for project evaluation. Table 8–4 provides a sample of the results of a large survey of CFOs. Notice that 75% of firms either always or almost always use NPV or IRR to evaluate projects. The dominance of these criteria is even stronger among larger, presumably more sophisticated, firms. Despite the clear advantages of discounted cash-flow methods, however, firms do use other investment criteria to evaluate projects. For example, just over half of corporations always or almost always compute a project's payback period. Profitability index is routinely computed by about 12% of firms.

TABLE 8–3 A comparison of investment decision rules

Criterion	Definition	Investment Rule	Comments
Net present value (NPV)	Present value of cash inflows minus present value of cash outflows	Accept project if NPV is positive. For mutually exclusive projects, choose the one with the highest (positive) NPV.	The "gold standard" of investment criteria. Only criterion necessarily consistent with maximizing the value of the firm. Provides proper rule for choosing among mutually exclusive investments. Only pitfall involves capital rationing, when one cannot accept all positive-NPV projects.
Internal rate of return (IRR)	The discount rate at which project NPV equals zero	Accept project if IRR is greater than opportunity cost of capital	If used properly, results in same accept-reject decision as NPV in the absence of project interactions. However, beware of the following pitfalls: IRR cannot rank mutually exclusive projects—the project with higher IRR may have lower NPV. The simple IRR rule cannot be used in cases of multiple IRRs or an upward-sloping NPV profile.
Payback period	Time until the sum of project cash flows equals the initial investment	Accept project if payback period is less than some specified number of years	A quick and dirty rule of thumb, with several critical pitfalls. Ignores cash flows beyond the acceptable payback period. Ignores discounting. Tends to improperly reject long-lived projects.
Profitability index	Ratio of net present value to initial investment	Accept project if profitability index is greater than 0. In case of capital rationing, accept projects with highest profitability index.	Results in same accept-reject decision as NPV in the absence of project interactions. Useful for ranking projects in case of capital rationing, but misleading in the presence of interactions. Cannot rank mutually exclusive projects.

Chapter 8   Net Present Value and Other Investment Criteria   **247**

TABLE 8–4 Capital budgeting techniques used in practice

Investment Criterion	Percentage of Firms That Always or Almost Always Use Criterion	Average Score on 0–4 Scale (0 = never use; 4 = always use)		
		All Firms	Small Firms	Large Firms
Internal rate of return	76	3.1	2.9	3.4
Net present value	75	3.1	2.8	3.4
Payback period	57	2.5	2.7	2.3
Profitability index	12	0.8	0.9	0.8

Source: Reprinted from the *Journal of Financial Economics,* Vol. 60, Issue 2-3, J. R. Graham and C. R. Harvey, "The Theory and Practice of Corporate Finance: Evidence from the Field," May 2001, pp. 187–243. © 2001 with permission from Elsevier Science.

What explains such wide use of presumably inferior decision rules? To some extent, these rules present rough reality checks on the project. As we noted in the introduction to the chapter, managers might want to consider some simple ways to describe project profitability, even if they present obvious pitfalls. For example, managers talk casually about quick-payback projects in the same way that investors talk about high-P/E stocks. The fact that they talk about payback does not mean that the payback rule governs their decisions.

SUMMARY

What is the net present value of an investment, and how do you calculate it? (*LO1*)

The **net present value** of a project measures the difference between its value and cost. NPV is therefore the amount that the project will add to shareholder wealth. A company maximizes shareholder wealth by accepting all projects that have a positive NPV.

How is the internal rate of return of a project calculated, and what must one look out for when using the internal rate of return rule? (*LO2*)

Instead of asking whether a project has a positive NPV, many businesses prefer to ask whether it offers a higher return than shareholders could expect to get by investing in the capital market. Return is usually defined as the discount rate that would result in a zero NPV. This is known as the **internal rate of return,** or **IRR.** The project is attractive if the IRR exceeds the **opportunity cost of capital.**

There are some pitfalls in using the internal rate of return rule. Be careful about using the IRR when (1) the early cash flows are positive, (2) there is more than one change in the sign of the cash flows, or (3) you need to choose between two **mutually exclusive projects.**

Why doesn't the payback rule always make shareholders better off? (*LO3*)

The net present value rule and the rate of return rule both properly reflect the time value of money. But companies sometimes use rules of thumb to judge projects. One is the **payback rule,** which states that a project is acceptable if you get your money back within a specified period. The payback rule takes no account of any cash flows that arrive after the payback period and fails to discount cash flows within the payback period.

How can the net present value rule be used to analyze three common problems that involve competing projects: when to postpone an investment expenditure; how to choose between projects with unequal lives; and when to replace equipment? (*LO4*)

Sometimes a project may have a positive NPV if undertaken today but an even higher NPV if the investment is delayed. Choose between these alternatives by comparing their NPVs *today.*

When you have to choose between projects with different lives, you should put them on an equal footing by comparing the **equivalent annual annuity** or benefit of the two projects. When you are considering whether to replace an aging machine with a new one, you should compare the annual cost of operating the old one with the equivalent annual annuity of the new one.

www.mhhe.com/bmm6e

How is the profitability index calculated, and how can it be used to choose between projects when funds are limited? (*LO5*)

If there is a shortage of capital, companies need to choose projects that offer the highest net present value per dollar of investment. This measure is known as the **profitability index**.

LISTING OF EQUATIONS

8.1   NPV = PV − required investment

8.2   Equivalent annual annuity = $\dfrac{\text{present value of costs}}{\text{annuity factor}}$

8.3   Profitability index = $\dfrac{\text{net present value}}{\text{initial investment}}$

QUESTIONS

QUIZ

Problems 1–8 refer to two projects with the following cash flows:

Year	Project A	Project B
0	−$200	−$200
1	80	100
2	80	100
3	80	100
4	80	

1. **IRR/NPV.** If the opportunity cost of capital is 11%, which of these projects is worth pursuing? (*LO1*)

2. **Mutually Exclusive Investments.** Suppose that you can choose only one of these projects. Which would you choose? The discount rate is still 11%. (*LO5*)

3. **IRR/NPV.** Which project would you choose if the opportunity cost of capital were 16%? (*LO1*)

4. **IRR.** What are the internal rates of return on projects A and B? (*LO2*)

5. **Investment Criteria.** In light of your answers to Quiz Questions 2–4, is there any reason to believe that the project with the higher IRR is the better project? (*LO2*)

6. **Profitability Index.** If the opportunity cost of capital is 11%, what is the profitability index for each project? Does the profitability index rank the projects correctly? (*LO5*)

7. **Payback.** What is the payback period of each project? (*LO3*)

8. **Investment Criteria.** Considering your answers to Quiz Questions 2, 3, and 7, is there any reason to believe that the project with the lower payback period is the better project? (*LO3*)

9. **NPV and IRR.** A project that costs $3,000 to install will provide annual cash flows of $800 for each of the next 6 years. Is this project worth pursuing if the discount rate is 10%? How high can the discount rate be before you would reject the project? (*LO1*)

10. **Payback.** A project that costs $2,500 to install will provide annual cash flows of $600 for the next 6 years. The firm accepts projects with payback periods of less than 5 years. Will

the project be accepted? *Should* this project be pursued if the discount rate is 2%? What if the discount rate is 12%? Will the firm's decision change as the discount rate changes? (*LO3*)

11. **Profitability Index.** What is the profitability index of a project that costs $10,000 and provides cash flows of $3,000 in years 1 and 2 and $5,000 in years 3 and 4? The discount rate is 9%. (*LO5*)

12. **NPV.** A proposed nuclear power plant will cost $2.2 billion to build and then will produce cash flows of $300 million a year for 15 years. After that period (in year 15), it must be decommissioned at a cost of $900 million. What is project NPV if the discount rate is 5%? What if it is 18%? (*LO1*)

PRACTICE PROBLEMS

13. **NPV/IRR.** Consider projects A and B:

Project	Cash Flows (dollars)			NPV at 10%
	C_0	C_1	C_2	
A	−30,000	21,000	21,000	+$6,446
B	−50,000	33,000	33,000	+ 7,273

Calculate IRRs for A and B. Which project does the IRR rule suggest is best? Which project is really best? (*LO2*)

14. **IRR.** You have the chance to participate in a project that produces the following cash flows:

C_0	C_1	C_2
+$5,000	+$4,000	−$11,000

The internal rate of return is 13.6%. If the opportunity cost of capital is 12%, would you accept the offer? (*LO2*)

15. **NPV/IRR.**

a. Calculate the net present value of the following project for discount rates of 0, 50, and 100%: (*LO1*)

C_0	C_1	C_2
−$6,750	+$4,500	+$18,000

b. What is the IRR of the project? (*LO2*)

16. **IRR.** Marielle Machinery Works forecasts the following cash flows on a project under consideration. It uses the internal rate of return rule to accept or reject projects. Should this project be accepted if the required return is 12%? (*LO2*)

C_0	C_1	C_2	C_3
−$10,000	0	+$7,500	+$8,500

17. **NPV/IRR.** A new computer system will require an initial outlay of $20,000, but it will increase the firm's cash flows by $4,000 a year for each of the next 8 years. Is the system worth installing if the required rate of return is 9%? What if it is 14%? How high can the discount rate be before you would reject the project? (*LO1*)

18. **Investment Criteria.** If you insulate your office for $10,000, you will save $1,000 a year in heating expenses. These savings will last forever.

a. What is the NPV of the investment when the cost of capital is 8%? 10%? (*LO1*)

b. What is the IRR of the investment? (*LO2*)

c. What is the payback period on this investment? (*LO3*)

www.mhhe.com/bmm6e

19. **NPV versus IRR.** Here are the cash flows for two mutually exclusive projects:

Project	C_0	C_1	C_2	C_3
A	−$20,000	+$8,000	+$8,000	+$ 8,000
B	− 20,000	0	0	+ 25,000

    a. At what interest rates would you prefer project A to B? (*Hint:* Try drawing the NPV profile of each project.). (*LO1*)

    b. What is the IRR of each project? (*LO2*)

20. **Payback and NPV.** A project has a life of 10 years and a payback period of 10 years. What must be true of project NPV? (*LO3*)

21. **IRR/NPV.** Consider this project with an internal rate of return of 13.1%. Should you accept or reject the project if the discount rate is 12%? (*LO2*)

Year	Cash Flow
0	+$100
1	−60
2	−60

22. **Payback and NPV.**

    a. What is the payback period on each of the following projects? (*LO3*)

Project	Year: 0	1	2	3	4
			Cash Flows (dollars)		
A	−5,000	+1,000	+1,000	+3,000	0
B	−1,000	0	+1,000	+2,000	+3,000
C	−5,000	+1,000	+1,000	+3,000	+5,000

    b. Given that you wish to use the payback rule with a cutoff period of 2 years, which projects would you accept? (*LO3*)

    c. If you use a cutoff period of 3 years, which projects would you accept? (*LO3*)

    d. If the opportunity cost of capital is 10%, which projects have positive NPVs? (*LO1*)

    e. "Payback gives too much weight to cash flows that occur after the cutoff date." True or false? (*LO3*)

23. **Profitability Index.** Consider the following projects: (*LO5*)

Project	C_0	C_1	C_2
A	−$2,100	+$2,000	+$1,200
B	− 2,100	+ 1,440	+ 1,728

    a. Calculate the profitability index for A and B assuming a 22% opportunity cost of capital.

    b. Use the profitability index rule to determine which project(s) you should accept (i) if you could undertake both and (ii) if you could undertake only one.

24. **Capital Rationing.** You are a manager with an investment budget of $8 million. You may invest in the following projects. Investment and cash-flow figures are in millions of dollars. (*LO5*)

Project	Discount Rate, %	Investment	Annual Cash Flow	Project Life, Years
A	10	3	1	5
B	12	4	1	8
C	8	5	2	4
D	8	3	1.5	3
E	12	3	1	6

a. Why might these projects have different discount rates?

b. Which projects should the manager choose?

c. Which projects will be chosen if there is no capital rationing?

25. **Profitability Index versus NPV.** Consider these two projects: (*LO5*)

Project	C_0	C_1	C_2	C_3
A	−$36	+$20	+$20	+$20
B	− 50	+ 25	+ 25	+ 25

a. Which project has the higher NPV if the discount rate is 10%?

b. Which has the higher profitability index?

c. Which project is most attractive to a firm that can raise an unlimited amount of funds to pay for its investment projects? Which project is most attractive to a firm that is limited in the funds it can raise?

26. **Mutually Exclusive Investments.** Here are the cash flow forecasts for two *mutually exclusive* projects: (*LO1*)

	Cash Flows (dollars)	
Year	Project A	Project B
0	−100	−100
1	30	49
2	50	49
3	70	49

a. Which project would you choose if the opportunity cost of capital is 2%?

b. Which would you choose if the opportunity cost of capital is 12%?

c. Why does your answer change?

27. **Equivalent Annual Annuity.** A precision lathe costs $10,000 and will cost $20,000 a year to operate and maintain. If the discount rate is 10% and the lathe will last for 5 years, what is the equivalent annual cost of the tool? (*LO4*)

28. **Equivalent Annual Annuity.** A firm can lease a truck for 4 years at a cost of $30,000 annually. It can instead buy a truck at a cost of $80,000, with annual maintenance expenses of $10,000. The truck will be sold at the end of 4 years for $20,000. Which is the better option if the discount rate is 10%? (*LO4*)

29. **Multiple IRR.** Consider the following cash flows: (*LO2*)

C_0	C_1	C_2	C_3	C_4
−$22	+$20	+$20	+$20	−$40

a. Confirm that one internal rate of return on this project is (a shade above) 7%, and that the other is (a shade below) 34%.

b. Is the project attractive if the discount rate is 5%?

c. What if it is 20%? 40%?

d. Why is the project attractive at midrange discount rates but not at very high or very low rates?

30. **Equivalent Annual Cost.** Econo-Cool air conditioners cost $300 to purchase, result in electricity bills of $150 per year, and last for 5 years. Luxury Air models cost $500, result in electricity bills of $100 per year, and last for 8 years. The discount rate is 21%. (*LO4*)

a. What are the equivalent annual costs of the Econo-Cool and Luxury Air models?

b. Which model is more cost-effective?

c. Now you remember that the inflation rate is expected to be 10% per year for the foreseeable future. Redo parts (a) and (b).

31. **Investment Timing.** You can purchase an optical scanner today for $400. The scanner provides benefits worth $60 a year. The expected life of the scanner is 10 years. Scanners are expected to decrease in price by 20% per year. Suppose the discount rate is 10%. Should you purchase the scanner today or wait to purchase? When is the best purchase time? (*LO4*)

www.mhhe.com/bmm6e

32. **Replacement Decision.** You are operating an old machine that is expected to produce a cash inflow of $5,000 in each of the next 3 years before it fails. You can replace it now with a new machine that costs $20,000 but is much more efficient and will provide a cash flow of $10,000 a year for 4 years. Should you replace your equipment now? The discount rate is 15%. (*LO4*)

33. **Replacement Decision.** A forklift will last for only 2 more years. It costs $5,000 a year to maintain. For $20,000 you can buy a new lift that can last for 10 years and should require maintenance costs of only $2,000 a year. (*LO4*)

    a. If the discount rate is 4% per year, should you replace the forklift?
    b. What if the discount rate is 12% per year? Why does your answer change?

CHALLENGE PROBLEMS

34. **NPV/IRR.** Growth Enterprises believes its latest project, which will cost $80,000 to install, will generate a perpetual growing stream of cash flows. Cash flow at the end of the first year will be $5,000, and cash flows in future years are expected to grow indefinitely at an annual rate of 5%.

    a. If the discount rate for this project is 10%, what is the project NPV? (*LO1*)
    b. What is the project IRR? (*LO2*)

35. **Investment Timing.** A classic problem in management of forests is determining when it is most economically advantageous to cut a tree for lumber. When the tree is young, it grows very rapidly. As it ages, its growth slows down. Why is the NPV-maximizing rule to cut the tree when its growth rate equals the discount rate? (*LO4*)

36. **Multiple IRRs.** Strip Mining Inc. can develop a new mine at an initial cost of $5 million. The mine will provide a cash flow of $30 million in 1 year. The land then must be reclaimed at a cost of $28 million in the second year. (*LO2*)

    a. What are the IRRs of this project?
    b. Should the firm develop the mine if the discount rate is 10%? 20%? 350%? 400%?

Please visit us at www.mhhe.com/bmm6e

37. **Investment Criteria.** A new furnace for your small factory will cost $27,000 a year to install and will require ongoing maintenance expenditures of $1,500 a year. But it is far more fuel-efficient than your old furnace and will reduce your consumption of heating oil by 2,400 gallons per year. Heating oil this year will cost $3 a gallon; the price per gallon is expected to increase by $.50 a year for the next 3 years and then to stabilize for the foreseeable future. The furnace will last for 20 years, at which point it will need to be replaced and will have no salvage value. The discount rate is 8%.

    a. What is the net present value of the investment in the furnace? (*LO1*)
    b. What is the IRR? (*LO2*)
    c. What is the payback period? (*LO3*)
    d. What is the equivalent annual cost of the furnace? (*LO4*)
    e. What is the equivalent annual savings derived from the furnace? (*LO4*)
    f. Compare the PV of the difference between the equivalent annual cost and savings to your answer to part (a). (*LO1*)

SOLUTIONS TO SELF-TEST QUESTIONS

8.1   Even if construction costs are $355,000, NPV is still positive:

$$\text{NPV} = \text{PV} - \$355,000 = \$357,143 - \$355,000 = \$2,143$$

Therefore, the project is still worth pursuing. The project is viable as long as construction costs are less than the PV of the future cash flow, that is, as long as construction costs are less than $357,143. However, if the opportunity cost of capital is 20%, the PV of the $400,000 sales price is lower and NPV is negative:

$$\text{PV} = \$400,000 \times \frac{1}{1.20} = \$333,333$$

$$\text{NPV} = \text{PV} - \$355,000 = -\$21,667$$

The present value of the future cash flow is not as high when the opportunity cost of capital is higher. The project would need to provide a higher payoff in order to be viable in the face of the higher opportunity cost of capital.

8.2 The payback period is $5,000/$660 = 7.6 years. Discounted payback is just over 11 years. Calculate NPV as follows. The present value of a $660 annuity for 20 years at 6% is

$$\text{PV annuity} = \$7,570$$
$$\text{NPV} = -\$5,000 + \$7,570 = +\$2,570$$

The project should be accepted.

8.3 The IRR is now about 8.9% because

$$\text{NPV} = -\$350,000 + \frac{\$16,000}{1.089} + \frac{\$16,000}{(1.089)^2} + \frac{\$416,000}{(1.089)^3} = 0$$

Note in Figure 8–6 that NPV falls to zero as the discount rate reaches 8.9%.

8.4 You want to be rich. The NPV of the long-lived investment is much larger.

$$\text{Short: NPV} = -\$1 + \frac{\$2}{1.075} = +\$.8605 \text{ million}$$
$$\text{Long: NPV} = -\$1 + \frac{\$.3}{.075} = +\$3 \text{ million}$$

8.5 You want to be richer. The second alternative generates greater value at any reasonable discount rate. Other risk-free investments offer 7.5%. Therefore

$$\text{NPV} = -\$1,000 + \frac{\$4,000}{1.075} = +\$2,721$$
$$\text{NPV} = -\$1,000,000 + \frac{\$1,500,000}{1.075} = +\$395,349$$

8.6

Year of Purchase	Cost of Computer	PV Savings	NPV at Year of Purchase	NPV Today
0	$50	$70	$20	$20
1	45	66	21	19.1
2	40	62	22	18.2
3	36	58	22	16.5
4	33	54	21	14.3
5	31	50	19	11.8

Purchase the new computer now.

FIGURE 8–6 NPV falls to zero at an interest rate of 8.9%.

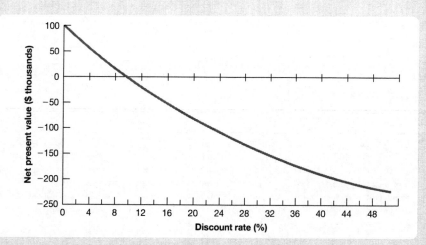

8.7

	Year:	0	1	2	3	PV of Costs
H Cash flows		$ 10,000	$1,100	$1,200		$11,992
Equivalent annual annuity			6,910	6,910		11,992
I Cash flows		12,000	1,100	1,200	$ 1,300	14,968
Equivalent annual annuity			6,019	6,019	6,019	14,968

Machine I is the better buy. However, it's still better to keep the old machine going for 1 more year. That costs $4,300, which is less than I's equivalent annual cost, $6,019.

8.8   Rank each project in order of profitability index as in the following table:

Project	Profitability Index	Investment
L	0.43	$7
J	0.33	3
M	0.33	6
N	0.25	4
K	0.20	5

Starting from the top, we run out of funds after accepting projects L and J. While J and M have equal profitability indexes, project M could not be chosen because it would force total investment above the limit of $10 million.

8.9   The profitability index gives the correct ranking for the first pair, but the incorrect ranking for the second:

Project	PV	Investment	NPV	Profitability Index (NPV/Investment)
Short	$1,860,500	$1,000,000	$ 860,500	0.86
Long	4,000,000	1,000,000	3,000,000	3.0
Small	3,721	1,000	2,721	2.7
Large	1,395,349	1,000,000	395,349	0.395

SOLUTIONS TO SPREADSHEET QUESTIONS

8.1   NPV would be calculated as £221.08 million.

8.2   This value, £221.08 million, is 1.13 times as great as the value in Table 8–1 because each cash flow is discounted for one fewer period. The Excel NPV function assumes the first cash flow comes after one period. In this example, the first cash flow actually comes immediately.

MINICASE

Flowton Products enjoys a steady demand for stainless steel infiltrators used in a number of chemical processes. Revenues from the infiltrator division are $50 million a year and production costs are $47.5 million. However, the 10 high-precision Munster stamping machines that are used in the production process are coming to the end of their useful life. One possibility is simply to replace each existing machine with a new Munster. These machines would cost $800,000 each and would not involve any additional operating costs. The alternative is to buy 10 centrally controlled Skilboro stampers. Skilboros cost $1.25 million each, but compared to the Munster, they would produce a total saving in operator and material costs of $500,000 a year. Moreover, the Skilboro is sturdily built and would last 10 years, compared with an estimated 7-year life for the Munster.

		Cash Flows (millions of dollars)				
	Year:	0	1–7	8	9	10
Munster						
Investment		−8.0				
Revenues			50.0	0	0	0
Costs			47.5	0	0	0
Net cash flow		−8.0	2.5	0	0	0
NPV at 15%		$2.40 million				
IRR		24.5%				
Payback period		3.2 years				
Skilboro						
Investment		−12.5				
Revenues			50.0	50.0	50.0	50.0
Costs			47.0	47.0	47.0	47.0
Net cash flow		−12.5	3.0	3.0	3.0	3.0
NPV at 15%		$2.56 million				
IRR		20.2%				
Payback period		4.2 years				

Analysts in the infiltrator division have produced the accompanying summary table, which shows the forecast total cash flows from the infiltrator business over the life of each machine. Flowton's standard procedures for appraising capital investments involve calculating net present value, internal rate of return, and payback, and these measures are also shown in the table.

As usual, Emily Balsam arrived early at Flowton's head office. She had never regretted joining Flowton. Everything about the place, from the mirror windows to the bell fountain in the atrium, suggested a classy outfit. Ms. Balsam sighed happily and reached for the envelope at the top of her in-tray. It was an analysis from the infiltrator division of the replacement options for the stamper machines. Pinned to the paper was the summary table of cash flows and a note from the CFO, which read, "Emily, I have read through 20 pages of excruciating detail and I still don't know which of these machines we should buy. The NPV calculation seems to indicate that the Skilboro is best, while IRR and payback suggest the opposite. Would you take a look and tell me what we should do and why."

Can you help Ms. Balsam by writing a memo to the CFO? You need to justify your solution and also to explain why some or all of the measures in the summary tables are inappropriate.

CAPITAL STRUCTURE AND COST OF CAPITAL

CHAPTER 6

Valuing Bonds

LEARNING OBJECTIVES

After studying this chapter, you should be able to:

1. Distinguish among a bond's coupon rate, current yield, and yield to maturity.

2. Find the market price of a bond given its yield to maturity, find a bond's yield given its price, and demonstrate why prices and yields vary inversely.

3. Show why bonds exhibit interest rate risk.

4. Understand why investors pay attention to bond ratings and demand a higher interest rate for bonds with low ratings.

Related Web sites for this chapter can be found at www.mhhe.com/bmm6e.

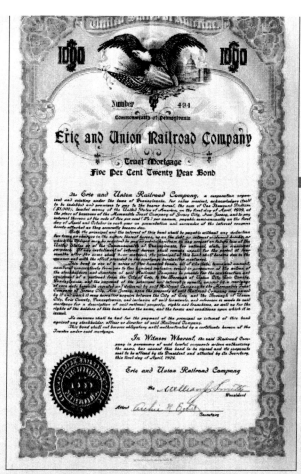

Bondholders once received a beautifully engraved certificate like this 1909 one for an Erie and Union Railroad bond. Nowadays their ownership is simply recorded on an electronic database.

Courtesy of Terry Cox

Investment in new plant and equipment requires money—often a lot of money. Sometimes firms may be able to save enough out of previous earnings to cover the cost of investments, but often they need to raise cash from investors. In broad terms, we can think of two ways to raise new money from investors: borrow the cash or sell additional shares of common stock.

If companies need the money only for a short while, they may borrow it from a bank; if they need it to make long-term investments, they generally issue bonds, which are simply long-term loans. When companies issue bonds, they promise to make a series of fixed interest payments and then

to repay the debt. As long as the company generates sufficient cash, the payments on a bond are certain. In this case bond valuation involves straightforward time-value-of-money computations. But there is some chance that even the most blue-chip company will fall on hard times and will not be able to repay its debts. Investors take this default risk into account when they price the bonds and demand a higher interest rate to compensate.

Companies are not the only bond issuers. State and local governments also raise money by selling bonds. So does the U.S. Treasury. There is always some risk that a company or municipality will not be able to come up with the cash to repay its bonds, but investors in Treasury issues can be confident that the government will make the promised payments. Therefore, in the first part of this chapter we focus on Treasury bonds and sidestep the issue of default. We show how bond prices are determined by market interest rates and how those prices respond to changes in rates. We also consider the yield to maturity and discuss why a bond's yield may vary with its time to maturity.

Later in the chapter we look at corporate bonds, where there is a possibility of default. We will see how bond ratings provide a guide to that default risk and how low-grade bonds offer higher promised yields.

In Chapter 14 we will look in more detail at the securities that companies issue, and we will see that there are many variations on bond design. But for now, we keep our focus on garden-variety bonds and general principles of bond valuation.

6.1 The Bond Market

bond
Security that obligates
the issuer to make
specified payments to the
bondholder.

Governments and corporations borrow money by selling **bonds** to investors. The market for these bonds is huge. In 2008 public holdings of U.S. government bonds totaled $3.5 trillion ($3,500,000,000,000).[1] Companies also raise very large sums of money by selling bonds. For example, General Motors once borrowed $17 billion by an issue of bonds. The market for all these bonds is sophisticated and active. Bond traders frequently make massive trades motivated by tiny price discrepancies.

When governments or companies issue bonds, they promise to make a series of interest payments and then to repay the debt. But don't get the idea that all bonds are alike. For example, most bonds make a fixed interest payment, but in other cases the payment may go up or down as short-term interest rates change. Bonds may also have different maturities. Sometimes a company may borrow for only a few years, but there have been a few occasions when bonds have been issued with maturities of 100 years or more.

Now and again you may encounter some exotic bonds. For example, managers of insurance companies constantly worry about the possibility of a major hurricane or earthquake that could prompt a flood of costly claims. In 2007 Travelers Companies shed part of this risk by issuing *catastrophe* (or *cat*) *bonds*. Travelers' cat bonds offered a tempting rate of interest, but if a hurricane strikes the northeast of the United States, the payments on the bonds are cut. Investors in the Travelers' bonds therefore share catastrophe risk with the insurer. Cat bonds and other such exotic issues are fairly rare; most corporate bonds are of the common or garden variety. But bond issuers are always on the lookout for innovative forms of debt that they hope will attract investors.

Bond Characteristics

face value
Payment at the maturity
of the bond. Also called
principal or *par value*.

coupon
The interest payments paid
to the bondholder.

In February 2001 the U.S. government made a typical issue of a Treasury bond. It auctioned off to investors $11 billion of 5% bonds maturing in 2011. The bonds have a **face value** (also called the *principal* or *par value*) of $1,000. Each year until the bond matures, the bondholder receives an interest payment of 5% of the face value, or $50. This 5% interest payment is called the bond's **coupon.** In the old days, most bonds used to have coupons that the investor clipped off and mailed to the bond issuer to claim their payment. When the 5% coupon bond matures in 2011, the government must pay the $1,000 face value of the bond in addition to the final coupon payment.

The prices at which you can buy and sell each Treasury bond are shown each day in the financial press and on the Web. At last count there were 190 different Treasury bonds. Table 6–1, which is compiled from *The Wall Street Journal*'s Web page, shows the prices for just a small sample of these issues. The entry for the 5% bond maturing in February 2011 is highlighted.

Prices are generally quoted in 32nds rather than decimals. Thus for the 5% bond, the *asked price*—that is, the price that investors need to pay to buy the bond—is shown as 108:06. This means that the price is 108 and 6/32, or 108.1875% of face value. Therefore, each bond costs $1,081.88. An investor who *already* owns the bond and wishes to *sell* it would receive the *bid price*, which is shown as 108:05. Just as the used-car dealer earns a living by reselling cars at higher prices than he paid for them, so the bond dealer needs to charge a *spread* between the bid and the asked price. Notice that the spread for these 5% bonds is only 1/32, or about .03% of the bond's value. Don't you wish that used-car dealers charged similar spreads?

The final column in the table shows the *asked yield to maturity*. This measures the return to investors if they buy the bond at the asked price and hold it to maturity in 2011. You can see that the 5% coupon Treasury bond offers a yield to maturity of 2.16%. We will explain shortly how this figure was calculated.

You can't buy Treasury bonds on the stock exchange. Instead, they are traded by a network of bond dealers, who quote bid and ask prices at which they are prepared to

---

[1] This figure includes Treasury notes (bonds maturing in 2 to 10 years) as well as long-term bonds maturing in more than 10 years.

TABLE 6–1 Sample Treasury bond quotes for February 15, 2008

Maturity	Coupon	Bid Price	Asked Price	Asked Yield %
2010 Feb 15	3.50	103:01	103:02	1.91
2011 Feb 15	**5.00**	**108:05**	**108:06**	**2.16**
2012 Feb 15	4.875	109:02	109:03	2.46
2013 Feb 15	3.875	105:02	105:03	2.77
2018 Feb 15	3.50	97:23	97:24	3.77
2023 Feb 15	7.125	130:04	130:05	4.36
2029 Feb 15	5.25	109:15	109:16	4.54
2037 Feb 15	4.75	102:25	102:26	4.57

Source: The Wall Street Journal Web site, **www.wsj.com**.

FIGURE 6–1 Cash flows to an investor in the 5% coupon bond maturing in the year 2011

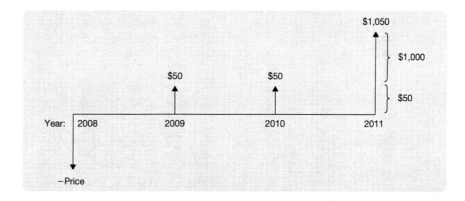

buy and sell. For example, suppose that in 2008 you decide to buy the "5s of 2011," that is, the 5% coupon bonds maturing in 2011. You approach a broker who checks the current price on her screen. If you are happy to go ahead with the purchase, your broker will contact a bond dealer and the trade is done.

If you plan to hold your bond until maturity, you can look forward to the cash flows shown in Figure 6–1. For the first 2 years, the cash flows equal the 5% coupon payment. Then, when the bond matures in 2011, you receive the $1,000 face value of the bond plus the final coupon payment.

Self-Test 6.1

Find the 3.50% coupon 2018 Treasury bond in Table 6–1.

a. How much does it cost to buy the bond?
b. If you already owned the bond, how much would a bond dealer pay you for it?
c. What annual interest payment does the bond make?
d. What is the bond's yield to maturity?

6.2 Interest Rates and Bond Prices

In Figure 6–1 we set out the cash flows from your 5% Treasury bond. The value of the bond is the present value of these cash flows. To find this value, you need to discount each future payment by the current interest rate.

The 5s were not the only Treasury bonds that matured in 2011. Almost identical bonds maturing at the same time offered an interest rate of about 2.15%. So, if the 5s had offered a lower return than 2.15%, no one would have been willing to hold them. Equally, if they had offered a *higher* return, everyone would have rushed to sell their other bonds and buy the 5s. In other words, if investors were on their toes, the 5s had to offer the same 2.15% rate of interest as similar Treasury bonds. You might recognize

2.15% as the opportunity cost of the funds invested in the bond, as we discussed in Chapter 2. This is the rate that investors could earn by placing their funds in similar securities rather than in this bond.

We can now calculate the present value of the 5s of 2011 by discounting the cash flows at 2.15%:

$$PV = \frac{\$50}{(1+r)} + \frac{\$50}{(1+r)^2} + \frac{\$1,050}{(1+r)^3}$$

$$= \frac{\$50}{(1.0215)} + \frac{\$50}{(1.0215)^2} + \frac{\$1,050}{(1.0215)^3} = \$1,081.95$$

Bond prices are usually expressed as a percentage of their face value. Thus we can say that your 5% Treasury bond is worth 108.195% of face value.[2]

Did you notice that your bond is like a package of two investments? The first provides a level stream of coupon payments of $50 a year for each of 3 years. The second consists of the final repayment of the $1,000 face value. Therefore, you can use the annuity formula to value the coupon payments and then add on the present value of the final payment of face value:

$$PV = PV(\text{coupons}) + PV(\text{face value})$$

$$= (\text{coupon} \times \text{annuity factor}) + (\text{face value} \times \text{discount factor}) \qquad (6.1)$$

$$= \$50 \times \left[\frac{1}{.0215} - \frac{1}{.0215(1.0215)^3} \right] + 1,000 \times \frac{1}{1.0215^3}$$

$$= \$143.77 + \$938.18 = \$1,081.95$$

If you need to value a bond with many years to run before maturity, it is usually easiest to value the coupon payments as an annuity and then add on the present value of the final payment.

Self-Test 6.2 Calculate the present value of a 6-year bond with a 9% coupon. The interest rate is 12%.

EXAMPLE 6.1 ▶ Bond Prices and Semiannual Coupon Payments

Thus far we've assumed that interest payments occur annually. This is the case for bonds in many European countries, but in the United States most bonds make coupon payments *semiannually*. So when you hear that a bond in the United States has a coupon rate of 5%, you can generally assume that the bond makes a payment of $50/2 = $25 every 6 months. Similarly, when investors in the United States refer to the bond's interest rate, they usually mean the semiannually compounded interest rate. Thus an interest rate quoted at 2.15% really means that the 6-month rate is 2.15/2 = 1.075%.[3]

---

[2] Our calculated value of $1081.95 (108.195%) is a little higher than the asked price of 108 6/32% quoted in Table 6–1. We discounted at 2.15%, which is rounded down slightly from the asked yield to maturity of 2.16%. Also, the bond's actual coupon is not $50 per year, but $25 every six months. In the next example, we'll show how to handle semiannual coupons.

[3] You may have noticed that the semiannually compounded interest rate on the bond is also the bond's APR, although this term is not generally used by bond investors. To find the effective rate, we can use a formula that we presented in Section 5.6:

$$\text{Effective annual rate} = \left(1 + \frac{\text{APR}}{m}\right)^m - 1$$

where m is the number of payments each year. In the case of our Treasury bond,

$$\text{Effective annual rate} = \left(1 + \frac{.0215}{2}\right)^2 - 1 = 1.01075^2 - 1 = .02162, \text{ or } 2.162\%$$

FIGURE 6–2 Cash flows to an investor in the 5% coupon bond maturing in 2011. The bond pays semiannual coupons, so there are two payments of $25 each year.

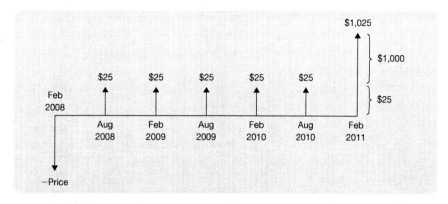

The actual cash flows on the Treasury bond are illustrated in Figure 6–2. To value the bond a bit more precisely, we should have discounted the series of semiannual payments by the semiannual rate of interest as follows:

$$PV = \frac{\$25}{(1.01075)} + \frac{\$25}{(1.01075)^2} + \frac{\$25}{(1.01075)^3} + \frac{\$25}{(1.01075)^4} + \frac{\$25}{(1.01075)^5} + \frac{\$1,025}{(1.01075)^6}$$
$$= \$1082.37$$

Thus, once we allow for the fact that coupon payments are semiannual, the value of the 5s is 108.237% of face value, which is slightly higher than the value that we obtained when we assumed annual coupon payments.[4] Since semiannual coupon payments just add to the arithmetic, we will stick for the most part to our simplification and assume annual interest payments.

How Bond Prices Vary with Interest Rates

Figure 6–3 plots the interest rate on 10-year Treasury bonds from 1900 to 2007. Notice how much the interest rate fluctuates. At the end of 1945 these bonds offered a measly 1.7% rate of interest. By the close of 1981 the interest rate on 10-year Treasuries had jumped to nearly 14%.

FIGURE 6–3 The interest rate on 10-year U.S. Treasury bonds

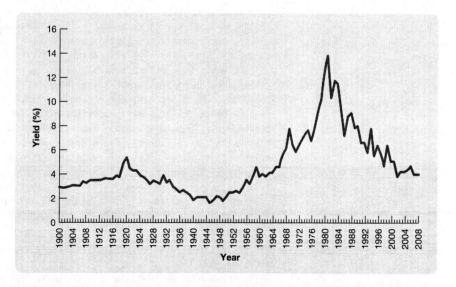

[4] Why is the present value a bit higher in this case? Because now we recognize that half the annual coupon payment is received only 6 months into the year, rather than at year-end. Since part of the coupon income is received earlier, its present value is higher.

As interest rates change, so do bond prices. For example, suppose that investors demanded an interest rate of 5% on 3-year Treasury bonds. What would be the price of the Treasury 5s of 2011? Just repeat our PV calculation with a discount rate of $r = .05$:

$$\text{PV at } 5\% = \frac{\$50}{(1.05)} + \frac{\$50}{(1.05)^2} + \frac{\$1,050}{(1.05)^3} = \$1,000.00$$

Thus when the interest rate is the same as the coupon rate (5% in our example), the bond sells for its face value.

We first valued the Treasury bond using an interest rate of 2.15%, which is lower than the coupon rate. In that case the price of the bond was *higher* than its face value. We then valued it using an interest rate that is equal to the coupon and found that bond price equaled face value. You have probably already guessed that when the cash flows are discounted at a rate that is *higher* than the bond's coupon rate, the bond is worth *less* than its face value. The following example confirms that this is the case.

EXAMPLE 6.2 ▶ Interest Rates and Bond Prices

Investors will pay $1,000 for a 5%, 3-year Treasury bond when the interest rate is 5%. Suppose that the interest rate is higher than the coupon rate at (say) 8%. Now what is the value of the bond? Simple! We just repeat our calculation but with $r = .08$:

$$\text{PV at } 8\% = \frac{\$50}{(1.08)} + \frac{\$50}{(1.08)^2} + \frac{\$1,050}{(1.08)^3} = \$922.69$$

The bond sells for 92.27% of face value.

This is a general result. When the market interest rate exceeds the coupon rate, bonds sell for less than face value. When the market interest rate is below the coupon rate, bonds sell for more than face value.

Suppose that interest rates rise. On hearing the news, bond investors appear disconsolate. Why? Don't they like higher interest rates? If you are not sure of the answer, look at Figure 6–4, which shows the present value of the 5% Treasury bond for different interest rates. For example, imagine yields soar from 2.15% to 8%. Our bond would then be worth only $922.69, creating a loss to bondholders of some 15%. Conversely, bondholders have reason to celebrate when market interest rates fall. You can see this also from Figure 6–4. For instance, if interest rates fall to 1%, the value of our 5% bond would increase to $1,117.64.

Figure 6–4 illustrates a fundamental relationship between interest rates and bond prices: **When the interest rate rises, the present value of the payments to be received by the bondholder falls and bond prices fall. Conversely, declines in the interest rate increase the present value of those payments and result in higher prices.**

A warning! People sometimes confuse the interest, or coupon, *payment* on the bond with the *interest rate*—that is, the return that investors require. The $50 coupon payments on our Treasury bond are *fixed* when the bond is issued. The **coupon rate**, 5%, measures the coupon payment ($50) as a percentage of the bond's face value ($1,000) and is therefore also fixed. **However, the interest rate changes from day to day. These changes affect the *present value* of the coupon payments but not the payments themselves.**

coupon rate
Annual interest payment as a percentage of face value.

Interest Rate Risk

We have just seen that bond prices fluctuate as interest rates change. In other words, bonds exhibit **interest rate risk.** Bond investors cross their fingers that market interest rates will fall, so that the price of their bond will rise. If they are unlucky and the market interest rate rises, the value of their investment falls.

interest rate risk
The risk in bond prices due to fluctuations in interest rates.

FIGURE 6–4 The value of the 5% bond falls as interest rates rise.

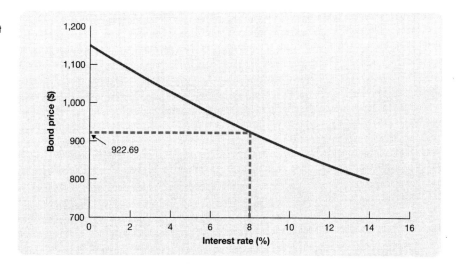

FIGURE 6–5 Plot of bond prices as a function of the interest rate. The price of long-term bonds is more sensitive to changes in the interest rate than is the price of short-term bonds.

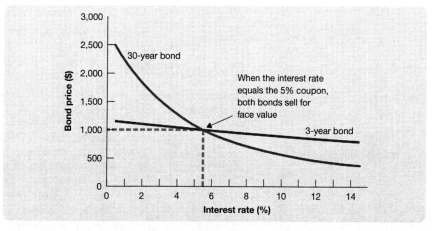

A change in interest rates has a greater effect on the prices of long-term bonds than on the prices of short-term bonds. For example, compare the two curves in Figure 6–5. The green line shows how the value of the 3-year, 5% coupon bond varies with the level of the interest rate. The purple line shows how the price of a 30-year, 5% bond varies with the level of interest rates. You can see that the 30-year bond is more sensitive to interest rate fluctuations than the 3-year bond. This should not surprise you. If you buy a 3-year bond when the market interest rate is 5% and rates then rise, you will be stuck with a bad deal—you have just loaned your money at a lower rate than you could have received if you had waited. However, think how much worse it would be if the loan had been for 30 years rather than 3 years. The longer the loan, the more income you have lost by accepting what turns out to be a low interest rate. This shows up in a bigger decline in the price of the longer-term bond. Of course, there is a flip side to this effect, which you can also see from Figure 6–5. When interest rates fall, the longer-term bond responds with a greater increase in price.

Self-Test 6.3

Suppose that the market interest rate rises overnight from 2.15% to 10%. Calculate the present values of the 5%, 3-year bond and of the 5%, 30-year bond both before and after this change in interest rates. Confirm that your answers correspond with Figure 6–5. Use your financial calculator or a spreadsheet. You can find a box on bond pricing using calculators on page 166 and using Excel on page 168.

6.3 Current Yield and Yield to Maturity

Suppose you are considering the purchase of a 3-year bond with a coupon rate of 10%. Your investment adviser quotes a price for the bond. How do you calculate the rate of return the bond offers?

For bonds priced at face value the answer is easy. The rate of return is the coupon rate. We can check this by setting out the cash flows on your investment:

	Cash Paid to You in Year:			
You Pay	1	2	3	Rate of Return
$1,000	$100	$100	$1,100	10%

Notice that in each year you earn 10% on your money ($100/$1,000). In the final year you also get back your original investment of $1,000. Therefore, your total return is 10%, the same as the coupon rate.

Now suppose that the market price of the 3-year bond is $1,136.16. Your cash flows are as follows:

	Cash Paid to You in Year:			
You Pay	1	2	3	Rate of Return
$1,136.16	$100	$100	$1,100	?

Notice that you are paying out $1,136.16 and receiving an annual income of $100. So your income as a proportion of the initial outlay is $100/$1,136.16 = .088, or 8.8%. This is sometimes called the bond's **current yield.**

However, your total return depends on both interest income and any capital gains or losses. A current yield of 8.8% may sound attractive only until you realize that the bond's price must fall. The price today is $1,136.16, but when the bond matures 3 years from now, the bond will sell for its face value, or $1,000. A price decline (i.e., a *capital loss*) of $136.16 is guaranteed, so the overall return over the next 3 years must be less than the 8.8% current yield.

Let us generalize. A bond that is priced above its face value is said to sell at a *premium.* Investors who buy a bond at a premium face a capital loss over the life of the bond, so the return on these bonds is always less than the bond's current yield. A bond priced below face value sells at a *discount.* Investors in discount bonds face a capital *gain* over the life of the bond; the return on these bonds is *greater* than the current yield: **Because it focuses only on current income and ignores prospective price increases or decreases, the** *current* **yield does not measure the bond's total rate of return. It overstates the return of premium bonds and understates that of discount bonds.**

We need a measure of return that takes account of both coupon payments and the change in a bond's value over its life. The standard measure is called **yield to maturity.** The yield to maturity is the answer to the following question: At what interest rate would the bond be correctly priced? **The yield to maturity is defined as the discount rate that makes the present value of the bond's payments equal to its price.**

If you can buy the 3-year bond at face value, the yield to maturity is the coupon rate, 10%. We can check this by noting that when we discount the cash flows at 10%, the present value of the bond is equal to its $1,000 face value:

current yield
Annual coupon payments divided by bond price.

yield to maturity
Interest rate for which the present value of the bond's payments equals the price.

$$PV \text{ at } 10\% = \frac{\$100}{(1.10)} + \frac{\$100}{(1.10)^2} + \frac{\$1,100}{(1.10)^3} = \$1,000.00$$

But suppose the price of the 3-year bond is $1,136.16. In this case the yield to maturity is only 5%. At that discount rate, the bond's present value equals its actual market price, $1,136.16:

$$\text{PV at } 5\% = \frac{\$100}{(1.05)} + \frac{\$100}{(1.05)^2} + \frac{\$1,100}{(1.05)^3} = \$1,136.16$$

EXAMPLE 6.3   ▶   Calculating Yield to Maturity for the Treasury Bond

We found the value of the 5% coupon Treasury bond by discounting at a 2.15% interest rate. We could have phrased the question the other way around: If the price of the bond is $1,081.95, what is the bond's yield to maturity? To calculate the yield, we need to find the discount rate r that solves the following equation:

$$\text{Price} = \frac{\$50}{(1+r)} + \frac{\$50}{(1+r)^2} + \frac{\$1,050}{(1+r)^3} = \$1,081.95$$

To compute the yield to maturity, most people use either a financial calculator or a spreadsheet. For your Treasury bond you would enter a PV on your calculator of $1,081.95.[5] The bond provides a regular payment of $50, entered as PMT = 50. The bond has a future value of $1,000, so FV = 1,000. The bond life is 3 years, so $n = 3$. Now compute the interest rate, and you will find that the yield to maturity is 2.15%. The nearby boxes review the use of spreadsheets and financial calculators in bond valuation problems.

The yield to maturity is a measure of a bond's total return, including both coupon income and capital gain. If you buy the bond today and hold it to maturity, your return will be the yield to maturity. Bond investors often refer loosely to a bond's "yield." It's a safe bet that they are talking about its yield to maturity rather than its current yield.

The only *general* procedure for calculating yield to maturity is trial and error. You guess at an interest rate and calculate the present value of the bond's payments. If the present value is greater than the actual price, your discount rate must have been too low, so you try a higher interest rate (since a higher rate results in a lower PV). Conversely, if PV is less than price, you must reduce the interest rate. When a financial calculator or spreadsheet program finds a bond's yield to maturity, it uses a similar trial-and-error process.

EXAMPLE 6.4   ▶   Yield to Maturity with Semiannual Coupon Payments

Let's redo Example 6.3, but this time we recognize that the coupons are paid semi-annually. Instead of three annual coupons of $50, the bond makes six semiannual payments of $25. We can find the *semiannual* yield to maturity on our calculators by using these inputs: $n = 6$ (semiannual) periods, PV = −1,081.95, FV = 1,000, PMT = 25. We then compute the interest rate to find that it is 1.082%. This of course is a 6-month, not an annual, rate. Bond dealers typically annualize the semiannual rate by doubling it, so the yield to maturity would be quoted as 1.082 × 2 = 2.164%. [In Excel (see the box on page 168), you can confirm that = YIELD(DATE(2008,2,15), DATE(2011,2,15),.05,108.195,100,2) = .02164.] A better way to annualize would be to account for compound interest. A dollar invested at 1.082% for two 6-month periods would grow to $1 × (1.01082)^2 = $1.0218. The *effective* annual yield is therefore 2.18%.

---

[5] Actually, on most calculators you would enter this as a negative number, −1,081.95, because the purchase of the bond represents a cash *outflow*. See the nearby box on financial calculators.

FINANCIAL CALCULATOR

Bond Valuation on a Financial Calculator

In Chapter 5 we saw that financial calculators can compute the present values of level annuities as well as the present values of one-time future cash flows. Coupon bonds present both of these characteristics: The coupon payments are level annuities, and the final payment of face value is an additional one-time payment. Thus for the coupon bond we looked at in Example 6.3, you would treat the periodic payment as PMT = $50, the final or future one-time payment as FV = $1,000, the number of periods as n = 3 years, and the interest rate as the yield to maturity of the bond, i = 2.15%. You would thus compute the value of the bond using the following sequence of keystrokes. By the way, the order in which the various inputs for the bond valuation problem are entered does not matter.

Hewlett-Packard HP-10B	Sharp EL-733A	Texas Instruments BA II Plus
50 PMT	50 PMT	50 PMT
1000 FV	1000 FV	1000 FV
3 N	3 N	3 N
2.15 I/YR	2.15 i	2.15 I/Y
PV	COMP PV	CPT PV

Your calculator should now display a value of −1,081.95. The minus sign reminds us that the initial cash flow is negative: You have to pay to buy the bond.

You can also use the calculator to find the yield to maturity of a bond. For example, if you buy this bond for $1,081.95, you should find that its yield to maturity is 2.15%. Let's check that this is so. You enter the PV as −1,081.95 because you buy the bond for this price. Thus to solve for the interest rate, use the following keystrokes:

Hewlett-Packard HP-10B	Sharp EL-733A	Texas Instruments BA II Plus
50 PMT	50 PMT	50 PMT
1000 FV	1000 FV	1000 FV
3 N	3 N	3 N
−1,081.95 PV	−1,081.95 PV	−1,081.95 PV
I/YR	COMP i	CPT I/Y

Your calculator should now display 2.15%, the yield to maturity of the bond.

Self-Test 6.4

A 4-year maturity bond with a 14% coupon rate can be bought for $1,200. What is the yield to maturity if the coupon is paid annually? What if it is paid semiannually? You will need a spreadsheet or a financial calculator to answer this question.

6.4 Bond Rates of Return

The yield to maturity is defined as the discount rate that equates the bond's price to the present value of all its promised future cash flows. It measures the rate of return that you will earn if you buy the bond today and hold it to maturity. However, as interest rates fluctuate, the return that you earn in the interim may be very different from the yield to maturity. If interest rates rise in a particular week, month, or year, the price of your bond will fall and your return for that period will be reduced. Conversely, if rates fall, the price of your bond will rise and your return will be increased. This is emphasized in the following example.

EXAMPLE 6.5 ▶ Rate of Return versus Yield to Maturity

Barron's called it the perfect storm. For bond investors, the spring of 2003 had been a period of fine weather and plain sailing. But in June, remarks by the Fed's chairman and an unexpectedly small interest rate cut by the Federal Reserve prompted a sharp fall in bond prices.

Suppose you had purchased the 5% bond in February 2003, just after it paid its coupon. Its yield to maturity in February was less than 3%, and the bond was selling for about $1,160. But by the end of the summer, the yield to maturity had increased to almost 4.1%. By the time it paid its next coupon in August, the bond's price had declined to $1,060. Over this 6-month period you would have collected $25 in coupon income (this is the semiannual payment on the 5% coupon bond with face value $1,000), but you would have suffered a capital loss of $100 on your investment. Your total dollar profit would have been $25 − $100 = −$75, and your 6-month **rate of return** would have been

rate of return

Total income per period per dollar invested.

$$\text{Rate of return} = \frac{\text{coupon income} + \text{price change}}{\text{investment}} \quad (6.2)$$

$$= \frac{\$25 - \$100}{1,160} = -.0647 = -6.47\%$$

Because yields rose during this period, bond prices fell, and investors earned negative returns. Do not confuse the bond's rate of return over a particular investment period with its yield to maturity.

It could have been worse; you could have owned long-term Treasury bonds, which were more affected by the rise in interest rates. For example, the price of Treasury 6.25% bonds of 2030 fell by nearly twice as much as the 5s of 2011.

Self-Test 6.5

Suppose that in February 2008 you had purchased the 5s of 2011 for $1,081.95, when they were yielding 2.15%, and that 12 months later the yield to maturity on the bond had fallen to 1.5%. Confirm that the rate of return on your bond would have been greater than the 2.15% yield to maturity.

Is there *any* connection between the yield to maturity and the rate of return during a particular period? Yes: If the bond's yield to maturity remains unchanged during the period, its rate of return will equal that yield. We can check this by assuming that the yield on the 5s of 2011 stays at 2.15%. If investors still demand an interest rate of 2.15% after 1 year, the value of the bond will be

$$PV = \frac{\$50}{1.0215} + \frac{\$1,050}{1.0215^2} = \$1,055.21$$

At the end of the 12 months you receive a coupon payment of $50 and have a bond worth $1,055.21, a bit less than you paid for it. The rate of return is therefore

$$\text{Rate of return} = \frac{\text{coupon income} + \text{price change}}{\text{investment}}$$

$$= \frac{50 + (1,055.21 - 1,081.95)}{1,081.95} = .0215, \text{ or } 2.15\%$$

The return on your investment is just equal to the yield to maturity.

When interest rates do not change, the bond price changes with time so that the total return on the bond is equal to the yield to maturity. The rate of return will be less than the yield to maturity if interest rates rise, and it will be greater than the yield to maturity if interest rates fall.

Self-Test 6.6

Suppose that in February 2009 you buy one of the 5s of 2011 for $1,055.21 and hold it for another year. At the end of that time the bond will have only 1 more year to maturity. Show that if the bond's yield to maturity remains at 2.15%, your return over the year will also be 2.15%.

The solid curve in Figure 6–6 plots the price of a 30-year maturity, 6% coupon Treasury bond over time assuming that its yield to maturity is currently 4% and remains at 4%. The price declines gradually until the maturity date, when it finally reaches face value. In each period, the price decline offsets the coupon income by just enough to reduce total return to 4%. The dashed curve in Figure 6–6 shows the corresponding price path for a bond with a 2% coupon that sells at a discount to face value. In this case, the coupon income would provide less than a competitive rate of return, so the

SPREADSHEET SOLUTIONS

Bond Valuation

Excel and most other spreadsheet programs provide built-in functions to compute bond values and yields. They typically ask you to input both the date you buy the bond (called the *settlement date*) and the maturity date of the bond.

The Excel function for bond value is
= PRICE(settlement date, maturity date, annual coupon rate, yield to maturity, final payment, number of coupon payments per year)

An interactive version of this spreadsheet can be found at **www.mhhe.com/bmm6e**.

For our 5% coupon bond, we would enter the values in column B in the spreadsheet below. Alternatively, we could simply enter the following function in Excel:

= PRICE(DATE(2008,02,15),DATE(2011,02,15), .05,.0215,100,1)

The DATE function in Excel, which we use for both the settlement and maturity date, uses the format DATE (year,month,day).

Notice that the coupon rate and yield to maturity are expressed as decimals, not percentages. In most cases, final payment will be 100 (i.e., 100% of face value), and the resulting price will be expressed as a percent of face value. Occasionally, however, you may encounter bonds that pay off at a premium or discount to face value.

The value of the bond, assuming annual coupon payments, is 108.195% of face value, or $1,081.95. If we wanted to assume semiannual coupon payments, we would simply change the entry in cell B12 to 2, and the bond value would change to 108.237% of face value, as we found in Example 6.1.

In this example, we assume that the first coupon payment comes in exactly one period (either a year or a half-year). In other words, the settlement date is precisely at the

	A	B	C	D	E	F
1						
2		Valuing bonds using a spreadsheet				
3						
4		5% coupon		6% coupon		
5		maturing Feb 2011		10-year maturity		
6						
7	Settlement date	2/15/2008		1/1/2000		
8	Maturity date	2/15/2011		1/1/2010		
9	Annual coupon rate	0.05		0.06		
10	Yield to maturity	0.0215		0.07		
11	Final payment (% of face value)	100		100		
12	Coupon payments per year	1		1		
13						
14	Bond price (% of par)	108.195		92.976		
15						
16						
17		The formula entered here is: =PRICE(B7,B8,B9,B10,B11,B12)				

Please visit us at www.mhhe.com/bmm6e

FIGURE 6–6 How bond prices change as they approach maturity, assuming an unchanged yield. Prices of both premium and discount bonds approach face value as their maturity date approaches.

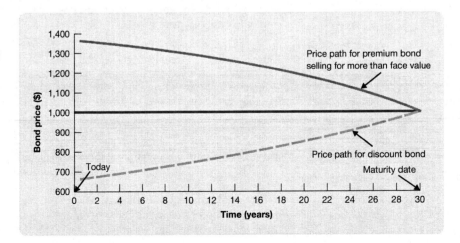

beginning of the period. However, the PRICE function will make the necessary adjustments for intraperiod purchase dates.

Suppose now that you wish to find the price of a 10-year maturity bond with a coupon rate of 6% (paid annually), selling at a yield to maturity of 7%. You are not given a specific settlement or maturity date. You can still use the PRICE function to value the bond. Simply choose an arbitrary settlement date (January 1, 2000 is convenient) and let the maturity date be 10 years hence. The appropriate inputs appear in column D of the spreadsheet on the previous page, with the resulting price, 92.976% of face value, appearing in cell D14. You can confirm this value on your calculator using the inputs: $n = 10$, $i = 7$, FV = 1000, PMT = 60.

Excel also provides a function for yield to maturity. It is = YIELD(settlement date, maturity date, annual coupon rate, bond price, final payment as percent of face value, number of coupon payments per year)

For example, to find the yield to maturity in Example 6.3, we would use column B in the spreadsheet below. If the coupons were paid semiannually, as in Example 6.4, we would change the entry for payments per year to 2 (see cell E12), and the yield would increase to 2.16%.

6.1 Suppose the yield to maturity on the February 2011 bond increases from 2.15% to 2.5% (assume annual coupon payments). What will happen to the bond's price? What is the percentage change in price?

6.2 Now assume the bond matures in February 2021. What is the price at an initial yield to maturity of 2.15% and the higher yield of 2.5%? What is the percentage change in price? Is the price of the longer-maturity bond more or less sensitive to changes in yields than that of the shorter-maturity bond?

6.3 If the price of the February 2011 bond decreases from 108.195 to 105, what happens to its yield to maturity?

	A	B	C	D	E	F	G
1							
2			Finding yield to maturity using a spreadsheet				
3			February 2011 maturity bond, coupon rate = 5%, maturity = 3 years				
4							
5			**Annual coupons**		Semiannual coupons		
6							
7	Settlement date		2/15/2008		2/15/2008		
8	Maturity date		2/15/2011		2/15/2011		
9	Annual coupon rate		0.05		0.05		
10	Bond price		108.195		108.195		
11	Redemption value (% of face value)		100		100		
12	Coupon payments per year		1		2		
13							
14	**Yield to maturity (decimal)**		0.0215		0.0216		
15							
16							
17			The formula entered here is: =YIELD(B7,B8,B9,B10,B11,B12)				

Please visit us at www.mhhe.com/bmm6e

bond sells below face value. Its price gradually approaches face value, however, and the price gain each year brings its total return up to the market interest rate.

6.5 The Yield Curve

When you bought your 5% bond of 2011, you bought a package of semiannual coupon payments plus the final repayment of face value. But sometimes it is inconvenient to buy things in packages. For example, perhaps you did not need a regular income and would have preferred to buy just the final repayment in 2011. That's not a problem. The Treasury is prepared to split its bonds into a series of mini-bonds, each of which makes a single payment. These single-payment bonds are called *strips*.

The prices of strips are shown regularly in the financial press or on the Web. For example, in February 2008 it would have cost you $934.08 to buy a strip that just paid out $1,000 in February 2011. The yield on this 3-year mini-bond was 2.30%. In other words, $934.08 \times 1.0230^3 = \$1,000$.

FIGURE 6–7 Treasury strips are bonds that make a single payment. The yields on Treasury strips in February 2008 show that investors received a higher yield on longer-term bonds.

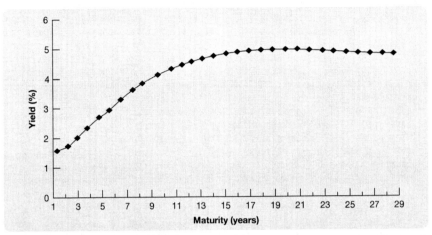

Source: Prepared from data in *The Wall Street Journal*, February 16, 2005. © 2005 by Dow Jones & Co. Inc, with permission of Dow Jones & Co. Inc. via Copyright Clearance Center.

yield curve

Plot of relationship between bond yields to maturity and time to maturity.

Bond investors often draw a plot of the relationship between bond yields and maturity. This is known as the **yield curve.** Treasury strips provide a convenient way to measure this yield curve. For example, if you look at Figure 6–7, you will see that in February 2008 one-year strips offered a yield to maturity of 1.7%; those with 20 or more years to run provided a yield of about 4.8%. In this case, the yield curve sloped upward.[6] This is usually the case, though sometimes long-term bonds offer *lower* yields, so the curve slopes downward.

But that raises a question. If long-term bonds offered much higher yields, why didn't everyone buy them? Who were the (foolish?) investors who put their money into short-term Treasuries at 2% or less?

Even when the yield curve is upward-sloping, investors might rationally stay away from long-term bonds for two reasons. First, the prices of long-term bonds fluctuate much more than prices of short-term bonds. We saw in Figure 6–5 that long-term bond prices are more sensitive to shifting interest rates. A sharp increase in interest rates could easily knock 20% or 30% off long-term bond prices. If investors don't like price fluctuations, they will invest their funds in short-term bonds unless they receive a higher yield to maturity on long-term bonds.

Second, short-term investors can profit if interest rates rise. Suppose you hold a 1-year bond. A year from now, when the bond matures, you can reinvest the proceeds and enjoy whatever rates the bond market offers then. These rates may be high enough to offset the first year's relatively low yield on the 1-year bond. Thus you often see an upward-sloping yield curve when future interest rates are expected to rise.

Self-Test 6.7   One-year Treasury bonds yield 5%, while 2-year bonds yield 6%. You are quite confident that in 1 year's time 1-year bonds will yield 8%. Would you buy the 2-year bond today?

Nominal and Real Rates of Interest

In Chapter 5 we drew a distinction between nominal and real rates of interest. The cash flows on the 5% Treasury bonds are fixed in nominal terms. Investors are sure to receive an interest payment of $50 each year, but they do not know what that money will buy them. The *real* interest rate on the Treasury bonds depends on the rate of

---

[6] Coupon bonds are like packages of strips. So investors often plot the yield curve using the yields on these packages. For example, you could plot the yields on the small sample of bonds in Table 6–1 against their maturity.

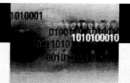

INTERNET INSIDER

Interest Rates and Bond Prices

Source: The Wall Street Journal Web site.

Bond Calculator

Log on to **www.smartmoney.com** to find a simple bond calculator that shows how prices change as interest rates change. Check whether a change in yield has a greater effect on the price of a long-term or a short-term bond.

Yield Curve

Look at the Living Yield Curve on **www.smartmoney.com.** This shows a moving picture of the yield curve. How does today's yield curve compare with yield curves in the past? Do short-term interest rates move more than long-term rates?

When we plotted the yield curve in Figure 6–7, we used the prices of Treasury strips. You can find current prices of strips by logging on to the Web site **www.wsj.com** and clicking on *Markets Data Center* and then *Bonds, Rates and Credit Markets.* Try plotting the yields on stripped coupons against maturity. Do they currently increase or decline with maturity? Can you explain why?

You can also use *The Wall Street Journal* site (**www.wsj.com**) to compare the yields on nominal Treasury bonds with those on TIPS. Suppose that you are confident that inflation will be 3% per year. Which bonds are the better buy?

inflation. For example, if the nominal rate of interest is 8% and the inflation rate is 4%, then the real interest rate is calculated as follows:

$$1 + \text{real interest rate} = \frac{1 + \text{nominal interest rate}}{1 + \text{inflation rate}} = \frac{1.08}{1.04} = 1.0385$$

$$\text{Real interest rate} = .0385 = 3.85\%$$

Since the inflation rate is uncertain, so is the real rate of interest on the Treasury bonds.

You *can* nail down a real rate of interest by buying an indexed bond, whose payments are linked to inflation. Indexed bonds have been available in some countries for many years, but they were almost unknown in the United States until 1997 when the U.S. Treasury began to issue inflation-indexed bonds known as *Treasury Inflation-Protected Securities,* or *TIPS.*[7] The real cash flows on TIPS are fixed, but the nominal cash flows (interest and principal) are increased as the consumer price index increases. For example, suppose the U.S. Treasury issues 3% coupon, 2-year TIPS. The *real* cash flows on the 2-year TIPS are therefore

	Year 1	Year 2
Real cash flows	$30	$1,030

The *nominal* cash flows on TIPS depend on the inflation rate. For example, suppose inflation turns out to be 5% in year 1 and a further 4% in year 2. Then the *nominal* cash flows would be

	Year 1	Year 2
Nominal cash flows	$30 × 1.05 = $31.50	$1,030 × 1.05 × 1.04 = $1,124.76

These cash payments are just sufficient to provide the holder with a 3% real rate of interest.

As we write this in early 2008, 10-year TIPS offer a yield of 1.5%. This yield is a *real* interest rate. It measures the amount of extra goods your investment will allow

---

[7] Indexed bonds were not completely unknown in the United States before 1997. For example, in 1780 American Revolution soldiers were compensated with indexed bonds that paid the value of "five bushels of corn, 68 pounds and four-sevenths part of a pound of beef, ten pounds of sheep's wool, and sixteen pounds of sole leather."

FIGURE 6–8 The bottom line shows the real yield on long-term indexed bonds issued by the U.K. government. The top line shows the yield on U.K. government long-term nominal bonds. Notice that the real yield has been much more stable than the nominal yield.

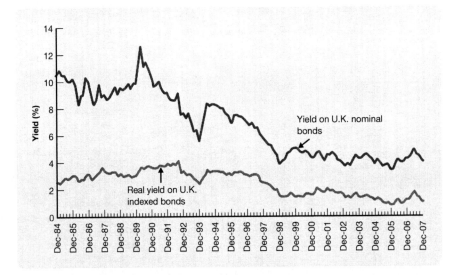

you to buy. The 1.5% real yield on TIPS is 2.3% less than the 3.8% yield on nominal 10-year Treasury bonds. If the annual inflation rate proves to be higher than 2.3%, you will earn a higher return by holding TIPS; if the inflation rate is lower than 2.3%, the reverse will be true.

Real interest rates depend on the supply of savings and the demand for new investment. As this supply-demand balance changes, real interest rates change. But they do so gradually. We can see this by looking at the United Kingdom, where the government has issued indexed bonds since 1982. The red line in Figure 6–8 shows that the (real) interest rate on these bonds has fluctuated within a relatively narrow range.

Suppose that investors revise upward their forecast of inflation by 1%. How will this affect interest rates? If investors are concerned about the purchasing power of their money, the changed forecast should not affect the real rate of interest. The *nominal* interest rate must therefore rise by 1% to compensate investors for the higher inflation prospects.

The blue line in Figure 6–8 shows the nominal rate of interest in the United Kingdom since 1985. You can see that the nominal rate is much more variable than the real rate. When investors were worried about inflation in the late 1980s, the nominal interest rate was about 7 percentage points above the real rate. As we write this in spring 2008, inflation fears have eased and the nominal interest rate in the United Kingdom is 3 percentage points above the real rate.

6.6 Corporate Bonds and the Risk of Default

Our focus so far has been on U.S. Treasury bonds. But the federal government is not the only issuer of bonds. State and local governments borrow by selling bonds.[8] So do corporations. Many foreign governments and corporations also borrow in the United States. At the same time U.S. corporations may borrow dollars or other currencies by issuing their bonds in other countries. For example, they may issue dollar bonds in London that are then sold to investors throughout the world.

There is an important distinction between bonds issued by corporations and those issued by the U.S. Treasury. National governments don't go bankrupt—they just print

---

[8] These *municipal bonds* enjoy a special tax advantage; investors are exempt from federal income tax on the coupon payments on state and local government bonds. As a result, investors are prepared to accept lower yields on this debt.

TABLE 6–2 Key to Moody's and Standard & Poor's bond ratings. The highest-quality bonds are rated triple A, then come double-A bonds, and so on.

Moody's	Standard & Poor's	Safety
Aaa	AAA	The strongest rating; ability to repay interest and principal is very strong.
Aa	AA	Very strong likelihood that interest and principal will be repaid.
A	A	Strong ability to repay, but some vulnerability to changes in circumstances.
Baa	BBB	Adequate capacity to repay; more vulnerability to changes in economic circumstances.
Ba	BB	Considerable uncertainty about ability to repay.
B	B	Likelihood of interest and principal payments over sustained periods is questionable.
Caa	CCC	Bonds that may already be in default or in danger of imminent default.
Ca	CC	
C	C	Little prospect for interest or principal on the debt ever to be repaid.

more money.[9] So investors do not worry that the U.S. Treasury will default on its bonds. However, there is some chance that corporations may get into financial difficulties and may default on their bonds. Thus the payments promised to corporate bondholders represent a best-case scenario: The firm will never pay more than the promised cash flows, but in hard times it may pay less.

default (or credit) risk
The risk that a bond issuer may default on its bonds.

The risk that a bond issuer may default on its obligations is called **default risk** (or **credit risk**). Companies need to compensate for this default risk by promising a higher rate of interest on their bonds. The difference between the promised yield on a corporate bond and the yield on a U.S. Treasury bond with the same coupon and maturity is called the **default premium.** The greater the chance that the company will get into trouble, the higher the default premium demanded by investors.

default premium
The additional yield on a bond that investors require for bearing credit risk.

The safety of most corporate bonds can be judged from bond ratings provided by Moody's, Standard & Poor's, or other bond-rating firms. Table 6–2 lists the possible bond ratings in declining order of quality. For example, the bonds that receive the highest Moody's rating are known as *Aaa* (or "triple A") bonds. Then come *Aa* ("double A"), *A, Baa* bonds, and so on. Bonds rated Baa and above are called **investment grade,** while those with a rating of Ba or below are referred to as *speculative grade, high-yield,* or **junk bonds.**

investment grade
Bonds rated Baa or above by Moody's or BBB or above by Standard & Poor's.

junk bond
Bond with a rating below Baa or BBB.

It is rare for highly rated bonds to default. For example, since 1971 fewer than 1 in 1,000 triple-A bonds have defaulted within 10 years of issue. However, when an investment-grade bond does default, the shock waves can be considerable. For example, in May 2001 WorldCom sold $11.8 billion of bonds with an investment-grade rating. Within little more than a year WorldCom filed for bankruptcy, and its bondholders lost more than 80% of their investment. For low-grade issues, defaults are more common. For example, over half of the bonds that were rated CCC by Standard & Poor's at issue have defaulted within 10 years.

As you would expect, the yield on corporate bonds varies with the bond rating. Figure 6–9 shows the extra yield on corporate bonds compared with U.S. Treasuries. You can see that the yield spreads rise as safety falls off. For example, as worries

---

[9] But they can't print money of other countries. Therefore, when a foreign government borrows dollars, investors worry that in some future crisis the government may not be able to come up with enough dollars to repay the debt. This worry shows up in the yield that investors demand on such debt. For example, in late 2001, the Argentine government defaulted on over $80 billion of debt. Bondholders were subsequently offered new bonds worth about a third of the face value of the defaulting bonds.

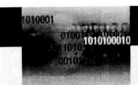

INTERNET INSIDER

Bond Ratings and Yields

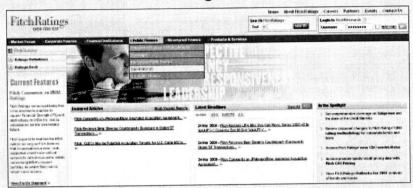

Source: Fitch Ratings Web site.

Bond Ratings
You can find the most recent bond rating for any company by logging on to the Web sites of one of the ratings companies. Try **www.fitch-ratings.com** (you need to register to use Moody's and Standard & Poor's sites, but not the Fitch Web site). Try finding the bond rating for some sample companies. Were they investment-grade or below?

Default Spreads
In Figure 6–9 we showed how bonds with greater credit risk have promised higher yields to maturity. This yield spread goes up when the economic outlook is particularly uncertain. You can check how much extra yield low-grade bonds offer today by looking at the entry for corporate bond spreads on **www.bondsonline.com.** Is the yield spread greater for short-term or long-term bonds? Can you explain why? Incidentally, the Bondsonline Web site also offers some useful explanations of bond markets.

about the economy intensified in 2008, the promised yield on junk bonds climbed to nearly 8% above the yield on Treasuries. You might have been tempted by the higher promised yields on the lower-grade bonds. But remember, these bonds do not always keep their promises.

EXAMPLE 6.6 ▶ Promised versus Expected Yield to Maturity

Bad Bet Inc. issued bonds several years ago with a coupon rate (paid annually) of 10% and face value of $1,000. The bonds are due to mature in 6 years. However, the firm is currently in bankruptcy proceedings, the firm has ceased to pay interest, and the bonds sell for only $200. Based on *promised* cash flow, the yield to maturity on the bond is 63.9%. (On your calculator, set PV = −200, FV = 1,000, PMT = 100, n = 6, and compute i.) But this calculation is based on the very unlikely possibility that the firm will resume paying interest and come out of bankruptcy. Suppose that the most likely outcome is that after 3 years of litigation, during which no interest will be paid, debt-holders will receive 27 cents on the dollar—that is, they will receive $270 for each

FIGURE 6–9 Yield spreads between corporate and 10-year Treasury bonds

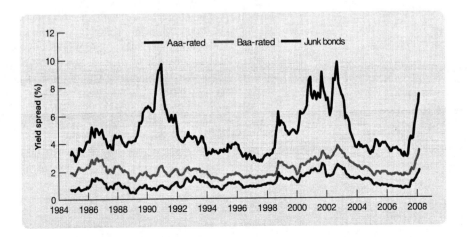

bond with $1,000 face value. In this case the expected return on the bond is 10.5%. (On your calculator, set PV = -200, FV = 270, PMT = 0, $n = 3$, and compute i.) When default is a real possibility, the promised yield can depart considerably from the expected return.

Variations in Corporate Bonds

Most corporate bonds are similar to the 5% Treasury bonds that we examined earlier in the chapter. In other words, they promise to make a fixed nominal coupon payment for each year until maturity, at which point they also promise to repay the face value. However, you will find that there is greater variety in the design of corporate bonds. We will return to this issue in Chapter 14, but here are a few types of corporate bonds that you may encounter.

Zero-Coupon Bonds Corporations sometimes issue zero-coupon bonds. In this case, investors receive $1,000 face value at the maturity date but do not receive a regular coupon payment. In other words, the bond has a coupon rate of zero. The bonds are like Treasury strips. They are issued at prices well below face value, and the investor's return comes from the difference between the purchase price and the payment of face value at maturity.

Floating-Rate Bonds Sometimes the coupon rate can change over time. For example, floating-rate bonds make coupon payments that are tied to some measure of current market rates. The rate might be reset once a year to the current short-term Treasury rate plus 2%. So if the Treasury rate at the start of the year is 6%, the bond's coupon rate over the next year is set at 8%. This arrangement means that the bond's coupon rate always approximates current market interest rates.

Convertible Bonds If you buy a convertible bond, you can choose later to exchange it for a specified number of shares of common stock. For example, a convertible bond that is issued at face value of $1,000 may be convertible into 50 shares of the firm's stock. Because convertible bonds offer the opportunity to participate in any price appreciation of the company's stock, investors will accept lower interest rates on convertible bonds.

Bond issuers are always trying to invent new types of bonds that they hope will appeal to a particular clientele of investors. In Section 6.1 we came across one example, the catastrophe bond, the payments on which are reduced if there is some natural disaster. Here, just for fun, is an example of another exotic bond.

Managers of life insurance companies agonize about the possibility of a pandemic or other disaster that results in a sharp increase in the death rate. In 2006 the French insurance company Axa sought to protect itself against this danger by issuing nearly €350 million of *mortality bonds*. Axa's bonds offered a tempting yield but the bondholders will lose their entire investment if death rates for 2 consecutive years are 10% or more above expectations.

SUMMARY

What are the differences between the bond's coupon rate, current yield, and yield to maturity? (*LO1*)

A bond is a long-term debt of a government or corporation. When you own a bond, you receive a fixed interest payment each year until the bond matures. This payment is known as the coupon. The **coupon rate** is the annual coupon payment expressed as a fraction of the bond's **face value.** At maturity the bond's face value is repaid. In the United States most bonds have a face value of $1,000. The **current yield** is the annual coupon payment expressed as a fraction of the bond's price. The **yield to maturity** measures the average rate of return to an investor who purchases the bond and holds it until maturity, accounting for coupon income as well as the difference between purchase price and face value.

How can one find the market price of a bond given its yield to maturity or find a bond's yield given its price? Why do prices and yields vary inversely? (*LO2*)

Bonds are valued by discounting the coupon payments and the final repayment by the yield to maturity on comparable bonds. The bond payments discounted at the bond's yield to maturity equal the bond price. You may also start with the bond price and ask what interest rate the bond offers. The interest rate that equates the present value of bond payments to the bond price is the yield to maturity. Because present values are lower when discount rates are higher, price and yield to maturity vary inversely.

Why do bonds exhibit interest rate risk? (*LO3*)

Bond prices are subject to **interest rate risk,** rising when market interest rates fall and falling when market rates rise. Long-term bonds exhibit greater interest rate risk than short-term bonds.

Why do investors pay attention to bond ratings and demand a higher interest rate for bonds with low ratings? (*LO4*)

Investors demand higher promised yields if there is a high probability that the borrower will run into trouble and default. **Credit risk** implies that the promised yield to maturity on the bond is higher than the expected yield. The additional yield investors require for bearing credit risk is called the **default premium.** Bond ratings measure the bond's credit risk.

LISTING OF EQUATIONS

6.1   Bond price = PV(coupons) + PV(face value)

$$= (\text{coupon} \times \text{annuity factor}) + (\text{face value} \times \text{discount factor})$$

6.2   Bond rate of return $= \dfrac{\text{coupon income} + \text{price change}}{\text{investment}}$

QUESTIONS

QUIZ

1. **Bond Yields.** A 30-year Treasury bond is issued with face value of $1,000, paying interest of $60 per year. If market yields increase shortly after the T-bond is issued, what happens to the bond's
   a. coupon rate? (*LO1*)
   b. price? (*LO1*)
   c. yield to maturity? (*LO1*)
   d. current yield? (*LO1*)

2. **Bond Yields.** If a bond with face value of $1,000 and a coupon rate of 8% is selling at a price of $970, is the bond's yield to maturity more or less than 8%? What about the current yield? (*LO1*)

3. **Bond Yields.** A bond with face value $1,000 has a current yield of 7% and a coupon rate of 8%. What is the bond's price? (*LO1*)

4. **Bond Pricing.** A 6-year Circular File bond pays interest of $80 annually and sells for $950. What are its coupon rate, current yield, and yield to maturity? (*LO2*)

5. **Bond Pricing.** If Circular File (see Quiz Question 4) wants to issue a new 6-year bond at face value, what coupon rate must the bond offer? (*LO2*)

6. **Bond Yields.** A bond has 10 years until maturity, a coupon rate of 8%, and sells for $1,100.
   a. What is the current yield on the bond? (*LO1*)
   b. What is the yield to maturity? (*LO2*)

7. **Coupon Rate.** General Matter's outstanding bond issue has a coupon rate of 10% and a current yield of 9.6%, and it sells at a yield to maturity of 9.25%. The firm wishes to issue additional bonds to the public at face value. What coupon rate must the new bonds offer in order to sell at face value? (*LO2*)

8. **Financial Pages.** Turn back to Table 6–1. What is the current yield of the 7.125% 2023 maturity bond? Why is this more than its yield to maturity? (*LO1*)

PRACTICE PROBLEMS

9. **Bond Prices and Returns.** One bond has a coupon rate of 8%, another a coupon rate of 12%. Both bonds have 10-year maturities and sell at a yield to maturity of 10%. If their yields to maturity next year are still 10%, what is the rate of return on each bond? Does the higher coupon bond give a higher rate of return? (*LO2*)

10. **Bond Returns.** (*LO2*)
    a. If the bond in Quiz Question 6 has a yield to maturity of 8% 1 year from now, what will its price be?
    b. What will be the rate of return on the bond?
    c. If the inflation rate during the year is 3%, what is the real rate of return on the bond?

11. **Bond Pricing.** A General Motors bond carries a coupon rate of 8%, has 9 years until maturity, and sells at a yield to maturity of 7%.
    a. What interest payments do bondholders receive each year? (*LO1*)
    b. At what price does the bond sell? (Assume annual interest payments.) (*LO2*)
    c. What will happen to the bond price if the yield to maturity falls to 6%? (*LO2*)

12. **Bond Pricing.** A 30-year maturity bond with face value of $1,000 makes annual coupon payments and has a coupon rate of 8%. What is the bond's yield to maturity if the bond is selling for
    a. $900? (*LO2*)
    b. $1,000? (*LO2*)
    c. $1,100? (*LO2*)

13. **Bond Pricing.** Repeat the previous problem assuming semiannual coupon payments. (*LO2*)

14. **Bond Pricing.** Fill in the table below for the following zero-coupon bonds. The face value of each bond is $1,000. (*LO2*)

Price	Maturity (years)	Yield to Maturity
$300	30	—
300	—	8%
—	10	10

15. **Consol Bonds.** Perpetual Life Corp. has issued consol bonds with coupon payments of $60. (Consols pay interest forever and never mature. They are perpetuities.) If the required rate of return on these bonds at the time they were issued was 6%, at what price were they sold to the public? If the required return today is 10%, at what price do the consols sell? (*LO2*)

16. **Bond Pricing.** Sure Tea Co. has issued 9% annual coupon bonds that are now selling at a yield to maturity of 10% and current yield of 9.8375%. What is the remaining maturity of these bonds? (*LO2*)

17. **Bond Pricing.** Large Industries bonds sell for $1,065.15. The bond life is 9 years, and the yield to maturity is 7%. What must be the coupon rate on the bonds? (*LO2*)

18. **Bond Prices and Yields.**
    a. Several years ago, Castles in the Sand, Inc., issued bonds at face value at a yield to maturity of 7%. Now, with 8 years left until the maturity of the bonds, the company has run into hard

www.mhhe.com/bmm6e

times and the yield to maturity on the bonds has increased to 15%. What has happened to the price of the bond? (*LO2*)

    b. Suppose that investors believe that Castles can make good on the promised coupon payments, but that the company will go bankrupt when the bond matures and the principal comes due. The expectation is that investors will receive only 80% of face value at maturity. If they buy the bond today, what yield to maturity do they expect to receive? (*LO4*)

19. **Bond Returns.** You buy an 8% coupon, 10-year maturity bond for $980. A year later, the bond price is $1,100. (*LO2*)

    a. What is the new yield to maturity on the bond?

    b. What is your rate of return over the year?

20. **Bond Returns.** You buy an 8% coupon, 20-year maturity bond when its yield to maturity is 9%. A year later, the yield to maturity is 10%. What is your rate of return over the year? (*LO3*)

21. **Interest Rate Risk.** Consider three bonds with 8% coupon rates, all selling at face value. The short-term bond has a maturity of 4 years, the intermediate-term bond has maturity 8 years, and the long-term bond has maturity 30 years. (*LO3*)

    a. What will happen to the price of each bond if their yields increase to 9%?

    b. What will happen to the price of each bond if their yields decrease to 7%?

    c. What do you conclude about the relationship between time to maturity and the sensitivity of bond prices to interest rates?

22. **Rate of Return.** A 2-year maturity bond with face value of $1,000 makes annual coupon payments of $80 and is selling at face value. What will be the rate of return on the bond if its yield to maturity at the end of the year is

    a. 6%? (*LO3*)

    b. 8%? (*LO3*)

    c. 10%? (*LO3*)

23. **Rate of Return.** A bond that pays coupons annually is issued with a coupon rate of 4%, maturity of 30 years, and a yield to maturity of 7%. What rate of return will be earned by an investor who purchases the bond and holds it for 1 year if the bond's yield to maturity at the end of the year is 8%? (*LO3*)

24. **Credit Risk.** A bond's credit rating provides a guide to its risk. Long-term bonds rated Aa currently offer yields to maturity of 7.5%. A-rated bonds sell at yields of 7.8%. If a 10-year bond with a coupon rate of 7% is downgraded by Moody's from Aa to A rating, what is the likely effect on the bond price? (*LO4*)

25. **Real Returns.** Suppose that you buy a 1-year maturity bond for $1,000 that will pay you back $1,000 plus a coupon payment of $60 at the end of the year. What real rate of return will you earn if the inflation rate is

    a. 2%? (*LO3*)

    b. 4%? (*LO3*)

    c. 6%? (*LO3*)

    d. 8%? (*LO3*)

26. **Real Returns.** Now suppose that the bond in the previous problem is a TIPS (inflation-indexed) bond with a coupon rate of 4%. What will the cash flow provided by the bond be for each of the four inflation rates? What will be the real and nominal rates of return on the bond in each scenario? (*LO1*)

27. **Real Returns.** Now suppose the TIPS bond in the previous problem is a 2-year maturity bond. What will be the bondholder's cash flows in each year in each of the inflation scenarios? (*LO1*)

CHALLENGE PROBLEMS

28. **Interest Rate Risk.** Suppose interest rates increase from 8% to 9%. Which bond will suffer the greater percentage decline in price: a 30-year bond paying annual coupons of 8% or a 30-year

Chapter 6 Valuing Bonds   179

zero-coupon bond? Can you explain intuitively why the zero exhibits greater interest rate risk even though it has the same maturity as the coupon bond? *(LO3)*

Please visit us at www.mhhe.com/bmm6e

29. **Interest Rate Risk.** Consider two 30-year maturity bonds. Bond A has a coupon rate of 4%, while bond B has a coupon rate of 12%. Both bonds pay their coupons semiannually. *(LO3)*

   a. Construct an Excel spreadsheet showing the prices of each of these bonds for yields to maturity ranging from 2% to 15% at intervals of 1%. Column A should show the yield to maturity (ranging from 2% to 15%), and columns B and C should compute the prices of the two bonds (using Excel's bond price function) at each interest rate.

   b. In columns D and E, compute the percentage difference between the bond price and its value when yield to maturity is 8%.

   c. Plot the values in columns D and E as a function of the interest rate. Which bond's price is proportionally more sensitive to interest rate changes?

   d. Can you explain the result you found in part (c)? *Hint:* Is there any sense in which a bond that pays a high coupon rate has lower "average" or "effective" maturity than a bond that pays a low coupon rate?

Please visit us at www.mhhe.com/bmm6e

30. **Yield Curve.** In Figure 6–7, we saw a plot of the yield curve on stripped Treasury bonds and pointed out that bonds of different maturities may sell at different yields to maturity. In principle, when we are valuing a stream of cash flows, each cash flow should be discounted by the yield appropriate to its particular maturity. Suppose the yield curve on (zero-coupon) Treasury strips is as follows:

Time to Maturity	YTM
1 year	4.0%
2	5.0
3–5	5.5
6–10	6.0

You wish to value a 10-year bond with a coupon rate of 10%, paid annually. *(LO2)*

   a. Set up an Excel spreadsheet to value each of the bond's annual cash flows using this table of yields. Add up the present values of the bond's 10 cash flows to obtain the bond price.

   b. What is the bond's yield to maturity?

   c. Compare the yield to maturity of the 10-year, 10% coupon bond to that of a 10-year zero-coupon bond or Treasury strip. Which is higher? Why does this result make sense given this yield curve?

STANDARD &POOR'S

1. Go to Market Insight (**www.mhhe.com/edumarketinsight**) and find the bond rating of Toyota (TM) and General Motors (GM) in the *Financial Highlights* section of Market Insight. Why is the bond rating (i.e., S&P Issuer Credit Rating) of Toyota superior to that of GM? Is one firm in better financial health? Compare the ratio of EBIT to interest payments for the two firms. Which has the "healthier" ratio? Which has the lower indebtedness, as measured by the ratio of debt to equity?

SOLUTIONS TO SELF-TEST QUESTIONS

6.1 a. The asked price is $97\frac{24}{32}\%$ of face value, or $977.50.

   b. The bid price is $97\frac{23}{32} = 97.7188\%$ of face value, or $977.188.

   c. The annual coupon is 3.5% of face value, or $35, paid in two semiannual installments.

   d. The yield to maturity, based on the asked price, is given as 3.77%.

6.2 The coupon is 9% of $1,000, or $90 a year. First value the 6-year annuity of coupons:

$$PV = \$90 \times (\text{6-year annuity factor})$$

$$= \$90 \times \left[\frac{1}{.12} - \frac{1}{.12(1.12)^6} \right]$$

$$= \$90 \times 4.1114 = \$370.03$$

Then value the final payment and add:

$$PV = \frac{\$1,000}{(1.12)^6} = \$506.63$$

$$PV \text{ of bond} = \$370.03 + \$506.63 = \$876.66$$

6.3 At an interest rate of 2.15%, the 3-year bond sells for $1,081.95. If the interest rate jumps to 10%, the bond price falls to $875.66, a decline of 19.1%. The 30-year bond sells for $1,625.33 when the interest rate is 2.15%, but its price falls to $528.65 at an interest rate of 10%, a much larger percentage decline of 67.5%.

6.4 The yield to maturity assuming annual coupons is about 8%, because the present value of the bond's cash returns is $1,199, almost exactly $1,200, when discounted at 8%:

$$PV = PV \text{ (coupons)} + PV \text{ (final payment)}$$

$$= (\text{coupon} \times \text{annuity factor}) + (\text{face value} \times \text{discount factor})$$

$$= \$140 \times \left[\frac{1}{.08} - \frac{1}{.08(1.08)^4} \right] + \$1,000 \times \frac{1}{1.08^4}$$

$$= \$463.70 + \$735.03 = \$1,199$$

To obtain a more precise solution on your calculator, these would be your inputs:

	Annual Payments	Semiannual Payments
n	4	8
PV	−1,200	−1,200
FV	1000	1000
PMT	140	70

Compute i to find yield to maturity (annual payments) = 7.97%. Yield to maturity (semiannual payments) = 4.026% per 6 months, which would be reported in the financial press as 8.05% annual yield.

6.5 The 5% coupon bond with maturity 2011 starts with 3 years left until maturity and sells for $1,081.95. At the end of the year, the bond has only 2 years to maturity and investors demand an interest rate of 1.5%. Therefore, the value of the bond becomes

$$PV \text{ at } 1.5\% = \frac{\$50}{(1.015)} + \frac{\$1,050}{(1.015)^2} = \$1,068.46$$

You invested $1,081.95. At the end of the year you receive a coupon payment of $50 and have a bond worth $1,068.46. Your rate of return is therefore

$$\text{Rate of return} = \frac{\$50 + (\$1,068.46 - \$1,081.95)}{\$1,081.95} = .0337, \text{ or } 3.37\%$$

The yield to maturity at the start of the year was 2.15%. However, because interest rates fell during the year, the bond price rose and the rate of return was greater than the yield to maturity.

6.6 By the end of this year, the bond will have only 1 year left until maturity. It will make only one more payment of coupon plus face value, so its price will be $1,050/1.0215 = $1,027.90. The rate of return is therefore

$$\frac{\$50 + (\$1,027.90 - \$1,055.21)}{\$1,055.21} = .0215, \text{ or } 2.15\%$$

6.7 If you invest in a 2-year bond, you will have $1,000 \times 1.06^2 = $1,123.60. If you are right in your forecast about 1-year rates, then an investment in 1-year bonds will produce $1,000 \times 1.05 \times 1.08 = $1,134.00 by the end of 2 years. You would do better to invest in the 1-year bond.

www.mhhe.com/bmm6e

SOLUTIONS TO SPREADSHEET QUESTIONS

6.1

Yield to maturity	Price (% of face value)
2.15%	108.195
2.50%	107.140

Decline in price of 0.98%

6.2

Yield to maturity	Price (% of face value)
2.15%	132.025
2.50%	127.458

Decline in price of 3.46%

6.3   3.22%

CHAPTER 7

Valuing Stocks

LEARNING OBJECTIVES

After studying this chapter, you should be able to:

1. Understand the stock trading reports in the financial pages of the newspaper.

2. Calculate the present value of a stock given forecasts of future dividends and future stock price.

3. Use stock valuation formulas to infer the expected rate of return on a common stock.

4. Interpret price-earnings ratios.

5. Understand what professionals mean when they say that there are no free lunches on Wall Street.

Share prices on the New York Stock Exchange. Watching the stock exchange ticker is fun but not informative. How do the buy and sell orders get to the floor? How are the trades actually executed? What underlying factors determine the values of traded stocks and bonds?

© Allan Schein Photography/Corbis

A corporation can raise cash for investment by borrowing or by selling new shares of common stock to investors. If it borrows, it has a fixed obligation to repay the lender. If it issues shares, there is no fixed obligation, but the new stockholders become partial owners of the firm. All old and new stockholders share in its fortunes, in proportion to the number of shares held. In this chapter, we take a first look at common stocks, the stock market, and the principles of stock valuation.

We start by looking at how stocks are bought and sold. Then we look at what determines stock prices and how stock valuation formulas can be used to infer the rate of return that investors are expecting. We will see how the firm's investment opportunities are reflected in its stock price and why stock market analysts focus so much attention on the price-earnings, or P/E, ratio of the company.

Why should you care how stocks are valued? After all, if you want to know the value of a firm's stock, you can look up the stock price in *The Wall Street Journal*. But you need to know what determines prices for at least two reasons. First, you may need to value the common stock of a business that is not traded on a stock exchange. Second, in order to make good capital budgeting decisions, corporations need to have some understanding of how the market values firms. A project is attractive if it increases shareholder wealth. But you can't judge that unless you know how shares are valued.

There may be a third reason why you would like to know how stocks are valued. You may be hoping that the knowledge will allow you to make a killing on Wall Street. It's a pleasant thought, but we will see that even professional investors find it difficult to outsmart the competition and earn consistently superior returns.

7.1 Stocks and the Stock Market

common stock
Ownership shares in a
publicly held corporation.

In Chapter 1, we saw how FedEx (Federal Express) was founded and how it has grown and thrived. Suppose that you're convinced that its best days are still to come, and you want a piece of the action. What should you do?

If you want to share in FedEx's future, you will want to buy **common stock** in the firm. Large firms sell or *issue* shares of stock to the public when they need to raise money, and as the name suggests, shareholders *share* the ownership of the firm in proportion to the number of shares they hold.[1] They benefit if the company prospers, and they suffer losses if it does not.

primary market
Market for the sale of new
securities by corporations.

initial public offering (IPO)
First offering of stock to the
general public.

FedEx and other firms sell new shares to the public only infrequently. These sales take place in the so-called **primary market.** The first time the company sells shares to the public is called its **initial public offering,** or **IPO.** Companies raise funds by selling these new shares, but the previous owners now have to share ownership (and profits) of the firm with their new co-owners. IPOs are often eagerly anticipated, as they are the first opportunity for the general public to buy shares in hot companies that to date have been owned solely by founders and their private backers.

The all-time star performer in an IPO was VA Linux Systems. In 1999 its shares were sold to investors at $30 each; by the end of the first day, they had reached $239, a gain of nearly 700%. But shares of stock can be risky investments. For example, less than 2 years after they were first sold to the public, the shares of VA Linux (now renamed VA Software Corporation) were priced at less than $1 each. If you had bought the shares when they first started trading, you would have lost 99% of your investment. You can understand why investors would be unhappy if forced to tie the knot with a particular company forever. So large companies usually arrange for their stock to be listed on a stock exchange, which allows investors to trade shares among themselves. Exchanges are really markets for secondhand stocks, but they prefer to describe themselves as **secondary markets,** which sounds more important.

secondary market
Market in which previously
issued securities are traded
among investors.

The two principal stock markets in the United States are the New York Stock Exchange (NYSE) and NASDAQ.[2] In addition, there are many computer networks called *electronic communication networks (ECNs),* that connect traders with each other. All of these markets compete vigorously for the business of traders and just as vigorously tout the advantages of their own trading venue. The volume of trades in these markets is immense. For example, every day the NYSE alone trades more than 3 billion shares with market value exceeding $100 billion.

Of course, there are stock exchanges in many other countries. Some are tiny, such as the Dar es Salaam exchange in Tanzania, which trades shares in just seven companies. Others, such as the London, Tokyo, Frankfurt, and pan-European Euronext exchanges, trade the shares of thousands of firms.

Suppose that Ms. Jones, a longtime FedEx shareholder, no longer wishes to hold her shares in the company. She can sell them via a stock exchange to Mr. Brown, who wishes to increase his stake in the firm. The transaction merely transfers (partial) ownership of the firm from one investor to another. No new shares are created, and FedEx usually will neither care nor even be aware that such a trade has taken place.[3]

Ms. Jones and Mr. Brown do not buy or sell FedEx shares themselves. Instead, each must hire a brokerage firm with trading privileges on an exchange to arrange the transaction for them. Not so long ago, such trades would have involved hands-on

---

[1] We use the terms "shares," "stock," and "common stock" interchangeably, as we do "shareholders" and "stockholders."

[2] This originally was an acronym for National Association of Security Dealers Automated Quotation system, but now is simply known as the NASDAQ market.

[3] Eventually, FedEx must know to whom it should send dividend checks, but this information is needed only when such payments are being prepared. In some cases, FedEx might care about a stock transaction, for example, if a large investor is building a big stake in the firm. But this is the exception.

negotiation. The broker would have had to agree on an acceptable price with a dealer in the stock or would have brought the trade to the floor of an exchange where a *specialist* in FedEx would have coordinated the transaction. But today the vast majority of trades are executed automatically and electronically, even on the more traditional exchanges.

When Ms. Jones and Mr. Brown decide to buy or sell FedEx stock, they need to give their brokers instructions about the price at which they are prepared to transact. Ms. Jones, who is anxious to sell quickly, might give her broker a *market order* to sell stock at the best available price. On the other hand, Mr. Brown might give his broker a price limit at which he is willing to buy FedEx stock. If his order cannot be executed immediately, it is recorded in the exchange's *limit order book* until it can be executed.

Figure 7–1 shows a portion of the limit order book for FedEx from the Archipelago Exchange, an electronic market run by the NYSE. The bid prices on the left are the prices (and numbers of shares) at which investors are willing to buy. The Ask column presents offers to sell. The prices are arranged from best to worst, so the highest bids and lowest asks are at the top of the list. The broker might electronically enter Ms. Jones's market order to sell 100 shares on the Archipelago Exchange, where it would be automatically matched or *crossed* with the best offer to buy, which at that moment was $103.23 a share. Similarly, a market order to buy would be crossed with the best ask price, $103.29. The *bid-ask spread* at that moment was therefore 6 cents per share.

Reading Stock Market Listings

If you are thinking about buying shares in FedEx, you will wish to see its current price. Until recently, you probably would have looked for that information in *The Wall Street Journal* or the financial pages of your local newspaper. But those pages contain less and less information about individual stocks, and most investors today turn to the Internet for their information. For example, if you go to **finance.yahoo.com**, enter FedEx's ticker symbol, FDX, and ask to "Get Quotes," you will find recent trading data such as that presented in Table 7–1.[4]

The last price at which the stock traded on October 30 was $103.23 per share, which was $.16 lower than its closing price the previous day, $103.39. The range of prices at which the stock traded that day, as well as over the previous 52 weeks, is provided. In the set of columns on the right, Yahoo tells us that 1,216,100 shares traded this

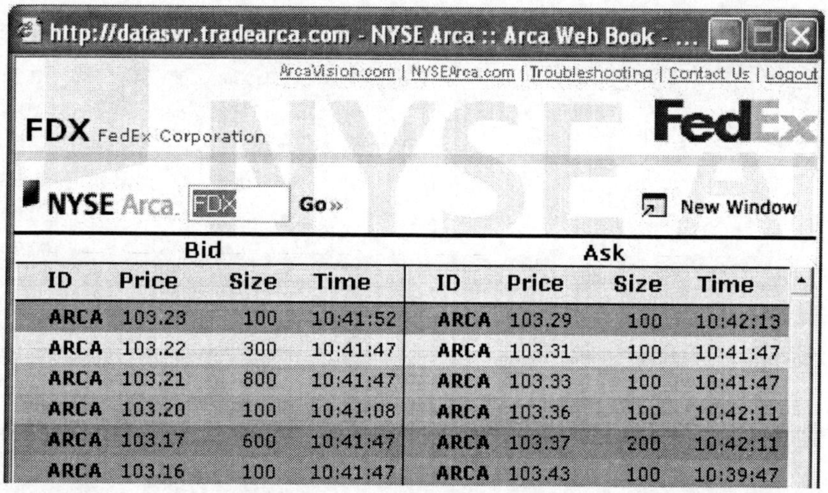

Bid				Ask			
ID	Price	Size	Time	ID	Price	Size	Time
ARCA	103.23	100	10:41:52	ARCA	103.29	100	10:42:13
ARCA	103.22	300	10:41:47	ARCA	103.31	100	10:41:47
ARCA	103.21	800	10:41:47	ARCA	103.33	100	10:41:47
ARCA	103.20	100	10:41:08	ARCA	103.36	100	10:42:11
ARCA	103.17	600	10:41:47	ARCA	103.37	200	10:42:11
ARCA	103.16	100	10:41:47	ARCA	103.43	100	10:39:47

FIGURE 7–1 A portion of the limit order book for Federal Express from the NYSE/Archipelago exchange

[4] Other good sources of trading data are **http://moneycentral.msn.com/investor/home.asp** or the online edition of *The Wall Street Journal* at **www.wsj.com** (look for the Market Data and Tools tab).

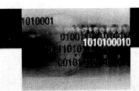

INTERNET INSIDER

The Limit Order Book

Find the limit order book for IBM stock by log on to the Arca Web site at **http://datasvr.tradearca.com/arcadataserver/Auction.php** and clicking on *Web Book*. What is the highest price at which you can sell IBM shares? What is the lowest price at which you can buy them?

day, compared to average volume of 2,108,570 shares over the last 3 months. FedEx's *market cap* (shorthand for market capitalization) is the total value of its outstanding shares of stock, $31.93 billion. You will frequently hear traders referring to large-cap or small-cap firms, which is a convenient way to summarize the size of the company.

FedEx earned $6.533 per share in the past year. (The abbreviation "ttm" in the parentheses stands for *trailing 12 months.*) Therefore, the ratio of price per share to earnings per share, known as the *price-earnings multiple* or, equivalently, **P/E ratio,** is 103.23/6.533 = 15.80. The P/E ratio is a key tool of stock market analysts, and we will have much to say about it later in the chapter.

The *dividend yield* tells you how much dividend income you would receive for every $100 invested in the stock. FedEx paid annual dividends of $.40 per share, so its yield was .40/103.23 = .0039 = .39%. For every $100 invested in the stock, you would have received $.39 in dividends. Of course, this would not be the total rate of return on your investment, as you would also hope for some increase in the stock price. The dividend yield is thus much like the current yield of a bond. Both ignore prospective capital gains or losses.

Of course, the price at which you can buy shares in FedEx changes day to day and minute to minute. Remember, each share represents partial ownership in the firm, and share values will wax or wane with investors' perceptions of the prospects of the company. Figure 7–2 shows the share price of FedEx over a 6-month period. Its price fell by 12% in just 2 months, from around $117 in mid-July 2007 to only $103 in mid-September. The lesson? Again, we see that stocks can be risky investments.

P/E ratio
Ratio of stock price to earnings per share.

TABLE 7–1 Trading data for FedEx, October 30, 2007

Last Trade:	103.23
Trade Time:	4:01PM ET
Change:	↓ 0.16 (0.15%)
Prev Close:	103.39
Open:	103.00
Day's Range:	102.70–103.86
52-wk Range:	99.30–121.42
Volume:	1,216,100
Avg Vol (3m):	2,108,570
Market Cap:	31.93B
P/E (ttm):	15.80
EPS (ttm):	6.533
Div & Yield:	0.40 (0.39%)

Source: Yahoo! Finance, October 30, 2007. Reproduced with permission of Yahoo! Inc. © 2007 by Yahoo! Inc. YAHOO! and the YAHOO! logo are trademarks of Yahoo! Inc.

FIGURE 7–2 Share price history for FedEx

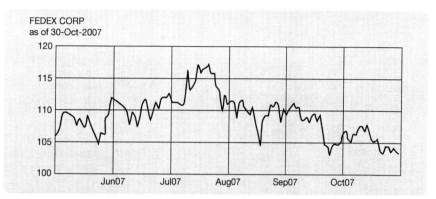

Source: Yahoo! Finance. Reproduced with permission of Yahoo! Inc. © 2007 by Yahoo! Inc. YAHOO! and the YAHOO! logo are trademarks of Yahoo! Inc.

7.2 Market Values, Book Values, and Liquidation Values

We've seen how FedEx's share price is determined by traders in the secondary stock markets, and also how volatile that price can be. But how do traders decide on the prices they are willing to pay for these shares? Why would they pay $117 for a share in July but only $103 just 2 months later? Why would they pay $103 a share for FedEx but only $35 a share for Microsoft? To answer these questions, we need to look at what determines the value.

Finding the value of FedEx stock may sound like a simple problem. Each quarter, the company publishes a balance sheet, which lists the value of the firm's assets and liabilities. The simplified balance sheet in Table 7–2 shows that in May 2007 the book value of all FedEx's assets—plant and machinery, inventories of materials, cash in the bank, and so on—was $24,000 million. FedEx's liabilities—money that it owes the banks, taxes that are due to be paid, and the like—amounted to $11,344 million. The difference between the value of the assets and the liabilities was $12,656 million. This was the **book value** of the firm's equity.[5] Book value records all the money that FedEx has raised from its shareholders plus all the earnings that have been plowed back on their behalf.

book value
Net worth of the firm according to the balance sheet.

Book value is a reassuringly definite number. Each year Ernst & Young, one of America's largest accounting firms, tells us:

> In our opinion, the financial reports . . . present fairly, in all material respects, the consolidated financial position of FedEx Corporation . . . , and the results of its operations and its cash flows . . . , in conformity with U.S. generally accepted accounting principles.[6]

But does the stock price equal book value? FedEx shares in November 2007 were selling at a bit more than $103, but as Table 7–3 shows, its book value per share was only $42.76. So the shares were worth about 2.4 times book value. This and the other cases shown in Table 7–3 tell us that investors in the stock market do *not* just buy and sell at book value per share.

TABLE 7–2

BALANCE SHEET FOR FedEx, MAY 31, 2007 (figures in millions of dollars)			
Assets		**Liabilities and Shareholders' Equity**	
Plant, equipment, and other assets	24,000	Liabilities	11,344
		Equity	12,656

Note: Shares of stock outstanding: 296 million. Book value of equity (per share): 12,656/296 = $42.76.

---

[5] "Equity" is still another word for stock. Thus, stockholders are often referred to as *equity investors.*

[6] When a major accounting firm makes such a statement and it proves not to be true, there can be hell to pay. Arthur Andersen discovered this when it certified the accounts of Enron Corporation before Enron went bankrupt.

INTERNET INSIDER

Stock Exchanges

Source: NYSE Euronext Web site.

The major stock exchanges have wonderful Web sites. Look first at the NYSE on **www.nyse.com**. Browse through this Web site. For example, look at how the trading floor works, and make sure you understand how stocks are bought and sold. Find *NYSE MarkeTrac*, and click on the DJIA ticker tape, which shows trades for the stocks in the Dow Jones Industrial Average. You can stop the tape at any point and click on the ticker symbol to find some data about the stock. Check that you know how the dividend yield and price-earnings (P/E) ratio were calculated. Go back to the main page and look at NYSE Facts and Figures. Find the value of the shares traded on the NYSE, and look at who owns them.

Now log on to **www.nasdaq.com**. Browse through the Market Activity pages, and load the Nasdaq ticker tape.

Make Some Trades

And you thought all stock exchanges traded stock! Check out the Hollywood Stock Exchange on **www.hsx.com**. Buy shares of your favorite actors, movies, and music artists and watch their values rise or fall based on the success of their careers and personal life. Stocks soar with a number-one film at the box office and plummet with a stay at the Betty Ford clinic. Join and play for free. It's 90 percent fun, but it will also get you used to some stock market jargon.

Real stock values are established with "votes," just like on the HSX, but the votes cost real money.

Investors know that accountants don't even try to estimate market values. The value of the assets reported on the firm's balance sheet is equal to their original (or "historical") cost less an allowance for depreciation. But that may not be a good guide to what the firm could sell its assets for today.

liquidation value

Net proceeds that could be realized by selling the firm's assets and paying off its creditors.

Well, maybe stock price equals **liquidation value** per share, that is, the amount of cash per share a company could raise if it sold off all its assets in secondhand markets and paid off all its debts. Wrong again. A successful company ought to be worth more than liquidation value. After all, that's the goal of bringing all those assets together in the first place.

TABLE 7–3 Market values versus book values, November 2007

Firm	Stock Price	Book Value per Share	Price-to-Book-Value Ratio
FedEx	103.61	42.76	2.4
Consolidated Edison	45.87	31.5	1.5
Wal-Mart	43.88	15.36	2.9
PepsiCo	72.74	10.10	7.2
U.S. Airways	23.08	14.43	1.6
Microsoft	36.15	3.38	10.7
Google	741.79	69.31	10.7
IBM	112.34	14.78	7.6
McDonald's	57.81	12.43	4.7
Exxon Mobil	89.64	21.31	4.2
Pfizer	23.31	9.71	2.4
Dow Chemical	43.84	19.05	2.3

Source: Yahoo! Finance Web site, **finance.yahoo.com**. Reproduced with permission of Yahoo! Inc. © 2007 by Yahoo! Inc. YAHOO! and the YAHOO! logo are trademarks of Yahoo! Inc.

The difference between a company's actual value and its book or liquidation value is often attributed to *going-concern value,* which refers to three factors:

1. *Extra earning power.* A company may have the ability to earn more than an adequate rate of return on assets. In this case the value of those assets will be higher than their book value or secondhand value.

2. *Intangible assets.* There are many assets that accountants don't put on the balance sheet. Some of these assets are extremely valuable. Take Pfizer, a pharmaceutical company. As you can see from Table 7–3, it sells at 2.4 times book value per share. Where did all that extra value come from? Largely from the cash flow generated by the drugs it has developed, patented, and marketed. These drugs are the fruits of a research and development (R&D) program that has grown to more than $7 billion per year. But U.S. accountants don't recognize R&D as an investment and don't put it on the company's balance sheet. Nevertheless, expertise, experience, and knowledge are crucial assets, and their values do show up in stock prices.

3. *Value of future investments.* If investors believe a company will have the opportunity to make very profitable investments in the future, they will pay more for the company's stock today. When eBay, the Internet auction house, first sold its stock to investors in 1998, the book value of shareholders' equity was about $100 million. Yet 1 day after the issue investors valued the equity at over $6 *billion.* In part, this difference reflected an intangible asset, eBay's unique platform for trading a wide range of goods over the Internet. But investors also judged that eBay was a *growth company.* In other words, they were betting that the company's know-how and brand name would allow it to expand internationally and make it easier for customers to trade and pay online.

Market price is not the same as book value or liquidation value. Market value, unlike book value and liquidation value, treats the firm as a going concern.

It is not surprising that stocks virtually never sell at book or liquidation values. Investors buy shares on the basis of present and *future* earning power. Two key features determine the profits the firm will be able to produce: first, the earnings that can be generated by the firm's current tangible and intangible assets, and second, the opportunities the firm has to invest in lucrative projects that will increase future earnings.

EXAMPLE 7.1 ▶	Amazon.com and Consolidated Edison

Amazon.com, like eBay, is a growth company. In 2007, its profit was $476 million. Yet investors at the time were prepared to pay about 76 times that amount, or $36.5 billion for Amazon's common stock. The value of the stock came from the company's market position, its highly regarded distribution system, and the promise of new related products that will generate increased future earnings. Amazon was a pure growth firm, because its market value depended almost entirely on intangible assets and the anticipated profitability of new investments.

Contrast this with Consolidated Edison (Con Ed), the electric utility servicing the New York City area. Con Ed is not a growth company. Its market is limited, and it is expanding capacity at a very deliberate pace. More important, it is a regulated utility, so its returns on present and future investments are constrained. Con Ed's value derives mostly from the stream of income generated by its *existing* assets. Therefore, while Amazon shares in 2007 sold for 30.5 times book value, Con Ed shares sold in 2007 at only about 1.5 times book value.

market-value balance sheet
Financial statement that uses the market value of all assets and liabilities.

Financial executives are not bound by generally accepted accounting principles, and they sometimes construct a firm's **market-value balance sheet.** Such a balance sheet helps them to think about and evaluate the sources of firm value. Take a look

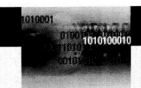

INTERNET INSIDER

Market versus Book Values

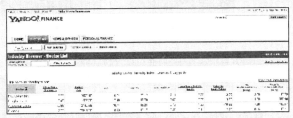

Log on to **http://finance.yahoo.com** and click on *Investing* and find the Industry Browser. You will see some financial ratios for different industries, including the ratio of market price to book value. Is the market value of equity usually higher or lower than book value? Why? Which industries have the highest ratios of market to book? Are there any industries where the market value is on average lower than book value?

Source: Reproduced with permission of Yahoo! Inc. © 2008 by Yahoo! Inc. YAHOO! and the YAHOO! logo are trademarks of Yahoo! Inc.

TABLE 7–4

A MARKET-VALUE BALANCE SHEET (figures in millions of dollars)	
Assets	**Liabilities and Shareholders' Equity**
Assets in place	Market value of debt and other obligations
Investment opportunities	Market value of shareholders' equity

at Table 7–4. A market-value balance sheet contains two classes of assets: (1) assets already in place, both tangible and intangible, and (2) opportunities to invest in attractive future ventures. Consolidated Edison's stock market value is dominated by tangible assets in place; Amazon's, by the value of future investment opportunities.

Other firms, like Microsoft, seem to have it all. Microsoft earns plenty from its current products. These earnings are part of what makes the stock attractive to investors. In addition, investors are willing to pay for the company's ability to invest profitably in new ventures that will increase future earnings.

Let's summarize. Just remember:

- *Book value* records what a company has paid for its assets, less a deduction for depreciation. It does not capture the true value of a business.
- *Liquidation value* is what the company could net by selling its assets and repaying its debts. It does not capture the value of a successful going concern.
- *Market value* is the amount that investors are willing to pay for the shares of the firm. This depends on the earning power of *today's* assets and the expected profitability of *future* investments.

Take a look at the nearby Internet Insider box for more on market versus book values. The next question is, What determines market value?

Self-Test 7.1

In the 1970s, the computer industry was growing rapidly. In the 1980s, many new competitors entered the market, and computer prices fell. Computer makers in the last decade such as Dell, struggled with thinning profit margins and intense competition. How has the industry's market-value balance sheet changed over time? Have assets in place become proportionately more or less important? Do you think this progression is unique to the computer industry?

7.3 Valuing Common Stocks

Valuation by Comparables

If book values are unreliable estimates of market value, then perhaps there are other, more useful indicators. *Valuation by comparables* is a common first approach. For example, if we were interested in valuing FedEx, we would divide its stock price by measures of assets or earnings and then see how these relations stack up against other firms in the same industry.

TABLE 7–5 Price-to-book-value ratios and P/E ratios for selected companies and their competitors, November 2007

Firm	Price-to-Book-Value Ratio		Price-Earnings Ratio	
	Company	Industry	Company	Industry
FedEx	2.4	3.4	15.7	18.1
Consolidated Edison	1.5	1.7	14.5	16.4
Wal-Mart	2.9	2.5	14.8	17.9
PepsiCo	7.2	2.4	19.5	20.8
U.S. Airways	1.6	2.3	4.6	9.4
Microsoft	10.7	3.7	24.1	29.4
Google	10.7	3.8	56.8	40.0
IBM	7.6	3.8	16.8	25.5
McDonald's	4.7	2.7	30.9	22.7
Exxon Mobil	4.2	2.5	12.5	11.6
Pfizer	2.4	4.3	11.2	21.7
Dow Chemical	2.3	3.8	12.5	17.7

Note: Industry figures are median ratios for companies in the corresponding industry.
Source: Yahoo! Finance, **finance.yahoo.com**. Reproduced with permission of Yahoo! Inc. © 2007 by Yahoo! Inc. YAHOO! and the YAHOO! logo are trademarks of Yahoo! Inc.

Look at the first row of Table 7–5. Notice that the typical stock in the air delivery and freight industry sells for 3.4 times its book value. Therefore, as a first stab at valuing FedEx, you might estimate that its stock would also sell at 3.4 times book. This would give you a value for FedEx of $145, quite a bit higher than its actual market price of $103.

An alternative would be to look at how much investors in the air delivery and freight industry are typically prepared to pay for $1 of earnings. The first row in Table 7–5 shows that the typical price-earnings ratio for these stocks is 18.1. You might therefore presume that FedEx stock should sell at a similar multiple of earnings. This would give a value for FedEx of $119, a bit closer to the actual figure but still an overestimate.

Table 7–5 sets out the ratios of price to book and price to earnings (P/E) for a sample of companies and their industry competitors. You can see, for example, that the price-to-book ratio works best for companies with plenty of fixed assets. It works poorly for firms like Google that have major investments in research and development or other intangible assets.

Price-to-earnings and price-to-book ratios are the most popular rules of thumb for judging the value of a common stock, but financial analysts sometimes look at other multiples. For example, infant firms often do not earn positive profits. So, rather than calculating a price-to-earnings ratio, analysts may look at the price-to-sales ratio for these firms. In the late 1990s, when dot-com companies were growing rapidly but losing lots of money, multiples were often based on the number of subscribers or Web-site visits.

There is nothing wrong with rules of thumb if intelligently applied. But all these ratios vary from stock to stock even for firms that are in the same line of business. So blind use of industry ratios is unlikely to produce an accurate estimate of the price that investors would be prepared to pay for any one stock. To understand why some firms sell at higher multiples than others, we need to dig deeper and look at what determines a stock's value.

Price and Intrinsic Value

In the previous chapter, we saw that the value of a bond is the present value of its coupon payments plus the present value of its final payment of face value. You can think of stocks in a similar way. Instead of receiving coupon payments, investors may receive dividends; and instead of receiving face value, they will receive the stock price at the time they sell their shares.

Consider, for example, an investor who buys a share of Blue Skies Inc. today and plans to sell it in 1 year. Call the predicted stock price in 1 year P_1, the expected dividend per share over the year DIV_1, and the discount rate for the stock's expected cash flows r. Then the present value of the cash flows the investor will receive from Blue Skies is

$$V_0 = \frac{DIV_1 + P_1}{1 + r} \tag{7.1}$$

intrinsic value
Present value of future cash flows from a stock or other security.

We call V_0 the **intrinsic value** of the share. Intrinsic value is just the present value of the cash flows anticipated by the investor in the stock.

To illustrate, suppose investors expect a cash dividend of $3 over the next year $(DIV_1 = \$3)$ and expect the stock to sell for $81 a year hence $(P_1 = \$81)$. If the discount rate is 12%, then intrinsic value is $75:

$$V_0 = \frac{3 + 81}{1.12} = \$75$$

You can think of intrinsic value as the "fair" price for the stock. If investors buy the stock for $75, their expected rate of return will precisely equal the discount rate—in other words, their investment will just compensate them for the opportunity cost of their money.

To confirm this, note that the expected rate of return over the next year is the expected dividend plus the expected increase in price, $P_1 - P_0$, all divided by price at the start of the year, P_0. If the investor buys the shares for intrinsic value, then $P_0 = \$75$ and

$$\text{Expected return} = \frac{DIV_1 + P_1 - P_0}{P_0} = \frac{3 + 81 - 75}{75} = .12, \text{ or } 12\%$$

Notice that this expected return comes in two parts, the dividend and the capital gain:

$$
\begin{aligned}
\text{Expected rate of return} &= \text{expected dividend yield} + \text{expected capital gain} \\
&= \frac{DIV_1}{P_0} + \frac{P_1 - P_0}{P_0} \\
&= \frac{3}{75} + \frac{81 - 75}{75} \\
&= .04 + .08 = .12, \text{ or } 12\%
\end{aligned}
$$

Of course, the actual return for Blue Skies may turn out to be more or less than investors expect. For example, in 2007, a year when oil prices soared and housing prices sank, one of the best-performing industries was oil and gas services, with a return of more than 40%. This was almost certainly better than investors expected at the start of the year. At the other extreme, shares of home-building companies dramatically fell in price, with the result that their rate of return was worse than −50%. No investor at the start of the year would have purchased these shares anticipating such a loss. Never confuse the actual outcome with the expected outcome.

The dream of every investor is to buy shares at a bargain price, that is, a price less than intrinsic value. But in competitive markets, no price other than intrinsic value could survive for long. To see why, imagine that Blue Skies' current price were above $75. Then the expected rate of return on Blue Skies stock would be *lower* than that on other securities of equivalent risk. (*Check this!*) Investors would bail out of Blue Skies stock and move into other securities. In the process they would force down the price of Blue Skies stock. If P_0 were less than $75, Blue Skies stock would offer a *higher* expected rate of return than equivalent-risk securities. (*Check this, too.*) Everyone would rush to buy, forcing the price up to $75. When the stock is priced correctly (that is, price equals present value), the *expected* rate of return on Blue Skies stock is also the rate of return that investors *require* to hold the stock. **At each point in time** all securities of the same risk are priced to offer the same expected rate of return. This is a fundamental characteristic of prices in well-functioning markets. It is also common sense.

Equation 7.1 is just a *definition* of intrinsic value, which works for any discount rate r. Now we can go beyond the definition and identify r as the expected rate of return on all securities at a given level of risk. If a stock is priced correctly, it will offer an expected rate of return equal to that of other equally risky stocks and price will equal intrinsic value:

$$P_0 = \frac{DIV_1 + P_1}{1 + r} \tag{7.2}$$

Thus today's price will equal the present value of dividend payments plus the present value of future price. But now we need to take a further step: How do we estimate the future price P_1?

Self-Test 7.2

Androscoggin Copper is increasing next year's dividend to $5 per share. The forecast stock price next year is $105. Equally risky stocks of other companies offer expected rates of return of 10%. What should Androscoggin common stock sell for?

The Dividend Discount Model

We have managed to explain today's stock price P_0 in terms of the dividend DIV_i and the expected stock price next year P_1. But future stock prices are not easy to forecast directly, though you may encounter individuals who claim to be able to do so. A formula that requires tomorrow's stock price to explain today's stock price is not generally helpful.

As it turns out, we can express a stock's intrinsic value (and, therefore, price) as the present value of all the forecasted future dividends paid by the company to its shareholders without referring to the future stock price. This is the **dividend discount model:**

dividend discount model
Discounted cash flow model which states that today's stock price equals the present value of all expected future dividends.

$$P_0 = \text{present value of } (DIV_1, DIV_2, DIV_3, \dots, DIV_t, \dots)$$
$$= \frac{DIV_1}{1 + r} + \frac{DIV_2}{(1+r)^2} + \frac{DIV_3}{(1+r)^3} + \dots + \frac{DIV_t}{(1+r)^t} + \dots$$

How far out in the future could we look? In principle, 40, 60, or 100 years or more—corporations are potentially immortal. However, far-distant dividends will not have significant present values. For example, the present value of $1 received in 30 years using a 10% discount rate is only $.057. Most of the value of established companies comes from dividends to be paid within a person's working lifetime.

How do we get from the one-period formula $P_0 = (DIV_1 + P_1)/(1 + r)$ to the dividend discount model? We look at increasingly long investment horizons.

Let's consider investors with different investment horizons. Each investor will value the share of stock as the present value of the dividends that she or he expects to receive plus the present value of the price at which the stock is eventually sold. Unlike bonds, however, the final horizon date for stocks is not specified—stocks do not "mature." Moreover, both dividends and final sales price can only be estimated. But the general valuation approach is the same. For a one-period investor, the valuation formula looks like this:

$$P_0 = \frac{DIV_1 + P_1}{1 + r}$$

A 2-year investor would value the stock as

$$P_0 = \frac{DIV_1}{1 + r} + \frac{DIV_2 + P_2}{(1+r)^2}$$

and a 3-year investor would use the formula

$$P_0 = \frac{DIV_1}{1+r} + \frac{DIV_2}{(1+r)^2} + \frac{DIV_3 + P_3}{(1+r)^3}$$

In fact we can look as far out into the future as we like. Suppose we call our horizon date H. Then the stock valuation formula would be

$$P_0 = \frac{DIV_1}{1+r} + \frac{DIV_2}{(1+r)^2} + \cdots + \frac{DIV_H + P_H}{(1+r)^H} \qquad (7.3)$$

In words, the value of a stock is the present value of the dividends it will pay over the investor's horizon plus the present value of the expected stock price at the end of that horizon.

Does this mean that investors with different horizons will come to different conclusions about the value of the stock? No! Regardless of the investment horizon, the stock value will be the same. This is because the stock price at the horizon date is determined by expectations of dividends from that date forward. Therefore, as long as investors agree about a firm's prospects, they will also agree on its present value. Let's confirm this with an example.

EXAMPLE 7.2   ▶   Valuing Blue Skies Stock

Take Blue Skies. The firm is growing steadily, and investors expect both the stock price and the dividend to increase at 8% per year. Now consider three investors, Erste, Zweiter, and Dritter. Erste plans to hold Blue Skies for 1 year; Zweiter, for 2; and Dritter, for 3. Compare their payoffs:

	Year 1	Year 2	Year 3
Erste	$DIV_1 = 3$		
	$P_1 = 81$		
Zweiter	$DIV_1 = 3$	$DIV_2 = 3.24$	
		$P_2 = 87.48$	
Dritter	$DIV_1 = 3$	$DIV_2 = 3.24$	$DIV_3 = 3.50$
			$P_3 = 94.48$

Remember, we assumed that dividends and stock prices for Blue Skies are expected to grow at a steady 8%. Thus $DIV_2 = \$3 \times 1.08 = \$3.24$, $DIV_3 = \$3.24 \times 1.08 = \$3.50$, and so on.

Each investor requires the same 12% expected return. So we can calculate present value over Erste's 1-year horizon:

$$PV = \frac{DIV_1 + P_1}{1+r} = \frac{\$3 + \$81}{1.12} = \$75$$

or Zweiter's 2-year horizon:

$$PV = \frac{DIV_1}{1+r} + \frac{DIV_2 + P_2}{(1+r)^2}$$

$$= \frac{\$3}{1.12} + \frac{\$3.24 + \$87.48}{(1.12)^2}$$

$$= \$2.68 + \$72.32 = \$75$$

or Dritter's 3-year horizon:

$$PV = \frac{DIV_1}{1+r} + \frac{DIV_2}{(1+r)^2} + \frac{DIV_3 + P_3}{(1+r)^3}$$

$$= \frac{\$3}{1.12} + \frac{\$3.24}{(1.12)^2} + \frac{\$3.50 + \$94.48}{(1.12)^3}$$

$$= \$2.68 + \$2.58 + \$69.74 = \$75$$

All agree the stock is worth $75 per share. This illustrates our basic principle: The value of a common stock equals the present value of dividends received out to the investment horizon plus the present value of the forecast stock price at the horizon. Moreover, when you move the horizon date, the stock's present value should not change. The principle holds for horizons of 1, 3, 10, 20, and 50 years or more.

Self-Test 7.3   Refer to Self-Test 7.2. Assume that Androscoggin Copper's dividend and share price are expected to grow at a constant 5% per year. Calculate the current value of Androscoggin stock with the dividend discount model using a 3-year horizon. You should get the same answer as in Self-Test 7.2.

Look at Table 7–6, which continues the Blue Skies example for various time horizons, still assuming that the dividends are expected to increase at a steady 8% compound rate. The expected price increases at the same 8% rate. Each row in the table represents a present value calculation for a different horizon year. Note that total present value does not depend on the investment horizon. Figure 7–3 presents the same data in a graph. Each column shows the present value of the dividends up to the horizon and the present value of the price at the horizon. As the horizon recedes, the dividend stream accounts for an increasing proportion of present value but the *total* present value of dividends plus terminal price always equals $75.

If the horizon is infinitely far away, then we can forget about the final horizon price—it has almost no present value—and simply say,

Stock price = PV(all future dividends per share)

This is the dividend discount model.

FIGURE 7–3 **Value of Blue Skies for different horizons**

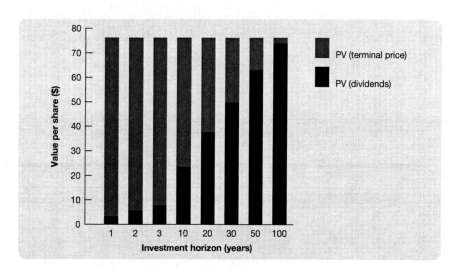

TABLE 7–6 Value of Blue Skies

Horizon, Years	PV (Dividends)	+	PV (Terminal Price)	=	Value per Share
1	$ 2.68		$72.32		$75
2	5.26		69.74		75
3	7.75		67.25		75
10	22.87		52.13		75
20	38.76		36.24		75
30	49.81		25.19		75
50	62.83		12.17		75
100	73.02		1.98		75

7.4 Simplifying the Dividend Discount Model

The Dividend Discount Model with No Growth

Consider a company that pays out all its earnings to its common shareholders. Such a company could not grow because it could not reinvest.[7] Stockholders might enjoy a generous immediate dividend, but they could not look forward to higher future dividends. The company's stock would offer a perpetual stream of equal cash payments, $DIV_1 = DIV_2 = \cdots = DIV_t = \cdots$.

The dividend discount model says that these no-growth shares should sell for the present value of a constant, perpetual stream of dividends. We learned how to do that calculation when we valued perpetuities in Chapter 5. Just divide the annual cash payment by the discount rate. The discount rate is the rate of return demanded by investors in other stocks with the same risk:

$$P_0 = \frac{DIV_1}{r}$$

Since our company pays out all its earnings as dividends, dividends and earnings are the same, and we could just as well calculate stock value by

$$\text{Value of a no-growth stock} = P_0 = \frac{EPS_1}{r}$$

where EPS_1 represents next year's earnings per share of stock. Thus some people loosely say, "Stock price is the present value of future earnings," and calculate value by this formula. Be careful—this is a special case.

Self-Test 7.4

Moonshine Industries has produced a barrel per week for the past 20 years but cannot grow because of certain legal hazards. It earns $25 per share per year and pays it all out to stockholders. The stockholders have alternative, equivalent-risk ventures yielding 20% per year on average. How much is one share of Moonshine worth? Assume the company can keep going indefinitely.

The Constant-Growth Dividend Discount Model

The dividend discount model requires a forecast of dividends for every year into the future, which poses a bit of a problem for stocks with potentially infinite lives. Unless we want to spend a lifetime forecasting dividends, we must use simplifying assumptions to reduce the number of estimates. As we have just seen, the simplest simplification assumes a no-growth perpetuity, which works only for no-growth shares.

---

[7] We assume it does not raise money by issuing new shares.

Here's another simplification that finds a good deal of practical use. Suppose forecasted dividends grow at a constant rate into the indefinite future. If dividends grow at a steady rate, then instead of forecasting an infinite number of dividends, we need to forecast only the next dividend and the dividend growth rate.

Recall Blue Skies Inc. It will pay a $3 dividend in 1 year. If the dividend grows at a constant rate of $g = .08$ (8%) thereafter, then dividends in future years will be

$$
\begin{aligned}
\text{DIV}_1 &= \$3 & &= \$3.00 \\
\text{DIV}_2 &= \$3 \times (1+g) = \$3 \times 1.08 &= \$3.24 \\
\text{DIV}_3 &= \$3 \times (1+g)^2 = \$3 \times 1.08^2 &= \$3.50
\end{aligned}
$$

Plug these forecasts of future dividends into the dividend discount model:

$$
\begin{aligned}
P_0 &= \frac{\text{DIV}_1}{1+r} + \frac{\text{DIV}_1(1+g)}{(1+r)^2} + \frac{\text{DIV}_1(1+g)^2}{(1+r)^3} + \frac{\text{DIV}_1(1+g)^3}{(1+r)^4} + \cdots \\
&= \frac{\$3}{1.12} + \frac{\$3.24}{(1.12)^2} + \frac{\$3.50}{(1.12)^3} + \frac{\$3.78}{(1.12)^4} + \cdots \\
&= \$2.68 + \$2.58 + \$2.49 + \$2.40 + \cdots
\end{aligned}
$$

Although there is an infinite number of terms, each term is proportionately smaller than the preceding one as long as the dividend growth rate g is less than the discount rate r. Because the present value of far-distant dividends will be ever closer to zero, the sum of all of these terms is finite despite the fact that an infinite number of dividends will be paid. The sum can be shown to equal

$$
P_0 = \frac{\text{DIV}_1}{r - g} \tag{7.4}
$$

constant-growth dividend discount model
Version of the dividend discount model in which dividends grow at a constant rate.

This equation is called the **constant-growth dividend discount model,** or the *Gordon growth model* after Myron Gordon, who did much to popularize it.[8]

EXAMPLE 7.3 ▶ Blue Skies Valued by the Constant-Growth Model

Let's apply the constant-growth model to Blue Skies. Assume a dividend has just been paid. The next dividend, to be paid in a year, is forecast at $\text{DIV}_1 = \$3$, the growth rate of dividends is $g = 8\%$, and the discount rate is $r = 12\%$. Therefore, we solve for the stock value as

$$
P_0 = \frac{\text{DIV}_1}{r - g} = \frac{\$3}{.12 - .08} = \$75
$$

The constant-growth formula is close to the formula for the present value of a perpetuity. Suppose you forecast no growth in dividends ($g = 0$). Then the dividend stream is a simple perpetuity, and the valuation formula is $P_0 = \text{DIV}_1/r$. This is precisely the formula you used in Self-Test 7.4 to value Moonshine, a no-growth common stock.

The constant-growth model generalizes the perpetuity formula to allow for constant growth in dividends. Notice that as g increases, the stock price also rises. However, the constant-growth formula is valid only when g is less than r. If someone forecasts

---

[8] Notice that the first dividend is assumed to come at the *end* of the first period and is discounted for a full period. If the stock has just paid a dividend DIV_0, then next year's dividend will be $(1 + g)$ times the dividend just paid. So another way to write the valuation formula is

$$
P_0 = \frac{\text{DIV}_1}{r - g} = \frac{\text{DIV}_0 \times (1 + g)}{r - g}
$$

perpetual dividend growth at a rate greater than investors' required return *r,* then two things happen:

1. The formula explodes. It gives crazy answers. (Try a numerical example.)
2. You know the forecast is wrong, because far-distant dividends would have incredibly high present values. (Again, try a numerical example. Calculate the present value of a dividend paid after 100 years, assuming $DIV_1 = \$3$, $r = .12$, but $g = .20$.)

Estimating Expected Rates of Return

We argued earlier, in Section 7.3, that in competitive markets, common stocks with the same risk are priced to offer the same expected rate of return. But how do you figure out what that expected rate of return is?

It's not easy. Consensus estimates of future dividends, stock prices, or overall rates of return are not published in *The Wall Street Journal* or reported by TV newscasters. Economists argue about which statistical models give the best estimates. There are nevertheless some useful rules of thumb that can give sensible numbers.

One rule of thumb is based on the constant-growth dividend discount model, which forecasts a constant growth rate *g* in both future dividends and stock prices. That means expected capital gains equal *g* per year.

We can calculate the expected rate of return by rearranging the constant-growth formula as

$$r = \frac{DIV_1}{P_0} + g \tag{7.5}$$
$$= \text{dividend yield} + \text{growth rate}$$

For Blue Skies, the expected first-year dividend is $3 and the growth rate is 8%. With an initial stock price of $75, the expected rate of return is

$$r = \frac{DIV_1}{P_0} + g$$
$$= \frac{\$3}{\$75} + .08 = .04 + .08 = .12, \text{ or } 12\%$$

Suppose we found another stock with the same risk as Blue Skies. It ought to offer the same expected total rate of return even if its immediate dividend or expected growth rate is very different. The required rate of return is not the unique property of Blue Skies or any other company; it is set in the worldwide market for common stocks. Blue Skies cannot change its value of *r* by paying higher or lower dividends or by growing faster or slower, unless these changes also affect the risk of the stock. When we use the rule-of-thumb formula, $r = DIV_1/P_0 + g$, we are *not* saying that *r,* the expected rate of return, is *determined by* DIV_1 or *g.* It is determined by the rate of return offered by other equally risky stocks. That return determines how much investors are willing to pay for Blue Skies' forecast future dividends:

$$\underbrace{\frac{DIV_1}{P_0} + g}_{\substack{\text{Given } DIV_1 \text{ and} \\ g, \text{ investors set} \\ \text{the stock price}}} = r = \underbrace{\text{expected rate of return offered}}_{\substack{\text{so that Blue Skies offers an} \\ \text{adequate expected rate of} \\ \text{return } r}} \text{by other, equally risky stocks}$$

EXAMPLE 7.4   ▶   Blue Skies Gets a Windfall

Blue Skies has won a lawsuit against its archrival, Nasty Manufacturing, which forces Nasty Manufacturing to withdraw as a competitor in a key market. As a result, Blue Skies is able to generate 9% per year future growth without sacrificing immediate dividends. Will that increase *r,* the expected rate of return?

Chapter 7   Valuing Stocks

This is very good news for Blue Skies stockholders. The stock price will jump to

$$P_0 = \frac{\text{DIV}_1}{r - g} = \frac{\$3}{.12 - .09} = \$100$$

But at the new price Blue Skies will offer the same 12% expected return:

$$r = \frac{\text{DIV}_1}{P_0} + g$$

$$= \frac{\$3}{\$100} + .09 = .12, \text{ or } 12\%$$

Blue Skies' good news is reflected in a higher stock price today, not in a higher expected rate of return in the future. The unchanged expected rate of return corresponds to Blue Skies' unchanged risk.

Self-Test 7.5

Androscoggin Copper can grow at 5% per year for the indefinite future. It's selling at $100, and next year's dividend is $5. What is the expected rate of return from investing in Carrabasset Mining common stock? Carrabasset and Androscoggin shares are equally risky.

Few real companies are expected to grow in such a regular and convenient way as Blue Skies or Androscoggin Copper. Nevertheless, in some mature industries, growth is reasonably stable and the constant-growth model approximately valid. In such cases the model can be turned around to infer the rate of return expected by investors.

Nonconstant Growth

Many companies grow at rapid or irregular rates for several years before finally settling down. Obviously in such cases we can't use the constant-growth model to estimate value. However, there is an alternative approach. Set the *investment horizon* (year *H*) at the future year by which you expect the company's growth to settle down. Calculate the present value of dividends from now to the horizon year. Forecast the stock price in that year, and discount it also to present value. Then add up to get the total present value of dividends plus the ending stock price. The formula is

$$P_0 = \underbrace{\frac{\text{DIV}_1}{1 + r} + \frac{\text{DIV}_2}{(1 + r)^2} + \cdots + \frac{\text{DIV}_H}{(1 + r)^H}}_{\substack{\text{PV of dividends from} \\ \text{year 1 to horizon}}} + \underbrace{\frac{P_H}{(1 + r)^H}}_{\substack{\text{PV of stock price} \\ \text{at horizon}}}$$

The stock price in the horizon year is often called *terminal value.*

EXAMPLE 7.5   ▶   Estimating the Value of PepsiCo Stock

In late 2007, the share price of PepsiCo's stock was about $72. The company earned about $3.40 a share and paid out about 40% of earnings as dividends. Let's see how we might use the dividend discount model to estimate Pepsi's intrinsic value.

Investors in 2007 were optimistic about the prospects for Pepsi and were forecasting that earnings would grow over the next 5 years by 11.5% a year.[9] This growth rate is almost certainly higher than the return, *r,* that investors required from Pepsi stock, and it is implausible to suppose that such rapid growth could continue indefinitely.

---

[9] Consensus analysts' forecasts are collected by Zack's, First Call, and IBES. They are available on the Web at **moneycentral.com** and **finance.yahoo.com**.

Therefore, we cannot use the simple perpetual-growth formula to value Pepsi. Instead, we will break the problem down into three steps:

Step 1. Value Pepsi's dividends over the period of rapid growth.
Step 2. Estimate Pepsi's stock price at the horizon year, when growth should have settled down.
Step 3. Calculate the present value of Pepsi stock by summing the present value of dividends up to the horizon year and the present value of the stock price at the horizon.

Step 1: Our first task is to value Pepsi's dividends over the next 5 years. If dividends keep pace with the growth in earnings, then forecast earnings and dividends are as follows:

Year	1	2	3	4	5
Earnings	$3.79	$4.23	$4.71	$5.25	$5.86
Dividends (40% of earnings)	1.52	1.69	1.88	2.10	2.34

We estimate that in 2007 investors required a return of about 8.5% from Pepsi stock.[10] Therefore, the present value of the forecast dividends for years 1 to 5 was

$$\text{PV of dividends years 1 to 5} = \frac{\$1.52}{1.085} + \frac{\$1.69}{(1.085)^2} + \frac{\$1.88}{(1.085)^3} + \frac{\$2.10}{(1.085)^4} + \frac{\$2.34}{(1.085)^5}$$
$$= \$7.38$$

Step 2: The trickier task is to estimate the price of Pepsi stock in the horizon year 5. The most likely scenario is that after year 5 growth will gradually start settling down to a sustainable rate, but to keep life simple, we will assume that in year 6 the growth rate falls *immediately* to 6% a year.[11] Thus the forecast dividend in year 6 is

$$\text{DIV}_6 = 1.06 \times \text{DIV}_5 = 1.06 \times \$2.34 = \$2.48$$

and the expected price at the end of year 5 is

$$P_5 = \frac{\text{DIV}_6}{r - g} = \frac{\$2.48}{.085 - .06} = \$99.20$$

Step 3: Remember, the value of Pepsi today is equal to the present value of forecast dividends up to the horizon date plus the present value of the price at the horizon. Thus,

$$P_0 = \text{PV (dividends years 1–5)} + \text{PV (price in year 5)}$$
$$= \$7.38 + \frac{\$99.20}{(1.085)^5} = \$73.35$$

Our estimate of Pepsi's intrinsic value is just about equal to its market price.

A Reality Check   Does it make you nervous to note that your estimate of the horizon price accounts for such a large proportion of the stock's value? It should. Only very

---

[10] For now, you can take this value purely as an assumption. In Chapter 12, we will show you how to estimate required returns. This value is about 3 percentage points higher than the 2007 yield to maturity on Pepsi's long-term bonds. Pepsi stock requires a higher discount rate because it is riskier than Pepsi bonds.

[11] We will show shortly that if a company plows back a constant proportion of earnings and earns a constant return on these new investments, then earnings and dividends will grow by g = plowback ratio × return on new investment. Thus, if from year 5 onward Pepsi continues to reinvest 60% of its earnings and earns an ROE of 10% on this investment, earnings and dividends will grow by .6 × .10 = .06, or 6%.

minor changes in your assumptions about growth beyond year 5 could change your estimate of this horizon price by 10, 20, or 30%.

In the case of Pepsi we *know* what the actual market price was in 2007, but suppose that you are using the dividend discount model to value a company that is going public for the first time or that you are wondering whether to buy Blue Skies' concatenator division. In such cases you do not have the luxury of looking up the market price in *The Wall Street Journal*. A valuation error of 30% could amount to serious money. Wise managers, therefore, check that their estimate of value is in the right ballpark by looking at what the market is prepared to pay for similar businesses. For example, suppose you can find mature, public companies whose scale, risk, and growth prospects today roughly match those projected for Pepsi at the investment horizon. You discover that their stocks tend to sell at multiples of 18 times recent earnings. Then you can reasonably guess that Pepsi's value in year 5 will be about 18 times current earnings, that is, $18 \times \$5.86 = \$105.48$. This is not too far from the $99.20 horizon value that we obtained from the dividend discount model.

Of course, these checks are just an application of the *valuation-by-comparables* method that we introduced earlier in the chapter.

Self-Test 7.6

Suppose that on further analysis you decide that after year 5 Pepsi's earnings and dividends will grow by a constant 5.5% a year. How does this affect your estimate of the value of Pepsi stock at year 0?

7.5 Growth Stocks and Income Stocks

We often hear investors speak of *growth stocks* and *income stocks*. They buy growth stocks primarily in the expectation of capital gains, and they are interested in the future growth of earnings rather than in next year's dividends. On the other hand, they buy income stocks principally for the cash dividends. Let us see whether these distinctions make sense.

Think back once more to Blue Skies. It is expected to pay a dividend next year of $3 ($DIV_1 = 3$), and this dividend is expected to grow at a steady rate of 8% a year ($g = .08$). If investors require a return of 12% ($r = .12$), then the price of Blue Skies should be $DIV_1/(r - g) = \$3/(.12 - .08) = \$75$.

But what determines the rate of dividend growth? Let's check. Suppose that Blue Skies starts year 1 with book equity of $25 a share and earns a return on this equity of 20% a year. Then Blue Skies' earnings per share are

Earnings per share = book equity per share $\times$ return on equity = $25 \times .20 = \$5$

payout ratio
Fraction of earnings paid out as dividends.

plowback ratio
Fraction of earnings retained by the firm.

Blue Skies proposes to pay a dividend in year 1 of $DIV_1 = \$3$ a share, which leaves $2 a share to be plowed back in new plant and equipment. The company's **payout ratio** (the fraction of earnings paid out as dividends) is, therefore, $3/$5 = .60, and its **plowback ratio** (the fraction of earnings reinvested in the firm) is $2/$5 = .40.

After reinvesting 40% of its earnings, Blue Skies will start year 2 with additional equity per share of

Earnings per share in year 1 $\times$ plowback ratio

= initial equity per share $\times$ return on equity $\times$ plowback ratio

= $\$25 \times .20 \times .40 = \$2$

Since Blue Skies started with assets of $25 a share, the growth rate of Blue Skies' equity is $2/$25 = .08, or 8%. The growth rate is

Growth rate = return on equity $\times$ plowback ratio

For example, for Blue Skies, the growth rate equals .20 × .40 = .08, or 8%.

If Blue Skies continues to earn a return of 20% on its equity and plows back 40% of its earnings in new plant and equipment, then earnings and dividends will also continue to grow by 8%. Financial managers sometimes refer to this as the company's **sustainable growth rate,** because it is the rate of growth that the company can sustain from reinvested earnings without changing its leverage.

sustainable growth rate
Steady rate at which firm can grow; return on equity × plowback ratio.

If a company earns a constant return on its equity and plows back a constant proportion of earnings, then

$$g = \text{sustainable growth rate} = \text{return on equity} \times \text{plowback ratio} \qquad (7.6)$$

What if Blue Skies did not plow back *any* of its earnings into new plant and equipment? In that case it would pay out all of its earnings, $5 a share, but would forgo any further growth in earnings and dividends:

$$g = \text{sustainable growth rate} = \text{return on equity} \times \text{plowback ratio} = .20 \times 0 = 0$$

We could recalculate value with $\text{DIV}_1 = \text{EPS}_1 = \$5$ and $g = 0$:

$$P_0 = \frac{\text{DIV}_1}{r - g} = \frac{\text{EPS}_1}{r} = \frac{\$5}{.12} = \$41.67$$

Thus, if Blue Skies did not reinvest any of its earnings, its stock price would not be $75 but $41.67. The $41.67 represents the value of earnings from assets that are already in place. The rest of the stock price ($75 − $41.67 = $33.33) is the net present value of the *future* investments that Blue Skies is expected to make.

What if Blue Skies kept to its policy of reinvesting 40% of its profits but the forecasted return on new investments was only 12%? In that case the sustainable growth rate would also be lower:

$$g = \text{sustainable growth rate} = \text{return on equity} \times \text{plowback ratio}$$
$$= .12 \times .40 = .048, \text{ or } 4.8\%$$

If we plug this new figure into our valuation formula, we come up again with a value of $41.67 for Blue Skies stock:

$$P_0 = \frac{\$3}{.12 - .048} = \$41.67$$

Plowing earnings back into new investments may result in growth in earnings and dividends but it does not add to the current stock price if that money is expected to earn only the return that investors require. Plowing earnings back *does* add value if investors believe that the reinvested earnings will earn a higher rate of return.

To repeat, if Blue Skies did not reinvest any of its earnings, the value of its stock would simply derive from the stream of earnings from the existing assets:

$$P_0 = \frac{\text{DIV}_1}{r} = \frac{\text{EPS}_1}{r} = \frac{\$5}{.12} = \$41.67$$

Equally, if the company *did* reinvest each year but earned only the return that investors require, then those new investments would not add any value. The price of the stock would still be $41.67. Fortunately, investors believe that Blue Skies has the opportunity to earn 20% on its new investments, well above the 12% return that investors require. This is reflected in the $75 that investors are prepared to pay for the stock. The total value of Blue Skies stock is equal to the value of its assets in place *plus* the **present value of its growth opportunities,** or **PVGO:**

present value of growth opportunities (PVGO)
Net present value of a firm's future investments.

Valuing Growth Opportunities

In April 2004 Google, the Internet search-engine provider, announced its plans to go public. Rather than selling shares at a fixed price, Google proposed to auction them to investors. Stock would be allotted to investors who were prepared to pay the most, but all those receiving stock would pay the same price.

The popularity of Google's sophisticated search technology created enormous interest in the issue, and investment managers and their advisers began to debate how much the stock was worth. Google's preliminary prospectus suggested a value of between $108 and $135 a share, which would have valued the equity at $29 billion to $36 billion.

If Google stock was sold at these prices, its share price would be more than 100 times its earnings. Clearly a stock price of $108 or more could not be justified by the stream of earnings generated by existing assets; it would make sense only if investors believed that Google had very valuable growth opportunities that would allow it to earn high returns on future investments. As *The Wall Street Journal* commented, "Sure, the company is making money hand over fist, and it has juicy margins and profits that are expanding rapidly. But . . . in the long run, Google likely will have to prove that it can continue to come up with new ways to profit from its dominant position in the Web-search business for its shares to be big winners."

It is notoriously difficult to guess what future opportunities may become available to a high-tech company. Rather than attempting to make detailed growth forecasts, many investors simply compared Google with rival companies such as Yahoo, whose stock was also trading at a price of around 100 times recent earnings.

As the date of the issue approached, a number of financial analysts expressed reservations about Google's suggested price range, and the company announced that it was reducing the number of shares on offer and cutting its estimate of the issue price to $85 from $95 a share. The auction took place in August, and after investors had submitted their bids, Google announced a sale price of $85, somewhat below the point at which the supply of shares equaled demand. It seemed that the pessimists had been right in their criticisms of the price range that Google had originally suggested. However, once trading started, investors rushed to buy. Google stock opened for trading at $100, within 5 months the price had doubled to just over $200, and in 2007 it reached $700 a share. At that price, it ranked fifth in total market capitalization among all U.S. firms, ahead of giants such as Procter & Gamble, whose earnings were three times those of Google. Pessimists argued that such valuations were crazy, but optimists responded that Google was growing far faster than P&G and would continue to do so. It seems that valuing growth stocks is far from an exact science.

Value of assets in place	$41.67
+ Present value of growth opportunities (PVGO)	33.33
= Total value of Blue Skies stock	$75.00

The superior prospects of Blue Skies are reflected in its price-earnings ratio. With a stock price of $75 and earnings of $5, the P/E ratio is $75/$5 = 15. If Blue Skies had no growth opportunities, its stock price would be only $41.67 and its P/E would be $41.67/$5 = 8.33. The P/E ratio is, therefore, an indicator of Blue Skies' rosy prospects.

Does this mean that the financial manager should celebrate if the firm's stock sells at a high P/E? The answer is usually yes. The high P/E suggests that investors think that the firm has good growth opportunities. However, firms can have high P/E ratios not because the price is high but because earnings are temporarily depressed. A firm that earns *nothing* in a particular period will have an *infinite* P/E.

Of course, valuing stocks is always harder in practice than in principle. Forecasting cash flows and settling on an appropriate discount rate require skill and judgment. The difficulties are often greatest in the case of companies like Blue Skies, whose value comes largely from growth opportunities rather than assets that are already in place. As the nearby box shows, in these cases there is plenty of room for disagreement about value.

Self-Test 7.7

Suppose that instead of plowing money back into lucrative ventures, Blue Skies' management is investing at an expected return on equity of 10%, which is *below* the return of 12% that investors could expect to get from comparable securities.

a. Find the sustainable growth rate of dividends and earnings in these circumstances. Assume a 60% payout ratio.

b. Find the new value of its investment opportunities. Explain why this value is negative despite the positive growth rate of earnings and dividends.

c. If you were a corporate raider, would Blue Skies be a good candidate for an attempted takeover?

7.6 There Are No Free Lunches on Wall Street

We have explained how common stocks are valued. Does that mean that we have just given the game away and told you how to make an instant fortune on the stock market? We are sorry to disappoint you. It is not so easy to beat the market, and even highly paid pros find it very difficult to do so with any consistency.

Look, for example, at Figure 7–4, which shows the average performance of equity mutual funds over three decades. You can see that in some years these mutual funds did beat the market, but as often as not (in fact, in 21 of the 37 years since 1970) it was the other way around. Of course, it would be surprising if some of the managers were not smarter than others and were able to earn superior returns. But it seems hard to spot the smart ones, and the top-performing managers one year have about an average chance of falling on their face the next year.

EXAMPLE 7.6   ▶   Performance of Money Managers

Forbes, a widely read investment magazine, publishes annually an "honor roll" of the most consistently successful mutual funds. Suppose that every year starting in 1975, you invested an equal sum in each of these successful funds when *Forbes* announced its honor roll. You would have outperformed the market in only 5 of the following 16 years, and your average annual return would have been more than 1% below the return on the market.[12]

As this kind of discouraging evidence has accumulated, many investors have given up the search for superior investment returns. Instead, they simply buy and hold index funds or exchange-traded portfolios (ETFs) that track the entire stock market. We discussed index funds and ETFs in Chapter 2. Recall that they provide maximum diversification, with very low management fees. Why pay higher fees to managers

FIGURE 7-4 Annual returns on the Wilshire 5000 Market Index and equity mutual funds, 1971-2007. The market index provided a higher return than the average mutual fund in 21 of the 37 years.

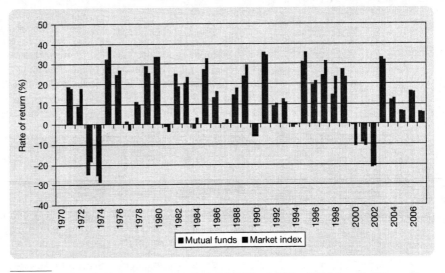

■ Mutual funds ■ Market index

---

[12] See B. G. Malkiel, "Returns from Investing in Equity Mutual Funds 1971 to 1991," *Journal of Finance* 50 (June 1995), pp. 549–572.

who attempt to "beat the market" but can't do so consistently? Corporate pension funds now invest over one-quarter of their U.S. equity holdings in index funds.

Why is it so difficult to beat the market consistently? Let's look at two possible ways that you might attempt to do so.

Method 1: Technical Analysis

Some investors try to achieve superior returns by spotting and exploiting patterns in stock prices. These investors are known as **technical analysts.**

Technical analysis sounds plausible. For example, you might hope to beat the market by buying stocks when they are on their way up and by selling them on their way down. Unfortunately, it turns out that such simple rules don't work. A large price rise in one period may be followed by a further rise in the next period, but it is just as likely to be followed by a fall.

Look, for example, at Figure 7–5*a*. The horizontal axis shows the return on the New York Composite Index in one week (5 business days), while the vertical axis shows the return in the following week. Each point in the chart represents a different week over a recent 20-year period. If a market rise one week tended to be followed by a rise the next week, the points in the chart would plot along an upward-sloping line. But you can see that there was no such tendency; the points are scattered randomly across the chart. Statisticians sometimes measure the relationship between these changes by the coefficient of correlation. In our example, the correlation between the market movements in successive weeks is $-.022$—in other words, effectively zero. Figure 7–5*b* shows a similar plot for monthly (20-business-day) moves. Again you can see that this month's change in the index gives you almost no clue as to the likely change next month. The correlation between successive monthly changes is $-.004$.

Financial economists and statisticians who have studied stock price movements have concluded that you won't get rich looking for consistent patterns in price changes. This seems to be so regardless of whether you look at the market as a whole (as we did in Figure 7–5) or at individual stocks. **Prices appear to wander randomly. They are equally likely to offer a high or low return on any particular day,** *regardless of what has occurred on previous days.* **In other words, prices seem to follow a random walk.**

technical analysts
Investors who attempt to identify undervalued stocks by searching for patterns in past stock prices.

random walk
Security prices change randomly, with no predictable trends or patterns.

FIGURE 7–5*a* **Each dot shows the returns on the New York Composite Index on two successive weeks between January 1968 and January 2007. The circled dot shows a weekly return of +3.1%, followed by +5.2% in the next week. The scatter diagram shows no significant relationship between returns on successive weeks.**

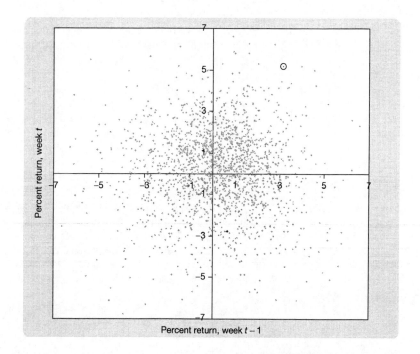

FIGURE 7–5b This scatter diagram shows that there is also no relationship between market returns in successive months.

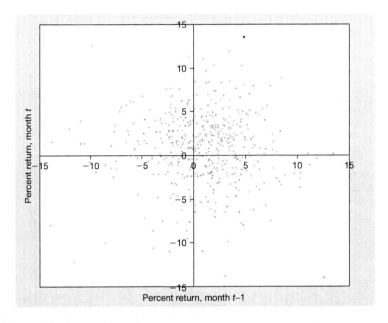

If you are not sure what we mean by "random walk," consider the following example: You are given $100 to play a game. At the end of each week a coin is tossed. If it comes up heads, you win 3% of your investment; if it is tails, you lose 2.5%. Therefore, your payoff at the end of the first week is either $103 or $97.50. At the end of the second week the coin is tossed again. Now the possible outcomes are as follows:

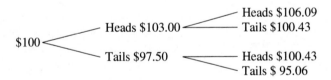

This process is a random walk because successive changes in the value of your stake are independent. That is, the odds of making money each week are the same, regardless of the value at the start of the week or the pattern of heads or tails in the previous weeks.

If a stock's price follows a random walk, the odds of an increase or decrease during any day, month, or year do not depend *at all* on the stock's previous price moves. The historical path of prices gives no useful information about the future—just as a long series of recorded heads and tails gives no information about the next toss.

If you find it difficult to believe that stock prices could behave like our coin-tossing game, then look at the two charts in Figure 7–6. One of these charts shows the outcome from playing our game for 5 years; the other shows the actual performance of the Standard & Poor's Index for a 5-year period. Can you tell which one is which?[13]

Does it surprise you that stocks seem to follow a random walk? If so, imagine that it were not the case and that changes in stock prices were expected to persist for several months. Figure 7–7 provides a hypothetical example of such a predictable cycle. You can see that an upswing in the market started when the index was 1,100 and is expected to carry the price to 1,300 next month. What will happen when investors perceive this bonanza? Since stocks are a bargain at their current level, investors will rush to buy

---
[13] The top chart in Figure 7–6 shows the real Standard & Poor's Index for the years 1980 through 1984. The bottom chart was generated by a series of random numbers. You may be among the 50% of our readers who guess right, but we bet it was just a guess.

FIGURE 7-6 One of these charts shows the Standard & Poor's Index for a 5-year period. The other shows the results of playing our coin-toss game for 5 years. Can you tell which is which? (The answer is given in footnote 13.)

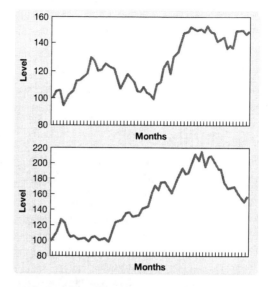

FIGURE 7-7 Cycles self-destruct as soon as they are recognized by investors. The stock price instantaneously jumps to the present value of the expected future price.

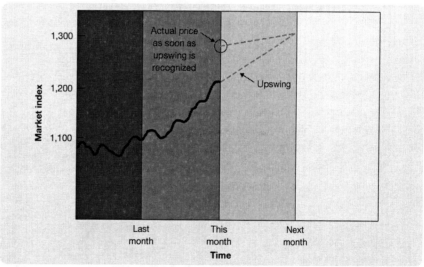

and, in so doing, will push up prices. They will stop buying only when stocks are fairly priced. **Thus, as soon as a cycle becomes apparent to investors, they immediately eliminate it by their trading.**

Self-Test 7.8   True or false: If stock prices follow a random walk,

a. Successive stock prices are not related.
b. Successive stock price changes are not related.
c. Stock prices fluctuate above and below a normal long-run price.
d. The history of stock prices cannot be used to predict future returns to investors.

Method 2: Fundamental Analysis

You may not be able to earn superior returns just by studying past stock prices, but what about other types of information? After all, most investors don't just look at past stock prices. Instead, they try to gauge a firm's business prospects by studying the

fundamental analysts
Investors who attempt to find mispriced securities by analyzing fundamental information, such as accounting data and business prospects.

financial and trade press, the company's financial accounts, the president's annual statements, and other items of news. These investors are called **fundamental analysts,** in contrast to technical analysts who focus on past stock price movements.

Fundamental analysts are paid to uncover stocks for which price does *not* equal intrinsic value. If intrinsic value exceeds price, for example, the stock is a bargain and will offer a superior expected return. But what happens if there are many talented and competitive fundamental analysts? If one of them uncovers a stock that appears to be a bargain, it stands to reason that others will as well, and there will be a wave of buying that pushes up the price. In the end, their actions will eliminate the original bargain opportunity. To profit, your insights must be *different* from those of your competitors, and you must act *faster* than they can. This is a tall order.

To illustrate the challenge facing stock market analysts, look at Figure 7–8, which shows how stock prices react to one particular item of news—the announcement of a takeover. In most takeovers the acquiring company is willing to pay a hefty premium to induce the shareholders of the target company to give up their shares. You can see from Figure 7–8 that the stock price of the target company typically jumps up on the day that the public becomes aware of a takeover attempt (day 0 in the graph). However, this adjustment in the stock price is immediate; thereafter there is no further drift in the stock price, either upward or downward. By the time the acquisition has been made public, it is too late to buy.

Researchers have looked at the stock price reaction to many other types of news, such as earnings and dividend announcements, and plans to issue additional stock or repurchase existing stock. All this information seems to be rapidly and accurately reflected in the price of the stock, so it is impossible to make superior returns by buying or selling after the announcement.

A Theory to Fit the Facts

Economists often refer to the stock market as an efficient market. By this they mean that the competition to find misvalued stocks is intense. So when new information comes out, investors rush to take advantage of it and thereby eliminate any profit opportunities. Professional investors express the same idea when they say that there are no free lunches on Wall Street.

It is useful to distinguish three types of information and three degrees of efficiency. The term *weak-form efficiency* describes a market in which prices already reflect all

efficient market
Market in which prices reflect all available information.

FIGURE 7–8 The performance of the stocks of target companies compared with that of the market. The prices of target stocks jump up on the announcement day, but from then on there are no unusual price movements. The announcement of the takeover attempt seems to be fully reflected in the stock price on the announcement day.

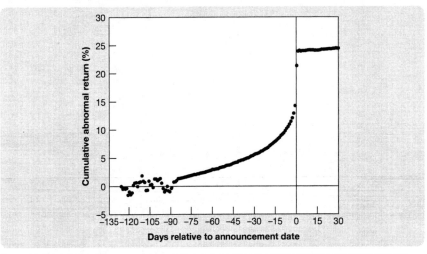

Source: Updated version of figure appearing in A. Keown and J. Pinkerton, "Merger Announcements and Insider Trading Activity," *Journal of Finance* 36 (September 1981); pp. 855–869. We are grateful to Jinghua Yan for updating the calculations to the period 1979–2004.

the information contained in past prices. In such a market, share price changes are random, and technical analysis that searches for patterns in past returns is valueless. Figure 7–5, which looked at successive weekly and monthly changes in the market index, is evidence in favor of weak-form efficiency.

Semistrong-form efficiency describes a market in which prices reflect not just the information contained in past prices but all publicly available information. In such a market it is impossible to earn consistently superior returns simply by reading the financial press, studying the company's financial statements, and so on. Figure 7–8, which looked at the market reaction to merger announcements, was just one piece of evidence in favor of semistrong efficiency. As soon as information about the mergers became public, the stock prices jumped.

Finally, *strong-form efficiency* refers to a market where prices impound all available information. In such a market no investor, however hardworking, could expect to earn superior profits. Figure 7–4, which showed the performance of mutual funds, was consistent with strong-form efficiency.

Self-Test 7.9   Technical analysts and fundamental analysts all try to earn superior returns in the stock market. Explain how their efforts help keep the market efficient.

7.7 Market Anomalies and Behavioral Finance

Market Anomalies

Few simple economic theories are as well supported by the evidence as the efficient-market theory. However, no theory this simple can be universally true; there are always some puzzles or apparent exceptions. Let us look at two examples.

The Earnings Announcement Puzzle   In an efficient stock market, a company's stock price should react instantly at the announcement of unexpectedly good or bad earnings. But, in fact, stocks with the best earnings news typically outperform the stocks with the worst earnings news. Figure 7–9 shows stock performance following the announcement of unexpectedly good or bad earnings during the years 1972 to 2001. The 10% of the stocks of firms with the best earnings news outperform those with the worst news by about 1% per month over the 6-month period following the announcement. It seems that investors underreact to the earnings announcement and become aware of the full significance only as further information arrives.

The New-Issue Puzzle   When firms issue stock to the public, investors typically rush to buy. On average, those lucky enough to be awarded stock receive an immediate capital gain. However, researchers have found that these early gains often turn into losses. For example, suppose that you bought stock immediately following each initial public offering and then held that stock for 5 years. Over the period 1970 to 2003 your average annual return would have been 4.1% less than the return on a portfolio of similar-sized stocks.[14]

The jury is still out on these studies of longer-term anomalies. We can't be sure whether they are important exceptions to the efficient-market theory or a coincidence that stems from the efforts of many researchers to find interesting patterns in the data. There may also be other explanations. Take, for example, the new-issue puzzle. Most new issues during the past 30 years have involved growth stocks with high market values and limited book assets. Perhaps the stocks performed badly not because they had just been issued but because all growth stocks happened to perform badly during

---

[14] An excellent resource for data and analysis of initial public offerings is Professor Jay Ritter's Web page, **http://bear.cba.ufl.edu/ritter**.

FIGURE 7-9 **Average stock returns over the 6 months following announcements of quarterly earnings. The 10% of stocks with the best earnings news (portfolio 10) outperformed those with the worst news (portfolio 1) by about 1% per month.**

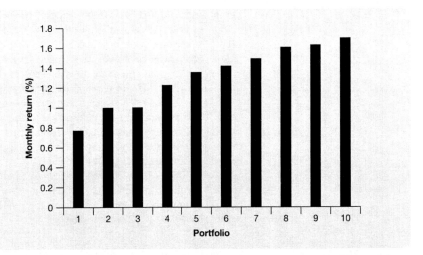

Source: T. Chordia and L. Shivakumar, "Inflation Illusion and the Post-earnings Announcement Drift," *Journal of Accounting Research* 43 (2005), pp. 521–556.

this period. Of course, if that is true, we need to address another question: Why have growth stocks performed poorly over such a long period of time? We will come back to this question in Chapter 12.

Behavioral Finance

Investors in technology stocks in the 1990s saw an extraordinary run-up in the value of their holdings. The NASDAQ market index, which is heavily weighted toward high-tech stocks, rose 580% from the start of 1995 to March 2000. But then even more rapidly than it began, the boom ended. By October 2002 the NASDAQ index had fallen 78%.

Some of the largest price gains and losses were experienced by the new "dot-com stocks." For example, Yahoo shares, which began trading in April 1996, appreciated by 1,400% in just 4 years. At this point Yahoo stock was valued at $124 billion, more than the market capitalizations of GM, Heinz, and Boeing combined. It was not, however, to last; just over a year later Yahoo's market capitalization was little more than $6 billion.

What caused the boom in high-tech stocks? Had there been a sharp improvement in the prospects for dividend growth? Or had investors decided that they did not need such high returns from common stocks? Neither explanation seemed capable of explaining the prices that investors were prepared to pay. Could it be that the theory of efficient markets was another casualty of the rise and fall of the dot-coms?

Some scholars believe that the answers to these questions lie in behavioral psychology. People are not 100% rational 100% of the time. This shows up in two broad areas—their attitudes to risk and the way that they assess probabilities:

1. *Attitudes toward risk.* Psychologists have observed that, when making risky decisions, people are particularly loath to incur losses, even if those losses are small. Losers are liable to regret their actions and kick themselves for having been so foolish. To avoid this unpleasant possibility, individuals will tend to shun those actions that may result in loss.

   The pain of a loss seems to depend on whether it comes on the heels of earlier losses. Once investors have suffered a loss, they may be even more cautious not to risk a further loss. Conversely, just as gamblers are known to be more willing to take large bets when they are ahead, so investors may be more prepared to run the risk of a stock market dip after they have experienced a period of substantial gains. If they do then suffer a small loss, they at least have the consolation of being up on the year.

You can see how this sort of behavior could lead to a stock price "bubble." The early investors in Yahoo and other dot-coms were big winners. They may have stopped worrying about the risk of loss. They may have thrown caution to the winds and piled even more investment into these companies, driving stock prices far above fundamental values. The day of reckoning came when investors woke up and realized how far above fundamental value prices had soared.

2. *Beliefs about probabilities.* Most investors do not have a Ph.D. in probability theory and may make common errors in assessing the probability of uncertain outcomes. Psychologists have found that, when judging the possible future outcomes, individuals commonly look back to what has happened in recent periods and then assume that this is representative of what may occur in the future. The temptation is to project recent experience into the future and to forget the lessons learned from the more distant past. For example, an investor who places too much weight on recent events may judge that glamorous growth companies are very likely to continue to grow rapidly, even though very high rates of growth cannot persist indefinitely.

A second common bias is overconfidence. Most of us believe that we are better-than-average drivers, and most investors think that they are better-than-average stockpickers. We know that two speculators who trade with one another cannot both make money from the deal; for every winner there must be a loser. But presumably investors are prepared to continue trading because each is confident that it is the other one who is the patsy.

You can see how such behavior may have reinforced the dot-com boom. As the bull market developed, it generated increased optimism about the future and stimulated demand for shares. The more that investors racked up profits on their stocks, the more confident they became in their views and the more willing they became to bear the risk that the next month might not be so good.

Now it is not difficult to believe that your uncle Harry or aunt Hetty may have become caught up in a scatty whirl of irrational exuberance,[15] but why didn't hard-headed professional investors bail out of the overpriced stocks and force their prices down to fair value? Perhaps they felt that it was too difficult to predict when the boom would end and that their jobs would be at risk if they moved aggressively into cash when others were raking up profits. In this case, sales of stock by the pros were simply not large enough to stem the tide of optimism that was sweeping the market.

It is too early to say how far behavioral finance scholars can help to sort out some of the puzzles and explain events like the dot-com boom. One thing, however, seems clear: It is relatively easy for statisticians to spot anomalies with the benefit of hindsight and for psychologists to provide an explanation for them. It is much more difficult for investment managers who are at the sharp end to spot and invest in mispriced securities. And that is the basic message of the efficient-market theory.

---

[15] The term "irrational exuberance" was coined by Alan Greenspan, former chairman of the Federal Reserve Board, to describe the dot-com boom. It was also the title of a book by Robert Shiller that examined the boom. See R. Shiller, *Irrational Exuberance* (New York City: Broadway Books, 2001).

SUMMARY

What information about company stocks is regularly reported in the financial pages of the newspaper? *(LO1)*

Firms that wish to raise new capital may either borrow money or bring new "partners" into the business by selling shares of **common stock**. Large companies usually arrange for their stocks to be traded on a stock exchange. The stock listings report the stock's price, price change, volume, **dividend yield,** and **price-earnings (P/E)** ratio.

www.mhhe.com/bmm6e

How can one calculate the present value of a stock given forecasts of future dividends and future stock price? *(LO2)*

Stockholders generally expect to receive (1) cash dividends and (2) capital gains or losses. The rate of return that they expect over the next year is defined as the expected dividend per share DIV_1 plus the expected increase in price $P_1 - P_0$, all divided by the price at the start of the year P_0.

Unlike the fixed interest payments that the firm promises to bondholders, the dividends that are paid to stockholders depend on the fortunes of the firm. That's why a company's common stock is riskier than its debt. The return that investors expect on any one stock is also the return that they demand on all stocks subject to the same degree of risk. The present value of a stock equals the present value of the forecast future dividends and future stock price, using that expected return as the discount rate.

The present value of a share is equal to the stream of expected dividends per share up to some horizon date plus the expected price at this date, all discounted at the return that investors require. If the horizon date is far away, we simply say that stock price equals the present value of all future dividends per share. This is the **dividend discount model.**

How can stock valuation formulas be used to infer the expected rate of return on a common stock? *(LO3)*

If dividends are expected to grow forever at a constant rate g, then the expected return on the stock is equal to the dividend yield (DIV_1/P_0) plus the expected rate of dividend growth. The value of the stock according to this **constant-growth dividend discount model** is $P_0 = DIV_1/(r - g)$.

How should investors interpret price-earnings ratios? *(LO4)*

You can think of a share's value as the sum of two parts—the value of the assets in place and the **present value of growth opportunities,** that is, of future opportunities for the firm to invest in high-return projects. The price-earnings (P/E) ratio reflects the market's assessment of the firm's growth opportunities.

How does competition among investors lead to efficient markets? *(LO5)*

Competition between investors will tend to produce an **efficient market**—that is, a market in which prices rapidly reflect new information and investors have difficulty making consistently superior returns. Of course, we all *hope* to beat the market, but if the market is efficient, all we can rationally *expect* is a return that is sufficient on average to compensate for the time value of money and for the risks we bear.

The efficient-market theory comes in three flavors. The *weak form* states that prices reflect all the information contained in the past series of stock prices. In this case it is impossible to earn superior profits simply by looking for past patterns in stock prices. The *semistrong form* of the theory states that prices reflect all published information, so it is impossible to make consistently superior returns just by reading the newspaper, looking at the company's annual accounts, and so on. The *strong form* states that stock prices effectively impound all available information. This form tells us that private information is hard to come by, because in pursuing it you are in competition with thousands—perhaps millions—of active and intelligent investors. The best you can do in this case is to assume that securities are fairly priced.

The evidence for market efficiency is voluminous, and there is little doubt that skilled professional investors find it difficult to win consistently. Nevertheless, there remain some puzzling instances where markets do not seem to be efficient. Some financial economists attribute these apparent anomalies to behavioral foibles.

LISTING OF EQUATIONS

7.1 $V_0 = \dfrac{DIV_1 + P_1}{1 + r}$

7.2 $P_0 = \dfrac{DIV_1 + P_1}{1 + r}$

7.3 $P_0 = \dfrac{\text{DIV}_1}{1+r} + \dfrac{\text{DIV}_2}{(1+r)^2} + \cdots + \dfrac{\text{DIV}_H + P_H}{(1+r)^H}$

7.4 $P_0 = \dfrac{\text{DIV}_1}{r-g}$

7.5 $r = \dfrac{\text{DIV}_1}{P_0} + g = \text{dividend yield} + \text{growth rate}$

7.6 $g = \text{sustainable growth rate} = \text{return on equity} \times \text{plowback ratio}$

QUESTIONS

QUIZ

1. **Dividend Discount Model.** Amazon.com has never paid a dividend, but in November 2007 the market value of its stock was $35 billion. Does this invalidate the dividend discount model? *(LO2)*

2. **Dividend Yield.** Favored stock will pay a dividend this year of $2.40 per share. Its dividend yield is 8%. At what price is the stock selling? *(LO1)*

3. **Preferred Stock.** Preferred Products has issued preferred stock with an $8 annual dividend that will be paid in perpetuity. *(LO2)*

    a. If the discount rate is 12%, at what price should the preferred sell?
    b. At what price should the stock sell 1 year from now?
    c. What is the dividend yield, the capital gains yield, and the expected rate of return of the stock?

4. **Constant-Growth Model.** Waterworks has a dividend yield of 8%. If its dividend is expected to grow at a constant rate of 5%, what must be the expected rate of return on the company's stock? *(LO3)*

5. **Dividend Discount Model.** How can we say that price equals the present value of all future dividends when many actual investors may be seeking capital gains and planning to hold their shares for only a year or two? Explain. *(LO2)*

6. **Rate of Return.** Steady As She Goes, Inc., will pay a year-end dividend of $3 per share. Investors expect the dividend to grow at a rate of 4% indefinitely.

    a. If the stock currently sells for $30 per share, what is the expected rate of return on the stock? *(LO3)*
    b. If the expected rate of return on the stock is 16.5%, what is the stock price? *(LO2)*

7. **Dividend Yield.** BMM Industries pays a dividend of $2 per quarter. The dividend yield on its stock is reported at 4.8%. What price is the stock selling at? *(LO1)*

8. **Forms of Efficient Markets.** Supply the missing words from the following list: *fundamental, semistrong, strong, technical, weak. (LO5)*

    There are three forms of the efficient market theory. Tests that have found there are no patterns in share price changes provide evidence for the _____ form of the theory. Evidence for the _____ form of the theory is provided by tests that look at how rapidly markets respond to new public information, and evidence for the _____ form of the theory is provided by tests that look at the performance of professionally managed portfolios. Market efficiency results from competition between investors. Many investors search for information about the company's business that would help them to value the stock more accurately. This is known as _____ analysis. Such research helps to ensure that prices reflect all available information. Other investors study past stock prices for recurrent patterns that would allow them to make superior profits. This is known as _____ analysis. Such research helps to eliminate any patterns.

9. **Information and Efficient Markets.** "It's competition for information that makes securities markets efficient." Is this statement correct? Explain. *(LO5)*

10. **Behavioral Finance.** Some finance scholars cite well-documented behavioral biases to explain apparent cases of market inefficiency. Describe two of these biases. *(LO5)*

PRACTICE PROBLEMS

11. **Stock Values.** Integrated Potato Chips paid a $1 per share dividend *yesterday*. You expect the dividend to grow steadily at a rate of 4% per year. *(LO2)*
    a. What is the expected dividend in each of the next 3 years?
    b. If the discount rate for the stock is 12%, at what price will the stock sell?
    c. What is the expected stock price 3 years from now?
    d. If you buy the stock and plan to hold it for 3 years, what payments will you receive? What is the present value of those payments? Compare your answer to (b).

12. **Constant-Growth Model.** A stock sells for $40. The next dividend will be $4 per share. If the rate of return earned on reinvested funds is 15% and the company reinvests 40% of earnings in the firm, what must be the discount rate? *(LO3)*

13. **Constant-Growth Model.** Gentleman Gym just paid its annual dividend of $3 per share, and it is widely expected that the dividend will increase by 5% per year indefinitely. *(LO2)*
    a. What price should the stock sell at? The discount rate is 15%.
    b. How would your answer change if the discount rate were only 12%? Why does the answer change?

14. **Constant-Growth Model.** Arts and Crafts, Inc., will pay a dividend of $5 per share in 1 year. It sells at $50 a share, and firms in the same industry provide an expected rate of return of 14%. What must be the expected growth rate of the company's dividends? *(LO2)*

15. **Constant-Growth Model.** Eastern Electric currently pays a dividend of about $1.64 per share and sells for $27 a share. *(LO3)*
    a. If investors believe the growth rate of dividends is 3% per year, what rate of return do they expect to earn on the stock?
    b. If investors' required rate of return is 10%, what must be the growth rate they expect of the firm?
    c. If the sustainable growth rate is 5% and the plowback ratio is .4, what must be the rate of return earned by the firm on its new investments?

16. **Constant-Growth Model.** You believe that the Non-stick Gum Factory will pay a dividend of $2 on its common stock next year. Thereafter, you expect dividends to grow at a rate of 6% a year in perpetuity. If you require a return of 12% on your investment, how much should you be prepared to pay for the stock? *(LO2)*

17. **Negative Growth.** Horse and Buggy Inc. is in a declining industry. Sales, earnings, and dividends are all shrinking at a rate of 10% per year. *(LO2)*
    a. If $r = 15\%$ and $\text{DIV}_1 = \$3$, what is the value of a share?
    b. What price do you forecast for the stock next year?
    c. What is the expected rate of return on the stock?
    d. Can you distinguish between "bad stocks" and "bad companies"? Does the fact that the industry is declining mean that the stock is a bad buy?

18. **Constant-Growth Model.** Metatrend's stock will generate earnings of $6 per share this year. The discount rate for the stock is 15%, and the rate of return on reinvested earnings also is 15%. *(LO2)*
    a. Find both the growth rate of dividends and the price of the stock if the company reinvests the following fraction of its earnings in the firm: (i) 0%; (ii) 40%; (iii) 60%.
    b. Redo part (a) now assuming that the rate of return on reinvested earnings is 20%. What is the present value of growth opportunities for each reinvestment rate?
    c. Considering your answers to parts (a) and (b), can you briefly state the difference between companies experiencing growth versus companies with growth opportunities?

19. **Nonconstant Growth.** You expect a share of stock to pay dividends of $1.00, $1.25, and $1.50 in each of the next 3 years. You believe the stock will sell for $20 at the end of the third year. *(LO2)*

a. What is the stock price if the discount rate for the stock is 10%?

b. What is the dividend yield?

20. **Constant-Growth Model.** Here are data on two stocks, both of which have discount rates of 15%: *(LO2)*

	Stock A	Stock B
Return on equity	15%	10%
Earnings per share	$2.00	$1.50
Dividends per share	$1.00	$1.00

a. What are the dividend payout ratios for each firm?

b. What are the expected dividend growth rates for each firm?

c. What is the proper stock price for each firm?

21. **P/E Ratios.** Web Cites Research projects a rate of return of 20% on new projects. Management plans to plow back 30% of all earnings into the firm. Earnings this year will be $3 per share, and investors expect a 12% rate of return on stocks facing the same risks as Web Cites. *(LO4)*

a. What is the sustainable growth rate?

b. What is the stock price?

c. What is the present value of growth opportunities?

d. What is the P/E ratio?

e. What would the price and P/E ratio be if the firm paid out all earnings as dividends?

f. What do you conclude about the relationship between growth opportunities and P/E ratios?

22. **Constant-Growth Model.** Fincorp will pay a year-end dividend of $2.40 per share, which is expected to grow at a 4% rate for the indefinite future. The discount rate is 12%. *(LO2)*

a. What is the stock selling for?

b. If earnings are $3.10 a share, what is the implied value of the firm's growth opportunities?

23. **P/E Ratios.** No-Growth Industries pays out all of its earnings as dividends. It will pay its next $4 per share dividend in a year. The discount rate is 12%. *(LO4)*

a. What is the price-earnings ratio of the company?

b. What would the P/E ratio be if the discount rate were 10%?

24. **Growth Opportunities.** Stormy Weather has no attractive investment opportunities. Its return on equity equals the discount rate, which is 10%. Its expected earnings this year are $4 per share. Find the stock price, P/E ratio, and growth rate of dividends for plowback ratios of

a. zero. *(LO2)*

b. .40. *(LO2)*

c. .80. *(LO2)*

25. **Growth Opportunities.** Trend-Line Inc. has been growing at a rate of 6% per year and is expected to continue to do so indefinitely. The next dividend is expected to be $5 per share. *(LO2)*

a. If the market expects a 10% rate of return on Trend-Line, at what price must it be selling?

b. If Trend-Line's earnings per share will be $8, what part of Trend-Line's value is due to assets in place, and what part to growth opportunities?

26. **P/E Ratios.** Castles in the Sand generates a rate of return of 20% on its investments and maintains a plowback ratio of .30. Its earnings this year will be $4 per share. Investors expect a 12% rate of return on the stock.

a. Find the price and P/E ratio of the firm. *(LO2)*

b. What happens to the P/E ratio if the plowback ratio is reduced to .20? Why? *(LO4)*

c. Show that if plowback equals zero, the earnings-price ratio, E/P, falls to the expected rate of return on the stock. *(LO4)*

27. **Dividend Growth.** Grandiose Growth has a dividend growth rate of 20%. The discount rate is 10%. The end-of-year dividend will be $2 per share. *(LO2)*

a. What is the present value of the dividend to be paid in year 1? Year 2? Year 3?

b. Could anyone rationally expect this growth rate to continue indefinitely?

28. **Stock Valuation.** Start-Up Industries is a new firm that has raised $200 million by selling shares of stock. Management plans to earn a 24% rate of return on equity, which is more than

the 15% rate of return available on comparable-risk investments. Half of all earnings will be reinvested in the firm. *(LO2)*

a. What will be Start-Up's ratio of market value to book value?

b. How would that ratio change if the firm can earn only a 10% rate of return on its investments?

29. **Nonconstant Growth.** Planned Obsolescence has a product that will be in vogue for 3 years, at which point the firm will close up shop and liquidate the assets. As a result, forecast dividends are $DIV_1 = \$2$, $DIV_2 = \$2.50$, and $DIV_3 = \$18$. What is the stock price if the discount rate is 12%? *(LO2)*

30. **Nonconstant Growth.** Tattletale News Corp. has been growing at a rate of 20% per year, and you expect this growth rate in earnings and dividends to continue for another 3 years. *(LO2)*

a. If the last dividend paid was $2, what will the next dividend be?

b. If the discount rate is 15% and the steady growth rate after 3 years is 4%, what should the stock price be today?

31. **Nonconstant Growth.** Reconsider Tattletale News from the previous problem.

a. What is your prediction for the stock price in 1 year? *(LO2)*

b. Show that the expected rate of return equals the discount rate. *(LO3)*

32. **Interpreting the Efficient-Market Theory.** How would you respond to the following comments? *(LO5)*

a. "Efficient market, my eye! I know lots of investors who do crazy things."

b. "Efficient market? Balderdash! I know at least a dozen people who have made a bundle in the stock market."

c. "The trouble with the efficient-market theory is that it ignores investors' psychology."

33. **Real versus Financial Investments.** Why do investments in financial markets almost always have zero NPVs, whereas firms can find many investments in their product markets with positive NPVs? *(LO5)*

34. **Investment Performance.** It seems that every month we read an article in *The Wall Street Journal* about a stockpicker with a marvelous track record. Do these examples mean that financial markets are not efficient? *(LO5)*

35. **Implications of Efficient Markets.** The president of Good Fortunes, Inc., states at a press conference that the company has a 30-year history of ever-increasing dividend payments. Good Fortunes is widely regarded as one of the best-run firms in its industry. Does this make the firm's stock a good buy? Explain. *(LO5)*

36. **Implications of Efficient Markets.** "Long-term interest rates are at record highs. Most companies, therefore, find it cheaper to finance with common stock or relatively inexpensive short-term bank loans." Discuss. *(LO5)*

37. **Expectations and Efficient Markets.** Geothermal Corp. just announced good news: Its earnings have increased by 20%. Most investors had anticipated an increase of 25%. Will Geothermal's stock price increase or decrease when the announcement is made? *(LO5)*

38. **Behavioral Finance.** In Section 7.7 we gave two examples of market anomalies (the earnings-announcement puzzle and the new-issue puzzle). Do you think that behavioral finance can help to explain these anomalies? *(LO5)*

CHALLENGE PROBLEMS

39. **Sustainable Growth.** Computer Corp. reinvests 60% of its earnings in the firm. The stock sells for $50, and the next dividend will be $2.50 per share. The discount rate is 15%. What is the rate of return on the company's reinvested funds? *(LO2)*

40. **Nonconstant Growth.** A company will pay a $2 per share dividend in 1 year. The dividend in 2 years will be $4 per share, and it is expected that dividends will grow at 5% per year thereafter. The expected rate of return on the stock is 12%. *(LO2)*

a. What is the current price of the stock?

   b. What is the expected price of the stock in a year?

   c. Show that the expected return, 12%, equals dividend yield plus capital appreciation.

41. **Nonconstant Growth.** Phoenix Industries has pulled off a miraculous recovery. Four years ago it was near bankruptcy. Today, it announced a $1 per share dividend to be paid a year from now, the first dividend since the crisis. Analysts expect dividends to increase by $1 a year for another 2 years. After the third year (in which dividends are $3 per share) dividend growth is expected to settle down to a more moderate long-term growth rate of 6%. If the firm's investors expect to earn a return of 14% on this stock, what must be its price? *(LO2)*

42. **Nonconstant Growth.** Compost Science, Inc. (CSI), is in the business of converting Boston's sewage sludge into fertilizer. The business is not in itself very profitable. However, to induce CSI to remain in business, the Metropolitan District Commission (MDC) has agreed to pay whatever amount is necessary to yield CSI a 10% return on investment. At the end of the year, CSI is expected to pay a $4 dividend. It has been reinvesting 40% of earnings and growing at 4% a year. *(LO2)*

   a. Suppose CSI continues on this growth trend. What is the expected rate of return for an investor who purchases the stock at the market price of $100?

   b. What part of the $100 price is attributable to the present value of growth opportunities?

   c. Now the MDC announces a plan for CSI to also treat Cambridge sewage. CSI's plant will therefore be expanded gradually over 5 years. This means that CSI will have to reinvest 80% of its earnings for 5 years. Starting in year 6, however, it will again be able to pay out 60% of earnings. What will be CSI's stock price once this announcement is made and its consequences for CSI are known?

Please visit us at www.mhhe.com/bmm6e

43. **Nonconstant Growth.** Better Mousetraps has come out with an improved product, and the world is beating a path to its door. As a result, the firm projects growth of 20% per year for 4 years. By then, other firms will have copycat technology, competition will drive down profit margins, and the sustainable growth rate will fall to 5%. The most recent annual dividend was $DIV_0 = \$1$ per share. *(LO2)*

   a. What are the expected values of DIV_1, DIV_2, DIV_3, and DIV_4?

   b. What is the expected stock price 4 years from now? The discount rate is 10%.

   c. What is the stock price today?

   d. Find the dividend yield, DIV_1/P_0.

   e. What will next year's stock price, P_1, be?

   f. What is the expected rate of return to an investor who buys the stock now and sells it in 1 year?

Please visit us at www.mhhe.com/bmm6e

44. **Nonconstant Growth.** *(LO2)*

   a. Return to the previous problem, and compute the value of Better Mousetraps for assumed sustainable growth rates of 6% through 9%, in increments of .5%.

   b. Compute the percentage change in the value of the firm for each 1-percentage-point increase in the assumed final growth rate, g.

   c. What happens to the sensitivity of intrinsic value to changes in g? What do you conclude about the reliability of the dividend growth model when the assumed sustainable growth rate begins to approach the discount rate?

45. **Yield Curve and Efficient Markets.** If the yield curve is downward-sloping, meaning that long-term interest rates are lower than short-term interest rates, what might investors believe about future short-term interest rates? *(LO5)*

STANDARD &POOR'S

1. Go to **www.mhhe.com/edumarketinsight**. Review Table 7–3, which lists the market values of several firms. Update the table. Which company's value changed by the greatest percentage since 2007, when the table was created? *(Hint:* Look for the price per share and the number of shares outstanding. The product of the two is total market capitalization.) Now calculate book value per share. Have the book values for any firm changed? Which seems to be more stable, book or market value? Why?

2. Using the constant dividend growth stock valuation model, estimate the current required rate of return, r, of H. J. Heinz (HNZ). Using the information from Market Insight's Company Profile and Financial Highlights reports, estimate next year's dividend DIV_1 by using the current dividend and the 5-year dividend growth rate. Use the current price, DIV_1, and the growth rate to estimate the return required by investors.

3. From the Financial Highlights and Company Profile links of Market Insight, obtain the price-earnings ratios of Adobe Systems (ADBE) and American Electric Power (AEP). Which of these two firms seems to be more of a "growth stock"? Now obtain a forecast of each firm's expected earnings per share in the coming year from a site such as **finance.yahoo.com**. What is the present value of growth opportunities for each firm as a fraction of the stock price? (Assume, for simplicity, that the required rate of return on the stocks is $r = 12\%$.) Are the relative values you obtain for PVGO consistent with the P/E ratios?

SOLUTIONS TO SELF-TEST QUESTIONS

7.1 Expected industry profitability has fallen. Thus the value of future investment opportunities has fallen relative to the value of assets in place. This happens in all growth industries sooner or later, as competition increases and profitable new investment opportunities shrink.

7.2 $$P_0 = \frac{DIV_1 + P_1}{1 + r} = \frac{\$5 + \$105}{1.10} = \$100$$

7.3 Since dividends and share price grow at 5%,

$$DIV_2 = \$5 \times 1.05 = \$5.25, \quad DIV_3 = \$5 \times 1.05^2 = \$5.51$$

$$P_3 = \$100 \times 1.05^3 = \$115.76$$

$$P_0 = \frac{DIV_1}{1 + r} + \frac{DIV_2}{(1 + r)^2} + \frac{DIV_3 + P_3}{(1 + r)^3}$$

$$= \frac{\$5.00}{1.10} + \frac{\$5.25}{(1.10^2)} + \frac{\$5.51 + \$115.76}{(1.10)^3} = \$100$$

7.4 $$P_0 = \frac{DIV}{r} = \frac{\$25}{.20} = \$125$$

7.5 The two firms have equal risk, so we can use the data for Androscoggin to find the expected return on either stock:

$$r = \frac{DIV_1}{P_0} + g = \frac{\$5}{\$100} + .05 = .10, \text{ or } 10\%$$

7.6 We've already calculated the present value of dividends through year 5 as $7.39. We can also forecast the dividend in year 6 as

$$DIV_6 = 1.055 \times DIV_5 = 1.055 \times \$2.34 = \$2.4687$$

Price in year 5 is

$$P_5 = \frac{\$2.4687}{.085 - .055} = \$82.29$$

$$P_0 = PV(\text{dividends through year 5}) + PV(P_5)$$

$$= \$7.39 + \frac{\$82.29}{(1.085)^5}$$

$$= \$62.12$$

7.7 a. The sustainable growth rate is

$$g = \text{return on equity} \times \text{plowback ratio}$$
$$= 10\% \times .40 = 4\%$$

b. First value the company. At a 60% payout ratio, $DIV_1 = \$3$ as before. Using the constant-growth model,

www.mhhe.com/bmm6e

$$P_0 = \frac{\$3}{.12 - .04} = \$37.50$$

which is $4.17 per share less than the company's no-growth value of $41.67. In this example Blue Skies is throwing away $4.17 of potential value by investing in projects with unattractive rates of return.

c. Sure. A raider could take over the company and generate a profit of $4.17 per share just by halting all investments offering less than the 12% rate of return demanded by investors. This assumes the raider could buy the shares for $37.50.

7.8 a. False. The *levels* of successive stock prices are related. If a stock is selling for $100 per share today, the best guess of its price tomorrow is $100.

   b. True. *Changes* in stock prices are unrelated. Whether a stock price increases or decreases today has no bearing on whether it will do so tomorrow.

   c. False. There is no such thing as a "normal" price. If there were, you could make easy profits by buying shares selling below their normal prices (which would tend to be rising back toward those normal levels) and selling shares currently selling above their normal prices. Under a random walk, prices are equally likely to rise or fall.

   d. True. Under a random walk, prices are equally likely to over- or underperform regardless of their past history.

7.9 Fundamental analysts ensure that stock prices reflect all publicly available information about the underlying value of the firm. If share prices deviate from their fundamental values, such analysts will generate buying or selling pressure that will return prices to their proper levels. Similarly, technical analysts ensure that if there is useful information in stock price history, it will be reflected in current share prices.

MINICASE

Terence Breezeway, the CEO of Prairie Home Stores, wondered what retirement would be like. It was almost 20 years to the day since his uncle Jacob Breezeway, Prairie Home's founder, had asked him to take responsibility for managing the company. Now it was time to spend more time riding and fishing on the old Lazy Beta Ranch.

Under Mr. Breezeway's leadership Prairie Home had grown slowly but steadily and was solidly profitable. (Table 7–7 shows earnings, dividends, and book asset values for the last 5 years.) Most of the company's supermarkets had been modernized and its brand name was well known.

Mr. Breezeway was proud of this record, although he wished that Prairie Home could have grown more rapidly. He had passed up several opportunities to build new stores in adjacent counties. Prairie Home was still just a family company. Its common stock was distributed among 15 grandchildren and nephews of Jacob Breezeway, most of whom had come to depend on generous regular dividends. The commitment to high dividend payout[17] had reduced the earnings available for reinvestment and thereby constrained growth.

Mr. Breezeway believed the time had come to take Prairie Home public. Once its shares were traded in the public market, the Breezeway descendants who needed (or just wanted) more cash to spend could sell off part of their holdings. Others with more interest in the business could hold on to their shares and be rewarded by higher future earnings and stock prices.

But if Prairie Home did go public, what should its shares sell for? Mr. Breezeway worried that shares would be sold, either by Breezeway family members or by the company itself, at too low a price. One relative was about to accept a private offer for $200, the current book value per share, but Mr. Breezeway had intervened and convinced the would-be seller to wait.

Prairie Home's value depended not just on its current book value or earnings but on its future prospects, which were good. One financial projection (shown in the top panel of Table 7–8) called for growth in earnings of over 100% by 2019. Unfortunately, this plan would require reinvestment of all of Prairie Home's earnings from 2013 to 2016. After that the company could resume its normal dividend payout and growth rate. Mr. Breezeway believed this plan was feasible.

He was determined to step aside for the next generation of top management. But before retiring, he had to decide whether to recommend that Prairie Home Stores "go public"—and before that decision he had to know what the company was worth.

The next morning he rode thoughtfully to work. He left his horse at the south corral and ambled down the dusty street to Mike Gordon's Saloon, where Francine Firewater, the company's CFO, was having her usual steak-and-beans breakfast. He asked Ms. Firewater to prepare a formal report to Prairie Home stockholders, valuing the company on the assumption that its shares were publicly traded.

Ms. Firewater asked two questions immediately. First, what should she assume about investment and growth? Mr. Breezeway suggested two valuations, one assuming more rapid expansion (as in the top panel of Table 7–8) and another just projecting past growth (as in the bottom panel of Table 7–8).

Second, what rate of return should she use? Mr. Breezeway said that 15%, Prairie Home's usual return on book equity, sounded right to him, but he referred her to an article in the *Journal of Finance* indicating that investors in rural supermarket chains, with risks similar to Prairie Home Stores, expected to earn about 11% on average.

---

[17] The company traditionally paid out cash dividends equal to 10% of start-of-period book value. See Table 7–7.

TABLE 7-7 Financial data for Prairie Home Stores, 2008–2012 (figures in millions)

	2008	2009	2010	2011	2012
Book value, start of year	$62.7	$66.1	$69.0	$73.9	$76.5
Earnings	9.7	9.5	11.8	11.0	11.2
Dividends	6.3	6.6	6.9	7.4	7.7
Retained earnings	3.4	2.9	4.9	2.6	3.5
Book value, end of year	66.1	69.0	73.9	76.5	80.0

Notes:
1. Prairie Home Stores has 400,000 common shares.
2. The company's policy is to pay cash dividends equal to 10% of start-of-year book value.

TABLE 7-8 Financial projections for Prairie Home Stores, 2013–2018 (figures in millions)

	2013	2014	2015	2016	2017	2018
Rapid-Growth Scenario						
Book value, start of year	$80	$ 92	$105.8	$121.7	$139.9	$146.9
Earnings	12	13.8	15.9	18.3	21.0	22.0
Dividends	0	0	0	0	14	14.7
Retained earnings	12	13.8	15.9	18.3	7.0	7.4
Book value, end of year	92	105.8	121.7	139.9	146.9	154.3
Constant-Growth Scenario						
Book value, start of year	$80	$ 84	$88.2	$92.6	$ 97.2	$102.1
Earnings	12	12.6	13.2	13.9	14.6	15.3
Dividends	8	8.4	8.8	9.3	9.7	10.2
Retained earnings	4	4.2	4.4	4.6	4.9	5.1
Book value, end of year	84	88.2	92.6	97.2	102.1	107.2

Notes:
1. Both panels assume earnings equal to 15% of start-of-year book value. This profitability rate is constant.
2. The top panel assumes all earnings are reinvested from 2013 to 2016. In 2017 and later years, two-thirds of earnings are paid out as dividends and one-third reinvested.
3. The bottom panel assumes two-thirds of earnings are paid out as dividends in all years.
4. Columns may not add up because of rounding.

www.mhhe.com/bmm6e

CHAPTER 17

Payout Policy

LEARNING OBJECTIVES

After studying this chapter, you should be able to:

1. Describe how dividends are paid and how corporations decide how much to pay.

2. Explain how stock repurchases are used to distribute cash to investors.

3. Explain why dividend increases and repurchases are good news for investors and why dividend cuts are bad news.

4. Explain why payout policy would not affect firm value in an ideal world.

5. Show how differences in the tax treatment of dividends and capital gains might affect payout policy.

Related Web sites for this chapter can be found at www.mhhe.com/bmm6e.

This investor is obviously delighted with his extra cash, but can companies increase share value simply by increasing their dividend payout?

Everett Collection

Shareholders invest in the corporation when they buy newly issued shares and when the corporation reinvests earnings on the shareholders' behalf. The shareholders do not usually demand a prompt cash return on their investment. Some long-established companies have never yet paid a cash dividend. Sooner or later, however, most corporations do pay out cash to their shareholders. They pay dividends, or they use cash to buy back previously issued shares.

How much should a corporation pay out in a given year? Should the payout come as dividends or share repurchases? The answers to these two questions are the corporation's *payout policy*.

We start the chapter with a discussion of how dividends are paid and how firms repurchase their stock. We then show that in an ideal world, the value of a firm would be independent of its payout policy. This demonstration is in the same spirit as the Modigliani and Miller debt-irrelevance proposition of the previous chapter.

That leads us to look at the real-world complications that might favor one policy over another. These complications include transaction costs, taxes, and the signals that investors might read into the firm's payout decisions.

17.1 How Corporations Pay Out Cash to Shareholders

Corporations pay out cash to their shareholders in two ways. They can pay a cash dividend or repurchase some outstanding shares. Figure 17–1 shows that dividends and repurchases absorb a significant fraction of earnings. Between 2002 and 2006, U.S. corporations paid out 40% of earnings as dividends and a further 46% as repurchases.

Stock repurchases were rare before the mid-1980s, but have since become far more common. In 2006, a record year for repurchases, five U.S. companies each bought back more than $10 billion. They included Microsoft ($19.2 billion), Procter & Gamble ($16.8 billion), and Time Warner ($13.7 billion). The repurchase champion is ExxonMobil, which has repurchased $68 billion of its shares since 2002.

Most mature, profitable companies pay cash dividends. Growth companies typically pay small or no dividends. The no-dividend group includes household names such as Sun Microsystems, Cisco, Oracle, Amazon, and Google. The no-dividend group also includes companies that used to pay dividends but have fallen on hard times and been forced to cut back dividends to conserve cash. An example is Ford Motor Company, which paid regular dividends for decades but cut its dividend to zero in 2006.

Paying Dividends

cash dividend

Payment of cash by the firm to its shareholders.

In November 2007, Union Pacific's board of directors met and decided to authorize a regular quarterly **cash dividend** of $.44 per share, an increase of $.09 from the previous year's quarterly dividend of $.35. The term *regular* indicated that the directors expected to maintain or increase the dividend in the future. Instead of increasing the regular dividend, they could have kept it at $.35 and authorized a *special* dividend. Investors realize that special dividends probably won't be repeated.

Some of Union Pacific's shareholders may have welcomed the cash, but others preferred to reinvest the dividend in the company. To help these investors, Union Pacific offered an automatic dividend reinvestment plan. If a shareholder belonged to this plan, his or her dividends were automatically used to buy additional shares.[1]

Who receives the Union Pacific dividend? That may seem an obvious question, but shares trade constantly, and the firm's records of who owns its shares are never fully up to date. So corporations have to specify a particular day's roster of shareholders who qualify to receive each dividend. Union Pacific announced that it would send a dividend check on January 2 (the *payment date*) to all shareholders recorded in its books on November 29 (the *record date*).

FIGURE 17–1 Dividends and stock repurchases in the United States, 1980–2006

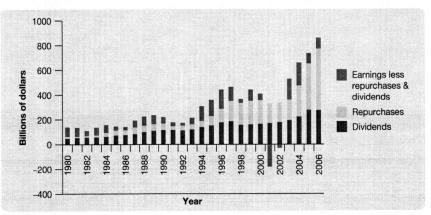

Source: Compustat.

---

[1] Often the new shares in an automatic dividend investment plan are issued at a small discount from the market price; the firm offers this sweetener because it saves the underwriting costs of a regular share issue. Sometimes 10% or more of total dividends are reinvested under such plans.

FIGURE 17–2 The key dates for Union Pacific's quarterly dividend.

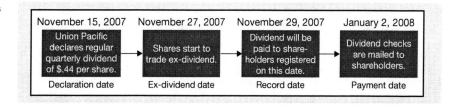

On November 27, two days before the record date, Union Pacific stock began to trade **ex-dividend.** Investors who bought shares on that date did not have their purchases registered by the record date and were not entitled to the dividend. Other things equal, a stock is worth less if you miss out on the dividend. So when a stock "goes ex-dividend," its price falls by about the amount of the dividend.

Figure 17–2 illustrates the sequence of the key dividend dates. This sequence is the same whenever companies pay a dividend (though of course the actual dates will differ).

ex-dividend
Without dividend. Buyer of a stock after the ex-dividend date does not receive the most recently declared dividend.

Self-Test 17.1

Mick Milekin buys 100 shares of Junk Bombs, Inc., on Tuesday, June 2. The company has declared a dividend of $1 per share payable on June 30 to shareholders of record as of Wednesday, June 3. If the ex-dividend date is June 1, is Mick entitled to the dividend? When will the checks go out in the mail?

Limitations on Dividends

Suppose that an unscrupulous board decided to sell all the firm's assets and distribute the money as dividends. That would not leave anything in the kitty to pay the firm's debts.

State law helps to protect the firm's creditors against excessive dividend payments. For example, most states prohibit a company from paying dividends if doing so would make the company insolvent.[2] Also, companies are not allowed to pay a dividend if it cuts into legal capital. *Legal capital* is generally defined as the par value of the outstanding shares.[3]

Banks and other lenders may also demand dividend restrictions, particularly if they are worried about the borrower's creditworthiness. We mentioned that Ford eliminated its dividend in 2006. Ford has lost billions and has been forced to borrow heavily to finance its recovery plan. Its loan agreements prohibit dividends. Thus Ford's stockholders can forget about dividends until the company's health improves and its debt can be paid off or renegotiated.

Stock Dividends and Stock Splits

stock dividend
Distribution of additional shares to a firm's stockholders.

stock split
Issue of additional shares to firm's stockholders.

Union Pacific's dividend was in cash, but companies sometimes declare **stock dividends.** For example, the firm could declare a stock dividend of 10%. In this case it would send each shareholder one additional share for each 10 that the shareholder owns.

A stock dividend is very much like a **stock split.** In both cases the shareholder is given a fixed number of new shares for each one held. For example, in a two-for-one stock split, each investor would receive one additional share for each share already held. The investor ends up with two shares rather than one. A two-for-one stock split is therefore like a 100% stock dividend. Both result in a doubling of the number

---

[2] The statutes define insolvency in different ways. In some cases, it just means an inability to meet immediate obligations; in other cases, it means a deficiency of assets compared with all outstanding fixed liabilities.

[3] Where there is no par value, legal capital consists of part or all of the receipts from the issue of shares.

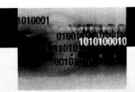

INTERNET INSIDER

Dividend Payments

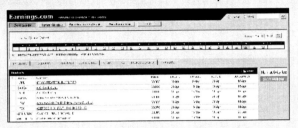

Log on to **www.earnings.com** and click on *Dividends* to find a recent list of dividend declarations. Can you explain what each of the dates means? What is the typical interval between each event?

of outstanding shares, but they do not affect the company's assets, profits, or total value.[4]

More often than not, however, the announcement of a stock split does result in a rise in the market price of the stock, even though investors are aware that the company's business is not affected. The reason: Investors take the decision as a signal of management's confidence in the future.[5]

EXAMPLE 17.1 ▶   Stock Dividends and Splits

Amoeba Products has issued 2 million shares currently selling at $15 each. Thus investors place a total market value on Amoeba of $30 million. The company now declares a 50% stock dividend. This means that each shareholder will receive one new share for every two shares that are currently held. So the total number of Amoeba shares will increase from 2 million to 3 million. The company's assets are not changed by this paper transaction and are still worth $30 million. The value of each share after the stock dividend is therefore $30/3 = $10.

If Amoeba split its stock three for two, the effect would be the same.[6] In this case two shares would split into three. (Amoeba's motto is "Divide and conquer.") So each shareholder has 50% more shares with the same total value. Share price must decline by a third.

17.2 Stock Repurchases

Another way for the firm to hand back cash to its stockholders is to repurchase some of its shares. For example, when Union Pacific announced its dividend increase in 2007, it also announced plans to repurchase up to 20 million of its shares over the following 2 years. The company can keep these reacquired shares in its treasury and resell them if it needs money later.[7]

---

[4] One survey of managers indicated that 94% of splits are motivated by the desire to bring the stock price into an acceptable "trading range." They seem to believe that if the price is too high, investors won't be able to afford to buy a "round lot" of 100 shares. Of course that might be a problem for you or us, but it isn't a worry for the Prudential or GM pension fund. See J. Lakonishok and B. Lev, "Stock Splits and Stock Dividends: Why, Who, and When," *Journal of Finance* 42 (September 1987), pp. 913–932.

[5] See E. F. Fama, L. Fisher, M. Jensen, and R. Roll, "The Adjustment of Stock Prices to New Information," *International Economic Review* 10 (February 1969), pp. 1–21. For evidence that companies which split their stock have above-average earnings prospects, see P. Asquith, P. Healy, and K. Palepu, "Earnings and Stock Splits," *Accounting Review* 64 (July 1989), pp. 387–403.

[6] The distinction between stock dividends and stock splits is a technical one. A stock dividend is shown on the balance sheet as a transfer from retained earnings to par value and additional paid-in capital. A split is shown as a proportional reduction in the par value of each share. Neither affects the total book value of stockholders' equity.

[7] Companies also keep treasury shares for issue to managers who exercise stock options.

stock repurchase
Firm buys back stock from
its shareholders.

There are four main ways to implement a **stock repurchase**:

1. *Open-market repurchase.* The firm announces that it plans to buy stock in the secondary market, just like any other investor. This is by far the most common method. There are limits on how many of its own shares a firm can purchase on a given day, so repurchases are spread out over several months or years.
2. *Tender offer.* The firm offers to buy back a stated number of shares at a fixed price. If enough shareholders accept the offer, the deal is done.
3. *Auction.* The firm states a range of prices at which it is prepared to repurchase. Shareholders submit offers declaring how many shares they are prepared to sell at each price, and the firm calculates the lowest price at which it can buy the desired number of shares.
4. *Direct negotiation.* The firm may negotiate repurchase of a block of shares from a major shareholder. The most notorious examples are *greenmail transactions,* in which the target of an attempted takeover buys out the hostile bidder. "Greenmail" means that the shares are repurchased at a generous price that makes the bidder happy to leave the target alone.

Why Repurchases Are Like Dividends

To see why share repurchase is similar to a dividend, look at panel A of Table 17–1, which shows the market value of Hewlard Pocket's assets and liabilities. Shareholders hold 100,000 shares worth in total $1 million, so the price per share equals $1 million/100,000 = $10. This is the price just before the current dividend is paid.

Pocket is proposing to pay a dividend of $1 a share. With 100,000 shares outstanding, that amounts to a total payout of $100,000. Panel B shows the effect of this dividend payment. The cash account is reduced by $100,000, and the market value of the firm's assets falls to $900,000. Since there are still 100,000 shares outstanding, share price falls to $9. Suppose that before the dividend payment you owned 1,000 shares of Pocket worth $10,000. After the payment you would have $1,000 in cash and 1,000 shares worth $9,000.

TABLE 17–1 Cash dividend
versus share repurchase.
Hewlard Pocket's market-
value balance sheet.

Assets		Liabilities and Shareholders' Equity	
A. Original balance sheet			
Cash	$ 150,000	Debt	$ 0
Other assets	850,000	Equity	1,000,000
Value of firm	$1,000,000	Value of firm	$1,000,000
Shares outstanding = 100,000			
Price per share = $1,000,000/100,000 = $10			
B. After cash dividend			
Cash	$ 50,000	Debt	$ 0
Other assets	850,000	Equity	900,000
Value of firm	$ 900,000	Value of firm	$ 900,000
Shares outstanding = 100,000			
Price per share = $900,000/100,000 = $9			
C. After stock repurchase			
Cash	$ 50,000	Debt	$ 0
Other assets	850,000	Equity	900,000
Value of firm	$ 900,000	Value of firm	$ 900,000
Shares outstanding = 90,000			
Price per share = $900,000/90,000 = $10			

Rather than paying out $100,000 as a dividend, Pocket could use the cash to buy back 10,000 shares at $10 each. Panel C shows what happens. The firm's assets fall to $900,000, just as in panel B, but only 90,000 shares remain outstanding, so the price per share remains at $10. If you owned 1,000 shares before the repurchase, you would own 1% of the company. If you then sold 100 of your shares to Pocket, you would still own 1% of the company. Your sales would put $1,000 of cash in your wallet, and you would keep 900 shares worth $9,000. Your position is exactly the same with the share repurchase (panel C of Table 17–1) as with the cash dividend (panel B): Shares worth $9,000 and cash of $1,000.

It's not surprising that a cash dividend and a share repurchase are equivalent transactions. In both cases the firm pays out cash, which goes into shareholders' wallets. The assets left in the company are the same in each case. The number of shares is reduced by repurchases, however, and the price per share is higher than it is when the cash is paid out as dividends.

Self-Test 17.2   What would Table 17–1 look like if the dividend changes to $1.50 per share and the share repurchase to $150,000?

Repurchases and Share Valuation

Now here is a question that often causes confusion. We stated in Chapter 7 that the value of a share of stock is equal to the discounted value of the stream of dividends paid on that stock. If companies also hand back cash to their shareholders in the form of repurchases, does our simple dividend discount model still hold?

The answer is yes, but we need to explain why. Here's a simple example. Look back to panel B of Table 17–1, and note that the share price is $9 immediately after the current $1 dividend is paid. Let's calculate that price as the PV of subsequent dividends. We'll suppose that Hewlard Pocket is expected to earn and continue to pay out a constant $100,000 per year in perpetuity. If the cost of equity is 11.1%, the overall equity value (market capitalization) of Pocket stock is

$$\text{Market capitalization} = 100,000/.111 = \$900,000$$

The expected dividend per share is $1, the price per share is $1/.111 = \$9$, and your 1,000 shares are worth $9,000. Of course, you have just received $1,000 in dividends, so your total stake is $10,000.

Now move to panel C, and suppose that Pocket's current payout of $100,000 is not a dividend but a one-time share repurchase. Starting next year, Pocket will resume cash dividends and pay out $100,000 per year overall.

Panel C shows the post-repurchase price of $10, which makes sense because there are now only 90,000 shares outstanding. Future dividends per share are not $1 but $100,000/90,000 = \$1.11$. The PV of these dividends is $1.11/.111 = \$10$. This is Pocket's share price immediately after the repurchase.

If you sell shares back to Pocket's repurchase program, you get $10 per share. If you don't sell, you get no cash immediately but you get higher future dividends per share. Either way you have $10 per share.

So our dividend discount model still holds. The price of a share is the PV of future dividends *per share*. The only trick is to remember that share repurchases reduce the number of shares and increase future dividends per share. You can also calculate PV per share by first calculating the firm's overall market capitalization, which depends on aggregate cash paid out to all present and future shareholders, and then dividing by the number of shares currently outstanding.

17.3 How Do Corporations Decide How Much to Pay Out?

In 2004 a survey asked senior executives about their firms' dividend policies.[8] Figure 17–3 summarizes the executives' responses. Three features stand out:

1. Managers are reluctant to make dividend changes that may have to be reversed, and they are willing to raise new financing if necessary to maintain payout.
2. Managers "smooth" dividends and hate to cut them back. Dividends tend to follow trends in long-run, sustainable earnings. Transitory fluctuations in earnings rarely affect dividend payouts.
3. Managers focus more on dividend *changes* than on absolute levels. Thus paying a $2 dividend is an important financial decision if last year's dividend was $1, but it's no big deal if last year's dividend was $2.

Corporations that pay regular dividends sometimes act as though they have a *target payout ratio,* say 40% of earnings. A 40% target ratio does *not* imply that each year's dividends equal 40% of each year's earnings, however. Dividends in that case would be just as volatile as earnings. We know, on the contrary, that dividends are smoothed.

Think instead of the *target dividend* as a percentage of *expected* or *normal* earnings, not this year's actual earnings. For example, suppose that the financial manager forecasts average income of $5 per share over the next 2 or 3 years. If the target payout ratio is 40%, the target dividend is 40% of $5, or $2.

If the current dividend is less than the target, then the dividend is increased gradually toward the target. But what if the firm hits hard times and expected earnings fall, leaving the current dividend *higher* than the target dividend? In this case, the dividend would probably not be cut immediately, but just be left alone. Financial managers don't cut regular dividends unless the cut is forced by heavy losses or dangerously high debt.

Repurchase Decisions

Repurchases do not replace dividends. Most companies that repurchase are mature and profitable and *also* pay dividends.

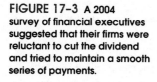

FIGURE 17–3 A 2004 survey of financial executives suggested that their firms were reluctant to cut the dividend and tried to maintain a smooth series of payments.

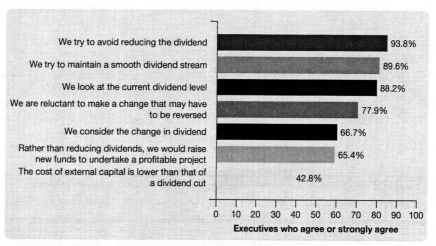

Source: A. Brav, J. R. Graham, C. R. Harvey, and R. Michaely, "Payout Policy in the 21st Century," *Journal of Financial Economics* 77 (September 2005), pp. 483–527. © 2005 Elsevier Science, with permission.

---

[8] See A. Brav, J. R. Graham, C. R. Harvey, and R. Michaely, "Payout Policy in the 21st Century," *Journal of Financial Economics* 77 (September 2005), pp. 483–527.

Repurchases are used to distribute excess cash. For example, by 2004 Texas Instruments (TI) had accumulated $6.4 billion of cash and short-term investments, far more than the book value of its plant and equipment. TI decided to return the surplus cash to shareholders by a major repurchase program. Companies also use repurchases to replace equity with debt financing. The proceeds of debt issues are used to repurchase shares.

Repurchase programs are not long-term commitments. Therefore, repurchases are much less stable and predictable than dividends. Repurchases mushroom in booms and wither in recessions. You can see this from Figure 17–1, which shows that repurchases fell sharply during the early 1990s and then again following the end of the dotcom bubble in 2000.

The Information Content of Dividends and Repurchases

When a corporation announces a dividend increase, its stock price usually jumps up. For example, Healy and Palepu found that the announcement of a company's first dividend caused an immediate price increase of 4% on average.[9] Such announcements are obviously good news for investors. The news is good not because investors simply "like dividends." It is good because announcements of dividend increases send positive signals about future income. **Managers don't increase dividends unless they are confident that income will be high enough to cover the dividend with room to spare. A dividend increase conveys that confidence to investors. A dividend cut, on the other hand, conveys a *lack* of confidence.**

It is no surprise, therefore, to find that announcements of dividend cuts are usually taken as bad news (stock price typically falls) and that dividend increases are good news (stock price rises). This is called the **information content of dividends.** The stock price responses to dividend cuts or increases do not mean that investors like dividends for their own sake. A dividend initiation or increase may be welcomed only as a sign that the company is doing well. Even investors who otherwise prefer low-payout policies might find that a cut in the dividend is unwelcome news about the firm's prospects.

Notice that investors do not get excited about the *level* of a company's dividend; they worry about the *change,* which they view as an important indicator of the company's ability to generate cash. The nearby box illustrates how an unexpected change in dividends can cause the stock price to bounce back and forth as investors struggle to interpret its significance.

**information content
of dividends**
Dividend increases send
good news about future
cash flow and earnings.
Dividend cuts send bad
news.

Self-Test 17.3

In January 2004 GATX, a specialized leasing company, announced that although earnings for the latest quarter were higher than a year earlier, it was cutting its regular quarterly dividend from $.32 a share to $.20. It pointed out that this new dividend level better reflected current earnings and recovery expectations. The next day, 10 times the normal number of shares changed hands, and the stock price fell by 16%. Why would the dividend cut result in such a sharp fall in price?

Announcements of share repurchase programs are also good news for investors. But repurchase programs are short-lived and may not be repeated, unlike dividend increases, which imply a longer-run commitment. Therefore, the information content of a repurchase program can be different from the information content of dividends. For example, a repurchase announcement may signal only that the manager thinks that the firm's stock is undervalued and a "good buy."

---

[9] See P. Healy and K. Palepu, "Earnings Information Conveyed by Dividend Initiations and Omissions," *Journal of Financial Economics* 21 (1988), pp. 149–175.

Companies repurchase shares when they have accumulated more cash than they can invest profitably or when they undertake to substitute debt for equity. Shareholders are often relieved to see companies paying out the excess cash rather than frittering it away on unprofitable investments. Of course, investors would be less thrilled if their favorite growth company suddenly announced a repurchase program because its managers could not think of anything better to do with its cash.

17.4 Why Payout Policy Should Not Matter

MM's dividend-irrelevance proposition

Under ideal conditions, the value of the firm is unaffected by dividend policy.

Franco Modigliani and Merton Miller (MM), who proved that financing doesn't matter in perfect financial markets, also proved that dividend policy doesn't matter in perfect financial markets.[10] We have already seen the common sense of MM's argument in Table 17–1, which shows that investors should not care whether a firm distributes cash by dividends or share repurchases.

MM would admit that payout policy *may* matter, not just because of the information content of dividends and repurchases but also because of taxes and market imperfections. But first we take a more thorough look at **MM's dividend-irrelevance proposition.**

Payout decisions are often intertwined with other financing or investment decisions. Some firms pay out little cash because management is optimistic about the firm's future and wishes to retain earnings for expansion. In this case the payout decision is a by-product of the firm's capital budgeting decision. Another firm might finance capital expenditures largely by borrowing. This frees up cash that can be paid out to shareholders. In this case the payout decision is a by-product of the borrowing decision.

We wish to isolate payout policy from other problems of financial management. The precise question we should ask is, What is the effect of a change in payout policy, *given the firm's capital budgeting and borrowing decisions?*

Suppose that the firm proposes to increase its dividend. The cash to finance that dividend increase has to come from somewhere. If we fix the firm's investment outlays and borrowing, there is only one possible source—an issue of stock. What if the firm decides to reduce its dividend? In that case it would have extra cash. If investment outlays and borrowing are fixed, there is only one possible way that this cash can be used—to repurchase stock. **Thus payout policy involves a trade-off between higher or lower cash dividends and the issue or repurchase of stock.**

One nice feature of economics is that it can accommodate not just two but three opposing points of view. And so it is with payout policy. On one side there is a group that believes high dividends increase value. On the other side there is a group that believes high dividends bring high taxes and therefore reduce firm value. And in the center there is MM's middle-of-the-road party, which believes payout policy makes no difference.

Payout Policy Is Irrelevant in Efficient Financial Markets

We can illustrate MM's views about payout policy by considering the Pickwick Paper Company, which had set aside $100 million in cash to construct a new paper mill. But Pickwick's directors now propose to use the $100 million to increase the dividend payment. If Pickwick is to continue to build its new mill, that cash needs to be replaced. If the borrowing is fixed, the money must come from the sale of new shares. The combination of the dividend payment and the new issue of shares leaves Pickwick and its shareholders in exactly the same position they started from. All that has happened is that Pickwick has put an extra $100 million in investors' pockets (the dividend payment) and then taken it out again (the share issue). In other words, Pickwick is simply

---

[10] M. H. Miller and F. Modigliani, "Dividend Policy, Growth and the Valuation of Shares," *Journal of Business* 34 (October 1961), pp. 411–433.

FINANCE IN PRACTICE

The Dividend Cut Heard 'Round the World

On May 9, 1994, FPL Group, the parent company of Florida Power & Light Company, announced a 32% reduction in its quarterly dividend payout, from 62 cents per share to 42 cents. This was the first-ever dividend cut by a healthy utility. A number of utilities had reduced their dividends in the past, but only after cash flow problems—often associated with heavy investment in nuclear plants—had given them no other choice.

In its announcement, FPL stressed that it had studied the situation carefully and that, given the prospect of increased competition in the electric utility industry, the company's high dividend payout ratio (which had averaged 90% in the past 4 years) was no longer in the stockholders' best interests. The new policy resulted in a dividend payout of about 60% of the prior year's earnings. Management also announced that, starting in 1995, the dividend payout would be reviewed in February instead of May to reinforce the linkage between dividends and annual earnings. In doing so, the company wanted to minimize unintended "signaling effects" from any future changes in the dividend.

At the same time it announced this change in dividend policy, FPL Group's board authorized the repurchase of up to 10 million shares of common stock over the next 3 years. FPL's management said that 4 million shares would be repurchased over the next 12 months, depending on market conditions. In adopting this strategy, the company noted that changes in the U.S. tax code since 1990 had made capital gains more attractive than dividends to shareholders.

Besides providing a more tax-efficient means of distributing excess capital to its stockholders, FPL's substitution of stock repurchases for dividends was also designed to increase the company's financial flexibility in preparation for a new era of deregulation and heightened competition among utilities. Although much of the cash savings from the dividend cut would be returned to investors in the form of stock repurchases, the rest would be used to retire debt at Florida Power & Light and so reduce the company's leverage ratio. This deleveraging and strengthening of FPL's financial condition were intended to prepare the company for an increase in business risk and to provide the financial resources to take advantage of future growth opportunities.

The stock market's initial reaction to FPL's announcement was negative. On the day of the announcement, the company's stock price fell from $31.88 to $27.50, a drop of nearly 14%. But as analysts digested the news and considered the reasons for the reduction, they concluded that the action was not a signal of financial distress but rather a strategic decision that would improve the company's long-term financial flexibility and prospects for growth. This view spread throughout the financial community, and FPL's stock began to recover.

On May 31, less than a month after the announcement, FPL's stock closed at $32.17 (adjusted for the quarterly dividend of 42 cents), or about 30 cents higher than the pre-announcement price. By the middle of June, at least 15 major brokerage houses had placed FPL's common stock on their "buy" lists. On May 9, 1995—exactly 1 year after the announcement of the cut—FPL's stock price closed at $37.75, giving stockholders a 1-year postannouncement return (including dividends) of 23.8%, more than double the 11.2% of the S&P Index and well above the 14.2% of the S&P utilities index over the same period.

Source: Modified from D. Soter, E. Brigham, and P. Evanson, "The Dividend Cut Heard 'Round the World': The Case of FPL," *Journal of Applied Corporate Finance* 9 (Spring 1996), pp. 4–15. Used with permission.

recycling cash. To suggest that this makes investors better off is like advising the cook to cool the kitchen by leaving the refrigerator door open.

After Pickwick pays the additional dividend and replaces the cash by selling new shares, the company value is unchanged. The old shareholders now have an extra $100 million of cash in their pockets, but they have given up a stake in the firm to those investors who buy the newly issued shares. The new stockholders are putting up $100 million and therefore will demand to receive shares *worth* $100 million. Since the total value of the company is the same, the value of the old stockholders' stake in the company falls by this $100 million. Thus the extra dividend that the old stockholders receive just offsets the loss in the value of the shares that they hold.

Does it make any difference to the old stockholders that they receive an extra dividend payment plus an offsetting capital loss? It might if that were the only way they could get their hands on the cash. But as long as there are efficient capital markets, they can raise cash by selling shares. Thus Pickwick's old shareholders can "cash in" either by persuading the management to pay a higher dividend or by selling some of their shares. In either case there will be the same transfer of value from the old to the new stockholders. **Because investors do not need dividends to convert their shares to cash, they will not pay higher prices for firms with higher dividend payouts. In other words, payout policy will have no impact on the value of the firm. This is MM's argument.**

The example of the Pickwick Paper Company showed that the firm cannot make shareholders better off simply by increasing the proportion of earnings paid out as dividends. But the same argument also works in reverse: If investment and borrowing are held constant, any *reduction* in dividends must be balanced by a *purchase* of stock. For example, suppose that Old Curiosity Shops has $100 million surplus cash which it had been proposing to pay out to shareholders as a dividend. If Old Curiosity now decides not to pay this dividend, then the surplus cash can be used to buy back some of the company's shares. The shareholders miss out on $100 million of dividend payments but they receive $100 million from the sale to the company of part of their shareholdings.

Thus MM's irrelevance argument holds both for increases in dividends and for reductions. **As these examples illustrate, payout policy is a trade-off between cash dividends and the issue or repurchase of common stock. In a perfect capital market, the payout decision would have no impact on firm value.**

These examples may seem artificial at first, for we do not observe firms scheduling a stock issue with every dividend payment. But there are many firms that pay dividends and also issue stock from time to time. They could avoid the stock issues by paying lower dividends and retaining more funds in the firm. Many other firms use unwanted cash to repurchase shares. They could instead use the cash to increase the dividend.

Of course our examples of dividend irrelevance have ignored taxes, issue costs, and a variety of other real-world complications. We will turn to these intricacies shortly, but before we do, we note that the crucial assumption in our proof is that the sale or purchase of shares occurs at a fair price. The shares that Pickwick sells to raise $100,000 must actually be worth $100,000; those that Old Curiosity buys for $100,000 must also be worth that figure. In other words, dividend irrelevance assumes efficient capital markets.

EXAMPLE 17.2 ▶ Dividend Irrelevance

The columns labeled "Old Dividend Plan" in Table 17–2 show that Consolidated Pasta is currently expected to pay annual dividends of $10 a share in perpetuity. Shareholders expect a 10% rate of return from Consolidated stock, and therefore the value of each share is

$$PV = \frac{10}{1.10} + \frac{10}{(1.10)^2} + \frac{10}{(1.10)^3} + \cdots = \frac{10}{.10} = \$100$$

Consolidated has issued 1 million shares. So the total forecast dividend payment in each year is 1 million × $10 = $10 million, and the total value of Consolidated Pasta equity is 1 million × $100 = $100 million. The president, Al Dente, has read that the value of a share depends on the dividends it pays. That suggests an easy way to keep shareholders happy—increase next year's dividend to $20 per share. That way, he

TABLE 17–2 Consolidated Pasta is currently expected to pay a dividend of $10 million in perpetuity. However, the president is proposing to pay a one-time bumper dividend of $20 million in year 1. To replace the lost cash, the firm will need to issue more shares, and the dividends that will need to be diverted to the new shareholders will exactly offset the effect of the higher dividend in year 1.

	Old Dividend Plan		Revised Dividend Plan	
	Year 1	Year 2 On	Year 1	Year 2 On
Total dividend payments ($ million)	10	10	20	10
Total dividends paid to old shareholders ($ million)	10	10	20	9
Total dividends paid to new shareholders ($ million)	—	—	—	1

Note: New shareholders are putting up $10 million of cash at the end of year 1. Since they require a return of 10%, the total dividends paid to the new shares (starting in year 2) must be 10% of $10 million, or $1 million.

reasons, share price should rise by the present value of the increase in the first-year dividend to a new value of

$$PV = \frac{20}{1.10} + \frac{10}{(1.10)^2} + \frac{10}{(1.10)^3} + \cdots = \frac{10}{1.10} + \frac{10}{.10} = \$109.91$$

The president's heart is obviously in the right place. Unfortunately, his head isn't. Let's see why.

Consolidated is proposing to pay out an extra $10 million in dividends. It can't do that *and* earn the same profits in the future, unless it also replaces the lost cash by an issue of shares. The new shareholders who provide this cash will require a return of 10% on their investment. So Consolidated will need to pay $1 million a year of dividends to the new shareholders ($1 million/$10 million = .10, or 10%). This is shown in the last line of Table 17–2.

As long as the company replaces the extra cash it pays out, it will continue to earn the same profits and to pay out $10 million of dividends each year from year 2. However, $1 million of this total will be needed to satisfy the new shareholders, leaving only $9 million (or $9 a share) for the original shareholders. Now recalculate the value of the original shares under the revised dividend plan:

$$PV = \frac{20}{1.10} + \frac{9}{(1.10)^2} + \frac{9}{(1.10)^3} + \cdots = \frac{11}{1.10} + \frac{9}{.10} = \$100$$

The value of the shares is unchanged. The extra cash dividend in year 1 is exactly offset by the reduction of dividends per share in later years. This reduction is necessary because some of the money paid out as dividends in later years is diverted to the new shareholders.[11]

The Assumptions behind Dividend Irrelevance

Many stockholders and businesspeople find it difficult to accept the suggestion that dividend policy is irrelevant. When faced with MM's argument, they often reply that dividends are cash in hand while capital gains are at best in the bush. It may be true, they say, that the recipient of an extra cash dividend forgoes an equal capital gain, but if the dividend is safe and the capital gain is risky, isn't the stockholder ahead?

It's correct that dividends are more predictable than capital gains. Managers can stabilize dividends but they cannot control stock price. From this it seems a small step to conclude that increased dividends make the firm less risky.[12] But the important point is, once again, that as long as investment policy and borrowing are held constant, a firm's *overall* cash flows are the same regardless of payout policy. The risks borne by *all* the firm's stockholders are likewise fixed by its investment and borrowing policies and unaffected by dividend policy.

If we really believed that existing stockholders are better off by trading a risky asset for cash, then we would also have to argue that the new stockholders—those who

---

[11] Notice that at the end of year 1, when the new shareholders purchase their shares, the dividend per share they can look forward to receiving will be $9; since this dividend is expected to be a perpetuity, the share price at that time will be $9/.10 = $90. So the new shareholders will receive $10,000,000/$90 = 111,111 shares. Consistent with Table 17–2, the new shareholders therefore will receive total dividend payments of 111,111 × $9 = $1 million and the old shareholders will receive total dividend payments of 1 million × $9 = $9 million. Notice also that after the extra $10 million dividend is paid in year 1, the share price falls to $90, and the value of the shares held by the original shareholders falls by exactly $10 million to $90 million.

[12] In that case one might also argue that interest payments are even more predictable, so a company's risk would be reduced by increasing the proportion of profits paid out as interest. How would you respond to that suggestion?

trade cash for the newly issued shares—are worse off. But this doesn't make sense: The new stockholders are bearing risk, but they are getting paid for it. They are willing to buy because the new shares are priced to offer an expected return adequate to compensate for the risk.

MM's argument for the irrelevance of dividend policy does not assume a world of certainty; it assumes an efficient capital market. Market efficiency means that the transfers of ownership created by shifts in dividend policy are carried out on fair terms. And since the *overall* value of (old and new) stockholders' equity is unaffected, nobody gains or loses.

17.5 Why Dividends May Increase Value

Market Imperfections

Most economists agree that MM's conclusions are correct, given their assumptions of perfect and efficient capital markets. However, nobody claims their model is an exact description of the so-called real world. Thus the impact of payout policy finally boils down to arguments about imperfections and inefficiencies.

Those who believe that dividends are good argue that some investors have a natural preference for high-payout stocks. For example, some financial institutions are legally restricted from holding stocks lacking established dividend records. Trusts and endowment funds may prefer high-dividend stocks because dividends are regarded as spendable "income," whereas capital gains are "additions to principal," which may not be spent.

In addition, there is a natural clientele of investors, including the elderly, who look to their stock portfolios for a steady source of cash to live on. In principle this cash can be generated from stocks paying no dividends at all; the investors can just sell off a small fraction of their holdings from time to time. But that can be inconvenient and lead to heavy transaction costs.

Behavioral psychology may also help to explain why some investors prefer to receive regular dividends rather than sell small amounts of stock. We are all liable to succumb to temptation. Some of us may hanker after fattening foods, while others may be dying for a drink. We could seek to control these cravings by willpower, but that can be a painful struggle. Instead, it may be easier to set simple rules for ourselves ("cut out chocolate," or "wine only with meals"). In just the same way, we may welcome the self-discipline that comes from limiting our spending to dividend income.

All this may well be true, but it does not follow that you can increase the value of *your* firm by increasing dividend payout. Smart managers already have recognized that there is a clientele of investors who would be prepared to pay a premium for high-payout stocks. **There are natural clienteles for high-payout stocks, but it does not follow that any particular firm can benefit by increasing its dividends. The high-dividend clienteles already have plenty of high-dividend stocks to choose from.**

You don't hear businesspeople argue that because there is a clientele of car buyers, their company should manufacture cars. So why should you believe that because there is a clientele of investors who like high payouts, your company can increase value by manufacturing a high payout? That clientele was probably satisfied long ago.

Self-Test 17.4   The Altria Group pays a generous cash dividend. Suppose an investor in Altria does not need a regular income. What could she do? If there were no trading costs, would she have any reason to care about Altria's payout policy? What if there is a brokerage fee on the purchase of new shares? What if Altria has a dividend reinvestment plan that allows the investor to buy shares at a 5% discount?

17.6 Why Dividends May Reduce Value

The low-dividend creed is simple. Companies can convert dividends into capital gains by shifting their dividend policy. If dividends are taxed more heavily than capital gains, such financial alchemy should be welcomed by any taxpaying investor. Firms should pay the lowest cash dividend they can get away with. Surplus cash should be used to repurchase shares.

Table 17–3 illustrates this. It assumes that dividends are taxed at a rate of 40% but that capital gains are taxed at only 20%. The stocks of firms A and B are equally risky, and investors demand an expected *after-tax* rate of return of 10% on each. Investors expect A to be worth $112.50 per share next year. The share price of B is expected to be only $102.50, but a $10 dividend is also forecast, so the total pretax payoff is the same, $112.50.

Both stocks offer the same pretax dollar payoff. Yet B's stock sells for less than A's. The reason is obvious: Investors are willing to pay more for stock A because its return comes in the form of low-taxed capital gains. After tax, both stocks offer the same 10% expected return despite the fact that B's *pretax* return is higher.

Suppose the management of firm B eliminates the $10 dividend and uses the cash to repurchase stock instead. We saw earlier that a stock repurchase is equivalent to a cash dividend, but it is treated differently by the tax authorities. Stockholders who sell shares back to their firm pay tax only on any capital gains realized in the sale. By substituting a repurchase for a dividend, B's new policy would reduce the taxes paid by stockholders, and its stock price should rise.

Self-Test 17.5   Look again at Table 17–3. What would happen to the price and pretax rate of return on stock B if the tax on capital gains were eliminated?

Why Pay Any Dividends at All?

If dividends are taxed more heavily than capital gains, why should any firm ever pay a cash dividend? If cash is to be distributed to stockholders, isn't share repurchase the best channel for doing so?

Few would go that far. The Internal Revenue Service has attempted to prevent firms from disguising dividends as repurchases. A firm that eliminates dividends and starts repurchasing stock on a regular basis may find that the IRS would recognize the

TABLE 17–3 Effects of a shift in dividend policy when dividends are taxed more heavily than capital gains. The high-payout stock (firm B) must sell at a lower price in order to provide the same after-tax return.

	Firm A	Firm B
Next year's price	$112.50	$102.50
Dividend	$ 0	$ 10.00
Total *pretax* payoff	$112.50	$112.50
Today's stock price	$100	$ 97.78
Capital gain	$ 12.50	$ 4.72
Before-tax rate of return (%)	$\frac{12.5}{100} = .125 = 12.5\%$	$\frac{14.72}{97.78} = .1505 = 15.05\%$
Tax on dividend at 40%	$0	.40 × $10 = $4.00
Tax on capital gain at 20%	.20 × $12.50 = $2.50	.20 × $4.72 = $.94
Total after-tax income (dividends plus capital gains less taxes)	(0 + 12.50) − 2.50 = $10.00	(10 + 4.72) − (4.00 + .94) = $9.78
After-tax rate of return (%)	$\frac{10}{100} = .10 = 10\%$	$\frac{9.78}{97.78} = .10 = 10\%$

Microsoft's Payout Bonanza

By 2004 Microsoft had amassed a $61 billion pile of cash. The company's operations were throwing off a further $15 billion of cash each year, far in excess of the company's opportunities for new profitable investments. So, unless Microsoft took some strong action, it looked as if its cash mountain could only continue to grow.

Microsoft's solution was to announce the largest cash distribution in corporate history, involving a total payout of $75 billion over 4 years. The company doubled its regular dividend to about $3.5 billion a year. In addition, the company proposed a one-off special dividend costing $32 billion. Finally, up to $30 billion of cash was to be used to buy back stock over a period of 4 years.

repurchase program for what it really is and tax the payments accordingly. That is why financial managers seldom announce that they are repurchasing stock to save stockholders taxes; they give some other reason.[13]

Taxation of Dividends and Capital Gains under Current Tax Law

In the United States the case for low dividends was strongest before 1986. The top rate of tax on dividends was then 50%, while realized capital gains were taxed at 20%.

As we write this in 2008, the top rate of tax on both dividends and capital gains is 15%. There is, however, one way that tax law continues to favor capital gains. Taxes on dividends have to be paid immediately, but taxes on capital gains can be deferred until shares are sold and the capital gains are realized. Stockholders can choose when to sell their shares and thus when to pay the capital gains tax.[14] The longer they wait, the less the present value of the capital gains tax liability.[15] Thus the *effective* capital gains tax rate can be less than the statutory rate.

The distinction between dividends and capital gains is less important for financial institutions, many of which operate free of all taxes and therefore have no reason to prefer capital gains to dividends or vice versa. Only corporations have a tax reason to *prefer* dividends. They pay corporate income tax on only 30% of any dividends received.[16] Thus the effective tax rate on dividends received by large corporations is 30% of 35% (the marginal rate of corporate income tax), or 10.5%. But they have to pay a 35% tax on the full amount of any capital gain.

The implications of these tax rules for payout policy are pretty simple. Capital gains have advantages to many investors, but they are far less advantageous than they were 30 or 40 years ago. Consequently, it is less easy today to make convincing arguments in favor of one kind of payout rather than another.

Look, for example, at the nearby box, which discusses Microsoft's plan to pay out $75 billion of cash to its stockholders. Microsoft opted to split this huge payout between a special dividend and stock repurchases. Would the company have chosen to pay such a large dividend if it still attracted tax of 40% or 50%? We doubt it. It seems that today companies can be much more relaxed about differences in the tax treatment of dividends and stock repurchases.

---

[13] They might say, "Our stock is a good investment," or "We want to have the shares available to finance acquisitions of other companies." What do you think of these rationales?

[14] If the stock is willed to your heirs, capital gains escape taxation altogether.

[15] Suppose the discount rate is 8%, and an investor in a 15% capital gains tax bracket has a $100 capital gain. If the stock is sold today, the capital gains tax will be $15. If sale is deferred 1 year, the tax due on that $100 gain still will be $15, but by virtue of delaying the sale for a year, the present value of the tax falls to $15/1.08 = $13.89. The effective tax rate falls to 13.89%. The longer the sale is deferred, the lower the effective tax rate.

[16] Actually, the percentage of dividend income on which tax is paid depends on the firm's ownership share in the company paying the dividend. If the share is less than 20%, taxes are paid on 30% of dividends received.

www.mhhe.com/bmm6e

SUMMARY

How are dividends paid, and how do companies decide how much to pay? *(LO1)*

Dividends come in many forms. The most common is the regular **cash dividend,** but sometimes companies pay a special cash dividend, and sometimes they pay a **stock dividend.** A firm is not free to pay dividends at will. For example, it may have accepted restrictions on dividends as a condition for borrowing money.

Dividends do not go up and down with every change in the firm's earnings. Instead, managers aim for smooth dividends and increase dividends gradually as earnings grow.

How are repurchases used to distribute cash to shareholders? *(LO2)*

Corporations also distribute cash by repurchasing shares. **Stock repurchases** have grown rapidly in recent years, but they do not replace dividends. Firms that repurchase usually also pay dividends.

Repurchases are used to distribute excess cash. Firms also use repurchases to replace equity with debt financing. In this case, the proceeds of new debt issues are paid out to equity investors via repurchases.

Why are dividend increases and repurchases usually good news for investors? Why are dividend cuts bad news? *(LO3)*

Managers do not increase dividends unless they are confident that the firm will generate enough earnings to cover the payout. Announcement of a dividend increase conveys the managers' confidence to investors. This **information content of dividends** is the main reason that stock price usually increases when a dividend increase is announced.

Repurchases are also good news for investors. Announcement of a repurchase program can reveal the managers' view that the stock is a "good buy" at its current price. Repurchases can also reassure investors who worry that managers will spend excess cash on unprofitable investments.

Why would payout policy not affect firm value in an ideal world? *(LO4)*

If we hold the company's investment policy and capital structure constant, then payout policy is a trade-off between cash dividends and the issue or repurchase of common stock. In an ideally simple and perfect world, the choice would have no effect on market value. This is the **MM dividend-irrelevance proposition.** MM's proposition is controversial in some quarters. A common—though by no means universal—view is that high dividends enhance share price. This could be true if there were a restricted supply of high-payout stocks.

How might differences in the tax treatment of dividends and capital gains affect payout policy? *(LO5)*

In the United States, individual investors pay tax on dividend income at a top rate of 15%. The top capital gains rate is also 15%, but the investor pays no tax until his or her shares are actually sold. The longer the wait before the sale, the lower the present value of the tax. Thus capital gains have a tax advantage for investors. The advantage was much greater in the 1970s and early 1980s, when the top tax rate on dividends was 50% and the top rate on capital gains only 20%.

If dividend income is taxed more heavily than capital gains, investors should demand a higher pretax rate of return on high-dividend stocks. Instead of paying high dividends, corporations should shift to repurchases. Taxes are one reason for the rapid growth of repurchases.

QUESTIONS

QUIZ

1. **Dividend Sequence.** Cash Cow International paid a regular quarterly dividend of $.075 a share. *(LO1)*

    a. Connect each of the following dates to the correct term:

May 7	Record date
June 6	Payment date
June 7	Ex-dividend date
June 11	Last with-dividend date
July 2	Declaration date

b. On one of these dates the stock price is likely to fall by about the amount of the dividend. Why?

c. The stock price in early January was $27. What was the prospective dividend yield?

d. The earnings per share were forecast at around $1.90. What was the percentage payout ratio?

2. **Splits and Dividends.** Shares in Raven Products are selling for $80 per share. There are 1 million shares outstanding. What will be the share price in each of the following situations? Ignore taxes. *(LO1)*

   a. The stock splits five for four.

   b. The company pays a 25% stock dividend.

   c. The company repurchases 100,000 shares.

3. **Institutional Background.** True or false? If false, correct the statement. *(LO1)*

   a. A corporation cannot pay a dividend if its legal capital is impaired or if it is insolvent.

   b. There is no important difference between a regular and a special dividend.

   c. The effective tax rate on capital gains can be less than the stated rate.

   d. Corporations settle on a target payout ratio and in every year pay out that fraction of the year's earnings.

   e. Managers and investors are more concerned with dividend changes than dividend levels.

   f. Stock price will be higher when a corporation distributes cash by repurchases rather than cash dividends.

4. **Dividend Irrelevance.** You own 2,000 shares of Patriot Corporation, which is about to double its dividend from $.75 to $1.50 per share. You do not need the extra dividend income, but you don't want to sell out. What would you do to offset the dividend increase? *(LO4)*

5. **Dividend Policy.** Big Bend Tubing's dividend was $2.20 last year. Big Bend's target payout ratio is 50%. This year's earnings per share are $5. But Pablo Donoso, the CFO, worries about higher raw-material costs and forecasts average future earnings of only $4 per share over the next 3 years. Should Mr. Donoso cut or increase this year's dividend? How does your answer change if forecast average earnings are $3, $5, or $7? *(LO1)*

6. **Information Content of Dividends.** Why are dividend increases typically good news for investors and dividend cuts bad news? Explain briefly. *(LO3)*

7. **Dividends versus Repurchases.** What is the tax reason for *not* paying generous cash dividends? *(LO5)*

PRACTICE PROBLEMS

8. **DRIPs.** A firm considers initiating an aggressive dividend reinvestment plan (DRIP) in which it allows its investors to use dividends to buy shares at a discount of 40% from current market value. The firm's financial manager argues that the policy will benefit shareholders by giving them the opportunity to buy additional shares at a deep discount and will benefit the firm by providing a source of cash. Is the manager correct? *(LO4)*

9. **Cash Dividends.** The stock of Payout Corp. will go ex-dividend tomorrow. The dividend will be $0.50 per share, and there are 20,000 shares of stock outstanding. The market-value balance sheet for Payout is shown on the following table. *(LO1)*

   a. What price is Payout stock selling for today?

   b. What price will it sell for tomorrow? Ignore taxes.

Assets		Liabilities and Equity	
Cash	$100,000	Equity	$1,000,000
Fixed assets	900,000		

10. **Repurchases.** Now suppose that Payout from Practice Problem 9 announces its intention to repurchase $10,000 worth of stock instead of paying out the dividend. *(LO2)*

    a. What effect will the repurchase have on an investor who currently holds 100 shares and sells 1 of those shares back to the company in the repurchase?

    b. Compare the effects of the repurchase to the effects of the cash dividend that you worked out in problem 9.

11. **Stock Dividend.** Now suppose that Payout again changes its mind and decides to issue a 1% stock dividend instead of either issuing the cash dividend or repurchasing 1% of the outstanding stock. How would this action affect a shareholder who owns 100 shares of stock? Compare with your answers to Practice Problems 9 and 10. *(LO1)*

12. **Dividend Irrelevance.** Suppose Al Dente from Example 17.2 changes his mind and cuts out Consolidated's year-1 dividend entirely, instead spending $10 million to buy back stock. Are shareholders any better or worse off than if Consolidated had paid out $10 million as cash dividends? *(Hints:* How many shares will be repurchased? The purchase price at year 1 will be $110.) *(LO4)*

13. **Information.** Which of the following newspaper headlines would have the greatest positive impact on stock price? Explain. *(LO3)*

    a. "Growler Corporation announces a $1 increase in its regular dividend."

    b. "Growler Corporation announces a $1 special dividend."

    c. "Growler Corporation wins lawsuit and collects cash amounting to $1 per Growler share. Growler plans to use the cash in a stock buyback program."

14. **Stock Dividends and Splits.** Suppose that you own 1,000 shares of Nocash Corp. and the company is about to pay a 25% stock dividend. The stock currently sells at $100 per share. *(LO1)*

    a. What will be the number of shares that you hold and the total value of your equity position after the dividend is paid?

    b. What will happen to the number of shares that you hold and the value of your equity position if the firm splits five for four instead of paying the stock dividend?

15. **Dividend Policy.** In 2008, Arborio Farms earned $3.60 per share and paid a cash dividend of $1.20 per share, exactly in line with its target payout ratio of 33%. Arborio's earnings per share in the next 6 years were $3.30 in 2009, $3.60 in 2010, $4.00 in 2011, $4.68 in 2012, $4.00 in 2013, and $4.05 in 2014. Make a prediction of Arborio's dividends per share in these years. You can make additional assumptions if that is helpful, but make sure your prediction is reasonable. *(LO1)*

16. **Dividends and Taxes.** Good Values, Inc., is all-equity-financed. The total market value of the firm currently is $100,000, and there are 2,000 shares outstanding. Ignore taxes. *(LO1)*

    a. The firm has declared a $5 per share dividend. The stock will go ex-dividend tomorrow. At what price will the stock sell today? Tomorrow?

    b. Now assume that the tax rate on dividend income is 30%, and the tax rate on capital gains is zero. At what price will the stock sell, taking account of the taxation of dividends?

17. **Repurchases and Taxes.** Now suppose that instead of paying a dividend Good Values (from the previous problem) plans to repurchase $10,000 worth of stock. *(LO5)*

    a. What will be the stock price before and after the repurchase?

    b. Suppose an investor who holds 200 shares sells 20 of her shares back to the firm. If there are no taxes on dividends or capital gains, show that she should be indifferent between the repurchase and the dividend.

    c. Show that if dividends are taxed at 30% and capital gains are not taxed, the value of the firm is higher if it pursues the share repurchase instead of the dividend.

18. **Dividends and Taxes.** Investors require an after-tax rate of return of 10% on their stock investments. Assume that the tax rate on dividends is 30% while capital gains escape taxation. A firm

will pay a $2 per share dividend 1 year from now, after which it is expected to sell at a price of $20. *(LO5)*

a. Find the current price of the stock.

b. Find the expected before-tax rate of return for a 1-year holding period.

c. Now suppose that the dividend will be $3 per share. If the expected after-tax rate of return is still 10%, and investors still expect the stock to sell at $20 in 1 year, at what price must the stock now sell?

d. What is the before-tax rate of return? Why is it now higher than in part (b)?

19. **Dividends and Taxes.** The expected pretax return on three stocks is divided between dividends and capital gains in the following way: *(LO5)*

Stock	Expected Dividend	Expected Capital Gain
A	$ 0	$10
B	5	5
C	10	0

a. If each stock is priced at $100, what are the expected net returns on each stock to (i) a pension fund that does not pay taxes, (ii) a corporation paying tax at 35%, and (iii) an individual with an effective tax rate of 15% on dividends and 10% on capital gains?

b. Suppose that investors pay 50% tax on dividends and 20% tax on capital gains. If stocks are priced to yield an 8% return *after tax,* what would A, B, and C each sell for? Assume the expected dividend is a level perpetuity.

20. **Signaling.** It is well documented that stock prices tend to rise when firms announce an increase in their dividend payouts. How then can it be said that dividend policy is irrelevant? *(LO3)*

21. **Dividend Irrelevance.** Respond to the following two statements. *(LO4)*

a. "MM say that investors are equally happy with a dollar of dividends and a dollar of capital gains. That's crazy. Everyone knows that dividends are stable and capital gains risky. I'll take the dividend any day."

b. "Safer companies tend to pay more generous dividends. Therefore a company can reduce the risk of its shares by increasing dividend payout."

22. **Dividends versus Repurchases.** Prowler Corporation wants to increase its debt ratio without changing its operations or capital investment outlays. Obviously Prowler will have to increase borrowing, but how should it reduce equity? What would you recommend? *(LO5)*

CHALLENGE PROBLEMS

23. **Dividends versus Repurchases.** Big Industries has the following market-value balance sheet. The stock currently sells for $20 a share, and there are 1,000 shares outstanding. The firm will either pay a $1 per share dividend or repurchase $1,000 worth of stock. Ignore taxes. *(LO4)*

Assets		Liabilities and Equity	
Cash	$ 2,000	Debt	$10,000
Fixed assets	28,000	Equity	20,000

a. What will be the price per share under each alternative (dividend versus repurchase)?

b. If total earnings of the firm are $2,000 a year, find earnings per share under each alternative.

c. Find the price-earnings ratio under each alternative.

d. Adherents of the "dividends-are-good" school sometimes point to the fact that stocks with high-dividend-payout ratios tend to sell at above-average price-earnings multiples. Is this evidence convincing? Discuss this argument with regard to your answers to parts (a) to (c).

Please visit us at www.mhhe.com/bmm6e

24. **Dividends and Taxes.** Shares in Growth Products Inc. are priced at $100. Investors expect the total *pretax* rate of return to be 10%. The tax rate on both capital gains and dividends is 15%. *(LO5)*

   a. If the entire return on the shares is in the form of dividends, what is the investor's annualized *after-tax* rate of return for a holding period of 1 year? 5 years? 10 years? 20 years?

   b. What is the investor's annualized *after-tax* rate of return for each holding period if all of the pretax return is in the form of capital gains?

   c. Explain why capital gains may be preferred to dividends even if the tax rate on the two are equal.

STANDARD &POOR'S

1. Go to Market Insight at **www.mhhe.com/edumarketinsight**. Review the dividend policy of Harley-Davidson (HOG), General Electric (GE), Citigroup (C), and Hawaiian Electric Industries (HE) in the S&P Stock Reports. Review the dividend yield, dividend payout ratio, and retention rate for each firm. What factors might explain the differences in dividend policies among the companies? Review the Financial Highlights page.

2. Go to Market Insight at **www.mhhe.com/edumarketinsight**. Go to the Industry tab and find three firms in the semiconductor industry and three in the electric utility industry. Now use the Excel Analytics section to find the average dividend-payout ratios of the firms in each industry. What do you conclude from the differences in their average payouts?

SOLUTIONS TO SELF-TEST QUESTIONS

17.1 The ex-dividend date is June 1. Therefore, Mick buys the stock ex-dividend and will not receive the dividend. The checks will be mailed on June 30.

17.2

Assets		Liabilities and Equity	
After cash dividend			
Cash	$ 0	Debt	$ 0
Other assets	850,000	Equity	850,000
Value of firm	$850,000	Value of firm	$850,000
Shares outstanding = 100,000			
Price per share = $850,000/100,000 = $8.50			
After stock repurchase			
Cash	$ 0	Debt	$ 0
Other assets	850,000	Equity	850,000
Value of firm	$850,000	Value of firm	$850,000
Shares outstanding = 85,000			
Price per share = $850,000/85,000 = $10			

If a dividend is paid, the stock price falls by the amount of the dividend. If the company instead uses the cash for a share repurchase, the stock price remains unchanged but, with fewer shares left outstanding, the market value of the firm falls by the same amount as it would have if the dividend had been paid.

17.3 The stock price dropped despite the increase in earnings because investors interpreted the dividend cut as a signal that future earnings would be lower than investors had previously expected. The dividend cut conveyed bad news about the future prospects of the firm.

17.4 An investor who prefers a zero-dividend policy can reinvest any dividends received. This will cause the value of the shares held to be unaffected by payouts. The price drop on the ex-dividend date is offset by the reinvestment of the dividends. However, if the investor had to pay brokerage fees on the newly purchased shares, she would be harmed by a high-payout policy since part of the proceeds of the dividends would go toward paying the broker. On the other hand, if the firm offers a dividend reinvestment plan (DRIP) with a 5% discount, she is better off with a high-dividend policy. The DRIP is like a "negative trading cost." She can increase the value of her stock by 5% of the dividend just by participating in the DRIP. Of course, her gain is at the expense of shareholders that do not participate in the DRIP.

17.5   The price of the stock will equal the after-tax cash flows discounted by the required (after-tax) rate of return:

$$P = \frac{102.50 + 10 \times (1 - .4)}{1.10} = 98.64$$

Notice that the after-tax proceeds from the stock would increase by the amount that previously went to pay capital gains taxes, $.20 \times \$4.72 = \$.944$. The present value of this tax saving is $\$.944/1.10 = \$.86$. Therefore, the price increases to $\$97.78 + \$.86 = \$98.64$. The pretax rate of return falls to $(102.50 - 98.64 + 10)/98.64 = .1405$, or 14.05%, but the after-tax rate of return remains at 10%.

MINICASE

George Liu, the CEO of Penn Schumann, was a creature of habit. Every month he and Jennifer Rodriguez, the company's chief financial officer, met for lunch and an informal chat at Pierre's. Nothing was ever discussed until George had finished his favorite *escalope de foie gras chaude*. At their last meeting in March he had then toyed thoughtfully with his glass of Chateau Haut-Brion Blanc before suddenly asking, "What do you think we should be doing about our payout policy?"

Penn Schumann was a large and successful pharmaceutical company. It had an enviable list of highly profitable drugs, many of which had 5 or more further years of patent protection. Earnings in the latest 4 years had increased rapidly, but it was difficult to see that such rates of growth could continue. The company had traditionally paid out about 40% of earnings as dividends, though the figure in 2008 was only 35%. Penn was spending over $4 billion a year on R&D, but the strong operating cash flow and conservative dividend policy had resulted in a buildup of cash. Penn's recent income statements, balance sheets, and cash-flow statements are summarized in Tables 17–4 to 17–6.

The problem, as Mr. Liu explained, was that Penn's dividend policy was more conservative than that of its main competitors. "Share prices depend on dividends," he said. "If we raise our dividend, we'll raise our share price, and that's the name of the game." Ms. Rodriguez suggested that the real issue was how much cash the company wanted to hold. The current cash holding was more than adequate for the company's immediate needs. On the other hand, the research staff had been analyzing a number of new compounds with promising applications in the treatment of liver diseases. If this research were to lead to a marketable product, Penn would need to make a large investment. In addition, the company might require cash for possible acquisitions in the biotech field. "What worries me," Ms. Rodriguez said, "is that investors don't give us credit for this and think that we are going to fritter away the cash on negative-NPV investments or easy living. I don't think we should commit to paying out high dividends, but perhaps we could use some of our cash to repurchase stock."

"I don't know where anyone gets the idea that we fritter away cash on easy living," replied Mr. Liu, as he took another sip of wine, "but I like the idea of buying back our stock. We can tell shareholders that we are so confident about the future that we believe buying our own stock is the best investment we can make." He scribbled briefly on his napkin. "Suppose we bought back 50 million shares at $105. That would reduce the shares outstanding to 488 million. Net income last year was nearly $4.8 billion, so earnings per share would increase to $9.84. If the price-earnings

TABLE 17–4 Penn Schumann, Inc., balance sheet (figures in millions of dollars)

	2008	2007
Cash and short-term investments	7,061	5,551
Receivables	2,590	2,214
Inventory	1,942	2,435
Total current assets	11,593	10,200
Property, plant, & equipment	21,088	19,025
Less accumulated depreciation	5,780	4,852
Net fixed assets	15,308	14,173
Total assets	26,901	24,373
Payables	6,827	6,215
Short-term debt	1,557	2,620
Total current liabilities	8,384	8,835
Long-term debt	3,349	3,484
Shareholders' equity	15,168	12,054
Total liabilities and equity	26,901	24,373
Note:		
Shares outstanding, millions	538	516
Market price per share ($)	105	88

www.mhhe.com/bmm6e

TABLE 17-5 Penn Schumann, Inc., income statement
(figures in millions of dollars)

	2008	2007
Revenue	16,378	13,378
Costs	8,402	7,800
Depreciation	928	850
EBIT	7,048	4,728
Interest	323	353
Tax	1,933	1,160
Net income	4,792	3,215
Dividends	1,678	1,350
Earnings per share ($)	8.91	6.23
Dividends per share ($)	3.12	2.62

TABLE 17-6 Penn Schumann, Inc., statement of cash flows
(figures in millions of dollars)

	2008
Net income	4,792
Depreciation	928
Decrease (increase) in receivables	(376)
Decrease (increase) in inventories	493
Increase (decrease) in payables	612
Total cash from operations	6,449
Capital expenditures	(2,063)
Increase (decrease) in short-term debt	(1,063)
Increase (decrease) in long-term debt	(135)
Dividends paid	(1,678)
Cash provided by financing activities	(2,876)
Net increase in cash	1,510

multiple stays at 11.8, the stock price should rise to $116. That's an increase of over 10%." A smile came over Mr. Liu's face. "Wonderful, he exclaimed, "here comes my *homard à la nage*. Let's come back to this idea over dessert."

Evaluate the arguments of Jennifer Rodriguez and George Liu. Do you think the company is holding too much cash? If you do, how do you think it could be best paid out?

www.mhhe.com/bmm6e

PART 3

Risk

CHAPTER

11

Introduction to Risk, Return, and the Opportunity Cost of Capital

LEARNING OBJECTIVES

After studying this chapter, you should be able to:

1. Estimate the opportunity cost of capital for an "average-risk" project.

2. Calculate returns and standard deviation of returns for individual common stocks or for a stock portfolio.

3. Understand why diversification reduces risk.

4. Distinguish between unique risk, which can be diversified away, and market risk, which cannot.

Related Web sites for this chapter can be found at www.mhhe.com/bmm6e.

Investing in risky assets is not the same as gambling.
After reading this chapter, you should be able to explain
the difference.
© Rainer Holz/Zefa/Corbis

We have thus far skirted the issue of project risk; now it is time to confront it head-on. We can no longer be satisfied with vague statements like "The opportunity cost of capital depends on the risk of the project." We need to know how to measure risk, and we need to understand the relationship between risk and the cost of capital. These are the topics of the next two chapters.

Think for a moment what the cost of capital for a project means. It is the rate of return that shareholders could expect to earn if they invested in equally risky securities. So one way to estimate the cost of capital is to find securities that have the same risk as the project and then estimate the expected rate of return on these securities.

We start our analysis by looking at the rates of return earned in the past from different investments, concentrating on the *extra* return that investors have received for investing in risky rather than safe securities. We then show how to measure the risk of a portfolio by calculating its standard deviation, and we look again at past history to find out how risky it is to invest in the stock market.

Finally, we explore the concept of diversification. Most investors do not put all their eggs into one basket—they diversify. Thus investors are not concerned with the risk of each security in isolation; instead, they are concerned with how much it contributes to the risk of a diversified portfolio. We therefore need to distinguish between the risk that can be eliminated by diversification and the risk that cannot be eliminated.

11.1 Rates of Return: A Review

When investors buy a stock or a bond, their return comes in two forms: (1) a dividend or interest payment and (2) a capital gain or a capital loss. For example, suppose you bought the stock of ExxonMobil at the beginning of 2007 when its price was $75.06 a share. By the end of the year the value of that investment had appreciated to $93.29, giving a capital gain of $93.29 − $75.06 = $18.23. In addition, in 2007 Exxon paid a dividend of $1.37 a share.

The *percentage* return on your investment was therefore

$$\text{Percentage return} = \frac{\text{capital gain} + \text{dividend}}{\text{initial share price}} \qquad\qquad \textbf{(11.1)}$$

$$= \frac{\$18.23 + \$1.37}{\$75.06} = .261, \text{ or } 26.1\%$$

The percentage return can also be expressed as the sum of the *dividend yield* and *percentage capital gain.* The dividend yield is the dividend expressed as a percentage of the stock price at the beginning of the year:

$$\text{Dividend yield} = \frac{\text{dividend}}{\text{initial share price}}$$

$$= \frac{\$1.37}{\$75.06} = .018, \text{ or } 1.8\%$$

Similarly, the percentage capital gain is

$$\text{Percentage capital gain} = \frac{\text{capital gain}}{\text{initial share price}}$$

$$= \frac{\$18.23}{\$75.06} = 0.243, \text{ or } 24.3\%$$

Thus the total return is the sum of 1.8% + 24.3% = 26.1%.

Remember that in Chapter 5 we made a distinction between the *nominal* rate of return and the *real* rate of return. The nominal return measures how much more money you will have at the end of the year if you invest today. The return that we just calculated for Exxon stock is therefore a nominal return. The real rate of return tells you how much more you will be able to *buy* with your money at the end of the year. To convert from a nominal to a real rate of return, we use the following relationship:

$$1 + \text{real rate of return} = \frac{1 + \text{nominal rate of return}}{1 + \text{inflation rate}}$$

In 2007 inflation was 4.1%. So we calculate the real rate of return on Exxon stock as follows:

$$1 + \text{real rate of return} = \frac{1.261}{1.041} = 1.211$$

Therefore, the real rate of return equals .211, or 21.1%.

Self-Test 11.1   Suppose you buy a bond for $1,020 with a 15-year maturity paying an annual coupon of $80. A year later interest rates have dropped and the bond's price has increased to $1,050. What are your nominal and real rates of return? Assume the inflation rate is 4%.

11.2 A Century of Capital Market History

When you invest in a stock, you don't know what return you will earn. But by looking at the history of security returns, you can get some idea of the return that investors might reasonably expect from investments in different types of securities and of the risks that they face. Let us look, therefore, at the risks and returns that investors have experienced in the past.

Market Indexes

market index
Measure of the investment performance of the overall market.

Dow Jones Industrial Average
Index of the investment performance of a portfolio of 30 "blue-chip" stocks.

Standard & Poor's Composite Index
Index of the investment performance of a portfolio of 500 large stocks. Also called the *S&P 500.*

Investors can choose from an enormous number of different securities. For example, currently, about 2,800 common stocks trade on the New York Stock Exchange, and a further 3,100 are traded on the NASDAQ Stock Market.

Financial analysts can't track every stock, so they rely on **market indexes** to summarize the return on different classes of securities. The best-known stock market index in the United States is the **Dow Jones Industrial Average,** generally known as the *Dow.* The Dow tracks the performance of a portfolio that holds one share in each of 30 large firms. For example, suppose that the Dow starts the day at a value of 12,000 and then rises by 120 points to a new value of 12,120. Investors who own one share in each of the 30 companies make a capital gain of $120/12,000 = .01$, or 1%.[1]

The Dow Jones Industrial Average was first computed in 1896. Most people are used to it and expect to hear it on the 6 o'clock news. However, it is far from the best measure of the performance of the stock market. First, with only 30 large industrial stocks, it is not representative of the performance of stocks generally. Second, investors don't usually hold an equal number of shares in each company. For example, in 2008 there were 10.1 billion shares in General Electric and about 1 billion in Du Pont. So on average investors did *not* hold the same number of shares in the two firms. Instead, they held over 10 times as many shares in General Electric as in Du Pont. It doesn't make sense, therefore, to look at an index that measures the performance of a portfolio with an equal number of shares in the two firms.

The **Standard & Poor's Composite Index,** better known as the *S&P 500,* includes the stocks of 500 major companies and is therefore a more comprehensive index than the Dow. Also, it measures the performance of a portfolio that holds shares in each firm in proportion to the number of shares that have been issued to investors. For example, the S&P portfolio would hold 10 times as many shares in General Electric as Du Pont. Thus the S&P 500 shows the *average* performance of investors in the 500 firms.

Only a small proportion of the publicly traded companies are represented in the S&P 500. However, these firms are among the largest in the country, and they account for about 75% of the market value of traded stocks. Therefore, success for professional investors usually means "beating the S&P."

Some stock market indexes, such as the Dow Jones Wilshire 5000, include an even larger number of stocks, while others focus on special groups of stocks such as the stocks of small companies. There are also stock market indexes for other countries, such as the Nikkei Index for Tokyo and the Financial Times (FT) Index for London. Morgan Stanley Capital International (MSCI) even computes a world stock market index. The Financial Times Company and Standard & Poor's have combined to produce their own world index.

The Historical Record

The historical returns of stock or bond market indexes can give us an idea of the typical performance of different investments. For example, Elroy Dimson, Paul Marsh,

---

[1] Stock market indexes record the market value of the portfolio. To calculate the total return on the portfolio, we need to add in any dividends that are paid.

and Mike Staunton have compiled measures of the investment performance of three portfolios of securities since 1900:

1. A portfolio of 3-month loans issued each week by the U.S. government. These loans are known as *Treasury bills.*
2. A portfolio of long-term *Treasury bonds* issued by the U.S. government and maturing in about 10 years.
3. A diversified portfolio of common stocks.

These portfolios are not equally risky. Treasury bills are about as safe an investment as you can make. Because they are issued by the U.S. government, you can be sure that you will get your money back. Their short-term maturity means that their prices are relatively stable. In fact, investors who wish to lend money for 3 months can achieve a certain payoff by buying 3-month bills. Of course, they can't be sure what that money will buy; there is still some uncertainty about inflation.

Long-term Treasury bonds are also certain to be repaid when they mature, but the prices of these bonds fluctuate more as interest rates vary. When interest rates fall, the value of long-term bonds rises; when rates rise, the value of the bonds falls.

Common stocks are the riskiest of the three groups of securities. When you invest in common stocks, there is no promise that you will get your money back. As a part-owner of the corporation, you receive what is left over after the bonds and any other debts have been repaid.

Figure 11–1 shows the performance of the three groups of securities assuming that all dividends or interest income had been reinvested in the portfolios. You can see that the performance of the portfolios fits our intuitive risk ranking. Common stocks were the riskiest investment, but they also offered the greatest gains. One dollar invested at the start of 1900 in a portfolio of common stocks would have grown to $22,745 by the end of 2007. At the other end of the spectrum, an investment in Treasury bills would have accumulated to only $69.

Table 11–1 shows the average of the annual returns from each of these portfolios. These returns are comparable to the return that we calculated for ExxonMobil. In other words, they include (1) dividends or interest and (2) any capital gains or losses.

The safest investment, Treasury bills, had the lowest rates of return—they averaged 4% a year. Long-term government bonds gave slightly higher returns than Treasury bills. This difference is called the **maturity premium.** Common stocks were in a class by themselves. Investors who accepted the risk of common stocks received on

maturity premium
Extra average return from investing in long- versus short-term Treasury securities.

FIGURE 11–1 How an investment of $1 at the start of 1900 would have grown by the end of 2007 (index values plotted on log scale)

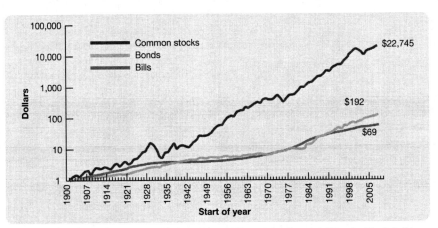

Source: Author's calculations using data from E. Dimson, P. R. Marsh, and M. Staunton, *Triumph of the Optimists: 101 Years of Global Investment Returns* (Princeton, NJ: Princeton University Press, 2002), with updates kindly provided by *Triumph's* authors.

TABLE 11–1 Average rates of return on Treasury bills, government bonds, and common stocks, 1900–2007 (figures in percent per year)

Portfolio	Average Annual Rate of Return	Average Premium (Extra Return versus Treasury Bills)
Treasury bills	4.0	
Treasury bonds	5.3	1.2
Common stocks	11.6	7.6

Source: Authors' calculations using data from Elroy Dimson, Paul Marsh, and Mike Staunton, *Triumph of the Optimists: 101 Years of Global Equity Returns* (Princeton, NJ: Princeton University Press, 2002), with updates kindly provided by *Triumph's* authors.

risk premium

Expected return in excess of risk-free return as compensation for risk.

average an extra return of 7.6% a year over the return on Treasury bills. This compensation for taking on the risk of common stock ownership is known as the market **risk premium:**

$$\frac{\text{Rate of return}}{\text{on common stocks}} = \frac{\text{interest rate on}}{\text{Treasury bills}} + \frac{\text{market risk}}{\text{premium}}$$

The historical record shows that investors have received a risk premium for holding risky assets. Average returns on high-risk assets are higher than those on low-risk assets.

You may ask why we look back over such a long period to measure average rates of return. The reason is that annual rates of return for common stocks fluctuate so much that averages taken over short periods are extremely unreliable. In some years investors in common stocks had a disagreeable shock and received a substantially lower return than they expected. In other years they had a pleasant surprise and received a higher-than-expected return. By averaging the returns across both the rough years and the smooth, we should get a fair idea of the typical return that investors might justifiably expect.

While common stocks have offered the highest average returns, they have also been riskier investments. Figure 11–2 shows the 108 annual rates of return on common stocks. The fluctuations in year-to-year returns on common stocks are remarkably wide. There were 2 years (1933 and 1954) when investors earned a return of more than 50%. However, Figure 11–2 shows that you can also lose money by investing in the stock market. The most dramatic case was the stock market crash of 1929–1932. Shortly after President Coolidge joyfully observed that stocks were "cheap at current

FIGURE 11–2 Rates of return on common stocks, 1900–2007

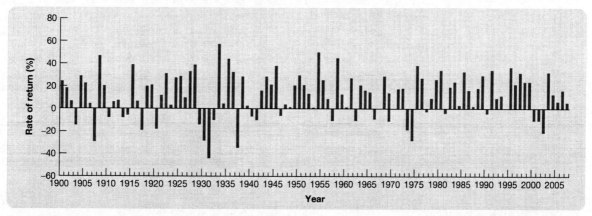

Source: Author's calculations using data from E. Dimson, P. R. Marsh, and M. Staunton, *Triumph of the Optimists: 101 Years of Global Investment Returns* (Princeton, NJ: Princeton University Press, 2002), with updates kindly provided by *Triumph's* authors.

prices," stocks rapidly became even cheaper. By July 1932 the Dow Jones Industrial Average had fallen in a series of slides by 89%.

You don't have to look that far back to see that the stock market is a risky place. Investors who had bought at the stock market peak in March 2000 would have seen little but falling stock prices over the next 2½ years. By October 2002 the S&P 500 had declined by 49%, while the tech-heavy NASDAQ market fell by 78%.

Bond prices also fluctuate, but far less than stock prices. The worst year for investors in our portfolio of Treasury bonds was 1967; their return that year was −9.2%.

Self-Test 11.2

Here are the average rates of return for common stocks and Treasury bills for four different periods:

	1900–1924	1925–1949	1950–1974	1975–2007
Stocks	9.5%	10.2%	11.1%	14.7%
Treasury bills	4.9	1.1	3.5	6.0

What was the risk premium on stocks for each of these periods?

Using Historical Evidence to Estimate Today's Cost of Capital

Think back now to Chapter 8, where we showed how firms calculate the present value of a new project by discounting the expected cash flows by the opportunity cost of capital. The opportunity cost of capital is the return that the firm's shareholders are giving up by investing in the project rather than in comparable risk alternatives.

Measuring the cost of capital is easy if the project is a sure thing. Since shareholders can obtain a surefire payoff by investing in a U.S. Treasury bill, the firm should invest in a risk-free project only if it can at least match the rate of interest on such a loan. If the project is risky—and most projects are—then the firm needs to at least match the return that shareholders could expect to earn if they invested in securities of similar risk. It is not easy to put a precise figure on this, but our skim through history provides an idea of the average return an investor might expect to earn from an investment in risky common stocks.

Suppose there is an investment project that you *know*—don't ask how—has the same risk as an investment in a diversified portfolio of U.S. common stocks. We will say that it has the same degree of risk as the *market portfolio*.

Instead of investing in the project, your shareholders could invest directly in this market portfolio. Therefore, the opportunity cost of capital for your project is the return that the shareholders could expect to earn on the market portfolio. This is what they are giving up by investing money in your project.

The problem of estimating the project cost of capital boils down to estimating the currently expected rate of return on the market portfolio. One way to estimate the expected market return is to assume that the future will be like the past and that today's investors expect to receive the average rates of return shown in Table 11–1. In this case, you would judge that the expected market return today is 11.6%, the average of past market returns.

Unfortunately, this is *not* the way to do it. Investors are not likely to demand the same return each year on an investment in common stocks. For example, we know that the interest rate on safe Treasury bills varies over time. At their peak in 1981, Treasury bills offered a return of 14%, nearly 10 percentage points above the 4% average return on bills shown in Table 11–1.

What if you were called upon to estimate the expected return on common stocks in 1981? Would you have said 11.6%? That doesn't make sense. Who would invest in the risky stock market for an expected return of 11.6% when you could get a safe 14% from Treasury bills?

A better procedure is to take the *current* interest rate on Treasury bills plus 7.6%, the average *risk premium* shown in Table 11–1. In 1981, when the rate on Treasury bills was 14%, that would have given

$$\text{Expected market return (1981)} = \text{interest rate on Treasury bills (1981)} + \text{normal risk premium}$$
$$= 14 + 7.6 = 21.6\%$$

The first term on the right-hand side tells us the time value of money in 1981; the second term measures the compensation for risk. **The expected return on an investment provides compensation to investors both for waiting (the time value of money) and for worrying (the risk of the particular asset).**

What about today? As we write this in early 2008, Treasury bills offer a return of only 2.2%. This suggests that investors in common stocks are looking for a return of 9.8%:[2]

$$\text{Expected market return (2008)} = \text{interest rate on Treasury bills (2008)} + \text{normal risk premium}$$
$$= 2.2 + 7.6 = 9.8\%$$

These calculations assume that there is a normal, stable risk premium on the market portfolio, so the expected *future* risk premium can be measured by the average past risk premium. But even with 100 years of data, we can't estimate the market risk premium exactly; nor can we be sure that investors today are demanding the same reward for risk that they were in the early 1900s. All this leaves plenty of room for argument about what the risk premium *really* is.[3]

Many financial managers and economists believe that long-run historical returns are the best measure available. Others have a gut instinct that investors don't need such a large risk premium to persuade them to hold common stocks. For example, recent surveys of financial economists revealed that they expected a risk premium in the region of 6%, while surveys of chief financial officers have suggested an average risk premium of 5.6%.[4]

We may be able to gain some further insights into the question by looking at the experience of other countries. Figure 11–3 shows that the United States is roughly average in terms of the risk premium. Danish common stocks come bottom of the league; the average risk premium in Denmark is only 4.8%. Top of the form is Italy with a premium of 10.8%. Some of these variations between countries may reflect differences in risk. For example, Italian stocks have been particularly variable and investors may have required a higher return to compensate. But remember how difficult it is to make precise estimates of what investors expected. You probably would not be too far out if you concluded that the *expected* risk premium was the same in each country.

---

[2] In practice, things might be a bit more complicated. We've mentioned the yield curve, the relationship between bond maturity and yield. When firms consider investments in long-lived projects, they usually think about risk premiums relative to long-term bonds. In this case, the risk-free rate would be taken as the current long-term bond yield less the average maturity premium on such bonds.

[3] Often the disagreements simply reflect the fact that the *risk premium* is defined in different ways. For example, some measure the average difference between stock returns and the returns (or yields) on long-term bonds.

[4] These figures are derived from surveys reported in I. Welch, "The Consensus Estimate for the Equity Premium By Academic Financial Economists in December 2007," Brown University, Department of Economics, January 2008; and J. R. Graham and C. R. Harvey, "The Equity Risk Premium in January 2007: Evidence from the Global CFO Outlook Survey," working paper, Fuqua School of Business, Duke University, January 25, 2007.

FIGURE 11–3 The risk premium in 17 countries, 1900–2007. The return on common stocks has averaged about 7.1% more than the interest rate on bills.

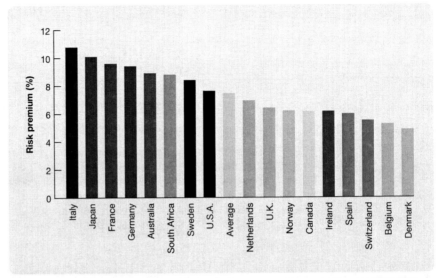

Source: Author's calculations using data from E. Dimson, P. R. Marsh, and M. Staunton, *Triumph of the Optimists: 101 Years of Global Investment Returns* (Princeton, NJ: Princeton University Press, 2002), with updates kindly provided by *Triumph*'s authors.

11.3 Measuring Risk

You now have some benchmarks. You know that the opportunity cost of capital for safe projects must be the rate of return offered by safe Treasury bills, and you know that the opportunity cost of capital for "average-risk" projects must be the expected return on the market portfolio. But you *don't* know how to estimate the cost of capital for projects that do not fit these two simple cases. Before you can do this, you need to understand more about investment risk.

The average fuse time for army hand grenades is 7 seconds, but that average hides a lot of potentially relevant information. If you are in the business of throwing grenades, you need some measure of the variation around the average fuse time.[5] Similarly, if you are in the business of investing in securities, you need some measure of how far the returns may differ from the average.

One way to present the spread of possible investment returns is by using histograms, such as the ones in Figure 11–4. The bars in each histogram show the number of years between 1900 and 2007 that the investment's return fell within a specific range. Look first at the performance of common stocks. Their risk shows up in the wide spread of outcomes. For example, you can see that in one year the return was between +55% and +60%, but there was also one year that investors lost between 40% and 45%.

The corresponding histograms for Treasury bonds and bills show that unusually high or low returns are much less common. Investors in these securities could have been much more confident of the outcome than common stockholders.

Variance and Standard Deviation

Investment risk depends on the dispersion or spread of possible outcomes. For example, Figure 11–4 showed that on past evidence there is greater uncertainty about the possible returns from common stocks than about the returns from bills or bonds. Sometimes a picture like Figure 11–4 tells you all you need to know about (past) dispersion. But in general, pictures do not suffice. The financial manager needs a

---
[5] We can reassure you; the variation around the standard fuse time is very small.

FIGURE 11–4 Historical returns on major asset classes, 1900–2007

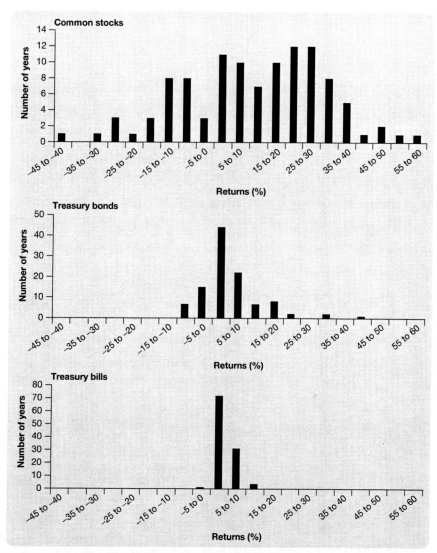

Source: Author's calculations using data from E. Dimson, P. R. Marsh, and M. Staunton, *Triumph of the Optimists: 101 Years of Global Investment Returns* (Princeton, NJ: Princeton University Press, 2002), with updates kindly provided by *Triumph*'s authors.

variance
Average value of squared deviations from mean. A measure of volatility.

standard deviation
Square root of variance. Another measure of volatility.

numerical measure of dispersion. The standard measures are **variance** and **standard deviation.** More variable returns imply greater investment risk. This suggests that some measure of dispersion will provide a reasonable measure of risk, and dispersion is precisely what is measured by variance and standard deviation.

Here is a very simple example showing how variance and standard deviation are calculated: Suppose that you are offered the chance to play the following game. You start by investing $100. Then two coins are flipped. For each head that comes up your starting balance will be *increased* by 20%, and for each tail that comes up your starting balance will be *reduced* by 10%. Clearly there are four equally likely outcomes:

- Head + Head: You make 20 + 20 = 40%
- Head + Tail: You make 20 − 10 = 10%
- Tail + Head: You make −10 + 20 = 10%
- Tail + Tail: You make −10 − 10 = −20%

There is a chance of 1 in 4, or .25, that you will make 40%; a chance of 2 in 4, or .5, that you will make 10%; and a chance of 1 in 4, or .25, that you will lose 20%. The game's expected return is therefore a weighted average of the possible outcomes:

$$\text{Expected return} = \text{probability-weighted average of possible outcomes}$$
$$= (.25 \times 40) + (.5 \times 10) + (.25 \times -20) = +10\%$$

If you play the game a very large number of times, your average return should be 10%.

Table 11–2 shows how to calculate the variance and standard deviation of the returns on your game. Column 1 shows the four equally likely outcomes. In column 2 we calculate the difference between each possible outcome and the expected outcome. You can see that at best the return could be 30% higher than expected; at worst it could be 30% lower.

These deviations in column 2 illustrate the spread of possible returns. But if we want a measure of this spread, it is no use just averaging the deviations in column 2—the average is always going to be zero because the positive and negative deviations cancel out. To get around this problem, we *square* the deviations in column 2 before averaging them. These squared deviations are shown in column 3. The variance is the average of these squared deviations and therefore is a natural measure of dispersion:

$$\text{Variance} = \text{average of squared deviations around the average} \qquad \textbf{(11.2)}$$
$$= \frac{1,800}{4} = 450$$

When we squared the deviations from the expected return, we changed the units of measurement from *percentages* to *percentages squared.* Our last step is to get back to percentages by taking the square root of the variance. This is the standard deviation:

$$\text{Standard deviation} = \text{square root of variance} \qquad \textbf{(11.3)}$$
$$= \sqrt{450} = 21\%$$

Because standard deviation is simply the square root of variance, it too is a natural measure of risk. If the outcome of the game had been certain, the standard deviation would have been zero because there would then be no deviations from the expected outcome. The actual standard deviation is positive because we *don't* know what will happen.

Now think of a second game. It is the same as the first except that each head means a 35% gain and each tail means a 25% loss. Again there are four equally likely outcomes:

- Head + Head: You gain 70%
- Head + Tail: You gain 10%
- Tail + Head: You gain 10%
- Tail + Tail: You lose 50%

TABLE 11–2 The coin-toss game; calculating variance and standard deviation

(1) Percent Rate of Return	(2) Deviation from Expected Return	(3) Squared Deviation
+40	+30	900
+10	0	0
+10	0	0
−20	−30	900

Notes:
1. Variance = average of squared deviations = 1,800/4 = 450.
2. Standard deviation = square root of variance = $\sqrt{450}$ = 21.2, about 21%.

TABLE 11–3 The coin-toss game; calculating variance and standard deviation when there are different probabilities of each outcome

(1) Percent Rate of Return	(2) Probability of Return	(3) Deviation from Expected Return	(4) Probability × Squared Deviation
+40	.25	+30	.25 × 900 = 225
+10	.50	0	.50 × 0 = 0
−20	.25	−30	.25 × 900 = 225

Notes:
1. Variance = sum of squared deviations weighted by probabilities = 225 + 0 + 225 = 450.
2. Standard deviation = square root of variance = $\sqrt{450}$ = 21.2, about 21%.

For this game, the expected return is 10%, the same as that of the first game, but it is more risky. For example, in the first game, the worst possible outcome is a loss of 20%, which is 30% worse than the expected outcome. In the second game the downside is a loss of 50%, or 60% below the expected return. This increased spread of outcomes shows up in the standard deviation, which is double that of the first game, 42% versus 21%. By this measure the second game is twice as risky as the first.

A Note on Calculating Variance

When we calculated variance in Table 11–2 we recorded separately each of the four possible outcomes. An alternative would have been to recognize that in two of the cases the outcomes were the same. Thus there was a 50% chance of a 10% return from the game, a 25% chance of a 40% return, and a 25% chance of a −20% return. We can calculate variance by weighting each squared deviation by the probability and then summing the results. Table 11–3 confirms that this method gives the same answer.

Self-Test 11.3   Calculate the variance and standard deviation of the second (higher-risk) coin-tossing game in the same formats as Tables 11–2 and 11–3.

Measuring the Variation in Stock Returns

When estimating the spread of possible outcomes from investing in the stock market, most financial analysts start by assuming that the spread of returns in the past is a reasonable indication of what could happen in the future. Therefore, they calculate the standard deviation of past returns. To illustrate, suppose that you were presented with the data for stock market returns shown in Table 11–4. The average return over the 6 years from 2002 to 2007 was 8.50%. This is just the sum of the returns over the 6 years divided by 6 (51.0/6 = 8.50%).

Column 2 in Table 11–4 shows the difference between each year's return and the average return. For example, in 2002 the return of −20.9% on common stocks was below the 6-year average by 29.4% (−20.9 − 8.5 = −29.4%). In column 3 we square these deviations from the average. The variance is then the average of these squared deviations:[6]

$$\text{Variance} = \text{average of squared deviations}$$
$$= \frac{1,480.08}{6} = 246.68$$

---

[6] *Technical note:* When variance is estimated from a sample of observed returns, it is common to add the squared deviations and divide by $N - 1$, rather than N, where N is the number of observations. This procedure adjusts the estimate for what is called *the loss of a degree of freedom*. We will ignore this fine point, emphasizing the interpretation of variance as an average squared deviation. In any event, the correction for the lost degree of freedom is negligible when there are plentiful observations. For example, with 100 years of data, the difference between dividing by 99 or 100 will affect the estimated variance by only 1% (i.e., a factor of 1.01).

TABLE 11-4 The average return and standard deviation of stock market returns, 2002-2007

Year	Rate of Return, %	Deviation from Average Return, %	Squared Deviation
2002	−20.9	−29.4	864.36
2003	31.6	23.1	533.61
2004	12.5	4.0	16.00
2005	6.4	−2.1	4.41
2006	15.8	7.3	53.29
2007	5.6	−2.9	8.41
Total	51.0		1,480.08
Average return = 51.0/6 = 8.50%			
Variance = average of squared deviations = 1,480.08/6 = 246.68			
Standard deviation = square root of variance = 15.71%			

Source: Authors' calculations using data from E. Dimson, P. R. Marsh, and M. Staunton, *Triumph of the Optimists: 101 Years of Global Equity Returns* (Princeton, NJ: Princeton University Press, 2002), with updates kindly provided by *Triumph's* authors.

Since standard deviation is the square root of the variance,

$$\text{Standard deviation} = \text{square root of variance}$$
$$= \sqrt{246.68} = 15.71\%$$

It is difficult to measure the risk of securities on the basis of just six past outcomes. Therefore, Table 11–5 lists the annual standard deviations for our three portfolios of securities over the period 1900–2007. As expected, Treasury bills were the least variable security, and common stocks were the most variable. Treasury bonds hold the middle ground.

Of course, there is no reason to believe that the market's variability should stay the same over many years. Indeed many people believe that in recent years the stock market has become more volatile due to irresponsible speculation by . . . (fill in here the name of your preferred guilty party). Figure 11–5 provides a chart of the volatility of the U.S. stock market for each year from 1900 to 2007.[7] You can see that there are periods of unusually high variability, but there is no long-term upward trend.

FIGURE 11-5 Annualized standard deviation of weekly changes in the Dow Jones Industrial Average, 1900-2007

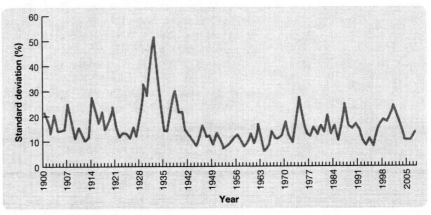

Source: Ibbotson Associates.

---

[7] We converted the weekly variance to an annual variance by multiplying by 52. In other words, the variance of annual returns is 52 times that of weekly returns. The longer you hold a security, the more risk you have to bear.

TABLE 11–5 **Standard deviation of returns, 1900–2007**

Portfolio	Standard Deviation, %
Treasury bills	2.8
Long-term government bonds	8.1
Common stocks	19.7

Source: Authors' calculations using data from Elroy Dimson, Paul Marsh, and Mike Staunton, *Triumph of the Optimists: 101 Years of Global Equity Returns* (Princeton, NJ: Princeton University Press, 2002), with updates kindly provided by *Triumph*'s authors.

11.4 Risk and Diversification

Diversification

We can calculate our measures of variability equally well for individual securities and portfolios of securities. Of course, the level of variability over 100 years is less interesting for specific companies than for the market portfolio because it is a rare company that faces the same business risks today as it did a century ago.

Table 11–6 presents estimated standard deviations for some well-known common stocks for a recent 5-year period.[8] The standard deviation of the market portfolio in these years was only 8.6%, well below the long-term average. However, the standard deviation of the returns on each of our stocks was much higher than 8.6%. Most stocks are substantially more variable than the market portfolio; only a handful are less variable.

This raises an important question: The market portfolio is made up of individual stocks, so why isn't its variability equal to the average variability of its components? The answer is that **diversification** *reduces variability.*

diversification
Strategy designed to reduce risk by spreading the portfolio across many investments.

Selling umbrellas is a risky business; you may make a killing when it rains, but you are likely to lose your shirt in a heat wave. Selling ice cream is no safer; you do well in the heat wave, but business is poor in the rain. Suppose, however, that you invest in

TABLE 11–6 **Standard deviations for selected common stocks, January 2003–December 2007**

Amazon.com	48.0%
Ford	34.6
Newmont	28.6
Intel	27.5
Microsoft	24.8
Dell Computer	23.4
Boeing	21.6
McDonald's	20.3
Pfizer	18.7
Du Pont	18.2
Disney	17.9
ExxonMobil	17.8
IBM	17.4
Wal-Mart	15.8
Campbell Soup	15.1
Heinz	13.5

---

[8] We pointed out earlier that five annual observations are insufficient to give a reliable estimate of variability. Therefore, these estimates are derived from 60 monthly rates of return, and then the monthly variance is multiplied by 12.

Corporate Finance

both an umbrella shop and an ice cream shop. By diversifying your investment across the two businesses, you make an average level of profit come rain or shine.

Portfolio diversification works because prices of different stocks do not move exactly together. Statisticians make the same point when they say that stock price changes are less than perfectly correlated. Diversification works best when the returns are negatively correlated, as is the case of our umbrella and ice cream businesses. When one business does well, the other does badly. Unfortunately, in practice, stocks that are negatively correlated are as rare as pecan pie in Budapest.

Asset versus Portfolio Risk

The history of returns on different asset classes provides compelling evidence of a risk–return trade-off and suggests that the variability of the rates of return on each asset class is a useful measure of risk. However, volatility of returns can be a misleading measure of risk for an individual asset held as part of a portfolio. To see why, consider the following example.

Suppose there are three equally likely outcomes, or *scenarios,* for the economy: a recession, normal growth, and a boom. An investment in an auto stock will have a rate of return of −8% in a recession, 5% in a normal period, and 18% in a boom. Auto firms are *cyclical:* They do well when the economy does well. In contrast, gold firms are often said to be *countercyclical,* meaning that they do well when other firms do poorly. Suppose that stock in a gold mining firm will provide a rate of return of 20% in a recession, 3% in a normal period, and −20% in a boom. These assumptions are summarized in Table 11–7.

It appears that gold is the more volatile investment. The difference in return across the boom and bust scenarios is 40% (−20% in a boom versus +20% in a recession), compared to a spread of only 26% for the auto stock. In fact, we can confirm the higher volatility by measuring the variance or standard deviation of returns of the two assets. The calculations are set out in Table 11–8.

TABLE 11–7 Rate of return assumptions for two stocks

		Rate of Return, %	
Scenario	Probability	Auto Stock	Gold Stock
Recession	1/3	−8	+20
Normal	1/3	+5	+3
Boom	1/3	+18	−20

TABLE 11–8 Expected return and volatility for two stocks

	Auto Stock			Gold Stock		
Scenario	Rate of Return, %	Deviation from Expected Return, %	Squared Deviation	Rate of Return, %	Deviation from Expected Return, %	Squared Deviation
Recession	−8	−13	169	+20	+19	361
Normal	+5	0	0	+3	+2	4
Boom	+18	+13	169	−20	−21	441
Expected return	$\frac{1}{3}(-8+5+18)=5\%$			$\frac{1}{3}(+20+3-20)=1\%$		
Variance*	$\frac{1}{3}(169+0+169)=112.7$			$\frac{1}{3}(361+4+441)=268.7$		
Standard deviation (= $\sqrt{\text{variance}}$)	$\sqrt{112.7}=10.6\%$			$\sqrt{268.7}=16.4\%$		

* Variance = average of squared deviations from the expected value.

Since all three scenarios are equally likely, the expected return on each stock is simply the average of the three possible outcomes.[9] For the auto stock the expected return is 5%; for the gold stock it is 1%. The variance is the average of the squared deviations from the expected return, and the standard deviation is the square root of the variance.

Self-Test 11.4

Suppose the probability of the recession or boom is .30, while the probability of a normal period is .40. Would you expect the variance of returns on these two investments to be higher or lower? Why? Confirm by calculating the standard deviation of the auto stock. (Refer back to "A Note on Calculating Variance" in Section 11.3 if you are unsure of how to do this.)

The gold mining stock offers a lower expected rate of return than the auto stock and *more* volatility—a loser on both counts, right? Would anyone be willing to hold gold mining stocks in an investment portfolio? The answer is a resounding yes.

To see why, suppose you do believe that gold is a lousy asset, and therefore you hold your entire portfolio in the auto stock. Your expected return is 5% and your standard deviation is 10.6%. We'll compare that portfolio to a partially diversified one, invested 75% in autos and 25% in gold. For example, if you have a $10,000 portfolio, you could put $7,500 in autos and $2,500 in gold.

First, we need to calculate the return on this portfolio in each scenario. The portfolio return is the weighted average of returns on the individual assets with weights equal to the proportion of the portfolio invested in each asset. For a portfolio formed from only two assets,

$$\begin{aligned}\text{Portfolio rate} \atop \text{of return} = &\left(\begin{matrix}\text{fraction of portfolio} \\ \text{in first asset}\end{matrix} \times \begin{matrix}\text{rate of return} \\ \text{on first asset}\end{matrix}\right) \\ &+\left(\begin{matrix}\text{fraction of portfolio} \\ \text{in second asset}\end{matrix} \times \begin{matrix}\text{rate of return} \\ \text{on second asset}\end{matrix}\right)\end{aligned} \quad (11.4)$$

For example, autos have a weight of .75 and a rate of return of −8% in the recession, and gold has a weight of .25 and a return of 20% in a recession. Therefore, the portfolio return in the recession is the following weighted average:[10]

$$\text{Portfolio return in recession} = [.75\times(-8\%)]+(.25\times20\%)$$
$$=-1\%$$

Table 11–9 expands Table 11–7 to include the portfolio of the auto stock and the gold mining stock. The expected returns and volatility measures are summarized at the bottom of the table. The surprising finding is this: When you shift funds from the auto stock to the more volatile gold mining stock, your portfolio variability actually *decreases*. In fact, the volatility of the auto-plus-gold stock portfolio is considerably less than the volatility of *either* stock separately. This is the payoff to diversification.

We can understand this more clearly by focusing on asset returns in the two extreme scenarios, boom and recession. In the boom, when auto stocks do best, the poor return

[9] If the probabilities were not equal, we would need to weight each outcome by its probability in calculating the expected outcome and the variance.

[10] Let's confirm this. Suppose you invest $7,500 in autos and $2,500 in gold. If the recession hits, the rate of return on autos will be −8%, and the value of the auto investment will fall by 8% to $6,900. The rate of return on gold will be 20%, and the value of the gold investment will rise 20% to $3,000. The value of the total portfolio falls from its original value of $10,000 to $6,900 + $3,000 = $9,900, which is a rate of return of −1%. This matches the rate of return given by the formula for the weighted average.

TABLE 11-9 Rates of return for two stocks and a portfolio

| | | Rate of Return, % | | |
Scenario	Probability	Auto Stock	Gold Stock	Portfolio Return, %*
Recession	1/3	−8	+20	−1.0
Normal	1/3	+5	+3	+4.5
Boom	1/3	+18	−20	+8.5
Expected return		5	1	4
Variance		112.7	268.7	15.2
Standard deviation		10.6	16.4	3.9

* Portfolio return = (.75 × auto stock return) + (.25 × gold stock return)

on gold reduces the performance of the overall portfolio. However, when auto stocks are stalling in a recession, gold shines, providing a substantial positive return that boosts portfolio performance. The gold stock offsets the swings in the performance of the auto stock, reducing the best-case return but improving the worst-case return. The inverse relationship between the returns on the two stocks means that the addition of the gold mining stock to an all-auto portfolio stabilizes returns.

A gold stock is really a *negative-risk* asset to an investor starting with an all-auto portfolio. Adding it to the portfolio reduces the volatility of returns. The *incremental* risk of the gold stock (that is, the *change* in overall risk when gold is added to the portfolio) is *negative* despite the fact that gold returns are highly volatile.

In general, the incremental risk of a stock depends on whether its returns tend to vary with or against the returns of the other assets in the portfolio. Incremental risk does not just depend on a stock's volatility. If returns do not move closely with those of the rest of the portfolio, the stock will reduce the volatility of portfolio returns.

We can summarize as follows:

1. **Investors care about the expected return and risk of their *portfolio* of assets. The risk of the overall portfolio can be measured by the volatility of returns, that is, the variance or standard deviation.**
2. **The standard deviation of the returns of an individual security measures how risky that security would be if held in isolation. But an investor who holds a portfolio of securities is interested only in how each security affects the risk of the entire portfolio. The contribution of a security to the risk of the portfolio depends on how the security's returns vary with the investor's other holdings. Thus a security that is risky if held in isolation may nevertheless serve to reduce the variability of the portfolio if its returns do not move in lockstep with the rest of the portfolio.**

EXAMPLE 11.1   ▶   Ford and Newmont Mining

Our example of the auto and gold mining stocks was entirely fanciful. But we can make the same point by looking at real auto and gold mining companies. For instance, suppose that in August 2004 you invested your savings in the stock of Ford Motor Company. The red line in Figure 11–6 shows how the value of your portfolio would have fluctuated over the following 40 months. The risk shows up in the wide spread of monthly returns. For example, in almost one month in seven you would have lost more than 10% of your capital. The standard deviation of Ford's returns during this period amounted to 30.4% a year.

The blue line in Figure 11–6 shows a similar picture of the performance of Newmont Mining stock over the same period. The fluctuations in this stock were almost as large as those of Ford. The standard deviation of the returns on Newmont stock was 28.2% a year.

How Diversification Reduces Risk

Source: Fidelity Web site.

1. A large mutual fund group such as Fidelity offers a variety of funds. Some, called *sector funds,* specialize in particular industries; others, known as *index funds,* simply invest in the market index. Log on to **www.fidelity.com** and find first the standard deviation of returns on the Fidelity Spartan 500 Index Fund, which replicates the S&P 500. Now find the standard deviation of fund returns for different industry (sector) funds. Are they larger or smaller than the index fund? How do you interpret your findings?

2. The power of diversification depends on the correlation between the assets. You can see this by logging on to Campbell Harvey's home page at **www.duke.edu/~charvey** and following the link from *Finance Tools* to *Two-Assets Mean Variance Graph.* See what happens to portfolio risk if you hold different proportions of two stocks chosen from Table 11–6. Enter the standard deviation for each stock, assuming a different expected return for each. Look first at the levels of portfolio risk if the returns move in perfect lockstep (correlation = 1.0). Now progressively reduce the correlation between the two stocks. You will find that portfolio risk falls. When the correlation is −1 (i.e., the stocks move in exactly opposite directions), diversification can potentially get rid of all risk.

FIGURE 11–6 The values of investments in the stock of Newmont Mining or Ford have been very variable. But the two stocks have not moved in lockstep. Investors could have reduced variability by dividing their money equally between the two stocks.

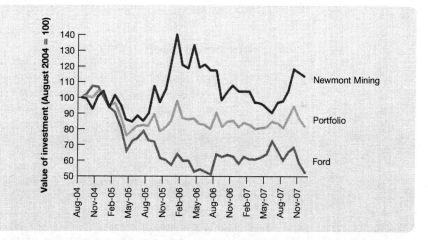

Although both stocks had their ups and downs, the two stocks have not moved in exact lockstep.[11] As often as not, a decline in the value of Ford stock was offset by a rise in the price of Newmont. So if you had split your portfolio between the two stocks, you could have reduced the monthly fluctuations in the value of your savings. You can see from the green line in Figure 11–6 that if your portfolio had been evenly divided between Ford and Newmont Mining, there would have been many more months when the return was just middling and far fewer cases of extreme returns. By diversifying between the two stocks, you would have reduced the standard deviation of the returns on your investment to 22.4% a year.

---

[11] Statisticians calculate a *correlation coefficient* as a measure of how closely two series move together. If Ford's and Newmont's stock moved in perfect lockstep, the correlation coefficient between the returns would be 1.0. If their returns were completely unrelated, the correlation would be zero. If the returns on two stocks tend to move inversely, that is, if one stock usually is up when the other is down, the correlation coefficient will be negative. If returns move in perfect but inverse lockstep, the correlation coefficient will be −1.0. But negative correlations are unusual. Because most firms have a common dependence on the overall economy, correlations between stock returns are typically positive. The average correlation between the returns on the stocks shown in Table 11–6 was .17.

FIGURE 11–7 The risk (standard deviation) of portfolios containing different numbers of New York Stock Exchange stocks. Notice that diversification reduces risk rapidly at first and then more slowly.

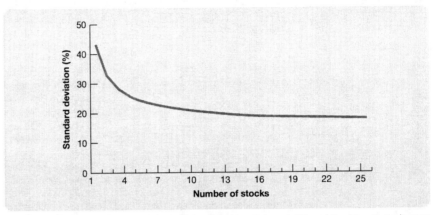

Source: M. Statman, "How Many Stocks Make a Diversified Portfolio?" *Journal of Financial and Quantitative Analysis* 22 (September 1987), pp. 353–363.

Self-Test 11.5

An investor is currently fully invested in gold mining stocks. Which action would do more to reduce portfolio risk: diversification into silver mining stocks or into automotive stocks? Why?

Market Risk versus Unique Risk

Our examples illustrate that even a little diversification can provide a substantial reduction in variability. Suppose you calculate and compare the standard deviations of randomly chosen one-stock portfolios, two-stock portfolios, five-stock portfolios, and so on. You can see from Figure 11–7 that diversification can cut the variability of returns by about half. But you can get most of this benefit with relatively few stocks: The improvement is slight when the number of stocks is increased beyond, say, 15 or 20.

Figure 11–7 also illustrates that no matter how many securities you hold, you cannot eliminate all risk. There remains the danger that the market—including your portfolio—will plummet.

unique risk
Risk factors affecting only that firm. Also called *diversifiable risk.*

market risk
Economywide (macroeconomic) sources of risk that affect the overall stock market. Also called *systematic risk.*

The risk that can be eliminated by diversification is called **unique risk.** The risk that you can't avoid regardless of how much you diversify is generally known as **market risk** or *systematic risk. Unique risk arises because many of the perils that surround an individual company are peculiar to that company and perhaps its direct competitors. Market risk stems from economywide perils that threaten all businesses. Market risk explains why stocks have a tendency to move together, so even well-diversified portfolios are exposed to market movements.*

Figure 11–8 divides risk into its two parts—unique risk and market risk. If you have only a single stock, unique risk is very important; but once you have a portfolio of 30 or more stocks, diversification has done most of what it can to eliminate risk. **For a reasonably well-diversified portfolio, only market risk matters.**

11.5 Thinking about Risk

How can you tell which risks are unique and diversifiable? Where do market risks come from? Here are three messages to help you think clearly about risk.

Message 1: Some Risks Look Big and Dangerous but Really Are Diversifiable

Managers confront risks "up close and personal." They must make decisions about particular investments. The failure of such an investment could cost a promotion, bonus, or otherwise steady job. Yet that same investment may not seem risky to an

FIGURE 11–8 **Diversification eliminates unique risk. But there is some risk that diversification cannot eliminate. This is called market risk.**

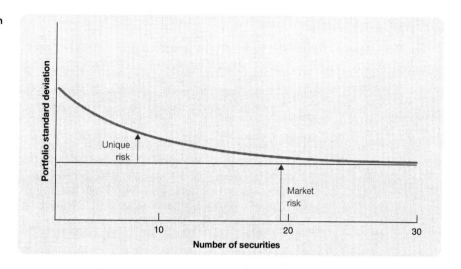

investor who can stand back and combine it in a diversified portfolio with many other assets or securities.

EXAMPLE 11.2 ▶ Wildcat Oil Wells

You have just been promoted to director of exploration, Western Hemisphere, of MPS Oil. The manager of your exploration team in far-off Costaguana has appealed for $20 million extra to drill in an even steamier part of the Costaguanan jungle. The manager thinks there may be an "elephant" field worth $500 million or more hidden there. But the chance of finding it is at best 1 in 10, and yesterday MPS's CEO sourly commented on the $100 million already "wasted" on Costaguanan exploration.

Is this a risky investment? For you it probably is; you may be a hero if oil is found and a goat otherwise. But MPS drills hundreds of wells worldwide; for the company as a whole, it's the *average* success rate that matters. Geologic risks (is there oil or not?) should average out. The risk of a worldwide drilling program is much less than the apparent risk of any single wildcat well.

Back up one step, and think of the investors who buy MPS stock. The investors may hold other oil companies too, as well as companies producing steel, computers, clothing, cement, and breakfast cereal. They naturally—and realistically—assume that your successes and failures in drilling oil wells will average out with the thousands of independent bets made by the companies in their portfolio.

Therefore, the risks you face in Costaguana do not affect the rate of return they demand for investing in MPS Oil. Diversified investors in MPS stock will be happy if you find that elephant field, but they probably will not notice if you fail and lose your job. In any case, they will not demand a higher *average* rate of return for worrying about geologic risks in Costaguana.

EXAMPLE 11.3 ▶ Fire Insurance

Would you be willing to write a $100,000 fire insurance policy on your neighbor's house? The neighbor is willing to pay you $100 for a year's protection, and experience shows that the chance of fire damage in a given year is substantially less than 1 in 1,000. But if your neighbor's house is damaged by fire, you would have to pay up.

Few of us have deep enough pockets to insure our neighbors, even if the odds of fire damage are very low. Insurance seems a risky business if you think policy by policy. But a large insurance company, which may issue a million policies, is concerned only with average losses, which can be predicted with excellent accuracy.

Self-Test 11.6

Imagine a laboratory at IBM, late at night. One scientist speaks to another.

"You're right, Watson, I admit this experiment will consume all the rest of this year's budget. I don't know what we'll do if it fails. But if this yttrium–magnoosium alloy superconducts, the patents will be worth millions."

Would this be a good or bad investment for IBM? Can't say. But from the ultimate investors' viewpoint this is *not* a risky investment. Explain why.

Message 2: Market Risks Are Macro Risks

We have seen that diversified portfolios are not exposed to the unique risks of individual stocks but are exposed to the uncertain events that affect the entire securities market and the entire economy. These are macroeconomic, or "macro," factors such as changes in interest rates, industrial production, inflation, foreign exchange rates, and energy costs. These factors affect most firms' earnings and stock prices. When the relevant macro risks turn generally favorable, stock prices rise and investors do well; when the same variables go the other way, investors suffer.

You can often assess relative market risks just by thinking through exposures to the business cycle and other macro variables. The following businesses have substantial macro and market risks:

- *Airlines.* Because business travel falls during a recession, and individuals postpone vacations and other discretionary travel, the airline industry is subject to the swings of the business cycle. On the positive side, airline profits really take off when business is booming and personal incomes are rising.
- *Machine tool manufacturers.* These businesses are especially exposed to the business cycle. Manufacturing companies that have excess capacity rarely buy new machine tools to expand. During recessions, excess capacity can be quite high.

Here, on the other hand, are two industries with less than average macro exposures:

- *Food companies.* Companies selling staples, such as breakfast cereal, flour, and dog food, find that demand for their products is relatively stable in good times and bad.
- *Electric utilities.* Business demand for electric power varies somewhat across the business cycle, but by much less than demand for air travel or machine tools. Also, many electric utilities' profits are regulated. Regulation cuts off upside profit potential but also gives the utilities the opportunity to increase prices when demand is slack.

Remember, investors holding diversified portfolios are mostly concerned with macroeconomic risks. They do not worry about microeconomic risks peculiar to a particular company or investment project. Micro risks wash out in diversified portfolios. Company managers may worry about both macro and micro risks, but only the former affect the cost of capital.

Self-Test 11.7

Which company of each of the following pairs would you expect to be more exposed to macro risks?

a. A luxury Manhattan restaurant or an established Burger Queen franchise?

b. A paint company that sells through small paint and hardware stores to do-it-yourselfers or a paint company that sells in large volumes to Ford, GM, and Chrysler?

Message 3: Risk Can Be Measured

Delta Airlines clearly has more exposure to macro risks than food companies such as Kellogg or General Mills. These are easy cases. But is IBM stock a riskier investment than ExxonMobil? That's not an easy question to reason through. We can, however, *measure* the risk of IBM and ExxonMobil by looking at how their stock prices fluctuate.

We've already hinted at how to do this. Remember that diversified investors are concerned with market risks. The movements of the stock market sum up the net effects of all relevant macroeconomic uncertainties. If the market portfolio of all traded stocks is up in a particular month, we conclude that the net effect of macroeconomic news is positive. Remember, the performance of the market is barely affected by a firm-specific event. These cancel out across thousands of stocks in the market.

How do we measure the risk of a single stock, like IBM or ExxonMobil? We do not look at the stocks in isolation, because the risks that loom when you're up close to a single company are often diversifiable. Instead we measure the individual stock's sensitivity to the fluctuations of the overall stock market. We will show you how this works in the next chapter.

SUMMARY

How can one estimate the opportunity cost of capital for an "average-risk" project? *(LO1)*

Over the past century the return on the **Standard & Poor's Composite Index** of common stocks has averaged 7.6% a year higher than the return on safe Treasury bills. This is the **risk premium** that investors have received for taking on the risk of investing in stocks. Long-term bonds have offered a higher return than Treasury bills but less than stocks.

If the risk premium in the past is a guide to the future, we can estimate the expected return on the market today by adding that 7.6% expected risk premium to today's interest rate on Treasury bills. This would be the opportunity cost of capital for an average-risk project, that is, one with the same risk as a typical share of common stock.

How is the standard deviation of returns for individual common stocks or for a stock portfolio calculated? *(LO2)*

The spread of outcomes on different investments is commonly measured by the **variance** or **standard deviation** of the possible outcomes. The variance is the average of the squared deviations around the average outcome, and the standard deviation is the square root of the variance. The standard deviation of the returns on a market portfolio of common stocks has averaged around 20% a year.

Why does diversification reduce risk? *(LO3)*

The standard deviation of returns is generally higher on individual stocks than it is on the market. Because individual stocks do not move in exact lockstep, much of their risk can be diversified away. By spreading your portfolio across many investments, you smooth out the risk of your overall position. The risk that can be eliminated through diversification is known as **unique risk.**

What is the difference between unique risk, which can be diversified away, and market risk, which cannot? *(LO4)*

Even if you hold a well-diversified portfolio, you will not eliminate all risk. You will still be exposed to macroeconomic changes that affect most stocks and the overall stock market. These macro risks combine to create **market risk**—that is, the risk that the market as a whole will slump.

Stocks are not all equally risky. But what do we mean by a "high-risk stock"? We don't mean a stock that is risky if held in isolation; we mean a stock that makes an above-average contribution to the risk of a diversified portfolio. In other words, investors don't need to worry much about the risk that they can diversify away; they *do* need to worry about risk that can't be diversified. This depends on the stock's sensitivity to macroeconomic conditions.

www.mhhe.com/bmm6e

LISTING OF EQUATIONS

11.1   Percentage return $= \dfrac{\text{capital gain} + \text{dividend}}{\text{initial share price}}$

11.2   Variance = average of squared deviations around the average

11.3   Standard deviation = square root of variance

11.4 $\begin{aligned}\text{Portfolio rate of return} =& \left(\begin{array}{c}\text{fraction of portfolio} \\ \text{in first asset}\end{array} \times \begin{array}{c}\text{rate of return} \\ \text{on first asset}\end{array}\right) \\ +& \left(\begin{array}{c}\text{fraction of portfolio} \\ \text{in second asset}\end{array} \times \begin{array}{c}\text{rate of return} \\ \text{on second asset}\end{array}\right)\end{aligned}$

QUESTIONS

QUIZ

1. **Rate of Return.** A stock is selling today for $40 per share. At the end of the year, it pays a dividend of $2 per share and sells for $44. What is the total rate of return on the stock? What are the dividend yield and percentage capital gain? (*LO2*)

2. **Rate of Return.** Return to Quiz Question 1. Suppose the year-end stock price after the dividend is paid is $36. What are the dividend yield and percentage capital gain in this case? Why is the dividend yield unaffected? (*LO2*)

3. **Real versus Nominal Returns.** You purchase 100 shares of stock for $40 a share. The stock pays a $2 per share dividend at year-end. What is the rate of return on your investment for the end-of-year stock prices listed below? What is your real (inflation-adjusted) rate of return? Assume an inflation rate of 4%. (*LO2*)
    a. $38
    b. $40
    c. $42

4. **Real versus Nominal Returns.** The Costaguanan stock market provided a rate of return of 95%. The inflation rate in Costaguana during the year was 80%. In the United States, in contrast, the stock market return was only 12%, but the inflation rate was only 2%. Which country's stock market provided the higher real rate of return? (*LO2*)

5. **Real versus Nominal Returns.** The inflation rate in the United States in the twentieth century averaged around 3%. What was the average real rate of return on Treasury bills, Treasury bonds, and common stocks in that period? Use the data in Table 11–1. (*LO2*)

6. **Real versus Nominal Returns.** Do you think it is possible for risk-free Treasury bills to offer a negative nominal interest rate? Might they offer a negative real expected rate of return? (*LO2*)

7. **Market Indexes.** The accompanying table shows quarterly stock prices on the Dar es Salaam Stock Exchange for 2006–2007. Construct two stock market indexes, one using weights as in the Dow Jones Industrial Average, the other using weights as in the Standard & Poor's Composite Index. (*LO2*)

Quarterly Prices in Tanzanian Shillings for Trading on the Dar es Salaam Stock Exchange (Only six stocks were traded at the start of 2006.)						
	Tanzania Breweries, 276 million*	TOL 32 million*	Tanzania Tea Packers, 16.4 million*	Tanzania Cigarette Company, 100 million*	Simba, 64 million*	Swissport, 36 million*
Mar. 2006	1500	295	440	1580	830	610
Jun. 2006	1500	275	440	1500	820	610
Sep. 2006	1600	300	440	1540	890	670
Dec. 2006	1580	330	440	1480	960	680

* Number of shares outstanding.

8. **Stock Market History.** (*LO1*)
   a. What was the average rate of return on large U.S. common stocks from 1900 to 2007?
   b. What was the average risk premium on large stocks?
   c. What was the standard deviation of returns on the market portfolio?

PRACTICE PROBLEMS

9. **Risk Premiums.** Here are stock market and Treasury bill percentage returns between 2003 and 2007: (*LO1*)

Year	Stock Market Return	T-Bill Return
2003	31.64	1.02
2004	12.62	1.20
2005	6.38	2.98
2006	15.77	4.80
2007	5.62	4.66

   a. What was the risk premium on common stock in each year?
   b. What was the average risk premium?
   c. What was the standard deviation of the risk premium?

10. **Market Indexes.** In 1990, the Dow Jones Industrial Average was at a level of about 2,600. In 2007, it was about 12,000. Would you expect the Dow in 2007 to be more or less likely to move up or down by more than 40 points in a day than in 1990? Does this mean the market was riskier in 2007 than it was in 1990? (*LO2*)

11. **Maturity Premiums.** Investments in long-term government bonds produced a negative average return during the period 1977–1981. How should we interpret this? Did bond investors in 1977 expect to earn a negative maturity premium? What do these 5 years' bond returns tell us about the normal future maturity premium? (*LO1*)

12. **Risk Premiums.** What will happen to the opportunity cost of capital if investors suddenly become especially conservative and less willing to bear investment risk? (*LO1*)

13. **Risk Premiums and Discount Rates.** Top hedge fund manager Diana Sauros believes that a stock with the same market risk as the S&P 500 will sell at year-end at a price of $50. The stock will pay a dividend at year-end of $2. What price should she be willing to pay for the stock today? (*Hint:* Start by checking today's 1-year Treasury rates.) (*LO1*)

14. **Scenario Analysis.** The common stock of Leaning Tower of Pita, Inc., a restaurant chain, will generate the following payoffs to investors next year: (*LO1*)

	Dividend	Stock Price
Boom	$5	$195
Normal economy	2	100
Recession	0	0

    The company goes out of business if a recession hits. Calculate the expected rate of return and standard deviation of return to Leaning Tower of Pita shareholders. Assume for simplicity that the three possible states of the economy are equally likely. The stock is selling today for $80.

15. **Portfolio Risk.** Who would view the stock of Leaning Tower of Pita (see Practice Problem 14) as a risk-reducing investment—the owner of a gambling casino or a successful bankruptcy lawyer? Explain. (*LO3*)

16. **Scenario Analysis.** The common stock of Escapist Films sells for $25 a share and offers the following payoffs next year: (*LO3*)

	Dividend	Stock Price
Boom	0	$18
Normal economy	$1	26
Recession	3	34

www.mhhe.com/bmm6e

Calculate the expected return and standard deviation of Escapist. All three scenarios are equally likely. Then calculate the expected return and standard deviation of a portfolio half invested in Escapist and half in Leaning Tower of Pita (from Practice Problem 14). Show that the portfolio standard deviation is lower than either stock's. Explain why this happens.

17. **Scenario Analysis.** Consider the following scenario analysis: (*LO2*)

Scenario	Probability	Rate of Return	
		Stocks	**Bonds**
Recession	.20	−5%	+14%
Normal economy	.60	+15	+8
Boom	.20	+25	+4

    a. Is it reasonable to assume that Treasury bonds will provide higher returns in recessions than in booms?

    b. Calculate the expected rate of return and standard deviation for each investment.

    c. Which investment would *you* prefer?

18. **Portfolio Analysis.** Use the data in the previous problem and consider a portfolio with weights of .60 in stocks and .40 in bonds. (*LO3*)

    a. What is the rate of return on the portfolio in each scenario?

    b. What are the expected rate of return and standard deviation of the portfolio?

    c. Would you prefer to invest in the portfolio, in stocks only, or in bonds only?

19. **Risk Premium.** If the stock market return in 2013 turns out to be −20%, what will happen to our estimate of the "normal" risk premium? Does this make sense? (*LO1*)

20. **Diversification.** In which of the following situations would you get the largest reduction in risk by spreading your portfolio across two stocks? (*LO3*)

    a. The stock returns vary with each other.

    b. The stock returns are independent.

    c. The stock returns vary against each other.

21. **Market Risk.** Which firms of each pair below would you expect to have greater market risk? (*LO4*)

    a. General Steel or General Food Supplies.

    b. Club Med or General Cinemas.

22. **Risk and Return.** A stock will provide a rate of return of either −20% or +28%.

    a. If both possibilities are equally likely, calculate the expected return and standard deviation. (*LO2*)

    b. If Treasury bills yield 4% and investors believe that the stock offers a satisfactory expected return, what must the market risk of the stock be? (*LO4*)

23. **Unique versus Market Risk.** Sassafras Oil is staking all its remaining capital on wildcat exploration off the Côte d'Huile. There is a 10% chance of discovering a field with reserves of 50 million barrels. If it finds oil, it will immediately sell the reserves to Big Oil, at a price depending on the state of the economy. Thus the possible payoffs are as follows: (*LO4*)

	Value of Reserves, per Barrel	Value of Reserves, 50 Million Barrels	Value of Dryholes
Boom	$4	$200,000,000	0
Normal economy	5	250,000,000	0
Recession	6	300,000,000	0

Is Sassafras Oil a risky investment for a diversified investor in the stock market—compared, say, to the stock of Leaning Tower of Pita, described in Practice Problem 14? Explain.

24. **Diversification.** Go to our Online Learning Center at **www.mhhe.com/bmm6e**, and link to the material for Chapter 11, where you will find a spreadsheet containing 5 years of monthly rates of return on Shell Oil, BP (British Petroleum), and Wal-Mart. (*LO3*)

    a. What was the average return and standard deviation of returns for each firm?

Please visit us at www.mhhe.com/bmm6e

www.mhhe.com/bmm6e

b. What was the correlation of returns between each pair of firms? Try using Excel's CORREL function, which calculates the correlation between two series of numbers. Which pair of firms exhibits the highest correlation of returns? Is this surprising?

c. Now imagine that you held an equally weighted portfolio of Shell and Wal-Mart (that is, a portfolio with equal dollar investments in each stock). Compute the portfolio's rate of return for each month, and calculate the standard deviation of the portfolio's monthly rate of return. How does the portfolio standard deviation compare to the average of the standard deviations of each component stock?

d. Repeat part (c), but this time calculate the results for a portfolio of Shell and BP. Comparing your answers to (c) and (d), which pair of firms provides greater benefits from diversification? Relate your answer to the correlation coefficients you found in part (a).

STANDARD &POOR'S

1. Using Market Insight at **www.mhhe.com/edumarketinsight**, find the monthly rates of return over a 2-year period for five companies of your choice. Now assume you form an equally weighted portfolio of the five firms (i.e., a portfolio with equal investments in each firm). What is the rate of return each month on your portfolio? Compare the standard deviation of the monthly portfolio return to that of each firm and to the average standard deviation across the five firms. What do you conclude about portfolio diversification?

2. Return to the monthly returns of the five companies you chose in the previous question.

a. Using the Excel functions for average (AVERAGE) and sample standard deviation (STDEV), calculate the average and the standard deviation of the returns for each of the firms.

b. Using Excel's correlation function (CORREL), find the correlations between each pair of five stocks. What are the highest and lowest correlations?

c. Try finding correlations between pairs of stocks in the same industry. Are the correlations higher than those you found in part (b)? Is this surprising?

SOLUTIONS TO SELF-TEST QUESTIONS

11.1 The bond price at the end of the year is \$1,050. Therefore, the capital gain on each bond is \$1,050 − \$1,020 = \$30. Your dollar return is the sum of the income from the bond, \$80, plus the capital gain, \$30, or \$110. The rate of return is

$$\frac{\text{Income plus capital gain}}{\text{Original price}} = \frac{80+30}{1,020} = .108, \text{ or } 10.8\%$$

Real rate of return is

$$\frac{1+\text{nominal return}}{1+\text{inflation rate}} - 1 = \frac{1.108}{1.04} - 1 = .065, \text{ or } 6.5\%$$

11.2 The risk premium on stocks is the average return in excess of Treasury bills. It was 4.6% in period 1, 9.1% in period 2, 7.6% in period 3, and 8.7% in period 4.

11.3

Rate of Return	Deviation	Squared Deviation
+70%	+60%	3,600
+10	0	0
+10	0	0
−50	−60	3,600

Variance = average of squared deviations = 7,200/4 = 1,800

Standard deviation = square root of variance = $\sqrt{1,800}$ = 42.4, about 42%

11.4   The standard deviation should decrease because there is now a lower probability of the more extreme outcomes. The expected rate of return on the auto stock is now

$$[.3\times(-8\%)]+(.4\times5\%)+(.3\times18\%)=5\%$$

The variance is

$$[.3\times(-8-5)^2]+[.4\times(5-5)^2]+[.3\times(18-5)^2]=101.4$$

The standard deviation is $\sqrt{101.4}=10.07\%,$ which is lower than the value assuming equal probabilities of each scenario.

11.5   The gold mining stock's returns are more highly correlated with the silver mining company than with a car company. As a result, the automotive firm will offer a greater diversification benefit. The power of diversification is lowest when rates of return are highly correlated, performing well or poorly in tandem. Shifting part of the portfolio from one such firm to another has little impact on overall risk.

11.6   The success of this project depends on the experiment. Success does *not* depend on the performance of the overall economy. The experiment creates a diversifiable risk. A portfolio of many stocks will embody "bets" on many such unique risks. Some bets will work out and some will fail. Because the outcomes of these risks do not depend on common factors, such as the overall state of the economy, the risks will tend to cancel out in a well-diversified portfolio.

11.7   a. The luxury restaurant will be more sensitive to the state of the economy because expense account meals will be curtailed in a recession. Burger Queen meals should be relatively recession-proof.

b. The paint company that sells to the auto producers will be more sensitive to the state of the economy. In a downturn, auto sales fall dramatically as consumers stretch the lives of their cars. In contrast, in a recession, more people "do it themselves," which makes paint sales through small stores more stable and less sensitive to the economy.

www.mhhe.com/bmm6e

CHAPTER **12**

Risk, Return, and Capital Budgeting

LEARNING OBJECTIVES

After studying this chapter, you should be able to:

1. Measure and interpret the market risk, or beta, of a security.

2. Relate the market risk of a security to the rate of return that investors demand.

3. Calculate the opportunity cost of capital for a project.

Professor William F. Sharpe receiving the Nobel Prize in Economics. The prize was for Sharpe's development of the capital asset pricing model. This model shows how risk should be measured and provides a formula relating risk to the opportunity cost of capital.

Leif Jansson/Pica Pressfoto

In Chapter 11 we began to come to grips with the topic of risk. We made the distinction between *unique* risk and macro, or *market,* risk. Unique risk arises from events that affect only the individual firm or its immediate competitors; it can be eliminated by diversification. But regardless of how much you diversify, you cannot avoid the macroeconomic events that create market risk. This is why investors do not require a higher rate of return to compensate for unique risk but do need a higher return to persuade them to take on market risk.

How can you measure the market risk of a security or a project? We will see that market risk is usually measured by the sensitivity of the investment's returns to fluctuations in the market. We will also see that the risk premium investors demand should be proportional to this sensitivity. This relationship between risk and return is a useful way to estimate the return that investors expect from investing in common stocks.

Finally, we will distinguish between the risk of the company's securities and the risk of an individual project. We will also consider what managers should do when the risk of the project is different from that of the company's existing business.

12.1 Measuring Market Risk

market portfolio

Portfolio of all assets in the economy. In practice a broad stock market index is used to represent the market.

Changes in interest rates, government spending, oil prices, foreign exchange rates, and other macroeconomic events affect almost all companies and the returns on almost all stocks. We can therefore assess the impact of "macro" news by tracking the rate of return on a **market portfolio** of all securities. If the market is up on a particular day, then the net impact of macroeconomic changes must be positive. We know the performance of the market reflects only macro events, because firm-specific events—that is, unique risks—average out when we look at the combined performance of thousands of companies and securities.

In principle the market portfolio should contain all assets in the world economy—not just stocks but bonds, foreign securities, real estate, and so on. In practice, however, financial analysts make do with indexes of the stock market, such as the Standard & Poor's Composite Index (the S&P 500).[1]

Our task here is to define and measure the risk of *individual* common stocks. You can probably see where we are headed. Risk depends on exposure to macroeconomic events and can be measured as the sensitivity of a stock's returns to fluctuations in returns on the market portfolio. This sensitivity is called the stock's **beta.** Beta is often written as the Greek letter β.

beta

Sensitivity of a stock's return to the return on the market portfolio.

Measuring Beta

In the last chapter we looked at the variability of several individual securities. Amazon. com had the highest standard deviation and Wal-Mart had nearly the lowest. If you had held Amazon on its own, your returns would have varied three times as much as if you had held Wal-Mart. But wise investors don't put all their eggs in just one basket: They reduce their risk by diversification. An investor with a diversified portfolio will be interested in the effect each stock has on the risk of the entire portfolio.

Diversification can eliminate the risk that is unique to individual stocks but not the risk that the market as a whole may decline, carrying your stocks with it.

Some stocks are less affected than others by market fluctuations. Investment managers talk about "defensive" and "aggressive" stocks. Defensive stocks are not very sensitive to market fluctuations and therefore have low betas. In contrast, aggressive stocks amplify any market movements and have higher betas. If the market goes up, it is good to be in aggressive stocks; if it goes down, it is better to be in defensive stocks (and better still to have your money in the bank).

Aggressive stocks have high betas, betas greater than 1.0, meaning that their returns tend to respond more than one for one to changes in the return of the overall market. The betas of defensive stocks are less than 1.0. The returns of these stocks vary less than one for one with market returns. The average beta of all stocks is—no surprises here—1.0 exactly.

Now we'll show you how betas are measured.

EXAMPLE 12.1 ▶   Measuring Beta for Turbot-Charged Seafoods

Suppose we look back at the trading history of Turbot-Charged Seafoods and pick out 6 months when the return on the market portfolio was plus or minus 1%.

Month	Market Return, %	Turbot-Charged Seafood's Return, %	
1	+1	+ .8	
2	+1	+1.8	Average = .8%
3	+1	− .2	
4	−1	−1.8	
5	−1	+ .2	Average = −.8%
6	−1	− .8	

[1] We discussed the most popular stock market indexes in Section 11.2.

FIGURE 12–1 This figure is a plot of the data presented in the table in Example 12.1. Each point shows the performance of Turbot-Charged Seafoods stock when the overall market is either up or down by 1%. On average, Turbot-Charged moves in the same direction as the market, but not as far. Therefore, Turbot-Charged's beta is less than 1.0. We can measure beta by the slope of a line fitted to the points in the figure. In this case it is .8.

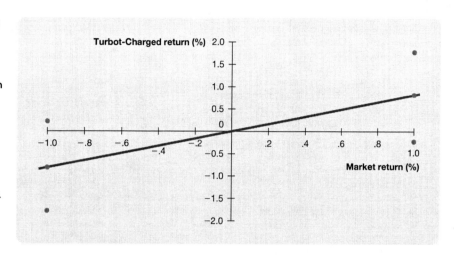

Look at Figure 12–1, where these observations are plotted. We've drawn a line through the average performance of Turbot when the market is up or down by 1%. *The slope of this line is Turbot's beta.* You can see right away that the beta is .8, because on average Turbot stock gains or loses .8% when the market is up or down by 1%. Notice that a 2-percentage-point difference in the market return (-1 to $+1$) generates on average a 1.6-percentage-point difference for Turbot shareholders ($-.8$ to $+.8$). The ratio, $1.6/2 = .8$, is beta.

In 4 months, Turbot's returns lie above or below the line in Figure 12–1. The distance from the line shows the response of Turbot's stock returns to news or events that affected Turbot but did *not* affect the overall market. For example, in month 2, investors in Turbot stock benefited from good macroeconomic news (the market was up 1%) and also from some favorable news specific to Turbot. The market rise gave a boost of .8% to Turbot stock (beta of .8 times the 1% market return). Then firm-specific news gave Turbot stockholders an extra 1% return, for a total return that month of 1.8%.

As this example illustrates, we can break down common stock returns into two parts: the part explained by market returns and the firm's beta, and the part due to news that is specific to the firm. Fluctuations in the first part reflect market risk; fluctuations in the second part reflect unique risk.

Of course, diversification can get rid of the unique risks. That's why wise investors, who don't put all their eggs in one basket, will look to Turbot's less-than-average beta and call its stock "defensive."

Self-Test 12.1

Here are 6 months' returns to stockholders in the Anchovy Queen restaurant chain:

Month	Market Return, %	Anchovy Queen Return, %
1	+1	+2.0
2	+1	+0
3	+1	+1.0
4	−1	−1.0
5	−1	+0
6	−1	−2.0

Draw a figure like Figure 12–1 and check the slope of the fitted line. What is Anchovy Queen's beta?

SPREADSHEET SOLUTIONS

Calculating Risk

Excel and most other spreadsheet programs provide built-in functions for computing a stock's beta. In columns B and C of the following spreadsheet we have entered returns for Standard & Poor's 500 Index (the S&P 500) and Ford for 6 months in 2007. (In practice, estimates based on just 6 months would be *very* unreliable. Most estimates of standard deviation and beta use something like 5 years of monthly data.)

Here are some points to note about the spreadsheet:

1. *Columns B and C.* Notice that these columns show monthly *returns* for the market index and the stock. Sometimes people mistakenly enter prices instead of returns and get nonsensical results.
2. *Row 10.* Footnote 6 in the previous chapter (see page 321) pointed out that in estimating variability from a sample of observations, it is common to make an adjustment for what is called *the loss of a degree of freedom*. In this case the appropriate formula for standard deviation would be STDEV(C3:C8).
3. *Row 11.* We have converted monthly standard deviations to annual figures by multiplying by the square root of 12 (the number of months in a year).

4. *Row 12.* In calculating beta, it is important to enter first the addresses for the stock returns (C3:C8) and then those for the market returns (B3:B8).

Spreadsheet Questions

12.1. Suppose that Ford's return in November 2007 had been −12%, and its return in September 2007 had been 5.1%. Would you expect its beta to be more or less than the value obtained in the spreadsheet? Reestimate beta with these new data, and confirm your intuition.
12.2. Suppose that Ford's return in each month had been 1% higher than the values presented in the accompanying spreadsheet. Would Ford's beta differ from the value obtained in the spreadsheet? Reestimate beta with these new data, and confirm your intuition.
12.3. Suppose that you add 1 more month of data to your spreadsheet and find that in January 2008, Ford was down 5% while the market was up 5%. Would you expect Ford's beta to be more or less than the value obtained in the spreadsheet? Reestimate beta with this new data point, and confirm your intuition.

Please visit us at www.mhhe.com/bmm6e

	A	B	C	D
1		Returns, percent		Formula used in
2	Month	S&P 500	Ford	Column C
3	Dec-07	−0.86	−10.39	
4	Nov-07	−4.40	−15.33	
5	Oct-07	1.48	4.48	
6	Sep-07	3.58	8.71	
7	Aug-07	1.29	−8.23	
8	Jul-07	−3.20	−9.66	
9				
10	Standard deviation (monthly)	2.78	8.62	=STDEVP(C3:C8)
11	Standard deviation, annualized	9.62	29.86	=C10*SQRT(12)
12	Beta		2.68	=SLOPE(C3:C8,B3:B8)
13	Correlation		0.86	=CORREL(C3:C8,B3:B8)

Real life doesn't serve up numbers quite as convenient as those in our examples so far. However, the procedure for measuring real companies' betas is exactly the same:

1. Observe rates of return, usually monthly, for the stock and the market.
2. Plot the observations as in Figure 12–1.
3. Fit a line showing the average return to the stock at different market returns.

Beta is the slope of the fitted line.

This may sound like a lot of work, but in practice computers do it for you. The nearby box shows how to use the SLOPE function in Excel to calculate a beta. Here are two real examples.

Betas for Amazon.com and Wal-Mart

Each point in Figure 12–2a shows the return on Amazon.com stock and the return on the market index in a different month. For example, the circled point shows that in July 2005, Amazon stock price rose by 36.4%, whereas the market index rose by 3.6%. Notice that more often than not Amazon outperformed the market when the index rose and underperformed the market when the index fell. Thus Amazon was a relatively aggressive, high-beta stock.

FIGURE 12–2 (a) Each point in this figure shows the returns on Amazon.com common stock and the overall market in a particular month between January 2003 and December 2007. Amazon's beta is the slope of the line fitted to these points. Amazon has a very high beta of 2.39. (b) In this plot of 60 months' returns for Wal-Mart and the overall market, the slope of the fitted line is much less than Amazon's beta in (a). Wal-Mart has a relatively low beta of .24.

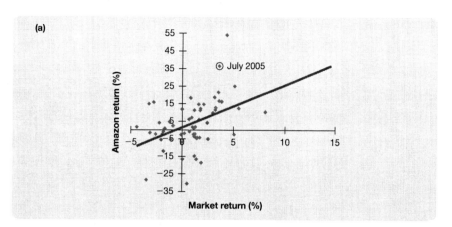

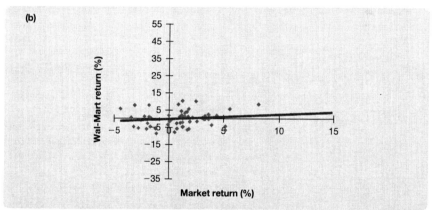

We have drawn a line of best fit through the points in the figure.[2] The slope of this line is 2.39. For each extra 1% rise in the market, Amazon stock price moved on average an extra 2.39%. For each extra 1% fall in the market, Amazon stock price fell an extra 2.39%. Thus Amazon's beta was 2.39.

Of course, Amazon's stock returns are not perfectly related to market returns. The company was also subject to unique risk, which shows up in the scatter of points around the line. Sometimes Amazon flew south while the market went north, or vice versa.

Figure 12–2*b* shows a similar plot of the monthly returns for Wal-Mart. In contrast to Amazon, Wal-Mart was a defensive, low-beta stock. It was not highly sensitive to market movements, usually lagging when the market rose and yet doing better (or less badly) when the market fell. The slope of the line of best fit shows that on average an extra 1% change in the index resulted in an extra .24% change in the price of Wal-Mart stock. Thus Wal-Mart's beta was .24.

Estimates of beta can be accessed easily, for example, at **finance.yahoo.com**, but you may find it interesting to look at Table 12–1, which shows how past market movements have affected several well-known stocks. Wal-Mart had the lowest beta: Its stock return was .24 times as sensitive as the average stock to market movements. Amazon was near the other extreme: Its return was 2.39 times as sensitive as the average stock to market movements.

---

[2] The line of best fit is usually known as a *regression* line. The slope of the line can be calculated using *ordinary least squares* regression. The dependent variable is the return on the stock (Amazon.com). The independent variable is the return on the market index, in this case the S&P 500.

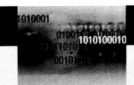

INTERNET INSIDER

Risk and Return

Source: Yahoo! Finance Web site. Reproduced with permission of Yahoo! Inc. © 2008 Yahoo! Inc. Yahoo! and the Yahoo! logo are trademarks of Yahoo! Inc.

Betas and Expected Stock Returns

You can find estimates of stock betas by logging on to **finance.yahoo.com** and looking at a company's profile. Try comparing the stock betas of Eastman Kodak (EK), The Home Depot (HD), Du Pont (DD), Altria Group (MO), and Caterpillar (CAT). Once you have read Section 12.2, use the capital asset pricing model to estimate the expected return for each of these stocks. You will need a figure for the current Treasury bill rate. You can find this also on **finance.yahoo.com** by clicking on *Bonds—Rates*. Assume for your estimates a market risk premium of 7%.

Fund Betas

Log on to **www.fidelity.com** and look at the list of mutual funds that are managed by Fidelity. Some of these funds, such as the Aggressive Growth Fund, appear from their names to be high-risk. Others, such as the Balanced Fund, appear to be low-risk. Pick several apparent high- and low-risk funds and then check whether their betas really do match the fund's name.

Total Risk and Market Risk

Ford and Amazon.com top our list of betas in Table 12–1. They were also at the top of Table 11–6, which showed the total variability of the same group of stocks. But total risk is not the same as market risk. Some of the most variable stocks have below-average betas, and vice versa.

Consider, for example, Newmont Mining. Newmont is the world's largest gold producer. The company cites the many risks that the company faces as "gold and other metals' price volatility, increased costs and variances in ore grade or recovery rates from those assumed in mining plans, as well as political and operational risks in the countries in which we operate and governmental regulation and judicial outcomes."

TABLE 12–1 Betas for selected common stocks, January 2003–December 2007

	Beta
Amazon.com	2.39
Ford	2.46
Newmont Mining	0.84
Intel	1.59
Microsoft	1.04
Dell Computer	1.27
Boeing	1.23
McDonald's	1.44
Pfizer	0.67
Du Pont	1.24
Disney	1.00
ExxonMobil	0.81
IBM	1.13
Wal-Mart	0.24
Campbell Soup	0.46
Heinz	0.59

Note: Betas are calculated from 5 years of monthly returns.

These risks are considerable and are reflected in the high standard deviation of the returns on Newmont's stock (see Table 11–6). But they are not macro risks. When the U.S. economy is booming, gold prices are just as likely to slump, and a mine in some distant part of the world may well be hit by political unrest. So, while Newmont stock has above-average volatility, it has a relatively low beta.

Portfolio Betas

Diversification decreases variability from unique risk but not from market risk. The beta of a portfolio is just an average of the betas of the securities in the portfolio, weighted by the investment in each security. For example, a portfolio comprising only two stocks would have a beta as follows:

$$\text{Beta of portfolio} = (\text{fraction of portfolio in first stock} \times \text{beta of first stock}) \quad \textbf{(12.1)}$$
$$+ (\text{fraction of portfolio in second stock}$$
$$\times \text{beta of second stock})$$

Thus a portfolio invested 50-50 in Amazon and Wal-Mart would have a beta of $(.5 \times 2.39) + (.5 \times .24) = 1.315$.

A well-diversified portfolio of stocks all with betas of 2.39, like Amazon, would still have a portfolio beta of 2.39. However, most of the individual stocks' unique risk would be diversified away. The market risk would remain, and such a portfolio would end up 2.39 times as variable as the market. For example, if the market has an annual standard deviation of 15%, a fully diversified portfolio with beta of 2.39 has a standard deviation of $2.39 \times 15 = 35.9\%$.

Portfolios with betas between 0 and 1.0 tend to move in the same direction as the market but not as far. A well-diversified portfolio of low-beta stocks like Wal-Mart all with betas of .24, has almost no unique risk and is relatively unaffected by market movements. Such a portfolio is .24 times as variable as the market.

Of course, on average stocks have a beta of 1.0. A well-diversified portfolio including all kinds of stocks, with an average beta of 1.0, has the same variability as the market index.

Self-Test 12.2

Suppose you invested an equal amount in each of the stocks shown in Table 12–1. Calculate the beta of your portfolio.

EXAMPLE 12.2 ▶   How Risky Are Mutual Funds?

You don't have to be wealthy to own a diversified portfolio. You can buy shares in one of the more than 8,000 mutual funds in the United States.

Investors buy shares of the funds, and the funds use the money to buy portfolios of securities. The returns on the portfolios are passed back to the funds' owners in proportion to their shareholdings. Therefore, the funds act like investment cooperatives, offering even the smallest investors diversification and professional management at low cost.

Let's look at the betas of two mutual funds that invest in stocks. Figure 12–3a plots the monthly returns of Vanguard's Explorer mutual fund and of the S&P index for 5 years ending in December 2007. You can see that the stocks in the Explorer fund had above-average sensitivity to market changes: They had on average a beta of 1.39.

If the Explorer fund had no unique risk, its portfolio would have been 1.39 times as variable as the market portfolio. But the fund manager wanted to beat the market, not to hold it. So the fund had not diversified away all the unique risk; there is still some scatter about the line in Figure 12–3a. As a result, the variability of the fund was somewhat more than 1.39 times that of the market.

Figure 12–3b shows the same sort of plot for Vanguard's Index Trust 500 Portfolio mutual fund. Notice that this fund has a beta of 1.0 and only a tiny residual of unique risk—the fitted line fits almost exactly because an *index fund* is designed to track the market as closely as possible. The managers of the fund do not attempt to pick good

FIGURE 12–3a The slope of the fitted line shows that investors in the Vanguard Explorer mutual fund bore market risk greater than that of the S&P 500 portfolio. Explorer's beta was 1.39. This was the average beta of the individual common stocks held by the fund. Investors also bore some unique risk, however; note the scatter of Explorer's returns above and below the fitted line.

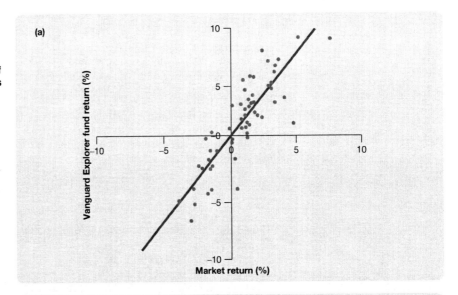

FIGURE 12–3b The Vanguard 500 Portfolio is a fully diversified index fund designed to track the performance of the market. Note the fund's beta (1.0) and the absence of unique risk. The fund's returns lie almost precisely on the fitted line relating its returns to those of the S&P 500 portfolio.

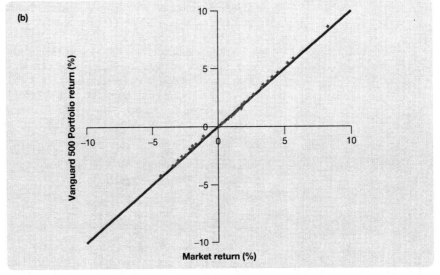

stocks but just work to achieve full diversification at very low cost. (The Vanguard index fund takes investments of as little as $3,000 and the total expenses of the fund are less than .20% of the fund's assets.) The index fund is *fully diversified*. Investors in this fund buy the market as a whole and don't have to worry at all about unique risk.

Self-Test 12.3   Suppose you could achieve full diversification in a portfolio constructed from stocks with an average beta of .5. If the standard deviation of the market is 20% per year, what is the standard deviation of the portfolio return?

12.2 Risk and Return

In Chapter 11 we looked at past returns on selected investments. The least risky investment was U.S. Treasury bills. Since the return on Treasury bills is fixed, it is unaffected by what happens to the market. Thus the beta of Treasury bills is zero. The *most* risky investment that we considered was the market portfolio of common stocks. This has average market risk: Its beta is 1.0.

FIGURE 12–4 (a) Here we begin the plot of expected rate of return against beta. The first benchmarks are Treasury bills (beta = 0) and the market portfolio (beta = 1.0). We assume a Treasury bill rate of 3% and a market return of 10%. The market risk premium is 10 − 3 = 7%. (b) A portfolio split evenly between Treasury bills and the market will have beta = .5 and an expected return of 6.5% (point X). A portfolio invested 20% in the market and 80% in Treasury bills has beta = .2 and an expected rate of return of 4.4% (point Y). Note that the expected rate of return on any portfolio mixing Treasury bills and the market lies on a straight line. The risk premium is proportional to the portfolio beta.

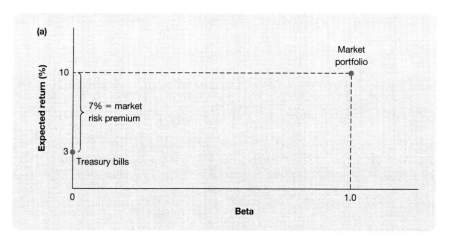

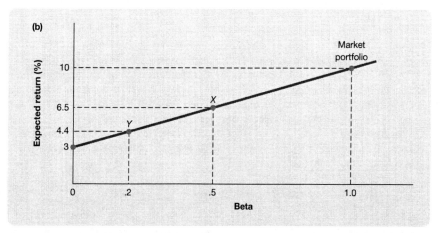

Wise investors don't run risks just for fun. They are playing with real money and therefore require a higher return from the market portfolio than from Treasury bills. The difference between the return on the market and the interest rate on bills is termed the **market risk premium.** Over the past century the average market risk premium has been 7.6% a year. Of course, there is plenty of scope for argument as to whether the past century constitutes a typical period, but we will just assume here that the normal risk premium is a nice round 7%, that is, 7% is the additional return that an investor could reasonably expect from investing in the stock market rather than Treasury bills.

In Figure 12–4a we have plotted the risk and expected return from Treasury bills and the market portfolio. You can see that Treasury bills have a beta of zero and a risk-free return; we'll assume that return is 3%. The market portfolio has a beta of 1.0 and an assumed expected return of 10%.[3]

Now, given these two benchmarks, what expected rate of return should an investor require from a portfolio that is equally divided between Treasury bills and the market? Halfway between, of course. Thus in Figure 12–4b we have drawn a straight line through the Treasury bill return and the expected market return. The portfolio (marked with an X) would have a beta of .5 and an expected return of 6.5%. This includes a risk premium of 3.5% above the Treasury bill return of 3%.

You can calculate this return as follows: Start with the difference between the expected market return r_m and the Treasury bill rate r_f. This is the expected market risk premium:

$$\text{Market risk premium} = r_m - r_f = 10\% - 3\% = 7\%$$

market risk premium
Risk premium of market portfolio. Difference between market return and return on risk-free Treasury bills.

---

[3] We assumed that the risk premium on the market is about 7%. With a 3% Treasury bill rate, the expected market return would be 3 + 7 = 10%.

Beta measures risk relative to the market. Therefore, the expected risk premium equals beta times the market risk premium:

$$\text{Risk premium} = r - r_f = \beta(r_m - r_f)$$

With a beta of .5 and a market risk premium of 7%,

$$\text{Risk premium} = \beta(r_m - r_f) = .5 \times 7\% = 3.5\%$$

The total expected rate of return is the sum of the risk-free rate and the risk premium:

$$\text{Expected return} = \text{risk-free rate} + \text{risk premium} \qquad (12.2)$$
$$r = r_f + \beta(r_m - r_f)$$
$$= 3\% + 3.5\% = 6.5\%$$

You could have calculated the expected rate of return in one step from this formula:

$$\text{Expected return} = r = r_f + \beta(r_m - r_f)$$
$$= 3\% + (.5 \times 7\%) = 6.5\%$$

capital asset pricing model (CAPM)
Theory of the relationship between risk and return which states that the expected risk premium on any security equals its beta times the market risk premium.

This basic relationship should hold not only for our portfolios of Treasury bills and the market, but for *any* asset. This conclusion is known as the **capital asset pricing model**, or **CAPM**. The CAPM has a simple interpretation: **The expected rates of return demanded by investors depend on two things: (1) compensation for the time value of money (the risk-free rate r_f) and (2) a risk premium, which depends on beta and the market risk premium.**

Note that the expected rate of return on an asset with $\beta = 1.0$ is just the market return. With a risk-free rate of 3% and market risk premium of 7%,

$$r = r_f + \beta(r_m - r_f)$$
$$= 3\% + (1 \times 7\%) = 10\%$$

Self-Test 12.4

What are the risk premium and expected rate of return on a stock with $\beta = 1.5$? Assume a Treasury bill rate of 6% and a market risk premium of 7%.

Why the CAPM Makes Sense

The CAPM assumes that the stock market is dominated by well-diversified investors who are concerned only with market risk. That is reasonable in a stock market where trading is dominated by large institutions and even small fry can diversify at very low cost. The following example shows why in this case the CAPM makes sense.

EXAMPLE 12.3 ▶   How Would You Invest $1 Million?

Have you ever daydreamed about receiving a $1 million check, no strings attached, from an unknown benefactor? Let's daydream about how you would invest it.

We have two good candidates: Treasury bills, which offer an absolutely safe return, and the market portfolio (possibly via the Vanguard index fund discussed earlier in this chapter). The market has generated superior returns on average, but those returns have fluctuated a lot. (Look back to Figure 11–4.) So your investment policy is going to depend on your tolerance for risk.

If you're a wimp, you may invest only part of your money in the market portfolio and lend the remainder to the government by buying Treasury bills. Suppose that you invest 20% of your money in the market portfolio and put the other 80% in U.S. Treasury bills.

Then the beta of your portfolio will be a mixture of the beta of the market ($\beta_{\text{market}} = 1.0$) and the beta of the T-bills ($\beta_{\text{T-bills}} = 0$):

$$\text{Beta of portfolio} = \left(\begin{array}{c}\text{proportion} \\ \text{in market}\end{array} \times \begin{array}{c}\text{beta of} \\ \text{market}\end{array}\right) + \left(\begin{array}{c}\text{proportion} \\ \text{in T-bills}\end{array} \times \begin{array}{c}\text{beta of} \\ \text{T-bills}\end{array}\right)$$

$$\beta = (.2 \times \beta_{\text{market}}) \qquad\qquad + (.8 \times \beta_{\text{T-bills}})$$
$$= (.2 \times 1.0) \qquad\qquad + (.8 \times 0) = .20$$

The fraction of funds that you invest in the market also affects your expected return. If you invest your entire million in the market portfolio, you earn the full market risk premium. But if you invest only 20% of your money in the market, you earn only 20% of the risk premium.

$$\begin{array}{c}\text{Expected} \\ \text{risk premium} \\ \text{on portfolio}\end{array} = \left(\begin{array}{c}\text{proportion in} \\ \text{market}\end{array} \times \begin{array}{c}\text{market risk} \\ \text{premium}\end{array}\right) + \left(\begin{array}{c}\text{proportion in} \\ \text{T-bills}\end{array} \times \begin{array}{c}\text{risk premium} \\ \text{on T-bills}\end{array}\right)$$

$$= (.2 \times \text{expected market risk premium}) + (.8 \times 0)$$
$$= .2 \times \text{expected market risk premium}$$
$$= .2 \times 7 = 1.4\%$$

The expected return on your portfolio is equal to the risk-free interest rate plus the expected risk premium:

$$\text{Expected portfolio return} = r_{\text{portfolio}} = 3 + 1.4 = 4.4\%$$

In Figure 12–4b we show the beta and expected return on this portfolio by the letter Y.

The Security Market Line

Example 12.3 illustrates a general point: By investing some proportion of your money in the market portfolio and lending (or borrowing)[4] the balance, you can obtain any combination of risk and expected return along the sloping line in Figure 12–5. This line is generally known as the **security market line.**

security market line
Relationship between
expected return and beta.

Self-Test 12.5

How would you construct a portfolio with a beta of .25? What is the expected return to this strategy? Assume Treasury bills yield 6% and the market risk premium is 7%.

The security market line describes the expected returns and risks from investing different fractions of your funds in the market. It also sets a standard for other investments. Investors will be willing to hold other investments only if they offer equally

---

[4] Notice that the security market line extends above the market return at $\beta = 1.0$. How would you generate a portfolio with, say, $\beta = 2.0$? It's easy, but it's risky. Suppose you borrow \$1 million and invest the loan plus \$1 million in the market portfolio. That gives you \$2 million invested and a \$1 million liability. Your portfolio now has a beta of 2.0:

$$\text{Beta of portfolio} = (\text{proportion in market} \times \text{beta of market}) + (\text{proportion in loan} \times \text{beta of loan})$$
$$\beta = (2 \times \beta_{\text{market}}) + (-1 \times \beta_{\text{loan}})$$
$$= (2 \times 1.0) + (-1 \times 0) = 2$$

Notice that the proportion in the loan is negative because you are borrowing, not lending money.

By the way, borrowing from a bank or stockbroker would not be difficult or unduly expensive as long as you put up your \$2 million stock portfolio as security for the loan.

Can you calculate the risk premium and the expected rate of return on this borrow-and-invest strategy?

FIGURE 12–5 The security market line shows how expected rate of return depends on beta. According to the capital asset pricing model, expected rates of return for all securities and all portfolios lie on this line.

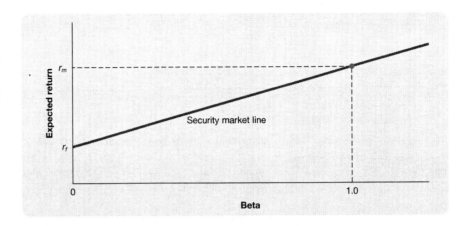

good prospects. Thus the required risk premium for *any* investment is given by the security market line:

Risk premium on investment = beta × expected market risk premium

Look back to Figure 12–4*b*, which suggests that an individual common stock with $\beta = .5$ must offer a 6.5% expected rate of return when Treasury bills yield 3% and the market risk premium is 7%. You can now see why this has to be so. If that stock offered a lower rate of return, nobody would buy even a little of it—they could get 6.5% just by investing 50–50 in Treasury bills and the market. And if nobody wants to hold the stock, its price has to drop. A lower price means a better buy for investors, that is, a higher rate of return. The price will fall until the stock's expected rate of return is pushed up to 6.5%. At that price and expected return the CAPM holds.

If, on the other hand, our stock offered more than 6.5%, diversified investors would want to buy more of it. That would push the price up and the expected return down to the levels predicted by the CAPM.

This reasoning holds for stocks with any beta. That's why the CAPM makes sense, and why the expected risk premium on an investment should be proportional to its beta.

Self-Test 12.6

Suppose you invest $400,000 in Treasury bills and $600,000 in the market portfolio. What is the return on your portfolio if bills yield 6% and the expected return on the market is 13%? What does the return on this portfolio imply for the expected return on individual stocks with betas of .6?

How Well Does the CAPM Work?

The basic idea behind the capital asset pricing model is that investors expect a reward for both waiting and worrying. The greater the worry, the greater the expected return. If you invest in a risk-free Treasury bill, you just receive the rate of interest. That's the reward for waiting. When you invest in risky stocks, you can expect an extra return or risk premium for worrying. The capital asset pricing model states that this risk premium is equal to the stock's beta times the market risk premium. Therefore,

Expected return on stock = risk-free interest rate + (beta × market risk premium)
$$r = r_f + \beta(r_m - r_f)$$

How well does the CAPM work in practice? Do the returns on stocks with betas of .5 on average lie halfway between the return on the market portfolio and the interest rate on Treasury bills? Unfortunately, the evidence is conflicting. Let's look back to the actual returns earned by investors in low-beta stocks and in high-beta stocks.

FIGURE 12–6 The capital asset pricing model states that the expected risk premium from any investment should lie on the security market line. The dots show the actual average risk premium from portfolios with different betas. The high-beta portfolios generated higher returns, just as predicted by the CAPM. But the high-beta portfolios plotted below the market line and four of the five low-beta portfolios plotted above. A line fitted to the 10 portfolio returns would be "flatter" than the security market line.

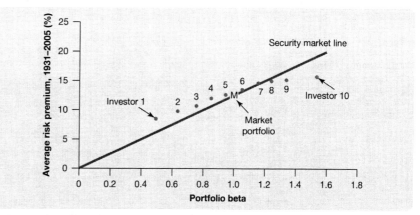

Source: F. Black, "Beta and Return," *Journal of Portfolio Management* 20 (Fall 1993), pp. 8–18. We are grateful to Adam Kolasinski for recalculating and extending the plots.

Imagine that in 1931 ten investors gathered together in a Wall Street bar and agreed to establish investment trust funds for their children. Each investor decided to follow a different strategy. Investor 1 opted to buy the 10% of the New York Stock Exchange stocks with the lowest estimated betas; investor 2 chose the 10% with the next-lowest betas; and so on, up to investor 10, who proposed to buy the stocks with the highest betas. They also planned that at the end of each year they would reestimate the betas of all NYSE stocks and reconstitute their portfolios. And so they parted with much cordiality and good wishes.

In time the 10 investors all passed away, but their children agreed to meet in early 2006 in the same bar to compare the performance of their portfolios. Figure 12–6 shows how they fared. Investor 1's portfolio turned out to be much less risky than the market; its beta was only .49. However, investor 1 also realized the lowest return, 8.5% above the risk-free rate of interest. At the other extreme, the beta of investor 10's portfolio was 1.53, about three times that of investor 1's portfolio. But investor 10 was rewarded with the highest return, averaging 15.6% a year above the interest rate. So over this 75-year period returns did indeed increase with beta.

As you can see from Figure 12–6, the market portfolio over the same 75-year period provided an average return of 12.5% above the interest rate[5] and (of course) had a beta of 1.0. The CAPM predicts that the risk premium should increase in proportion to beta, so the returns of each portfolio should lie on the upward-sloping security market line in Figure 12–6. Since the market provided a risk premium of 12.5%, investor 1's portfolio, with a beta of .49, should have provided a risk premium of about 6% and investor 10's portfolio, with a beta of 1.53, should have given a premium of over 19%. You can see that, while high-beta stocks performed better than low-beta stocks, the difference was not as great as the CAPM predicts.

Figure 12–6 provides broad support for the CAPM, though it suggests that the line relating return to beta has been too flat. But recent years have been less kind to the CAPM. For example, if the 10 friends had invested their cash in 1966 rather than 1931, there would have been very little relation between their portfolio returns and beta.[6] Does this imply that there has been a fundamental change in the relation between risk and return in the last 40 years, or did high-beta stocks just happen to perform worse during these years than investors expected? It is hard to be sure.

---

[5] In Figure 12–6 the stocks in the "market portfolio" are weighted equally. Since the stocks of small firms have provided higher average returns than those of large firms, the risk premium on an equally weighted index is higher than that on a value-weighted index. This is one reason for the difference between the 12.5% market risk premium in Figure 12–6 and the 7.6% premium reported in Table 11–1.

[6] During this later period, the returns to the first seven investors increased in line with beta. However, the highest beta portfolios performed poorly.

352   **Part Three**   Risk

FIGURE 12–7 The purple
line shows the cumulative
difference between the returns
on small-firm and large-firm
stocks from 1926 to September
2007. The orange line shows
the cumulative difference
between the returns on high-
book-to-market-value stocks
and low-book-to-market-
value stocks.

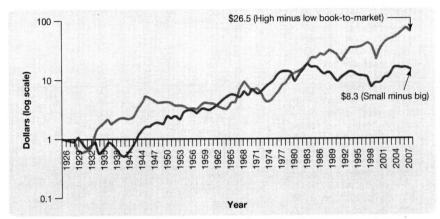

Source: **mba.tuck.dartmouth.edu/pages/faculty/ken.french/data_library.html.** Used by permission of
Kenneth R. French.

There is little doubt that the CAPM is too simple to capture everything that is going
on in the market. For example, look at Figure 12–7. The purple line shows the cumulative difference between the returns on small-firm stocks and large-firm stocks. If you
had bought the shares with the smallest market capitalizations and sold those with the
largest capitalizations, this is how your wealth would have changed. You can see that
small-cap stocks did not always do well, but over the long haul their owners have made
substantially higher returns. Since the end of 1926 the average annual difference between
the returns on the two groups of stocks has been 3.7%. Now look at the orange line in
Figure 12–7, which shows the cumulative difference between the returns on value stocks
and growth stocks. *Value stocks* here are defined as those with high ratios of book value
to market value. *Growth stocks* are those with low ratios of book to market. Notice that
value stocks have provided a higher long-run return than growth stocks. Since 1926 the
average annual difference between returns on value and growth stocks has been 5.3%.

The superior performance of small-firm stocks and value stocks does not fit well
with the CAPM, which predicts that beta is the *only* reason that expected returns differ. If investors *expected* the returns to depend on firm size or book-to-market ratios,
then the simple version of the capital asset pricing model cannot be the whole truth.

What's going on here? It is hard to say. Defenders of the capital asset pricing model
emphasize that it is concerned with *expected* returns, whereas we can observe only *actual*
returns. Actual returns reflect expectations, but they also embody lots of "noise"—the
steady flow of surprises that conceal whether on average investors have received the
returns that they expected. Thus, when we observe that in the past small-firm stocks and
value stocks have provided superior performance, we can't be sure whether this was simply a coincidence or whether investors have required a higher return to hold these stocks.

Such debates have prompted headlines like "Is Beta Dead?" in the business press. It
is not the first time that beta has been declared dead, but the CAPM remains the leading model for estimating required returns. Only strong theories can have more than
one funeral.

The CAPM is not the only model of risk and return. It has several brothers and
sisters as well as second cousins. However, the CAPM captures in a simple way two
fundamental ideas. First, almost everyone agrees that investors require some extra
return for taking on risk. Second, investors appear to be concerned principally with the
market risk that they cannot eliminate by diversification. That is why financial managers rely on the capital asset pricing model as a good rule of thumb.

Using the CAPM to Estimate Expected Returns

To calculate the returns that investors are expecting from particular stocks, we need
three numbers—the risk-free interest rate, the expected market risk premium, and

TABLE 12–2 Expected rates of return

	Beta	Expected Return
Amazon.com	2.39	19.8
Ford	2.46	20.2
Newmont Mining	0.84	8.9
Intel	1.59	14.1
Microsoft	1.04	10.3
Dell Computer	1.27	11.9
Boeing	1.23	11.6
McDonald's	1.44	13.1
Pfizer	0.67	7.7
Du Pont	1.24	11.7
Disney	1.00	10.0
ExxonMobil	0.81	8.7
IBM	1.13	10.9
Wal-Mart	0.24	4.7
Campbell Suop	0.46	6.2
Heinz	0.59	7.1

Note: Expected return $= r = r_f + \beta(r_m - r_f) = 3\% + \beta \times 7\%$.

beta. Suppose that the interest rate on Treasury bills is about 3% and that the market risk premium is about 7%. Now look back to Table 12–1, where we gave you betas of several stocks. Table 12–2 puts these numbers together to give an estimate of the expected return from each stock. Let's take Dell Computer as an example:

$$\text{Expected return on Dell} = \text{risk-free interest rate} + \left(\text{beta} \times \begin{array}{c}\text{expected market}\\\text{risk premium}\end{array}\right)$$

$$r = 3\% + (1.27 \times 7\%) = 11.9\%$$

Of our sample of companies, Ford and Amazon had the highest betas. Investors in these two stocks required compensation for taking on the extra market risk. Table 12–2 suggests that the expected rate of return from Ford and Amazon was around 20%, not far from double the figure for Dell.

12.3 Capital Budgeting and Project Risk

We have seen that the firm faces a trade-off. It can either buy new plant and equipment or return cash to its shareholders, who can then invest the money for themselves in the capital market. When the company invests the cash, shareholders can't invest these funds in the capital market. The return that shareholders give up by keeping their money in the company is therefore called the *opportunity cost of capital.* Shareholders need the company to earn at least the opportunity cost of capital on its investments.

We have referred loosely to the return that investors could expect to earn by buying securities. But there are thousands of different securities that investors can buy. The expected return on each of these securities depends on its risk. So we need to redefine the opportunity cost of capital for a project, *r*, as the expected return on a security that has a similar level of risk to that of the project. The capital asset pricing model tells us how to calculate this.

company cost of capital
Expected rate of return demanded by investors in a company, determined by the average risk of the company's securities.

Company versus Project Risk

Many companies estimate the rate of return required by investors in their securities and use this **company cost of capital** to discount the cash flows on all new projects.

Because investors require a higher rate of return from a risky company, risky firms will have a higher company cost of capital and will set a higher discount rate for their new investment opportunities. For example, on past evidence Dell has a beta of 1.27; the corresponding expected rate of return is about 11.9% (see Table 12–2). According to the company cost of capital rule, Dell should use an 11.9% cost of capital to calculate project NPVs.

This is a step in the right direction, but we must take care when the firm has issued securities other than equity.[7] Moreover, this approach can get a firm in trouble if its new projects do not have the same risk as its existing business. Dell's beta reflects investors' estimate of the risk of the computer hardware business, and its company cost of capital is the return that investors require for taking on this risk. If Dell is considering an expansion of its regular business, it makes sense to discount expected cash flows by the company cost of capital. But suppose Dell is wondering whether to branch out into production of pharmaceuticals. Its beta tells us nothing about the **project cost of capital.** That depends on the risk of the pharmaceutical business and the return that shareholders require from investing in such a business.

project cost of capital
Minimum acceptable expected rate of return on a project given its risk.

Self-Test 12.7

Dell is contemplating an expansion of its existing business. The investment is forecast to produce cash flows of $50 million a year for each of 10 years. What is its present value? Use data from Table 12–2.

The project cost of capital depends on the use to which that capital is put. Therefore, it depends on the risk of the project—not on the risk of the company. If a company invests in a low-risk project, it should discount the cash flows at a correspondingly low cost of capital. If it invests in a high-risk project, those cash flows should be discounted at a high cost of capital. Many companies use the company cost of capital as a measure of the return that they require on a "typical" capital investment. They then adjust the required return up or down depending on the risk of the particular project.

Self-Test 12.8

The company cost of capital for Dell Computer is about 11.9% (see Table 12–2); for Pfizer it is about 7.7%. What would be the more reasonable discount rate for Dell to use for a proposed move into pharmaceutical production? Why?

EXAMPLE 12.4 ▶ Estimating the Opportunity Cost of Capital for a Project

Suppose that Dell is contemplating investment in a new project. You have forecast the cash flows on the project and calculated that the internal rate of return is 11%. We assume that Treasury bills offer a return of 3% and that the expected market risk premium is 7%. Should Dell go ahead with the project?

To answer this question, you need the opportunity cost of capital, r. You start with the *project's* beta. For example, if the project is a sure thing, its beta is zero and the cost of capital equals the interest rate on Treasury bills:

$$r = r_f + \beta(r_m - r_f) = 3 + (0 \times 7) = 3\%$$

If the project offers an expected return of 11% when the cost of capital is 3%, Dell should obviously go ahead.[8] But if you had compared this project's return with

---

[7] We could ignore this complication in the case of Dell, because Dell is financed primarily by common stock. Therefore, the risk of its assets equals the risk of its stock. But most companies issue a mix of debt and common stock.

[8] In Chapter 8 we described some special cases where you should prefer projects that offer a *lower* internal rate of return than the cost of capital. We assume here that your project is a "normal" one and that you prefer high IRRs to low ones.

Dell's 11.9% *company* cost of capital, you would have wrongly concluded that it was not worthwhile.

Surefire projects rarely occur outside finance texts. So let's think about the cost of capital if the project has the same risk as the market portfolio. In this case beta is 1.0, and the cost of capital is the expected return on the market:

$$r = 3 + (1.0 \times 7) = 10\%$$

The project appears less attractive than before but still worth doing.

The project is attractive because, as Figure 12–8 shows, its expected rate of return lies above the security market line. The project offers a higher return than investors can reasonably expect elsewhere on equally risky investments. Therefore, it is a positive-NPV investment.

The security market line provides a standard for project acceptance. If the project's expected return lies above the security market line, then it is higher than investors could expect to earn by investing their funds in the capital market, and the project is an attractive investment opportunity.

Determinants of Project Risk

We have seen that the company cost of capital is the correct discount rate for projects that have the same risk as the company's existing business but *not* for those projects that are safer or riskier than the company's average. How do we know whether a project is unusually risky? Estimating project risk is never going to be an exact science, but here are two things to bear in mind.

First, we saw in Chapter 10 that operating leverage increases the risk of a project. When a large fraction of your costs is fixed, any change in revenues can have a dramatic effect on earnings. Therefore, projects that involve high fixed costs tend to have higher betas.

Second, many people intuitively associate risk with the variability of earnings. But much of this variability reflects diversifiable risk. Lone prospectors in search of gold look forward to extremely uncertain future earnings, but whether they strike it rich is not likely to depend on the performance of the rest of the economy. These investments (like Newmont Mining) have a high standard deviation but a low beta.

What matters is the strength of the relationship between the firm's earnings and the aggregate earnings of all firms. Cyclical businesses, whose revenues and earnings are strongly dependent on the state of the economy, tend to have high betas and a high cost of capital. By contrast, businesses that produce essentials, such as food, beer, and cosmetics, are less affected by the state of the economy. They tend to have low betas and a low cost of capital.

FIGURE 12–8 The expected return of this project is more than the expected return one could earn on stock market investments with the same market risk (beta). Therefore, the project's expected return lies above the security market line, and the project should be accepted.

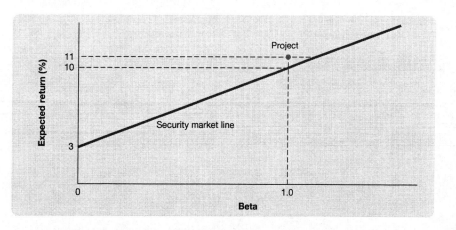

Don't Add Fudge Factors to Discount Rates

Risk to an investor arises because an investment adds to the spread of possible portfolio returns. To a diversified investor, risk is predominantly market risk. But in everyday usage *risk* simply means "bad outcome." People think of the "risks" of a project as the things that can go wrong. For example,

- A geologist looking for oil worries about the risk of a dry hole.
- A pharmaceutical manufacturer worries about the risk that a new drug which reverses balding may not be approved by the Food and Drug Administration.
- The owner of a hotel in a politically unstable part of the world worries about the political risk of expropriation.

Managers sometimes add fudge factors to discount rates to account for worries such as these.

This sort of adjustment makes us nervous. First, the bad outcomes we cited appear to reflect diversifiable risks that would not affect the expected rate of return demanded by investors. Second, the need for an adjustment in the discount rate usually arises because managers fail to give bad outcomes their due weight in cash-flow forecasts. They then try to offset that mistake by adding a fudge factor to the discount rate. For example, if a manager is worried about the possibility of a bad outcome such as a dry hole in oil exploration, he or she may reduce the value of the project by using a higher discount rate. That's not the way to do it. Instead, the possibility of the dry hole should be included in the calculation of the expected cash flows to be derived from the well. Suppose that there is a 50% chance of a dry hole and a 50% chance that the well will produce oil worth $20 million. Then the *expected* cash flow is not $20 million but $(.5 \times 0) + (.5 \times 20) = \$10$ million. You should discount the $10 million expected cash flow at the opportunity cost of capital; it does not make sense to discount the $20 million using a fudged discount rate.

Expected cash-flow forecasts should already reflect the probabilities of *all* possible outcomes, good and bad. If the cash-flow forecasts are prepared properly, the discount rate should reflect only the market risk of the project. It should not be fudged to offset errors or biases in the cash-flow forecast.

SUMMARY

How can you measure and interpret the market risk, or beta, of a security? *(LO1)*

The contribution of a security to the risk of a diversified portfolio depends on its market risk. But not all securities are equally affected by fluctuations in the market. The sensitivity of a stock to market movements is known as **beta.** Stocks with a beta greater than 1.0 are particularly sensitive to market fluctuations. Those with a beta of less than 1.0 are not so sensitive to such movements. The average beta of all stocks is 1.0.

What is the relationship between the market risk of a security and the rate of return that investors demand of that security? *(LO2)*

The extra return that investors require for taking risk is known as the risk premium. The **market risk premium**—that is, the risk premium on the **market portfolio**—averaged 7.6% between 1900 and 2007. The **capital asset pricing model** states that the expected risk premium of an investment should be proportional to both its beta and the market risk premium. The expected rate of return from any investment is equal to the risk-free interest rate plus the risk premium, so the **CAPM** boils down to

$$r = r_f + \beta(r_m - r_f)$$

The **security market line** is the graphical representation of the CAPM equation. The security market line relates the expected return investors demand of a security to its beta.

How can a manager calculate the opportunity cost of capital for a project? *(LO3)*

The opportunity cost of capital is the return that investors give up by investing in the project rather than in securities of equivalent risk. Financial managers use the capital asset pricing model to estimate the opportunity cost of capital. The **company cost of capital** is the expected rate of return demanded by investors in a company. It depends on the *average* risk of the company's assets and operations.

The opportunity cost of capital is determined by the use to which the capital is put. Therefore, required rates of return depend on the risk of the project, not on the risk of the firm's existing business. The **project cost of capital** is the minimum acceptable expected rate of return on a project given its risk.

Your cash-flow forecasts should already factor in the chances of pleasant and unpleasant surprises. Potential bad outcomes should be reflected in the discount rate only to the extent that they affect beta.

LISTING OF EQUATIONS

12.1 Beta of portfolio = (fraction of portfolio in first stock × beta of first stock)
+ (fraction of portfolio in second stock × beta of second stock)

12.2 Expected return = risk-free rate + risk premium
$$r = r_f + \beta(r_m - r_f)$$

QUESTIONS

QUIZ

1. **Risk and Return.** True or false? Explain or qualify as necessary. (*LO2*)
   a. Investors demand higher expected rates of return on stocks with more variable rates of return.
   b. The capital asset pricing model predicts that a security with a beta of zero will provide an expected return of zero.
   c. An investor who puts $10,000 in Treasury bills and $20,000 in the market portfolio will have a portfolio beta of 2.0.
   d. Investors demand higher expected rates of return from stocks with returns that are highly exposed to macroeconomic changes.
   e. Investors demand higher expected rates of return from stocks with returns that are very sensitive to fluctuations in the stock market.

2. **Diversifiable Risk.** In light of what you've learned about market versus diversifiable (unique) risks, explain why an insurance company has no problem in selling life insurance to individuals but is reluctant to issue policies insuring against flood damage to residents of coastal areas. Why don't the insurance companies simply charge coastal residents a premium that reflects the actuarial probability of damage from hurricanes and other storms? (*LO1*)

3. **Unique versus Market Risk.** Figure 12–9 plots monthly rates of return from 2003 to 2007 for the Snake Oil mutual fund. Was this fund well-diversified? Explain. (*LO1*)

FIGURE 12–9 Monthly rates of return for the Snake Oil mutual fund and the Standard & Poor's Composite Index. See Quiz Question 3.

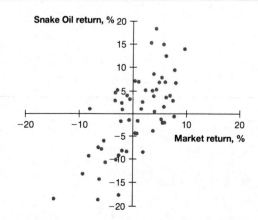

4. **Risk and Return.** Suppose that the risk premium on stocks and other securities did in fact rise with total risk (that is, the variability of returns) rather than just market risk. Explain how investors could exploit the situation to create portfolios with high expected rates of return but low levels of risk. (*LO2*)

5. **CAPM and Hurdle Rates.** A project under consideration has an internal rate of return of 14% and a beta of .6. The risk-free rate is 4%, and the expected rate of return on the market portfolio is 14%. (*LO3*)

    a. Should the project be accepted?
    b. Should the project be accepted if its beta is 1.6?
    c. Why does your answer change?

PRACTICE PROBLEMS

6. **CAPM and Valuation.** You are considering acquiring a firm that you believe can generate expected cash flows of $10,000 a year forever. However, you recognize that those cash flows are uncertain. (*LO2*)

    a. Suppose you believe that the beta of the firm is .4. How much is the firm worth if the risk-free rate is 4% and the expected rate of return on the market portfolio is 11%?
    b. By how much will you overvalue the firm if its beta is actually .6?

7. **CAPM and Expected Return.** If the risk-free rate is 6% and the expected rate of return on the market portfolio is 13%, is a security with a beta of 1.25 and an expected rate of return of 16% overpriced or underpriced? (*LO2*)

8. **Using Beta.** Investors expect the market rate of return this year to be 14%. A stock with a beta of .8 has an expected rate of return of 12%. If the market return this year turns out to be 10%, what is your best guess as to the rate of return on the stock? (*LO1*)

9. **Unique versus Market Risk.** Figure 12–10 shows plots of monthly rates of return on three stocks versus the stock market index. The beta and standard deviation of each stock is given beside its plot. (*LO1*)

    a. Which stock is safest for a diversified investor?
    b. Which stock is safest for an undiversified investor who puts all her funds in one of these stocks?
    c. Consider a portfolio with equal investments in each stock. What would this portfolio's beta have been?
    d. Consider a well-diversified portfolio made up of stocks with the same beta as Ford. What are the beta and standard deviation of this portfolio's return? The standard deviation of the market portfolio's return is 20%.
    e. What is the expected rate of return on each stock? Use the capital asset pricing model with a market risk premium of 8%. The risk-free rate of interest is 4%.

10. **Calculating Beta.** Following are several months' rates of return for Tumblehome Canoe Company. Prepare a plot like Figure 12–1. What is Tumblehome's beta? (*LO1*)

Month	Market Return, %	Tumblehome Return, %
1	0	+1
2	0	−1
3	−1	−2.5
4	−1	−0.5
5	+1	+2
6	+1	+1
7	+2	+4
8	+2	+2
9	−2	−2
10	−2	−4

www.mhhe.com/bmm6e

FIGURE 12–10 These plots show monthly rates of return for (a) Ford, (b) Newmont Mining, and (c) McDonald's, plus the market portfolio. See Practice problem 9.

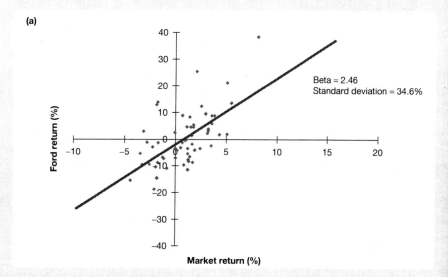

(a)

Beta = 2.46
Standard deviation = 34.6%

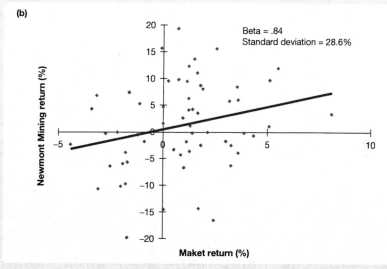

(b)

Beta = .84
Standard deviation = 28.6%

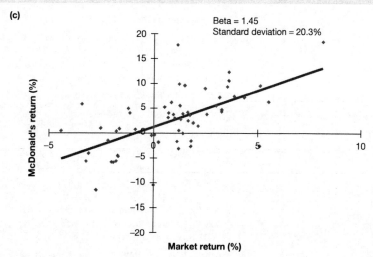

(c)

Beta = 1.45
Standard deviation = 20.3%

11. **Expected Returns.** Consider the following two scenarios for the economy and the returns in each scenario for the market portfolio, an aggressive stock A, and a defensive stock D. (*LO2*)

	Rate of Return		
Scenario	Market	Aggressive Stock A	Defensive Stock D
Bust	−8%	−10%	−6%
Boom	32	38	24

a. Find the beta of each stock. In what way is stock D defensive?

b. If each scenario is equally likely, find the expected rate of return on the market portfolio and on each stock.

c. If the T-bill rate is 4%, what does the CAPM say about the fair expected rate of return on the two stocks?

d. Which stock seems to be a better buy on the basis of your answers to (a) through (c)?

12. **CAPM and Cost of Capital.** Draw the security market line when the Treasury bill rate is 4% and the market risk premium is 7%. What are the project costs of capital for new ventures with betas of .75 and 1.75? Which of the following capital investments have positive NPVs? (*LO3*)

Project	Beta	Internal Rate of Return, %
P	1.0	14
Q	0	6
R	2.0	18
S	0.4	7
T	1.6	20

13. **CAPM and Valuation.** You are a consultant to a firm evaluating an expansion of its current business. The cash-flow forecasts (in millions of dollars) for the project are as follows: (*LO3*)

Years	Cash Flow
0	−100
1–10	+ 15

On the basis of the behavior of the firm's stock, you believe that the beta of the firm is 1.4. Assuming that the rate of return available on risk-free investments is 4% and that the expected rate of return on the market portfolio is 12%, what is the net present value of the project?

14. **CAPM and Cost of Capital.** Reconsider the project in the preceding problem. What is the project IRR? What is the cost of capital for the project? Does the accept–reject decision using IRR agree with the decision using NPV? (*LO3*)

15. **CAPM and Valuation.** A share of stock with a beta of .75 now sells for $50. Investors expect the stock to pay a year-end dividend of $2. The T-bill rate is 4%, and the market risk premium is 7%. If the stock is perceived to be fairly priced today, what must be investors' expectation of the price of the stock at the end of the year? (*LO2*)

16. **CAPM and Expected Return.** Reconsider the stock in the preceding problem. Suppose investors actually believe the stock will sell for $52 at year-end. Is the stock a good or bad buy? What will investors do? At what point will the stock reach an "equilibrium" at which it again is perceived as fairly priced? (*LO2*)

17. **Portfolio Risk and Return.** Suppose that the S&P 500, with a beta of 1.0, has an expected return of 13% and T-bills provide a risk-free return of 5%. (*LO2*)

a. What would be the expected return and beta of portfolios constructed from these two assets with weights in the S&P 500 of (i) 0; (ii) .25; (iii) .5; (iv) .75; (v) 1.0?

b. On the basis of your answer to (a), what is the trade-off between risk and return, that is, how does expected return vary with beta?

c. What does your answer to (b) have to do with the security market line relationship?

18. **Portfolio Risk and Return.** Suppose that the S&P 500, with a beta of 1.0, has an expected return of 10% and T-bills provide a risk-free return of 4%. (*LO1*)

a. How would you construct a portfolio from these two assets with an expected return of 8%?

b. How would you construct a portfolio from these two assets with a beta of .4?

c. Show that the risk premiums of the portfolios in (a) and (b) are proportional to their betas.

19. **CAPM and Valuation.** You are considering the purchase of real estate that will provide perpetual income that should average $50,000 per year. How much will you pay for the property if you believe its market risk is the same as the market portfolio's? The T-bill rate is 5%, and the expected market return is 12.5%. (*LO3*)

20. **Risk and Return.** According to the CAPM, would the expected rate of return on a security with a beta less than zero be more or less than the risk-free interest rate? Why would investors be willing to invest in such a security? (*Hint:* Look back to the auto and gold example in Chapter 11). (*LO2*)

21. **CAPM and Expected Return.** The following table shows betas for several companies. Calculate each stock's expected rate of return using the CAPM. Assume the risk-free rate of interest is 5%. Use a 7% risk premium for the market portfolio. (*LO2*)

Company	Beta
Cisco	1.54
Citigroup	1.21
Merck	1.23
Coca-Cola	.66

22. **CAPM and Expected Return.** Stock A has a beta of .5, and investors expect it to return 5%. Stock B has a beta of 1.5, and investors expect it to return 13%. Use the CAPM to find the market risk premium and the expected rate of return on the market. (*LO2*)

23. **CAPM and Expected Return.** If the expected rate of return on the market portfolio is 13% and T-bills yield 6%, what must be the beta of a stock that investors expect to return 10%? (*LO2*)

24. **Project Cost of Capital.** Suppose Cisco is considering a new investment in the common stock of a pharmaceutical company. Which of the betas shown in the table in problem 21 is most relevant in determining the required rate of return for this venture? Explain why the expected return to Cisco stock is *not* the appropriate required return. (*LO3*)

25. **Risk and Return.** True or false? Explain or qualify as necessary. (*LO2*)

a. The expected rate of return on an investment with a beta of 2.0 is twice as high as the expected rate of return of the market portfolio.

b. The contribution of a stock to the risk of a diversified portfolio depends on the market risk of the stock.

c. If a stock's expected rate of return plots below the security market line, it is underpriced.

d. A diversified portfolio with a beta of 2.0 is twice as volatile as the market portfolio.

e. An undiversified portfolio with a beta of 2.0 is twice as volatile as the market portfolio.

26. **CAPM and Expected Return.** A mutual fund manager expects her portfolio to earn a rate of return of 11% this year. The beta of her portfolio is .8. If the rate of return available on risk-free assets is 4% and you expect the rate of return on the market portfolio to be 14%, should you invest in this mutual fund? (*LO2*)

27. **Required Rate of Return.** Reconsider the mutual fund manager in the previous problem. Explain how you would use a stock index mutual fund and a risk-free position in Treasury bills (or a money market mutual fund) to create a portfolio with the same risk as the manager's but with a higher expected rate of return. What is the rate of return on that portfolio? (*LO2*)

28. **Required Rate of Return.** In view of your answer to the preceding problem, explain why a mutual fund must be able to provide an expected rate of return in excess of that predicted by the security market line for investors to consider the fund an attractive investment opportunity. (*LO2*)

29. **CAPM.** We Do Bankruptcies is a law firm that specializes in providing advice to firms in financial distress. It prospers in recessions when other firms are struggling. Consequently, its beta is negative, −.2. (*LO2*)

a. If the interest rate on Treasury bills is 5% and the expected return on the market portfolio is 15%, what is the expected return on the shares of the law firm according to the CAPM?

b. Suppose you invested 90% of your wealth in the market portfolio and the remainder of your wealth in the shares in the law firm. What would be the beta of your portfolio?

CHALLENGE PROBLEMS

30. **Leverage and Portfolio Risk.** Footnote 4 in the chapter asks you to consider a borrow-and-invest strategy in which you use $1 million of your own money and borrow another $1 million to invest $2 million in a market index fund. If the risk-free interest rate is 4% and the expected rate of return on the market index fund is 12%, what is the risk premium and expected rate of return on the borrow-and-invest strategy? Why is the risk of this strategy twice that of simply investing your $1 million in the market index fund? (*LO2*)

eX**cel**

Please visit us at www.mhhe.com/bmm6e

31. **Beta.** Go to our Online Learning Center at **www.mhhe.com/bmm6e**, and link to the material for Chapter 12, where you will find a spreadsheet containing 5 years of monthly rates of return on Dell Computer (DELL), Consolidated Edison (ED), and the S&P 500. (*LO1*)

   a. Calculate the beta of each firm. Use Excel's SLOPE function, which fits a regression line through a scatter diagram of two series of numbers.
   b. Does the relative magnitude of each beta make sense in terms of the business risk of the two firms? Explain.

STANDARD
&POOR'S

1. Use data from Market Insight (**www.mhhe.com/edumarketinsight**) to calculate the beta of General Motors (GM). Start by obtaining the monthly rates of return of GM and the S&P 500 over the most recent 3 years. Enter these returns in an Excel spreadsheet. Plot the returns and then draw by eye the best line through the points. What is the slope of the line? How much does GM's return increase on average given a 1-percentage-point increase in the market return? Now use the regression (slope) function in Excel, calculate a regression with GM's return as the dependent variable and the S&P 500 return as the explanatory variable. What is GM's beta?

2. Go to Market Insight at **www.mhhe.com/edumarketinsight.** Enter the ticker symbol "GOOG" for Google. In the Excel Analytics section, click on *Monthly Valuation Data*. Save the monthly returns for Google and the S&P 500 in a new spreadsheet. Now calculate the beta of Google as in the previous question. Then repeat the procedure to obtain data for Anheuser-Busch (BUD), JP Morgan Chase (JPM), Union Pacific (UNP), and FedEx (FDX).

   a. Which of the stocks would you classify as defensive? Which would be classified as aggressive?
   b. Do the beta coefficients for the low-beta firms make sense given the industries in which these firms operate? Briefly explain.

SOLUTIONS TO SELF-TEST QUESTIONS

12.1 See Figure 12–11. Anchovy Queen's beta is 1.0.

12.2 A portfolio's beta is just a weighted average of the betas of the securities in the portfolio. In this case the weights are equal, since an equal amount is assumed invested in each of the stocks in Table 12–1. The average beta of these stocks is 1.15.

12.3 The standard deviation of a fully diversified portfolio's return is proportional to its beta. The standard deviation in this case is $.5 \times 20 = 10\%$.

12.4 $r = r_f + \beta(r_m - r_f) = 6 + (1.5 \times 7) = 16.5\%$

12.5 Put 25% of your money in the market portfolio and the rest in Treasury bills. The portfolio's beta is .25 and its expected return is

$$r_{portfolio} = (.75 \times 6) + (.25 \times 13) = 7.75\%$$

The expected return also may be computed as

$$r_f + \beta(r_m - r_f) = 6 + .25 \times 7 = 7.75\%$$

FIGURE 12–11 Each point shows the performance of Anchovy Queen stock when the market is up or down by 1%. On average, Anchovy Queen stock follows the market; it has a beta of 1.0.

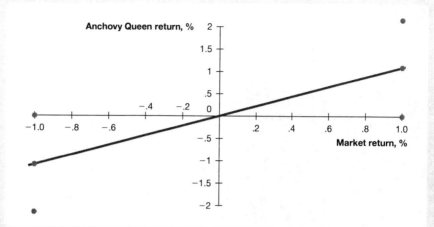

12.6 $r_{\text{portfolio}} = (.4 \times 6) + (.6 \times 13) = 10.2\%$. This portfolio's beta is .6, since \$600,000, which is 60% of the investment, is in the market portfolio. Investors in a stock with a beta of .6 would not buy it unless it also offered a rate of return of 10.2% and would rush to buy if it offered more. The stock price would adjust until the stock's expected rate of return was 10.2%.

12.7   Present value = \$50 million × 10-year annuity factor at 11.9% = \$283.7 million.

12.8   Dell should use Pfizer's cost of capital, 7.7%. Dell's company cost of capital tells us what expected rate of return investors demand from the computer hardware business. This is not the appropriate project cost of capital for its proposed venture into pharmaceuticals.

SOLUTIONS TO SPREADSHEET QUESTIONS

12.1   We would expect beta to fall from the value obtained in the spreadsheet. Ford's return in November (when the market fell) is not as bad as originally assumed, and its return in September (when the market rose) is not as good as originally assumed. In both cases, Ford's returns are less responsive to the market. In fact, beta falls to 2.07.

12.2   Ford's beta is precisely the same as the original value. Increasing the assumed return in each month by a constant does not change the typical *responsiveness* of Ford to variation in the return of the market index.

12.3   If in the additional month of data Ford is down 5% while the market is up 5%, we would expect beta to fall. In this month, Ford's stock moved in opposition to the market index. Adding this observation therefore reduces our estimate of Ford's typical response to market movements. In fact, beta falls to 1.75.

www.mhhe.com/bmm6e

CHAPTER 14

Introduction to Corporate Financing

LEARNING OBJECTIVES

After studying this chapter, you should be able to:

1. Explain why managers should assume that the securities they issue are fairly priced.

2. Interpret shareholder equity accounts in the firm's financial statements.

3. Describe voting procedures for the election of a firm's board of directors and other matters.

4. Describe the major classes of securities sold by the firm.

5. Summarize the changing ways that U.S. firms have financed their growth.

Related Web sites for this chapter can be found at www.mhhe.com/bmm6e.

There are more than 57 different kinds of securities that a company can issue.

Scott Goodwin Photography

Up to this point we have concentrated almost exclusively on the firm's capital expenditure decision. Now we move to the other side of the balance sheet to look at how the firm can finance those capital expenditures. To put it crudely, you have learned how to spend money; now you must learn how to raise it. In the next few chapters, therefore, we assume that the firm has already decided on which investment projects to accept, and we focus on the best way to finance these projects.

You will find that in some ways financing decisions are more complicated than investment decisions. You'll need to learn about the wide variety of securities that companies can issue and

the financial institutions that may buy these securities. But there are also ways in which financing decisions are easier than investment decisions. For example, financing decisions do not have the same degree of finality as investment decisions. When Ford Motor Company decides to issue a bond, it knows that it can buy it back later if second thoughts arise. It would be far more difficult for Ford to dismantle or sell an auto factory that is no longer needed.

In later chapters we will look at some of the classic finance problems, such as how much firms should borrow and what dividends they should pay their shareholders. In this chapter we set the scene with a brief overview of the types of long-term finance.

We begin our discussion of financing with a basic conceptual point. It is easier to make shareholders wealthier through your investment decisions than by your financing decisions. As we explain, competition between investors makes it difficult to find misvalued securities.

We then introduce you to the principal sources of finance, and we show how they are used by corporations. It is customary to classify these sources of finance as debt or equity. However, we will see that a simple division of sources of finance into debt and equity would miss the enormous variety of financing instruments that companies use today. For example, Table 14-1 shows the many long-term securities issued by H. J. Heinz. Yet Heinz has not come close to exhausting the menu of possible securities.

14.1 Creating Value with Financing Decisions

Smart investment decisions make shareholders wealthier. So do smart financing decisions. For example, if your company can borrow at 3% when the going rate is 4%, you have done your shareholders a good turn.

Unfortunately, this is more easily said than done. The problem is that competition in financial markets is more intense than in most product markets. In product markets, companies regularly find competitive advantages that allow positive-NPV investments. For example, a company may have only a few competitors that specialize in the same line of business in the same geographical area. Or it may be able to capitalize on patents or technology or on customer recognition and loyalty. All this opens up the opportunity to make superior profits and find projects with positive NPVs.

But there are few protected niches in *financial* markets. You can't patent the design of a new security. Moreover, in these markets you always face fast-moving competition, including all the other corporations seeking funds, to say nothing of the state, local, and federal governments, financial institutions, individuals, and foreign firms and governments that also come to New York, London, or Tokyo for financing. The investors who supply financing are numerous, and they are smart. Most likely, these investors can assess values of securities at least as well as you can.

Of course, when you borrow, you would like to pay less than the going rate of interest. But if the loan is a good deal for your shareholders, it must be a bad deal for the lenders. So what are the chances that your firm could consistently trick investors into overpaying for its securities? Pretty slim. In general, firms should assume that the securities they issue sell for their true values.

But what do we mean by *true value?* It is a potentially slippery phrase. True value does not mean ultimate future value—we do not expect investors to be fortune-tellers. It means a price that incorporates all the information *currently* available to investors. We came across this idea in Chapter 7, when we introduced the concept of *efficient capital markets* and showed how difficult it is for investors to obtain consistently superior performance. In an efficient capital market all securities are fairly priced given the information available to investors. In that case the sale of securities at their market price can never be a positive-NPV transaction.

All this means that it's harder to make or lose money by smart or stupid financing strategies. It is difficult to make money—that is, to find cheap financing—because the investors who supply the financing demand fair terms. At the same time, it's harder to lose money because competition among investors prevents any one of them from demanding more than fair terms.

TABLE 14-1 Large firms use many different kinds of securities. Look at the variety of sources of finance for H. J. Heinz.

Equity
Common stock
Preferred stock
Debt
Commercial paper
Debentures
Guaranteed notes
Remarketable debt
Euro notes
Sterling notes
New Zealand dollar notes
Bank loans

> Just remember as you read the following chapters: There are no free lunches on Wall Street. . . . and no easy answers for the financial manager who must decide which securities to issue.

14.2 Common Stock

treasury stock
Stock that has been repurchased by the company and held in its treasury.

issued shares
Shares that have been issued by the company.

outstanding shares
Shares that have been issued by the company and are held by investors.

authorized share capital
Maximum number of shares that the company is permitted to issue.

par value
Value of security shown in the company's accounts.

additional paid-in capital
Difference between issue price and par value of stock. Also called *capital surplus*.

We will illustrate the characteristics of different securities by looking at how H. J. Heinz has financed its capital expenditures. We start with common stock.

Most major corporations are far too large to be owned by one investor. For example, you would need to lay your hands on about $16 billion if you wanted to own the whole of Heinz. Heinz is owned by about 39,000 different investors, each of whom holds a number of shares of common stock. These investors are therefore known as *shareholders,* or *stockholders.* Altogether in May 2007 Heinz had outstanding about 322 million shares of common stock. Thus, if you were to buy one Heinz share, you would own 1/322,000,000, or about .0000003%, of the company. Of course, a large pension fund might hold many thousands of Heinz shares.

The 322 million shares held by investors are not the only shares that have been issued by Heinz. The company has also issued a further 109 million shares, which it later bought back from investors. These repurchased shares are held in the company's treasury and are known as **treasury stock.** The shares held by investors are said to be **issued and outstanding shares.** By contrast, the 109 million treasury shares are said to be *issued but not outstanding.*

If Heinz wishes to raise more money, it can sell more shares. However, there is a limit to the number that it can issue without getting the approval of the current shareholders. The maximum number of shares that can be issued is known as the **authorized share capital**—for Heinz, this is 600 million shares. Since Heinz has already issued 431 million shares, it can issue 169 million more without shareholders' approval.

Table 14–2 shows how the investment by Heinz's common stockholders is recorded in the company's books. The price at which each share is recorded is known as its **par value.** In Heinz's case each share has a par value of $.25. Thus the total par value of the issued shares is 431 million shares × $.25 per share = $108 million. Par value has little economic significance.[1]

The price at which new shares are sold to investors almost always exceeds par value. The difference is entered into the company's accounts as **additional paid-in capital,** or *capital surplus.* For example, if Heinz sold an additional 1 million shares at

TABLE 14–2 Book value of common stockholders' equity of H. J. Heinz Company, May 2, 2007 (figures in millions)

Common shares ($.25 par value per share)	$ 108
Additional paid-in capital	581
Retained earnings	5,779
Treasury shares at cost	(4,406)
Other	(219)
Net common equity	1,843
Note:	
Authorized shares	600
Issued shares, of which	431
Outstanding shares	322
Treasury shares	109

---

[1] Because some states do not allow companies to sell new shares below par value, par value is generally set at a low figure. Some companies even issue shares with no par value, in which case the stock is listed in the accounts at an arbitrarily determined figure.

$40 a share, the par value of the common stock would increase by 1 million × $.25 = $250,000 and additional paid-in capital would increase by 1 million × ($40 − $.25) = $39,750,000. You can see from this example that the funds raised from the stock issue are divided between par value and additional paid-in capital. Since the choice of par value in the first place was immaterial, so is the allocation between par value and additional paid-in capital.

Besides buying new stock, shareholders also indirectly contribute new capital to the firm whenever profits that could be paid out as dividends are instead plowed back into the company. Table 14–2 shows that the cumulative amount of such **retained earnings** is $5,779 million.

Heinz's books also show the amount that the company has spent to repurchase its own stock. The repurchase of the 109 million shares cost Heinz $4,406 million. This is money that has in effect been returned to shareholders.

The sum of the par value, additional paid-in capital, and retained earnings, less repurchased stock and some miscellaneous other adjustments, is known as the *net common equity* of the firm. It equals the total amount contributed directly by shareholders when the firm issued new stock and indirectly when it plowed back part of its earnings. The book value of Heinz's net common equity is $1,843 million. With 322 million shares outstanding this is equivalent to 1,843/322 = $5.72 a share. But, the market value of Heinz's stock is about $46, much higher than its book value. Evidently investors believe that Heinz's assets are worth much more than they originally cost.

retained earnings
Earnings not paid out as dividends.

Self-Test 14.1

Generic Products has had one stock issue in which it sold 100,000 shares to the public at $15 per share. Can you fill in the following table?

Common shares ($1 par value per share)	_____
Additional paid-in capital	_____
Retained earnings	_____
Net common equity	$4,500,000

Ownership of the Corporation

A corporation is owned by its common stockholders. Some of its stock is held directly by individual investors, but, as we saw in Chapter 2, the greater proportion belongs to financial institutions such as mutual funds, pension funds, and insurance companies. Their holdings are summarized again in Figure 14–1. You can see that in the United

FIGURE 14–1 Holdings of corporate equities, third quarter, 2007

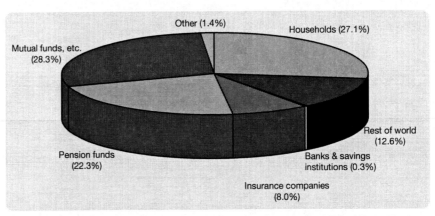

Source: Board of Governors of the Federal Reserve System, Division of Research and Statistics, "Flow of Funds Accounts," table L.213 at **www.federalreserve.gov/releases/z1/current/data.htm**.

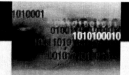

Book Value of Common Equity

In Table 14–2 we showed the book value of Heinz's common equity. You can construct a similar table for another company by looking up its annual report on the Web. An easy way to do this is to log on to **www.annualreports.com.** What is the difference between the company's outstanding and issued shares? Explain. Has the company in the past raised more money by issuing new shares or by plowing back earnings? Is that typical of U.S. public companies (see Section 14.6)?

Source: IR Solutions & Annualreports.com.

States just over 70% of common stock is held by foreign investors or U.S. financial institutions, with pension funds and mutual funds each holding over 20%.

What do we mean when we say that the stockholders *own* the corporation? First, the stockholders are entitled to whatever profits are left over after the lenders have received their entitlement. Usually the company pays out part of these profits as dividends and plows back the remainder into new investments. Shareholders hope that these investments will enable the company to earn higher profits and pay higher dividends in the future.

Second, shareholders have the ultimate control over how the company is run. Occasionally, the company must get shareholder approval before it can take certain actions. For example, it needs shareholder agreement to increase the authorized capital or to merge with another company. On most other matters, shareholder control boils down to the right to vote on appointments to the board of directors.

The board of directors usually consists of the company's top management as well as *outside directors,* who are not employed by the firm. The board is there to look after shareholders' interests. It appoints and oversees the management of the firm and meets to vote on such matters as a new share issue or the payment of a dividend. Most of the time the board will go along with the management, but in crisis situations it can be very independent. For example, when the management of RJR Nabisco announced that it wanted to take over the company, the outside directors stepped in to make sure that the company was sold to the highest bidder.

Voting Procedures

majority voting
Voting system in which each director is voted on separately.

cumulative voting
Voting system in which all votes that one shareholder is allowed to cast can be cast for one candidate for the board of directors.

In most companies stockholders elect directors by a system of **majority voting.** In this case each director is voted on separately, and stockholders can cast one vote for each share they own. In some companies directors are elected by **cumulative voting.** The directors are then voted on jointly, and the stockholders can, if they choose, cast all their votes for just one candidate. For example, suppose that there are five directors to be elected and you own 100 shares. You therefore have a total of $5 \times 100 = 500$ votes. Under majority voting you can cast a maximum of 100 votes for any one candidate. With a cumulative voting system you can cast all 500 votes for your favorite candidate. Cumulative voting makes it easier for a minority group of the stockholders to elect a director to represent their interests. That is why minority groups devote so much effort to campaigning for cumulative voting.

On many issues a simple majority of the votes cast is enough to carry the day, but there are some decisions that require a "supermajority" of, say, 75% of those eligible to vote. For example, a supermajority vote is sometimes needed to approve a merger. This makes it difficult for the firm to be taken over and therefore helps to protect the incumbent management.

Shareholders can either vote in person or appoint a proxy to vote. The issues on which they are asked to vote are rarely contested, particularly in the case of large publicly traded firms. Occasionally, however, there are **proxy contests** in which outsiders compete with the firm's existing management and directors for control of the corporation. But the odds are stacked against the outsiders, for the insiders can get the firm to pay all the costs of presenting their case and obtaining votes.

proxy contest
Takeover attempt in which outsiders compete with management for shareholders' votes.

Classes of Stock

Most companies in the United States issue just one class of common stock. But a few, such as Ford Motor and Google, have issued two classes of shares with different voting rights. For example, suppose that a firm needs fresh capital, but its management does not want to give up its controlling interest. The existing shares could be labeled "class A," and then "class B" shares with limited voting rights could be issued to outside investors.

In some countries it is fairly common for firms to issue two classes of stock with different voting rights. That may be a good thing if the controlling shareholders then use their influence to improve profitability. However, you can see the dangers here. If an idle or incompetent management has a large block of votes, it may use these votes to stay in control. Or if another corporation has a controlling stake, it may exercise its influence to gain a business advantage.

14.3 Preferred Stock

preferred stock
Stock that takes priority over common stock in regard to dividends.

net worth
Book value of common stockholders' equity plus preferred stock.

Usually when investors talk about equity or stock, they are referring to common stock. But companies may also issue **preferred stock,** and this too is part of the company's equity. The sum of Heinz's common equity and preferred stock is known as its **net worth.**

For most companies preferred stock is much less important than common stock. However, it can be a useful method of financing in mergers and certain other special situations.

Like debt, preferred stock promises a series of fixed payments to the investor and with relatively rare exceptions preferred dividends are paid in full and on time. Nevertheless, preferred stock is legally an equity security. This is because payment of a preferred dividend is within the discretion of the directors. The only obligation is that no dividends can be paid on the common stock until the preferred dividend has been paid.[2] If the company goes out of business, the preferred stockholders get in the queue after the debtholders but before the common stockholders.

Preferred stock rarely confers full voting privileges. This is an advantage to firms that want to raise new money without sharing control of the firm with the new shareholders. However, if there is any matter that affects their place in the queue, preferred stockholders usually get to vote on it. Most issues also provide the holder with some voting power if the preferred dividend is skipped.

Companies cannot deduct preferred dividends when they calculate taxable income. Like common stock dividends, preferred dividends are paid from after-tax income. For most industrial firms this is a serious deterrent to issuing preferred. However, regulated public utilities can take tax payments into account when they negotiate with regulators the rates they charge customers. So they can effectively pass the tax disadvantage of preferred on to the consumer. Preferred stock also has a particular attraction for banks, for regulators allow banks to lump preferred in with common stock when calculating whether they have sufficient equity capital.

Preferred stock does have one tax advantage. If one corporation buys another's stock, only 30% of the dividends it receives is taxed. This rule applies to dividends

---

[2] These days this obligation is usually cumulative. In other words, before the common stockholders get a cent, the firm must pay any preferred dividends that have been missed in the past.

on both common and preferred stock, but it is most important for preferred, for which returns are dominated by dividends rather than capital gains.

Suppose that your firm has surplus cash to invest. If it buys a bond, the interest will be taxed at the company's tax rate of 35%. If it buys a preferred share, it owns an asset like a bond (the preferred dividends can be viewed as "interest"), but the effective tax rate is only 30% of 35%, $.30 \times .35 = .105$, or 10.5%. It is no surprise that most preferred shares are held by corporations.

If you invest your firm's spare cash in a preferred stock, you will want to make sure that when it is time to sell the stock, it won't have plummeted in value. One problem with garden-variety preferred stock that pays a fixed dividend is that the preferred's market prices go up and down as interest rates change (because present values fall when rates rise). So one ingenious banker thought up a wrinkle: Why not link the dividend on the preferred stock to interest rates so that it goes up when interest rates rise and vice versa? The result is known as **floating-rate preferred.** If you own floating-rate preferred, you know that any change in interest rates will be counterbalanced by a change in the dividend payment, so the value of your investment is protected.

floating-rate preferred
Preferred stock paying
dividends that vary with
short-term interest rates.

Self-Test 14.2

A company in a 35% tax bracket can buy a bond yielding 10% or a preferred stock of the same firm that is priced to yield 8%. Which will provide the higher after-tax yield?

14.4 Corporate Debt

When they borrow money, companies promise to make regular interest payments and to repay the principal (that is, the original amount borrowed). **However, corporations have limited liability. By this we mean that the promise to repay the debt is not always kept. If the company gets into deep water, the company has the right to default on the debt and to hand over the company's assets to the lenders.**

Clearly it will choose bankruptcy only if the value of the assets is less than the amount of the debt. In practice, when companies go bankrupt, this handover of assets is far from straightforward. For example, when Pacific Gas and Electric filed for bankruptcy in 2004, the bankruptcy court was faced with several thousand creditors all jostling for a better place in the queue. By the time the company had emerged from bankruptcy 3 years later, it had agreed to make 2,100 separate payments resolving $8.4 billion of agreed claims and had set aside a further $1.8 billion for claims that were still under dispute.

Because lenders are not regarded as owners of the firm, they don't normally have any voting power. Also, the company's payments of interest are regarded as a cost and are therefore deducted from taxable income. Thus interest is paid out of *before-tax* income, whereas dividends on common and preferred stock are paid out of *after-tax* income. This means that the government provides a tax subsidy on the use of debt, which it does not provide on stock.

Debt Comes in Many Forms

Some orderly scheme of classification is essential to cope with the almost endless variety of debt issues. We will walk you through the major distinguishing characteristics.

Interest Rate The interest payment, or *coupon,* on most long-term loans is fixed at the time of issue. If a $1,000 bond is issued with a coupon of 10%, the firm continues to pay $100 a year regardless of how interest rates change. As we pointed out in Chapter 5, you sometimes encounter zero-coupon bonds. In this case the firm does not make a regular interest payment. It just makes a single payment at maturity. Obviously, investors pay less for zero-coupon bonds.

prime rate
Benchmark interest rate charged by banks.

Most loans from a bank and some long-term loans carry a *floating interest rate.* For example, your firm may be offered a loan at "1 percent over prime." The **prime rate** is the benchmark interest rate charged by banks to large customers with good to excellent credit. (But the largest and most creditworthy corporations can, and do, borrow at *less* than prime.) The prime rate is adjusted up and down with the general level of interest rates. When the prime rate changes, the interest on your floating-rate loan also changes.

Floating-rate loans are not always tied to the prime rate. Often they are tied to the rate at which international banks lend to one another. This is known as the *London Interbank Offered Rate,* or *LIBOR.*

Self-Test 14.3

Would you expect the price of a 10-year floating-rate bond to be more or less sensitive to changes in interest rates than the price of a 10-year maturity fixed-rate bond?

funded debt
Debt with more than 1 year remaining to maturity.

Maturity   **Funded debt** is any debt repayable more than 1 year from the date of issue. Debt due in less than a year is termed *unfunded* and is carried on the balance sheet as a current liability. Unfunded debt is often described as short-term debt, and funded debt is described as long-term, although it is clearly artificial to call a 364-day debt short-term and a 366-day debt long-term (except in leap years).

There are corporate bonds of nearly every conceivable maturity. For example, Bristol Myers Squibb has issued bonds that do not mature until 2097. Some British banks have issued perpetuities—that is, bonds which may survive forever. At the other extreme we find firms borrowing literally overnight.

Repayment Provisions   Long-term loans are commonly repaid in a steady regular way, perhaps after an initial grace period. For bonds that are publicly traded, this is done by means of a **sinking fund.** Each year the firm puts aside a sum of cash into a sinking fund that is then used to buy back the bonds. When there is a sinking fund, investors are prepared to lend at a lower rate of interest. They know that they are more likely to be repaid if the company sets aside some cash each year than if the entire loan has to be repaid on one specified day.

sinking fund
Fund established to retire debt before maturity.

Suppose that a company issues a 6%, 30-year bond at a price of $1,000. Five years later interest rates have fallen to 4%, and the price of the bond has risen dramatically. If you were the company's treasurer, wouldn't you like to be able to retire the bonds and issue some new bonds at the lower interest rate? Well, with some bonds, known as **callable bonds,** the company does have the option to buy them back for the *call price.*[3] Of course, holders of these callable bonds know that the company will wish to buy the issue back if interest rates fall, and therefore the price of the bond will not rise above the call price.

callable bond
Bond that may be repurchased by firm before maturity at specified call price.

Figure 14–2 shows the risk of a call to the bondholder. The purple line is the value of a 30-year, 6.5% "straight," that is, noncallable, bond; the orange line is the value of a bond with the same coupon rate and maturity but callable at $1,060 (i.e., 106% of face value). At very high interest rates the risk that the company will call the bonds is negligible, and the values of the two bonds are nearly identical. As rates fall, the straight bond continues to increase steadily in value, but since the capital appreciation of the callable bond is limited by the call price, its capital appreciation will lag behind that of the straight bond.

A callable bond gives the *company* the option to retire the bonds early. But some bonds give the *investor* the right to demand early repayment. During the 1990s many loans to Asian companies gave the lenders a repayment option. Consequently, when the Asian crisis struck in 1997, these companies were faced by a flood of lenders

---

[3] Sometimes callable bonds specify a period during which the firm is not allowed to call the bond if the purpose is simply to issue another bond at a lower interest rate.

FIGURE 14–2 Prices of callable versus straight debt. When interest rates fall, bond prices rise. But the price of the callable bond (orange line) is limited by the call price.

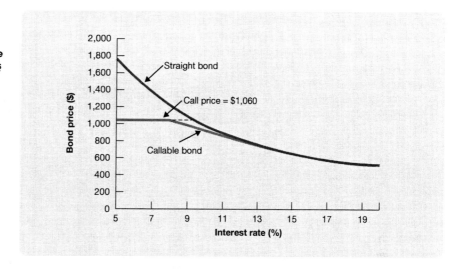

demanding their money back. Needless to say, companies that were already struggling to survive did not appreciate this additional burden.

Self-Test 14.4

Suppose Heinz is considering two issues of 20-year maturity coupon bonds; one issue will be callable, the other not. For a given coupon rate, will the callable or non-callable bond sell at the higher price? If the bonds are both to be sold to the public at face value, which bond must have the higher coupon rate?

subordinated debt
Debt that may be repaid in bankruptcy only after senior debt is paid.

Seniority   Some debts are **subordinated.** In the event of default the subordinated lender gets in line behind the firm's general creditors. The subordinated lender holds a junior claim and is paid only after all senior creditors are satisfied.

When you lend money to a firm, you can assume that you hold a senior claim unless the debt agreement says otherwise. However, this does not always put you at the front of the line, for the firm may have set aside some of its assets specifically for the protection of other lenders. That brings us to our next classification.

Security   When you borrow to buy your home, the savings and loan company will take out a mortgage on the house. The mortgage acts as security for the loan. If you default on the loan payments, the S&L can seize your home.

secured debt
Debt that has first claim on specified collateral in the event of default.

When companies borrow, they also may set aside certain assets as security for the loan. These assets are termed *collateral,* and the debt is said to be **secured.** In the event of default, the secured lender has first claim on the collateral; unsecured lenders have a general claim on the rest of the firm's assets but only a junior claim on the collateral.

Default Risk   Seniority and security do not guarantee payment. A debt can be senior and secured but still as risky as a dizzy tightrope walker—it depends on the value and the risk of the firm's assets. In Chapter 6 we showed how the safety of most corporate bonds can be judged from bond ratings provided by rating agencies such as Moody's and Standard & Poor's. Bonds that are rated "triple-A" seldom default. At the other extreme, many speculative-grade (or "junk") bonds may be teetering on the brink.

As you would expect, investors demand a high return from low-rated bonds. We saw evidence of this in Chapter 6, where Figure 6–9 compares the yields on default-free U.S. Treasury bonds with those on corporate bonds in various rating classes. The lower-rated bonds do in fact offer higher promised yields to maturity.

Country and Currency   These days capital markets know few national boundaries and many large firms in the United States borrow abroad. For example, an American company may choose to finance a new plant in Switzerland by borrowing Swiss francs from a Swiss bank, or it may expand its Dutch operation by issuing a bond in Holland. Also many foreign companies come to the United States to borrow dollars, which are then used to finance their operations throughout the world.

In addition to these national capital markets, there is also an international capital market centered mainly in London. Banks from all over the world have branches in London. They include such giants as Citicorp, UBS, Deutsche Bank, Bank of Tokyo–Mitsubishi, HSBC, and BNP Paribas. One reason they are there is to collect deposits in the major currencies. For example, suppose an Arab sheikh has just received payment in dollars for a large sale of oil to the United States. Rather than depositing the check in the United States, he may choose to open a dollar account with a bank in London. Dollars held in a bank outside the United States came to be known as **eurodollars.** Similarly, yen held outside Japan were termed euroyen, and so on.

eurodollars
Dollars held on deposit in a bank outside the United States.

The London bank branch that is holding the sheikh's dollar deposit may temporarily lend those dollars to a company, in the same way that a bank in the United States may relend dollars that have been deposited with it. Thus a company can either borrow dollars from a bank in the United States or borrow dollars from a bank in London.[4]

If a firm wants to make an issue of long-term bonds, it can choose to do so in the United States. Alternatively, it can sell the bonds to investors in several countries. Because these international issues have usually been marketed by the London branches of international banks, they have traditionally been known as **eurobonds.** A eurobond may be denominated in dollars, yen, or any other currency. Unfortunately, when the single European currency was established it was called the *euro.* It is easy, therefore, to confuse a *eurobond* (a bond that is sold internationally) with a bond that is denominated in *euros.*

eurobond
Bond that is marketed internationally.

Public versus Private Placements   Publicly issued bonds are sold to anyone who wishes to buy, and once they have been issued, they can be freely traded in the securities markets. In a **private placement,** the issue is sold directly to a small number of banks, insurance companies, or other investment institutions. Privately placed bonds cannot be resold to individuals in the United States and can be resold only to other qualified institutional investors. However, there is increasingly active trading *among* these investors.

private placement
Sale of securities to a limited number of investors without a public offering.

We will have more to say about the difference between public issues and private placements in the next chapter.

Protective Covenants   When investors lend to a company, they know that they might not get their money back. But they expect that the company will use their money well and not take unreasonable risks. To help ensure this, lenders usually impose a number of conditions, or **protective covenants,** on companies that borrow from them. An honest firm is willing to accept these conditions because it knows that they enable the firm to borrow at a reasonable rate of interest.

protective covenant
Restriction on a firm to protect bondholders.

Companies that borrow in moderation are less likely to get into difficulties than those that are up to the gunwales in debt. So lenders usually restrict the amount of extra debt that the firm can issue. Lenders are also eager to prevent others from pushing ahead of them in the queue if trouble occurs. So they will not allow the company to create new debt that is senior to them or to put aside assets for other lenders.

In June 2006 Heinz announced plans to raise its dividend and buy back $1 billion of its shares. Holders of Heinz's bonds were unhappy with the news, since it meant

---

[4] Because the Federal Reserve requires banks in the United States to keep interest-free reserves, there is in effect a tax on dollar deposits in the United States. Overseas dollar deposits are free of this tax, and therefore banks can afford to charge the borrower slightly lower interest rates.

FINANCE IN PRACTICE

Marriott Plan Enrages Holders of Its Bonds

Marriott Corp. has infuriated bond investors with a restructuring plan that may be a new way for companies to pull the rug out from under bondholders.

Prices of Marriott's existing bonds have plunged as much as 30% in the past two days in the wake of the hotel and food-services company's announcement that it plans to separate into two companies, one burdened with virtually all of Marriott's debt.

On Monday, Marriott said that it will divide its operations into two separate businesses. One, Marriott International Inc., is a healthy company that will manage Marriott's vast hotel chain; it will get most of the old company's revenue, a larger share of the cash flow and will be nearly debt-free.

The second business, called Host Marriott Corp., is a debt-laden company that will own Marriott hotels along with other real estate and retain essentially all of the old Marriott's $3 billion of debt.

The announcement stunned and infuriated bondholders, who watched nervously as the value of their Marriott bonds tumbled and as Moody's Investors Service Inc. downgraded the bond to the junk-bond category from investment-grade.

Price Plunge

In trading, Marriott's 10% bonds that mature in 2012, which Marriott sold to investors just six months ago, were quoted yesterday at about 80 cents on the dollar, down from 110 Friday. The price decline translates into a stunning loss of $300 for a bond with a $1,000 face amount.

Marriott officials concede that the company's spinoff plan penalizes bondholders. However, the company notes that, like all public corporations, its fiduciary duty is to stockholders, not bondholders. Indeed, Marriott's stock jumped 12% Monday. (It fell a bit yesterday.)

Bond investors and analysts worry that if the Marriott spinoff goes through, other companies will soon follow suit by separating debt-laden units from the rest of the company. "Any company that fears it has underperforming divisions that are dragging down its stock price is a possible candidate" for such a restructuring, says Dorothy K. Lee, an assistant vice president at Moody's.

If the trend heats up, investors said, the Marriott restructuring could be the worst news for corporate bondholders since RJR Nabisco Inc.'s managers shocked investors in 1987 by announcing they were taking the company private in a record $25 billion leveraged buy-out. The move, which loaded RJR with debt and tanked the value of RJR bonds, triggered a deep slump in prices of many investment-grade corporate bonds as investors backed away from the market.

Strong Covenants May Re-Emerge

Some analysts say the move by Marriott may trigger the re-emergence of strong covenants, or written protections, in future corporate bond issues to protect bondholders against such restructurings as the one being engineered by Marriott. In the wake of the RJR buy-out, many investors demanded stronger covenants in new corporate bond issues.

Some investors blame themselves for not demanding stronger covenants. "It's our own fault," said Robert Hickey, a bond fund manager at Van Kampen Merritt. In their rush to buy bonds in an effort to lock in yields, many investors have allowed companies to sell bonds with covenants that have been "slim to none," Mr. Hickey said.

Source: "Marriott Plan Engages Holders of Its Bonds," *The Wall Street Journal*, October 7, 1992. Copyright 1992 by Dow Jones & Co. Inc. Reproduced with permission of Dow Jones & Co., Inc. via Copyright Clearance Center.

that there would be less cash available to service their debt. By August the price of Heinz's bonds had drifted down by 5%. Debtholders are aware that bumper payments to shareholders can reduce the value of their debt, and they often protect themselves by limiting the amount of cash that can be paid out as dividends or repurchases.

The story of Marriott in the nearby box is a more dramatic example of what can happen when bondholders are not sufficiently careful about the conditions they impose.

Self-Test 14.5

In 1987 RJR Nabisco, the food and tobacco giant, had $5 billion of A-rated debt outstanding. In that year the company was taken over, and $19 billion of debt was issued and used to buy back equity. The debt ratio skyrocketed, and the debt was downgraded to a BB rating. The holders of the previously issued debt were furious, and one filed a lawsuit claiming that RJR had violated an *implicit* obligation not to undertake major financing changes at the expense of existing bondholders. Why did these bondholders believe they had been harmed by the massive issue of new debt? What type of *explicit* restriction would you have wanted if you had been one of the original bondholders?

A Debt by Any Other Name   The word *debt* sounds straightforward, but companies enter into a number of financial arrangements that look suspiciously like debt yet are treated differently in the accounts. Some of these obligations are easily identifiable. For example, accounts payable are simply obligations to pay for goods that have already been delivered and are therefore like a short-term debt.

Other arrangements are not so easy to spot. For example, instead of borrowing money to buy equipment, many companies **lease** or rent it on a long-term basis. In this case the firm promises to make a series of payments to the lessor (the owner of the equipment). This is just like the obligation to make payments on an outstanding loan. What if the firm can't make the payments? The lessor can then take back the equipment, which is precisely what would happen if the firm had *borrowed* money from the lessor, using the equipment as collateral for the loan.

lease
Long-term rental agreement.

There is nothing underhanded about entering into long-term leases. They are clearly shown on the company's balance sheet as a liability. Sometimes, however, companies go to considerable lengths to ensure that investors do not know how much they have borrowed. For example, Enron was able to borrow $658 million by setting up *special-purpose entities (SPEs),* which raised cash by a mixture of equity and debt and then used that debt to help fund the parent company. None of this debt showed up on Enron's balance sheet.

EXAMPLE 14.1 ▶   The Terms of Heinz's Bond Issue

Now that you are familiar with some of the jargon, you might like to look at an example of a bond issue. Table 14–3 is a summary of the terms of a bond issue by Heinz taken from *Mergent's Industrial Manual.* We have added some explanatory notes.

Innovation in the Debt Market

We have discussed domestic bonds and eurobonds, fixed-rate and floating-rate loans, secured and unsecured loans, senior and junior loans, and much more. You might think that this gives you all the choice you need. Yet almost every day companies and their advisers dream up new types of debt. We described some unusual bonds in Chapter 6. Here are a couple more examples.

Indexed Bonds   We saw in Chapter 6 how the United States government has issued bonds whose payments rise in line with inflation. Occasionally borrowers have linked the payments on their bonds to the price of a particular commodity. For example, Mexico, which is a large oil producer, has issued billions of dollars worth of bonds that provide an extra payoff if oil prices rise. Mexico reasons that oil-linked bonds reduce its risk. If the price of oil is high, it can afford the higher payments on the bond. If oil prices are low, its interest payments will also be lower.

Asset-Backed Bonds   The rock star David Bowie earns royalties from a number of successful albums such as *The Rise and Fall of Ziggy Stardust* and *Diamond Dogs.* But instead of waiting to receive these royalties, Bowie decided that he would prefer the money up front. The solution was to issue $55 million of 10-year bonds and to set aside the future royalty payments from the singer's albums to make the payments on these bonds. Such bonds are known as *asset-backed securities;* the borrower sets aside a group of assets and the income from these assets is then used to service the debt. The Bowie bonds are an unusual example of an asset-backed security, but billions of dollars of house mortgages and credit card loans are packaged each year and resold as asset-backed bonds.

These two examples illustrate the great variety of potential security designs. As long as you can convince investors of its attractions, you can issue a callable, subordinated, floating-rate bond denominated in euros. Rather than combining features of existing securities, you may be able to create an entirely new one. We can imagine a copper mining company issuing preferred shares on which the dividend fluctuates with the world copper price. We know of no such security, but it is perfectly legal to issue it and—who knows?—it might generate considerable interest among investors.

Variety is intrinsically good. People have different tastes, levels of wealth, rates of tax, and so on. Why not offer them a choice? Of course, the problem is the expense

TABLE 14-3 Heinz's bond issue

Comment	Description of Bond
1. A debenture is an unsecured bond.	**H. J. Heinz Company 6.375% debentures, due 2028**
2. Coupon is 6.375%. Thus each bond makes an annual interest payment of .06375 × $1,000 = $63.75.	
3. Moody's bond rating is A, the third-highest quality rating.	**Rating—A**
4. Heinz is authorized to issue (and has outstanding) $250 million of the bonds.	AUTH. $250,000,000: outstg. $250,000,000.
5. The bond was issued in July 1998 and is to be repaid in July 2028.	DATED July 10, 1998. DUE July 15, 2028.
6. Interest is payable at 6-month intervals on January and July 15.	INTEREST J&J 15.
7. A trustee is appointed to look after the bondholders' interest.	TRUSTEE First National Bank of Chicago.
8. The bonds are registered. The registrar keeps a record of who owns the bonds.	DENOMINATION Fully registered. $1,000 and integral multiples thereof. Transferable and exchangable without service charge.
9. The bond can be held in multiples of $1,000.	
10. Unlike some bond issues, the Heinz issue does not give the company an option to call (i.e., repurchase) the bonds before maturity at specified prices. Also Heinz does not set aside money each year in a sinking fund that is then used to redeem the bonds.	EARLY REDEMPTION The debentures are not redeemable prior to maturity.
11. The bonds are not secured, that is, no assets have been set aside to protect the bondholders in the event of default.	SECURITY Not secured. Ranks equally with all other unsecured and unsubordinated indebtedness of the Company. Company or any affiliate will not create as security for any indebtedness for borrowed money, any mortgage, pledge, security interest, or lien on any stock or any indebtedness of any affiliate . . . without effectively providing that the debentures shall be secured equally and ratably with such indebtedness, unless such secured debt would not exceed 10% of Consolidated Net Assets.
12. However, if Heinz sets aside assets to protect any other bondholders, the debenture will also be secured on these assets. This is termed a *negative pledge clause*.	
13. The bonds were sold at a price of 99.549% of face value. After deducting the payment to the underwriters the company received $986.74 per bond. The bonds could be bought from the listed underwriters.	OFFERED $250,000,000 at 99.549 plus accrued interest (proceeds to Company 98.674) thru Goldman, Sachs & Co., J. P. Morgan & Co., Warburg Dillon Read LLC.

of designing and marketing new securities. But if you can think of a new security that will appeal to investors, you may be able to issue it on especially favorable terms and thus increase the value of your company.

14.5 Convertible Securities

warrant
Right to buy shares from a company at a stipulated price before a set date.

We have seen that companies sometimes have the option to repay an issue of bonds before maturity. There are also cases in which *investors* have an option. The most dramatic case is provided by a **warrant,** which is *nothing but* an option. Companies often issue warrants and bonds in a package.

EXAMPLE 14.2 ▶ Warrants

Macaw Bill wishes to make a bond issue, which could include some warrants as a "sweetener." Each warrant might allow you to purchase one share of Macaw stock at a price of $50 any time during the next 5 years. If Macaw's stock performs well, that option could turn out to be very valuable. For instance, if the stock price at the end of the 5 years is $80, then you pay the company $50 and receive in exchange a share worth $80. Of course, an investment in warrants also has its perils. If the price of Macaw stock fails to rise above $50, then the warrants expire worthless.

convertible bond
Bond that the holder may exchange for a specified amount of another security

A **convertible bond** gives its owner the option to exchange the bond for a predetermined number of common shares. The convertible bondholder hopes that the company's share price will zoom up so that the bond can be converted at a big profit. But if the shares zoom down, there is no obligation to convert; the bondholder remains just that. Not surprisingly, investors value this option to keep the bond or exchange it for shares, and therefore a convertible bond sells at a higher price than a comparable bond that is not convertible.

The convertible is rather like a package of a bond and a warrant. But there is an important difference: When the owners of a convertible wish to exercise their options to buy shares, they do not pay cash—they just exchange the bond for shares of the stock.

Companies may also issue convertible preferred stock. In this case the investor receives preferred stock with fixed dividend payments but has the option to exchange this preferred stock for the company's common stock. The preferred stock issued by Heinz is convertible into common stock.

These examples do not exhaust the options encountered by the financial manager. In fact, once you read Chapter 23 and learn how to analyze options, you will find that they are all around you.

14.6 Patterns of Corporate Financing

Firms have two broad sources of cash: They can raise money from external sources by an issue of shares or debt, or they can plow back part of their profits. Shareholders are happy for companies to plow this money back into the firm, so long as it goes to positive-NPV investments. Every positive-NPV investment generates a higher price for their shares.

internally generated funds
Cash reinvested in the firm: depreciation plus earnings not paid out as dividends

Figure 14–3 summarizes the sources of capital for U.S. corporations. Notice the importance of **internally generated funds,** defined as depreciation plus earnings that are not paid out as dividends.[5] Over these 12 years, internally generated cash covered 83% of firms' capital requirements.

Do Firms Rely Too Heavily on Internal Funds?

Some observers worry that companies rely so much on internal funds. They argue that managers might think more carefully about spending money if they have to ask investors for it. Think back to Chapter 1, where we pointed out that a firm is a team,

FIGURE 14–3 Sources of funds for U.S. nonfinancial corporations, 1995–2006

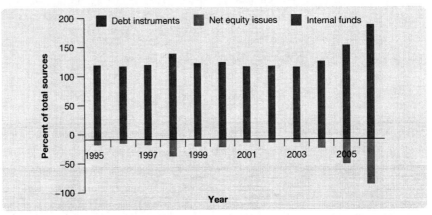

Source: Board of Governors of the Federal Reserve System, Division of Research and Statistics, "Flow of Funds Accounts," Table F.102 at **www.federalreserve.gov/releases/z1/current/data.htm.**

_____
[5] Remember that depreciation is a noncash expense.

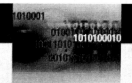

INTERNET INSIDER

Patterns of Corporate Financing

F.102 Nonfarm Nonfinancial Corporate Business			
Billions of dollars			
	2005	2006	2007
1 Profits before tax (book)	959.9	1016.5	1046.8
2 − Taxes on corporate income	262.7	287.1	311.6
3 − Net dividends	196.1	415.1	374.8
4 − Capital consumption allowance (3)	554.0	574.5	755.1
5 − U.S. internal funds, book	1061.3	981.7	859.9
6 − Foreign earnings retained abroad	−30.4	147.4	153.6
7 − Inventory valuation adjustment (IVA)	56.2	35.3	37.6
8 − Net capital transfers (2)	0.0	0.0	0.6
9 − Total internal funds + IVA	995.0	962.3	936.2

Source: Federal Reserve Web site.

In Figure 14–3 we summarized the sources and uses of funds for U.S. nonfinancial corporations. The data for this figure can be found on **www.federalreserve.gov/releases/z1/current/data.htm.** Look at Table F.102 for the latest year. Don't be put off by its complexity. Just find "total internal funds" (which appeared in row 9 at the time we last looked) and "net funds raised in markets" (row 37). What proportion of the funds that companies needed in the latest year was generated internally, and how much had to be raised on the financial markets? Is this the usual pattern? Now look at "net new equity issues" (row 38). Were companies on average issuing new equity or buying their shares back?

---

consisting of managers, shareholders, debtholders, and so on. The shareholders and debtholders would like to monitor management to make sure that it is pulling its weight and truly maximizing market value, but it is costly for individual investors to keep check on management. However, large financial institutions are specialists in monitoring, so when the firm goes to the bank for a large loan or makes a public issue of stock or bonds, managers know that they had better have all the answers. If they want a quiet life, they will avoid going to the capital market to raise money and they will retain sufficient earnings to be able to meet unanticipated demands for cash.

We do not mean to paint managers as loafers. There are also rational reasons for relying on internally generated funds. For example, the costs of issuing new securities are avoided. Moreover, the announcement of a new equity issue is usually bad news for investors, who worry that management may be trying to sell overpriced stock.[6] Raising equity capital from internal sources, then, avoids the costs and the bad omens associated with equity issues.

Self-Test 14.6

"Since internal funds provide the bulk of industry's needs for capital, the securities markets serve little function." Does the speaker have a point?

External Sources of Capital

Of course, firms don't rely exclusively on internal funds. In most years there is a gap between the cash that companies need and the cash that they generate internally. This gap is the **financial deficit.** To make up the deficit, companies must either sell new equity or borrow.

financial deficit
Difference between the cash companies need and the amount generated internally.

Look again at Figure 14–3, which shows how corporate America has made up the deficit. Notice that for most of this period firms were making large issues of debt and using the money to buy back common stock. In Figure 14–3 these repurchases show up as negative issues of equity.

Has this policy resulted in an increase in the proportion of debt that companies use? Figure 14–4 shows that the answer partly depends on how you measure the debt ratio. You can see that in book-value terms the debt ratio has crept fairly steadily upward over the last 50 years (though it actually dipped a little during the 1990s). However, the picture is rather different in terms of market values. Booming stock prices until 1999 ensured that for two decades the amount of long-term debt grew less rapidly than the market value of equity.

---

[6] Managers do have insiders' insights and naturally are tempted to issue stock when the stock price looks good to them, that is, when they are less optimistic than outside investors. The outside investors realize all this and will buy a new issue only at a discount from the preannouncement price. Stock issues are discussed further in the next chapter.

408   **Part Four** Financing

FIGURE 14–4 The ratio of debt to debt plus equity for the nonfinancial corporate sector

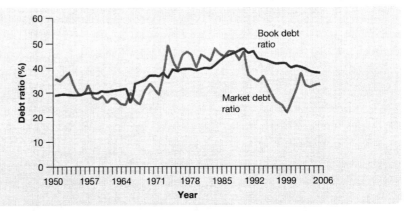

Source: Board of Governors of the Federal Reserve System, Division of Research and Statistics, "Flow of Funds Accounts," Table B.102 at **www.federalreserve.gov/releases/z1/current/data.htm**.

Should we be worried that book debt ratios are higher today than they were 50 years ago? It is true that high debt ratios mean that more companies are likely to fall into financial distress when a serious recession hits the economy. But all companies live with this to some degree, and it does not always follow that less risk is better. Finding the optimal debt ratio is like finding the optimal speed limit; we can agree that accidents at 30 miles per hour are less dangerous, other things being equal, than accidents at 60 miles per hour, but we do not therefore set the national speed limit at 30. Speed has benefits as well as risks. So does debt, as we will see in Chapter 16.

SUMMARY

www.mhhe.com/bmm6e

Why should firms assume that the securities they issue are fairly priced? *(LO1)*

Managers want to raise money at the lowest possible cost, but their ability to find cheap financing is limited by the intense competition between investors. As a result of this competition, securities are likely to be fairly priced given the information available to investors. Such a market is said to be *efficient.*

What information is contained in the shareholders' equity account in the firm's financial statements? *(LO2)*

The stockholders' equity account breaks down the book value of equity into **par value, additional paid-in capital, retained earnings,** and **treasury stock.** For most purposes, the allocation among the first three categories is not important. These accounts also show the total number of shares issued as well as shares repurchased by the company.

What procedures are used for elections to a firm's board of directors and other matters put to shareholders? *(LO3)*

Most companies use a **majority voting** system in which each director is voted on separately and stockholders cast one vote for each share they own. Less commonly, firms employ **cumulative voting,** which means that all directors are voted on jointly and stockholders may cast all their votes for just one candidate. On most issues put to the shareholders, a majority of votes is usually enough to prevail, but for some decisions a supermajority is required.

What are the major classes of securities issued by firms to raise capital? *(LO4)*

A company can issue a variety of securities such as common stock, preferred stock, and bonds. The **common stockholders** own the company. By this we mean that they are entitled to whatever profits are left over after other investors have been paid and that they have the ultimate control over how the company is run. Because shareholdings in the United States are usually widely dispersed, managers get to make most of the decisions. Managers may be given strong financial incentives to perform well, and their actions are monitored by the board of directors.

www.mhhe.com/bmm6e

Preferred stock offers a fixed dividend but the company has the discretion not to pay it. It can't, however, then pay a dividend on the common stock. Despite its name, preferred stock is not a popular source of finance, but it is useful in special situations.

When companies issue **bonds,** they promise to make a series of interest payments and to repay the principal. However, this liability is limited. Stockholders have the right to default on their obligation and to hand over the assets to the debtholders. Unlike dividends on common stock and preferred stock, the interest payments on debt are regarded as a cost and therefore they are paid out of before-tax income. Here are some forms of debt:

- *Fixed-rate* and *floating-rate* debt.
- *Funded (long-term)* and *unfunded (short-term)* debt.
- *Callable* and *sinking-fund* debt.
- *Senior* and *subordinated* debt.
- *Secured* and *unsecured* debt.
- *Investment grade* and *junk* debt.
- *Domestic bonds* and *eurobonds.*
- *Publicly traded* debt and *private placements.*

The fourth source of finance consists of options and optionlike securities. The simplest option is a **warrant,** which gives its holder the right to buy a share from the firm at a set price by a set date. Warrants are often sold in combination with other securities. **Convertible bonds** give their holder the right to convert the bond to shares. They therefore resemble a package of straight debt and a warrant.

What are recent trends in firms' use of different sources of finance? *(LO5)*

Internally generated cash is the principal source of company funds. Some people worry about that; they think that if management does not go to the trouble of raising money, it may be profligate in spending it.

In recent years, net equity issues have often been negative; that is, companies have repurchased more equity than they have issued. At the same time companies have issued large quantities of debt. However, large levels of **internally generated funds** in this period allowed book equity to increase despite the share repurchases, with the result that the ratio of long-term debt to book value of equity was fairly stable.

QUESTIONS

QUIZ

1. **Equity Accounts.** The authorized share capital of the Alfred Cake Company is 100,000 shares. The equity is currently shown in the company's books as follows: *(LO2)*

Common stock ($1 par value)	$ 60,000
Additional paid-in capital	10,000
Retained earnings	30,000
Common equity	100,000
Treasury stock (2,000 shares)	5,000
Net common equity	$ 95,000

a. How many shares are issued?

b. How many are outstanding?

c. How many more shares can be issued without the approval of shareholders?

2. **Equity Accounts.** *(LO2)*

a. Look back at Quiz Question 1. Suppose that the company issues 10,000 shares at $4 a share. Which of the above figures would change?

b. What would happen to the company's books if instead it bought back 1,000 shares at $4 per share?

3. **Financing Terms.** Fill in the blanks by choosing the appropriate term from the following list: *lease, funded, floating-rate, eurobond, convertible, subordinated, call, sinking fund, prime rate, private placement, public issue, senior, unfunded, eurodollar rate, warrant, debentures, term loan. (LO4)*

   a. Debt maturing in more than 1 year is often called _____ debt.

   b. An issue of bonds that is sold simultaneously in several countries is traditionally called a(n) _____.

   c. If a lender ranks behind the firm's general creditors in the event of default, the loan is said to be _____.

   d. In many cases a firm is obliged to make regular contributions to a(n) _____, which is then used to repurchase bonds.

   e. Most bonds give the firm the right to repurchase or _____ the bonds at specified prices.

   f. The benchmark interest rate that banks charge to their customers with good credit is generally termed the _____.

   g. The interest rate on bank loans is often tied to short-term interest rates. These loans are usually called _____ loans.

   h. Where there is a(n) _____, securities are sold directly to a small group of institutional investors. These securities cannot be resold to individual investors. In the case of a(n) _____, debt can be freely bought and sold by individual investors.

   i. A long-term rental agreement is called a(n) _____.

   j. A(n) _____ bond can be exchanged for shares of the issuing corporation.

   k. A(n) _____ gives its owner the right to buy shares in the issuing company at a predetermined price.

4. **Financing Trends.** True or false? Explain. *(LO5)*

   a. In several recent years, nonfinancial corporations in the United States have repurchased more stock than they have issued.

   b. A corporation pays tax on only 30% of the common or preferred dividends it receives from other corporations.

   c. Because of the tax advantage, a large fraction of preferred shares is held by corporations.

5. **Preferred Stock.** In what ways is preferred stock like long-term debt? In what ways is it like common stock? *(LO4)*

PRACTICE PROBLEMS

6. **Voting for Directors.** If there are 10 directors to be elected and a shareholder owns 100 shares, indicate the maximum number of votes that he or she can cast for a favorite candidate under

   a. majority voting. *(LO3)*

   b. cumulative voting. *(LO3)*

7. **Voting for Directors.** The shareholders of the Pickwick Paper Company need to elect five directors. There are 400,000 shares outstanding. How many shares do you need to own to *ensure* that you can elect at least one director if the company has

   a. majority voting? *(LO3)*

   b. cumulative voting? *(LO3)*

   (*Hint:* How many votes in total will be cast? How many votes are required to ensure that at least one-fifth of votes are cast for your choice?)

8. **Equity Accounts.** Look back at Table 14–2. *(LO2)*

   a. Suppose that Heinz issues 10 million shares at $40 a share. Rework Table 14–2 to show the company's equity after the issue.

   b. Suppose that Heinz *subsequently* repurchased 500,000 shares at $50 a share. Rework part (a) to show the effect of the further change.

9. **Equity Accounts.** Common Products has just made its first issue of stock. It raised $2 million by selling 200,000 shares of stock to the public. These are the only shares outstanding. The par value of each share was $2. Fill in the following table: *(LO2)*

www.mhhe.com/bmm6e

Common shares (par value)	_____
Additional paid-in capital	_____
Retained earnings	_____
Net common equity	$2,500,000

10. **Protective Covenants.** Why might a bond agreement limit the amount of assets that the firm can lease? *(LO4)*

11. **Bond Yields.** Other things equal, will the following provisions increase or decrease the yield to maturity at which a firm can issue a bond? *(LO4)*

    a. A call provision.

    b. A restriction on further borrowing.

    c. A provision of specific collateral for the bond.

    d. An option to convert the bonds into shares.

12. **Income Bonds.** *Income bonds* are unusual. Interest payments on such bonds may be skipped or deferred if the firm's income is insufficient to make the payment. In what way are these bonds like preferred stock? Why might a firm choose to issue an income bond instead of preferred stock? *(LO4)*

13. **Preferred Stock.** Preferred stock of financially strong firms sometimes sells at lower yields than the bonds of those firms. For weaker firms, the preferred stock has a higher yield. What might explain this pattern? *(LO4)*

STANDARD
&POOR'S

1. Go to Market Insight at **www.mhhe.com/edumarketinsight**. Anheuser-Busch Inc. (BUD) used internal and external sources to fund its recent growth. Examine Anheuser-Busch's internal and external sources of funds, and then compare your findings with Figure 14–3 in this chapter. (See Annual Cash Flow Statement.) What was Anheuser-Busch's primary use of funds?

2. What has happened to the book debt ratios (Ratios Report) of Anheuser-Busch Inc. (BUD) in the last few years? How has the debt ratio changed if one calculates debt ratios using the market value of equity?

3. Compare the major sources and uses of funds (Annual Cash Flow Report and Balance Sheet) for General Mills (GIS) and Heinz (HNZ). What factors might explain the differences in financing patterns for the two companies?

SOLUTIONS TO SELF-TEST QUESTIONS

14.1 Par value of common shares must be $1 × 100,000 shares = $100,000. Additional paid-in capital is ($15 − $1) × 100,000 = $1,400,000. Since book value is $4,500,000, retained earnings must be $3,000,000. Therefore, the accounts look like this:

Common shares ($1 par value per share)	$100,000
Additional paid-in capital	1,400,000
Retained earnings	3,000,000
Net common equity	$4,500,000

14.2 The corporation's after-tax yield on the bonds is 10% − (.35 × 10%) = 6.5%. The after-tax yield on the preferred is 8% − [.35 × (.30 × 8%)] = 7.16%. The preferred stock provides the higher after-tax rate despite its lower before-tax rate.

14.3 Because the coupon on floating-rate debt adjusts periodically to current market conditions, the bondholder is less vulnerable to changes in market yields. The coupon rate paid by the bond is

412

Part Four Financing

not locked in for as long a period of time. Therefore, prices of floaters should be less sensitive to changes in market interest rates.

14.4 The callable bond will sell at a lower price. Investors will not pay as much for the callable bond since they know that the firm may call it away from them if interest rates fall. Thus they know that their capital gains potential is limited, which makes the bond less valuable. If both bonds are to sell at face value, the callable bond must pay a higher coupon rate as compensation to the investor for the firm's right to call the bond.

14.5 The extra debt makes it more likely that the firm will not be able to make good on its promised payments to its creditors. If the new debt is not junior to the already-issued debt, then the original bondholders suffer a loss when their bonds become more susceptible to default risk. A protective covenant limiting the amount of new debt that the firm can issue would have prevented this problem. Investors, having witnessed the problems of the RJR bondholders, generally demanded the covenant on future debt issues.

14.6 Capital markets provide liquidity for investors. Because individual stockholders can always lay their hands on cash by selling shares, they are prepared to invest in companies that retain earnings rather than pay them out as dividends. Well-functioning capital markets allow the firm to serve all its stockholders simply by maximizing value. Capital markets also provide managers with information. Without this information, it would be very difficult to determine opportunity costs of capital or to assess financial performance.

CHAPTER 15

Venture Capital, IPOs, and Seasoned Offerings

LEARNING OBJECTIVES

After studying this chapter, you should be able to:

1. Understand how venture capital firms design successful deals.
2. Understand how firms make initial public offerings and the costs of such offerings.
3. Know what is involved when established firms make a general cash offer or a private placement of securities.
4. Explain the role of the underwriter in an issue of securities.
5. Describe the terms of a rights issue.

Related Web sites for this chapter can be found at www.mhhe.com/bmm6e.

Trading opens on Nasdaq for shares in Google.
© Getty Images

Bill Gates and Paul Allen founded Microsoft in 1975, when both were around 20 years old. Eleven years later Microsoft shares were sold to the public for $21 a share and immediately zoomed to $35. The largest shareholder was Bill Gates, whose shares in Microsoft then were worth $350 million.

In 1976 two college dropouts, Steve Jobs and Steve Wozniak, sold their most valuable possessions, a van and a couple of calculators, and used the cash to start manufacturing computers in a garage. In 1980, when Apple Computer went public, the shares were offered to investors at $22 and jumped to $36. At that point, the shares owned by the company's two founders were worth $414 million.

In 1996 two Stanford computer science students, Larry Page and Sergey Brin, decided to collaborate to develop a Web search engine. To help turn their idea into a commercial product, the two friends succeeded in raising almost $1 million from several wealthy investors, and this was later supplemented by funding from two *venture capital* firms that specialized in helping young start-up businesses. The company, now named Google, went public in 2004 at a price of $85 a share, putting a value on the enterprise of $23 billion.

Such stories illustrate that the most important asset of a new firm may be a good idea. But that is not all you need. To take an idea from the drawing board to a prototype and through to large-scale production requires ever greater amounts of capital.

To get a new company off the ground, entrepreneurs may rely on their own savings and personal bank loans. But this is unlikely to be sufficient to build a successful enterprise. *Venture capital* firms specialize in providing new equity capital to help firms over the awkward adolescent period before they are large enough to "go public." In the first part of this chapter we will explain how venture capital firms do this.

If the firm continues to be successful, there is likely to come a time when it needs to tap a wider source of capital. At this point it will make its first public issue of common stock. This is known as an *initial public offering,* or *IPO.* In the second section of the chapter we will describe what is involved in an IPO.

A company's initial public offering is seldom its last. In Chapter 14 we saw that internally generated cash is not usually sufficient to satisfy the firm's needs. Established companies make up the deficit by issuing more equity or debt. The remainder of this chapter looks at this process.

15.1 Venture Capital

venture capital
Money invested to finance a new firm.

You have taken a big step. With a couple of friends, you have formed a corporation to open a number of fast-food outlets, offering innovative combinations of national dishes such as sushi with sauerkraut, curry Bolognese, and chow mein with York-shire pudding. Breaking into the fast-food business costs money, but, after pooling your savings and borrowing to the hilt from the bank, you have raised $100,000 and purchased 1 million shares in the new company. At this *zero-stage* investment, your company's assets are $100,000 plus the *idea* for your new product.

That $100,000 is enough to get the business off the ground, but if the idea takes off, you will need more capital to pay for new restaurants. Many start-ups continue to grow with funds provided directly by managers or by their friends and families. Some thrive using bank loans and reinvested earnings. But, particularly if your start-up combines high-risk, sophisticated technology and substantial investment, you will probably need to find an investor who is prepared to back an untried company in return for part of the profits. Equity capital in young businesses is known as **venture capital,** and it is provided by specialist venture capital firms, wealthy individuals, and investment institutions such as pension funds.

Most entrepreneurs are able to spin a plausible yarn about their company. But it is as hard to convince a venture capitalist to invest in your business as it is to get a first novel published. Your first step is to prepare a *business plan.* This describes your product, the potential market, the production method, and the resources—time, money, employees, plant, and equipment—needed for success. It helps if you can point to the fact that you are prepared to put your money where your mouth is. By staking all your savings in the company, you *signal* your faith in the business.

The venture capital company knows that the success of a new business depends on the effort its managers put in. Therefore, it will try to structure any deal so that you have a strong incentive to work hard. For example, if you agree to accept a modest salary (and look forward instead to increasing the value of your investment in the company's stock), the venture capital company knows you will be committed to working hard. However, if you insist on a watertight employment contract and a fat salary, you won't find it easy to raise venture capital.

You are unlikely to persuade a venture capitalist to give you all at once as much money as you need. Rather, the firm will probably offer you enough to reach the next major checkpoint. Suppose you can convince the venture capital company to buy 1 million new shares for $.50 each. This will give it one-half ownership of the firm: It owns 1 million shares, and you and your friends also own 1 million shares. Because the venture capitalist is paying $500,000 for a claim to half your firm, it is placing a $1 million value on the business. After this *first-stage* financing, your company's balance sheet looks like this:

FIRST-STAGE MARKET-VALUE BALANCE SHEET (figures in millions)			
Assets		**Liabilities and Shareholders' Equity**	
Cash from new equity	$ .5	New equity from venture capital	$ .5
Other assets	.5	Your original equity	.5
Value	$1.0	Value	$1.0

Self-Test 15.1

Why might the venture capital company prefer to put up only part of the funds up front? Would this affect the amount of effort put in by you, the entrepreneur? Is your willingness to accept only part of the venture capital that will eventually be needed a good signal of the likely success of the venture?

Suppose that 2 years later your business has grown to the point at which it needs a further injection of equity. This *second-stage* financing might involve the issue of a further 1 million shares at $1 each. Some of these shares might be bought by the original backers and some by other venture capital firms. The balance sheet after the new financing would then be as follows:

SECOND-STAGE MARKET-VALUE BALANCE SHEET (figures in millions)			
Assets		**Liabilities and Shareholders' Equity**	
Cash from new equity	$1	New equity from second-stage financing	$1
Other assets	2	Equity from first stage	1
		Your original equity	1
Value	$3	Value	$3

Notice that the value of the initial 1 million shares owned by you and your friends has now been marked up to $1 million. Does this begin to sound like a money machine? It was so only because you have made a success of the business and new investors are prepared to pay $1 to buy a share in the business. When you started out, it wasn't clear that sushi and sauerkraut would catch on. If it hadn't caught on, the venture capital firm could have refused to put up more funds.

You are not yet in a position to cash in on your investment, but your gain is real. The second-stage investors have paid $1 million for a one-third share in the company. (There are now 3 million shares outstanding, and the second-stage investors hold 1 million shares.) Therefore, at least these impartial observers—who are willing to back up their opinions with a large investment—must have decided that the company was worth at least $3 million. Your one-third share is therefore also worth $1 million.

Venture Capital Companies

Some young companies grow with the aid of equity investment provided by wealthy individuals known as *angel investors*. Many others raise capital from specialist venture capital firms, which pool funds from a variety of investors, seek out fledgling companies to invest in, and then work with these companies as they try to grow. In addition, some large technology firms such as Intel, Johnson and Johnson, and Sun Microsystems, act as *corporate venturers* by providing capital to new innovative companies.

Most venture capital funds are organized as limited private partnerships with a fixed life of about 10 years. Pension funds and other investors are the limited partners. The management company, which is the general partner, is responsible for making and overseeing the investments and, in return, receives a fixed fee as well as a share of the profits. You will find that these venture capital partnerships are often lumped together with similar partnerships that provide funds for companies in distress or that buy out whole companies and then take them private. The general term for these activities is *private equity investing*.

Venture capital firms are not passive investors. They are usually represented on each company's board of directors, they help to recruit senior managers for the company, and they provide ongoing advice. This advice can be very valuable to businesses in their early years and helps them to bring their products more quickly to market.

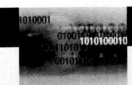

INTERNET INSIDER

Venture Capital

To find out what is happening in the venture capital industry, log on to **www.pwcmoneytree.com.** Look at the recent national data. How does the level of deals compare with levels in recent years? Which industries are attracting the most venture capital? Is the money going into new start-ups or expansion of existing businesses?

For every 10 first-stage venture capital investments, only 2 or 3 may survive as successful, self-sufficient businesses, and only 1 may pay off big. From these statistics come two rules of success in venture capital investment. First, don't shy away from uncertainty; accept a low probability of success. But don't buy into a business unless you can see the *chance* of a big, public company in a profitable market. There's no sense taking a big risk unless the reward is big if you win. Second, cut your losses; identify losers early, and if you can't fix the problem—by replacing management, for example—don't throw good money after bad.

Very few new businesses make it big, but those that do can be very profitable. For example, an investor who provided $1,000 of first-stage financing for Intel would have reaped over $25 million by 2007. So venture capitalists keep sane by reminding themselves of the success stories—those who got in on the ground floor of firms like Genentech, Sun Microsystems, and Federal Express.[1]

15.2 The Initial Public Offering

initial public offering (IPO)
First offering of stock to the general public.

For many successful start-ups there comes a time when they need more capital than can comfortably be provided by a small number of individuals or venture capitalists. At this point one solution is to sell the business to a larger firm. But many entrepreneurs do not fit easily into a corporate bureaucracy and would prefer instead to remain the boss. In this case, the company may choose to raise money by selling shares to the public. **A firm is said to *go public* when it sells its first issue of shares in a general offering to investors. This first sale of stock is called an initial public offering, or IPO.**

An IPO is called a *primary* offering when new shares are sold to raise additional cash for the company. It is a *secondary* offering when the company's founders and the venture capitalist cash in on some of their gains by selling shares. A secondary offer therefore is no more than a sale of shares from the early investors in the firm to new investors, and the cash raised in a secondary offer does not flow to the company. Of course, IPOs can be and commonly are both primary and secondary: The firm raises new cash at the same time that some of the already existing shares in the firm are sold to the public.

Some of the biggest secondary offerings have involved governments selling off stock in nationalized enterprises. For example, the Japanese government raised $12.6 billion by selling its stock in Nippon Telegraph and Telephone, and the Italian government took in $19.3 billion from the sale of its shares in the electricity company Enel. Even these two issues were dwarfed by the 2006 IPO of the state-owned Industrial and Commercial Bank of China, which raised $22 billion.

---

[1] Fortunately, the successes seem to have outweighed the failures. The National Venture Capital Association (NVCA) estimated that net returns on early-stage venture capital funds averaged over 16% a year for the 20 years ending in June 2007.

We have seen that companies may make an IPO to raise new capital or to enable the existing shareholders to cash out, but there may be other benefits to going public. For example, the company's stock price provides a readily available yardstick of performance and allows the firm to reward the management team with stock options. And, because information about the company becomes more widely available, the firm can diversify its sources of finance and reduce its borrowing cost.

While there are advantages to having a market for your shares, we should not give the impression that firms everywhere aim to go public. In many countries it is common for businesses to remain privately owned. Even in the United States many firms choose to remain as private, unlisted companies. They include some very large operations, such as Bechtel and Levi Strauss. Also, you should not think of the issue process in the United States as a one-way street; public firms often go into reverse and return to being privately owned. For a somewhat extreme example, consider the food service company Aramark. It began life in 1936 as a private company and went public in 1960. In 1984 the management bought out the company and took it private, and it remained private until 2001, when it had its second public offering. But the experiment did not last long, for 6 years later Aramark was the object of yet another buyout that took the company private once again.

Managers often chafe at the red tape involved in running a public company and at the unrelenting pressure from shareholders to report increasing earnings. These complaints have become more vocal since the passage of the Sarbanes-Oxley Act. This act has sought to prevent a repeat of the corporate scandals that brought about the collapse of Enron and WorldCom, but a consequence has been an increased reporting burden on small public companies and a rise in the number of companies reverting to private ownership.

Arranging a Public Issue

underwriter

Firm that buys an issue of securities from a company and resells it to the public.

Once a firm decides to go public, the first task is to select the underwriters. **Underwriters are investment banking firms that act as financial midwives to a new issue. Usually they play a triple role—first providing the company with procedural and financial advice, then buying the stock, and finally reselling it to the public.** A small IPO may have only one underwriter, but larger issues usually require a syndicate of underwriters who buy the issue and resell it.

spread

Difference between public offer price and price paid by underwriter.

In the typical underwriting arrangement, called a *firm commitment*, the underwriters buy the securities from the firm and then resell them to the public. The underwriters receive payment in the form of a **spread**—that is, they are allowed to sell the shares at a slightly higher price than they paid for them. But the underwriters also accept the risk that they won't be able to sell the stock at the agreed offering price. If that happens, they will be stuck with unsold shares and must get the best price they can for them. In the more risky cases, the underwriter may not be willing to enter into a firm commitment and handles the issue on a *best efforts* basis. In this case the underwriter agrees to sell as much of the issue as possible but does not guarantee the sale of the entire issue.

Before any stock can be sold to the public, the company must register the issue with the Securities and Exchange Commission (SEC). This involves preparation of a detailed and sometimes cumbersome registration statement, which contains information about the proposed financing and the firm's history, existing business, and plans for the future. The SEC does not evaluate the wisdom of an investment in the firm, but it does check the registration statement for accuracy and completeness. The firm must also comply with the "blue-sky" laws of each state, so named because they seek to protect the public against firms that fraudulently promise the blue sky to investors.[2]

---

[2] Sometimes states go beyond blue-sky laws in their efforts to protect their residents. When Apple Computer Inc. made its first public issue, the Massachusetts state government decided the offering was too risky for its residents and therefore banned the sale of the shares to investors in the state. The state relented later, after the issue was out and the price had risen. Massachusetts investors obviously did not appreciate this "protection."

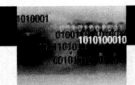

INTERNET INSIDER

Initial Public Offerings (IPOs)

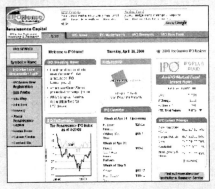

Source: IPOHome Web site.

1. In the appendix to this chapter we provide a flavor of an IPO prospectus, but you can see what an actual prospectus or registration statement looks like by using the SEC's huge database on **www.sec.gov/edgar/searchedgar/webusers.htm.** Edgar can be a bit complicated, however. We suggest instead that you first log on to **finance.yahoo.com,** look up Market Overview and IPO Calendar to find a recent IPO, and then click on *Filings,* which will take you to the correct SEC form. (Registration statements are shown as SEC Form S-1.) On the basis of this prospectus, do you think the stock looks like an attractive investment? Which parts of the statement appear most useful? Which seem the least useful?

2. When markets are booming, there tend to be more IPOs. Find out what has been happening to the market for IPOs recently by logging on to **www.ipohome.com.** Has there been an unusually large volume of IPOs recently? What have been the largest issues? How have IPOs performed recently?

3. We describe underpricing as part of the costs of a new issue. Jay Ritter's home page (**bear.cba.ufl.edu/ritter**) is a mine of information on IPO underpricing. Look up his table of underpricing by year. Is underpricing now less of a problem than in the boom IPO years of 1998–2000? Now look at Jay Ritter's table of "money-left-on-the-table." Which company provided the greatest 1-day dollar gains to investors?

---

prospectus
Formal summary that provides information on an issue of securities.

The first part of the registration statement is distributed to the public in the form of a preliminary **prospectus.** One function of the prospectus is to warn investors about the risks involved in any investment in the firm. Some investors have joked that if they read prospectuses carefully, they would never dare buy any new issue. In the nearby Internet Insider box we show how you can find real IPO prospectuses on the Web. However, if you find the prospect intimidating, you can instead turn to the appendix to this chapter, which provides a streamlined version of a possible prospectus for your restaurant business.

The company and its underwriters also need to set the issue price. To gauge how much the stock is worth, they may undertake discounted cash-flow calculations like those described in Chapter 7. They also look at the price-earnings ratios of the shares of the firm's principal competitors.

Before settling on the issue price, the underwriters generally arrange a "roadshow," which gives the underwriters and the company's management an opportunity to talk to potential investors. These investors may then offer their reaction to the issue, suggest what they think is a fair price, and indicate how much stock they would be prepared to buy. This allows the underwriters to build up a book of likely orders. Although investors are not bound by their indications, they know that if they want to maintain a good relationship with the underwriters, they must be careful not to renege on their expressions of interest.

The managers of the firm are eager to secure the highest possible price for their stock, but the underwriters are likely to be cautious because they will be left with any unsold stock if they overestimate investor demand. As a result, underwriters typically try to underprice the initial public offering. **Underpricing,** they argue, is needed to tempt investors to buy stock and to reduce the cost of marketing the issue to customers. **Underpricing represents a cost to the existing owners since the new investors are allowed to buy shares in the firm at a favorable price.**

underpricing
Issuing securities at an offering price set below the true value of the security.

Sometimes new issues are dramatically underpriced. For example, when the prospectus for the IPO of eBay was first published, the underwriters indicated that the company would sell 3.5 million shares at a price between $14 and $16 each. However, the enthusiasm for eBay's Web-based auction system was such that the underwriters increased the issue price to $18. The next morning dealers were flooded with orders to buy eBay; over 4.5 million shares traded, and the stock closed the day at a price of $47.375.

The experience of eBay is not typical, but it is common to see the stock price increase significantly from the issue price in the days following the sale. For example, one study of new issues between 1990 and 2007 found an average first-day price rise of 23%.[3] Such immediate price jumps suggest that investors would have been prepared to pay much more than they did for the shares.

| EXAMPLE 15.1 ▶ | Underpricing of IPOs |

Suppose an IPO is a secondary issue and the firm's founders sell part of their holding to investors. Clearly, if the shares are sold for less than their true worth, the founders will suffer an opportunity loss.

But what if the IPO is a primary issue that raises new cash for the company? Do the founders care whether the shares are sold for less than their market value? The following example illustrates that they do care.

Suppose Cosmos.com has 2 million shares outstanding and now offers a further 1 million shares to investors at $50. On the first day of trading the share price jumps to $80, so the shares that the company sold for $50 million are now worth $80 million. The total market capitalization of the company is 3 million × $80 = $240 million.

The value of the founders' shares is equal to the total value of the company less the value of the shares that have been sold to the public—in other words, $240 million − $80 million = $160 million. The founders might justifiably rejoice at their good fortune. However, if the company had issued shares at a higher price, it would have needed to sell fewer shares to raise the $50 million that it needs and the founders would have retained a larger share of the company. For example, suppose that the outside investors, who put up $50 million, received shares that were *worth* only $50 million. In that case the value of the founders' shares would be $240 million − $50 million = $190 million.

The effect of selling shares below their true value is to transfer $30 million of value from the founders to the investors who buy the new shares.

Unfortunately, underpricing does not mean that anyone can become wealthy by buying stock in IPOs. If an issue is underpriced, everybody will want to buy it and the underwriters will not have enough stock to go around. You are therefore likely to get only a small share of these hot issues. If it is overpriced, other investors are unlikely to want it and the underwriter will be only too delighted to sell it to you. This phenomenon is known as the *winner's curse*.[4] It implies that, unless you can spot which issues are underpriced, you are likely to receive a small proportion of the cheap issues and a large proportion of the expensive ones. Since the dice are loaded against uninformed investors, they will play the game only if there is substantial underpricing on average.

| EXAMPLE 15.2 ▶ | Underpricing of IPOs and Investor Returns |

Suppose that an investor will earn an immediate 10% return on underpriced IPOs and lose 5% on overpriced IPOs. But because of high demand, you may get only half the shares you bid for when the issue is underpriced. Suppose you bid for $1,000 of shares in two issues, one overpriced and the other underpriced. You are awarded the full $1,000 of the overpriced issue but only $500 worth of shares in the underpriced issue. The net gain on your two investments is (.10 × $500) − (.05 × $1,000) = 0. Your net profit is zero, despite the fact that, on average, the IPOs are underpriced

---

[3] These figures are provided on Jay Ritter's home page, **bear.cba.ufl.edu/ritter**.

[4] The highest bidder in an auction is the participant who places the highest value on the auctioned object. Therefore, it is likely that the winning bidder has an overly optimistic assessment of true value. Winning the auction suggests that you have overpaid for the object—this is the winner's curse. In the case of IPOs, your ability to "win" an allotment of shares may signal that the stock is overpriced.

(10% underpricing versus 5% overpricing). You have suffered the winner's curse: You "win" a larger allotment of shares when they are overpriced.

Self-Test 15.2

What is the percentage profit earned by an investor who can identify the underpriced issues in Example 15.2? Who are such investors likely to be?

---

flotation costs

The costs incurred when a firm issues new securities to the public.

The costs of a new issue are termed **flotation costs.** Underpricing is not the only flotation cost. In fact, when people talk about the cost of a new issue, they often think only of the *direct costs* of the issue. For example, preparation of the registration statement and prospectus involves management, legal counsel, and accountants, as well as underwriters and their advisers. There is also the underwriting spread. (Remember, underwriters make their profit by selling the issue at a higher price than they paid for it.) For most issues between $20 million and $80 million, the spread is 7%.

Look at the green bars (corresponding to IPOs) in Figure 15–1. These show the direct costs of going public.[5] For a small IPO of no more than $10 million, the underwriting spread and administrative costs are likely to absorb 15% to 20% of the proceeds from the issue. For the very largest IPOs, these direct costs may amount to only 5% of the proceeds.

EXAMPLE 15.3   ▶   Costs of an IPO

When the investment bank Goldman Sachs went public in 1999, the sale was partly a primary issue (the company sold new shares to raise cash) and partly a secondary one (two large existing shareholders cashed in some of their shares). The syndicate of 129 underwriters acquired a total of 69 million Goldman Sachs shares for $50.75 each and sold them to the public at an offering price of $53.[6] The underwriters' spread was therefore $53 − $50.75 = $2.25. The firm and its shareholders also paid

---

FIGURE 15–1 Total direct costs as a percentage of gross proceeds. The total direct costs for initial public offerings (IPOs), seasoned equity offerings (SEOs), convertible bonds, and straight bonds are composed of underwriter spreads and other direct expenses.

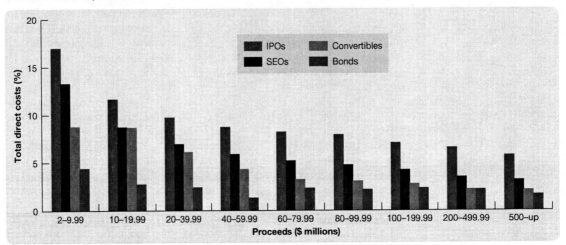

Source: Immoo Lee, Scott Lochhead, Jay Ritter, and Quanshui Zhao, "The Costs of Raising Capital," *Journal of Financial Research* 19 (Spring 1996), pp. 59–74. Copyright © 1996. Reprinted by permission.

---

[5] These figures do not capture all administrative costs. For example, they do not include management time spent on the issue.

[6] No prizes for guessing which investment bank acted as lead underwriter.

a total of $9.2 million in legal fees and other costs. By the end of the first day's trading Goldman's stock price had risen to $70.

Here are the direct costs of the Goldman Sachs issue:

Direct Expenses	
Underwriting spread	69 million × $2.25 = $155.25 million
Other expenses	9.2
Total direct expenses	$164.45 million

The total amount of money raised by the issue was 69 million × $53 = $3,657 million. Of this sum 4.5% was absorbed by direct expenses (that is, 164.45/3,657 = .045).

In addition to these direct costs, there was underpricing. The market valued each share of Goldman Sachs at $70, so the cost of underpricing was 69 million × ($70 − $53) = $1,173 million, resulting in total costs of $164.45 + $1,173 = $1,337.45 million. Therefore, while the total market value of the issued shares was 69 million × $70 = $4,830 million, direct costs and the costs of underpricing absorbed nearly 28% of the market value of the shares.

Self-Test 15.3

Suppose that the underwriters acquired Goldman Sachs shares for $60 and sold them to the public at an offering price of $64. If all other features of the offer were unchanged (and investors still valued the stock at $70 a share), what would have been the direct costs of the issue and the costs of underpricing? What would have been the total costs as a proportion of the market value of the shares?

Other New-Issue Procedures

Almost all IPOs in the United States use the bookbuilding method. In other words, the underwriters build up a book of likely orders, buy the issue from the company at a discount, and then resell it to investors. This method is in some ways like an auction, since potential buyers indicate how many shares they are prepared to buy at given prices. However, the indications are not binding and are used only as a guide to fix the price of the issue. The advantage of the bookbuilding method is that it allows underwriters to give preference to those investors whose bids are most helpful in setting the issue price and to offer them a reward in the shape of underpricing. But critics of the method point to the dangers of allowing the underwriters to decide who is allotted stock.

An alternative way to issue stock is by means of an open auction. In this case, investors are invited to submit their bids, stating both an offering price and how many shares they wish to buy. The securities are then sold to the highest bidders. Most governments, including the U.S. Treasury, sell their bonds by auction. In the United States, auctions of common stock are fairly rare. However, in 2004 Google simultaneously raised eyebrows and $1.7 billion in the world's largest IPO to be sold by auction.

15.3 The Underwriters

We have described underwriters as playing a triple role—providing advice, buying a new issue from the company, and reselling it to investors. Underwriters don't just help the company to make its initial public offering; they are called in whenever a company wishes to raise cash by selling securities to the public.

Successful underwriting requires considerable experience and financial muscle. If a large issue fails to sell, the underwriters may be left with a loss of several hundred million dollars and some very red faces. Underwriting in the United States is therefore

How Scandal Hit the Investment Banking Industry

For investment banks, 1999 looked like a wonderful year. Not only did they underwrite a near-record number of IPOs, but the stocks that they sold leaped by an average of 71% on their first day of trading, earning the underwriters some very grateful clients. Just 3 years later the same investment banks were in disgrace. Probing by then New York State Attorney General Eliot Spitzer uncovered a chronicle of unethical and shameful behavior during the boom years.

As the dot-com stock market boom developed, investment banking analysts had begun to take on the additional role of promoters of the shares they analyzed, in the process becoming celebrities with salaries to match. The early run-up in the stock price of dot-com IPOs therefore owed much to hype by the underwriters' analysts, who strongly promoted stocks that they sometimes privately thought were overpriced. One superstar Internet analyst was revealed in internal e-mails to have believed that stocks he was peddling to investors were "junk" and "a piece of crap." In many cases the stocks were indeed junk, and the underwriters who had puffed the IPOs soon found themselves sued by disgruntled investors who had bought at the inflated prices.

The underwriters' troubles deepened further when it was disclosed that in a number of cases they had allocated stock in hot new issues to the personal brokerage accounts of the CEOs of major corporate clients. This stock could then be sold, or "spun," for quick profits. Five senior executives of leading telecom companies were disclosed to have received a total of $28 million in profits from their allocation of stocks in IPOs underwritten by one bank. Over the same period the bank received over $100 million of business from these five companies. Eliot Spitzer argued that such lucrative perks were really attempts by the banks to buy future business and that the profits therefore belonged to the companies' shareholders rather than the executives. Soon top executives of several other companies were facing demands from disgruntled shareholders that they return to their companies the profits they had pocketed from hot initial public offerings.

These scandals that engulfed the investment banking industry resulted in a $1.4 billion payout by the banks and an agreement to separate investment banking and research departments, hire independent consultants, and select independent research providers. But the revelations also raised troubling questions about ethical standards and the pressures that can lead employees to unscrupulous behavior.

---

dominated by the major investment banking firms, which specialize in underwriting new issues, dealing in securities, and arranging mergers. Large commercial banks, including a number of foreign banks, are also heavily involved in underwriting. Table 15–1 lists some of the largest firms, ranked by total volume of issues in the first 9 months of 2007. Citigroup, the winner, raised a total of $511 billion. Of course, only a small proportion of this sum involved companies that were coming to the market for the first time.

Underwriting is not always fun. On October 15, 1987, the British government finalized arrangements to sell its holding of British Petroleum (BP) shares at £3.30 a share. This huge issue involving more than $12 billion was underwritten by an international group of underwriters and simultaneously marketed in a number of countries. Four days after the underwriting arrangement was finalized, the October stock market crash occurred and stock prices nose-dived. The underwriters appealed to the British government to cancel the issue, but the government hardened its heart and pointed out that the underwriters knew the risks when they agreed to handle the sale.[7] By the closing date of the offer, the price of BP stock had fallen to £2.96 and the underwriters had lost more than $1 billion.

Companies get to make only one IPO, but underwriters are in the business all the time. Wise underwriters, therefore, realize that their reputation is on the line and will not handle an issue unless they believe the facts have been presented fairly to investors. If a new issue goes wrong and the stock price crashes, the underwriters can find themselves very unpopular with their clients. For example, in 1999 the software company VA Linux went public at $30 a share. The next day trading opened at $299 a share, but then the price began to sag. Within 2 years it had fallen below $2. Disgruntled VA Linux investors sued the underwriters for overhyping the issue. VA Linux investors were not the only ones to feel aggrieved. Investment banks soon found themselves embroiled in a major scandal as evidence emerged that they had deliberately oversold

---

[7] The government's only concession was to put a floor on the underwriters' losses by giving them the option to resell their stock to the government at £2.80 a share. The BP offering is described and analyzed in C. Muscarella and M. Vetsuypens, "The British Petroleum Stock Offering: An Application of Option Pricing," *Journal of Applied Corporate Finance* 1 (1989), pp. 74–80.

TABLE 15–1 Top 10 managing underwriters of global debt and equity issues January–September 2007 (figures in billions)

Underwriter	Value of Issues	Market Share, %
Citigroup	$511	8.5
J.P. Morgan	443	7.4
Deutsche Bank	405	6.7
Merrill Lynch	364	6.1
Morgan Stanley	348	5.8
Lehman Brothers	315	5.2
Barclays Capital	297	4.9
Goldman Sachs	275	4.6
Credit Suisse	257	4.3
UBS	248	4.1

Source: Thomson Reuters Web site, **www.thomsonreuters.com.**

many of the issues that they underwrote during the dot-com boom years. As the nearby box explains, there was further embarrassment when it emerged that several well-known underwriters had engaged in "spinning"—that is, allocating stock in popular new issues to managers of their important corporate clients. The underwriter's seal of approval for a new issue no longer seemed as valuable as it once had.

15.4 General Cash Offers by Public Companies

seasoned offering
Sale of securities by a firm that is already publicly traded.

rights issue
Issue of securities offered only to current stockholders.

After the initial public offering a successful firm will continue to grow, and from time to time it will need to raise more money by issuing stock or bonds. An issue of additional stock by a company whose stock already is publicly traded is called a **seasoned offering.** Any issue of securities needs to be formally approved by the firm's board of directors. If a stock issue requires an increase in the company's authorized capital, it also needs the consent of the stockholders.

Public companies can issue securities either by making a general cash offer to investors at large or by making a **rights issue,** which is limited to existing shareholders. In the latter case, the company offers the shareholders the opportunity, or *right,* to buy more shares at an "attractive" price. For example, if the current stock price is $100, the company might offer investors an additional share at $50 for each share they hold. Suppose that before the issue an investor has one share worth $100 and $50 in the bank. If the investor takes up the offer of a new share, that $50 of cash is transferred from the investor's bank account to the company's. The investor now has two shares that are a claim on the original assets worth $100 and on the $50 cash that the company has raised. So the two shares are worth a total of $150, or $75 each.

EXAMPLE 15.4 ▶   Rights Issues

In 2007 banks around the world were battered by heavy losses on their real estate loans. The Royal Bank of Scotland, the U.K.'s second-largest bank, was no exception, and in April 2008 it announced that to rebuild its capital it would raise a record £12.22 billion (or about $24 billion) by an equity rights issue. If you were a shareholder of RBS, you received the right to buy 11 additional shares for every 18 shares that you initially owned. The purchase price was set at £2 a share.

Before the issue, the bank had approximately 10 billion shares outstanding, which were priced at £3.725 each. So investors valued the bank at $10 \times £3.725 = £37.25$ billion. The new issue increased the total number of shares by $10 \times 11/18 = 6.11$ billion and therefore raised $6.11 \times £2 = £12.22$ billion. In effect, the issue increased the total value of the bank to $37.25 + 12.22 = £49.47$ billion and reduced the value of each share to $£49.47/16.11 = £3.071$.

Suppose that you owned 18 shares in the bank before the issue. Your holding would have been worth $18 \times £3.725 = £67.05$. If you decided to take up the rights offer, you would have needed to lay out $11 \times £2 = £22$ and the value of your shareholding would have increased by exactly £22 to $29 \times £3.071 = £89.05$.

In some countries the rights issue is the most common or only method for issuing stock, but in the United States rights issues are now very rare. We therefore will concentrate on the mechanics of the general cash offer.

General Cash Offers and Shelf Registration

general cash offer
Sale of securities open to all investors by an already-public company.

When a public company makes a **general cash offer** of debt or equity, it essentially follows the same procedure used when it first went public. This means that it must first register the issue with the SEC and draw up a prospectus.[8] Before settling on the issue price, the underwriters will usually contact potential investors and build up a book of likely orders. The company will then sell the issue to the underwriters, and they in turn will offer the securities to the public.

Companies do not need to prepare a separate registration statement every time they issue new securities. Instead, they are allowed to file a single registration statement covering financing plans for up to 2 years into the future. The actual issues can then be sold to the public with scant additional paperwork, whenever the firm needs cash or thinks it can issue securities at an attractive price. This is called **shelf registration**—the registration is put "on the shelf," to be taken down, dusted off, and used as needed.

shelf registration
A procedure that allows firms to file one registration statement for several issues of the same security.

Think of how you might use shelf registration when you are a financial manager. Suppose that your company is likely to need up to $200 million of new long-term debt over the next year or so. It can file a registration statement for that amount. It now has approval to issue up to $200 million of debt, but it isn't obliged to issue any. Nor is it required to work through any *particular* underwriters—the registration statement may name the underwriters the firm thinks it may work with, but others can be substituted later.

Now you can sit back and issue debt as needed, in bits and pieces if you like. Suppose Merrill Lynch comes across an insurance company with $10 million ready to invest in corporate bonds, priced to yield, say, 7.3%. If you think that's a good deal, you say OK and the deal is done, subject to only a little additional paperwork. Merrill Lynch then resells the bonds to the insurance company, hoping for a higher price than it paid for them.

Here is another possible deal. Suppose you think you see a window of opportunity in which interest rates are "temporarily low." You invite bids for $100 million of bonds. Some bids may come from large investment bankers acting alone, others from ad hoc syndicates. But that's not your problem; if the price is right, you just take the best deal offered.

Thus shelf registration offers several advantages:

1. Securities can be issued in dribs and drabs without incurring excessive costs.
2. Securities can be issued on short notice.
3. Security issues can be timed to take advantage of "market conditions" (although any financial manager who can reliably identify favorable market conditions could make a lot more money by quitting and becoming a bond or stock trader instead).
4. The issuing firm can make sure that underwriters compete for its business.

Not all companies eligible for shelf registration actually use it for all their public issues. Sometimes they believe they can get a better deal by making one large

---

[8] The procedure is similar when a company makes an international issue of bonds or equity, but as long as these issues are not sold publicly in the United States, they do not need to be registered with the SEC.

issue through traditional channels, especially when the security to be issued has some unusual feature or when the firm believes it needs the investment banker's counsel or stamp of approval on the issue. Thus shelf registration is less often used for issues of common stock than for garden-variety corporate bonds.

Costs of the General Cash Offer

Whenever a firm makes a cash offer, it incurs substantial administrative costs. Also, the firm needs to compensate the underwriters by selling them securities below the price that they expect to receive from investors. Look back at Figure 15–1, which shows the average underwriting spread and administrative costs for several types of security issues in the United States.

The figure clearly shows that the costs are proportionately smaller for large issues. Costs may absorb 13% of a $5 million seasoned equity issue but less than 4% of a $500 million issue.

Figure 15–1 also shows that issue costs are higher for equity than for debt securities. Issue costs are higher for equity than for debt because administrative costs are somewhat higher and also because underwriting stock is riskier than underwriting bonds. The underwriters demand additional compensation for the greater risk they take in buying and reselling equity.

Self-Test 15.4

Use Figure 15–1 to compare the costs of 10 issues of $15 million of stock in a seasoned offering versus 1 issue of $150 million.

Market Reaction to Stock Issues

Because stock issues usually throw a sizable number of new shares onto the market, it is widely believed that they must temporarily depress the stock price. If the proposed issue is very large, this price pressure may, it is thought, be so severe as to make it almost impossible to raise money.

This belief in price pressure implies that a new issue depresses the stock price temporarily below its true value. However, that view doesn't appear to fit very well with the notion of market efficiency. If the stock price falls solely because of increased supply, then that stock would offer a higher return than comparable stocks and investors would be attracted to it as ants to a picnic.

Economists who have studied new issues of common stock have generally found that the announcement of the issue does result in a decline in the stock price. For industrial issues in the United States this decline amounts to about 3%.[9] While this may not sound overwhelming, such a price drop can be a large fraction of the money raised. Suppose that a company with a market value of equity of $5 billion announces its intention to issue $500 million of additional equity and thereby causes the stock price to drop by 3%. The loss in value is .03 × $5 billion, or $150 million. That's 30% of the amount of money raised (.30 × $500 million = $150 million).

What's going on here? Is the price of the stock simply depressed by the prospect of the additional supply? Possibly, but here is an alternative explanation.

Suppose managers (who have better information about the firm than outside investors) know that their stock is undervalued. If the company sells new stock at this low price, it will give the new shareholders a good deal at the expense of the old

---

[9] See, for example, P. Asquith and D. W. Mullins, "Equity Issues and Offering Dilution," *Journal of Financial Economics* 15 (January–February 1986), pp. 61–90; R. W. Masulis and A. N. Korwar, "Seasoned Equity Offerings: An Empirical Investigation," *Journal of Financial Economics* 15 (January–February 1986), pp. 91–118; and W. H. Mikkelson and M. M. Partch, "Valuation Effects of Security Offerings and the Issuance Process," *Journal of Financial Economics* 15 (January–February 1986), pp. 31–60.

shareholders. In these circumstances managers might be prepared to forgo the new investment rather than sell shares at too low a price.

If managers know that the stock is *overvalued,* the position is reversed. If the company sells new shares at the high price, it will help its existing shareholders at the expense of the new ones. Managers might be prepared to issue stock even if the new cash were just put in the bank.

Of course investors are not stupid. They can predict that managers are more likely to issue stock when they think it is overvalued, and therefore they mark the price of the stock down accordingly. **The tendency for stock prices to decline at the time of an issue may have nothing to do with increased supply. Instead, the stock issue may simply be a *signal* that well-informed managers believe the market has overpriced the stock.**[10]

15.5 The Private Placement

private placement
Sale of securities to a limited number of investors without a public offering.

Whenever a company makes a public offering, it must register the issue with the SEC. It could avoid this costly process by selling the issue privately. There are no hard-and-fast definitions of a **private placement,** but the SEC has insisted that the security should be restricted largely to knowledgeable investors.

One disadvantage of a private placement is that the investor cannot easily resell the security. This is less important to institutions such as life insurance companies, which invest huge sums of money in corporate debt for the long haul. In 1990 the SEC relaxed its restrictions on who could buy unregistered issues. Under the new rule, Rule 144a, large financial institutions can trade unregistered securities among themselves.

As you would expect, it costs less to arrange a private placement than to make a public issue. That might not be so important for the very large issues where costs are less significant, but it is a particular advantage for companies making smaller issues.

Another advantage of the private placement is that the debt contract can be custom-tailored for firms with special problems or opportunities. Also, if the firm wishes later to change the terms of the debt, it is much simpler to do this with a private placement where only a few investors are involved.

Therefore, it is not surprising that private placements occupy a particular niche in the corporate debt market, namely, loans to small and medium-sized firms. These are the firms that face the highest costs in public issues, that require the most detailed investigation, and that may require specialized, flexible loan arrangements.

We do not mean that large, safe, and conventional firms should rule out private placements. Enormous amounts of capital are sometimes raised by this method. For example, in 2005, Berkshire Hathaway, the investment company controlled by Warren Buffett, borrowed $3.75 billion in a private placement. Nevertheless, the advantages of private placement—avoiding registration costs and establishing a direct relationship with the lender—are generally more important to smaller firms.

Of course these advantages are not free. Lenders in private placements have to be compensated for the risks they face and for the costs of research and negotiation. They also have to be compensated for holding an asset that is not easily resold. All these factors are rolled into the interest rate paid by the firm. It is difficult to generalize about the differences in interest rates between private placements and public issues, but a typical yield differential is on the order of half a percentage point.

---

[10] This explanation was developed in S. C. Myers and N. S. Majluf, "Corporate Financing and Investment Decisions When Firms Have Information That Investors Do Not Have," *Journal of Financial Economics* 13 (1984), pp. 187–222.

www.mhhe.com/bmm6e

SUMMARY

How do venture capital firms design successful deals? *(LO1)*

Infant companies raise **venture capital** to carry them through to the point at which they can make their first public issue of stock. Venture capital firms try to structure the financing to avoid conflicts of interest. If both the entrepreneur and the venture capital investors have an important equity stake in the company, they are likely to pull in the same direction. The entrepreneur's willingness to take that stake also *signals* management's confidence in the company's future. In addition, most venture capital is provided in stages that keep the firm on a short leash and force it to prove at each stage that it deserves the additional funds.

How do firms make initial public offerings, and what are the costs of such offerings? *(LO2)*

The **initial public offering** is the first sale of shares in a general offering to investors. The sale of the securities is usually managed by an underwriting firm that buys the shares from the company and resells them to the public. The **underwriter** helps to prepare a **prospectus,** which describes the company and its prospects. The costs of an IPO include direct costs, such as legal and administrative fees, as well as the **underwriting spread**—the difference between the price the underwriter pays to acquire the shares from the firm and the price the public pays the underwriter for those shares. Another major implicit cost is the **underpricing** of the issue—that is, shares are typically sold to the public somewhat below the true value of the security. This discount is reflected in abnormally high average returns to new issues on the first day of trading.

What are some of the significant issues that arise when established firms make a general cash offer or a private placement of securities? *(LO3)*

There are always economies of scale in issuing securities. It is cheaper to go to the market once for $100 million than to make two trips for $50 million each. Consequently, firms "bunch" security issues. This may mean relying on short-term financing until a large issue is justified. Or it may mean issuing more than is needed at the moment to avoid another issue later.

A **seasoned offering** may depress the stock price. The extent of this price decline varies, but for issues of common stocks by industrial firms the fall in the value of the existing stock may amount to a significant proportion of the money raised. The likely explanation for this pressure is the information the market reads into the company's decision to issue stock.

Shelf registration often makes sense for debt issues by blue-chip firms. Shelf registration reduces the time taken to arrange a new issue, it increases flexibility, and it may cut underwriting costs. It seems best suited for debt issues by large firms that are happy to switch between investment banks. It seems least suited for issues of unusually risky securities or for issues by small companies that most need a close relationship with an investment bank.

Private placements are well-suited for small, risky, or unusual firms. The special advantages of private placement stem from avoiding registration expenses and a more direct relationship with the lender. These are not worth as much to blue-chip borrowers.

What is the role of the underwriter in an issue of securities? *(LO4)*

Underwriters manage the sale of the securities and advise on the price at which the issue is sold. They then buy the securities from the issuing company, and resell them to the public. The difference between the price at which the underwriter buys the securities and the price at which they are resold is the underwriter's spread. Underwriting firms have expertise in such sales because they are in the business all the time, whereas the company raises capital only occasionally.

What is a rights issue? *(LO5)*

Unlike a general cash offering, a rights issue is an offer to buy shares that is made only to existing shareholders. The shares are priced at a substantial discount to current market value, which ensures that the shareholders will either exercise the rights themselves or sell them to other investors. In either case, the firm raises funds when the right is exercised.

QUESTIONS

QUIZ

1. **Underwriting.** *(LO3)*
   a. Is a rights issue more likely to be used for an initial public offering or for subsequent issues of stock?
   b. Is a private placement more likely to be used for issues of seasoned stock or seasoned bonds by an industrial company?
   c. Is shelf registration more likely to be used for issues of unseasoned stocks or bonds by a large industrial company?

2. **Underwriting.** Each of the following terms is associated with one of the events beneath. Can you match them up? *(LO4)*
   a. Shelf registration
   b. Firm commitment
   c. Rights issue

   A. The underwriter agrees to buy the issue from the company at a fixed price.
   B. The company offers to sell stock to existing stockholders.
   C. Several issues of the same security may be sold under the same registration.

3. **Underwriting Costs.** For each of the following pairs of issues, state which issue you would expect would involve the lower proportionate underwriting and administrative costs, other things equal. *(LO3)*
   a. A large issue/a small issue.
   b. A bond issue/a common stock issue.
   c. A small private placement of bonds/a small general cash offer of bonds.

4. **IPO Costs.** Why are the issue costs for debt issues generally less than those for equity issues? *(LO2)*

5. **Venture Capital.** Why do venture capital companies prefer to advance money in stages? *(LO1)*

6. **IPOs.** Your broker calls and says that you can get 500 shares of an imminent IPO at the offering price. Should you buy? Are you worried about the fact that your broker called *you*? *(LO2)*

PRACTICE PROBLEMS

7. **IPO Underpricing.** Having heard about IPO underpricing, I put in an order to my broker for 1,000 shares of every IPO he can get for me. After 3 months, my investment record is as follows: *(LO2)*

IPO	Shares Allocated to Me	Price per Share	Initial Return
A	500	$10	7%
B	200	20	12
C	1,000	8	–2
D	0	12	23

   a. What is the average underpricing of this sample of IPOs?
   b. What is the average initial return on my "portfolio" of shares purchased from the four IPOs I bid on? Calculate the average initial return, weighting by the amount of money invested in each issue.
   c. Why have I performed so poorly relative to the average initial return on the full sample of IPOs? What lessons do you draw from my experience?

8. **IPO Costs.** Moonscape has just completed an initial public offering. The firm sold 3 million shares at an offer price of $8 per share. The underwriting spread was $.50 a share. The price of the stock closed at $12 per share at the end of the first day of trading. The firm incurred $100,000 in legal, administrative, and other costs. What were flotation costs as a fraction of funds raised? Were flotation costs for Moonscape higher or lower than is typical for IPOs of this size (see Figure 15–1)? *(LO2)*

9. **IPO Costs.** Look at the illustrative new issue prospectus in the appendix. *(LO2)*

   a. Is this issue a primary offering, a secondary offering, or both?

   b. What are the direct costs of the issue as a percentage of the total proceeds? Are these more than the average for an issue of this size?

   c. Suppose that on the first day of trading the price of Hotch Pot stock is $15 a share. What are the *total* costs of the issue as a percentage of the market price?

   d. After paying her share of the expenses, how much will the firm's president, Emma Lucullus, receive from the sale? What will be the value of the shares that she retains in the company?

10. **Flotation Costs.** "For small issues of common stock, the costs of flotation amount to about 15% of the proceeds. This means that the opportunity cost of external equity capital is about 15 percentage points higher than that of retained earnings." Does this follow? *(LO2)*

11. **Flotation Costs.** When Microsoft went public, the company sold 2 million new shares (the primary issue). In addition, existing shareholders sold .8 million shares (the secondary issue) and kept 21.1 million shares. The new shares were offered to the public at $21, and the underwriters received a spread of $1.31 a share. At the end of the first day's trading the market price was $35 a share. *(LO2)*

   a. How much money did the company receive before paying its portion of the direct costs?

   b. How much did the existing shareholders receive from the sale before paying their portion of the direct costs?

   c. If the issue had been sold to the underwriters for $30 a share, how many shares would the company have needed to sell to raise the same amount of cash?

   d. How much better off would the existing shareholders have been?

12. **Flotation Costs.** The market value of the marketing research firm Fax Facts is $600 million. The firm issues an additional $100 million of stock, but as a result the stock price falls by 2%. What is the cost of the price drop to existing shareholders as a fraction of the funds raised? *(LO2)*

13. **Flotation Costs.** Young Corporation stock currently sells for $30 per share. There are 1 million shares currently outstanding. The company announces plans to raise $3 million by offering shares to the public at a price of $30 per share. *(LO2)*

   a. If the underwriting spread is 6%, how many shares will the company need to issue in order to be left with net proceeds of $3 million?

   b. If other administrative costs are $60,000, what is the dollar value of the total direct costs of the issue?

   c. If the share price falls by 3% at the announcement of the plans to proceed with a seasoned offering, what is the dollar cost of the announcement effect?

14. **Private Placements.** You need to choose between the following types of issues: *(LO3)*

   • *A public issue of $10 million face value of 10-year debt.* The interest rate on the debt would be 8.5%, and the debt would be issued at face value. The underwriting spread would be 1.5%, and other expenses would be $80,000.

   • *A private placement of $10 million face value of 10-year debt.* The interest rate on the private placement would be 9%, but the total issuing expenses would be only $30,000.

   a. What is the difference in the proceeds to the company net of expenses?

   b. Other things equal, which is the better deal?

   c. What other factors beyond the interest rate and issue costs would you wish to consider before deciding between the two offers?

15. **Rights.** In 2008 Pandora, Inc., makes a rights issue at a subscription price of $5 a share. One new share can be purchased for every four shares held. Before the issue there were 10 million shares outstanding and the share price was $6. *(LO5)*

   a. What is the total amount of new money raised?

   b. What is the expected stock price after the rights are issued?

16. **Rights.** Practice Problem 15 contains details of a rights offering by Pandora. Suppose that the company had decided to issue the new stock at $4 instead of $5 a share. How many new shares would it have needed to raise the same sum of money? Recalculate the answers to Practice Problem 15. Show that Pandora's shareholders are just as well off if it issues the shares at $4 a share rather than the $5 assumed in Practice Problem 15. *(LO5)*

17. **Rights.** Consolidated Jewels needs to raise $2 million to pay for its Diamonds in the Rough campaign. It will raise the funds by offering 200,000 rights, each of which entitles the owner to buy one new share. The company currently has outstanding 1 million shares priced at $20 each. *(LO5)*

    a. What must be the subscription price on the rights the company plans to offer?
    b. What will be the share price after the rights issue?
    c. What is the value of a right to buy one share?
    d. How many rights would be issued to an investor who currently owns 1,000 shares?
    e. Show that the investor who currently holds 1,000 shares is unaffected by the rights issue. Specifically, show that the value of the rights plus the value of the 1,000 shares after the rights issue equals the value of the 1,000 shares before the rights issue.

18. **Rights.** Associated Breweries is planning to market unleaded beer. To finance the venture, it proposes to make a rights issue with a subscription price of $10. One new share can be purchased for each two shares held. The company currently has outstanding 100,000 shares priced at $40 a share. Assuming that the new money is invested to earn a fair return, give values for the following: *(LO5)*

    a. Number of new shares.
    b. Amount of new investment.
    c. Total value of company after issue.
    d. Total number of shares after issue.
    e. Share price after the issue.

CHALLENGE PROBLEMS

Please visit us at www.mhhe.com/bmm6e

19. **Venture Capital.** Here is a difficult question. Pickwick Electronics is a new high-tech company financed entirely by 1 million ordinary shares, all of which are owned by George Pickwick. The firm needs to raise $1 million now for stage 1 and, assuming all goes well, a further $1 million at the end of 5 years for stage 2.

    First Cookham Venture Partners is considering two possible financing schemes:

    · Buying 2 million shares now at their current valuation of $1.
    · Buying 1 million shares at the current valuation and investing a further $1 million at the end of 5 years at whatever the shares are worth.

    The outlook for Pickwick is uncertain, but as long as the company can secure the additional finance for stage 2, it will be worth either $2 million or $12 million after completing stage 2. (The company will be valueless if it cannot raise the funds for stage 2.) Show the possible payoffs for Mr. Pickwick and First Cookham, and explain why one scheme might be preferred. Assume an interest rate of zero. *(LO1)*

SOLUTIONS TO SELF-TEST QUESTIONS

15.1 Unless the firm can secure second-stage financing, it is unlikely to succeed. If the entrepreneur is going to reap any reward on his own investment, he needs to put in enough effort to get further financing. By accepting only part of the necessary venture capital, management increases its own risk and reduces that of the venture capitalist. This decision would be costly and foolish if management lacked confidence that the project would be successful enough to get past the first stage. A credible signal by management is one that only managers who are truly confident can afford to provide. However, words are cheap and there is little to be lost by saying that you are confident (although if you are proved wrong, you may find it difficult to raise money a second time).

15.2 If an investor can distinguish between overpriced and underpriced issues, she will bid only on the underpriced ones. In this case she will purchase only issues that provide a 10% gain. However, the ability to distinguish these issues requires considerable insight and research. The return to the informed IPO participant may be viewed as a return on the resources expended to become informed.

15.3 Direct expenses:

Underwriting spread = 69 million × $4	$ 276.0 million
Other expenses	9.2
Total direct expenses	$ 285.2 million
Underpricing = 69 million × ($70 − $64)	414.0
Total expenses	$ 699.2 million
Market value of issue = 69 million × $70	$4,830.0 million

Expenses as proportion of market value = 699.2/4,830 = .145 = 14.5%.

15.4 Ten issues of $15 million each will cost about 9% of proceeds, or .09 × $150 million = $13.5 million. One issue of $150 million will cost only about 4% of $150 million, or $6 million.

MINICASE

Mutt.Com was founded in 2006 by two graduates of the University of Wisconsin with help from Georgina Sloberg, who had built up an enviable reputation for backing new start-up businesses. Mutt.Com's user-friendly system was designed to find buyers for unwanted pets. Within 3 years the company was generating revenues of $3.4 million a year and, despite racking up sizable losses, was regarded by investors as one of the hottest new e-commerce businesses. The news that the company was preparing to go public therefore generated considerable excitement.

The company's entire equity capital of 1.5 million shares was owned by the two founders and Ms. Sloberg. The initial public offering involved the sale of 500,000 shares by the three existing shareholders, together with the sale of a further 750,000 shares by the company in order to provide funds for expansion.

The company estimated that the issue would involve legal fees, auditing, printing, and other expenses of $1.3 million, which would be shared proportionately between the selling shareholders and the company. In addition, the company agreed to pay the underwriters a spread of $1.25 per share (this cost also would be shared).

The roadshow had confirmed the high level of interest in the issue, and indications from investors suggested that the entire issue could be sold at a price of $24 a share. The underwriters, however, cautioned about being too greedy on price. They pointed out that indications from investors were not the same as firm orders. Also, they argued, it was much more important to have a successful issue than to have a group of disgruntled shareholders. They therefore suggested an issue price of $18 a share.

That evening Mutt.Com's financial manager decided to run through some calculations. First, she worked out the net receipts to the company and the existing shareholders assuming that the stock was sold for $18 a share. Next, she looked at the various costs of the IPO and tried to judge how they stacked up against the typical costs for similar IPOs. That brought her up against the question of underpricing. When she had raised the matter with the underwriters that morning, they had dismissed the notion that the initial day's return on an IPO should be considered part of the issue costs. One of the members of the underwriting team had asked: "The underwriters want to see a high return and a high stock price. Would Mutt.Com prefer a low stock price? Would that make the issue less costly?" Mutt.Com's financial manager was not convinced but felt that she should have a good answer. She wondered whether underpricing was only a problem because the existing shareholders were selling part of their holdings. Perhaps the issue price would not matter if they had not planned to sell.

www.mhhe.com/bmm6e

APPENDIX

Hotch Pot's New-Issue PROSPECTUS[11]

Prospectus

800,000 Shares
Hotch Pot, Inc.
Common Stock ($.01 par value)

Of the 800,000 shares of Common Stock offered hereby, 500,000 shares are being sold by the Company and 300,000 shares are being sold by the Selling Stockholders. See "Principal and Selling Stockholders." The Company will not receive any of the proceeds from the sale of shares by the Selling Stockholders.

Before this offering there has been no public market for the Common Stock. **These securities involve a high degree of risk. See "Certain Factors."**

THESE SECURITIES HAVE NOT BEEN APPROVED OR DISAPPROVED BY THE SECURITIES AND EXCHANGE COMMISSION NOR HAS THE COMMISSION PASSED ON THE ACCURACY OR ADEQUACY OF THIS PROSPECTUS. ANY REPRESENTATION TO THE CONTRARY IS A CRIMINAL OFFENSE.

	Price to Public	Underwriting Discount	Proceeds to Company*	Proceeds to Selling Shareholders†
Per share	$12.00	$1.30	$10.70	$10.70
Total†	$9,600,000	$1,040,000	$5,350,000	$3,210,000

* Before deducting expenses payable by the Company estimated at $400,000, of which $250,000 will be paid by the Company and $150,000 by the Selling Stockholders.
† The Company and the Selling Shareholders have granted to the Underwriters options to purchase up to 120,000 additional shares at the initial public offering price less the underwriting discount, solely to cover overallotment.

The Common Stock is offered, subject to prior sale, when, as, and if delivered to and accepted by the Underwriters and subject to approval of certain legal matters by their counsel and by counsel for the Company and the Selling Shareholders. The Underwriters reserve the right to withdraw, cancel, or modify such offer and reject orders in whole or in part.

Silverman Pinch Inc.   April 1, 2009

No person has been authorized to give any information or to make any representations, other than as contained therein, in connection with the offer contained in this Prospectus, and, if given or made, such information or representations must not be relied upon. This Prospectus does not constitute an offer of any securities other than the registered securities to which it relates or an offer to any person in any jurisdiction where such an offer would be unlawful. The delivery of this Prospectus at any time does not imply that information herein is correct as of any time subsequent to its date.

IN CONNECTION WITH THIS OFFERING, THE UNDERWRITER MAY OVERALLOT OR EFFECT TRANSACTIONS WHICH STABILIZE OR MAINTAIN THE MARKET PRICE OF THE COMMON STOCK OF THE COMPANY AT A LEVEL ABOVE THAT WHICH MIGHT OTHERWISE PREVAIL IN THE OPEN MARKET. SUCH STABILIZING, IF COMMENCED, MAY BE DISCONTINUED AT ANY TIME.

Prospectus Summary

The following summary information is qualified in its entirety by the detailed information and financial statements appearing elsewhere in this Prospectus.

---

[11] Real prospectuses would be much longer than our simple example. You can get a better impression of the contents of a prospectus by looking at some real ones. These are available on the SEC's site **www.sec.gov/edgar/searchedgar/webusers.htm** and are shown as Form S-1. For example, take a look at the prospectus dated 11/14/01 for the IPO of Bam!Entertainment, the publisher of games software. Notice the mixture of useful information and redundant qualification.

The Company: Hotch Pot, Inc., operates a chain of 140 fast-food outlets in the United States offering unusual combinations of dishes.

The Offering: Common Stock offered by the Company 500,000 shares; Common Stock offered by the Selling Stockholders 300,000 shares; Common Stock to be outstanding after this offering 3,500,000 shares.

Use of Proceeds: For the construction of new restaurants and to provide working capital.

The Company

Hotch Pot, Inc., operates a chain of 140 fast-food outlets in Illinois, Pennsylvania, and Ohio. These restaurants specialize in offering an unusual combination of foreign dishes.

The Company was organized in Delaware in 1999.

Use of Proceeds

The Company intends to use the net proceeds from the sale of 500,000 shares of Common Stock offered hereby, estimated at approximately $5 million, to open new outlets in midwest states and to provide additional working capital. It has no immediate plans to use any of the net proceeds of the offering for any other specific investment.

Dividend Policy

The Company has not paid cash dividends on its Common Stock and does not anticipate that dividends will be paid on the Common Stock in the foreseeable future.

Certain Factors

Investment in the Common Stock involves a high degree of risk. The following factors should be carefully considered in evaluating the Company:

Substantial Capital Needs   The Company will require additional financing to continue its expansion policy. The Company believes that its relations with its lenders are good, but there can be no assurance that additional financing will be available in the future.

Competition   The Company is in competition with a number of restaurant chains supplying fast food. Many of these companies are substantially larger and better capitalized than the Company.

Capitalization

The following table sets forth the capitalization of the Company as of December 31, 2008, and as adjusted to reflect the sale of 500,000 shares of Common Stock by the Company.

	Actual	As Adjusted
	(in thousands)	
Long-term debt	$ –	$ –
Stockholders' equity	30	35
Common stock—$.01 par value, 3,000,000 shares outstanding, 3,500,000 shares outstanding, as adjusted		
Paid-in capital	1,970	7,315
Retained earnings	3,200	3,200
Total stockholders' equity	5,200	10,550
Total capitalization	$5,200	$10,550

Selected Financial Data

[*The Prospectus typically includes a summary income statement and balance sheet.*]

Management's Analysis of Results of Operations and Financial Condition

Revenue growth for the year ended December 31, 2008, resulted from the opening of ten new restaurants in the Company's existing geographic area and from sales of a new range of desserts, notably crepe suzette with custard. Sales per customer increased by 20% and this contributed to the improvement in margins.

During the year the Company borrowed $600,000 from its banks at an interest rate of 2% above the prime rate.

Business

Hotch Pot, Inc., operates a chain of 140 fast-food outlets in Illinois, Pennsylvania, and Ohio. These restaurants specialize in offering an unusual combination of foreign dishes. 50% of company's revenues derived from sales of two dishes, sushi and sauerkraut and curry bolognese. All dishes are prepared in three regional centers and then frozen and distributed to the individual restaurants.

Management

The following table sets forth information regarding the Company's directors, executive officers, and key employees:

Name	Age	Position
Emma Lucullus	28	President, Chief Executive Officer, & Director
Ed Lucullus	33	Treasurer & Director

Emma Lucullus Emma Lucullus established the Company in 1999 and has been its Chief Executive Officer since that date.

Ed Lucullus Ed Lucullus has been employed by the Company since 1999.

Executive Compensation

The following table sets forth the cash compensation paid for services rendered for the year 2008 by the executive officers:

Name	Capacity	Cash Compensation
Emma Lucullus	President and Chief Executive Officer	$130,000
Ed Lucullus	Treasurer	$ 95,000

Certain Transactions

At various times between 1999 and 2008 First Cookham Venture Partners invested a total of $1.5 million in the Company. In connection with this investment, First Cookham Venture Partners was granted certain rights to registration under the Securities Act of 1933, including the right to have their shares of Common Stock registered at the Company's expense with the Securities and Exchange Commission.

Principal and Selling Stockholders

The following table sets forth certain information regarding the beneficial ownership of the Company's voting Common Stock as of the date of this prospectus by (i) each person known by the Company to be the beneficial owner of more than 5% of its voting Common Stock, and (ii) each director of the Company who beneficially owns voting Common Stock. Unless otherwise indicated, each owner has sole voting and dispositive power over his shares.

Name of Beneficial Owner	Shares Beneficially Owned prior to Offering		Shares to Be Sold	Shares Beneficially Owned after Offering	
	Number	Percent		Number	Percent
Emma Lucullus	400,000	13.3	25,000	375,000	12.9
Ed Lucullus	400,000	13.3	25,000	375,000	12.9
First Cookham Venture Partners	1,700,000	66.7	250,000	1,450,000	50.0
Hermione Kraft	200,000	6.7	—	200,000	6.9

Lock-Up Agreements

The holders of the Common Stock have agreed with the Underwriter not to sell, pledge, or otherwise dispose of their shares, other than as specified in this Prospectus, for a period of 180 days after the date of the Prospectus without the prior consent of Silverman Pinch.

Description of Capital Stock

The Company's authorized capital stock consists of 10,000,000 shares of voting Common Stock.

As of the date of this Prospectus, there are 4 holders of record of the Common Stock.

Under the terms of one of the Company's loan agreements, the Company may not pay cash dividends on Common Stock except from net profits without the written consent of the lender.

Underwriting

Subject to the terms and conditions set forth in the Underwriting Agreement, the Underwriter, Silverman Pinch Inc., has agreed to purchase from the Company and the Selling Stockholders 800,000 shares of Common Stock.

There is no public market for the Common Stock. The price to the public for the Common Stock was determined by negotiation between the Company and the Underwriter and was based on, among other things, the Company's financial and operating history and condition, its prospects, and the prospects for its industry in general, the management of the Company, and the market prices of securities for companies in businesses similar to that of the Company.

Legal Matters

The validity of the shares of Common Stock offered by the Prospectus is being passed on for the Company by Brown, Merkel, and Sarkozy and for the Underwriter by Harper Rudd.

Legal Proceedings

Hotch Pot was served in January 2009 with a summons and complaint in an action commenced by a customer who alleges that consumption of the Company's products caused severe nausea and loss of feeling in both feet. The Company believes that the complaint is without foundation.

Experts

The consolidated financial statements of the Company have been so included in reliance on the reports of Hooper Firebrand, independent accountants, given on the authority of that firm as experts in auditing and accounting.

Financial Statements

[Text and tables omitted.]

CHAPTER 16

Debt Policy

LEARNING OBJECTIVES

After studying this chapter, you should be able to:

1. Show why capital structure does not affect firm value in perfect capital markets.

2. Show why the tax system encourages debt finance, and derive the value of interest tax shields.

3. Show how costs of financial distress can lead to an optimal capital structure.

4. Explain why financial slack is valuable and might influence optimal capital structure.

5. Summarize bankruptcy procedures for firms that cannot pay their creditors.

Related Web sites for this chapter can be found at www.mhhe.com/bmm6e.

"Neither a borrower nor a lender be." So says Polonius in Shakespeare's *Hamlet*. Is this sound advice for the modern corporation?

Everett Collection

A firm's basic financial resource is the stream of cash flows produced by its assets and operations. When the firm is financed entirely by common stock, all those cash flows belong to the stockholders. When it issues both debt and equity, the firm splits the cash flows into two streams, a relatively safe stream that goes to the debtholders and a more risky one that goes to the stockholders.

The firm's mix of securities is known as its *capital structure*. Look at Table 16–1. You can see that in some industries companies borrow much more heavily than in others. Most high-tech firms, such as Intel and Microsoft, rely almost wholly on equity finance. So do most biotech, software and Internet companies. At the other extreme, debt accounts for a substantial part of the market value of airlines and utilities.

Capital structure is not immutable. Firms change their capital structure, sometimes almost overnight. Later in the chapter you will see how Sealed Air Corporation did just that.

Shareholders want management to choose the mix of securities that maximizes firm value. But is there an optimal capital structure? We must consider the possibility that no combination has any greater appeal than any other. Perhaps the really important decisions concern the company's assets, and decisions about capital structure are mere details—matters to be attended to but not worried about.

In the first part of the chapter we will look at examples in which capital structure *doesn't* matter. After that we will put back some of the things that do make a difference, such as taxes, bankruptcy, and the signals that your financing decisions may send to investors. We will then draw up a checklist for financial managers who need to decide on the firm's capital structure. We conclude the chapter with a brief discussion of what happens when firms cannot pay their debts and enter bankruptcy proceedings.

TABLE 16–1 Median book debt ratios for a sample of nonfinancial industries

Industry	Debt Ratio
Internet information	0.07
Biotech	0.12
Communications equipment	0.19
Semiconductors	0.21
Oil exploration	0.29
Aerospace/defense	0.32
Beverages (alcoholic)	0.36
Consumer appliances	0.40
Hotels and motels	0.53
Gas utilities	0.53
Airlines	0.73

Note: Debt ratio = $D/(D + E)$ where D and E refer to the book values of long-term debt and equity, respectively.
Source: **finance.yahoo.com**, February 2008.

16.1 How Borrowing Affects Value in a Tax-Free Economy

It is after the ball game and the pizza man is delivering a pizza to Yogi Berra. "Should I cut it into four slices as usual, Yogi?" asks the pizza man. "No," replies Yogi, "Cut it into eight; I'm hungry tonight."

capital structure
The mix of long-term debt and equity financing.

If you understand why more slices won't sate Yogi's appetite, you will have no difficulty understanding why a company's choice of **capital structure** can't increase the underlying value of the firm.

Think of a simple balance sheet, with all entries expressed as current market values:

Assets	Liabilities and Stockholders' Equity
Value of cash flows from the firm's real assets and operations	Market value of debt
	Market value of equity
Value of firm	Value of firm

The right- and left-hand sides of a balance sheet are always equal. (Balance sheets have to balance!) Therefore, if you add up the market values of all the firm's debt and equity securities, you can calculate the value of the future cash flows from the real assets and operations.

In fact, the value of those cash flows *determines* the value of the firm and therefore determines the aggregate value of all the firm's outstanding debt and equity securities. If the firm changes its capital structure, say, by using more debt and less equity financing, overall value should not change.

Think of the left-hand side of the balance sheet as the size of the pizza; the right-hand side determines how it is sliced. A company can slice its cash flow into as many parts as it likes, but the value of those parts will always sum back to the value of the unsliced cash flow. (Of course, we have to make sure that none of the cash-flow stream is lost in the slicing. We cannot say "The value of a pizza is independent of how it is sliced" if the slicer is also a nibbler.)

The basic idea here (the value of a pizza does not depend on how it is sliced) has various applications. Yogi Berra got friendly chuckles for his misapplication. Franco Modigliani and Merton Miller received Nobel Prizes for applying it to corporate financing. Modigliani and Miller, always referred to as "MM," showed in 1958 that the value of a firm does not depend on how its cash flows are "sliced." More precisely, they demonstrated the following proposition: **When there are no taxes and capital**

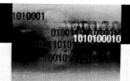

INTERNET INSIDER

Book- and Market-Value Balance Sheets

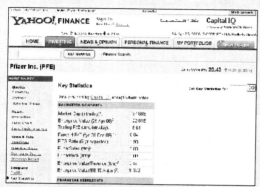

Log on to **finance.yahoo.com** and find the key statistics for Pfizer (PFE) and Coca-Cola (KO). Construct the debt ratio, debt/(debt + equity), for both firms. Now calculate their debt ratios by using the market value of equity but assuming that book value of debt approximates its market value. How does debt as a proportion of firm value change as you switch from book to market values?

Source: Yahoo! Finance Web site. Reproduced with permission of Yahoo! Inc. © 2008 by Yahoo! Inc. Yahoo! and the Yahoo! logo are trademarks of Yahoo! Inc.

markets function well, the market value of a company does not depend on its capital structure. In other words, financial managers cannot increase value by changing the mix of securities used to finance the company.

Of course, this MM proposition rests on some important simplifying assumptions. For example, capital markets have to be "well functioning." This means that investors can trade securities without restrictions and can borrow or lend on the same terms as the firm. It also means that capital markets are efficient, so securities are fairly priced given the information available to investors. (We discussed market efficiency in Chapter 7.) MM's proposition also assumes that there are no distorting taxes, and it ignores the costs encountered if a firm borrows too much and lands in financial distress.

The firm's capital structure decision can matter if these assumptions are not true or if other practical complications are encountered. But the best way to *start* thinking about capital structure is to work through MM's argument. *To keep things as simple as possible, we will ignore taxes until further notice.*

MM's Argument

Cleo, the president of River Cruises, is reviewing that firm's capital structure with Antony, the financial manager. Table 16–2 shows the current position. The company has no debt and all its operating income is paid as dividends to the shareholders. The *expected* earnings and dividends per share are $1.25, but this figure is by no means certain—it could turn out to be more or less than $1.25. For example, earnings could fall to $.75 in a slump or they could jump to $1.75 in a boom.

The price of each share is $10. The firm expects to produce a level stream of earnings and dividends in perpetuity. With no growth forecast, stockholders' expected return

TABLE 16–2 River Cruises is entirely equity-financed. Although it expects to have an income of $125,000 in perpetuity, this income is not certain. This table shows the return to the stockholder under different assumptions about operating income. We assume no taxes.

Data			
Number of shares	100,000		
Price per share	$10		
Market value of shares	$1 million		
		State of the Economy	
	Slump	Normal	Boom
Operating income	$75,000	125,000	175,000
Earnings per share	$.75	1.25	1.75
Return on shares	7.5%	12.5%	17.5%
		Expected outcome	

is equal to the dividend yield—that is, the expected dividend per share divided by the price, $1.25/$10.00 = .125, or 12.5%.

Cleo has come to the conclusion that shareholders would be better off if the company had equal proportions of debt and equity. She therefore proposes to issue $500,000 of debt at an interest rate of 10% and to use the proceeds to repurchase 50,000 shares.

restructuring
Process of changing the firm's capital structure without changing its real assets.

This is called a **restructuring**. Notice that the $500,000 raised by the new borrowing does not stay in the firm. It goes right out the door to shareholders in order to repurchase and retire 50,000 shares. Therefore, the assets and investment policy of the firm are not affected. Only the financing mix changes.

What would MM say about this new capital structure? Suppose the change is made. Operating income is the same, so the value of the "pie" is fixed at $1 million. With $500,000 in new debt outstanding, the remaining common shares must be worth $500,000, that is, 50,000 shares at $10 per share. The total value of the debt and equity is still $1 million.

Since the value of the firm is the same, common shareholders are no better or worse off than before. River Cruises shares still trade at $10 each. The overall value of River Cruises's equity falls from $1 million to $500,000, but shareholders have also received $500,000 in cash.

Antony points all this out: "The restructuring doesn't make our stockholders any richer or poorer, Cleo. Why bother? Capital structure doesn't matter."

Self-Test 16.1

Suppose River Cruises issues $350,000 of new debt (rather than $500,000) and uses the proceeds to repurchase and retire common stock. How does this affect price per share? How many shares will be left outstanding?

How Borrowing Affects Earnings per Share

Cleo is unconvinced. She prepares Table 16–3 and Figure 16–1 to show how borrowing $500,000 could increase earnings per share. Comparison of Tables 16–2 and 16–3 shows that "normal" earnings per share increase to $1.50 (versus $1.25) after the restructuring. Table 16–3 also shows more "upside" (earnings per share of $2.50 versus $1.75) and more "downside" ($.50 versus $.75).

The orange line in Figure 16–1 shows how earnings per share would vary with operating income under the firm's current all-equity financing. It is therefore simply

TABLE 16–3 River Cruises is wondering whether to issue $500,000 of debt at an interest rate of 10% and repurchase 50,000 shares. This table shows the return to the shareholder under different assumptions about operating income. Returns to shareholders are increased in normal and boom times but fall more in slumps.

Data			
Number of shares	50,000		
Price per share	$10		
Market value of shares	$500,000		
Market value of debt	$500,000		

Outcomes			
		State of the Economy	
	Slump	Normal	Boom
Operating income	$75,000	125,000	175,000
Interest	$50,000	50,000	50,000
Equity earnings	$25,000	75,000	125,000
Earnings per share	$.50	1.50	2.50
Return on shares	5%	15%	25%
		Expected outcome	

FIGURE 16-1 Borrowing increases River Cruises's earnings per share (EPS) when operating income is greater than $100,000 but reduces it when operating income is less than $100,000. Expected EPS rises from $1.25 to $1.50.

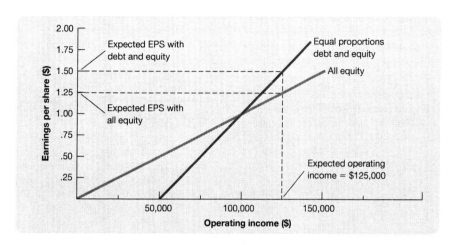

a plot of the data in Table 16–2. The purple line shows how earnings per share would vary if the company moves to equal proportions of debt and equity. It is therefore a plot of the data in Table 16–3.

Cleo reasons as follows: "It is clear that debt could either increase or reduce the return to the equityholder. In a slump the return to the equityholder is reduced by the use of debt, but otherwise it is *increased*. We could be heading for a recession but it doesn't look likely. Maybe we could help our shareholders by going ahead with the debt issue."

As financial manager, Antony replies as follows: "I agree that borrowing will increase earnings per share as long as there's no slump. But we're not really doing anything for shareholders that they can't do on their own. Suppose River Cruises does *not* borrow. In that case an investor could go to the bank, borrow $10, and then invest $20 in two shares. Such an investor would put up only $10 of her own money. Table 16–4 shows how the payoffs on this $10 investment vary with River Cruises's operating income. You can see that these payoffs are exactly the same as the investor would get by buying one share in the company after the restructuring. (Compare the last two lines of Tables 16–3 and 16–4.) It makes no difference whether shareholders borrow directly or whether River Cruises borrows on their behalf. Therefore, if River Cruises goes ahead and borrows, it will not allow investors to do anything that they could not do already, and so it cannot increase the value of the firm.

"We can run the same argument in reverse and show that investors also won't be any *worse* off after the restructuring. Imagine an investor who owns two shares in the company before the restructuring. If River Cruises borrows money, there is some chance that the return on the shares will be lower than before. If that possibility is not to our investor's taste, he can buy one share in the restructured company and also invest $10 in the firm's debt. Table 16–5 shows how the payoff on this investment varies with River Cruises's operating income. You can see that these payoffs

TABLE 16-4 Individual investors can replicate River Cruises's borrowing by borrowing on their own. In this example we assume that River Cruises has not restructured. However, the investor can put up $10 of her own money, borrow $10 more, and buy two shares at $10 apiece. This generates the same rates of return as in Table 16–3.

	State of the Economy		
	Slump	**Normal**	**Boom**
Earnings on two shares	$1.50	2.50	3.50
Less interest at 10%	$1.00	1.00	1.00
Net earnings on investment	$.50	1.50	2.50
Return on $10 investment	5%	15%	25%
		Expected outcome	

TABLE 16–5 Individual investors can also undo the effects of River Cruises's borrowing. Here the investor buys one share for $10 and lends out $10 more. Compare these rates of return to the original returns of River Cruises in Table 16–2.

	State of the Economy		
	Slump	Normal	Boom
Earnings on one share	$.50	1.50	2.50
Plus interest at 10%	$1.00	1.00	1.00
Net earnings on investment	$1.50	2.50	3.50
Return on $20 investment	7.5%	12.5%	17.5%
		Expected outcome	

are exactly the same as the investor got before the restructuring. (Compare the last lines of Tables 16–2 and 16–5.) By lending half of his capital (by investing in River Cruises's debt), the investor exactly offsets the company's borrowing. So if River Cruises goes ahead and borrows, it won't *stop* investors from doing anything that they could previously do."

This re-creates MM's original argument.[1] As long as investors can borrow or lend on their own account on the same terms as the firm, they are not going to pay more for a firm that has borrowed on their behalf. The value of the firm after the restructuring must be the same as before. **In other words, the value of the firm must be unaffected by its capital structure.**

This conclusion is widely known as **MM's proposition I.** It is also called the **MM debt-irrelevance proposition,** because it shows that under ideal conditions the firm's debt policy shouldn't matter to shareholders.

MM's proposition I (debt-irrelevance proposition)
The value of a firm is unaffected by its capital structure.

Self-Test 16.2

Suppose that River Cruises had issued $750,000 of debt, using the proceeds to buy back stock.

a. What would be the impact of a $50,000 change in operating income on earnings per share?
b. Show how a conservative investor could "undo" the change in River Cruises's capital structure by varying the investment strategy shown in Table 16–5. *Hint:* The investor will have to lend $3 for every dollar invested in River Cruises's stock.

How Borrowing Affects Risk and Return

Figure 16–2 summarizes the implications of MM's debt irrelevance proposition for River Cruises. The upper circles represent firm value; the lower circles, expected, or "normal," operating income. Restructuring does not affect the size of the circles, because the amount and risk of operating income are unchanged. Thus if the firm raises $500,000 in debt and uses the proceeds to repurchase and retire shares, the remaining shares *must* be worth $500,000, and the total value of debt and equity *must* stay at $1 million.

The two bottom circles in Figure 16–2 are also the same size. But notice that the bottom right circle shows that shareholders can expect to earn more than half of River Cruises's normal operating income. They get more than half of the expected income "pie." Does that mean shareholders are better off? MM say no. Why? Because shareholders bear more risk.

Look again at Tables 16–2 and 16–3. Restructuring does not affect operating income, regardless of the state of the economy. Therefore, debt financing does not affect the **operating risk** or, equivalently, the **business risk** of the firm. But with less equity outstanding, a change in operating income has a greater impact on earnings per

operating risk (business risk)
Risk in firm's operating income.

---
[1] There are many more general—and technical—proofs of the MM proposition. We will not pursue them here.

FIGURE 16-2 "Slicing the pie" for River Cruises. The circles on the left assume the company has no debt. The circles on the right reflect the proposed restructuring. The restructuring splits firm value (top circles) 50-50. Shareholders get more than 50% of expected, or "normal," operating income (bottom circles), but only because they bear financial risk. Note that restructuring does not affect total firm value or operating income.

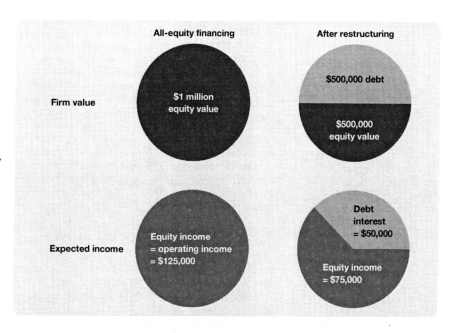

share. Suppose operating income drops from $125,000 to $75,000. Under all-equity financing, there are 100,000 shares; so earnings per share fall by $.50. With 50% debt, there are only 50,000 shares outstanding; so the same drop in operating income reduces earnings per share by $1.

You can see now why the use of debt finance is known as **financial leverage** and a firm that has issued debt is described as a *levered firm*. The debt increases the uncertainty about percentage stock returns. If the firm is financed entirely by equity, a decline of $50,000 in operating income reduces the return on the shares by 5 percentage points. If the firm issues debt, then the same decline of $50,000 in operating income reduces the return on the shares by 10 percentage points. (Compare Tables 16–2 and 16–3.) In other words, the effect of leverage is to double the magnitude of the upside and downside in the return on River Cruises's shares. Whatever the beta of the firm's shares before the restructuring, it would be twice as high afterward.

Debt finance does not affect the operating risk but it does add financial risk. With only half the equity to absorb the same amount of operating risk, risk per share must double.[2]

Consider now the implications of MM's proposition I for the expected return on River Cruises's stock. Before the proposed debt issue, the expected stream of earnings and dividends per share is $1.25. Since investment in the shares is risky, the shareholders require a return of 12.5%, or 2.5% above the interest rate. So the share price (which for a perpetuity is equal to the expected dividend divided by the required return) is $1.25/.125 = $10. The good news is that after the debt issue, expected earnings and dividends rise to $1.50. The bad news is that the risk of the shares has now doubled. So instead of being content with a return of 2.5% above the interest rate, shareholders now demand a return of 5% more than the interest rate—that is, a required return of 10 + 5 = 15%. The benefit from the rise in dividends is exactly canceled out by the

financial leverage
Debt financing to amplify the effects of changes in operating income on the returns to stockholders.

financial risk
Risk to shareholders resulting from the use of debt.

---

[2] Think back to Section 10.3, where we showed that fixed costs increase the variability in a firm's profits. These fixed costs are said to provide *operating leverage*. It is exactly the same with debt. Debt interest is a fixed cost, and therefore debt magnifies the variability of profits after interest. These fixed interest charges create financial leverage.

rise in the required return. The share price after the debt issue is $1.50/.15 = $10—exactly the same as before.

	Current Structure: All Equity	Proposed Structure: Equal Debt and Equity
Expected earnings per share	$1.25	$1.50
Share price	$10	$10
Expected return on share	12.5%	15.0%

Thus leverage increases the expected return to shareholders, but it also increases the risk. The two effects cancel, leaving shareholder value unchanged.

Debt and the Cost of Equity

What is River Cruises's cost of capital? With all-equity financing, the answer is easy. Stockholders pay $10 per share and expect earnings per share of $1.25. If the earnings per share are paid out in a perpetual stream, the expected return is $1.25/10 = .125, or 12.5%. This is the cost of equity capital, r_{equity}, and also r_{assets}, the expected return and cost of capital for the firm's assets.

Since the restructuring does not change operating earnings or firm value, it should not change the cost of capital either. Suppose the restructuring takes place. Also, by a grand stroke of luck you simultaneously become a real estate billionaire. Flush with cash, you decide to buy *all* the outstanding debt and equity of River Cruises. What rate of return should you expect on this investment? The answer is 12.5%, because once you own all the debt and equity, you will effectively own all the assets and receive all the operating income.

You will indeed get 12.5%. Table 16–3 shows expected earnings per share of $1.50, and share price is still $10. Therefore, the expected return on equity is $1.50/$10 = .15, or 15% (r_{equity} = .15). The return on debt is 10% (r_{debt} = .10). Your overall return is

$$(.5 \times .10) + (.5 \times .15) = .125 = r_{assets}$$

There is obviously a general principle here: the appropriate weighted average of r_{debt} and r_{equity} takes you to r_{assets}, the opportunity cost of capital for the company's assets. The formula is

$$r_{assets} = (r_{debt} \times D/V) + (r_{equity} \times E/V)$$

where D and E are the amounts of outstanding debt and equity and V equals overall firm value, the sum of D and E. Remember that D, E, and V are market values, not book values.

This formula does not match the weighted-average cost of capital (WACC) formula presented in Chapter 13.[3] Don't worry, we'll get to WACC in a moment. (Remember, we're still ignoring taxes.) First let's look at the implications of MM's debt-irrelevance proposition for the cost of equity.

MM's proposition I states that the firm's choice of capital structure does not affect the firm's operating income or the value of its assets. So r_{assets}, the expected return on the package of debt and equity, is unaffected.

However, we have just seen that leverage does increase the risk of the equity and the return that shareholders demand. To see how the expected return on equity varies with leverage, we simply rearrange the formula for the company cost of capital as follows:

$$r_{equity} = r_{assets} + \frac{D}{E}(r_{assets} - r_{debt}) \qquad (16.1)$$

---

[3] See Sections 13.1 and 13.2.

which in words says that

$$
\begin{matrix}
\text{Expected} \\
\text{return} \\
\text{on equity}
\end{matrix}
=
\begin{matrix}
\text{expected} \\
\text{return} \\
\text{on assets}
\end{matrix}
+
\left[
\begin{matrix}
\text{debt-} \\
\text{equity} \\
\text{ratio}
\end{matrix}
\times
\left(
\begin{matrix}
\text{expected} \\
\text{return on} \\
\text{assets}
\end{matrix}
-
\begin{matrix}
\text{expected} \\
\text{return on} \\
\text{debt}
\end{matrix}
\right)
\right]
$$

MM's proposition II
The required rate of return on equity increases as the firm's debt-equity ratio increases.

This is **MM's proposition II.** It states that the expected rate of return on the common stock of a levered firm increases in proportion to the debt-equity ratio (D/E), expressed in market values. Note that $r_{equity} = r_{assets}$ if the firm has no debt.

EXAMPLE 16.1 ▶   River Cruises's Cost of Equity

We can check out MM's proposition II for River Cruises. Before the decision to borrow,

$$
r_{equity} = r_{assets} = \frac{\text{expected operating income}}{\text{market value of all securities}}
$$
$$
= \frac{125,000}{1,000,000} = .125, \text{ or } 12.5\%
$$

If the firm goes ahead with its plan to borrow, the expected return on assets, r_{assets}, is still 12.5%. So the expected return on equity is

$$
r_{equity} = r_{assets} + \frac{D}{E}(r_{assets} - r_{debt})
$$
$$
= .125 + \frac{500,000}{500,000}(.125 - .10)
$$
$$
= .15, \text{ or } 15\%
$$

We pointed out in Chapter 13 that you can think of a debt issue as having an explicit cost and an implicit cost. The explicit cost is the rate of interest charged on the firm's debt. **But debt also increases financial risk and causes shareholders to demand a higher return on their investment. Once you recognize this implicit cost, debt is no cheaper than equity—the return that investors require on their assets is unaffected by the firm's borrowing decision.**

Self-Test 16.3

When the firm issues debt, why does r_{assets}, the company cost of capital, remain fixed while the expected return on equity, r_{equity}, changes? Why is it not the other way around?

The implications of MM's proposition II are shown in Figure 16–3. No matter how much the firm borrows, the expected return on the package of debt and equity, r_{assets}, is unchanged, but the expected rate of return on the separate parts of the package does change. How is this possible? Because the proportions of debt and equity in the package are also changing. More debt means that the cost of equity increases, but at the same time the *amount* of equity is less.

In Figure 16–3 we have drawn the rate of interest on the debt as constant no matter how much the firm borrows. That is not wholly realistic. It is true that most large, conservative companies could borrow a little more or less without noticeably affecting the interest rate that they pay. But at higher debt levels lenders become concerned that they may not get their money back and they demand higher rates of interest. Figure 16–4 modifies Figure 16–3 to take account of this. You can see that as the firm borrows more, the risk of default increases and the firm has to pay higher rates of interest. Proposition II continues to predict that the expected return on the package of debt and equity does not change. However, the slope of the r_{equity} line now tapers off as D/E increases. Why? Essentially because holders of risky debt begin to bear part of the

FIGURE 16–3 MM's proposition II with a fixed interest rate on debt. The expected return on River Cruises's equity rises in line with the debt-equity ratio. The weighted average of the expected returns on debt and equity is constant, equal to the expected return on assets.

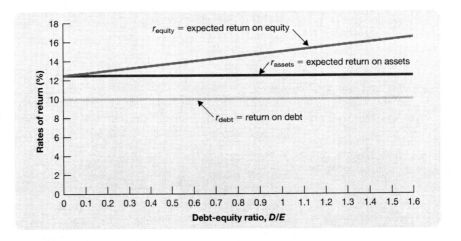

FIGURE 16–4 MM's proposition II when debt is not risk-free. As the debt-equity ratio increases, debtholders demand a higher expected rate of return to compensate for the risk of default. The expected return on equity increases more slowly when debt is risky because the debtholders take on part of the risk. The expected return on the package of debt and equity, r_{assets}, remains constant.

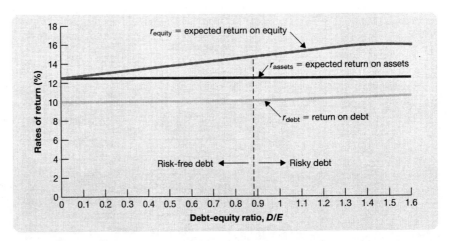

firm's operating risk. As the firm borrows more, more of that risk is transferred from stockholders to bondholders.

Figures 16–3 and 16–4 wrap up our discussion of MM's leverage-irrelevance proposition. Because overall firm value is constant, the average return on the firm's debt and equity securities is also constant, regardless of the fraction of debt financing. This result follows from MM's assumptions that capital markets are well functioning and taxes are absent. Now it's time to put taxes back into the picture.

16.2 Capital Structure and Corporate Taxes

The MM propositions suggest that debt policy should not matter. Yet financial managers do worry about debt policy, and for good reasons. Now we are ready to see why.

If debt policy were *completely* irrelevant, actual debt ratios would vary randomly from firm to firm and from industry to industry. Yet almost all airlines, utilities, and real estate development companies rely heavily on debt. And so do many firms in capital-intensive industries like steel, aluminum, chemicals, and mining. On the other hand, it is rare to find a drug or software company that is not predominantly equity-financed. Glamorous growth companies seldom use much debt, despite rapid expansion and often heavy requirements for capital.

TABLE 16–6 Since debt interest is tax-deductible, River Cruises's debtholders and equityholders expect to receive a higher combined income when the firm is leveraged

	Zero Debt	$500,000 of Debt
Expected operating income	$125,000	$125,000
Debt interest at 10%	0	50,000
Before-tax income	125,000	75,000
Tax at 35%	43,750	26,250
After-tax income	81,250	48,750
Combined debt and equity income (debt interest + after-tax income)	81,250	98,750

The explanation of these patterns lies partly in the things that we have so far left out of our discussion. Now we will put all these things back in, starting with taxes.

Debt and Taxes at River Cruises

Debt financing has one important advantage: The interest that the company pays is a tax-deductible expense, but equity income is subject to corporate tax.

To see the advantage of debt finance, let's look once again at River Cruises. Table 16–6 shows how expected income is reduced if profits are taxed at a rate of 35%. The left-hand column sets out the position if River Cruises is financed entirely by equity. The right-hand column shows what happens if the firm issues $500,000 of debt at an interest rate of 10%.

Notice that the combined income of the debtholders and equityholders is higher by $17,500 when the firm is levered. This is because the interest payments are tax-deductible. Thus every dollar of interest reduces taxes by $.35. The total amount of tax savings is simply .35 × interest payments. In the case of River Cruises, the **interest tax shield** is .35 × $50,000 = $17,500 each year. In other words, the "pie" of after-tax income that is shared by debt and equity investors increases by $17,500 relative to the zero-debt case. Since the debtholders receive no more than the going rate of interest, all the benefit of this interest tax shield is captured by the shareholders.

The interest tax shield is a valuable asset. Let's see how much it could be worth. Suppose that River Cruises plans to replace its bonds when they mature and to keep "rolling over" the debt indefinitely. It therefore looks forward to a permanent stream of tax savings of $17,500 per year. These savings depend only on the corporate tax rate and on the ability of River Cruises to earn enough to cover interest payments. So the risk of the tax shield is likely to be small. If we wish to compute the present value of all the future tax savings associated with permanent debt, we should discount the interest tax shields at a relatively low rate.

But what rate? The most common assumption is that the risk of the tax shields is the same as that of the interest payments generating them. Thus we discount at 10%, the expected rate of return demanded by investors who are holding the firm's debt. If the debt is permanent, then the firm can look forward to annual savings of $17,500 in perpetuity. Their present value is

interest tax shield
Tax savings resulting from deductibility of interest payments.

$$\text{PV tax shield} = \frac{\$17,500}{.10} = \$175,000$$

This is what the tax savings are worth to River Cruises.

How does company value change? We continue to assume that if the firm is all-equity-financed, the shareholders will demand a 12.5% return and therefore the company will be valued at $81,250/.125 = $650,000.[4] But if River Cruises issues $500,000

---

[4] The firm was worth $1 million when the corporate tax rate was zero (see Table 16–2). It is worth only $650,000 when all-equity-financed because 35% of income is lost to taxes.

of permanent debt, the package of all the firm's securities increases by the value of the tax shield to $650,000 + $175,000 = $825,000.

Let us generalize. The interest payment each year equals the rate of interest times the amount borrowed, or $r_{\text{debt}} \times D$. The annual tax saving is the corporate tax rate T_c times the interest payment. Therefore,

$$\text{Annual tax shield} = \text{corporate tax rate} \times \text{interest payment}$$
$$= T_c \times (r_{\text{debt}} \times D)$$

If the tax shield is perpetual, we use the perpetuity formula to calculate its present value:

$$\text{PV tax shields} = \frac{\text{annual tax shield}}{r_{\text{debt}}} = \frac{T_c \times (r_{\text{debt}} \times D)}{r_{\text{debt}}} = T_c D \qquad \textbf{(16.2)}$$

Of course the present value of the tax shield is less if the firm does not plan to borrow permanently or if it may not be able to use the tax shields in the future. This present value ($T_c D$) is actually the maximum possible value. However, we will continue to use this value in the rest of the chapter in order to keep the argument and illustrations simple.

Self-Test 16.4

In the year ending October 2007, Wal-Mart paid out $1,929 million as debt interest. How much more tax would Wal-Mart have paid if the firm had been entirely equity-financed? What would be the present value of Wal-Mart's interest tax shield if the company planned to keep its borrowing permanently at the 2007 level? Assume an interest rate of 6% and a corporate tax rate of 35%.

How Interest Tax Shields Contribute to the Value of Stockholders' Equity

MM's proposition I amounts to saying that "the value of the pizza does not depend on how it is sliced." The pizza is the firm's assets, and the slices are the debt and equity claims. If we hold the pizza constant, then a dollar more of debt means a dollar less of equity value.

But there is really a third slice—the government's. MM would still say that the value of the pizza—in this case the company value *before* taxes—is not changed by slicing. But anything the firm can do to reduce the size of the government's slice obviously leaves more for the others. One way to do this is to borrow money. This reduces the firm's tax bill and increases the cash payments to the investors. The value of their investment goes up by the present value of the tax savings.

In a no-tax world, MM's proposition I states that the value of the firm is unaffected by capital structure. But MM also modified proposition I to recognize corporate taxes:

Value of levered firm = value if all-equity-financed + present value of tax shield

In the special case of permanent debt,

$$\text{Value of levered firm} = \text{value if all-equity-financed} + T_c D \qquad \textbf{(16.3)}$$

This "corrected" formula is illustrated in Figure 16–5. It implies that borrowing increases firm value and shareholders' wealth.

Corporate Taxes and the Weighted-Average Cost of Capital

We have shown that when there are corporate taxes, debt provides the company with a valuable tax shield. Few companies explicitly calculate the present value of interest tax shields associated with a particular borrowing policy. The tax shields are not forgotten, however, because they show up in the discount rate used to evaluate capital investments.

FIGURE 16–5 The heavy purple line shows how the interest tax shields affect the market value of the firm. Additional borrowing decreases corporate income tax payments and increases the cash flows available to investors. Thus market value increases.

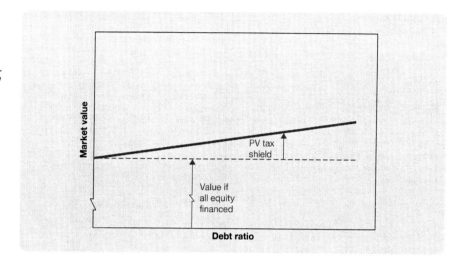

Since debt interest is tax-deductible, the government in effect pays 35% of the interest cost. So to keep its investors happy, the firm has to earn the *after-tax* rate of interest on its debt and the return required by shareholders. Once we recognize the tax benefit of debt, the weighted-average cost of capital formula (see Chapter 13 for a review if you need one) becomes

$$\text{WACC} = (1 - T_c)\, r_{\text{debt}} \left(\frac{D}{D+E} \right) + r_{\text{equity}} \left(\frac{E}{D+E} \right)$$

Notice that when we allow for the tax advantage of debt, the weighted-average cost of capital depends on the *after-tax* rate of interest $(1 - T_c) \times r_{\text{debt}}$.

EXAMPLE 16.2 ▶ **WACC and Debt Policy**

We can use the weighted-average cost of capital formula to see how leverage affects River Cruises's cost of capital if the company pays corporate tax. When a company has no debt, the weighted-average cost of capital and the return required by shareholders are identical. In the case of River Cruises the WACC with all-equity financing is 12.5%, and the value of the firm is $650,000.

Now let us calculate the weighted-average cost of capital if River Cruises issues $500,000 of permanent debt ($D = \$500,000$). Company value increases by PV tax shield = $175,000, from $650,000 to $825,000 (meaning that $D + E = \$825,000$). Therefore the value of equity must be $825,000 − $500,000 = $325,000 ($E = \$325,000$).

Table 16–6 shows that when River Cruises borrows, the expected equity income is $48,750. So the expected return to shareholders is 48,750/325,000 = 15% ($r_{\text{equity}} = .15$). The interest rate is 10% ($r_{\text{debt}} = .10$), and the corporate tax rate is 35% ($T_c = .35$). This is all the information we need to see how leverage affects River Cruises's weighted-average cost of capital:

$$\text{WACC} = (1 - T_c) r_{\text{debt}} \left(\frac{D}{D+E} \right) + r_{\text{equity}} \left(\frac{E}{D+E} \right)$$

$$= (1 - .35).10 \left(\frac{500,000}{825,000} \right) + .15 \left(\frac{325,000}{825,000} \right) = .0985, \text{ or } 9.85\%$$

We saw earlier that if there are no corporate taxes, the weighted-average cost of capital is unaffected by borrowing. But when there are corporate taxes, debt provides

408   Corporate Finance

FIGURE 16–6 Changes in River Cruises's cost of capital with increased leverage when there are corporate taxes. The after-tax cost of debt is assumed to be constant at $(1 - .35)10\% = 6.5\%$. With increased borrowing the cost of equity rises, but more slowly than in the no-tax case (see Figure 16–3). The weighted-average cost of capital (WACC) declines as the firm borrows more.

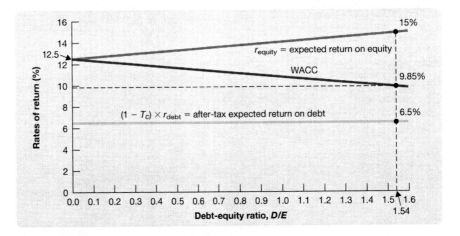

the company with a new benefit—the interest tax shield. In this case leverage reduces the weighted-average cost of capital (in River Cruises's case from 12.5% to 9.85%).

Figure 16–6 repeats Figure 16–3 except that now we have allowed for the effect of taxes on River Cruises's cost of capital. You can see that as the company borrows more, the expected return on equity rises, but the rise is less rapid than in the absence of taxes. The after-tax cost of debt is only 6.5%. As a result, the weighted-average cost of capital declines. For example, if the company has debt of $500,000, the equity is worth $325,000 and the debt/equity ratio (D/E) is $500,000/$325,000 = 1.54. Figure 16–6 shows that with this amount of debt the weighted-average cost of capital is 9.85%, the same figure that we calculated above.

The Implications of Corporate Taxes for Capital Structure

If borrowing provides an interest tax shield, the implied optimal debt policy appears to be embarrassingly extreme: All firms should borrow to the hilt. This maximizes firm value and minimizes the weighted-average cost of capital.

MM were not that fanatical about it. No one would expect the gains to apply at extreme debt ratios. For example, if a firm borrows heavily, all its operating income may go to pay interest and therefore there are no corporate taxes to be paid. There is no point in such firms borrowing any more.

There may also be some tax *disadvantages* to borrowing, for bondholders have to pay personal income tax on any interest they receive. The top rate of tax on bond interest is 35%. Stockholders, on the other hand, are taxed at only 15% on both dividends and capital gains. Capital gains have the additional advantage that they are not taxed until the stock is sold.[5]

All this suggests that there may come a point at which the tax savings from debt level off and may even decline. But it doesn't explain why highly profitable companies with large tax bills often thrive with little or no debt. There are clearly factors besides tax to consider. One such factor is the likelihood of financial distress.

16.3 Costs of Financial Distress

Financial distress occurs when promises to creditors are broken or honored with difficulty. Sometimes financial distress leads to bankruptcy. Sometimes it means only skating on thin ice.

---

[5] The delay reduces the present value of the tax payment.

As we will see, financial distress is costly. Investors know that levered firms may run into financial difficulty, and they worry about the **costs of financial distress.** That worry is reflected in the current market value of the levered firm's securities. Even the most blue-chip firms are concerned about how their debt is perceived by investors. They know that they will be charged a lower rate of interest if the probability of default is minimal, and they are therefore anxious to maintain an investment-grade rating.

Even if the firm is not now in financial distress, investors factor the potential for future distress into their assessment of current value. This means that the overall value of the firm is

$$\text{Overall market value} = \text{value if all-equity-financed} + \text{PV tax shield} - \text{PV costs of financial distress}$$

The present value of the costs of financial distress depends both on the probability of distress and on the magnitude of the costs encountered if distress occurs.

Figure 16–7 shows how the trade-off between the tax benefits of debt and the costs of distress determines optimal capital structure. Think of a firm like River Cruises, which starts with no debt but considers moving to higher and higher debt levels, holding its assets and operations constant.

At moderate debt levels the probability of financial distress is trivial, and therefore the tax advantages of debt dominate. But at some point additional borrowing causes the probability of financial distress to increase rapidly and the potential costs of distress begin to take a substantial bite out of firm value. The theoretical optimum is reached when the present value of tax savings from further borrowing is just offset by increases in the present value of costs of distress.

This is called the **trade-off theory** of optimal capital structure. The theory says that managers will try to increase debt levels to the point where the value of additional interest tax shields is exactly offset by the additional costs of financial distress.

Now let's take a closer look at financial distress.

Bankruptcy Costs

In principle, bankruptcy is merely a legal mechanism for allowing creditors (that is, lenders) to take over the firm when the decline in the value of its assets triggers a default on outstanding debt. If the company cannot pay its debts, the company is turned over to the creditors, who become the new owners; the old stockholders are left with nothing. Bankruptcy is not the *cause* of the decline in the value of the firm. It is the result.

In practice, of course, anything involving courts and lawyers cannot be free. The fees involved in a bankruptcy proceeding are paid out of the remaining value of the

costs of financial distress Costs arising from bankruptcy or distorted business decisions before bankruptcy.

trade-off theory Debt levels are chosen to balance interest tax shields against the costs of financial distress.

FIGURE 16–7 The trade-off theory of capital structure. The curved orange line shows how the market value of the firm at first increases as the firm borrows but finally decreases as the costs of financial distress become more and more important. The optimal capital structure balances the costs of financial distress against the value of the interest tax shields generated by borrowing.

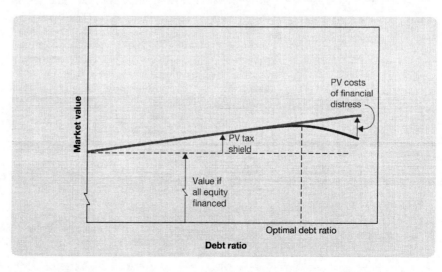

firm's assets. Creditors end up with only what is left after paying the lawyers and other court expenses. If there is a possibility of bankruptcy, the current market value of the firm is reduced by the present value of these potential costs.

It is easy to see how increased leverage affects the costs of financial distress. The more the firm owes, the higher the chance of default and therefore the greater the expected value of the associated costs. This reduces the current market value of the firm.

Creditors foresee the costs and realize that if default occurs, the bankruptcy costs will come out of the value of the firm. For this they demand compensation in advance in the form of a higher promised interest rate. This reduces the possible payoffs to stockholders and reduces the current market value of their shares.

Self-Test 16.5   Suppose investors foresee $2 million of legal costs if the firm defaults on its bonds. How does this affect the value of the firm's bonds if bankruptcy occurs? How does the possibility of default affect the interest rate demanded by bondholders *today*? How does this possibility affect today's value of the firm's common stock?

When large firms file for bankruptcy, they usually do so under an arrangement called *Chapter 11*. The purpose of Chapter 11 is to nurse the firm back to health and enable it to face the world again. This requires approval of a reorganization plan for who gets what; under the plan each class of creditors needs to give up its claim in exchange for new securities or a mixture of new securities and cash. The challenge is to design a new capital structure that will satisfy the creditors and allow the firm to solve the business problems that got it into trouble in the first place. Sometimes it proves possible to satisfy both demands and the patient emerges fit and healthy. Often, however, the proceedings involve costly delays and legal tangles, and the business continues to deteriorate.

Bankruptcy costs can add up fast. Failed energy giant Enron set a record with legal, accounting, and other professional costs of $1 billion. And WorldCom paid between $800 million and $1 billion in fees during the 21 months that it spent in Chapter 11.[6]

Of course, these are exceptional cases, for only the largest firms can lay their hands on a billion dollars when bankrupt. But daunting as such numbers may seem, bankruptcy costs average only about 3% of the value of a firm in the year before bankruptcy.[7] The proportion is typically higher for small firms than for large ones; it seems that there are significant economies of scale in going bankrupt.

Thus far we have discussed only the *direct* (that is, legal and administrative) costs of bankruptcy. The *indirect* costs reflect the difficulties of running a company while it is going through bankruptcy. When Eastern Airlines entered bankruptcy in 1989, it was in severe financial trouble, but it still had some valuable, profit-making routes and some readily salable assets such as planes and terminal facilities. These assets were more than sufficient to repay in full its liabilities of $3.7 billion. However, the bankruptcy judge was determined to keep Eastern flying. Unfortunately, Eastern's losses continued to pile up. After the airline spent nearly 2 years under the "protection" of the bankruptcy court, the judge called it a day, the assets were sold off, and the creditors received less than $.9 billion. The unsuccessful attempt at resuscitation had cost Eastern's creditors $2.8 billion.

We don't know how much these indirect costs add to the expenses of bankruptcy. We suspect it is a significant number, particularly when bankruptcy proceedings are prolonged. Perhaps the best evidence is the reluctance of creditors to force a firm into bankruptcy. In principle, they would be better off to end the agony and seize the assets as soon as possible. But, instead, creditors often overlook defaults in the hope of nursing the firm over a difficult period. They do this in part to avoid the costs of

---

[6] See "Enron Bankruptcy Specialist to File for Additional Payment," *The Wall Street Journal*, September 3, 2004, p. A2, and "Weil Gotshal Leads Pack as Firms Gobble $50 Million MCI Fees," *The Lawyer*, April 26, 2004, p. 5.
[7] See, for example, L. A. Weiss, "Bankruptcy Resolution: Direct Costs and Violation of Priority of Claims," *Journal of Financial Economics* 27 (October 1990), pp. 285–314.

bankruptcy. There is an old financial saying, "Borrow $1,000 and you've got a banker. Borrow $10,000,000 and you've got a partner."

Financial Distress without Bankruptcy

Not every firm that gets into trouble goes bankrupt. As long as the firm can scrape up enough cash to pay the interest on its debt, it may be able to postpone bankruptcy for many years. Eventually the firm may recover, pay off its debt, and escape bankruptcy altogether.

A narrow escape from bankruptcy does *not* mean that costs of financial distress are avoided. When a firm is in trouble, suppliers worry that they may not be paid, potential customers fear that the firm will not be able to honor its warranties, and employees start slipping out for job interviews. The firm's bondholders and stockholders both want it to recover, but in other respects their interests may be in conflict. In times of financial distress the security holders are like many political parties—united on generalities but threatened by squabbling on any specific issue. **Financial distress is costly when these conflicts get in the way of running the business. Stockholders are tempted to forsake the usual objective of maximizing the overall market value of the firm and to pursue narrower self-interest instead. They are tempted to play games at the expense of their creditors. These games add to the costs of financial distress.**

Think of a company—call it Double-R Nutting—which is teetering on the brink of bankruptcy. It has large debts and large losses. Double-R's assets have little value, and if its debts were due today, Double-R would default, leaving the firm bankrupt. The debtholders would perhaps receive a few cents on the dollar, and the shareholders would be left with nothing.

But suppose the debts are not due yet. That grace period explains why Double-R's shares still have value. There could be a stroke of luck that will rescue the firm and allow it to pay off its debts with something left over. That's a long shot—unless firm value increases sharply, the stock will be valueless. But the owners have a secret weapon: They control investment and operating strategy.

The First Game: Bet the Bank's Money   Suppose Double-R has the opportunity to take a wild gamble. If it does not come off, the shareholders will be no worse off; the company will probably go under anyway. But if the gamble does succeed, there will be more than enough assets to pay off the debt and the surplus will go into the shareholders' pockets. You can see why management might want to take the chance. In taking the gamble, they are essentially betting the debtholders' money, but if Double-R does hit the jackpot, the equityholders get most of the loot.

One owner-manager of a small bankrupt company called KenDavis Industries put the point this way: "Everyone agrees there is no shareholder equity—so *we've* got *nothing* to lose. The *banks* have it all on the line now—not us." This was essentially the situation facing Federal Express while it was still struggling in 1974. It had only $5,000 left in its checking account but needed $24,000 for its weekly jet fuel payment. Fred Smith took the incentive to gamble literally. He took the firm's remaining $5,000 and boarded a plane for Las Vegas, where he won $27,000. When asked how he had mustered the nerve to do this, he replied, "What difference did it make? Without the funds for the fuel companies, we couldn't have flown anyway."[8] The effects of such distorted incentives to take on risk are usually not this blatant, but the results can be the same. For example, Sambo's Restaurants borrowed while in bankruptcy proceedings and used the funds to pay for a risky marketing initiative, changing the name and concept of its restaurants. When the gamble failed, unsecured creditors suffered most of the loss: They received only 11 cents of each dollar owed them.[9]

---

[8] Roger Frock, *Changing How the World Does Business, FedEx's Incredible Journey to Success: The Inside Story* (San Francisco: Berrett-Koehler Publishers, 2006).

[9] The KenDavis and Sambo's cases are cited in Lynn M. LoPucki, "The Trouble with Chapter 11," *Wisconsin Law Review*, 1993, pp. 729–760.

These kinds of warped capital investment strategies are costly for the bondholders and for the firm as a whole. Why are they associated with financial distress? Because the temptation to follow such strategies is strongest when the odds of default are high. A healthy firm would never invest in Double-R's lousy gamble, since it would be gambling with its own money, not the bondholders'. A healthy firm's creditors would not be vulnerable to this type of game.

The Second Game: Don't Bet Your Own Money   We have just seen how shareholders, acting in their narrow self-interest, may take on risky, unprofitable projects. These are errors of commission. We will now illustrate how conflicts of interest may also lead to errors of omission.

Suppose Double-R uncovers a relatively safe project with a positive NPV. Unfortunately, the project requires a substantial investment. Double-R will need to raise this extra cash from its shareholders. Although the project has a positive NPV, the profits may not be sufficient to rescue the company from bankruptcy. If that is so, all the profits from the new project will be used to help pay off the company's debt, and the shareholders will get no return on the cash they put up. Although it is in the firm's interest to go ahead with the project, it is not in the *owners'* interest, and the project will be passed up.

Again, our example illustrates a general point. The value of any investment opportunity to the firm's *stockholders* is reduced because project benefits must be shared with the bondholders. Thus it may not be in the stockholders' self-interest to contribute fresh equity capital even if that means forgoing positive-NPV opportunities.

These two games illustrate potential conflicts of interest between stockholders and debtholders. The conflicts, which theoretically affect all levered firms, become much more serious when firms are staring bankruptcy in the face. **If the probability of default is high, managers and stockholders will be tempted to take on excessively risky projects. At the same time, stockholders may refuse to contribute more equity capital even if the firm has safe, positive-NPV opportunities. Stockholders would rather take money out of the firm than put new money in.**

The company knows that lenders will demand a higher rate of interest if they are worried that games will be played at their expense. So to reassure lenders that its intentions are honorable, the firm will commonly agree to **loan covenants.** For example, it may promise to limit future borrowing and not to pay excessive dividends. Of course, no amount of fine print can cover every possible game that the company might play. For instance, no contract can ensure that companies will accept all positive-NPV investments and reject negative ones.

We do not mean to leave the impression that managers and stockholders always succumb to temptation unless restrained. Usually they refrain voluntarily, not only because of a sense of fair play but also on pragmatic grounds: A firm or individual that makes a killing today at the expense of a creditor will be coldly received when the time comes to borrow again. Aggressive game playing is done only by out-and-out crooks and by firms in extreme financial distress. Firms limit borrowing precisely because they don't wish to land in distress and be exposed to the temptation to play.

loan covenant
Agreement between firm and lender requiring the firm to fulfill certain conditions to safeguard the loan.

Self-Test 16.6   We have described two games that might be played by firms in financial distress. Why are the games costly? How does the possibility that the game might be played at some point in the future affect today's capital structure decisions?

Costs of Distress Vary with Type of Asset

Suppose your firm's only asset is a large downtown hotel, mortgaged to the hilt. A recession hits, occupancy rates fall, and the mortgage payments cannot be met. The lender takes over and sells the hotel to a new owner and operator. The stock is worthless and you use the firm's stock certificates for wallpaper.

What is the cost of bankruptcy? In this example, probably very little. The value of the hotel is, of course, much less than you hoped, but that is due to the lack of guests, not to bankruptcy. Bankruptcy does not damage the hotel itself. The direct bankruptcy costs are restricted to items such as legal and court fees, real estate commissions, and the time the lender spends sorting things out.

Suppose we repeat the story of Heartbreak Hotel for Fledgling Electronics. Everything is the same, except for the underlying assets. Fledgling is a high-tech going concern, and much of its value reflects investors' belief that its research team will come up with profitable ideas. Fledgling is a "people business"; its most important assets go down in the elevator and into the parking lot every night.

If Fledgling gets into trouble, the stockholders may be reluctant to put up money to cash in on those profitable ideas—why should they put up cash which will simply go to pay off the banks? Failure to invest is likely to be much more serious for Fledgling than for a company like Heartbreak Hotel.

If Fledgling finally defaults on its debt, the lender would find it much more difficult to cash in by selling off the assets. In fact, if trouble comes, many of those assets may drive into the sunset and never come back.

Some assets, like good commercial real estate, can pass through bankruptcy and reorganization largely unscathed; the values of other assets are likely to be considerably diminished. The losses are greatest for intangible assets that are linked to the continuing prosperity of the firm. That may be why debt ratios are low in the pharmaceutical industry, where company values depend on continued success in research and development. It may also explain the low debt ratios in many service companies, whose main asset is their skilled labor. The moral of these examples is this: **Do not think only about whether borrowing is likely to bring trouble. Think also of the value that may be lost if trouble comes.**

Self-Test 16.7

For which of the following companies would the costs of financial distress be most serious? Why?

- A 3-year-old biotech company. So far the company has no products approved for sale, but its scientists are hard at work developing a breakthrough drug.
- An oil production company with 50 producing wells and 20 million barrels of proven oil reserves.

We have now completed our review of the building blocks of the trade-off theory of optimal capital structure. In the next section we will sum up that theory and briefly cover a competing "pecking order" theory.

16.4 Explaining Financing Choices

The Trade-Off Theory

Financial managers often think of the firm's debt-equity decision as a trade-off between interest tax shields and the costs of financial distress. Of course, there is controversy about how valuable interest tax shields are and what kinds of financial trouble are most threatening, but these disagreements are only variations on a theme. Thus Figure 16–7 illustrates the debt-equity trade-off.

This trade-off theory predicts that target debt ratios will vary from firm to firm. Companies with safe, tangible assets and plenty of taxable income to shield ought to have high target ratios. Unprofitable companies with risky, intangible assets ought to rely primarily on equity financing.

All in all, this trade-off theory of capital structure tells a comforting story. It avoids extreme predictions and rationalizes moderate debt ratios. But what are the facts? Can the trade-off theory of capital structure explain how companies actually behave?

The answer is yes and no. On the yes side, the trade-off theory successfully explains many industry differences in capital structure. For example, high-tech growth companies, whose assets are risky and mostly intangible, normally use relatively little debt. Utilities or retailers can and do borrow heavily because their assets are tangible and relatively safe.

On the no side, there are other things the trade-off theory cannot explain. It cannot explain why some of the most successful companies thrive with little debt. Consider, for example, the large pharmaceutical company Johnson & Johnson, which is basically all-equity-financed. Granted, Johnson & Johnson's most valuable assets are intangible: the fruits of its research and development. We know that intangible assets and conservative capital structures should go together. But Johnson & Johnson also has a very large corporate income tax bill ($2.7 billion in 2007) and the highest possible credit rating. It could borrow enough to save tens of millions of tax dollars without raising a whisker of concern about possible financial distress.

Our example illustrates an odd fact about real-life capital structures: The most profitable companies generally borrow the least. Here the trade-off theory fails, for it predicts exactly the reverse. Under the trade-off theory, high profits should mean more debt-servicing capacity and more taxable income to shield and therefore should result in a *higher* debt ratio.

Self-Test 16.8
Rank these industries in order of predicted debt ratios under the trade-off theory of capital structure: (a) Internet software; (b) auto manufacturing; (c) regulated electric utilities.

A Pecking Order Theory

There is an alternative theory which could explain why profitable companies borrow less. It is based on *asymmetric information*—managers know more than outside investors about the profitability and prospects of the firm. Thus investors may not be able to assess the true value of a new issue of securities by the firm. They may be especially reluctant to buy newly issued common stock, because they worry that the new shares will turn out to be overpriced.

Such worries can explain why the announcement of a stock issue can drive down the stock price.[10] If managers know more than outside investors, they will be tempted to time stock issues when their companies' stock is *overpriced*—in other words, when the managers are relatively pessimistic. On the other hand, optimistic managers will see their companies' shares as *underpriced* and decide *not* to issue. You can see why investors would learn to interpret the announcement of a stock issue as a "pessimistic manager" signal and mark down the stock price accordingly. You can also see why optimistic financial managers—and most managers *are* optimistic!—would view a common stock issue as a relatively expensive source of financing.

All these problems are avoided if the company can finance with internal funds, that is, with earnings retained and reinvested. But if external financing is required, the path of least resistance is debt, not equity. Issuing debt seems to have a trifling effect on stock prices. There is less scope for debt to be misvalued and therefore a debt issue is a less worrisome signal to investors.

pecking order theory
Firms prefer to issue debt rather than equity if internal finance is insufficient.

These observations suggest a **pecking order theory** of capital structure. It goes like this:

1. Firms prefer internal finance, since these funds do not send any adverse signals that may lower the stock price.
2. If external finance is required, firms issue debt first and issue equity only as a last resort. This pecking order arises because an issue of debt is less likely than an equity issue to be interpreted by investors as a bad omen.

---

[10] We described this "announcement effect" in Chapter 15.

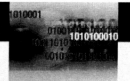

Capital Structure

1. On **finance.yahoo.com** find the profile for PepsiCo (PEP) and IBM (IBM), and then look at each firm's annual balance sheet and income statement under Financials. Calculate the present value of the interest tax shield contributed by each company's long-term debt. Now suppose that each issues $3 billion more of long-term debt and uses the proceeds to repurchase equity. How would the interest tax shield change?

2. Go back to the Yahoo! home page, click on *Industries,* and find the *Industry Browser.* This will give you a table of financial ratios for different industries. Compare the debt-equity ratios for different industries. Can you account for the differences? Are they better explained by the trade-off theory or the pecking order theory?

Source: Yahoo! Finance Web site. Reproduced with permission of Yahoo! Inc. © 2008 by Yahoo! Inc. Yahoo! and the Yahoo! logo are trademarks of Yahoo! Inc.

In this story, there is no clear target debt-equity mix, because there are two kinds of equity, internal and external. The first is at the top of the pecking order, and the second is at the bottom. The pecking order explains why the most profitable firms generally borrow less; it is not because they have low target debt ratios but because they don't need outside money. Less profitable firms issue debt because they do not have sufficient internal funds for their capital investment program and because debt is first in the pecking order for *external* finance.

The pecking order theory does not deny that taxes and financial distress can be important factors in the choice of capital structure. However, the theory says that these factors are less important than managers' preference for internal over external funds and for debt financing over new issues of common stock.

For most U.S. corporations, internal funds finance the majority of new investment, and most external financing comes from debt. These aggregate financing patterns are consistent with the pecking order theory. Yet the pecking order seems to work best for mature firms. Fast-growing high-tech firms often resort to a series of common stock issues to finance their investments. For this type of firm common stock often comes at the *top* of the pecking order. The reasons why the pecking order theory works for some firms and not others are not well understood.

The Two Faces of Financial Slack

Other things equal, it's better to be at the top of the pecking order than at the bottom. Firms that have worked down the pecking order and need external equity may end up living with excessive debt or bypassing good investments because shares can't be sold at what managers consider a fair price.

financial slack
Ready access to cash or debt financing.

When asked about what factors are uppermost in their minds when they think about debt policy, financial managers commonly mention the tax advantage of debt and the importance of maintaining the firm's credit rating. But they place even greater emphasis on the need to retain flexibility so that the company has access to funds for pursuing new projects when they come along.[11] In other words, they place a high value on **financial slack.** Having financial slack means having cash, marketable securities,

---

[11] J. R. Graham and C. R. Harvey, "The Theory and Practice of Corporate Finance: Evidence from the Field." *Journal of Financial Economics* 61 (2001), pp. 187–243.

and ready access to the debt markets or to bank financing. Ready access basically requires conservative financing so that potential lenders see the company's debt as a safe investment.

In the long run, a company's value rests more on its capital investment and operating decisions than on financing. Therefore, you want to make sure your firm has sufficient financial slack so that financing is quickly available for good investments. Financial slack is most valuable to firms with plenty of positive-NPV growth opportunities. That is another reason why growth companies usually aspire to conservative capital structures.

However, there is also a dark side to financial slack. Too much of it may encourage managers to take it easy, expand their perks, or empire-build with cash that should be paid back to stockholders. Michael Jensen has stressed the tendency of managers with ample free cash flow (or unnecessary financial slack) to plow too much cash into mature businesses or ill-advised acquisitions. "The problem," Jensen says, "is how to motivate managers to disgorge the cash rather than investing it below the cost of capital or wasting it in organizational inefficiencies."[12]

If that's the problem, then maybe debt is an answer. Scheduled interest and principal payments are contractual obligations of the firm. Debt forces the firm to pay out cash. Perhaps the best debt level would leave just enough cash in the bank, after debt service, to finance all positive-NPV projects, with not a penny left over.

We do not recommend this degree of fine-tuning, but the idea is valid and important. For some firms, the threat of financial distress may have a good effect on managers' incentives. After all, skating on thin ice can be useful if it makes the skater concentrate. Likewise, managers of highly levered firms are more likely to work harder, run a leaner operation, and think more carefully before they spend money.

The nearby box tells the story of how Sealed Air Corporation borrowed more than $300 million, using the proceeds of the loan to pay a special cash dividend to shareholders. The net effect was an increase in debt from a trivial level to fully 65% of the total value of the firm. The dramatic increase in debt committed the firm to pay out large sums of money as interest, leaving it with little opportunity to fritter its cash away in pursuit of a comfortable life. Sealed Air showed great improvements in efficiency after the change in capital structure.

16.5 Bankruptcy Procedures

workout

Agreement between a company and its creditors establishing the steps the company must take to avoid bankruptcy.

bankruptcy

The reorganization or liquidation of a firm that cannot pay its debts.

Firms that issue debt always bear a risk that when the debt comes due, they will not be able to pay their creditors. At that point, the firm may be forced into bankruptcy. We conclude this chapter with a brief overview of the bankruptcy process.

A corporation that cannot pay its debts will often try to come to an informal agreement with its creditors. This is known as a **workout.** A workout may take several forms. For example, the firm may negotiate an *extension,* that is, an agreement with its creditors to delay payments. Or the firm may negotiate a *composition,* in which the firm makes partial payments to its creditors in exchange for relief of its debts.

The advantage of a negotiated agreement is that the costs and delays of formal bankruptcy are avoided. However, the larger the firm and the more complicated its capital structure, the less likely it is that a negotiated settlement can be reached.

If the firm cannot get an agreement, then it may have no alternative but to file for **bankruptcy.**[13] Under the federal bankruptcy system the firm has a choice of procedures. In about two-thirds of the cases a firm will file for, or be forced into, bankruptcy

---

[12] M. C. Jensen, "Agency Costs of Free Cash Flow, Corporate Finance and Takeovers," *American Economic Review* 26 (May 1986), p. 323.

[13] Occasionally creditors will allow the firm to petition for bankruptcy after it has reached an agreement with the creditors. This is known as a *prepackaged bankruptcy.* The court simply approves the agreed workout plan.

FINANCE IN PRACTICE

How Sealed Air's Change in Capital Structure Acted as a Catalyst to Organizational Change

Sealed Air Corporation manufactures a wide variety of packaging materials such as plastic packing bubbles and Jiffy padded envelopes.

As it entered 1989, Sealed Air was very conservatively financed with $33 million in total debt and over $54 million in cash. Thus, rather than borrowing cash, the company was actually a net lender. However, in June of that year Sealed Air dramatically changed its capital structure by paying a special one-time dividend of $40 a share. With about 8.25 million shares trading, the total cash payout amounted to almost $330 million, or close to 90% of the total market value of the firm's common stock. To help finance this special dividend, the company borrowed a total of $307 million. Thus, the company went overnight from being a net lender to being a very heavy borrower. Debt now amounted to 125% of the book value of the assets and 65% of their market value.

Until the change in capital structure Sealed Air's performance was no better than that of the industry as a whole. But the change was a prelude to a sharp improvement in the company's operating performance. In the following 5 years, operating profit increased by 70% while the asset base grew by only 9%. This improvement in profitability was more than matched by the company's stock market performance. The initial effect of Sealed Air's announced change in capital structure was a jump of 10% in the stock price. Over the next 5½ years the stock outperformed the market by 400%.

What then motivated the change in capital structure and what role, if any, did this change play in the company's subsequent performance?

Some of the gains from the change in capital structure may have come from the fact that the company was able to offset the interest payments against tax. But this does not appear to have been a primary motive. Instead, the change appears to have been management's response to the realization that life at Sealed Air was in many respects too comfortable. For years patents had insulated the company from competition. Cash was plentiful. So the company never needed to think hard about requests to invest in new projects, and there was no sense of urgency in removing inefficiencies. In the management's view it would take nothing less than a "crisis" to shake employees out of their complacency. The change in capital structure was just such a crisis.

The sharp increase in debt levels meant that cash was no longer abundant for it was now needed to pay the debtholders and was literally essential to the company's survival. Thus managers now felt under pressure to make those efficiency gains that previously had not seemed worthwhile. As employees became aware of the need for more effective operations, it was possible to decentralize decision making within the company and to install a more effective system of performance measurement and compensation. The result was a sharp increase in profit margins and a reduction in the working capital and fixed assets employed to generate each dollar of sales. It seemed that the capital structure change had succeeded in kickstarting a remarkable improvement in Sealed Air's performance.

Source: Adapted from K. H. Wruck, "Financial Policy as a Catalyst for Organizational Change: Sealed Air Corporation's Leveraged Special Dividend," *Journal of Applied Corporate Finance* 7 (Winter 1995), pp. 20–37. Used with permission.

---

liquidation
Sale of bankrupt firm's assets.

under Chapter 7 of the 1978 Bankruptcy Reform Act. Then the firm's assets are **liquidated**—that is, sold—and the proceeds are used to pay creditors.

There is a pecking order of unsecured creditors.[14] First come claims for expenses that arise after bankruptcy is filed, such as attorneys' fees or employee compensation earned after the filing. If such postfiling claims did not receive priority, no firm in bankruptcy proceedings could continue to operate. Next come claims for wages and employee benefits earned in the period immediately prior to the filing. Taxes are next in line, together with debts to some government agencies such as the Small Business Administration or the Pension Benefit Guarantee Corporation. Finally come general unsecured claims such as bonds or unsecured trade debt.

reorganization
Restructuring of financial claims on failing firm to allow it to keep operating.

The alternative to a liquidation is to seek a **reorganization,** which keeps the firm as a going concern and usually compensates creditors with new securities in the reorganized firm. Such reorganizations are generally in the shareholders' interests—they have little to lose if things deteriorate further and everything to gain if the firm recovers.

Firms attempting reorganization seek refuge under Chapter 11 of the Bankruptcy Reform Act. Chapter 11 is designed to keep the firm alive and operating and to protect the value of its assets while a plan of reorganization is worked out. During this period, other proceedings against the firm are halted and the company is operated by existing management or by a court-appointed trustee.

---

[14] Secured creditors have the first priority to the collateral pledged for their loans.

The responsibility for developing a plan of reorganization may fall on the debtor firm. If no trustee is appointed, the firm has 120 days to present a plan to creditors. If this deadline is *not* met, or if a trustee is appointed, anyone can submit a plan—the trustee, for example, or a committee of creditors.

The reorganization plan is basically a statement of who gets what; each class of creditors gives up its claim in exchange for new securities. (Sometimes creditors receive cash as well.) The problem is to design a new capital structure for the firm that will (1) satisfy the creditors and (2) allow the firm to solve the *business* problems that got the firm into trouble in the first place. Sometimes only a plan of baroque complexity can satisfy these two requirements.

The reorganization plan goes into effect if it is accepted by creditors and confirmed by the court. Acceptance requires approval by a majority of each class of creditor. Once a plan is accepted, the court normally approves it, provided that *each* class of creditors has approved it and that the creditors will be better off under the plan than if the firm's assets were liquidated and distributed. The court may, under certain conditions, confirm a plan even if one or more classes of creditors vote against it. This is known as a *cram-down*.

The interests of the different classes of creditors do not always coincide. For example, junior creditors may threaten to slow the process as a way of extracting concessions from senior creditors. The senior creditors may take less than 100 cents on the dollar and give something to junior creditors in order to expedite the process and reach an agreement.

Chapter 11 proceedings are often successful, and the patient emerges fit and healthy. But in other cases cure proves impossible and the assets are liquidated. Sometimes the firm may emerge from Chapter 11 for a brief period before it is once again submerged by disaster and back in bankruptcy. For example, TWA came out of bankruptcy at the end of 1993 and was back again less than 2 years later, prompting jokes about "Chapter 22." TWA has plenty of company in this regard. In recent years, about 80% of large firms have emerged from bankruptcy proceedings with a second life, but nearly one-third of those reorganized firms met with failure within 5 years.[15] Among other notable "serial failures" are Planet Hollywood, Grand Union, Memorex, Continental Airlines, and Harvard Industries, which had the rare distinction of achieving a "Chapter 44."

The Choice between Liquidation and Reorganization

Here is an idealized view of the bankruptcy decision. Whenever a payment is due to creditors, management checks the value of the firm. If the firm is worth more than the promised payment, the firm pays up (if necessary, raising the cash by an issue of shares). If not, the equity is worthless, and the firm defaults on its debt and petitions for bankruptcy. If in the court's judgment the assets of the bankrupt firm can be put to better use elsewhere, the firm is liquidated and the proceeds are used to pay off the creditors. Otherwise, the creditors simply become the new owners and the firm continues to operate.

In practice, matters are rarely so simple. For example, we observe that firms often petition for bankruptcy even when the equity has a positive value. Moreover, the bankruptcy court may decide to keep the firm on life support even when the assets could be used more efficiently elsewhere. There are several reasons for this.

First, although the reorganized firm is legally a new entity, it is entitled to any tax-loss carry-forwards belonging to the old firm. If the firm is liquidated rather than reorganized, any tax-loss carry-forwards disappear. Thus there is an incentive to continue in operation even if assets are better used by another firm.

Second, if the firm's assets are sold off, it is easy to determine what is available to pay the creditors. However, when the company is reorganized, it needs to conserve cash as far as possible. Therefore, claimants are generally paid in a mixture of cash and securities. This makes it less easy to judge whether they have received their entitlement. For example, each bondholder may be offered $300 in cash and $700 in

---

[15] "The Firms That Can't Stop Failing," *The Economist,* September 7, 2002.

a new bond which pays no interest for the first 2 years and a low rate of interest there-after. A bond of this kind in a company that is struggling to survive may not be worth much, but the bankruptcy court usually looks at the face value of the new bonds and may therefore regard the bondholders as paid in full.

Senior creditors who know they are likely to get a raw deal in a reorganization are likely to press for a liquidation. Shareholders and junior creditors prefer a reorganiza-tion. They hope that the court will not interpret the pecking order too strictly and that they will receive some crumbs.

Third, although shareholders and junior creditors are at the bottom of the pecking order, they have a secret weapon: they can play for time. Bankruptcies of large companies often take several years before a plan is presented to the court and agreed to by each class of creditor. (The bankruptcy proceedings of the Missouri Pacific Railroad took a total of 22 years.) When they use delaying tactics, the junior claimants are betting on a turn of fortune that will rescue their investment. On the other hand, the senior creditors know that time is working against them, so they may be prepared to accept a smaller payoff as part of the price for getting a plan accepted. Also, prolonged bankruptcy cases are costly. (While their cases are extreme, we've seen that the WorldCom and Enron bankruptcies each generated about $1 billion in legal and administrative costs.) Senior claimants may see their money seeping into lawyers' pockets and therefore decide to settle quickly.

Fourth, while a reorganization plan is being drawn up, the company is allowed to buy goods on credit and borrow money. Postpetition creditors (those who extend credit to a firm already in bankruptcy proceedings) have priority over the old creditors, and their debt may even be secured by assets that are already mortgaged to existing debtholders. This also gives the prepetition creditors an incentive to settle quickly, before their claim on assets is diluted by the new debt.

Finally, profitable companies may file for Chapter 11 bankruptcy to protect them-selves against "burdensome" suits. For example, in 1982 Manville Corporation was threatened by 16,000 damage suits alleging injury from asbestos. Manville filed for bankruptcy under Chapter 11, and the bankruptcy judge agreed to put the damage suits on hold until the company was reorganized. This took 6 years. Of course, legislators worry that these actions are contrary to the original intent of the bankruptcy acts.

The U.S. bankruptcy system is often described as debtor-friendly. In some other countries, the bankruptcy regime is designed to recover as much cash as possible for the lenders. While critics of Chapter 11 complain about the costs of saving businesses that are not worth saving, commentators elsewhere bemoan the fact that their bank-ruptcy laws are causing the breakup of potentially healthy businesses.

SUMMARY

What is the goal of the capital structure decision? What is the financial manager trying to do? When would capital structure *not* matter? *(LO1)*

The goal is to maximize the overall market value of all the securities issued by the firm. Think of the financial manager as taking all the firm's real assets and selling them to investors as a package of securities. Some financial managers choose the simplest package possible: all-equity financing. Others end up issuing dozens of types of debt and equity securities. The financial manager must try to find the particular combination that maxi-mizes the market value of the firm. If firm value increases, common stockholders will benefit.

But capital structure does not necessarily affect firm value. Modigliani and Miller's (MM's) famous **debt-irrelevance proposition** states that firm value can't be increased by changing **capital structure.** Therefore, the proportions of debt and equity financing don't matter. **Financial leverage** does increase the expected rate of return to shareholders, but the risk of their shares increases proportionally. MM show that the extra return and extra risk balance out, leaving shareholders no better or worse off.

www.mhhe.com/bmm6e

www.mhhe.com/bmm6e

Of course, MM's argument rests on simplifying assumptions. For example, it assumes efficient, well-functioning capital markets and ignores taxes and costs of financial distress. But even if these assumptions are incorrect in practice, MM's proposition is important. It exposes logical traps that financial managers sometimes fall into, particularly the idea that debt is "cheap financing" because the explicit cost of debt (the interest rate) is less than the cost of equity. Debt has an implicit cost too, because increased borrowing increases **financial risk** and the cost of equity. When both costs are considered, debt is not cheaper than equity. MM show that if there are no corporate income taxes, the firm's weighted-average cost of capital does not depend on the amount of debt financing.

How do corporate income taxes modify MM's leverage-irrelevance proposition? *(LO2)*

Debt interest is a tax-deductible expense. Thus borrowing creates an **interest tax shield,** which equals the marginal corporate tax rate T_c times the interest payment $r_{debt} \times D$. Future interest tax shields are usually valued by discounting at the borrowing rate r_{debt}. In the special case of permanent debt,

$$\text{PV tax shield} = \frac{T_c(r_{debt} \times D)}{r_{debt}} = T_c D$$

Of course, interest tax shields are valuable only for companies that are making profits and paying taxes.

If interest tax shields are valuable, why don't all taxpaying firms borrow as much as possible? *(LO3)*

The more they borrow, the higher the odds of financial distress. The **costs of financial distress** can be broken down as follows:

- Direct bankruptcy costs, primarily legal and administrative costs.
- Indirect bankruptcy costs, reflecting the difficulty of managing a company when it is in bankruptcy proceedings.
- Costs of the threat of bankruptcy, such as poor investment decisions resulting from conflicts of interest between debtholders and stockholders.

Combining interest tax shields and costs of financial distress leads to a **trade-off theory** of optimal capital structure. The trade-off theory says that financial managers should increase debt to the point where the value of additional interest tax shields is just offset by additional costs of possible financial distress.

The trade-off theory says that firms with safe, tangible assets and plenty of taxable income should operate at high debt levels. Less profitable firms, or firms with risky, intangible assets, ought to borrow less.

What's the pecking order theory? *(LO4)*

The **pecking order theory** says that firms prefer internal financing (that is, earnings retained and reinvested) over external financing. If external financing is needed, they prefer to issue debt rather than issue new shares. The pecking order theory starts with the observation that managers know more than outside investors about the firm's value and prospects. Investors realize that firms may seek to issue equity when their stock is overvalued and therefore mark down the stock price when an equity issue is announced. Internal financing avoids this problem. If external financing is necessary, debt is the first choice.

The pecking order theory says that the amount of debt a firm issues will depend on its need for external financing. The theory also suggests that financial managers should try to maintain at least some **financial slack,** that is, a reserve of ready cash or unused borrowing capacity.

On the other hand, too much financial slack may lead to slack managers. High debt levels (and the threat of financial distress) can create strong incentives for managers to work harder, conserve cash, and avoid negative-NPV investments.

Is there a rule for finding optimal capital structure? *(LO3, 4)*

Sorry, there are no simple answers for capital structure decisions. Debt may be better than equity in some cases, worse in others. But there are at least four dimensions for the financial manager to think about.

- *Taxes.* How valuable are interest tax shields? Is the firm likely to continue paying taxes over the full life of a debt issue? Safe, consistently profitable firms are most likely to stay in a taxpaying position.
- *Risk.* Financial distress is costly even if the firm survives it. Other things equal, financial distress is more likely for firms with high business risk. That is why risky firms typically issue less debt.

www.mhhe.com/bmm6e

- *Asset type.* If distress does occur, the costs are generally greatest for firms whose value depends on intangible assets. Such firms generally borrow less than firms with safe, tangible assets.
- *Financial slack.* How much is enough? More slack makes it easy to finance future investments, but it may weaken incentives for managers. More debt, and therefore less slack, increases the odds that the firm may have to issue stock to finance future investments.

What happens when firms cannot pay their creditors? *(LO5)*

A firm that cannot meet its obligations may try to arrange a **workout** with its creditors to enable it to settle its debts. If this is unsuccessful, the firm may file for **bankruptcy,** in which case the business may be liquidated or reorganized. **Liquidation** means that the firm's assets are sold and the proceeds used to pay creditors. **Reorganization** means that the firm is maintained as an ongoing concern and creditors are compensated with securities in the reorganized firm. Ideally, reorganization should be chosen over liquidation when the firm as a going concern is worth more than its liquidation value. However, the conflicting interests of the different parties can result in violations of this principle.

LISTING OF EQUATIONS

16.1 $r_{\text{equity}} = r_{\text{assets}} + \dfrac{D}{E}(r_{\text{assets}} - r_{\text{debt}})$

16.2 PV tax shields $= \dfrac{\text{annual tax shield}}{r_{\text{debt}}} = \dfrac{T_c \times (r_{\text{debt}} \times D)}{r_{\text{debt}}} = T_c D$

16.3 Value of levered firm = value if all-equity-financed $+ T_c D$

QUESTIONS

QUIZ

1. **MM's Leverage-Irrelevance Proposition.** True or false? MM's leverage-irrelevance proposition says: *(LO1)*
   a. The value of the firm does not depend on the fraction of debt versus equity financing.
   b. As financial leverage increases, the value of the firm increases by just enough to offset the additional financial risk absorbed by equity.
   c. The cost of equity increases with financial leverage only when the risk of financial distress is high.
   d. If the firm pays no taxes, the weighted-average cost of capital does not depend on the debt ratio.

2. **Effects of Leverage.** Increasing financial leverage can increase both the cost of debt (r_{debt}) and the cost of equity (r_{equity}). How can the overall cost of capital stay constant? (Assume the firm pays no taxes.) *(LO1)*

3. **Tax Shields.** What is an interest tax shield? How does it increase the size of the "pie" for after-tax income stockholders? Explain. (*Hint:* Construct a simple numerical example showing how financial leverage affects the total cash flow available to debt and equity investors. Be sure to hold pretax operating income constant.) *(LO2)*

4. **Value of Tax Shields.** Establishment Industries borrows $800 million at an interest rate of 7.6%. It expects to maintain this debt level into the far future. What is the present value of interest tax shields? Establishment will pay tax at an effective rate of 35%. *(LO2)*

5. **Bankruptcy.** True or false? *(LO5)*
   a. When a company becomes bankrupt, it is usually in the interests of the equityholders to seek a liquidation rather than a reorganization.
   b. A reorganization plan must be presented for approval by each class of creditor.
   c. The Internal Revenue Service has first claim on the company's assets in the event of bankruptcy.
   d. In a reorganization, creditors may be paid off with a mixture of cash and securities.
   e. When a company is liquidated, one of the most valuable assets to be sold is often the tax-loss carry-forward.

6. **Trade-Off Theory.** What is the trade-off theory of optimal capital structure? How does it define the optimal debt ratio? *(LO3)*

7. **Financial Distress.** Give three examples of the types of costs incurred by firms in financial distress. *(LO3)*

8. **Pecking Order Theory.** What is the pecking order theory of optimal capital structure? If the theory is correct, what types of firms would you expect to operate at high debt levels? *(LO4)*

9. **Financial Slack.** Why is financial slack valuable? *(Hint:* What does the pecking order theory say about financial slack? Are there circumstances where too much financial slack might actually reduce the market value of the firm?) *(LO4)*

10. **Earnings and Leverage.** Suppose that River Cruises, which currently is all-equity-financed, issues $250,000 of debt and uses the proceeds to repurchase 25,000 shares. Assume that the firm pays no taxes and that debt finance has no impact on its market value. Rework Table 16–3 to show how earnings per share and share return now vary with operating income. *(LO1)*

11. **Debt Irrelevance.** Suppose an investor is unhappy with River Cruises's decision to borrow $250,000 (see the previous question). What modifications can she make to her own investment portfolio to offset the effects of the firm's additional borrowing? *(LO1)*

12. **Leverage and P/E Ratio.** Calculate the ratio of price to expected earnings for River Cruises both before and after it borrows the $250,000. Why does the P/E ratio fall after the increase in leverage? *(LO1)*

13. **Tax Shields.** Now suppose that the corporate tax is $T_c = .35$. Demonstrate that when River Cruises borrows the $250,000, the combined after-tax income of its debtholders and equityholders increases (compared to all-equity financing) by 35% of the firm's interest expense regardless of the state of the economy. *(LO2)*

PRACTICE PROBLEMS

14. **Equity Return and Leverage.** The common stock and debt of Northern Sludge are valued at $70 million and $30 million, respectively. Investors currently require a 16% return on the common stock and an 8% return on the debt. If Northern Sludge issues an additional $10 million of common stock and uses this money to retire debt, what happens to the expected return on the stock? Assume that the change in capital structure does not affect the risk of the debt and that there are no taxes. *(LO1)*

15. **Earnings and Leverage.** Reliable Gearing currently is all-equity-financed. It has 10,000 shares of equity outstanding, selling at $100 a share. The firm is considering a capital restructuring. The low-debt plan calls for a debt issue of $200,000 with the proceeds used to buy back stock. The high-debt plan would exchange $400,000 of debt for equity. The debt will pay an interest rate of 10%. The firm pays no taxes. *(LO1)*

a. What will be the debt-to-equity ratio after each contemplated restructuring?

b. If earnings before interest and tax (EBIT) will be either $90,000 or $130,000, what will be earnings per share for each financing mix for both possible values of EBIT? If both scenarios are equally likely, what is expected (i.e., average) EPS under each financing mix? Is the high-debt mix preferable?

c. Suppose that EBIT is $100,000. What is EPS under each financing mix? Why are they the same in this particular case?

16. **Leverage and Risk Premiums.** Astromet is financed entirely by common stock and has a beta of 1.0. The firm pays no taxes. The stock has a price-earnings multiple of 10 and is priced to offer a 10% expected return. The company decides to repurchase half the common stock and substitute an equal value of debt. *(LO1)*

Assume that the debt yields a *risk-free* 5%. Calculate

a. the beta of the common stock after the refinancing.

b. the required return and risk premium on the common stock before the refinancing.

c. the required return and risk premium on the common stock after the refinancing.

d. the required return on the debt.

e. the required return on the company (i.e., stock and debt combined) after the refinancing.

Assume that the operating profit of the firm is expected to remain constant. Give

f. the percentage increase in earnings per share after the refinancing.

g. the new price-earnings multiple. *(Hint:* Has anything happened to the stock price?)

17. **Leverage and Capital Costs.** Hubbard's Pet Foods is financed 80% by common stock and 20% by bonds. The expected return on the common stock is 12%, and the rate of interest on the bonds is 6%. Assume that the bonds are default-free and that there are no taxes. Now assume that Hubbard's issues more debt and uses the proceeds to retire equity. The new financing mix is 60% equity and 40% debt. If the debt is still default-free, what happens to the expected rate of return on equity? What happens to the expected return on the package of common stock and bonds? *(LO2)*

18. **Leverage and Capital Costs.** "MM totally ignore the fact that as you borrow more, you have to pay higher rates of interest." Explain carefully whether this is a valid objection. *(LO1)*

19. **Debt Irrelevance.** What's wrong with the following arguments? *(LO1)*

    a. As the firm borrows more and debt becomes risky, both stock- and bondholders demand higher rates of return. Thus by *reducing* the debt ratio we can reduce *both* the cost of debt and the cost of equity, making everybody better off.

    b. Moderate borrowing doesn't significantly affect the probability of financial distress or bankruptcy. Consequently, moderate borrowing won't increase the expected rate of return demanded by stockholders.

    c. A capital investment opportunity offering a 10% internal rate of return is an attractive project if it can be 100% debt-financed at an 8% interest rate.

    d. The more debt the firm issues, the higher the interest rate it must pay. That is one important reason why firms should operate at conservative debt levels.

20. **Leverage and Capital Costs.** A firm currently has a debt-equity ratio of 1/2. The debt, which is virtually riskless, pays an interest rate of 6%. The expected rate of return on the equity is 12%. What would happen to the expected rate of return on equity if the firm reduced its debt-equity ratio to 1/3? Assume the firm pays no taxes. *(LO1)*

21. **Leverage and Capital Costs.** If an increase in the debt-equity ratio makes both debt and equity more risky, how can the cost of capital remain unchanged? *(LO1)*

22. **Tax Shields.** Look back to Table 3–3 where we provided a summary 2006 income statement for PepsiCo, Inc. If the tax rate is 35%, what is PepsiCo's annual interest tax shield? What is the present value of the annual tax shield if the company plans to maintain its current debt level indefinitely? Assume a discount rate of 8%. *(LO2)*

23. **WACC.** Here is Establishment Industries's market-value balance sheet (figures in millions):

Net working capital	$ 550	Debt	$ 800
Long-term assets	2,150	Equity	1,900
Value of firm	$2,700		$2,700

The debt is yielding 7%, and the cost of equity is 14%. The tax rate is 35%. Investors expect this level of debt to be permanent. *(LO2)*

a. What is Establishment's WACC?

b. Write out a market-value balance sheet assuming Establishment has no debt. Use your answer to Quiz Question 4.

24. **Tax Shields and WACC.** Here are book- and market-value balance sheets of the United Frypan Company:

BOOK-VALUE BALANCE SHEET			
Net working capital	$ 20	Debt	$ 40
Long-term assets	80	Equity	60
	$ 100		$ 100

MARKET-VALUE BALANCE SHEET			
Net working capital	$ 20	Debt	$ 40
Long-term assets	140	Equity	120
	$ 160		$ 160

Assume that MM's theory holds except for taxes. There is no growth, and the $40 of debt is expected to be permanent. Assume a 35% corporate tax rate. *(LO2)*

a. How much of the firm's value is accounted for by the debt-generated tax shield?

b. What is United Frypan's after-tax WACC if $r_{debt} = 8\%$ and $r_{equity} = 15\%$?

c. Now suppose that Congress passes a law that eliminates the deductibility of interest for tax purposes after a grace period of 5 years. What will be the new value of the firm, other things equal? Assume an 8% borrowing rate.

25. **Bankruptcy.** What are the drawbacks of operating a firm that is close to bankruptcy? Give some examples. *(LO5)*

26. **Bankruptcy.** Explain why equity can sometimes have a positive value even when companies petition for bankruptcy. *(LO5)*

27. **Costs of Financial Distress.** The Salad Oil Storage Company (SOS) has financed a large part of its facilities with long-term debt. There is a significant risk of default, but the company is not on the ropes yet. Explain *(LO3)*

   a. why SOS stockholders could lose by investing in a positive-NPV project financed by an equity issue.

   b. why SOS stockholders could gain by investing in a highly risky, negative-NPV project.

28. **Financial Distress.** Explain how financial distress can lead to conflicts of interest between debt and equity investors. Then explain how these conflicts can lead to costs of financial distress. *(LO3)*

29. **Costs of Financial Distress.** For which of the following firms would you expect the costs of financial distress to be highest? Explain briefly. *(LO3)*

   a. A computer software company that depends on skilled programmers to produce new products.

   b. A shipping company that operates a fleet of modern oil tankers.

30. **Trade-Off Theory.** Smoke and Mirrors currently has EBIT of $25,000 and is all-equity-financed. EBIT is expected to stay at this level indefinitely. The firm pays corporate taxes equal to 35% of taxable income. The discount rate for the firm's projects is 10%. *(LO3)*

   a. What is the market value of the firm?

   b. Now assume the firm issues $50,000 of debt paying interest of 6% per year, using the proceeds to retire equity. The debt is expected to be permanent. What will happen to the total value of the firm (debt plus equity)?

   c. Recompute your answer to (b) under the following assumptions: The debt issue raises the probability of bankruptcy. The firm has a 30% chance of going bankrupt after 3 years. If it does go bankrupt, it will incur bankruptcy costs of $200,000. The discount rate is 10%. Should the firm issue the debt?

31. **Pecking Order Theory.** Alpha Corp. and Beta Corp. both produce turbo encabulators. Both companies' assets and operations are growing at the same rate, and their annual capital expenditures are about the same. However, Alpha Corp. is the more efficient producer and is consistently more profitable. According to the pecking order theory, which company should have the higher debt ratio? Explain. *(LO4)*

32. **Financial Slack.** Look back to the Sealed Air example in the box in Section 16.4. What was the value of financial slack to Sealed Air before its restructuring? What does the success of the restructuring say about optimal capital structure? Would you recommend that all firms restructure as Sealed Air did? *(LO4)*

CHALLENGE PROBLEMS

33. **Costs of Financial Distress.** Let's go back to the Double-R Nutting Company. Suppose that Double-R's bonds have a face value of $50. Its current *market-value* balance sheet is

Assets		Liabilities and Equity	
Net working capital	$20	Bonds outstanding	$25
Fixed assets	10	Common stock	5
Total assets	$30	Total liabilities and shareholders' equity	$30

Who would gain or lose from the following maneuvers? *(LO3)*

a. Double-R pays a $10 cash dividend.

b. Double-R halts operations, sells its fixed assets for $6, and converts net working capital into $20 cash. It invests its $26 in Treasury bills.

c. Double-R encounters an investment opportunity requiring a $10 initial investment with NPV = $0. It borrows $10 to finance the project by issuing more bonds with the same security, seniority, and so on, as the existing bonds.

d. Double-R finances the investment opportunity in part (c) by issuing more common stock.

34. **Trade-Off Theory.** Ronald Masulis[16] has analyzed the stock price impact of *exchange offers* of debt for equity or vice versa. In an exchange offer, the firm offers to trade freshly issued securities for seasoned securities in the hands of investors. Thus a firm that wanted to move to a higher debt ratio could offer to trade new debt for outstanding shares. A firm that wanted to move to a more conservative capital structure could offer to trade new shares for outstanding debt securities. Masulis found that debt-for-equity exchanges were good news (stock price increased on announcement) and equity-for-debt exchanges were bad news. *(LO4)*

a. Are these results consistent with the trade-off theory of capital structure?

b. Are the results consistent with the evidence that investors regard announcements of (i) stock issues as bad news, (ii) stock repurchases as good news, and (iii) debt issues as no news or, at most, trifling disappointments?

35. **Pecking Order Theory.** Construct a simple example to show that a firm's existing stockholders gain if it can sell overpriced stock to new investors and invest the cash in a zero-NPV project. Who loses from these actions? If investors are aware that managers are likely to issue stock when it is overpriced, what will happen to the stock price when the issue is announced? *(LO4)*

36. **Pecking Order Theory.** When companies announce an issue of common stock, the share price typically falls. When they announce an issue of debt, there is typically only a negligible change in the stock price. Can you explain why? *(LO4)*

37. **Taxes.** MM's proposition I suggests that in the absence of taxes it makes no difference whether the firm borrows on behalf of its shareholders or whether they borrow directly. However, if there are corporate taxes, this is no longer the case. Construct a simple example to show that with taxes it is better for the firm to borrow than for the shareholders to do so. *(LO2)*

38. **Taxes.** MM's proposition I, when modified to recognize corporate taxes, suggests that there is a tax advantage to firm borrowing. If there is a tax advantage to firm borrowing, there is also a tax *disadvantage* to firm lending. Explain why. *(LO2)*

eXcel

Please visit us at www.mhhe.com/bmm6e

39. **Tax Shields and WACC.** River Cruises's management now understands that the trade-off theory of optimal capital structure implies managers will increase debt as long as the value of additional interest tax shields exceeds the additional costs of potential financial distress. This trade-off gives rise to the hump-shaped curve in Figure 16–7, where the value of the firm is maximized at the optimal debt level. What will the curve of WACC as a function of debt level look like? *(LO1)*

a. Start with a no-tax economy. Continue to assume that River Cruises's required return on assets is 12.5% and return on debt is 10%. In a spreadsheet, calculate r_{equity}, WACC, and r_{debt} for debt-equity ratios ranging from 0 to 2.5 in increments of .1. Does WACC vary with the *D/E* ratio? Compare your plot to Figure 16–3.

b. Now assume the corporate tax rate is 35%. Repeat part (a). What happens to WACC as *D/E* increases? What seems to be the optimal capital structure?

c. What considerations are missing that would affect the optimal capital structure seemingly implied by part (b)?

STANDARD &POOR'S

1. Go to Market Insight at **www.mhhe.com/edumarketinsight**. Review the Ratio and Profitability reports for one or more of the following companies: UAL Corp. (UAL), Interstate Bakeries (IBCIQ), and Kmart (KM). Are you able to see a trend toward financial distress for these companies? What factors seem to be associated with their financial distress?

2. Go to Market Insight at **www.mhhe.com/edumarketinsight**. In the Excel Analytics section, find the long-term debt ratio for Georgia Pacific (GP) and Microsoft (MSFT). Do the comparative ratios make sense in terms of the trade-off theory of debt policy?

3. Now look at the debt ratio for Merck (MRK). Look as well at Merck's coverage ratios (cash coverage, times interest earned). Does Merck's debt policy seem more consistent with the trade-off or pecking order theory?

---

[16] R. W. Masulis, "The Effects of Capital Structure Change on Security Prices: A Study of Exchange Offers," *Journal of Financial Economics* 8 (June 1980), pp. 139–77, and "The Impact of Capital Structure Change on Firm Value," *Journal of Finance* 38 (March 1983), pp. 107–26.

SOLUTIONS TO SELF-TEST QUESTIONS

16.1   Price per share will stay at $10, so with $350,000, River Cruises can repurchase 35,000 shares, leaving 65,000 outstanding. The remaining value of equity will be $650,000. Overall firm value stays at $1 million. Shareholders' wealth is unchanged: They start with shares worth $1 million, receive $350,000, and retain shares worth $650,000.

16.2   a.

Data			
Number of shares	25,000		
Price per share	$10		
Market value of shares	$250,000		
Market value of debt	$750,000		
		State of the Economy	
	Slump	**Normal**	**Boom**
Operating income, dollars	75,000	125,000	175,000
Interest, dollars	75,000	75,000	75,000
Equity earnings, dollars	0	50,000	100,000
Earnings per share, dollars	0	2.00	4.00
Return on shares	0%	20%	40%

Every change of $50,000 in operating income leads to a change in the return to equityholders of 20%. This is double the swing in equity returns when debt was only $500,000.

b.   The stockholder should lend out $3 for every $1 invested in River Cruises's stock. For example, he could buy one share for $10 and then lend $30. The payoffs are:

	State of the Economy		
	Slump	**Normal**	**Boom**
Earnings on one share, dollars	0	2.00	4.00
Plus interest at 10%, dollars	3.00	3.00	3.00
Net earnings, dollars	3.00	5.00	7.00
Return on $40 investment	7.5%	12.5%	17.5%

16.3   Business risk is unaffected by capital structure. As the financing mix changes, whatever equity is outstanding must absorb the fixed business risk of the firm. The less equity, the more risk absorbed per share. Therefore, as capital structure changes, r_{assets} is held fixed while r_{equity} adjusts.

16.4   Wal-Mart's borrowing reduced taxable profits by $1,929 million. With a tax rate of 35%, tax was reduced by .35 × $1,929 = $675.2 million. If the borrowing is permanent, Wal-Mart will save this amount of tax each year. The present value of the tax savings would be $675.2/.06 = $11,253 million.

16.5   In bankruptcy bondholders will receive $2 million less. This lowers the expected cash flow from the bond and reduces its present value. Therefore, the bonds will be priced lower and must offer a higher interest rate. This higher rate is paid by the firm today. It comes out of stockholders' income. Thus common stock value falls.

16.6   The conflicts are costly because they lead to poor investment decisions. The more debt the firm has today, the greater the chance of poor decisions in the future. Investors foresee this possibility and reduce today's market value of the firm.

16.7   The biotech company. Its assets are all intangible. If bankruptcy threatens and the best scientists accept job offers from other firms, there may not be much value remaining for the biotech company's debt and equity investors. On the other hand, bankruptcy would have little or no effect on the value of 50 producing oil wells and of the oil reserves still in the ground.

16.8   The electric utility has the most stable cash flow. It also has the highest reliance on tangible assets that would not be impaired by a bankruptcy. It should have the highest debt ratio. The software firm has the least dependence on tangible assets and the most on assets that have value only if the firm continues as an ongoing concern. It probably also has the most unpredictable cash flows. It should have the lowest debt ratio.

www.mhhe.com/bmm6e

MINICASE

In March 2010 the management team of Londonderry Air (LA) met to discuss a proposal to purchase five shorthaul aircraft at a total cost of $25 million. There was general enthusiasm for the investment, and the new aircraft were expected to generate an annual cash flow of $4 million for 20 years.

The focus of the meeting was on how to finance the purchase. LA had $20 million in cash and marketable securities (see table), but Ed Johnson, the chief financial officer, pointed out that the company needed at least $10 million in cash to meet normal outflow and as a contingency reserve. This meant that there would be a cash deficiency of $15 million, which the firm would need to cover either by the sale of common stock or by additional borrowing. While admitting that the arguments were finely balanced, Mr. Johnson recommended an issue of stock. He pointed out that the airline industry was subject to wide swings in profits and the firm should be careful to avoid the risk of excessive borrowing. He estimated that in market value terms the long-term debt ratio was about 62% and that a further debt issue would raise the ratio to 64%.

Mr. Johnson's only doubt about making a stock issue was that investors might jump to the conclusion that management believed the stock was overpriced, in which case the announcement might prompt an unjustified selloff by investors. He stressed therefore that the company needed to explain carefully the reasons for the issue. Also, he suggested that demand for the issue would be enhanced if at the same time LA increased its dividend payment. This would provide a tangible indication of management's confidence in the future.

These arguments cut little ice with LA's chief executive. "Ed," she said, "I know that you're the expert on all this, but everything you say flies in the face of common sense. Why should we want

to sell more equity when our stock has fallen over the past year by nearly a fifth? Our stock is currently offering a dividend yield of 6.5%, which makes equity an expensive source of capital. Increasing the dividend would simply make it more expensive. What's more, I don't see the point of paying out more money to the stockholders at the same time that we are asking *them* for cash. If we hike the dividend, we will need to increase the amount of the stock issue; so we will just be paying the higher dividend out of the shareholders' own pockets. You're also ignoring the question of dilution. Our equity currently has a book value of $12 a share; it's not playing fair by our existing shareholders if we now issue stock for around $10 a share.

"Look at the alternative. We can borrow today at 5%. We get a tax break on the interest, so the after-tax cost of borrowing is .65 × 5 = 3.25%. That's about half the cost of equity. We expect to earn a return of 15% on these new aircraft. If we can raise money at 3.25% and invest it at 15%, that's a good deal in my book.

"You finance guys are always talking about risk, but as long as we don't go bankrupt, borrowing doesn't add any risk at all. In any case my calculations show that the debt ratio is only 45%, which doesn't sound excessive to me.

"Ed, I don't want to push my views on this—after all, you're the expert. We don't need to make a firm recommendation to the board until next month. In the meantime, why don't you get one of your new business graduates to look at the whole issue of how we should finance the deal and what return we need to earn on these planes?"

Evaluate Mr. Johnson's arguments about the stock issue and dividend payment as well as the reply of LA's chief executive. Who is correct? What is the required rate of return on the new planes?

Summary financial statements for Londonderry Air, 2009 (figures are book values, in millions of dollars)

Balance Sheet			
Bank debt	$ 50	Cash	$ 20
Other current liabilities	20	Other current assets	20
10% bond, due 2029*	100	Fixed assets	250
Stockholders' equity†	120		
Total liabilities	$ 290	Total assets	$ 290
Income Statement			
Gross profit	$57.5		
Depreciation	20.0		
Interest	7.5		
Pretax profit	30.0		
Tax	10.5		
Net profit	19.5		
Dividend	6.5		

* The yield to maturity on LA debt currently is 5%.
† LA has 10 million shares outstanding, with a market price of $10 a share. LA's equity beta is estimated at 1.25, the market risk premium is 8%, and the Treasury bill rate is 4%.

INVESTMENT AND FINANCING

CHAPTER 13

The Weighted-Average Cost of Capital and Company Valuation

LEARNING OBJECTIVES

After studying this chapter, you should be able to:

1. Calculate a firm's capital structure.

2. Estimate the required rates of return on the securities issued by the firm.

3. Calculate the weighted-average cost of capital.

4. Understand when the weighted-average cost of capital is—or isn't—the appropriate discount rate for a new project.

5. Use the weighted-average cost of capital to value a business given forecasts of its future cash flows.

Related Web sites for this chapter can be found at www.mhhe.com/bmm6e.

Jo Ann Cox explains the cost of capital to Geothermal's top management.

© McGraw-Hill Companies, Inc./Jill Braaten, photographer

In the last chapter you learned how to use the capital asset pricing model to estimate the expected return on a company's common stock. If the firm is financed wholly by common stock, then the stockholders own all the firm's assets and are entitled to all the cash flows. In this case, the expected return required by investors in the common stock equals the company cost of capital.[1]

Most companies, however, are financed by a mixture of securities, including common stock, bonds, preferred stock, or other securities. Each of these securities has different risks and therefore investors in them look for different rates of return. In these circumstances, the company cost of capital is no longer the same as the expected return on the common stock. It depends on the expected return from all the securities that the company has issued. It also depends on taxes,

because interest payments made by a corporation are tax-deductible expenses.

Therefore, the company cost of capital is usually calculated as a weighted average of the *after-tax* cost of debt interest and the "cost of equity," that is, the expected rate of return on the firm's common stock. The weights are the fractions of debt and equity in the firm's capital structure. Managers refer to the firm's *weighted-average cost of capital*, or *WACC* (rhymes with "quack").

Managers use the weighted-average cost of capital to evaluate average-risk capital investment projects. "Average risk" means that the project's risk matches the risk of the firm's existing assets and operations. This chapter explains how the weighted-average cost of capital is calculated in practice.

Managers calculating WACC can get bogged down in formulas. We want you to understand *why* WACC works, not just how to calculate it. Let's start with "Why?" We'll listen in as a young financial manager struggles to recall the rationale for project discount rates.

---

[1] Investors will invest in the firm's securities only if they offer the same expected return as other equally risky securities. When securities are properly priced, the return that investors can expect from their investments is therefore also the return that they *require*.

13.1 Geothermal's Cost of Capital

Jo Ann Cox, a recent graduate of a prestigious eastern business school, poured a third cup of black coffee and tried again to remember what she once knew about project hurdle rates. Why hadn't she paid more attention in Finance 101? Why had she sold her finance text the day after passing the finance final?

Costas Thermopolis, her boss and CEO of Geothermal Corporation, had told her to prepare a financial evaluation of a proposed expansion of Geothermal's production. She was to report at 9:00 Monday morning. Thermopolis, whose background was geophysics, not finance, not only expected a numerical analysis but also expected her to explain it to him.

Thermopolis had founded Geothermal in 1996 to produce electricity from geothermal energy trapped deep under Nevada. The company had pioneered this business and had obtained perpetual production rights for a large tract on favorable terms from the United States government. When the 2007 oil shock drove up energy prices worldwide, Geothermal became an exceptionally profitable company. It was currently reporting a rate of return on book assets of 25% per year.

Now, in 2010, production rights were no longer cheap. The proposed expansion would cost $30 million and should generate a perpetual after-tax cash flow of $4.5 million annually. The projected rate of return was 4.5/30 = .15, or 15%, much less than the profitability of Geothermal's existing assets. However, once the new project was up and running, it would be no riskier than Geothermal's present business.

Jo Ann realized that 15% was not necessarily a bad return—though of course 25% would have been better. Fifteen percent might still exceed Geothermal's cost of capital, that is, exceed the expected rate of return that outside investors would demand to invest money in the project. If the cost of capital was less than the 15% expected return, expansion would be a good deal and would generate net value for Geothermal and its stockholders.

Jo Ann remembered how to calculate the cost of capital for companies that used only common stock financing. Briefly she sketched the argument.

"I need the expected rate of return investors would require from Geothermal's real assets—the wells, pumps, generators, etc. That rate of return depends on the assets' risk. However, the assets aren't traded in the stock market, so I can't observe how risky they have been. I can only observe the risk of Geothermal's common stock.

"But if Geothermal issues only stock—no debt—then owning the stock means owning the assets, and the expected return demanded by investors in the stock must also be the cost of capital for the assets." She jotted down the following identities:

Value of business = value of stock
Risk of business = risk of stock
Rate of return on business = rate of return on stock
Investors' required return from business = investors' required return from stock

Unfortunately, Geothermal had borrowed a substantial amount of money; its stockholders did *not* have unencumbered ownership of Geothermal's assets. The expansion project would also justify some extra debt finance. Jo Ann realized that she would have to look at Geothermal's **capital structure**—its mix of debt and equity financing—and consider the expected rates of return required by debt as well as equity investors.

capital structure
The mix of long-term debt and equity financing.

Geothermal had issued 22.65 million shares, now trading at $20 each. Thus shareholders valued Geothermal's equity at $20 × 22.65 million = $453 million. In addition, the company had issued bonds with a market value of $194 million. The market value of the company's debt and equity was therefore $194 + $453 = $647 million. Debt was 194/647 = .3, or 30% of the total.

"Geothermal's worth more to investors than either its debt or its equity," Jo Ann mused. "But I ought to be able to find the overall value of Geothermal's business by adding up the debt and equity." She sketched a rough balance sheet:

Assets		Liabilities and Shareholders' Equity		
Market value of assets = value of Geothermal's existing business	$647	Market value of debt	$194	(30%)
		Market value of equity	453	(70%)
Total value	$647	Total value	$647	(100%)

"Holy Toledo, I've got it!" Jo Ann exclaimed. "If I bought *all* the securities issued by Geothermal, debt as well as equity, I'd own the entire business. That means . . ." She jotted again:

$$\text{Value of business} = \text{value of portfolio of all the firm's debt and equity securities}$$

$$\text{Risk of business} = \text{risk of portfolio}$$

$$\text{Rate of return on business} = \text{rate of return on portfolio}$$

$$\text{Investors' required return on business (company cost of capital)} = \text{investors' required return on portfolio}$$

"All I have to do is calculate the expected rate of return on a portfolio of all the firm's securities. That's easy. The debt's yielding 8%, and Fred, that nerdy banker, says that equity investors want 14%. Suppose he's right. The portfolio would contain 30% debt and 70% equity, so . . ."

$$\text{Portfolio return} = (.3 \times 8\%) + (.7 \times 14\%) = 12.2\%$$

It was all coming back to her now. The company cost of capital is just a weighted average of returns on debt and equity, with weights depending on relative market values of the two securities.

"But there's one more thing. Interest is tax-deductible. If Geothermal pays $1 of interest, taxable income is reduced by $1, and the firm's tax bill drops by 35 cents (assuming a 35% tax rate). The net cost is only 65 cents. So the after-tax cost of debt is not 8%, but $.65 \times 8 = 5.2\%$.

"Now I can finally calculate the weighted-average cost of capital:

$$\text{WACC} = (.3 \times 5.2\%) + (.7 \times 14\%) = 11.4\%$$

"Looks like the expansion's a good deal. Fifteen's better than 11.4. But I sure need a break."

13.2 The Weighted-Average Cost of Capital

Jo Ann's conclusions were important. It should be obvious by now that the choice of the discount rate can be crucial, especially when the project involves large capital expenditures or is long-lived. The nearby box describes how a major investment in a power station—an investment with both a large capital expenditure and very long life—turned on the choice of the discount rate.

Think again what the company cost of capital is, and what it is used for. We *define* it as the opportunity cost of capital for the firm's existing assets; we *use* it to value new assets that have the same risk as the old ones. The company cost of capital is the minimum acceptable rate of return when the firm expands by investing in average-risk projects.

FINANCE IN PRACTICE

Choosing the Discount Rate

Shortly before the British government began to sell off the electricity industry to private investors, controversy erupted over the industry's proposal to build a 1,200-megawatt nuclear power station known as Hinkley Point C. The government argued that a nuclear station would both diversify the sources of electricity generation and reduce sulfur dioxide and carbon dioxide emissions. Protesters emphasized the dangers of nuclear accidents and attacked the proposal as "bizarre, dated and irrelevant."

At the public inquiry held to consider the proposal, opponents produced some powerful evidence that the nuclear station was also a very high cost option. Their principal witness, Professor Elroy Dimson, argued that the government-owned power company had employed an unrealistically low figure for the opportunity cost of capital. Had the company used a more plausible figure, the cost of building and operating the nuclear station would have been higher than that of a comparable station based on fossil fuels.

The reason why the choice of discount rate was so important was that nuclear stations are expensive to build but cheap to operate. If capital is cheap (i.e., the discount rate is low), then the high up-front cost is less serious. But if the cost of capital is high, then the high initial cost of nuclear stations made them uneconomic.

Evidence produced at the inquiry suggested that the construction cost of a nuclear station was £1,527 million (or about $2.3 billion), while the cost of a comparable nonnuclear station was only £895 million. However, power stations last about 40 years, and, once built, nuclear stations cost much less to operate than nonnuclear stations. If operated at 75% of theoretical capacity, the running costs of the nuclear station would be about £63 million a year, compared with running costs of £168 million a year for the nonnuclear station.

The following table shows the cost advantage of the nuclear power station at different (real) discount rates. At a 5% discount rate, which was the figure used by the government, the present value of the costs of the nuclear option was

nearly £1 billion lower than that of a station based on fossil fuels. But with a discount rate of 16%, which was the figure favored by Professor Dimson, the position was almost exactly reversed, so the government could save nearly £1 billion by refusing the power company permission to build Hinkley Point C and relying instead on new fossil-fuel power stations.

Eight years after the inquiry, the proposal to construct Hinkley Point C continued to gather dust, and British Energy, the privatized electric utility, declared that it had no plans to build a new nuclear power station in the near future.

Present value of the cost advantage to a nuclear rather than a fossil-fuel station (figures in billions of pounds)

Real Discount Rate	Present Value of the Cost Advantage of the Nuclear Station
5%	0.9
8	0.2
10	−0.1
12	−0.4
14	−0.7
16	−0.9
18	−1.2

Technical Notes:
1. Present values are measured at the date that the power station comes into operation.
2. The above table assumes for simplicity that construction costs for nuclear stations are spread evenly over the 8 years before the station comes into operation, while the costs for fossil-fuel stations are assumed to be spread evenly over the 4 years before operation. As a result the present value of the costs of the two stations may differ slightly from the more precise estimates produced by Professor Dimson.

Source: Adapted from *Energy Economics,* Volume 11, Issue 3, E. Dimson, "The Discount Rate for a Power Station," pp. 175–180. © 1989 with permission from Elsevier Science.

We first introduced the opportunity cost of capital in the last section of Chapter 2. "Opportunity cost" is a shorthand reminder that, when the firm invests rather than returning cash to shareholders, the shareholders lose the opportunity to invest in financial markets. If the corporation acts in the shareholders' interests, it will invest their money only if it can find projects that offer higher rates of return than investors could achieve on their own. Therefore, the expected rates of return on investments in financial markets determine the cost of capital for corporate investments.

The company cost of capital is the opportunity cost of capital for the company as a whole. We discussed the company cost of capital in Chapter 12, but did not explain how to measure it when the firm has raised different types of debt and equity financing or how to adjust it for the tax-deductibility of interest payments. The weighted-average cost of capital formula handles these complications.

Calculating Company Cost of Capital as a Weighted Average

Calculating the company cost of capital is straightforward, though not always easy, when only common stock is outstanding. For example, a financial manager could estimate beta and calculate shareholders' required rate of return using the capital asset pricing model (CAPM). This would be the expected rate of return investors require on the company's existing assets and operations and also the expected return they will require on new investments that do not change the company's market risk.

But most companies issue debt as well as equity. **The company cost of capital is a** *weighted average* **of the returns demanded by debt and equity investors. The weighted average is the expected rate of return investors would demand on a portfolio of all the firm's outstanding securities.**

Let's review Jo Ann Cox's calculations for Geothermal. To avoid complications, we'll ignore taxes for the next two or three pages. The total market value of Geothermal, which we denote as V, is the sum of the values of the outstanding debt D and the equity E. Thus firm value is $V = D + E = \$194$ million $+ \$453$ million $= \$647$ million. Debt accounts for 30% of the value and equity accounts for the remaining 70%. If you held all the shares and all the debt, your investment in Geothermal would be $V = \$647$ million. Between them, the debt- and equityholders own *all* the firm's assets. So V is also the value of these assets—the value of Geothermal's existing business.

Suppose that Geothermal's equity investors require a 14% rate of return on their investment in the stock. What rate of return must a new project provide in order that all investors—both debtholders and stockholders—earn a fair rate of return? The debtholders require a rate of return of $r_{\text{debt}} = 8\%$. So each year the firm will need to pay interest of $r_{\text{debt}} \times D = .08 \times \$194$ million $= \$15.52$ million. The shareholders, who have invested in a riskier security, require an expected return of $r_{\text{equity}} = 14\%$ on their investment of \$453 million. Thus in order to keep shareholders happy, the company needs additional income of $r_{\text{equity}} \times E = .14 \times \$453$ million $= \$63.42$ million. To satisfy both the debtholders and the shareholders, Geothermal needs to earn \$15.52 million $+ \$63.42$ million $= \$78.94$ million. This is equivalent to earning a return of $r_{\text{assets}} = 78.94/647 = .122$, or 12.2%.

Figure 13–1 illustrates the reasoning behind our calculations. The figure shows the amount of income needed to satisfy the debt and equity investors. Notice that debtholders account for 30% of Geothermal's capital structure but receive less than 30% of its expected income. On the other hand, they bear less than a 30% share of risk, since they have first cut at the company's income and also first claim on its assets if the company gets in trouble. Shareholders expect a return of more than 70% of Geothermal's income because they bear correspondingly more risk.

However, if you buy *all* Geothermal's debt and equity, you own its assets lock, stock, and barrel. You receive all the income and bear all the risks. The expected rate of return you'd require on this portfolio of securities is the same return you'd require from unencumbered ownership of the business. This rate of return—12.2%, ignoring

FIGURE 13–1 Geothermal's debtholders account for 30% of the company's capital structure, but they get a smaller share of income because their return is guaranteed by the company. Geothermal's stockholders bear more risk and receive, on average, greater return. Of course, if you buy all the debt and all the equity, you get all the income.

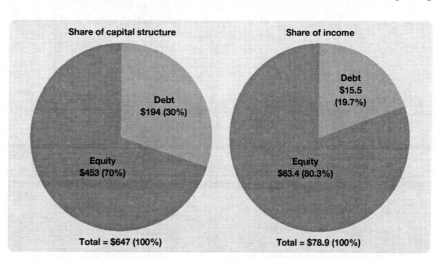

taxes—is therefore the company cost of capital and the required rate of return from an equal-risk expansion of the business.

The bottom line (still ignoring taxes) is

Company cost of capital = weighted average of debt and equity returns

The underlying algebra is simple. Debtholders need income of ($r_{\text{debt}} \times D$), and the equity investors need expected income of ($r_{\text{equity}} \times E$). The *total* income that is needed is ($r_{\text{debt}} \times D$) + ($r_{\text{equity}} \times E$). The amount of their combined existing investment in the company is V. So to calculate the return that is needed on the assets, we simply divide the income by the investment:

$$r_{\text{assets}} = \frac{\text{total income}}{\text{value of investment}}$$

$$= \frac{(D \times r_{\text{debt}}) + (E \times r_{\text{equity}})}{V} = \left(\frac{D}{V} \times r_{\text{debt}}\right) + \left(\frac{E}{V} \times r_{\text{equity}}\right)$$

For Geothermal,

$$r_{\text{assets}} = (.30 \times 8\%) + (.70 \times 14\%) = 12.2\%$$

This figure is the expected return demanded by investors in the firm's assets.

Self-Test 13.1

Hot Rocks Corp., one of Geothermal's competitors, has issued long-term bonds with a market value of $50 million and an expected return of 9%. It has 4 million shares outstanding trading for $10 each. At this price the shares offer an expected return of 17%. What is the weighted-average cost of capital for Hot Rocks's assets and operations? Assume Hot Rocks pays no taxes.

Use Market Weights, Not Book Weights

The company cost of capital is the expected rate of return that investors demand from the company's assets and operations. **The cost of capital must be based on what investors are actually willing to pay for the company's outstanding securities—that is, based on the securities'** *market* **values.**

Market values usually differ from the values recorded by accountants in the company's books. The book value of Geothermal's equity reflects money raised in the past from shareholders or reinvested by the firm on their behalf. If investors recognize Geothermal's excellent prospects, the market value of equity may be much higher than book, and the debt ratio will be lower when measured in terms of market values rather than book values.

Financial managers use book debt-to-value ratios for various purposes, and sometimes they unthinkingly look to the book ratios when calculating weights for the company cost of capital. That's a mistake, because the company cost of capital measures what investors want from the company, and it depends on how *they* value the company's securities. That value depends on future profits and cash flows, not on accounting history. Book values, while useful for many other purposes, only measure net cumulative historical outlays; they don't generally measure market values accurately.

Self-Test 13.2

Here is a book balance sheet for Duane S. Burg Associates. Figures are in millions.

Assets		Liabilities and Shareholders' Equity	
Assets (book value)	$75	Debt	$25
		Equity	50
	$75		$75

Unfortunately, the company has fallen on hard times. The 6 million shares are trading for only $4 apiece, and the market value of its debt securities is 20% below the face (book) value. Because of the company's large cumulative losses, it will pay no taxes on future income.

Suppose shareholders now demand a 20% expected rate of return. The bonds are now yielding 14%. What is the weighted-average cost of capital?

Taxes and the Weighted-Average Cost of Capital

Thus far in this chapter our examples have ignored taxes. When you calculate a project's NPV, you need to discount the cash flows *after* tax assuming that the project is wholly equity-financed. That is exactly the approach that we used in Chapter 9, when we valued Blooper's investment in the magnoosium mine. Sometimes you may encounter companies that forecast cash flows *before* tax and then try to compensate for this by using a higher discount rate. It doesn't work; there is no simple adjustment to the discount rate that will allow you to discount pretax cash flows.

Taxes are also important because most companies are financed by both equity and debt. The interest payments on this debt are deducted from income before tax is calculated. Therefore, the cost to the company is reduced by the amount of this tax saving.

The interest rate on Geothermal's debt is $r_{\text{debt}} = 8\%$. However, with a corporate tax rate of $T_c = .35$, the government bears 35% of the cost of the interest payments. The government doesn't send the firm a check for this amount, but the income tax that the firm pays is reduced by 35% of its interest expense.

Therefore, Geothermal's after-tax cost of debt is only $100 - 35 = 65\%$ of the 8% pretax cost:

$$\text{After-tax cost of debt} = (1 - \text{tax rate}) \times \text{pretax cost}$$
$$= (1 - T_c) \times r_{\text{debt}}$$
$$= (1 - .35) \times 8\% = 5.2\%$$

We can now adjust our calculation of Geothermal's cost of capital to recognize the tax savings associated with interest payments:

$$\text{Company cost of capital, after-tax} = (.3 \times 5.2\%) + (.7 \times 14\%) = 11.4\%$$

Self-Test 13.3

Criss-Cross Industries has earnings before interest and taxes (EBIT) of $10 million. Interest payments are $2 million, and the corporate tax rate is 35%. Construct a simple income statement to show that the debt interest reduces the taxes the firm owes to the government. How much more tax would Criss-Cross pay if it were financed solely by equity?

---

weighted-average cost of capital (WACC)
Expected rate of return on a portfolio of all the firm's securities, adjusted for tax savings due to interest payments.

Now we're back to the **weighted-average cost of capital**, or **WACC**. The general formula is

$$\text{WACC} = \left[\frac{D}{V} \times (1 - T_c) r_{\text{debt}} \right] + \left(\frac{E}{V} \times r_{\text{equity}} \right) \tag{13.1}$$

EXAMPLE 13.1 ▶ Weighted-Average Cost of Capital for McDonald's

In Chapter 12 we showed how the capital asset pricing model can be used to estimate the expected return on McDonald's common stock. We will now use this estimate to figure out the company's weighted-average cost of capital.

Step 1. *Calculate the value of each security as a proportion of firm value.* The company has outstanding 1,182 million shares, which at the beginning of 2008 had a market value of about \$52 each. The total market value of McDonald's equity was $E = 1{,}182 \times \$52 = \$61{,}464$ million. The company's latest balance sheet showed that it had borrowed $D = \$9{,}543$ million. So the total value of McDonald's securities is $V = D + E = \$9{,}543 + \$61{,}464 = \$71{,}007$ million. Debt as a proportion of the total value is $D/V = \$9{,}543/\$71{,}007 = .134$, and equity as a proportion of the total is $\$61{,}464/\$71{,}007 = .866$.

Step 2. *Determine the required rate of return on each security.* In Chapter 12 we estimated that McDonald's shareholders required a return of 13.1%. The average yield on McDonald's debt was about 5.5%.

Step 3. *Calculate a weighted average of the after-tax return on the debt and the return on the equity.*[2] The weighted-average cost of capital is

$$\text{WACC} = \left[\frac{D}{V} \times (1 - T_c) r_{\text{debt}} \right] + \left(\frac{E}{V} \times r_{\text{equity}} \right)$$
$$= [.134 \times (1 - .35)5.5\%] + (.866 \times 13.1\%) = 11.8\%$$

Self-Test 13.4

Calculate WACC for Hot Rocks (Self-Test 13.1) and Burg Associates (Self-Test 13.2) assuming the companies face a 35% corporate income tax rate.

What If There Are Three (or More) Sources of Financing?

We have simplified our discussion of the cost of capital by assuming the firm has only two classes of securities: debt and equity. Even if the firm has issued other classes of securities, our general approach to calculating WACC remains unchanged. We simply calculate the weighted-average after-tax return of each security type.

For example, suppose the firm also has outstanding preferred stock. Preferred stock has some of the characteristics of both common stock and fixed-income securities. Like bonds, preferred stock promises to pay a given, usually level, stream of dividends. Unlike bonds, however, there is no maturity date for the preferred stock. The promised dividends constitute a perpetuity as long as the firm stays in business. Moreover, a failure to come up with the cash to pay the dividends does not push the firm into bankruptcy. Instead, any unpaid dividends simply cumulate; the common stockholders do not receive dividends until the accumulated preferred dividends have been paid. Finally, unlike interest payments, preferred stock dividends are not considered tax-deductible expenses.

How would we calculate WACC for a firm with preferred stock as well as common stock and bonds outstanding? Using P to denote the value of preferred stock, we simply generalize Equation 13.1 for WACC as follows:

$$\text{WACC} = \left[\frac{D}{V} \times (1 - T_c) r_{\text{debt}} \right] + \left(\frac{P}{V} \times r_{\text{preferred}} \right) + \left(\frac{E}{V} \times r_{\text{equity}} \right) \qquad \textbf{(13.1a)}$$

Wrapping Up Geothermal

We now turn one last time to Jo Ann Cox and Geothermal's proposed expansion. We want to make sure that she—and you—know how to *use* the weighted-average cost of capital.

---

[2] Financial managers often use "equity" to refer to common stock, even though a firm's equity strictly includes both common and preferred stock. We continue to use r_{equity} to refer specifically to the expected return on the common stock.

Remember that the proposed expansion costs $30 million and should generate a perpetual cash flow of $4.5 million per year. A simple cash-flow worksheet might look like this:[3]

Revenue	$10.00 million
− Operating expenses	− 3.08
= Pretax operating cash flow	6.92
− Tax at 35%	− 2.42
After-tax cash flow	$ 4.50 million

Note that these cash flows do not include the tax benefits of using debt. Geothermal's managers and engineers forecast revenues, costs, and taxes as if the project were to be all-equity financed. The interest tax shields generated by the project's actual debt financing are not forgotten, however. They are accounted for by using the *after-tax* cost of debt in the weighted-average cost of capital.

Project net present value is calculated by discounting the cash flow (which is a perpetuity) at Geothermal's 11.4% weighted-average cost of capital:

$$NPV = -30 + \frac{4.5}{.114} = +\$9.5 \text{ million}$$

Expansion will thus add $9.5 million to the net wealth of Geothermal's owners.

Checking Our Logic

Any project offering a rate of return more than 11.4% will have a positive NPV, assuming that the project has the same risk and financing as Geothermal's business. A project offering exactly 11.4% would just break even; it would generate just enough cash to satisfy both debtholders and stockholders.

Let's check that out. Suppose the proposed expansion had revenues of only $8.34 million and after-tax cash flows of $3.42 million:

Revenue	$8.34 million
− Operating expenses	− 3.08
= Pretax operating cash flow	5.26
− Tax at 35%	− 1.84
After-tax cash flow	$3.42 million

With an investment of $30 million, the internal rate of return on this perpetuity is exactly 11.4%:

$$\text{Rate of return} = \frac{3.42}{30} = .114, \text{ or } 11.4\%$$

and NPV is exactly zero:

$$NPV = -30 + \frac{3.42}{.114} = 0$$

When we calculated Geothermal's weighted-average cost of capital, we recognized that the company's debt ratio was 30%. When Geothermal's analysts use the weighted-average cost of capital to evaluate the new project, they are *assuming* that the $30 million additional investment would support the issue of additional debt equal to 30% of the investment, or $9 million. The remaining $21 million is provided by

---

[3] For this example we ignore depreciation, a noncash but tax-deductible expense. (If the project were really perpetual, why depreciate?)

the shareholders either in the form of reinvested earnings or through the issue of additional shares.

The following table shows how the cash flows would be shared between the debt-holders and shareholders assuming still that the project has zero NPV. We start with the pretax operating cash flow of $5.26 million:

Cash flow before tax and interest	$5.26 million
− Interest payment (.08 × $9 million)	− .72
= Pretax cash flow	4.54
− Tax at 35%	− 1.59
After-tax cash flow	$2.95 million

Project cash flows before tax and interest are forecast to be $5.26 million. Out of this figure, Geothermal needs to pay interest of 8% of $9 million, which comes to $.72 million. This leaves a pretax cash flow of $4.54 million, on which the company must pay tax. Taxes equal .35 × 4.54 = $1.59 million. Shareholders are left with $2.95 million, just enough to give them the 14% return that they need on their $21 million investment. (Note that 2.95/21 = .14, or 14%.) Therefore, everything checks out.

If a project has zero NPV when the expected cash flows are discounted at the weighted-average cost of capital, then the project's cash flows are just sufficient to give debtholders and shareholders the returns they require.

13.3 Measuring Capital Structure

We have explained the formula for calculating the weighted-average cost of capital. We will now look at some of the practical problems in applying that formula. Suppose that the financial manager of Big Oil has asked you to estimate the firm's weighted-average cost of capital. Your first step is to work out Big Oil's capital structure. But where do you get the data?

Financial managers usually start with the company's accounts, which show the book value of debt and equity, whereas the weighted-average cost of capital formula calls for their *market* values. A little work and a dash of judgment are needed to go from one to the other.

Table 13–1 shows the debt and equity issued by Big Oil. The firm has borrowed $200 million from banks and has issued a further $200 million of long-term bonds. These bonds have a coupon rate of 8% and mature at the end of 12 years. Finally, there are 100 million shares of common stock outstanding, each with a par value of $1. But the accounts also recognize that Big Oil has in past years plowed back into the firm $300 million of retained earnings. The total book value of the equity shown in the accounts is $100 million + $300 million = $400 million.

The figures shown in Table 13–1 are taken from Big Oil's annual accounts and are therefore book values. Sometimes the differences between book values and market values are negligible. For example, consider the $200 million that Big Oil owes the bank. The interest rate on bank loans is usually linked to the general level of interest rates. Thus if interest rates rise, the rate charged on Big Oil's loan also rises to maintain the loan's value. As long as Big Oil is reasonably sure to repay the loan, it is worth

TABLE 13–1 The *book* values of Big Oil's debt and equity (dollar figures in millions)

Bank debt	$200	25.0%
Long-term bonds (12-year maturity, 8% coupon)	200	25.0
Common stock (100 million shares, par value $1)	100	12.5
Retained earnings	300	37.5
Total	$800	100.0%

TABLE 13–2 The market values of Big Oil's debt and equity (dollar figures in millions)

Bank debt	$ 200.0	12.6%
Long-term bonds	185.7	11.7
Total debt	385.7	24.3
Common stock (100 million shares at $12)	1,200.0	75.7
Total	$1,585.7	100.0%

close to $200 million. Most financial managers most of the time are willing to accept the book value of bank debt as a fair approximation of its market value.

What about Big Oil's long-term bonds? Since the bonds were originally issued, long-term interest rates have risen to 9%.[4] We can calculate the value today of each bond as follows.[5] There are 12 coupon payments of $.08 \times 200 = \$16$ million and then repayment of face value 12 years out. Thus the final cash payment to the bondholders is $216 million. All the bond's cash flows are discounted back at the *current* interest rate of 9%:

$$PV = \frac{16}{1.09} + \frac{16}{(1.09)^2} + \frac{16}{(1.09)^3} + \cdots + \frac{216}{(1.09)^{12}} = \$185.7$$

Therefore, the bonds are worth only $185.7 million, 93% of their face value.

If you used the book value of Big Oil's long-term debt rather than its market value, you would be a little bit off in your calculation of the weighted-average cost of capital, but probably not seriously so.

The really big errors are likely to arise if you use the book value of equity rather than its market value. The $400 million book value of Big Oil's equity measures the total amount of cash that the firm has raised from shareholders in the past or has retained and invested on their behalf. But perhaps Big Oil has been able to find projects that were worth more than they originally cost, or perhaps the value of the assets has increased with inflation. Perhaps investors see great future investment opportunities for the company. All these considerations determine what investors are willing to pay for Big Oil's common stock.

Big Oil's stock price is $12 a share. Thus the total *market value* of the stock is

Number of shares $\times$ share price $= 100$ million $\times \$12 = \$1,200$ million

In Table 13–2 we show the market values of Big Oil's debt and equity. You can see that debt accounts for 24.3% of company value ($D/V = .243$) and equity accounts for 75.7% ($E/V = .757$). These are the proportions to use when calculating the weighted-average cost of capital. Notice that if you looked only at the book values shown in the company accounts, you would mistakenly conclude that debt and equity each accounted for 50% of value.

Self-Test 13.5

Here is the capital structure shown in Executive Fruit's *book* balance sheet:

Debt	$4.1 million	45.0%
Preferred stock	2.2	24.2
Common stock	2.8	30.8
Total	$9.1 million	100.0%

Explain why the percentage weights given above should *not* be used in calculating Executive Fruit's WACC.

---

[4] If Big Oil's bonds are traded, you can simply look up their price. But many bonds are not regularly traded, and in such cases you need to infer their price by calculating the bond's value using the rate of interest offered by similar bonds.

[5] We assume that coupon payments are annual. Most bonds in the United States actually pay interest twice a year.

13.4 Calculating Required Rates of Return

To calculate Big Oil's weighted-average cost of capital, you also need the rate of return that investors require from each security.

The Expected Return on Bonds

We know that Big Oil's bonds offer a yield to maturity of 9%. As long as the company does not go belly-up, that is the rate of return investors can expect to earn from holding Big Oil's bonds. If there is any chance that the firm may be unable to repay the debt, however, the yield to maturity of 9% represents the most favorable outcome and the *expected* return is lower than 9%.

For most large and healthy firms, the probability of bankruptcy is sufficiently low that financial managers are content to take the promised yield to maturity on the bonds as a measure of the expected return. But beware of assuming that the yield offered on the bonds of Fly-by-Night Corporation is the return that investors could *expect* to receive.

The Expected Return on Common Stock

Estimates Based on the Capital Asset Pricing Model   In the last chapter we showed you how to use the capital asset pricing model to estimate the expected rate of return on common stock. The capital asset pricing model tells us that investors demand a higher rate of return from stocks with high betas. The formula is

$$\text{Expected return on stock} = \text{risk-free interest rate} + \left(\text{stock's beta} \times \text{expected market risk premium} \right)$$

Financial managers and economists measure the risk-free rate of interest by the yield on Treasury bills. To measure the expected market risk premium, they usually look back at capital market history, which suggests that investors have received an extra 7% to 8% a year from investing in common stocks rather than Treasury bills. Yet wise financial managers use this evidence with considerable humility, for who is to say whether investors in the past received more or less than they expected or whether investors today require a higher or lower reward for risk than their parents did?

Let's suppose Big Oil's common stock beta is estimated at .85, the risk-free interest rate (r_f) is 6%, and the expected market risk premium ($r_m - r_f$) is 7%. Then the CAPM would put Big Oil's cost of equity at

$$\text{Cost of equity} = r_{\text{equity}} = r_f + \beta(r_m - r_f)$$
$$= 6\% + .85(7\%) = 12\%$$

Self-Test 13.6   Jo Ann Cox decides to check whether Fred, the nerdy banker, was correct in claiming that Geothermal's cost of equity is 14%. She estimates Geothermal's beta at 1.20. The risk-free interest rate in 2010 is 6%, and the long-run average market risk premium is 7.6%. What is the expected rate of return on Geothermal's common stock, assuming of course that the CAPM is true? Recalculate Geothermal's weighted-average cost of capital.

Estimates Based on the Dividend Discount Model   Whenever you are given an estimate of the expected return on a common stock, always look for ways to check whether it is reasonable. One check on the estimates provided by the CAPM can be obtained from the dividend discount model (DDM). In Chapter 7 we showed you how to use the constant-growth DDM formula to estimate the return that investors expect from different common stocks. Remember the formula: If dividends are expected to grow indefinitely at a constant rate g, then the price of the stock is equal to

$$P_0 = \frac{\text{DIV}_1}{r_{\text{equity}} - g}$$

where P_0 is the current stock price, DIV_1 is the forecast dividend at the end of the year, and r_{equity} is the expected return from the stock. We can rearrange this formula to provide an estimate of r_{equity}:

$$r_{\text{equity}} = \frac{\text{DIV}_1}{P_0} + g \tag{13.2}$$

In other words, the expected return on equity is equal to the dividend yield (DIV_1/P_0) plus the expected perpetual growth rate in dividends (g).

This constant-growth dividend discount model is widely used in estimating expected rates of return on common stocks of public utilities. Utility stocks have a fairly stable growth pattern and are therefore tailor-made for the constant-growth formula.

Remember that the constant-growth formula will get you into trouble if you apply it to firms with very high current rates of growth. Such growth cannot be sustained indefinitely. Using the formula in these circumstances will lead to an overestimate of the expected return.

Beware of False Precision   Do not expect estimates of the cost of equity to be precise. In practice you can't know whether the capital asset pricing model fully explains expected returns or whether the assumptions of the dividend discount model hold exactly. Even if your formulas were right, the required inputs would be noisy and subject to error. Thus a financial analyst who can confidently locate the cost of equity in a band of 2 or 3 percentage points is doing pretty well. In this endeavor it is perfectly OK to conclude that the cost of equity is, say, "about 15%" or "somewhere between 14% and 16%."[6]

Sometimes accuracy can be improved by estimating the cost of equity or WACC for an industry or a group of comparable companies. This cuts down the "noise" that plagues single-company estimates. Suppose, for example, that Jo Ann Cox is able to identify three companies with investments and operations similar to Geothermal's. The average WACC for these three companies would be a valuable check on her estimate of WACC for Geothermal alone.

Or suppose that Geothermal is contemplating investment in oil refining. For this venture Geothermal's existing WACC is probably not right; it needs a discount rate reflecting the risks of the refining business. It could therefore try to estimate WACC for a sample of oil refining companies. If too few "pure-play" refining companies were available—most oil companies invest in production and marketing as well as refining—an industry WACC for a sample of large oil companies could be a useful check or benchmark.

The Expected Return on Preferred Stock

Preferred stock that pays a fixed annual dividend can be valued from the perpetuity formula:

$$\text{Price of preferred} = \frac{\text{dividend}}{r_{\text{preferred}}}$$

---

[6] The calculations in this chapter have been done to one or two decimal places just to avoid confusion from rounding.

where $r_{preferred}$ is the appropriate discount rate for the preferred stock. Therefore, we can infer the required rate of return on preferred stock by rearranging the valuation formula to

$$r_{preferred} = \frac{dividend}{price\ of\ preferred} \qquad (13.3)$$

For example, if a share of preferred stock sells for $20 and pays a dividend of $2 per share, the expected return on preferred stock is $r_{preferred} = \$2/\$20 = 10\%$, which is simply the dividend yield.

13.5 Calculating the Weighted-Average Cost of Capital

Once you have worked out Big Oil's capital structure and estimated the expected return on its securities, you require only simple arithmetic to calculate the weighted-average cost of capital. Table 13–3 summarizes the necessary data. Now all you need to do is plug the data in Table 13–3 into the weighted-average cost of capital formula:

$$WACC = \left[\frac{D}{V} \times (1 - T_c)r_{debt}\right] + \left(\frac{E}{V} \times r_{equity}\right)$$

$$= [.243 \times (1 - .35)\ 9\%] + (.757 \times 12\%) = 10.5\%$$

Suppose that Big Oil needs to evaluate a project with the same risk as its existing business. If the project would also support a 24.3% debt ratio, the 10.5% weighted-average cost of capital is the appropriate discount rate for the cash flows.

Real-Company WACCs

Big Oil is entirely hypothetical. Therefore you might be interested to look at Table 13–4, which gives some estimates of the weighted-average cost of capital for a sample of real companies. As you do so, remember that any estimate of the cost of capital for a single company can be way off the true cost. You should always check your estimate by looking at the cost of capital for a group of similar companies.[7]

13.6 Interpreting the Weighted-Average Cost of Capital

When You Can and Can't Use WACC

The weighted-average cost of capital is the rate of return that the firm must expect to earn on its average-risk investments in order to provide a fair expected return to all its security holders. Strictly speaking, the weighted-average cost of capital is an appropriate discount rate only for a project that is a carbon copy of the firm's existing business. But often it is used as a companywide benchmark discount rate; the benchmark is adjusted upward for unusually risky projects and downward for unusually safe ones.

TABLE 13–3 Data needed to calculate Big Oil's weighted-average cost of capital (dollar figures in millions)

Security Type	Capital Structure		Required Rate of Return
Debt	D = $ 385.7	D/V = .243	r_{debt} = .09, or 9%
Common stock	E = $1,200.0	E/V = .757	r_{equity} = .12, or 12%
Total	V = $1,585.7		

Note: Corporate tax rate = T_c = .35.

---

[7] Notice the low WACC for Ford, which results from the company's very high debt ratio. Should Ford use a WACC of 6.1% when valuing a proposal to expand its operations? The answer is yes if a 93% debt ratio really is a sensible target capital structure. But if you believe that this debt ratio does not constitute a desirable long-term capital structure for Ford, then you would need to recalculate WACC with a different ratio.

Weighted-Average Cost of Capital

Source: BondsOnline Web site.

In the Internet Insider box on page 344 we showed how you can estimate expected stock returns for five companies by using the betas shown on **finance.yahoo.com.** You can now go on to estimate the weighted-average cost of capital for these companies. You need two extra items of data—the relative proportions of equity and debt and the expected return on debt. You can work out the proportions of equity and debt by using **finance.yahoo.com** and looking at each company's *profile.* Remember, though, to use the market value of the equity, not its book value. Finding the yield on the debt is a little trickier. Log on to **www.bondsonline.com** to find the current level of Treasury yields and the yield spreads (i.e., the extra yield for bonds with different ratings). As we write this, Moody's ratings for the five companies vary from B for Eastman Kodak, to Baa for Home Depot and Altria, to A for Caterpillar and Du Pont.

There is a good musical analogy here. Most of us, lacking perfect pitch, need a well-defined reference point, like middle C, before we can sing on key. But anyone who can carry a tune gets *relative* pitches right. Businesspeople have good intuition about *relative* risks, at least in industries they are used to, but not about absolute risk or required rates of return. Therefore, they set a company- or industrywide cost of capital as a benchmark. This is not the right hurdle rate for everything the company does, but judgmental adjustments can be made for more risky or less risky ventures.

Some Common Mistakes

One danger with the weighted-average formula is that it tempts people to make logical errors. Think back to your estimate of the cost of capital for Big Oil:

$$\text{WACC} = \left[\frac{D}{V} \times (1 - T_c) r_{debt} \right] + \left(\frac{E}{V} \times r_{equity} \right)$$
$$= [.243 \times (1 - .35)\ 9\%] + (.757 \times 12\%) = 10.5\%$$

TABLE 13-4 Calculating the weighted-average cost of capital for selected companies

	Expected Return on Equity, %	Interest Rate on Debt, %	Proportion of Equity (E/V)	Proportion of Debt (D/V)	WACC, %
Amazon.com	19.8	7.3	0.96	0.04	19.3
Ford	20.2	7.7	0.07	0.93	6.1
Newmont Mining	8.9	6.5	0.89	0.11	8.4
Intel	14.1	5.8	0.98	0.02	13.9
Microsoft	10.3	na	1.00	0.00	10.3
Dell Computer	11.9	6.0	0.99	0.01	11.8
Boeing	11.6	5.8	0.88	0.12	10.7
McDonald's	13.1	5.9	0.89	0.11	12.1
Pfizer	7.7	5.3	0.95	0.05	7.5
Du Pont	11.7	6.0	0.81	0.19	10.2
Disney	10.0	6.0	0.78	0.22	8.7
ExxonMobil	8.7	5.3	1.00	0.00	8.7
IBM	10.9	5.8	0.80	0.20	9.5
Wal-Mart	4.7	5.7	0.80	0.20	4.5
Campbell Soup	6.2	6.0	0.82	0.18	5.8
Heinz	7.1	6.7	0.73	0.27	6.4

Notes:

1. Expected return on equity is taken from Table 12–2.
2. Interest rate on debt is calculated from yields on similarly rated bonds.
3. *D* is the book value of the firm's debt, and *E* is the market value of equity.
4. WACC = $(1 - .35) \times r_{debt} \times (D/V) + r_{equity} \times (E/V)$.

Now you might be tempted to say to yourself: "Aha! Big Oil has a good credit rating. It could easily push up its debt ratio to 50%. If the interest rate is 9% and the required return on equity is 12%, the weighted-average cost of capital would be

$$\text{WACC} = [.50 \times (1-.35)\ 9\%] + (.50 \times 12\%) = 8.9\%$$

At a discount rate of 8.9%, we can justify a lot more investment."

That reasoning will get you into trouble. First, if Big Oil increased its borrowing, the lenders would almost certainly demand a higher rate of interest on the debt. Second, as the borrowing increased, the risk of the common stock would also increase and therefore the stockholders would demand a higher return.

There are actually two costs of debt finance. The explicit cost of debt is the rate of interest that bondholders demand. But there is also an implicit cost, because borrowing increases the required return to equity. When you jumped to the conclusion that Big Oil could lower its weighted-average cost of capital to 8.9% by borrowing more, you were recognizing only the explicit cost of debt and not the implicit cost.

Self-Test 13.7

Jo Ann Cox's boss has pointed out that Geothermal proposes to finance its expansion entirely by borrowing at an interest rate of 8%. He argues that this is therefore the appropriate discount rate for the project's cash flows. Is he right?

How Changing Capital Structure Affects Expected Returns

We will illustrate how changes in capital structure affect expected returns by focusing on the simplest possible case, where the corporate tax rate T_c is zero.

Think back to our earlier example of Geothermal. Geothermal, you may remember, has the following market-value balance sheet:

Assets		Liabilities and Shareholders' Equity		
Assets = value of Geothermal's existing business	$647	Debt	$194	(30%)
		Equity	453	(70%)
Total value	$647	Value	$647	(100%)

Geothermal's debtholders require a return of 8%, and the shareholders require a return of 14%. Since we assume here that Geothermal pays no corporate tax, its weighted-average cost of capital is simply the expected return on the firm's assets:

$$\text{WACC} = r_{\text{assets}} = (.3 \times 8\%) + (.7 \times 14\%) = 12.2\%$$

This is the return you would expect if you held all Geothermal's securities and therefore owned all its assets.

Now think what will happen if Geothermal borrows an additional $97 million and uses the cash to buy back and retire $97 million of its common stock. The revised market-value balance sheet is

Assets		Liabilities and Shareholders' Equity		
Assets = value of Geothermal's existing business	$647	Debt	$291	(45%)
		Equity	356	(55%)
Total value	$647	Value	$647	(100%)

If there are no corporate taxes, the change in capital structure does not affect the total cash that Geothermal pays out to its security holders and it does not affect the risk of those cash flows. Therefore, if investors require a return of 12.2% on the total package of debt and equity before the financing, they must require the same 12.2% return on the package afterward. The weighted-average cost of capital is therefore unaffected by the change in the capital structure.

Although the required return on the *package* of the debt and equity is unaffected, the change in capital structure does affect the required return on the individual securities. Since the company has more debt than before, the debt is riskier and debtholders are likely to demand a higher return. Increasing the amount of debt also makes the equity riskier and increases the return that shareholders require. We will return to this point in Chapter 16.

What Happens When the Corporate Tax Rate Is Not Zero

We have shown that when there are no corporate taxes, the weighted-average cost of capital is unaffected by a change in capital structure. Unfortunately, taxes can complicate the picture.[8] For the moment, just remember:

- **The weighted-average cost of capital is the right discount rate for average-risk capital investments.**
- **The weighted-average cost of capital is the return the company needs to earn after tax in order to satisfy all its security holders.**
- **If the firm increases its debt ratio, both the debt and the equity will become more risky. The debtholders and equityholders require a higher return to compensate for the increased risk.**

13.7 Valuing Entire Businesses

Investors routinely buy and sell shares of common stock. Companies frequently buy and sell entire businesses. Do the discounted cash-flow formulas that we used in Chapter 7 to value Blue Skies' stock also work for entire businesses?

Sure! As long as the company's debt ratio is expected to remain fairly constant, you can treat the company as one big project and discount its cash flows by the weighted-average cost of capital. The result is the combined value of the company's debt and equity. If you want to know just the value of the equity, you must remember to subtract the value of the debt from the company's total value.

Suppose that you are interested in buying Establishment Industry's concatenator manufacturing operation. The problem is to figure out what it is worth. Table 13–5 sets out your forecasts for the next 6 years. Row 8 shows the expected cash flow from operations. This is equal to the expected profit after tax plus depreciation. Remember, depreciation is not a cash outflow, and therefore you need to add it back when calculating the operating cash flow. Row 9 in the table shows the forecast investments in plant and working capital.

The operating cash flow *less* investment expenditures is the amount of cash that the business can pay out to investors after paying for all investments necessary for growth. This is the concatenator division's **free cash flow** (row 10 in the table). Notice that the free cash flow is negative in the early years. Is that a bad sign? Not really. The business is running a cash deficit not because it is unprofitable but because it is growing so fast. Rapid growth is good news, not bad, as long as the business is earning more than the cost of capital on its investments.

The forecast cash flows in Table 13–5 did not include a deduction for debt interest. But we will not forget that acquisition of the concatenator business will support

free cash flow

Cash flow that is not required for investment in fixed assets or working capital and is therefore available to investors.

[8] There's nothing wrong with our formulas and examples, *provided* that the tax deductibility of interest payments doesn't change the aggregate risk of the debt and equity investors. However, if the tax savings from deducting interest are treated as safe cash flows, the formulas get more complicated. If you really want to dive into the tax-adjusted formulas showing how WACC changes with capital structure, we suggest Chapter 20 in R. A. Brealey, S. C. Myers, and F. Allen, *Principles of Corporate Finance,* 9th ed. (New York: Irwin/McGraw-Hill, 2008).

TABLE 13–5 Forecasts of operating cash flow and investment for the concatenator manufacturing division (thousands of dollars). Rapid expansion means that free cash flow is negative in the early years, because investment outstrips the cash flow from operations. Free cash flow turns positive when growth slows down.

	Year					
	1	2	3	4	5	6
1. Sales	1,189	1,421	1,700	2,020	2,391	2,510
2. Costs	1,070	1,279	1,530	1,818	2,152	2,260
3. Earnings before interest, taxes, depreciation, and amortization (EBITDA) = 1 − 2	119	142	170	202	239	250
4. Depreciation	45	59	76	99	128	136
5. Profit before tax = 3 − 4	74	83	94	103	111	114
6. Tax at 35%	25.9	29.1	32.9	36.1	38.9	39.9
7. Profit after tax = 5 − 6	48.1	54.0	61.1	67.0	72.2	74.1
8. Operating cash flow = 4 + 7	93.1	113.0	137.1	166.0	200.2	210.1
9. Investment in plant and working capital	166.7	200.0	240.0	200.0	160.0	130.6
10. Free cash flow = 8 − 9	−73.6	−87.1	−102.9	−34.1	40.2	79.5

additional debt. We will recognize that fact by discounting the free cash flows by the weighted-average cost of capital, which reflects both the firm's capital structure and the tax deductibility of its interest payments.

Suppose that a sensible capital structure for the concatenator operation is 60% equity and 40% debt.[9] You estimate that the required rate of return on the equity is 12% and that the business could borrow at an interest rate of 5%. The weighted-average cost of capital is therefore

$$\text{WACC} = \left[\frac{D}{V} \times (1 - T_c) r_{\text{debt}}\right] + \left(\frac{E}{V} \times r_{\text{equity}}\right)$$
$$= [.4 \times (1 - .35)5\%] + (.6 \times 12\%) = 8.5\%$$

Calculating the Value of the Concatenator Business

The value of the concatenator operation is equal to the discounted value of the free cash flows (FCFs) out to a horizon year plus the forecasted value of the business at the horizon, also discounted back to the present. That is,

$$\text{PV} = \underbrace{\frac{\text{FCF}_1}{1 + \text{WACC}} + \frac{\text{FCF}_2}{(1 + \text{WACC})^2} + \cdots + \frac{\text{FCF}_H}{(1 + \text{WACC})^H}}_{\text{PV (free cash flows)}} + \underbrace{\frac{\text{PV}_H}{(1 + \text{WACC})^H}}_{+ \text{PV (horizon value)}}$$

Of course, the concatenator business will continue to grow after the horizon, but it's not practical to forecast free cash flow year by year to infinity. PV_H stands in for the value of free cash flows in periods $H + 1$, $H + 2$, and so on.

Horizon years are often chosen arbitrarily. Sometimes the boss tells everybody to use 10 years because that's a nice round number. We have picked year 5 as the horizon year because the business is expected to settle down to steady growth of 5% a year from then on.

There are several common formulas or rules of thumb for estimating horizon value. Let's try the constant-growth formula that we introduced in Chapter 7:

$$\text{Horizon value} = \frac{\text{free cash flow in year 6}}{r - g} = \frac{79.5}{.085 - .05} = \$2,271.4 \text{ thousand}$$

[9] By this we mean that it makes sense to finance 40% of the *present value* of the business by debt. Remember that we use market-value weights to compute WACC. Debt as a proportion of *book value* may be more or less than 40%.

We now have all we need to calculate the value of the concatenator business today. We add up the present values of the free cash flows in the first 5 years and that of the horizon value:

$$PV \text{ (business)} = PV \text{ (free cash flows years 1–5)} + PV \text{ (horizon value)}$$
$$= -\frac{73.6}{1.085} - \frac{87.1}{(1.085)^2} - \frac{102.9}{(1.085)^3} - \frac{34.1}{(1.085)^4} + \frac{40.2}{(1.085)^5} + \frac{2,271.4}{(1.085)^5}$$
$$= \$1,290.4 \text{ thousand}$$

Notice that when we use the weighted-average cost of capital to value a company, we are asking, "What is the combined value of the company's debt and equity?" If you need to value the equity, you must subtract the value of any outstanding debt. Suppose that the concatenator business has been partly financed with $516,000 of debt, 40% of the overall value of about $1,290,000. Then the equity in the business is worth only $1,290,000 − $516,000 = $774,000.

Self-Test 13.8

Managers often use rules of thumb to check their estimates of horizon value. Suppose you observe that the value of the debt plus equity of a typical mature concatenator producer is nine times its EBITDA. (EBITDA is defined at line 3 of Table 13–5.) If your operation sold in year 5 at a similar multiple of EBITDA, how would your estimate of the *present* value of the operation change?

SUMMARY

Why do firms compute weighted-average costs of capital? (*LO4*)

They need a standard discount rate for average-risk projects. An "average-risk" project is one that has the same risk as the firm's existing assets and operations.

What about projects that are not average? (*LO4*)

The **weighted-average cost of capital** can still be used as a benchmark. The benchmark is adjusted up for unusually risky projects and down for unusually safe ones.

How do firms compute weighted-average costs of capital? (*LO3*)

Here's the WACC formula one more time:

$$WACC = \left[\frac{D}{V} \times (1 - T_c)r_{debt}\right] + \left(\frac{E}{V} \times r_{equity}\right)$$

The WACC is the expected rate of return on the portfolio of debt and equity securities issued by the firm. The required rate of return on each security is weighted by its proportion of the firm's total market value (not book value). Since interest payments reduce the firm's income tax bill, the required rate of return on debt is measured after tax, as $r_{debt} \times (1 - T_c)$.

How do firms measure capital structure? (*LO1*)

Capital structure is the proportion of each source of financing in total market value. The WACC formula is usually written assuming the firm's capital structure includes just two classes of securities, debt and equity. If there is another class, say preferred stock, the formula expands to include it. In other words, we would estimate $r_{preferred}$, the rate of return demanded by preferred stockholders, determine P/V, the fraction of market value accounted for by preferred, and add $r_{preferred} \times P/V$ to the equation. Of course the weights in the WACC formula always add up to 1. In this case $D/V + P/V + E/V = 1$.

How are the costs of debt and equity calculated? (*LO3*)

The cost of debt (r_{debt}) is the market interest rate demanded by bondholders. In other words, it is the rate that the company would pay on *new* debt issued to finance its investment projects. The cost of preferred ($r_{preferred}$) is just the preferred dividend divided by the market price of a preferred share.

www.mhhe.com/bmm6e

The tricky part is estimating the cost of equity (r_{equity}), the expected rate of return on the firm's shares. Financial managers use the capital asset pricing model to estimate expected return. But for mature, steady-growth companies, it can also make sense to use the constant-growth dividend discount model. Remember, estimates of expected return are less reliable for a single firm's stock than for a sample of comparable-risk firms. Therefore, managers also consider WACCs calculated for industries.

What happens when capital structure changes? (*LO4*)

The rates of return on debt and equity will change. For example, increasing the debt ratio will increase the risk borne by both debt and equity investors and cause them to demand higher returns. However, this does *not* necessarily mean that the overall WACC will increase, because more weight is put on the cost of debt, which is less than the cost of equity. In fact, if we ignore taxes, the overall **cost of capital** will stay constant as the fractions of debt and equity change. This is discussed further in Chapter 16.

Can WACC be used to value an entire business? (*LO5*)

Just think of the business as a very large project. Forecast the business's operating cash flows (after-tax profits plus depreciation), and subtract the future investments in plant and equipment and in net working capital. The resulting **free cash flows** can then be discounted back to the present at the weighted-average cost of capital. Of course, the cash flows from a company may stretch far into the future. Financial managers therefore typically produce detailed cash flows only up to some horizon date and then estimate the remaining value of the business at the horizon.

LISTING OF EQUATIONS

13.1 $$\text{WACC} = \left[\frac{D}{V} \times (1 - T_c) r_{debt}\right] + \left(\frac{E}{V} \times r_{equity}\right)$$

13.1a $$\text{WACC} = \left[\frac{D}{V} \times (1 - T_c) r_{debt}\right] + \left(\frac{P}{V} \times r_{preferred}\right) + \left(\frac{E}{V} \times r_{equity}\right)$$

13.2 $$r_{equity} = \frac{\text{DIV}_1}{P_0} + g$$

13.3 $$r_{preferred} = \frac{\text{dividend}}{\text{price of preferred}}$$

QUESTIONS

QUIZ

1. **Cost of Debt.** Micro Spinoffs, Inc., issued 20-year debt a year ago at par value with a coupon rate of 8%, paid annually. Today, the debt is selling at $1,050. If the firm's tax bracket is 35%, what is its after-tax cost of debt? (*LO2*)

2. **Cost of Preferred Stock.** Micro Spinoffs also has preferred stock outstanding. The stock pays a dividend of $4 per share, and the stock sells for $40. What is the cost of preferred stock? (*LO2*)

3. **Calculating WACC.** Suppose Micro Spinoffs's cost of equity is 12%. What is its WACC if equity is 50%, preferred stock is 20%, and debt is 30% of total capital? (*LO3*)

4. **Cost of Equity.** Reliable Electric is a regulated public utility, and it is expected to provide steady growth of dividends of 5% per year for the indefinite future. Its last dividend was $5 per share; the stock sold for $60 per share just after the dividend was paid. What is the company's cost of equity? (*LO2*)

www.mhhe.com/bmm6e

5. **Calculating WACC.** Reactive Industries has the following capital structure. Its corporate tax rate is 35%. What is its WACC? (*LO3*)

Security	Market Value	Required Rate of Return
Debt	$20 million	6%
Preferred stock	10 million	8
Common stock	50 million	12

6. **Company versus Project Discount Rates.** Geothermal's WACC is 11.4%. Executive Fruit's WACC is 12.3%. Now Executive Fruit is considering an investment in geothermal power production. Should it discount project cash flows at 12.3%? Why or why not? (*LO4*)

7. **Company Valuation.** Icarus Airlines is proposing to go public, and you have been given the task of estimating the value of its equity. Management plans to maintain debt at 30% of the company's present value, and you believe that at this capital structure the company's debt-holders will demand a return of 6% and stockholders will require 11%. The company is forecasting that next year's operating cash flow (depreciation plus profit after tax at 40%) will be $68 million and that investment expenditures will be $30 million. Thereafter, operating cash flows and investment expenditures are forecast to grow by 4% a year. (*LO5*)

    a. What is the total value of Icarus?
    b. What is the value of the company's equity?

PRACTICE PROBLEMS

8. **WACC.** The common stock of Buildwell Conservation & Construction, Inc., has a beta of .90. The Treasury bill rate is 4%, and the market risk premium is estimated at 8%. BCCI's capital structure is 30% debt, paying a 5% interest rate, and 70% equity. What is BCCI's cost of equity capital? Its WACC? Buildwell pays tax at 40%. (*LO3*)

9. **WACC and NPV.** BCCI (see the previous problem) is evaluating a project with an internal rate of return of 12%. Should it accept the project? If the project will generate a cash flow of $100,000 a year for 8 years, what is the most BCCI should be willing to pay to initiate the project? (*LO5*)

10. **Company Valuation.** You need to estimate the value of Buildwell Conservation (see Practice Problem 8). You have the following forecasts (in millions of dollars) of Buildwell's profits and of its future investments in new plant and working capital: (*LO5*)

	Year			
	1	**2**	**3**	**4 . . .**
Earnings before interest, taxes, depreciation, and amortization (EBITDA)	80	100	115	120
Depreciation	20	30	35	40
Pretax profit	60	70	80	80
Investment	12	15	18	20

From year 5 onward, EBITDA, depreciation, and investment are expected to remain unchanged at year-4 levels. Estimate the company's total value and the separate values of its debt and equity.

11. **Calculating WACC.** Find the WACC of William Tell Computers. The total book value of the firm's equity is $10 million; book value per share is $20. The stock sells for a price of $30 per share, and the cost of equity is 15%. The firm's bonds have a face value of $5 million and sell at a price of 110% of face value. The yield to maturity on the bonds is 9%, and the firm's tax rate is 40%. (*LO3*)

12. **WACC.** Nodebt, Inc., is a firm with all-equity financing. Its equity beta is .80. The Treasury bill rate is 4%, and the market risk premium is expected to be 10%. What is Nodebt's asset beta? What is Nodebt's weighted-average cost of capital? The firm is exempt from paying taxes. (*LO3*)

13. **Cost of Debt.** A financial analyst at Dawn Chemical notes that the firm's total interest payments this year were $10 million while total debt outstanding was $80 million, and he concludes that the cost of debt was 12.5%. What is wrong with this conclusion? (*LO2*)

14. **Cost of Equity.** Bunkhouse Electronics is a recently incorporated firm that makes electronic entertainment systems. Its earnings and dividends have been growing at a rate of 30%, and the current dividend yield is 2%. Its beta is 1.2, the market risk premium is 8%, and the risk-free rate is 4%. (*LO2*)
    a. Calculate two estimates of the firm's cost of equity.
    b. Which estimate seems more reasonable to you? Why?

15. **Cost of Debt.** Olympic Sports has two issues of debt outstanding. One is a 9% coupon bond with a face value of $20 million, a maturity of 10 years, and a yield to maturity of 10%. The coupons are paid annually. The other bond issue has a maturity of 15 years, with coupons also paid annually, and a coupon rate of 10%. The face value of the issue is $25 million, and the issue sells for 94% of par value. The firm's tax rate is 35%. (*LO2*)
    a. What is the before-tax cost of debt for Olympic?
    b. What is Olympic's after-tax cost of debt?

16. **Capital Structure.** Examine the following book-value balance sheet for University Products, Inc. What is the capital structure of the firm on the basis of market values? The preferred stock currently sells for $15 per share and the common stock for $20 per share. There are 1 million common shares outstanding. (*LO1*)

BOOK VALUE BALANCE SHEET (all values in millions)			
Assets		**Liabilities and Net Worth**	
Cash and short-term securities	$ 1	Bonds, coupon = 8%, paid annually (maturity = 10 years, current yield to maturity = 9%)	$10.0
Accounts receivable	3	Preferred stock (par value $20 per share)	2.0
Inventories	7	Common stock (par value $.10)	.1
Plant and equipment	21	Additional paid-in stockholders' capital	9.9
		Retained earnings	10.0
Total	$32	Total	$32.0

17. **Calculating WACC.** Turn back to University Products's balance sheet from the previous problem. If the preferred stock pays a dividend of $2 per share, the beta of the common stock is .8, the market risk premium is 10%, the risk-free rate is 6%, and the firm's tax rate is 40%, what is University's weighted-average cost of capital? (*LO3*)

18. **Project Discount Rate.** University Products is evaluating a new venture into home computer systems (see Practice Problems 16 and 17). The internal rate of return on the new venture is estimated at 13.4%. WACCs of firms in the personal computer industry tend to average around 14%. Should the new project be pursued? Will University Products make the correct decision if it discounts cash flows on the proposed venture at the firm's WACC? (*LO4*)

19. **Cost of Capital.** The total market value of Okefenokee Real Estate Company is $6 million, and the total value of its debt is $4 million. The treasurer estimates that the beta of the stock currently is 1.2 and that the expected risk premium on the market is 10%. The Treasury bill rate is 4%. (*LO3*)
    a. What is the required rate of return on Okefenokee stock?
    b. What is the beta of the company's existing portfolio of assets? The debt is perceived to be virtually risk-free.
    c. Estimate the weighted-average cost of capital assuming a tax rate of 40%.
    d. Estimate the discount rate for an expansion of the company's present business.
    e. Suppose the company wants to diversify into the manufacture of rose-colored glasses. The beta of optical manufacturers with no debt outstanding is 1.4. What is the required rate of return on Okefenokee's new venture? (You should assume that the risky project will not enable the firm to issue any additional debt.)

CHALLENGE PROBLEMS

20. **Changes in Capital Structure.** Look again at our calculation of Big Oil's WACC. Suppose Big Oil is excused from paying taxes. How would its WACC change? Now suppose Big Oil makes a large stock issue and uses the proceeds to pay off all its debt. How would the cost of equity change? (*LO2*)

21. **Changes in Capital Structure.** Refer again to Challenge Problem 20. Suppose Big Oil starts from the financing mix in Table 13–3, and then borrows an additional $200 million from the bank. It then pays out a special $200 million dividend, leaving its assets and operations unchanged. What happens to Big Oil's WACC, still assuming it pays no taxes? What happens to the cost of equity? (*LO1*)

22. **WACC and Taxes.** "The after-tax cost of debt is lower when the firm's tax rate is higher; therefore, the WACC falls when the tax rate rises. Thus, with a lower discount rate, the firm must be worth more if its tax rate is higher." Explain why this argument is wrong. (*LO5*)

23. **Cost of Capital.** An analyst at Dawn Chemical notes that its cost of debt is far below that of equity. He concludes that it is important for the firm to maintain the ability to increase its borrowing because if it cannot borrow, it will be forced to use more expensive equity to finance some projects. This might lead it to reject some projects that would have seemed attractive if evaluated at the lower cost of debt. Comment on this reasoning. (*LO4*)

eXcel

Please visit us at www.mhhe.com/bmm6e

STANDARD &POOR'S

Go to Market Insight (**www.mhhe.com/edumarketinsight**). We will calculate the weighted-average cost of capital for Caterpillar (CAT) using the Market Insight data. First we estimate the required return on the company's long-term debt (bonds) and common stock. (All information is located on the Market Insight reports, except where noted.)

1. Find Caterpillar's S&P credit rating in Market Insight, and then find the current yields on similarly rated bonds at **www.bondsonline.com**. Find the after-tax cost of debt assuming a tax rate of 40%.

2. Use one of these estimates for the cost of equity:

   a. The constant-dividend-growth valuation model, given the current price, current dividend, and the 5-year dividend growth rate.

   b. The CAPM, using the U.S. Treasury bill rate as your risk-free rate (**www.bondsonline.com**). Find the company's beta, and use the historical market risk premium, 7.6%, from Table 11–1.

3. Now find the weights for WACC. Use the book value (from the balance sheet) of long-term debt as an estimate of the market value of debt. Then find total market capitalization (total market value of equity) from Financial Highlights. Finally, calculate the proportions of each.

4. Refer to Sections 13.4 and 13.5 of this chapter to calculate the WACC.

SOLUTIONS TO SELF-TEST QUESTIONS

13.1 Hot Rocks' 4 million common shares are worth $40 million. Its market value balance sheet is:

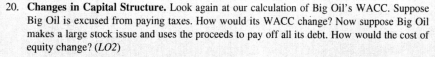
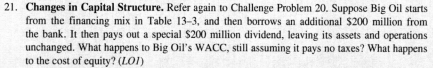

Assets		Liabilities and Shareholders' Equity		
Assets	$90	Debt	$50	(56%)
		Equity	40	(44%)
Value	$90	Value	$90	

$$\text{WACC} = (.56 \times 9\%) + (.44 \times 17\%) = 12.5\%$$

We use Hot Rocks' pretax return on debt because the company pays no taxes.

13.2 Burg's 6 million shares are now worth only 6 million × \$4 = \$24 million. The debt is selling for 80% of book, or \$20 million. The market value balance sheet is:

Assets		Liabilities and Shareholders' Equity		
Assets	\$44	Debt	\$20	(45%)
		Equity	24	(55%)
Value	\$44	Value	\$44	

$$\text{WACC} = (.45 \times 14\%) + (.55 \times 20\%) = 17.3\%$$

Note that this question ignores taxes.

13.3 Compare the two income statements, one for Criss-Cross Industries and the other for a firm with identical EBIT but no debt in its capital structure. (All figures in millions.)

	Criss-Cross	Firm with No Debt
EBIT	\$10.0	\$10.0
Interest expense	2.0	0.0
Taxable income	8.0	10.0
Taxes owed	2.8	3.5
Net income	5.2	6.5
Total income accruing to debt- & equityholders	7.2	6.5

Notice that Criss-Cross pays \$.7 million less in taxes than its debt-free counterpart. Accordingly, the total income available to debt- plus equityholders is \$.7 million higher.

13.4 For Hot Rocks,

$$\text{WACC} = [.56 \times 9 \times (1 - .35)] + (.44 \times 17) = 10.8\%$$

For Burg Associates,

$$\text{WACC} = [.45 \times 14 \times (1 - .35)] + (.55 \times 20) = 15.1\%$$

13.5 WACC measures the expected rate of return demanded by debt and equity investors in the firm (plus a tax adjustment capturing the tax-deductibility of interest payments). Thus the calculation must be based on what investors are actually paying for the firm's debt and equity securities. In other words, it must be based on market values.

13.6 From the CAPM:

$$r_{\text{equity}} = r_f + \beta_{\text{equity}}(r_m - r_f)$$
$$= 6\% + 1.20(7.6\%) = 15.1\%$$
$$\text{WACC} = .3(1 - .35)\ 8\% + .7(15.1\%) = 12.13\%$$

13.7 Jo Ann's boss is wrong. The ability to borrow at 8% does not mean that the cost of capital is 8%. The firm could not finance a stand-alone project with 8% debt. This analysis ignores the side effects of the borrowing, for example, that at the higher indebtedness of the firm the equity will be riskier and, therefore, the equityholders will demand a higher rate of return on their investment.

13.8 Estimated horizon value for the concatenator business is 9 × year-5 EBITDA = 9 × 239 = \$2,151 thousand. PV (horizon value) is $\$2,151/(1.085)^5 = \$1,430.5$ thousand. Adding in the PV of free cash flows for years 1 to 5 gives a present value for the business of \$1,210.3 thousand.

MINICASE

Bernice Mountaindog was glad to be back at Sea Shore Salt. Employees were treated well. When she had asked a year ago for a leave of absence to complete her degree in finance, top management promptly agreed. When she returned with an honors degree, she was promoted from administrative assistant (she had been secretary to Joe-Bob Brinepool, the president) to treasury analyst.

Bernice thought the company's prospects were good. Sure, table salt was a mature business, but Sea Shore Salt had grown steadily at the expense of its less well known competitors. The company's brand name was an important advantage, despite the difficulty most customers had in pronouncing it rapidly.

FIGURE 13-2 Mr. Brinepool's cost of capital memo

Sea Shore Salt Company
Spring Vacation Beach, Florida

CONFIDENTIAL MEMORANDUM

```
DATE:      January 15, 2009
TO:        S.S.S. Management
FROM:      Joe-Bob Brinepool, President
SUBJECT:   Cost of Capital
```

This memo states and clarifies our company's long-standing policy regarding hurdle rates for capital investment decisions. There have been many recent questions, and some evident confusion, on this matter.

Sea Shore Salt evaluates replacement and expansion investments by discounted cash flow. The discount or hurdle rate is the company's after-tax weighted-average cost of capital.

The weighted-average cost of capital is simply a blend of the rates of return expected by investors in our company. These investors include banks, bondholders, and preferred stock investors in addition to common stockholders. Of course many of you are, or soon will be, stockholders of our company.

The following table summarizes the composition of Sea Shore Salt's financing.

	Amount (in millions)	Percent of Total	Rate of Return
Bank loan	$120	20%	8%
Bond issue	80	13.3	7.75
Preferred stock	100	16.7	6
Common stock	300	50	16
	$600	100%	

The rates of return on the bank loan and bond issue are of course just the interest rates we pay. However, interest is tax-deductible, so the after-tax interest rates are lower than shown above. For example, the after-tax cost of our bank financing, given our 35% tax rate, is $8(1 - .35) = 5.2\%$.

The rate of return on preferred stock is 6%. Sea Shore Salt pays a $6 dividend on each $100 preferred share.

Our target rate of return on equity has been 16% for many years. I know that some newcomers think this target is too high for the safe and mature salt business. But we must all aspire to superior profitability.

Once this background is absorbed, the calculation of Sea Shore Salt's weighted-average cost of capital (WACC) is elementary:

$$\text{WACC} = 8(1 - .35)(.20) + 7.75(1 - .35)(.133) + 6(.167) + 16(.50) = 10.7\%$$

The official corporate hurdle rate is therefore 10.7%.

If you have further questions about these calculations, please direct them to our new Treasury Analyst, Ms. Bernice Mountaindog. It is a pleasure to have Bernice back at Sea Shore Salt after a year's leave of absence to complete her degree in finance.

Bernice started work on January 2, 2009. The first 2 weeks went smoothly. Then Mr. Brinepool's cost of capital memo (see Figure 13–2) assigned her to explain Sea Shore Salt's weighted-average cost of capital to other managers. The memo came as a surprise to Bernice, so she stayed late to prepare for the questions that would surely come the next day.

Bernice first examined Sea Shore Salt's most recent balance sheet, summarized in Table 13–6. Then she jotted down the following additional points:

- The company's bank charged interest at current market rates, and the long-term debt had just been issued. Book and market values could not differ by much.
- But the preferred stock had been issued 35 years ago, when interest rates were much lower. The preferred stock was now trading for only $70 per share.
- The common stock traded for $40 per share. Next year's earnings per share would be about $4 and dividends per share probably $2. Sea Shore Salt had traditionally paid out 50% of earnings as dividends and plowed back the rest.
- Earnings and dividends had grown steadily at 6% to 7% per year, in line with the company's sustainable growth rate:

$$\frac{\text{Sustainable}}{\text{growth rate}} = \frac{\text{return}}{\text{on equity}} \times \frac{\text{plowback}}{\text{ratio}}$$
$$= 4/30 \times .5$$
$$= .067, \text{ or } 6.7\%$$

- Sea Shore Salt's beta had averaged about .5, which made sense, Bernice thought, for a stable, steady-growth business. She made a quick cost of equity calculation by using the capital asset pricing model (CAPM). With current interest rates of about 7%, and a market risk premium of 7%,

$$\text{CAPM cost of equity} = r_E = r_f + \beta(r_m - r_f)$$
$$= 7\% + .5(7\%) = 10.5\%$$

This cost of equity was significantly less than the 16% decreed in Mr. Brinepool's memo. Bernice scanned her notes apprehensively. What if Mr. Brinepool's cost of equity was wrong? Was there some other way to estimate the cost of equity as a check on the CAPM calculation? Could there be other errors in his calculations?

Bernice resolved to complete her analysis that night. If necessary, she would try to speak with Mr. Brinepool when he arrived at his office the next morning. Her job was not just finding the right number. She also had to figure out how to explain it all to Mr. Brinepool.

TABLE 13–6 Sea Shore Salt's balance sheet, taken from the company's 2008 balance sheet (figures in millions)

Assets		Liabilities and Net Worth	
Working capital	$200	Bank loan	$120
Plant and equipment	360	Long-term debt	.80
Other assets	40	Preferred stock	100
		Common stock, including retained earnings	300
Total	$600	Total	$600

Notes:
1. At year-end 2008, Sea Shore Salt had 10 million common shares outstanding.
2. The company had also issued 1 million preferred shares with book value of $100 per share. Each share receives an annual dividend of $6.

APPENDIX A
Present Value and Future Value Tables

APPENDIX TABLE A-1 Future value of $1 after t years $= (1 + r)^t$

Number of Years							Interest Rate per Year								
	1%	2%	3%	4%	5%	6%	7%	8%	9%	10%	11%	12%	13%	14%	15%
1	1.0100	1.0200	1.0300	1.0400	1.0500	1.0600	1.0700	1.0800	1.0900	1.1000	1.1100	1.1200	1.1300	1.1400	1.1500
2	1.0201	1.0404	1.0609	1.0816	1.1025	1.1236	1.1449	1.1664	1.1881	1.2100	1.2321	1.2544	1.2769	1.2996	1.3225
3	1.0303	1.0612	1.0927	1.1249	1.1576	1.1910	1.2250	1.2597	1.2950	1.3310	1.3676	1.4049	1.4429	1.4815	1.5209
4	1.0406	1.0824	1.1255	1.1699	1.2155	1.2625	1.3108	1.3605	1.4116	1.4641	1.5181	1.5735	1.6305	1.6890	1.7490
5	1.0510	1.1041	1.1593	1.2167	1.2763	1.3382	1.4026	1.4693	1.5386	1.6105	1.6851	1.7623	1.8424	1.9254	2.0114
6	1.0615	1.1262	1.1941	1.2653	1.3401	1.4185	1.5007	1.5869	1.6771	1.7716	1.8704	1.9738	2.0820	2.1950	2.3131
7	1.0721	1.1487	1.2299	1.3159	1.4071	1.5036	1.6058	1.7138	1.8280	1.9487	2.0762	2.2107	2.3526	2.5023	2.6600
8	1.0829	1.1717	1.2668	1.3686	1.4775	1.5938	1.7182	1.8509	1.9926	2.1436	2.3045	2.4760	2.6584	2.8526	3.0590
9	1.0937	1.1951	1.3048	1.4233	1.5513	1.6895	1.8385	1.9990	2.1719	2.3579	2.5580	2.7731	3.0040	3.2519	3.5179
10	1.1046	1.2190	1.3439	1.4802	1.6289	1.7908	1.9672	2.1589	2.3674	2.5937	2.8394	3.1058	3.3946	3.7072	4.0456
11	1.1157	1.2434	1.3842	1.5395	1.7103	1.8983	2.1049	2.3316	2.5804	2.8531	3.1518	3.4785	3.8359	4.2262	4.6524
12	1.1268	1.2682	1.4258	1.6010	1.7959	2.0122	2.2522	2.5182	2.8127	3.1384	3.4985	3.8960	4.3345	4.8179	5.3503
13	1.1381	1.2936	1.4685	1.6651	1.8856	2.1329	2.4098	2.7196	3.0658	3.4523	3.8833	4.3635	4.8980	5.4924	6.1528
14	1.1495	1.3195	1.5126	1.7317	1.9799	2.2609	2.5785	2.9372	3.3417	3.7975	4.3104	4.8871	5.5348	6.2613	7.0757
15	1.1610	1.3459	1.5580	1.8009	2.0789	2.3966	2.7590	3.1722	3.6425	4.1772	4.7846	5.4736	6.2543	7.1379	8.1371
16	1.1726	1.3728	1.6047	1.8730	2.1829	2.5404	2.9522	3.4259	3.9703	4.5950	5.3109	6.1304	7.0673	8.1372	9.3576
17	1.1843	1.4002	1.6528	1.9479	2.2920	2.6928	3.1588	3.7000	4.3276	5.0545	5.8951	6.8660	7.9861	9.2765	10.7613
18	1.1961	1.4282	1.7024	2.0258	2.4066	2.8543	3.3799	3.9960	4.7171	5.5599	6.5436	7.6900	9.0243	10.5752	12.3755
19	1.2081	1.4568	1.7535	2.1068	2.5270	3.0256	3.6165	4.3157	5.1417	6.1159	7.2633	8.6128	10.1974	12.0557	14.2318
20	1.2202	1.4859	1.8061	2.1911	2.6533	3.2071	3.8697	4.6610	5.6044	6.7275	8.0623	9.6463	11.5231	13.7435	16.3665

Number of Years							Interest Rate per Year								
	16%	17%	18%	19%	20%	21%	22%	23%	24%	25%	26%	27%	28%	29%	30%
1	1.1600	1.1700	1.1800	1.1900	1.2000	1.2100	1.2200	1.2300	1.2400	1.2500	1.2600	1.2700	1.2800	1.2900	1.3000
2	1.3456	1.3689	1.3924	1.4161	1.4400	1.4641	1.4884	1.5129	1.5376	1.5625	1.5876	1.6129	1.6384	1.6641	1.6900
3	1.5609	1.6016	1.6430	1.6852	1.7280	1.7716	1.8158	1.8609	1.9066	1.9531	2.0004	2.0484	2.0972	2.1467	2.1970
4	1.8106	1.8739	1.9388	2.0053	2.0736	2.1436	2.2153	2.2889	2.3642	2.4414	2.5205	2.6014	2.6844	2.7692	2.8561
5	2.1003	2.1924	2.2878	2.3864	2.4883	2.5937	2.7027	2.8153	2.9316	3.0518	3.1758	3.3038	3.4360	3.5723	3.7129
6	2.4364	2.5652	2.6996	2.8398	2.9860	3.1384	3.2973	3.4628	3.6352	3.8147	4.0015	4.1959	4.3980	4.6083	4.8268
7	2.8262	3.0012	3.1855	3.3793	3.5832	3.7975	4.0227	4.2593	4.5077	4.7684	5.0419	5.3288	5.6295	5.9447	6.2749
8	3.2784	3.5115	3.7589	4.0214	4.2998	4.5950	4.9077	5.2389	5.5895	5.9605	6.3528	6.7675	7.2058	7.6686	8.1573
9	3.8030	4.1084	4.4355	4.7854	5.1598	5.5599	5.9874	6.4439	6.9310	7.4506	8.0045	8.5948	9.2234	9.8925	10.6045
10	4.4114	4.8068	5.2338	5.6947	6.1917	6.7275	7.3046	7.9259	8.5944	9.3132	10.0857	10.9153	11.8059	12.7614	13.7858
11	5.1173	5.6240	6.1759	6.7767	7.4301	8.1403	8.9117	9.7489	10.6571	11.6415	12.7080	13.8625	15.1116	16.4622	17.9216
12	5.9360	6.5801	7.2876	8.0642	8.9161	9.8497	10.8722	11.9912	13.2148	14.5519	16.0120	17.6053	19.3428	21.2362	23.2981
13	6.8858	7.6987	8.5994	9.5964	10.6993	11.9182	13.2641	14.7491	16.3863	18.1899	20.1752	22.3588	24.7588	27.3947	30.2875
14	7.9875	9.0075	10.1472	11.4198	12.8392	14.4210	16.1822	18.1414	20.3191	22.7374	25.4207	28.3957	31.6913	35.3391	39.3738
15	9.2655	10.5387	11.9737	13.5895	15.4070	17.4494	19.7423	22.3140	25.1956	28.4217	32.0301	36.0625	40.5648	45.5875	51.1859
16	10.7480	12.3303	14.1290	16.1715	18.4884	21.1138	24.0856	27.4462	31.2426	5.5271	40.3579	45.7994	51.9230	58.8079	66.5417
17	12.4677	14.4265	16.6722	19.2441	22.1861	25.5477	29.3844	33.7588	38.7408	44.4089	50.8510	58.1652	66.4614	75.8621	86.5042
18	14.4625	16.8790	19.6733	22.9005	26.6233	30.9127	35.8490	41.5233	48.0386	55.5112	64.0722	73.8698	85.0706	97.8622	112.4554
19	16.7765	19.7484	23.2144	27.2516	31.9480	37.4043	43.7358	51.0737	59.5679	69.3889	80.7310	93.8147	108.8904	126.2422	146.1920
20	19.4608	23.1056	27.3930	32.4294	38.3376	45.2593	53.3576	62.8206	73.8641	86.7362	101.7211	119.1446	139.3797	162.8524	190.0496

APPENDIX TABLE A-2 Discount factors: Present value of $1 to be received after t years $= 1/(1 + r)^t$

Number of Years	\multicolumn{15}{c}{Interest Rate per Year}														
	1%	2%	3%	4%	5%	6%	7%	8%	9%	10%	11%	12%	13%	14%	15%
1	0.9901	0.9804	0.9709	0.9615	0.9524	0.9434	0.9346	0.9259	0.9174	0.9091	0.9009	0.8929	0.8850	0.8772	0.8696
2	0.9803	0.9612	0.9426	0.9246	0.9070	0.8900	0.8734	0.8573	0.8417	0.8264	0.8116	0.7972	0.7831	0.7695	0.7561
3	0.9706	0.9423	0.9151	0.8890	0.8638	0.8396	0.8163	0.7938	0.7722	0.7513	0.7312	0.7118	0.6931	0.6750	0.6575
4	0.9610	0.9238	0.8885	0.8548	0.8227	0.7921	0.7629	0.7350	0.7084	0.6830	0.6587	0.6355	0.6133	0.5921	0.5718
5	0.9515	0.9057	0.8626	0.8219	0.7835	0.7473	0.7130	0.6806	0.6499	0.6209	0.5935	0.5674	0.5428	0.5194	0.4972
6	0.9420	0.8880	0.8375	0.7903	0.7462	0.7050	0.6663	0.6302	0.5963	0.5645	0.5346	0.5066	0.4803	0.4556	0.4323
7	0.9327	0.8706	0.8131	0.7599	0.7107	0.6651	0.6227	0.5835	0.5470	0.5132	0.4817	0.4523	0.4251	0.3996	0.3759
8	0.9235	0.8535	0.7894	0.7307	0.6768	0.6274	0.5820	0.5403	0.5019	0.4665	0.4339	0.4039	0.3762	0.3506	0.3269
9	0.9143	0.8368	0.7664	0.7026	0.6446	0.5919	0.5439	0.5002	0.4604	0.4241	0.3909	0.3606	0.3329	0.3075	0.2843
10	0.9053	0.8203	0.7441	0.6756	0.6139	0.5584	0.5083	0.4632	0.4224	0.3855	0.3522	0.3220	0.2946	0.2697	0.2472
11	0.8963	0.8043	0.7224	0.6496	0.5847	0.5268	0.4751	0.4289	0.3875	0.3505	0.3173	0.2875	0.2607	0.2366	0.2149
12	0.8874	0.7885	0.7014	0.6246	0.5568	0.4970	0.4440	0.3971	0.3555	0.3186	0.2858	0.2567	0.2307	0.2076	0.1869
13	0.8787	0.7730	0.6810	0.6006	0.5303	0.4688	0.4150	0.3677	0.3262	0.2897	0.2575	0.2292	0.2042	0.1821	0.1625
14	0.8700	0.7579	0.6611	0.5775	0.5051	0.4423	0.3878	0.3405	0.2992	0.2633	0.2320	0.2046	0.1807	0.1597	0.1413
15	0.8613	0.7430	0.6419	0.5553	0.4810	0.4173	0.3624	0.3152	0.2745	0.2394	0.2090	0.1827	0.1599	0.1401	0.1229
16	0.8528	0.7284	0.6232	0.5339	0.4581	0.3936	0.3387	0.2919	0.2519	0.2176	0.1883	0.1631	0.1415	0.1229	0.1069
17	0.8444	0.7142	0.6050	0.5134	0.4363	0.3714	0.3166	0.2703	0.2311	0.1978	0.1696	0.1456	0.1252	0.1078	0.0929
18	0.8360	0.7002	0.5874	0.4936	0.4155	0.3503	0.2959	0.2502	0.2120	0.1799	0.1528	0.1300	0.1108	0.0946	0.0808
19	0.8277	0.6864	0.5703	0.4746	0.3957	0.3305	0.2765	0.2317	0.1945	0.1635	0.1377	0.1161	0.0981	0.0829	0.0703
20	0.8195	0.6730	0.5537	0.4564	0.3769	0.3118	0.2584	0.2145	0.1784	0.1486	0.1240	0.1037	0.0868	0.0728	0.0611

Number of Years	\multicolumn{15}{c}{Interest Rate per Year}														
	16%	17%	18%	19%	20%	21%	22%	23%	24%	25%	26%	27%	28%	29%	30%
1	0.8621	0.8547	0.8475	0.8403	0.8333	0.8264	0.8197	0.8130	0.8065	0.8000	0.7937	0.7874	0.7813	0.7752	0.7692
2	0.7432	0.7305	0.7182	0.7062	0.6944	0.6830	0.6719	0.6610	0.6504	0.6400	0.6299	0.6200	0.6104	0.6009	0.5917
3	0.6407	0.6244	0.6086	0.5934	0.5787	0.5645	0.5507	0.5374	0.5245	0.5120	0.4999	0.4882	0.4768	0.4658	0.4552
4	0.5523	0.5337	0.5158	0.4987	0.4823	0.4665	0.4514	0.4369	0.4230	0.4096	0.3968	0.3844	0.3725	0.3611	0.3501
5	0.4761	0.4561	0.4371	0.4190	0.4019	0.3855	0.3700	0.3552	0.3411	0.3277	0.3149	0.3027	0.2910	0.2799	0.2693
6	0.4104	0.3898	0.3704	0.3521	0.3349	0.3186	0.3033	0.2888	0.2751	0.2621	0.2499	0.2383	0.2274	0.2170	0.2072
7	0.3538	0.3332	0.3139	0.2959	0.2791	0.2633	0.2486	0.2348	0.2218	0.2097	0.1983	0.1877	0.1776	0.1682	0.1594
8	0.3050	0.2848	0.2660	0.2487	0.2326	0.2176	0.2038	0.1909	0.1789	0.1678	0.1574	0.1478	0.1388	0.1304	0.1226
9	0.2630	0.2434	0.2255	0.2090	0.1938	0.1799	0.1670	0.1552	0.1443	0.1342	0.1249	0.1164	0.1084	0.1011	0.0943
10	0.2267	0.2080	0.1911	0.1756	0.1615	0.1486	0.1369	0.1262	0.1164	0.1074	0.0992	0.0916	0.0847	0.0784	0.0725
11	0.1954	0.1778	0.1619	0.1476	0.1346	0.1228	0.1122	0.1026	0.0938	0.0859	0.0787	0.0721	0.0662	0.0607	0.0558
12	0.1685	0.1520	0.1372	0.1240	0.1122	0.1015	0.0920	0.0834	0.0757	0.0687	0.0625	0.0568	0.0517	0.0471	0.0429
13	0.1452	0.1299	0.1163	0.1042	0.0935	0.0839	0.0754	0.0678	0.0610	0.0550	0.0496	0.0447	0.0404	0.0365	0.0330
14	0.1252	0.1110	0.0985	0.0876	0.0779	0.0693	0.0618	0.0551	0.0492	0.0440	0.0393	0.0352	0.0316	0.0283	0.0254
15	0.1079	0.0949	0.0835	0.0736	0.0649	0.0573	0.0507	0.0448	0.0397	0.0352	0.0312	0.0277	0.0247	0.0219	0.0195
16	0.0930	0.0811	0.0708	0.0618	0.0541	0.0474	0.0415	0.0364	0.0320	0.0281	0.0248	0.0218	0.0193	0.0170	0.0150
17	0.0802	0.0693	0.0600	0.0520	0.0451	0.0391	0.0340	0.0296	0.0258	0.0225	0.0197	0.0172	0.0150	0.0132	0.0116
18	0.0691	0.0592	0.0508	0.0437	0.0376	0.0323	0.0279	0.0241	0.0208	0.0180	0.0156	0.0135	0.0118	0.0102	0.0089
19	0.0596	0.0506	0.0431	0.0367	0.0313	0.0267	0.0229	0.0196	0.0168	0.0144	0.0124	0.0107	0.0092	0.0079	0.0068
20	0.0514	0.0433	0.0365	0.0308	0.0261	0.0221	0.0187	0.0159	0.0135	0.0115	0.0098	0.0084	0.0072	0.0061	0.0053

APPENDIX TABLE A-3 Annuity table: Present value of $1 per year for each of t years $= 1/r - 1/(r(1 + r)^t)$

Number of Years	1%	2%	3%	4%	5%	6%	7%	8%	9%	10%	11%	12%	13%	14%	15%
1	0.9901	0.9804	0.9709	0.9615	0.9524	0.9434	0.9346	0.9259	0.9174	0.9091	0.9009	0.8929	0.8850	0.8772	0.8696
2	1.9704	1.9416	1.9135	1.8861	1.8594	1.8334	1.8080	1.7833	1.7591	1.7355	1.7125	1.6901	1.6681	1.6467	1.6257
3	2.9410	2.8839	2.8286	2.7751	2.7232	2.6730	2.6243	2.5771	2.5313	2.4869	2.4437	2.4018	2.3612	2.3216	2.2832
4	3.9020	3.8077	3.7171	3.6299	3.5460	3.4651	3.3872	3.3121	3.2397	3.1699	3.1024	3.0373	2.9745	2.9137	2.8550
5	4.8534	4.7135	4.5797	4.4518	4.3295	4.2124	4.1002	3.9927	3.8897	3.7908	3.6959	3.6048	3.5172	3.4331	3.3522
6	5.7955	5.6014	5.4172	5.2421	5.0757	4.9173	4.7665	4.6229	4.4859	4.3553	4.2305	4.1114	3.9975	3.8887	3.7845
7	6.7282	6.4720	6.2303	6.0021	5.7864	5.5824	5.3893	5.2064	5.0330	4.8684	4.7122	4.5638	4.4226	4.2883	4.1604
8	7.6517	7.3255	7.0197	6.7327	6.4632	6.2098	5.9713	5.7466	5.5348	5.3349	5.1461	4.9676	4.7988	4.6389	4.4873
9	8.5660	8.1622	7.7861	7.4353	7.1078	6.8017	6.5152	6.2469	5.9952	5.7590	5.5370	5.3282	5.1317	4.9464	4.7716
10	9.4713	8.9826	8.5302	8.1109	7.7217	7.3601	7.0236	6.7101	6.4177	6.1446	5.8892	5.6502	5.4262	5.2161	5.0188
11	10.3676	9.7868	9.2526	8.7605	8.3064	7.8869	7.4987	7.1390	6.8052	6.4951	6.2065	5.9377	5.6869	5.4527	5.2337
12	11.2551	10.5753	9.9540	9.3851	8.8633	8.3838	7.9427	7.5361	7.1607	6.8137	6.4924	6.1944	5.9176	5.6603	5.4206
13	12.1337	11.3484	10.6350	9.9856	9.3936	8.8527	8.3577	7.9038	7.4869	7.1034	6.7499	6.4235	6.1218	5.8424	5.5831
14	13.0037	12.1062	11.2961	10.5631	9.8986	9.2950	8.7455	8.2442	7.7862	7.3667	6.9819	6.6282	6.3025	6.0021	5.7245
15	13.8651	12.8493	11.9379	11.1184	10.3797	9.7122	9.1079	8.5595	8.0607	7.6061	7.1909	6.8109	6.4624	6.1422	5.8474
16	14.7179	13.5777	12.5611	11.6523	10.8378	10.1059	9.4466	8.8514	8.3126	7.8237	7.3792	6.9740	6.6039	6.2651	5.9542
17	15.5623	14.2919	13.1661	12.1657	11.2741	10.4773	9.7632	9.1216	8.5436	8.0216	7.5488	7.1196	6.7291	6.3729	6.0472
18	16.3983	14.9920	13.7535	12.6593	11.6896	10.8276	10.0591	9.3719	8.7556	8.2014	7.7016	7.2497	6.8399	6.4674	6.1280
19	17.2260	15.6785	14.3238	13.1339	12.0853	11.1581	10.3356	9.6036	8.9501	8.3649	7.8393	7.3658	6.9380	6.5504	6.1982
20	18.0456	16.3514	14.8775	13.5903	12.4622	11.4699	10.5940	9.8181	9.1285	8.5136	7.9633	7.4694	7.0248	6.6231	6.2593

Number of Years	16%	17%	18%	19%	20%	21%	22%	23%	24%	25%	26%	27%	28%	29%	30%
1	0.8621	0.8547	0.8475	0.8403	0.8333	0.8264	0.8197	0.8130	0.8065	0.8000	0.7937	0.7874	0.7813	0.7752	0.7692
2	1.6052	1.5852	1.5656	1.5465	1.5278	1.5095	1.4915	1.4740	1.4568	1.4400	1.4235	1.4074	1.3916	1.3761	1.3609
3	2.2459	2.2096	2.1743	2.1399	2.1065	2.0739	2.0422	2.0114	1.9813	1.9520	1.9234	1.8956	1.8684	1.8420	1.8161
4	2.7982	2.7432	2.6901	2.6386	2.5887	2.5404	2.4936	2.4483	2.4043	2.3616	2.3202	2.2800	2.2410	2.2031	2.1662
5	3.2743	3.1993	3.1272	3.0576	2.9906	2.9260	2.8636	2.8035	2.7454	2.6893	2.6351	2.5827	2.5320	2.4830	2.4356
6	3.6847	3.5892	3.4976	3.4098	3.3255	3.2446	3.1669	3.0923	3.0205	2.9514	2.8850	2.8210	2.7594	2.7000	2.6427
7	4.0386	3.9224	3.8115	3.7057	3.6046	3.5079	3.4155	3.3270	3.2423	3.1611	3.0833	3.0087	2.9370	2.8682	2.8021
8	4.3436	4.2072	4.0776	3.9544	3.8372	3.7256	3.6193	3.5179	3.4212	3.3289	3.2407	3.1564	3.0758	2.9986	2.9247
9	4.6065	4.4506	4.3030	4.1633	4.0310	3.9054	3.7863	3.6731	3.5655	3.4631	3.3657	3.2728	3.1842	3.0997	3.0190
10	4.8332	4.6586	4.4941	4.3389	4.1925	4.0541	3.9232	3.7993	3.6819	3.5705	3.4648	3.3644	3.2689	3.1781	3.0915
11	5.0286	4.8364	4.6560	4.4865	4.3271	4.1769	4.0354	3.9018	3.7757	3.6564	3.5435	3.4365	3.3351	3.2388	3.1473
12	5.1971	4.9884	4.7932	4.6105	4.4392	4.2784	4.1274	3.9852	3.8514	3.7251	3.6059	3.4933	3.3868	3.2859	3.1903
13	5.3423	5.1183	4.9095	4.7147	4.5327	4.3624	4.2028	4.0530	3.9124	3.7801	3.6555	3.5381	3.4272	3.3224	3.2233
14	5.4675	5.2293	5.0081	4.8023	4.6106	4.4317	4.2646	4.1082	3.9616	3.8241	3.6949	3.5733	3.4587	3.3507	3.2487
15	5.5755	5.3242	5.0916	4.8759	4.6755	4.4890	4.3152	4.1530	4.0013	3.8593	3.7261	3.6010	3.4834	3.3726	3.2682
16	5.6685	5.4053	5.1624	4.9377	4.7296	4.5364	4.3567	4.1894	4.0333	3.8874	3.7509	3.6228	3.5026	3.3896	3.2832
17	5.7487	5.4746	5.2223	4.9897	4.7746	4.5755	4.3908	4.2190	4.0591	3.9099	3.7705	3.6400	3.5177	3.4028	3.2948
18	5.8178	5.5339	5.2732	5.0333	4.8122	4.6079	4.4187	4.2431	4.0799	3.9279	3.7861	3.6536	3.5294	3.4130	3.3037
19	5.8775	5.5845	5.3162	5.0700	4.8435	4.6346	4.4415	4.2627	4.0967	3.9424	3.7985	3.6642	3.5386	3.4210	3.3105
20	5.9288	5.6278	5.3527	5.1009	4.8696	4.6567	4.4603	4.2786	4.1103	3.9539	3.8083	3.6726	3.5458	3.4271	3.3158

APPENDIX TABLE A-4 Annuity table: Future value of $1 per year for each of t years $= ((1 + r)^t - 1)/r$

	Interest Rate per Year														
Number of Years	1%	2%	3%	4%	5%	6%	7%	8%	9%	10%	11%	12%	13%	14%	15%
1	1.0000	1.0000	1.0000	1.0000	1.0000	1.0000	1.0000	1.0000	1.0000	1.0000	1.0000	1.0000	1.0000	1.0000	1.0000
2	2.0100	2.0200	2.0300	2.0400	2.0500	2.0600	2.0700	2.0800	2.0900	2.1000	2.1100	2.1200	2.1300	2.1400	2.1500
3	3.0301	3.0604	3.0909	3.1216	3.1525	3.1836	3.2149	3.2464	3.2781	3.3100	3.3421	3.3744	3.4069	3.4396	3.4725
4	4.0604	4.1216	4.1836	4.2465	4.3101	4.3746	4.4399	4.5061	4.5731	4.6410	4.7097	4.7793	4.8498	4.9211	4.9934
5	5.1010	5.2040	5.3091	5.4163	5.5256	5.6371	5.7507	5.8666	5.9847	6.1051	6.2278	6.3528	6.4803	6.6101	6.7424
6	6.1520	6.3081	6.4684	6.6330	6.8019	6.9753	7.1533	7.3359	7.5233	7.7156	7.9129	8.1152	8.3227	8.5355	8.7537
7	7.2135	7.4343	7.6625	7.8983	8.1420	8.3938	8.6540	8.9228	9.2004	9.4872	9.7833	10.0890	10.4047	10.7305	11.0668
8	8.2857	8.5830	8.8923	9.2142	9.5491	9.8975	10.2598	10.6366	11.0285	11.4359	11.8594	12.2997	12.7573	13.2328	13.7268
9	9.3685	9.7546	10.1591	10.5828	11.0266	11.4913	11.9780	12.4876	13.0210	13.5795	14.1640	14.7757	15.4157	16.0853	16.7858
10	10.4622	10.9497	11.4639	12.0061	12.5779	13.1808	13.8164	14.4866	15.1929	15.9374	16.7220	17.5487	18.4197	19.3373	20.3037
11	11.5668	12.1687	12.8078	13.4864	14.2068	14.9716	15.7836	16.6455	17.5603	18.5312	19.5614	20.6546	21.8143	23.0445	24.3493
12	12.6825	13.4121	14.1920	15.0258	15.9171	16.8699	17.8885	18.9771	20.1407	21.3843	22.7132	24.1331	25.6502	27.2707	29.0017
13	13.8093	14.6803	15.6178	16.6268	17.7130	18.8821	20.1406	21.4953	22.9534	24.5227	26.2116	28.0291	29.9847	32.0887	34.3519
14	14.9474	15.9739	17.0863	18.2919	19.5986	21.0151	22.5505	24.2149	26.0192	27.9750	30.0949	32.3926	34.8827	37.5811	40.5047
15	16.0969	17.2934	18.5989	20.0236	21.5786	23.2760	25.1290	27.1521	29.3609	31.7725	34.4054	37.2797	40.4175	43.8424	47.5804
16	17.2579	18.6393	20.1569	21.8245	23.6575	25.6725	27.8881	30.3243	33.0034	35.9497	39.1899	42.7533	46.6717	50.9804	55.7175
17	18.4304	20.0121	21.7616	23.6975	25.8404	28.2129	30.8402	33.7502	36.9737	40.5447	44.5008	48.8837	53.7391	59.1176	65.0751
18	19.6147	21.4123	23.4144	25.6454	28.1324	30.9057	33.9990	37.4502	41.3013	45.5992	50.3959	55.7497	61.7251	68.3941	75.8364
19	20.8109	22.8406	25.1169	27.6712	30.5390	33.7600	37.3790	41.4463	46.0185	51.1591	56.9395	63.4397	70.7494	78.9692	88.2118
20	22.0190	24.2974	26.8704	29.7781	33.0660	36.7856	40.9955	45.7620	51.1601	57.2750	64.2028	72.0524	80.9468	91.0249	102.4436

	Interest Rate per Year														
Number of Years	16%	17%	18%	19%	20%	21%	22%	23%	24%	25%	26%	27%	28%	29%	30%
1	1.0000	1.0000	1.0000	1.0000	1.0000	1.0000	1.0000	1.0000	1.0000	1.0000	1.0000	1.0000	1.0000	1.0000	1.0000
2	2.1600	2.1700	2.1800	2.1900	2.2000	2.2100	2.2200	2.2300	2.2400	2.2500	2.2600	2.2700	2.2800	2.2900	2.3000
3	3.5056	3.5389	3.5724	3.6061	3.6400	3.6741	3.7084	3.7429	3.7776	3.8125	3.8476	3.8829	3.9184	3.9541	3.9900
4	5.0665	5.1405	5.2154	5.2913	5.3680	5.4457	5.5242	5.6038	5.6842	5.7656	5.8480	5.9313	6.0156	6.1008	6.1870
5	6.8771	7.0144	7.1542	7.2966	7.4416	7.5892	7.7396	7.8926	8.0484	8.2070	8.3684	8.5327	8.6999	8.8700	9.0431
6	8.9775	9.2068	9.4420	9.6830	9.9299	10.1830	10.4423	10.7079	10.9801	11.2588	11.5442	11.8366	12.1359	12.4423	12.7560
7	11.4139	11.7720	12.1415	12.5227	12.9159	13.3214	13.7396	14.1708	14.6153	15.0735	15.5458	16.0324	16.5339	17.0506	17.5828
8	14.2401	14.7733	15.3270	15.9020	16.4991	17.1189	17.7623	18.4300	19.1229	19.8419	20.5876	21.3612	22.1634	22.9953	23.8577
9	17.5185	18.2847	19.0859	19.9234	20.7989	21.7139	22.6700	23.6690	24.7125	25.8023	26.9404	28.1287	29.3692	30.6639	32.0150
10	21.3215	22.3931	23.5213	24.7089	25.9587	27.2738	28.6574	30.1128	31.6434	33.2529	34.9449	36.7235	38.5926	40.5564	42.6195
11	25.7329	27.1999	28.7551	30.4035	32.1504	34.0013	35.9620	38.0388	40.2379	42.5661	45.0306	47.6388	50.3985	53.3178	56.4053
12	30.8502	32.8239	34.9311	37.1802	39.5805	42.1416	44.8737	47.7877	50.8950	54.2077	57.7386	61.5013	65.5100	69.7800	74.3270
13	36.7862	39.4040	42.2187	45.2445	48.4966	51.9913	55.7459	59.7788	64.1097	68.7596	73.7506	79.1066	84.8529	91.0161	97.6250
14	43.6720	47.1027	50.8180	54.8409	59.1959	63.9095	69.0100	74.5280	80.4961	86.9495	93.9258	101.4654	109.6117	118.4108	127.9125
15	51.6595	56.1101	60.9653	66.2607	72.0351	78.3305	85.1922	92.6694	100.8151	109.6868	119.3465	129.8611	141.3029	153.7500	167.2863
16	60.9250	66.6488	72.9390	79.8502	87.4421	95.7799	104.9345	114.9834	126.0108	138.1085	151.3766	165.9236	181.8677	199.3374	218.4722
17	71.6730	78.9792	87.0680	96.0218	105.9306	116.8937	129.0201	142.4295	157.2534	173.6357	191.7345	211.7230	233.7907	258.1453	285.0139
18	84.1407	93.4056	103.7403	115.2659	128.1167	142.4413	158.4045	176.1883	195.9942	218.0446	242.5855	269.8882	300.2521	334.0074	371.5180
19	98.6032	110.2846	123.4135	138.1664	154.7400	173.3540	194.2535	217.7116	244.0328	273.5558	306.6577	343.7580	385.3227	431.8696	483.9734
20	115.3797	130.0329	146.6280	165.4180	186.6880	210.7584	237.9893	268.7853	303.6006	342.9447	387.3887	437.5726	494.2131	558.1118	630.1655

APPENDIX B
Solutions to Selected End-of-Chapter Problems

Chapter 1

1. Investment decisions: Purchase a new computer; conduct research to develop a new drug; shut down the factory. Financing decisions: Take out a bank loan or sell bonds; issue shares of stock to raise funds; buy or lease a new machine.

2. Unlike proprietorships, corporations are legally distinct from their owners, and so they have limited liability and pay taxes on their earnings. Shares of public corporations trade in stock markets, unlike those of private corporations.

6. a. financial
    b. financial
    c. real
    d. real
    e. real
    f. financial
    g. real
    h. financial

10. Takeover defences increase the target firm's agency problems. If management is protected against takeovers by takeover defences, it is more likely that managers will act in their own best interest, rather than in the interests of the firm and its stockholders.

19. The contingency arrangement aligns the interests of the lawyer and the client.

26. If you know that you will engage in business with another party on a repeated basis, you will be less likely to take advantage of your business partner should the opportunity to do so arise.

Chapter 2

4. Options markets, foreign exchange markets, futures markets, commodity markets, money market.

5. Buy shares in a mutual fund.

10. Look up the price of gold in commodity markets, and compare it to $1,500/6 = $250/ounce.

14. a. False
    b. False
    c. True
    d. False
    e. False
    f. False

19. These funds collect money from small investors and invest the money in the stock or bonds of large corporations, thus channeling funds from individuals to corporations. The advantages of mutual funds for individuals are diversification, professional investment management, and record keeping.

23. a. Find the rate of return available on other riskless investments, e.g., 1-year maturity U.S. Treasury notes.
    b. The opportunity cost is 20%. Not a worthwhile capital investment because the expected rate of return is 15%, less than the opportunity cost of capital.

Chapter 3

1.

Assets		Liabilities and Shareholders' Equity	
Cash	$ 10,000	Accounts payable	$ 17,000
Receivables	22,000	Long-term debt	170,000
Inventory	200,000		
Store and property	100,000	Shareholders' equity	145,000
Total assets	$332,000	Liabilities and share-holders' equity	$332,000

5. a. Taxes = $2,599
       Average tax rate = 13.0%
       Marginal tax rate = 15%
    b. Taxes = $8,844
       Average tax rate = 17.7%
       Marginal tax rate = 25%
    c. Taxes = $84,751
       Average tax rate = 28.3%
       Marginal tax rate = 33%
    d. Taxes = $1,009,556
       Average tax rate = 33.7%
       Marginal tax rate = 35%

9. Dividends = $600,000

10. Total taxes are reduced by $2,000.

11. a. Book value = $200,000
       Market value = $50,200,000
    b. Price per share = $25.10
       Book value per share = $.10

12.

Sales	$10,000
Cost of goods sold	6,500
G & A expenses	1,000
Depreciation expense	1,000
EBIT	1,500
Interest expense	500
Taxable income	1,000
Taxes (35%)	350
Net income	$ 650

Cash flow = net income + depreciation = $1,650

15. Cash flow will be $3,000 less than profits.

17. a. Cash flow = $3.95 million
       Net income = $1.95 million
    b. CF increases by $.35 million
       NI decreases by $.65 million
    c. Positive impact. Investors should care more about cash flow than book income.
    d. Both CF and NI decrease by $.65 million.

20. a. 2008: Equity = 890 − 650 = 240
       2009: Equity = 1,040 − 810 = 230
    b. 2008: NWC = 90 − 50 = 40
       2009: NWC = 140 − 60 = 80

c. Taxable income = 330
   Taxes paid = 115.50
d. Cash flow from operations = \$174.50
e. Gross investment = 450
f. Other current liabilities increased by 45.

22. Net working capital decreased by 50.

24. Earnings per share in 2005 = \$1.70
    Earnings per share in 2006 = \$1.52

28. Price per share = \$13.30

Chapter 4

1. a. Long-term debt ratio = .42
   b. Total debt ratio = .65
   c. Times interest earned = 3.75
   d. Cash coverage ratio = 7.42
   e. Current ratio = .74
   f. Quick ratio = .52
   g. Operating profit margin = 15.1%
   h. Inventory turnover = 17.06
   i. Days sales in inventory = 21.40 days
   j. Average collection period = 68.89 days
   k. ROE = 13.9%
   l. ROA = 7.2%
   m. payout ratio = .65

2. Gross investment = 2,576

8. a. ROE = 14.37%
   b. $\dfrac{\text{Assets}}{\text{Equity}} \times \dfrac{\text{sales}}{\text{assets}} \times \dfrac{\text{net income} + \text{interest}}{\text{sales}}$
      $\times \dfrac{\text{net income}}{\text{net income} + \text{interest}}$
      $= \dfrac{27,503}{9,121} \times \dfrac{13,193}{27,503} \times \dfrac{1,311 + 685}{13,193}$
      $\times \dfrac{1,311}{1,311 + 685} = .1437$

11. a. Debt-equity ratio = $\dfrac{\text{long-term debt}}{\text{equity at start of year}}$
    b. Return on equity = $\dfrac{\text{net income}}{\text{equity at start of year}}$
    c. Operating profit margin = $\dfrac{\text{net income} + \text{interest}}{\text{sales}}$
    d. Inventory turnover = $\dfrac{\text{cost of goods sold}}{\text{inventory at start of year}}$
    e. Current ratio = $\dfrac{\text{current assets}}{\text{current liabilities}}$
    f. Average collection period = $\dfrac{\text{receivables at start of year}}{\text{daily sales at start of year}}$
    g. Quick ratio
       $= \dfrac{\text{cash} + \text{marketable securities} + \text{accounts receivable}}{\text{current liabilities}}$

14. The current ratio is unaffected. The quick ratio falls.

16. Days sales in inventory = 2

18. a. Times interest earned = 1.25
    b. Cash coverage ratio = 1.5
    c. Fixed-payment coverage = 1.09

20. Total sales = \$54,750
    Asset turnover = .73
    ROA = 3.65%

22. $\dfrac{\text{Book debt}}{\text{Book equity}} = .5$

    $\dfrac{\text{Market equity}}{\text{Book equity}} = 2$

    $\dfrac{\text{Book debt}}{\text{Market equity}} = \dfrac{.5}{2} = .25$

24. Perhaps the firm has a lower ROA than its competitors; perhaps it pays a higher interest rate on its debt.

26. a. The shipping company
    b. United Foods
    c. The paper mill
    d. The power company
    e. Fledgling Electronics

Chapter 5

1. a. 46.32
   b. 21.45
   c. 67.56
   d. 45.64

3. $\$100 \times (1.04)^{113} = \$8,409$
   $\$100 \times (1.08)^{113} = \$598,252$

5. PV = \$548.47

9. PV = 796.56

10. a. $t = 23.36$
    b. $t = 11.91$
    c. $t = 6.17$

11. Effective annual rate
    a. 12.68%
    b. 8.24%
    c. 10.25%

13. $n = 11.9$ years

15. APR = 52%; EAR = 67.77%

20. The PV for the quarterback is \$11.37 million. The PV for the receiver is \$11.58 million.

24. a. EAR = 6.78%
    b. PMT = 573.14

28. APR = 19.19%

30. The value of the lease payments is \$38,132. It is cheaper to lease the truck.

34. a. PMT = 277.41
    b. PMT = 247.69

35. \$66,703.25

37. $79,079

46. $100 \times e^{.10 \times 8} = \$222.55$
    $100 \times e^{.08 \times 10} = \$222.55$

47. $n = 44.74$ months

48. The present value of your payments is $736. The present value of your receipts is $931. This is a good deal.

50. $r = 8\%$

53. a. The present value of the payoff is $1,117. This is a good deal.
    b. PV is $771. This is a bad deal.

60. $3,231

62. $2,964.53

66. a. Nominal rate = 3%
    b. Nominal rate = 7.12%
    c. Nominal rate = 9.18%

68. a. $79.38
    b. $91.51
    c. Real interest rate = 4.854%
    d. $91.51/(1.04854)^3 = \$79.38$

70. a. $228,107
    b. $13,950

71. 24 years. Real value increases by 58%

77. $.8418

78. $2,653.87

Chapter 6

1. a. Coupon rate remains unchanged.
   b. Price will fall.
   c. Yield to maturity increases.
   d. Current yield increases.

3. Bond price = $1,142.86

4. Coupon rate = 8%
   Current yield = 8.42%
   Yield to maturity = 9.12%

9. Rate of return on both bonds = 10%

10. a. Price will be $1,000.
    b. Rate of return = −1.82%
    c. Real return = −4.68%

11. a. Bondholder receives $80 per year.
    b. Price = $1,065.15
    c. The bond will sell for $1,136.03.

12. a. 8.97%
    b. 8%
    c. 7.18%

16. 20 years

18. a. Price = $641.01
    b. $r = 12.87\%$

19. a. Yield to maturity = 6.5%
    b. Rate of return = 20.41%

22. a. 9.89%
    b. 8%
    c. 6.18%

25. a. 3.92%
    b. 1.92%

c. 0
d. −1.85%

Chapter 7

3. a. $66.67
   b. $66.67
   c. Capital gains yield = 0
      Dividend yield = expected return = 12%

6. a. 14%
   b. $P_0 = \$24$

11. a. $DIV_1 = \$1.04$
       $DIV_2 = \$1.0816$
       $DIV_3 = \$1.1249$
    b. $P_0 = \$13$
    c. $P_3 = \$14.62$
    d. Your payments are:

	Year 1	Year 2	Year 3
DIV	1.04	1.0816	1.1249
Sales price			14.6232
Total cash flow	1.04	1.0816	15.7481
PV of cash flow	0.9286	0.8622	11.2092
Sum of PV = $13			

13. a. $P_0 = \$31.50$
    b. $P_0 = \$45$

16. $P_0 = \$33.33$

18. a. (i) Reinvest 0% of earnings.
           $g = 0$; $P_0 = \$40$
       (ii) Reinvest 40% of earnings.
           $g = 6\%$; $P_0 = \$40$
       (iii) Reinvest 60% of earnings.
           $g = 9\%$; $P_0 = \$40$
    b. (i) Reinvest 0% of earnings.
           $g = 0$; $P_0 = \$40$
       (ii) Reinvest 40% of earnings.
           $g = 8\%$; $P_0 = 51.43$
           PVGO = $11.43
       (iii) Reinvest 60% of earnings.
           $g = 12\%$; $P_0 = \$80$
           PVGO = $40
    c. In part (a), the return on reinvested earnings was equal to the discount rate.
       In part (b), the return on reinvested earnings was greater than the discount rate.

19. a. $P_0 = \$18.10$
    b. $DIV_1/P_0 = 5.52\%$

21. a. 6%
    b. $35
    c. $10
    d. 11.67
    e. 8.33

23. a. P/E = 33.33/4 = 8.33
    b. P/E increases to 10.

25. a. $P_0 = \$125$
    b. Assets in place = $80
       PVGO = $45

28. a. Market-to-book ratio = $800/$200 = 4
    b. Market-to-book ratio = ½

29. $16.59

40. a. $P_0 = \$52.80$
    b. $P_1 = \$57.14$
    c. Return = 3.78 + 8.22 = 12%

42. a. Expected return = 8%
    b. PVGO = $16.67
    c. $P_0 = \$106.22$

Chapter 8

1. Both projects are worth pursuing.

3. $NPV_A = \$23.85$ and $NPV_B = \$24.59$. Choose B.

5. No.

7. Project A has a payback period of 2.5 years.
   Project B has a payback period of 2 years.

11. .2680

13. $IRR_A = 25.7\%$
    $IRR_B = 20.7\%$

14. NPV = −$197.7. Reject.

15. a. $r = 0$ implies NPV = $15,750.
       $r = 50\%$ implies NPV = $4,250.
       $r = 100\%$ implies NPV = 0.
    b. IRR = 100%

17. $NPV_{9\%} = \$2,139.28$ and $NPV_{14\%} = -\$1,444.54$.
    The IRR is 11.81%.

20. NPV must be negative.

22. a.

Project	Payback
A	3
B	2
C	3

    b. Only B
    c. All three projects
    d.

Project	NPV
A	−1,011
B	3,378
C	2,405

    e. False

26. a. If $r = 2\%$, choose A.
    b. If $r = 12\%$, choose B.

27. $22,638

29. b. At 5% NPV = −$.443
    c. At 20% NPV = $.840
       At 40% NPV = −$.634

30. a. The equivalent annual cost of owning and operating Econo-cool is $252.53. The equivalent annual cost of Luxury Air is $234.21.
    b. Luxury Air.
    c. Econo-cool equivalent annual cost is $229.14. Luxury Air equivalent annual cost is $193.72.

33. a. The equivalent cost of owning and operating the new machine is $4,466. The old machine costs $5,000 a year to operate. You should replace.
    b. If $r = 12\%$, do not replace.

Chapter 9

3. $2.3 million

5. Increase in net cash flow = $106 million

6.

Revenue	$160,000
Rental costs	30,000
Variable costs	50,000
Depreciation	10,000
Pretax profit	$ 70,000
Taxes (35%)	24,500
Net income	$ 45,500

8. Cash flow = $3,300

10. Cash flow = $56,250

11. a.

Year	Depreciation	Book Value (end of year)
1	8,000	32,000
2	12,800	19,200
3	7,680	11,520
4	4,608	6,912
5	4,608	2,304
6	2,304	0

    b. After-tax proceeds are $18,332.

17. Cash flow = $3.705 million

18. a. Incremental operating CF = $1,300 in years 1 to 6
       Net after-tax cash flow at time 0 = −$4,800
    b. NPV = −4,800 + 1,300 × annuity factor (16%, 6 years) = −$9.84
    c. NPV = $137.09

21. a. Initial investment = $53,000
    b.

Year	Cash Flow ($000)
1	20.9
2	17.3
3	13.7
4	10.1

    c. NPV = − $4,377
    d. IRR = 7.50%

23. NPV = −10,894. Don't buy.

24. Equivalent annual (net-of-tax) costs:
    Quick and Dirty: $2.724 million
    Do-It-Right: $2.541 million
    Choose Do-It-Right.

26. NPV = −$349,773

30. a. −$71.75 million
    b. $40.25
    c. NPV = $28.35 million; IRR = 31.33%

Chapter 10

2. Variable costs = $.50 per burger
   Fixed costs = $2.5 million

5. a. $1.836 million
      $5.509 million

    b. $544,567
    c. $1.95 million

6. a. NPV = $5.6 million
   b. NPV = $2.9 million
   c. NPV = $6.8 million
   d. Price = $1.59 per jar

9. $1.50

12. Accounting break-even is unaffected. NPV break-even increases.

13. CF break-even is less than zero-profit break-even sales level.

15. a. Accounting break-even sales level is $6,400 per year. NPV break-even sales level is $7,166.
   b. Accounting break-even is unchanged. NPV break-even is $7,578.

16. a. Accounting break-even increases.
   b. NPV break-even falls.
   c. MACRS makes the project more attractive.

18. NPV will be negative.

21. DOL = 1

24. a. Average CF = 0
   b. Average CF = $15,000

27. a. NPV = −$681,728. The firm will reject the project.
   b. NPV = $69,855. The project is now worth pursuing.

Chapter 11

1. Return = 15%
   Dividend yield = 5%
   Capital gains yield = 10%

3. a. Rate of return = 0
   Real rate = −3.85%
   b. Rate of return = 5%
   Real rate = 0.96%
   c. Rate of return = 10%
   Real rate = 5.77%

5.

Asset Class	Real Rate
Treasury bills	.97%
Treasury bonds	2.23
Common stock	8.35

15. The bankruptcy lawyer

17. b. r_{stock} = 13%
   r_{bonds} = 8.4%
   Standard deviation (stocks) = 9.8%
   Standard deviation (bonds) = 3.2%

19. Our estimate of "normal" risk premiums will fall.

21. a. General Steel
   b. Club Med

23. Sassafras is *not* a risky investment to a diversified investor. Its return is better when the economy enters a recession. In contrast, the Leaning Tower of Pita has returns that are positively correlated with the rest of the economy.

Chapter 12

1. a. False
   b. False
   c. False
   d. True
   e. True

3. It is not well diversified.

7. Required return = $r_f + \beta(r_m - r_f)$ = 14.75%
   Expected return = 16%
   The security is underpriced.

11. a. β_A = 1.2
   β_D = .75
   b. r_m = 12%
   r_A = 14%
   r_D = 9%
   c. $r = r_f + \beta(r_m - r_f)$
   r_A = 13.6%
   r_D = 10%
   d. Stock A

13. NPV = −$25.29

15. P_1 = $52.625

19. $400,000

23. β = 4/7 = .571

25. a. False
   b. True
   c. False
   d. True
   e. False

26. $r = r_f + \beta(r_m - r_f)$ = 12%
   The 11% expected return is unattractive relative to its risk.

Chapter 13

1. 4.88%

4. 13.75%

8. The cost of equity capital is 11.2%.
   WACC = 8.74%

11. WACC = 12.4%

16.

	Dollars	Percent
Bonds	$ 9.36 million	30.3%
Preferred stock	1.50 million	4.9
Common stock	20.00 million	64.8
Total	$ 30.86 million	100.0%

17. 11.36%

18. The IRR is less than the WACC of firms in the computer industry. Reject the project.

19. a. r = 16%
   b. Weighted-average beta = .72
   c. WACC = 10.56%
   d. Discount rate = 10.56%
   e. r = 18%

Chapter 14

1. a. 60,000 shares issued
    b. Outstanding shares = 58,000
    c. 40,000

3. a. funded
    b. Eurobond
    c. subordinated
    d. sinking fund
    e. call
    f. prime rate
    g. floating rate
    h. private placement, public issue
    i. lease
    j. convertible
    k. warrant

6. a. 100 votes
    b. 1,000 votes

7. a. 200,001 shares
    b. 80,000 shares

9. Par value of common shares = $400,000
    Additional paid-in capital = $1,600,000
    Retained earnings = $500,000

12. Similarity: The firm promises to make specified payments. Advantage of income bonds: Interest payments are tax-deductible expenses.

Chapter 15

1. a. Subsequent issue
    b. Bond issue
    c. Bond issue

3. a. A large issue
    b. A bond issue
    c. Private placements

4. Less underwriter risk; less signaling effect from debt; easier to value.

7. a. 10%
    b. Average return = 3.94%
    c. I have suffered the winner's curse.

10. No

12. 12% of the value of funds raised.

14. a. Net proceeds of public issue = $9,770,000
       Net proceeds of private placement = $9,970,000
    b. The public issue
    c. The private placement can be custom-tailored, and its terms can be more easily renegotiated.

15. a. $12.5 million
    b. $5.80 per share

17. a. $10
    b. $18.333
    c. $8.333
    d. 200 rights

Chapter 16

4. $280 million

12. P/E = 10/1.25 = 8 (no leverage)
    P/E = 10/1.33 = 7.5 (leveraged)

15. a. Low-debt plan: $D/E = .25$
       High-debt plan: $D/E = .67$
    b.

	Low-Debt Plan		High-Debt Plan	
EPS	8.75	13.75	8.33	15.00
Expected EPS	$11.25		$11.67	

    c.

	Low-Debt	High-Debt
EPS	10	10

17. $r_{equity} = 14\%$

23. a. 11.2%
    b. The PV of the tax shield had been $.35 \times \$800 = \$280$ million. New market-value balance sheet:

Assets	Liabilities and Equity	
2,420	Debt	0
	Equity	2,420

25. Distorted investment decisions, impeded relations with other firms and creditors.

33. a. Stockholders gain; bondholders lose.
    b. Bondholders gain; stockholders lose.
    c. Bondholders lose; stockholders gain.
    d. Original stockholders lose; bondholders gain.

Chapter 17

1. a. May 7:   Declaration date
       June 6:   Last with-dividend date
       June 7:   Ex-dividend date
       June 11: Record date
       July 2:   Payment date
    b. The ex-dividend date, June 7.
    c. Dividend yield = 1.1%
    d. Payout ratio = 15.8%

2. a. Price = $64
    b. Price = $64
    c. Price = $80, unchanged

10. a. No effect on total wealth.
    b. No change: fewer shares, but higher price.

12. With a repurchase, shareholders will own fewer shares at a higher price. Their overall position is the same as with a dividend.

14. a. 1,250 shares. Value of equity remains at $100,000.
    b. Same effect as the stock dividend.

16. a. $50; $45
    b. $46.50

B-6   Appendix B

18. a. Price = $19.45
    b. Before-tax return = 13.1%
    c. Price = $20.09
    d. Before-tax return = 14.5%

19. a.

Stock	Pension	Corporation	Individual
A	10.00%	6.50%	9.00%
B	10.00	7.73	8.75
C	10.00	8.95	8.50

   b.

Stock	Price
A	$100
B	$ 81.25
C	$ 62.50

23. a. $20 per share.
    b. If the firm pays a dividend, EPS = $2. If the firm does the repurchase, EPS = $2.105.
    c. If the dividend is paid, the P/E ratio = 9.5. (Total market value = $19,000. Earnings = $2,000. Ratio = 9.5.) If the stock is repurchased, the P/E ratio = 9.5.

Chapter 18

1. a. False
   b. False
   c. True
   d. False
   e. True
   f. True
   g. False

6. Sales revenue will increase less than proportionally to output; costs and assets will increase roughly in proportion to output. Costs and assets will increase as a proportion of sales.

9. The balancing item is dividends. Dividends must be $200.

11. a. Internal growth rate = 10%
    b. Sustainable growth rate = 15%

13. a. Internal growth rate = 5.56%
    b. Sustainable growth rate = 8.33%

15. a.

Income Statement	20% Growth
Revenue	2,400
Cost of goods sold	2,160
EBIT	240
Interest expense	40
Earnings before taxes	200
State and federal taxes	80
Net income	120
Dividends	80
Retained earnings	40

Balance Sheet	
Assets	
Net working capital	240
Fixed assets	960
Net assets	1,200
Liabilities and Shareholders' Equity	
Long-term debt	400
Shareholders' equity	640
Total liabilities and shareholders' equity	1,040
Required external financing	160

   b.

Second-Stage Pro Forma Balance Sheet	
Assets	
Net working capital	240
Fixed assets	960
Net assets	1,200
Liabilities and Shareholders' Equity	
Long-term debt	560
Shareholders' equity	640
Total liabilities and shareholders' equity	1,200

17. a. $g = .025$
    b. Issue $1,000 in new debt.
    c. 1.5%

19. a. Internal growth rate = 10%
    b. External financing = $200,000
    c. Internal growth rate = 25%
    d. External financing = $50,000

21. Payout ratio can be at most .44.

23. Profit margin = 10%

25. $g = 12\%$

27. Required external financing is zero.

29. Higher

Chapter 19

1.

	Cash	Net Working Capital
a.	$2 million decline	$2 million decline
b.	$2,500 increase	Unchanged
c.	$5,000 decline	Unchanged
d.	Unchanged	$1 million increase
e.	Unchanged	Unchanged
f.	$5 million increase	Unchanged

2. a. Long-term financing, total capital requirement, marketable securities.
   b. Cash, cash, cash balance, marketable securities.

5. Lower inventory period and cash conversion cycle; reduce net working capital.

7. a. Cash conversion cycle falls.
   b. Cash conversion cycle increases.
   c. Cash conversion cycle falls.
   d. Cash conversion cycle increases.
   e. Cash conversion cycle falls.
   f. Cash conversion cycle increases.

9. Effective rate = 8.89%. If the compensating balance is 20%, the effective rate is 10%.

11. a. 6.38%
   b. 6.20%

15. The order is .75 times the following quarter's sales forecast:

Quarter	Order
1	270
2	252
3	288
4	288

17.

Quarter	Collections
1	348
2	368
3	352
4	352

19.

	Quarter			
	First	Second	Third	Fourth
Cash at start of period	$40	$10	$15	−$14
+ Net cash inflow (from problem 18)	−30	+5	−29	−41
= Cash at end of period	10	15	−14	−55
Minimum operating cash balance	30	30	30	30
Cumulative short-term financing required (minimum cash balance minus cash at end of period)	$20	$15	$44	$85

21.

	Quarter			
	First	Second	Third	Fourth
Cash requirements				
1. Cash required for operations	$50	$15	−$26	−$35
2. Interest on line of credit	0	0.9	0.9	0.7
3. Interest on stretched payables	0	0	0.8	0
4. Total cash required	$50	$15.9	−$24.3	−$34.3
Cash raised				
5. Line of credit (bank loan)	$45	$ 0	$ 0	$ 0
6. Stretched payables	0	15.9	0	0
7. Securities sold	5	0	0	0
8. Total cash raised	$50	$15.9	$0	$ 0
Repayments				
9. Of stretched payables	0	0	$15.9	0
10. Of line of credit (bank loan)	0	0	8.4	34.3
Increase in cash balances				
11. Addition to cash balances	$ 5	$ 0	$ 0	$ 0
Line of credit (bank loan)				
12. Beginning of quarter	$ 0	$45	$45	$36.6
13. End of quarter	45	45	36.6	2.3

22.

Sources of Cash	
Sale of marketable securities	2
Increase in bank loans	1
Increase in accounts payable	5
Cash from operations:	
Net income	6
Depreciation	2
Total	16
Uses of Cash	
Increase in inventories	6
Increase in accounts receivable	3
Investment in fixed assets	6
Dividend paid	1
Total	16
Change in cash balance	0

23.

	February	March	April
Sources of cash			
Collections on current sales	$ 100	$ 110	$ 90
Collections on accounts receivable	90	100	110
Total sources of cash	$ 190	$ 210	$ 200
Uses of cash			
Payments of accounts payable	$ 30	$ 40	$ 30
Cash purchases	70	80	60
Labor and administrative expenses	30	30	30
Capital expenditures	100	0	0
Taxes, interest, and dividends	10	10	10
Total uses of cash	$ 240	$ 160	$ 130
Net cash inflow (sources − uses)	−$ 50	+$ 50	+$70
Cash at start of period	$ 100	$ 50	$ 100
+ Net cash inflow	−50	+50	+70
= Cash at end of period	$ 50	$ 100	$ 170
Minimum operating cash balance	$ 100	$ 100	$ 100
Cumulative short-term financing required (minimum cash balance minus cash at end of period)	$ 50	$ 0	−$ 70

Chapter 20

1. a. $10
   b. 40 days
   c. 9.6%

4. a. Due lag and pay lag fall.
   b. Due lag and pay lag increase.
   c. Terms lag and pay lag increase.

6. Ledger balance = $215,000
   Net float = $15,000

8. a. Checks not yet cleared = $120,000
   Collections not yet available = 66,000
   Net float = $ 54,000
   b. Annual interest earnings = $1,320
   Present value of earnings = $22,000

11. a. 20 days
    b. $1.096 million
    c. Average days in receivables will fall.

13. a. The expected profit from a sale is −3. Do not extend credit.
    b. $p = .96$
    c. The present value of a sale, net of default, is positive, $365.28.
    d. $p = 19.35\%$

14. a. The expected profit of a sale is positive, $90.
    b. $p = .875$

19. a. Yes
    b. Credit should not be advanced.
    c. Net benefit from advancing credit = $50.

20. a. $30,000
    b. $6
    c. $180

22. Yes

23. Cash balances fall relative to sales.

24. PV(REV) = $1,200
    PV(COST) = $1,000
    Slow payers have a 70% probability of paying their bills. The expected profit of a sale to a slow payer is therefore .70($1,200 − $1,000) − .30($1,000) = −$160.
    Expected savings = $16. The credit check costs $5, so it is cost effective.

26. Sell only to groups 1, 2, and 3.

Chapter 21

1. a. Economies of scale is a valid reason.
   b. Diversification is not a valid reason.
   c. Possibly a valid reason.
   d. The bootstrap strategy is not a valid reason.

2. By merging, the firms can even out the workload over the year.

4. LBO: 5
   Poison pill: 3
   Tender offer: 4
   Shark repellent: 2
   Proxy contest: 1

6. $25 per share

8. a. $6.25 million
   b. $4 million
   c. NPV = $2.25 million

12. a. NPV = $10,000
    b. SCC will sell for $53.33; SDP will sell for $20.
    c. Price = $52.63
    d. NPV = $7,890

13. a. Total market value = $4,000,000 + 5,000,000 = $9,000,000
    Total earnings = $200,000 + 500,000 = $700,000
    Number of shares = 262,172
    Price per share = $9,000,000/262,172 = $34.33
    Price-earnings ratio = 34.33/2.67 = 12.9
    b. .81 share
    c. $567,365
    d. −$567,365

Chapter 22

1. a. 68.39 euros; $146.21
   b. 113.22 Swiss francs; $88.32
   c. Direct exchange rate will decrease and indirect exchange rate will increase.
   d. Canadian dollar is worth more.

3. a. $\dfrac{1 + r_x}{1 + r_\$} = \dfrac{f_{x/\$}}{s_{x/\$}}$

   b. $\dfrac{f_{x/\$}}{s_{x/\$}} = \dfrac{E(s_{x/\$})}{s_{x/\$}}$

   c. $\dfrac{E(1 + i_x)}{E(1 + i_\$)} = \dfrac{E(s_{x/\$})}{s_{x/\$}}$

   d. $\dfrac{1 + r_x}{1 + r_\$} = \dfrac{E(1 + i_x)}{E(1 + i_\$)}$

4. Foreign inflation rate
   Future exchange rates
   Domestic interest rates

6. a

8. Borrow the present value of 1 million Australian dollars, sell them for U.S. dollars in the spot market, and invest the proceeds in an 8-year U.S. dollar loan. In 8 years, it can repay the Australian loan with the anticipated Australian dollar payment.

10. a. 4%
    b. 14.4%
    c. −6.4%

14. Canadian dollar should be depreciating relative to the U.S. dollar.

16. Net present value = $.72 million

18. a. Depreciation of Trinidadian dollars
    b. Borrow in Trinidad.
    c. Its exposure is mitigated.

Chapter 23

1.

		Payoff	Profit
a.	Call option, $X = 620$	100	−1.32
b.	Put option, $X = 620$	0	−8.91
c.	Call option, $X = 720$	0	−55.50
d.	Put option, $X = 720$	0	−52.00
e.	Call option, $X = 820$	0	−17.90
f.	Put option, $X = 820$	100	−15.20

5. Figure 23.7a represents a call seller; Figure 23.7b represents a call buyer.

7. a. The exercise price of the put option.
   b. The value of the stock.

10. Lower bound is either zero or the stock price minus the exercise price, whichever is greater. The upper bound is the stock price.

14. You will be more tempted to choose the high-risk proposal.

16. a. Call option to pursue a project.
    b. Put option to sell the equipment.

18. Put option with exercise price equal to support price.

20. a. Option to put (sell) the stock to the underwriter.
    b. Volatility of the stock value; the length of the period for which the underwriter guarantees the issue; the interest rate; the price at which the underwriter is obligated to buy the stock; and the market value of the stock.

22. Put option on the bank assets with exercise price equal to the deposits owed to bank customers.

24. a. Buy a call option for $3. Exercise the call to purchase stock. Pay the $20 exercise price. Sell the share for $25.
    b. Buy a share and put option. Exercise the put. Riskless profit equals $1.

Chapter 24

1. They should insure against events that would result in financial distress and against risks that the insurance company can diversify away.

4. No

6. Advantages: liquidity, no storage costs, no spoilage. Disadvantages: no income or benefits that could accrue from holding asset in portfolio.

7.

	Gold Price		
	$800	**$860**	**$920**
a. Sales	$800,000	$860,000	$920,000
Futures contract cash flow	80,000	20,000	−40,000
b. Total revenues	$880,000	$880,000	$880,000
c. Sales	$800,000	$860,000	$920,000
+ Put option payoff	60,000	0	0
− Put option cost	−6,000	−6,000	−6,000
Total revenues	$854,000	$854,000	$914,000

9. Reject its offer. Instead borrow for 2 years at 7% and re-lend for 1 year at 6%.

11. The futures price for oil is $90 per barrel. Petrochemical will take a long position to hedge its cost of buying oil. Onnex will take a short position to hedge its revenue from selling oil.

	Oil Price ($ per barrel)		
	$80	**$90**	**$100**
Cost for Petrochemical:			
Cash flow to buy 1,000 barrels	−80,000	−90,000	−100,000
+ Cash flow on long futures position	−10,000	0	10,000
Total cash flow	−90,000	−90,000	−90,000
Revenue for Onnex:			
Revenue from 1,000 barrels	$80,000	$90,000	$100,000
+ Cash flow on short futures position	10,000	0	−10,000
Total cash flow	$90,000	$90,000	$90,000

The benefit of futures is the ability to lock in a riskless position without paying any money. The benefit of the option hedge is that you benefit if prices move in one direction without losing if they move in the other direction. However, this asymmetry comes at a price: the cost of the option.

12. The futures price is greater than the spot price for gold. This reflects the fact that the futures contract ensures your receipt of the gold without tying up your money now. The difference between the spot price and the futures price reflects compensation for the time value of money. Another way to put it is that the spot price must be lower than the futures price to compensate investors who buy and store gold for the opportunity cost of their funds until the futures maturity date.

14. A currency swap is an agreement to exchange a series of payments in one currency for a given series of payments in another currency. An interest rate swap is an exchange of a series of fixed payments for a series of payments that are linked to market interest rates.

Glossary

A

ACH See *Automated Clearing House*.

acquisition Takeover of a firm by purchase of that firm's common stock or assets.

additional paid-in capital Difference between issue price and par value of stock. Also called *capital surplus*.

agency problems Managers, acting as agents for stockholders, may act in their own interests rather than maximizing value.

aging schedule Classification of accounts receivable by time outstanding.

annual percentage rate (APR) Interest rate that is annualized using simple interest.

annuity Equally spaced level stream of cash flows with a finite maturity.

annuity due Level stream of cash flows starting immediately.

annuity factor Present value of a $1 annuity.

authorized share capital Maximum number of shares that the company is permitted to issue.

Automated Clearing House (ACH) An electronic network for cash transfers in the United States.

average tax rate Total taxes owed divided by total income.

B

balance sheet Financial statement that shows the value of the firm's assets and liabilities at a particular time.

balancing item Variable that adjusts to maintain the consistency of a financial plan. Also called *plug*.

bankruptcy The reorganization or liquidation of a firm that cannot pay its debts.

beta Sensitivity of a stock's return to the return on the market portfolio.

bond Security that obligates the issuer to make specified payments to the bondholder.

book value Net worth of the firm according to the balance sheet.

break-even analysis Analysis of the level of sales at which the project breaks even.

C

call option Right to buy an asset at a specified exercise price on or before the expiration date.

callable bond Bond that may be repurchased by the firm before maturity at a specified call price.

capital asset pricing model (CAPM) Theory of the relationship between risk and return which states that the expected risk premium on any security equals its beta times the market risk premium.

capital budget List of planned investment projects.

capital budgeting decision Decision to invest in tangible or intangible assets.

capital markets Markets for long-term financing.

capital rationing Limit set on the amount of funds available for investment.

capital structure The mix of long-term debt and equity financing.

CAPM See *capital asset pricing model*.

carrying costs Costs of maintaining current assets, including opportunity cost of capital.

cash conversion cycle Period between firm's payment for materials and collection on its sales.

cash dividend Payment of cash by the firm to its shareholders.

CEO Acronym for chief executive officer.

CFO See *chief financial officer*.

chief financial officer (CFO) Oversees the treasurer and controller and sets overall financial strategy.

collection policy Procedures to collect and monitor receivables.

commercial paper Short-term unsecured notes issued by firms.

common-size balance sheet Balance sheet that presents items as a percentage of total assets.

common-size income statement Income statement that presents items as a percentage of revenues.

common stock Ownership shares in a publicly held corporation.

company cost of capital Expected rate of return demanded by investors in a company, determined by the average risk of the company's securities.

compound interest Interest earned on interest.

concentration account System whereby customers make payments to a regional collection center which transfers funds to a principal bank.

constant-growth dividend discount model Version of the dividend discount model in which dividends grow at a constant rate.

consumer credit Bills awaiting payment from final customer to a company.

controller Officer responsible for budgeting, accounting, and taxes.

convertible bond Bond that the holder may exchange for a specified amount of another security.

corporation Business organized as a separate legal entity owned by stockholders.

cost of capital Minimum acceptable rate of return on capital investment.

costs of financial distress Costs arising from bankruptcy or distorted business decisions before bankruptcy.

coupon The interest payments paid to the bondholder.

coupon rate Annual interest payment as a percentage of face value.

credit analysis Procedure to determine the likelihood a customer will pay its bills.

credit policy Standards set to determine the amount and nature of credit to extend to customers.

credit risk See *default risk*.

cumulative voting Voting system in which all the votes one shareholder is allowed to cast can be cast for one candidate for the board of directors.

current yield Annual coupon payments divided by bond price.

D

decision tree   Diagram of sequential decisions and possible outcomes.

default premium   The additional yield that bond investors require for bearing credit risk.

default risk   The risk that a bond issuer may default on its bonds. Also called *credit risk.*

degree of operating leverage (DOL)   Percentage change in profits given a 1 percent change in sales.

depreciation tax shield   Reduction in taxes attributable to depreciation.

derivatives   Securities whose payoffs are determined by the values of other financial variables such as prices, exchange rates, or interest rates.

discount factor   Present value of a $1 future payment.

discount rate   Interest rate used to compute present values of future cash flows.

discounted cash flow (DCF)   Another term for the present value of a future cash flow.

diversification   Strategy designed to reduce risk by spreading the portfolio across many investments.

dividend   Periodic cash distribution from the firm to its shareholders.

dividend discount model   Discounted cash-flow model which states that today's stock price equals the present value of all expected future dividends.

dividend-payout ratio   Percentage of earnings paid out as dividends.

Dow Jones Industrial Average   Index of the investment performance of a portfolio of 30 "blue-chip" stocks.

Du Pont formula   A breakdown of ROE and ROA into component ratios.

E

economic value added (EVA)   Income that is measured after deduction of the cost of capital.

effective annual interest rate   Interest rate that is annualized using compound interest.

efficient markets   Markets in which prices reflect all available information.

equivalent annual annuity   The cash flow per period with the same present value as the cost of buying and operating a machine.

eurobond   Bond that is marketed internationally.

eurodollars   Dollars held on deposit in a bank outside the United States.

EVA   See *economic value added.*

exchange rate   Amount of one currency needed to purchase one unit of another.

ex-dividend   Without the dividend. Buyer of a stock after the ex-dividend date does not receive the most recently declared dividend.

expectations theory of exchange rates   Theory that expected spot exchange rate equals the forward rate.

F

face value   Payment at the maturity of the bond. Also called *par value* or *maturity value.*

financial assets   Claims to the income generated by real assets. Also called *securities.*

financial deficit   Difference between cash the companies need and the amount generated internally.

financial institution   A bank, insurance company, or similar financial intermediary.

financial intermediary   An organization that raises money from many investors and provides financing to individuals, corporations, or other organizations.

financial leverage   Debt financing to amplify the effects of changes in operating income on the returns to stockholders.

financial markets   Markets in which securities are issued and traded.

financial risk   Risk to shareholders resulting from the use of debt.

financial slack   Ready access to cash or debt financing.

financing decision   The form and amount of financing of a firm's investments.

fixed costs   Costs that do not depend on the level of output.

fixed-income market   Market for debt securities.

floating rate preferred   Preferred stock for which the dividend rate is linked to current market interest rates

floating-rate security   Security paying dividends or interest that vary with short-term interest rates.

flotation costs   The costs incurred when a firm issues new securities to the public.

forex   Abbreviation for foreign exchange; also abbreviated *fx.*

forward contract   Agreement to buy or sell an asset in the future at an agreed price.

forward exchange rate   Exchange rate agreed today for a future transaction.

free cash flow   Cash available for distribution to investors after the company has paid for any new capital investment or additions to working capital.

fundamental analysts   Analysts who attempt to find mispriced securities by analyzing fundamental information, such as accounting data and business prospects.

funded debt   Debt with more than 1 year remaining to maturity.

future value (FV)   Amount to which an investment will grow after earning interest.

futures contract   Exchange-traded promise to buy or sell an asset in the future at a prespecified price.

FV   See *future value.*

fx   Abbreviation for foreign exchange; also abbreviated *forex.*

G

GAAP   See *generally accepted accounting principles.*

general cash offer   Sale of securities open to all investors by an already-public company.

generally accepted accounting principles (GAAP)   Procedures for preparing financial statements.

H

hedge fund   A private investment pool, open to wealthy or institutional investors, that is only lightly regulated and therefore can pursue more speculative policies than mutual funds.

I

income statement   Financial statement that shows the revenues, expenses, and net income of a firm over a period of time.

inflation   Rate at which prices as a whole are increasing.

information content of dividends   Dividend increases send good news about future cash flow and earnings. Dividend cuts send bad news.

initial public offering (IPO)   First offering of stock to the general public.

interest rate parity   Theory that forward premium equals interest rate differential.

interest rate risk   The risk in bond prices dues to fluctuations in interest rates.

interest tax shield   Tax savings resulting from deductibility of interest payments.

internal growth rate   Maximum rate of growth without external financing.

internal rate of return (IRR)   Discount rate at which project NPV = 0.

internally generated funds   Cash reinvested in the firm; depreciation plus earnings not paid out as dividends.

international Fisher effect   Theory that real interest rates in all countries should be equal, with differences in nominal rates reflecting differences in expected inflation.

intrinsic value   The present value of the cash flows anticipated by an investor in a security.

investment grade   Bonds rated Baa or above by Moody's or BBB or above by Standard & Poor's.

IPO   See *initial public offering.*

IRR   See *internal rate of return.*

issued shares   Shares that have been issued by the company.

J

junk bond   Bond with a rating below Baa or BBB.

just-in-time approach   System of inventory management that requires minimum inventories of materials and very frequent deliveries by suppliers.

L

law of one price   Theory that prices of goods in all countries should be equal when translated to a common currency.

lease   Long-term rental agreement.

leveraged buyout (LBO)   Acquisition of a firm by a private group using substantial borrowed funds.

limited liability   The owners of the corporation are not personally responsible for its obligations.

line of credit   Agreement by a bank that a company may borrow at any time up to an established limit.

liquidation   Sale of bankrupt firm's assets.

liquidation value   Net proceeds that could be realized by selling the firm's assets and paying off its creditors.

liquidity   Ability to sell an asset for cash at short notice.

loan covenant   Agreement between firm and lender requiring the firm to fulfill certain conditions to safeguard the loan.

lock-box system   System whereby customers send payments to a post-office box and a local bank collects and processes checks.

M

majority voting   Voting system in which each director is voted on separately.

management buyout (MBO)   Acquisition of the firm by its own management in a leveraged buyout.

M&A   Abbreviation for mergers and acquisitions.

marginal tax rate   Additional taxes owed per dollar of additional income.

market capitalization   Total market value of equity, equal to share price times number of shares outstanding.

market index   Measure of the investment performance of the overall market.

market portfolio   Portfolio of all assets in the economy. In practice a broad stock market index is used to represent the market.

market risk   Economywide (macroeconomic) sources of risk that affect the overall stock market. Also called *systematic risk.*

market risk premium   Risk premium of market portfolio. Difference between market return and return on risk-free Treasury bills.

market-to-book ratio   Ratio of market value of equity to book value of equity

market value added   The difference between the market value of firm's equity and its book value.

market-value balance sheet   Financial statement that uses the market value of all assets and liabilities.

maturity premium   Extra average return from investing in long- versus short-term Treasury securities.

merger   Combination of two firms into one, with the acquirer assuming assets and liabilities of the target firm.

MM's dividend-irrelevance proposition   Under ideal conditions the value of the firm is unaffected by dividend policy.

MM's proposition I (debt irrelevance proposition)   The value of a firm is unaffected by its capital structure.

MM's proposition II   The required rate of return on equity increases as the firm's debt-equity ratio increases.

modified accelerated cost recovery system (MACRS)   Depreciation method that allows higher tax deductions in early years and lower deductions later.

money market   Market for short-term financing (less than 1 year).

mutual fund   An investment company that pools the savings of many investors and invests in a portfolio of securities.

mutually exclusive projects   Two or more projects that cannot be pursued simultaneously.

N

net present value (NPV)   Present value of cash flows minus investment.

net working capital   Current assets minus current liabilities.

net worth   Book value of common stockholders' equity plus preferred stock.

nominal interest rate   Rate at which money invested grows.

NPV   See *net present value.*

NPV break-even point   Minimum level of sales needed to cover all costs including the cost of capital.

NYSE   New York Stock Exchange.

O

open account   Agreement whereby sales are made with no formal debt contract.

operating leverage   Degree to which costs are fixed.

operating profit margin   Net income plus interest as a percentage of sales.

operating risk (business risk)   Risk in firm's operating income.

opportunity cost   Benefit or cash flow forgone as a result of an action.

opportunity cost of capital   Expected rate of return given up by investing in a project.

outstanding shares   Shares that have been issued by the company and are held by investors.

P

par value   Value of security shown in the company's accounts.

payback period   Time until cash flows recover the initial investment in the project.

payout ratio   Fraction of earnings paid out as dividends.

P/E   See *price-earnings multiple.*

pecking order theory   Firms prefer to issue debt rather than equity if internal finance is insufficient.

pension fund   Investment plan set up by an employer to provide for employees' retirement.

percentage of sales model   Planning model in which sales forecasts are the driving variables and most other variables are proportional to sales.

perpetuity   Stream of level cash payments that never ends.

planning horizon   Time horizon for a financial plan.

plowback ratio   Fraction of earnings retained by the firm.

poison pill   Measure taken by a target firm to avoid acquisition; for example, the right for existing shareholders to buy additional shares at an attractive price if a bidder acquires a large holding.

preferred stock   Stock that takes priority over common stock in regard to dividends.

present value (PV)   Value today of a future cash flow.

present value of growth opportunities (PVGO)   Net present value of a firm's future investments.

price-earnings multiple (P/E ratio)   Ratio of stock price to earnings per share.

primary market   Market for the sale of new securities by corporations.

prime rate   Benchmark interest rate charged by banks.

private placement   Sale of securities to a limited number of investors without a public offering.

pro formas   Projected or forecast financial statements.

profitability index   Ratio of net present value to initial investment.

project cost of capital   Minimum acceptable expected rate of return on a project given its risk.

prospectus   Formal summary that provides information on an issue of securities.

protective covenant   Restriction on a firm to protect bondholders.

proxy contest   Takeover attempt in which outsiders compete with management for shareholders' votes. Also called *proxy fight.*

purchasing power parity (PPP)   Theory that the cost of living in different countries is equal, and exchange rates adjust to offset inflation differentials across countries.

put option   Right to sell an asset at a specified exercise price on or before the expiration date.

PV   See *present value.*

R

random walk   Security prices change randomly, with no predictable trends or patterns.

rate of return   Total income and capital appreciation per period per dollar invested.

real assets   Assets used to produce goods and services.

real interest rate   Rate at which the purchasing power of an investment increases.

real options   Options to invest in, modify, or dispose of a capital investment project.

real value of $1   Purchasing power-adjusted value of a dollar.

reorganization   Restructuring of financial claims on failing firm to allow it to keep operating.

residual income   Also called economic value added or EVA. Profit minus cost of capital employed.

restructuring   Process of changing the firm's capital structure without changing its assets.

retained earnings   Earnings not paid out as dividends.

return on assets (ROA)   Net income plus interest as a percentage of total assets.

return on capital (ROC)   Net income plus interest as a percentage of long-term capital.

return on equity (ROE)   Net income as a percentage of shareholders' equity.

rights issue   Issue of securities offered only to current stockholders.

risk premium   Expected return in excess of risk-free return as compensation for risk.

ROA   See *return on assets.*

ROC   See *return on capital.*

ROE   See *return on equity.*

S

S&P   Abbreviation for Standard & Poor's stock market index.

scenario analysis   Project analysis given a particular combination of assumptions.

seasoned offering   Sale of securities by a firm that is already publicly traded.

secondary market   Market in which previously issued securities are traded among investors.

secured debt   Debt that has first claim on specified collateral in the event of default.

security market line   Relationship between expected return and beta.

sensitivity analysis   Analysis of the effects on project profitability of changes in sales, costs, and so on.

shark repellent   Amendments to a company charter made to forestall takeover attempts.

shelf registration   A procedure that allows firms to file one registration statement for several issues of the same security.

shortage costs   Costs incurred from shortages in current assets.

simple interest   Interest earned only on the original investment; no interest is earned on interest.

simulation analysis   Estimation of the probabilities of different possible outcomes, e.g., from an investment project.

sinking fund   Fund established to retire debt before maturity.

spot price   Price paid for immediate delivery

spot rate of exchange   Exchange rate for an immediate transaction.

spread   Difference between public offer price and price paid by underwriter.

stakeholder   Anyone with a financial interest in the firm.

Standard & Poor's Composite Index   Index of the investment performance of a portfolio of 500 large stocks. Also called the *S&P 500*.

standard deviation   Square root of variance. Another measure of volatility.

statement of cash flows   Financial statement that shows the firm's cash receipts and cash payments over a period of time.

stock dividend   Distribution of additional shares to a firm's stockholders.

stock repurchase   Firm buys back stock from its shareholders.

stock split   Issue of additional shares to firm's stockholders.

straight-line depreciation   Constant depreciation for each year of the asset's accounting life.

subordinated debt   Debt that may be repaid in bankruptcy only after senior debt is paid.

sunk costs   Costs that have been incurred and cannot be recovered.

sustainable growth rate   Steady rate at which a firm can grow without changing leverage; return on equity × plowback ratio.

swap   Arrangement by two counterparties to exchange one stream of cash flows for another.

T

technical analysts   Investors who attempt to identify undervalued stocks by searching for patterns in past prices.

tender offer   Takeover attempt in which outsiders directly offer to buy the stock of the firm's shareholders.

terms of sale   Credit, discount, and payment terms offered on a sale.

trade credit   Bills awaiting payment from one company to another.

trade-off theory   Debt levels are chosen to balance interest tax shields against the costs of financial distress.

treasurer   Manager responsible for financing, cash management, and relationships with banks and other financial institutions.

treasury stock   Stock that has been repurchased by the company and held in its treasury.

U

underpricing   Issuing securities at an offering price set below the true value of the security.

underwriter   Firm that buys an issue of securities from a company and resells it to the public.

unique risk   Risk factors affecting only that firm. Also called *diversifiable risk.*

V

variable costs   Costs that change as the level of output changes.

variance   Average value of squared deviations from mean. A measure of volatility.

venture capital   Money invested to finance a new firm.

W

WACC   See *weighted-average cost of capital.*

warrant   Right to buy shares from a company at a stipulated price before a set date.

weighted-average cost of capital (WACC)   Expected rate of return on a portfolio of all the firm's securities, adjusted for tax savings due to interest payments.

workout   Agreement between a company and its creditors establishing the steps the company must take to avoid bankruptcy.

Y

yield curve   Graph of the relationship between time to maturity and yield to maturity.

yield to maturity   Interest rate for which the present value of the bond's payments equals the price.

Global Index

Page numbers followed by n indicate material found in notes.

Global Index

Subject Index

Page numbers followed by n indicate material found in notes.